MAGILL'S SURVEY OF WORLD LITERATURE

Revised Edition

Magill's Survey of World Literature

Revised Edition

Volume 1

Abe—Carey

Edited by

Steven G. Kellman
University of Texas, San Antonio

SALEM PRESS, INC.
Pasadena, California   Hackensack, New Jersey

Editor in Chief: Dawn P. Dawson *Acquisitions Editor:* Mark Rehn
Editorial Director: Christina J. Moose *Research Supervisor:* Jeffry Jensen
Project Editor: Tracy Irons-Georges *Research Assistant:* Keli Trousdale
Copy Editor: Rebecca Kuzins *Production Editor:* Joyce I. Buchea
Editorial Assistant: Dana Garey *Design and Graphics:* James Hutson
Photo Editor: Cynthia Breslin Beres *Layout:* Mary Overell

Cover photo: Chinua Achebe (AP/Wide World Photos/Craig Ruttle)

Library of Congress Cataloging-in-Publication Data

Magill's survey of world literature / edited by Steven G. Kellman. — Rev. ed.
    p. cm.
  Includes bibliographical references and index.
  ISBN 978-1-58765-431-2 (set : alk. paper) — ISBN 978-1-58765-432-9 (vol. 1 : alk. paper) —
ISBN 978-1-58765-433-6 (vol. 2 : alk. paper) — ISBN 978-1-58765-434-3 (vol. 3 : alk. paper) —
ISBN 978-1-58765-435-0 (vol. 4 : alk. paper) — ISBN 978-1-58765-436-7 (vol. 5 : alk. paper) —
ISBN 978-1-58765-437-4 (vol. 6 : alk. paper) 1. Literature—History and criticism. 2. Literature—
Stories, plots, etc. 3. Literature—Bio-bibliography. 4. Authors—Biography—Dictionaries. I. Kellman,
Steven G., 1947- II. Magill, Frank N. (Frank Northen), 1907-1997.
  PN523.M29 2009
  809—dc22
                                                                                        2008046042

First Printing

CONTENTS

CONTENTS

PUBLISHER'S NOTE

Magill's Survey of World Literature offers profiles of major writers outside the United States from all time periods, accompanied by analyses of their significant titles of fiction, drama, poetry, and nonfiction. Originally published in 1993 with a 1995 supplement with Marshall Cavendish Corporation, this revised six-volume edition covers 380 writers at the heart of literary studies for middle and high school students and at the center of book discussions among library patrons. It is currently the only set from Salem Press that brings together information on the lives and works of writers from around the world in all genres. Its companion set, *Magill's Survey of American Literature*, was published in 2007 to wide acclaim and named an Editor's Choice by *Booklist* and a Best Reference, 2007, by *Library Journal*.

EXPANDING THE SCOPE

For this edition of *Magill's Survey of World Literature*, 87 new authors were added to the 293 already profiled, including Douglas Adams, Julian Barnes, Roberto Bolaño, Mikhail Bulgakov, Paul Celan, Roald Dahl, Rubén Darío, Roddy Doyle, Buchi Emecheta, Laura Esquivel, Helen Fielding, Gao Xingjian, Seamus Heaney, James Herriot, Primo Levi, Malcolm Lowry, Ian McEwan, A. A. Milne, Haruki Murakami, Ben Okri, J. K. Rowling, Françoise Sagan, Zadie Smith, Rabindranath Tagore, and Irvine Welsh. These new writers span both the globe, representing forty-five different countries, and time, from the sixth century B.C.E. to the twenty-first century. An effort was also made to add more women writers and authors of children's and young adult literature.

BRINGING THINGS UP TO DATE

All the original essays were evaluated for their currency, and 71 were given substantial revision, in many cases by the original contributor. The "Biography," "Analysis," and "Summary" sections were updated to include recent developments: new titles or awards, changes in residence or employment, and alterations in critical and popular reception. For these essays, one or more sections on specific works (novels, poems, short stories) were added. For all essays, the bibliographies—lists of the author's works and sources for further consultation—were revised to provide readers with the latest information.

A new feature for this edition is a sidebar in each essay called "Discussion Topics." They may address the writer's body of work, specific works, or life as it relates to his or her literature. Aimed at students, teachers, and members of reading groups, they can be used as paper topics or conversation points.

In addition, phonetic pronunciation is now provided for a profiled author's foreign-language or unusual last name upon its first mention in the main text—for example, Aeschylus (EHS-kuh-luhs). A Key to Pronunciation appears at the beginning of all six volumes.

FORMAT AND CONTENT

Magill's Survey of World Literature is arranged in an A-Z format, beginning with Japanese novelist and playwright Kōbō Abe and ending with French novelist Émile Zola. The essays vary from approximately six to thirteen pages in length. Each one begins with a block of reference information in a standard order:

- Name by which the author is best known
- **Born:** place and date
- **Died:** place and date
- A statement explaining the writer's literary importance

The main text is divided into the following sections:

- **Biography**—a chronological overview of the author's life, in many cases with a phonetic pronunciation of the author's name
- **Analysis**—a discussion about the author's style, dominant themes, and literary characteristics
- **Works**—profiles of one or more individual titles (novels, novellas, plays, poems, short stories, essays)

- **Summary**—one or two brief paragraphs summarizing the author's legacy

Each title section lists the year in which the work was first published. For short stories, poems, essays, or other short pieces, a collection of the author's works in which the reader can find the title is also indicated.

Every essay ends with a bibliography listing both the author's works in all genres (**By the Author**) and sources for further study (**About the Author**) and contains the thought-provoking "Discussion Topics" sidebar. All essays include the byline of the expert who wrote the entry. In addition, hundreds of author portraits and thumbnail photographs of book covers illustrate the text.

REFERENCE FEATURES

At the beginning of each volume are the Table of Contents for that volume, including the works featured in the title sections, and a Complete List of Contents for the entire set.

Five reference features can be found at the end of volume 6. A Glossary defines crucial literary terms for the reader, with examples from world literature. A Category List groups authors by genre, gender, and identity:

- Children's and Young Adult Literature Writers
- Gay or Bisexual Writers
- Jewish Writers
- Mystery and Detective Writers
- Nonfiction Writers
- Novelists
- Playwrights
- Poets
- Science-Fiction and Fantasy Writers
- Screenwriters
- Short-Story Writers
- Women

A Geographical List groups authors by country. The Title Index lists all featured works, while the Author Index lists all authors profiled in the set, along with their profiled works.

ACKNOWLEDGMENTS

We would like to thank our Editor, Steven G. Kellman, professor of literature at the University of Texas at San Antonio, for his invaluable expertise. We also owe our gratitude to all the outstanding writers who contributed material for this *Revised Edition* of *Magill's Survey of World Literature* and for the original set and its supplement. A list of their names and affiliations can be found in the front of volume 1.

CONTRIBUTORS

Randy L. Abbott
University of Evansville

Michael Adams
*City University of New York
Graduate Center*

Patrick Adcock
Henderson State University

Betty Alldredge
Angelo State University

M. D. Allen
University of Wisconsin—Fox Valley

Emily Alward
Henderson, Nevada, District Libraries

Anu Aneja
Ohio Wesleyan University

Raymond M. Archer
Indiana University, Kokomo

Stanley Archer
Texas A&M University

Gerald S. Argetsinger
Rochester Institute of Technology

William Atkinson
Kennesaw State College

Bryan Aubrey
Fairfield, Iowa

Charles Avinger
Washtenaw Community College

Jim Baird
University of North Texas

L. Michelle Baker
Shepherd University

Carl L. Bankston III
Tulane University

Paula C. Barnes
Hampton University

Carol M. Barnum
Southern Polytechnic State University

Henry J. Baron
Calvin College

David Barratt
Montreat College

Jane Missner Barstow
University of Hartford

Melissa E. Barth
Appalachian State University

Cynthia S. Becerra
Humphreys College

Richard P. Benton
Trinity College

Stephen Benz
Barry University

Donna Berliner
University of Texas, Dallas

Dorothy M. Betz
Georgetown University

Ksenija Bilbija
University of Wisconsin—Madison

Cynthia A. Bily
Adrian College

Margaret Boe Birns
New York University

Nicholas Birns
The New School

Franz G. Blaha
University of Nebraska—Lincoln

Nancy Blake
University of Illinois

Julia B. Boken
*State University of New York at
Oneonta*

Brinda Bose
Boston University

Beth Adams Bowser
Glenville, North Carolina

William Boyle
State University of New York, New Paltz

Beauty Bragg
Georgia College and State University

Gerhard Brand
California State University, Los Angeles

Jean R. Brink
Henry E. Huntington Library

Keith H. Brower
Salisbury State University

James S. Brown
Bloomsburg University

Carl Brucker
Arkansas Tech University

Jeffrey L. Buller
Florida Atlantic University

Susan Butterworth
Salem State College

Lawrence Byrne
Barry University

Ann M. Cameron
Indiana University, Kokomo

Edmund J. Campion
University of Tennessee

Henry L. Carrigan, Jr.
Northwestern University

Warren J. Carson
*University of South Carolina,
Spartanburg*

Hal Charles
Eastern Kentucky University

Cida S. Chase
Oklahoma State University

Allan Chavkin
Texas State University—San Marcos

John Steven Childs
Polytechnic University

David W. Cole
University of Wisconsin Colleges

Daniel L. Colvin
Western Illinois University

Michael L. Coulter
Grove City College

John W. Crawford
Henderson State University

Lee B. Croft
Arizona State University

Zachary W. Czaia
Catholic University of America

Laura Dabundo
Kennesaw College

Dolores A. D'Angelo
*Montgomery County Public Schools
Bethesda, Maryland*

Frank Day
Clemson University

Bill Delaney
San Diego, California

Joseph Dewey
University of Pittsburgh—Johnstown

M. Casey Diana
*University of Illinois,
Urbana-Champaign*

Carolyn F. Dickinson
Columbia College

Thomas Drucker
University of Wisconsin—Whitewater

Sarah Smith Ducksworth
Kean University

Margaret Duggan
South Dakota State University

Gweneth A. Dunleavy
University of Louisville

K Edgington
Towson University

Nada Elia
Western Illinois University

Robert P. Ellis
*Northborough, Massachusetts,
Historical Society*

Thomas L. Erskine
Salisbury University

Charlene Taylor Evans
Texas Southern University

Jack Ewing
Boise, Idaho

Kevin Farrell
The Catholic University of America

Nettie Farris
University of Louisville

Gisele C. Feal
State University of New York at Buffalo

James Feast
Baruch College

Thomas R. Feller
Nashville, Tennessee

John W. Fiero
University of Louisiana, Lafayette

Edward Fiorelli
St. John's University

Robert J. Forman
St. John's University

Carol Franks
Portland State University

Rachel E. Frier
The Catholic University of America

Terri Frongia
Santa Rosa Junior College

Jean C. Fulton
Maharishi International University

James Gaasch
Humboldt State University

Robert L. Gale
University of Pittsburgh

Ann D. Garbett
Averett University

Pat Ingle Gillis
Georgia Southern University

Erlis Glass
Rosemont College

Irene E. Gnarra
Kean College of New Jersey

Sheldon Goldfarb
University of British Columbia

Roy Neil Graves
University of Tennessee, Martin

John L. Grigsby
*Appalachian Research and Defense
Fund of Kentucky, Inc.*

William E. Grim
Ohio University

Daniel L. Guillory
Millikin University

M. Martin Guiney
Kenyon College

Natalie Harper
Simon's Rock College of Bard

Melanie Hawthorne
Texas A&M University

Peter B. Heller
Manhattan College

Terry Heller
Coe College

Diane Andrews Henningfeld
Adrian College

John Higby
Appalachian State University

John R. Holmes
Franciscan University of Steubenville

Joan Hope
Palm Beach Gardens, Florida

Gregory D. Horn
Southwest Virginia Community College

Pierre L. Horn
Wright State University

E. D. Huntley
Appalachian State University

Earl G. Ingersoll
*State University of New York
    at Brockport*

Archibald E. Irwin
Indiana University Southeast

Barry Jacobs
Montclair State College

D. Barton Johnson
*University of California,
    Santa Barbara*

Isaac Johnson
Pacific Union College

Jeff Johnson
Brevard Community College

Sheila Golburgh Johnson
Santa Barbara, California

Eunice Pedersen Johnston
North Dakota State University

Richard Jones
Stephen F. Austin State University

Tina Kane
Warwick, New York

Richard Keenan
University of Maryland—Eastern Shore

Douglas Keesey
*California Polytechnic State University,
    San Luis Obispo*

Steven G. Kellman
University of Texas, San Antonio

Rebecca Kelly
Southern College of Technology

Richard Kelly
University of Tennessee, Knoxville

Pamela Kett-O'Connor
Fargo, North Dakota

Leigh Husband Kimmel
Indianapolis, Indiana

Grove Koger
Boise State University

Kathleen L. Komar
University of California, Los Angeles

Wendy Alison Lamb
South Pasadena, California

David H. J. Larmour
Texas Tech University

Eugene Larson
Los Angeles Pierce College

Linda Ledford-Miller
University of Scranton

L. L. Lee
Western Washington University

Steven Lehman
John Abbott College

Leon Lewis
Appalachian State University

Thomas Tandy Lewis
St. Cloud State University

Anna Lillios
University of Central Florida

James L. Livingston
Northern Michigan University

Dana Loewy
University of Southern California

Stanley Longman
University of Georgia

Janet Lorenz
Los Angeles, California

Bernadette Flynn Low
*Community College of
    Baltimore County-Dundalk*

R. C. Lutz
Madison Advisors

Janet McCann
Texas A&M University

Joanne McCarthy
Tacoma, Washington

Sandra C. McClain
James Madison University

James McCorkle
Hobart and William Smith Colleges

Andrew Macdonald
Loyola University, New Orleans

Gina Macdonald
Nicholls State University

Ron McFarland
University of Idaho

Richard D. McGhee
Arkansas State University

Edythe M. McGovern
West Los Angeles College

Ric S. Machuga
Butte College

Dennis Q. McInerny
Holy Apostles College

S. Thomas Mack
University of South Carolina, Aiken

John L. McLean
Missouri Valley College

Dan McLeod
San Diego State University

Jennifer McLeod
California State University, Chico

Marian B. McLeod
Trenton State College

Victoria E. McLure
Texas Tech University

Magdalena Maczynska
Marymount Manhattan College

David W. Madden
California State University, Sacramento

Darryl F. Mallett
Sahuarita, Arizona

Barry Mann
Alliance Theatre

Lawrence K. Mansour
University of Maryland

Joss Lutz Marsh
Stanford University

Karen M. Cleveland Marwick
Hemel Hempstead, Hertfordshire,
England

Charles E. May
California State University, Long Beach

Laurence W. Mazzeno
Alvernia College

Kenneth W. Meadwell
University of Winnipeg

Patrick Meanor
State University of New York
at Oneonta

Julia Meyers
Duquesne University

Seth Michelson
University of Southern California

Vasa D. Mihailovich
University of North Carolina

Barbara Miliaras
University of Massachusetts, Lowell

Timothy C. Miller
Millersville University

Leslie B. Mittleman
California State University, Long Beach

Christian H. Moe
Southern Illinois University,
Carbondale

Charmaine Allmon Mosby
Western Kentucky University

John M. Muste
Ohio State University

Carolyn A. Nadeau
Pennsylvania State University

D. Gosselin Nakeeb
Pace University

William Nelles
University of Massachusetts,
Dartmouth

Terry Nienhuis
Western Carolina University

Ernest I. Nolan
Madonna University

Herbert Northcote
Temple University

George O'Brien
Georgetown University

Robert O'Connor
North Dakota State University

Linda Rohrer Paige
Georgia Southern University

Janet T. Palmer
Caldwell Community College and
Technical Institute

Margaret Parks
Kansas State University

David B. Parsell
Furman University

Pamela Pavliscak
University of North Carolina

Robert W. Peckham
Sacred Heart Major Seminary

Larry H. Peer
Brigham Young University

Thomas Amherst Perry
Texas A&M University—Commerce

Marion Petrillo
Bloomsburg University

Lela Phillips
Andrew College

Susan L. Piepke
Bridgewater College

Troy Place
Western Michigan University

Julie D. Prandi
Illinois Wesleyan University

Victoria Price
Lamar University

Charles Pullen
Queen's University, Canada

Josef Raab
University of Southern California

Thomas Rankin
Concord, California

John D. Raymer
Holy Cross College

Rosemary M. Canfield Reisman
Charleston Southern University

Elizabeth Richmond
University of Texas

Edward A. Riedinger
Ohio State University

Dorothy Dodge Robbins
Louisiana Tech University

Claire Robinson
Maharishi International University

Bernard F. Rodgers, Jr.
Simon's Rock College of Bard

Peter S. Rogers
Loyola University, New Orleans

Carl Rollyson
*Baruch College, City University
    of New York*

Paul Rosefeldt
Delgado Community College

Robert L. Ross
University of Texas, Austin

John K. Roth
Claremont McKenna College

Susan Rusinko
Bloomsburg University

Chaman L. Sahni
Boise State University

Dale Salwak
Citrus College

Elizabeth Sanders
Nicholls State University

Victor A. Santi
University of New Orleans

Richard Sax
Lake Erie College

Elizabeth D. Schafer
Loachapoka, Alabama

Kenneth Seib
Reno, Nevada

Richard J. Sherry
Asbury College

R. Baird Shuman
*University of Illinois,
    Urbana-Champaign*

Jack Siemsen
College of Idaho

Charles L. P. Silet
Iowa State University

Carl Singleton
Fort Hays State University

Jan Sjåvik
University of Washington

Genevieve Slomski
New Britain, Connecticut

Clyde Curry Smith
University of Wisconsin—Emeritus

Roger Smith
Portland, Oregon

Ronald E. Smith
University of North Alabama

Ira Smolensky
Monmouth College

Marjorie Smolensky
Monmouth College

Jean M. Snook
Memorial University of Newfoundland

George Soule
Carleton College

Hartley S. Spatt
*State University New York,
    Maritime College*

Maureen Kincaid Speller
University of Kent at Canterbury

Brian Stableford
Reading, Berkshire, England

Isabel B. Stanley
East Tennessee State University

Jill Stapleton-Bergeron
University of Tennessee

Elisabeth Stein
Tallahassee Community College

Ingo R. Stoehr
Kilgore College

Louise M. Stone
Bloomsburg University

Gerald H. Strauss
Bloomsburg University

James Sullivan
California State University, Los Angeles

Catherine Swanson
Austin, Texas

Roy Arthur Swanson
University of Wisconsin—Milwaukee

Sherri Szeman
Central State University

Nancy Conn Terjesen
Kent State University

Terry Theodore
*University of North Carolina,
    Wilmington*

Maxine S. Theodoulou
The Union Institute

Konny Thompson
Gonzaga University

Lou Thompson
Texas Woman's University

Jonathan L. Thorndike
Belmont University

Evelyn Toft
Fort Hays State University

Linda Jordan Tucker
Kennesaw State University

Richard Tuerk
Texas A&M University—Commerce

Complete List of Contents

Volume 1

Volume 2

Volume 3

Volume 4

Volume 5

Volume 6

KEY TO PRONUNCIATION

Foreign and unusual or ambiguous English-language names of profiled authors may be unfamiliar to some users of *Magill's Survey of World Literature*. To help readers pronounce such names correctly, phonetic spellings using the character symbols listed below appear in parentheses immediately after the first mention of the author's name in the narrative text. Stressed syllables are indicated in capital letters, and syllables are separated by hyphens.

Vowel Sounds

Symbol	Spelled (Pronounced)
a	answer (AN-suhr), laugh (laf), sample (SAM-puhl), that (that)
ah	father (FAH-thur), hospital (HAHS-pih-tuhl)
aw	awful (AW-fuhl), caught (kawt)
ay	blaze (blayz), fade (fayd), waiter (WAYT-ur), weigh (way)
eh	bed (behd), head (hehd), said (sehd)
ee	believe (bee-LEEV), cedar (SEE-dur), leader (LEED-ur), liter (LEE-tur)
ew	boot (bewt), lose (lewz)
i	buy (bi), height (hit), lie (li), surprise (sur-PRIZ)
ih	bitter (BIH-tur), pill (pihl)
o	cotton (KO-tuhn), hot (hot)
oh	below (bee-LOH), coat (koht), note (noht), wholesome (HOHL-suhm)
oo	good (good), look (look)
ow	couch (kowch), how (how)
oy	boy (boy), coin (koyn)
uh	about (uh-BOWT), butter (BUH-tuhr), enough (ee-NUHF), other (UH-thur)

Consonant Sounds

Symbol	Spelled (Pronounced)
ch	beach (beech), chimp (chihmp)
g	beg (behg), disguise (dihs-GIZ), get (geht)
j	digit (DIH-juht), edge (ehj), jet (jeht)
k	cat (kat), kitten (KIH-tuhn), hex (hehks)
s	cellar (SEHL-ur), save (sayv), scent (sehnt)
sh	champagne (sham-PAYN), issue (IH-shew), shop (shop)
ur	birth (burth), disturb (dihs-TURB), earth (urth), letter (LEH-tur)
y	useful (YEWS-fuhl), young (yuhng)
z	business (BIHZ-nehs), zest (zehst)
zh	vision (VIH-zhuhn)

MAGILL'S SURVEY OF
WORLD LITERATURE

Revised Edition

KŌBŌ ABE

Born: Tokyo, Japan
March 7, 1924
Died: Tokyo, Japan
January 22, 1993

Among the outstanding literary figures of modern Japan, Abe is a novelist and playwright of international recognition who is an observant commentator on contemporary life.

Library of Congress

BIOGRAPHY

Kōbō Abe (ahb-eh) was born on March 7, 1924, in Tokyo, Japan, during an interval when his Japanese father, a physician associated with the Manchurian School of Medicine in Mukden (later Shenyang), China, was in Japan on a research assignment. The family went to China shortly after the child was a year old. Abe remained in Mukden until he was sixteen. The experience of living outside his native country appears to have had a deep and lasting effect on Abe. The idea of one's homeland, traditionally very deeply ingrained in the Japanese, seems to have scarcely existed for Abe, according to his own comment about his early years. As a matter of fact, official family documents show him to have registered as a native of Hokkaido, the northern island of Japan. It is true that he lived in Hokkaido for several years, but Tokyo was indisputably his birthplace. Thus, Tokyo, where he was born, Mukden, the principal place where he was reared, and Hokkaido, the place of his family's origin, seemed to have little connection in the writer's mind. Abe himself is said to have commented that he was a "man without a hometown."

In 1941, Abe's parents sent him to Tokyo for school and for military training. His academic achievements there were not particularly noteworthy. When World War II broke out, Abe had ambivalent feelings. On the one hand, he found fascism and militarism to be utterly repugnant; on the other hand, the sense of patriotism triggered within him a desire to be identified with defending his country. When the time approached for Abe to make important decisions regarding his higher education, Abe enrolled as a medical student at the Tokyo Imperial University in 1943. He was not highly interested in becoming a physician, but he had no driving ambition to enter any other field either. Furthermore, his family applied pressure on him to follow in his father's footsteps, so he yielded to their wishes. While in medical school, he elected to specialize in gynecology. Not having been highly motivated to become a physician, he was bored by his studies, and on his first attempt he did not do very well on his examinations. When his professor learned that Abe did not plan to practice medicine, however, he was given a passing grade.

As a young man, Abe was interested in mathematics, in collecting insects, and in reading Japanese translations of such writers as Edgar Allan Poe, Fyodor Dostoevski, Franz Kafka, and the German philosophers Friedrich Nietzsche and Martin Heidegger. He made the decision to pursue literature as a career while he was still a medical student. Abe's medical background has influenced his writing. He has, for example, written science fiction. One of his science-fiction novels is *Daiyon kampyōki* (1958-1959, serial, 1959, book; *Inter Ice Age 4*, 1970).

Abe had a collection of poems privately printed in 1947. His first published fiction, *Owarishi michi no shirube ni* (as a signpost for the road), appeared in 1948, the same year he was graduated from medical school. Abe was not only a gifted novelist and short-story writer; he was also a playwright and producer. His own theatrical company often produced his plays.

As do many writers, Abe makes literary use of experiences and facts of his own life. For example, in Manchuria, where he was reared, deserts were familiar to him, and the shifting sands of *Suna no onna* (1962; *The Woman in the Dunes*, 1964) show the writer's knowledge of life amid the sands.

While Abe was still a medical student, he married an accomplished artist and stage designer; the couple followed independent careers. They had one daughter, Neri. Machi, his wife, has provided superior illustrations for many of her husband's works.

Abe died of heart failure in Tokyo on January 22, 1993. One of the foremost writers in Japan, he received several literary prizes: One short story, "Akai mayu" (1950; "Red Cocoon," 1966), won the Postwar Literature Prize. The play *Tomodachi* (pr., pb. 1967; *Friends*, 1969) was awarded the Tanizaki Jūn'ichirō Prize.

ANALYSIS

While numerous themes are developed in Kōbō Abe's works, few of them fail to incorporate aspects of alienation and loss of identity. Sometimes, his characters are alienated from other persons or from society. On other occasions, his characters are alienated from their own emotions, as in the story "Suichū toshi" (1952; the city under water), in which a character asks himself how he feels, only to find that his answer turns into a "hard substance." This concern with the effects of isolation is a central theme in Abe's best-known novel *The Woman in the Dunes*. In the work, a schoolteacher who is an amateur insect collector leaves the city to look for beetles in an area of sand dunes. He becomes trapped at the bottom of a deep hole, where a woman lives. She and the members of a village in the dunes keep him prisoner. Survival of the group depends on their daily success in battling the encroaching dunes. While he resists captivity at first, he gradually comes to the realization that his perceived prison of sand offers a kind of freedom that the city never offered him.

Trying to escape from stifling urban life is also thematically important to Abe, who sees modern humanity as lost in the urban setting. Abe com-

pares the city to a labyrinth, because people in it are always seeking, but never finding, a key to freedom. *Hako otoko* (1973; *The Box Man*, 1974) is an absurdist novel in which the protagonist cuts himself off from his fellows by taking up residence in a box that provides an anonymity and freedom denied him in everyday life. In *Tanin no kao* (1964; *The Face of Another*, 1966), the hero endeavors to fashion a new identity by concealing himself with a mask that hides his badly scarred face. In all three of these novels the heroes are alienated from contemporary life as a result of smothering urbanization. Abe's message—that the business world fragments and compartmentalizes human life, depriving people of human contact and causing an overwhelming degree of frustration—is clear in these novels and in most of his work.

Themes related to the loss of identity are frequently developed through metamorphoses. It has been suggested that metamorphosis in Abe's works are of two types, depending on the effects of the transformation on the character. In one type, the change is ultimately positive and allows a character to make a fresh start. In the other, the metamorphosis is negative because it is destructive. Several of Abe's early stories are of the first type. Of the second type, "Red Cocoon," whose title reveals the kind of change that takes place, is typical. The prizewinning *Kabe* (1951; the wall), in which a man changes into a section of a thick wall, is also an example of the second type. These transformations also serve as symbols of the inability to communicate. In a three-act play *Bō ni natta otoko* (pr., pb. 1969; *The Man Who Turned into a Stick*, 1975), people turn into sticks, and in so doing, they are deprived of language and sounds. This is a common theme in Abe's work.

Another common theme is the feeling of homelessness or ambivalence about where home is, which reflects Abe's life experience. In *Kemonotachi wa kokyō o mezasu* (1957; the beasts go homeward), the wilderness of Manchuria provides the setting. The search for the roots of existence that will serve to ground one's identity and the conflict between two kinds of homeland shed light on Abe's own conflict in being born in Japan but living in China during his formative years.

Along with metamorphosis and absurdity, another of Abe's preferred literary devices is turnabout or inversion of roles. For example, in *The*

Woman in the Dunes, the insect collector who catches beetles and pins them to a board is himself caught by the villagers, forced into a hole in the sand, and observed in much the same way that he has observed his insects. Similarly, in *Moetsukita chizu* (1967; *The Ruined Map*, 1969) a detective who undertakes to trace someone's missing husband not only fails to find the man but also ends up missing himself.

Perhaps more than any other writer, Abe has been compared with Franz Kafka. Some of the Kafkaesque characteristics of Abe's writing include the mixture of realistic detail with fantasy and the juxtaposition of accurate, concrete detail with fantastic and nightmarish settings or situations. Such combinations have led to Abe's being termed an absurdist novelist. There is a tone of realism in otherwise fantastic works, and the style is objective and logical.

THE WOMAN IN THE DUNES

First published: *Suna no onna*, 1962
   (English translation, 1964)
Type of work: Novel

Searching for his identity in a world of shifting sands, Niki Jumpei comes to terms with himself.

The Woman in the Dunes is Abe's most popular novel, no doubt in part because it was made into a film in 1963. The film was awarded the Special Jury Prize at the Cannes Film Festival in 1964. The story begins with the disappearance of Niki Jumpei, a young teacher. It traces Niki's difficult journey into his own consciousness and his finding his identity. The sand dunes, with their sands constantly encroaching upon the residents of the village that abducts Jumpei, are a powerful metaphor of one's struggle to discover one's identity.

Niki Jumpei likes to collect insects, so he goes one day to the sand dunes in a remote area, hoping to find some unusual ones for his collection. Once there, he becomes trapped at the bottom of a sand pit, only to discover that a woman lives there. She appears to think of him as a substitute for her dead husband.

Although there seems to be little meaningful life there, in order to survive at all, Niki must, daily, shovel away the sand that accumulates. Abe skillfully uses minute detail to make the reader remain ever aware of the completely invasive nature of the sand into every part of daily existence. After adapting somewhat, Niki then rejects this absurd life and fights to escape. During this period, he often abuses the woman with whom he shares the sand-pit home because  she accepts so passively what he is fighting to escape. Ultimately, however, Niki not only comes to terms with the strange kind of freedom that he finds in the dunes but also condones this life and opts for it over returning to the city in which he felt alienated. The ever-changing forms of the sand provide a parallel to the shifting realities of Niki's life. The absurdity of the sandy village is like that of his own personal world. One fantastic and improbable event after another occurs, but Abe's description of them is so accurate and so detailed that even the most unrealistic of them is made believable.

One of Abe's best novels, *The Woman in the Dunes*, illustrates most of the themes and literary methods that he uses in his work. In addition to the methods already discussed, another is the use of metaphor. In the novel, settings and characters are metaphors of human alienation. Another literary technique is Abe's frequent use of irony, which may also be found in *The Woman in the Dunes*. For example, the schoolteacher, after being captured, finds his treatment "outlandish." After all, he is an employed, taxpaying, productive person. *The Woman in the Dunes* is not completely grim, however. Abe uses humor and commentary on some of the qualities of human nature to relieve the tone of despair that might otherwise pervade the novel.

THE FACE OF ANOTHER

First published: *Tanin no kao*, 1964 (English translation, 1966)
Type of work: Novel

When a laboratory accident disfigures a chemist's face, he discovers that substituting a mask does not work.

The theme of alienation and lost identity, so common to Abe's work, is the focus of his novel *The Face of Another*. In a laboratory accident, a chemist sustains facial disfigurement so severe that he never appears, even at home, without bandages. In time, because of his lack of communication with his wife, he decides to get a lifelike mask in an effort to recover what he believes is his lost identity. A plastic surgeon agrees to make a mask, but he reminds the chemist that the mask, however perfect technically, will impose a new personality on him.

The novel contains numerous ironies. For example, it is precisely because of the unfortunate disfigurement, causing the chemist to wear a mask, that he is able to discover that one's face is not, in fact, one's real identity. The normal face, in fact, is as unreal as the mask, for it can conceal a self that is as ugly as a face that the mask might conceal. While it is true that initially the mask affords the chemist a new and more confident independence, he soon realizes that there is a negative side to having the mask as well. His need for a more normal relationship with his wife spurs him to test her love for him by trying to seduce her while wearing the new mask. He arranges for a clandestine meeting with his wife in a house other than his own, and the novel actually begins with an account of his waiting for her arrival. Meanwhile, he has been keeping notes in his diary of events related to the mask and his reactions to them, and he leaves the diary at home where his wife can find and read the entries. It turns out, however, that his wife was never deceived at all. She does not show up at the planned rendezvous. Instead, she leaves a note for her husband to find when he returns home, accusing him of being totally selfish in trying to manipulate her. She suggests that he needs a mirror, not her. The chemist refuses to accept her evaluation. He believes that thinking of oneself is always a result, not a cause, defending his belief by pointing out that it is the outside world that passes judgment on a person's value and "guarantees him the right to live." As the book ends, the chemist dons his mask and goes out into the streets.

A central message of the novel is that a mask is false and can no more be a person's identity than can the face with which that person is born. Ironically, however, using a mask enables one to look inward and realize that one's real self may be ugly, lonely, and alienated with or without a mask, and that an ideal self does not exist.

FRIENDS

First produced: *Tomodachi*, 1967 (first published, 1967; English translation, 1969)
Type of work: Play

When a family moves in with a young bachelor to save him from loneliness, they succeed only in destroying him.

Friends shows anything but friendship, which is the point of Abe's absurdist play. Though best known for his novels, he is a masterful surrealist playwright. Abe's plays have been compared to those of Edward Albee and Samuel Beckett. One critic has commented that in this play there is an inversion of the Golden Rule, which admonishes one to treat others as one would like to be treated. In *Friends*, a family, whose mission in life is rescuing lonely people, suddenly appears and moves in on a thirty-one-year-old bachelor in his apartment. Utter strangers, the family consists of an eighty-year-old grandmother, a mother and father, two sons, and three daughters.

The man is unsuccessful in getting the intruders to leave. He finally calls the police, who insist that he has no proof that they are trespassing, and because there is no visible sign of physical violence, they are not considered dangerous. The sweet smiles pasted on the family's faces lead the policemen to infer that perhaps the man is suffering from a persecution complex. Once the policemen are gone, the family members resume their mental torture of the man. Throughout the play, the image of a broken necklace has important symbolic associations. The family consider themselves called to mend lonely hearts in the same way that a string holds the beads of a necklace together. Almost all the family members comment on their being the string for the necklace.

Soon, the eldest daughter tries to seduce the bachelor; however, it is really one of her younger sisters who at least thinks she is in love with him. Within only a few days, the man loses his fiancé when she is won over by the family, who succeed in making the man look foolish and weak. Deliberately and systematically, they break his spirit and take away his freedom. Ultimately, they put him into a cage. He begins to behave like an animal, and, as his mental condition deteriorates, he assumes a fetal position and soon dies. Only the middle daughter shows any grief, and even she considers that the young man has turned against them. This social satire on sentimentality and on family life is filled with dry humor, which contributes to its bizarre tone.

SUMMARY

Displacement is a key theme of Kōbō Abe's works. This displacement can take the form of a person's being forced out of his or her home, as happens to the young man in *Friends*. It can also take the form of one's being displaced from one's own identity, as happens in many of Abe's works, including *The Face of Another*. Perhaps most memorably, Abe's works often present a displacement of the rational, whereby the absurd, the illogical, and the surreal invade and distort everyday reality. In many of Abe's works, people become such things as sticks, cocoons, or walls; they are placed in situations that their rational minds tell them cannot be happening. Such displacement is, in Abe's works, the result of modern society's rationalized, ordered, and imposed understanding of the human experience.

Victoria Price

BIBLIOGRAPHY

By the Author

LONG FICTION:
Owarishi michi no shirube ni, 1948
Baberu no tō no tanuki, 1951
Mahō no chōku, 1951
Kiga dōmei, 1954
Kemonotachi wa kokyō o mezasu, 1957
Daiyon kampyōki, 1958-1959 (serial); 1959 (book; *Inter Ice Age 4,* 1970)
Ishi no me, 1960
Suna no onna, 1962 (*The Woman in the Dunes,* 1964)
Tanin no kao, 1964 (*The Face of Another,* 1966)
Moetsukita chizu, 1967 (*The Ruined Map,* 1969)
Hako otoko, 1973 (*The Box Man,* 1974)
Mikkai, 1977 (*Secret Rendezvous,* 1979)
Hakobune sakura maru, 1984 (*The Ark Sakura,* 1988)
Kangarū nōto, 1991 (*The Kangaroo Notebook,* 1996)
Tobu otoko, 1994

DISCUSSION TOPICS

- Kōbō Abe was twenty-one years old when the atomic bombs were exploded in two Japanese cities. What effects of this experience do you detect in his literary works?

- In *The Face of Another,* to what extent is the chemist's attempt to test his wife's love for him unfair to her?

- Does the humor in *The Woman in the Dunes* successfully relieve the tone of despair? Justify your answer.

- Compare Abe's use of such devices as a man who turns into a wall or a stick with some of the transformations in Franz Kafka's fiction.

- How does Abe understand the concept of freedom?

DRAMA:

Seifuku, pr., pb. 1955

Yūrei wa koko ni iru, pr. 1958 (*The Ghost Is Here*, 1993)

Omae ni mo tsumi ga aru, pr., pb. 1965 (*You, Too, Are Guilty*, 1978)

Tomodachi, pr., pb. 1967 (*Friends*, 1969)

Bō ni natta otoko, pr., pb. 1969 (*The Man Who Turned into a Stick*, 1975)

Gikyoku zenshū, pb. 1970

Gaido bukku, pr. 1971

Imeji no tenrankai, pr. 1971 (pr. in the U.S. as *The Little Elephant Is Dead*, 1979)

Mihitsu no koi, pr., pb. 1971 (*Involuntary Homicide*, 1993)

Midoriiro no sutokkingu, pr., pb. 1974 (*The Green Stockings*, 1993)

Ue: Shin doreigari, pr., pb. 1975

Three Plays, pb. 1993

SHORT FICTION:

Kabe, 1951

Suichū toshi, 1964

Yume no tōbō, 1968

Four Stories by Kōbō Abe, 1973

Beyond the Curve, 1991

POETRY:

Mumei shishū, 1947

NONFICTION:

Uchinaro henkyō, 1971

MISCELLANEOUS:

Abe Kobo zenshū, 1972-1997 (30 volumes)

About the Author

Hibbett, Howard, ed. *Contemporary Japanese Literature*. New York: Alfred A. Knopf, 1977.

Iles, Timothy. *Abe Kōbō: An Exploration of His Prose, Drama, and Theatre*. Florence, Italy: European Press Academic, 2000.

Keene, Donald. *Five Modern Japanese Novelists*. New York: Columbia University Press, 2003.

Kimball, Arthur G. *Crisis in Identity and Contemporary Japanese Novels*. Rutland, Vt.: Charles E. Tuttle, 1973.

Kokusai Bunka Shinkokai [Japan Cultural Society]. *Introduction to Contemporary Japanese Literature, 1956-1970*. Tokyo: University of Tokyo Press, 1972.

Martins Janiera, Armando. *Japanese and Western Literature: A Comparative Study*. Rutland, Vt.: Charles E. Tuttle, 1970.

Rubin, Jay, ed. *Modern Japanese Writers*. New York: Charles Scribner's Sons, 2001.

Shields, Nancy K. *Fake Fish: The Theater of Kōbō Abe*. New York: Weatherhill, 1996.

Tsuruta, Kinya, and Thomas E. Swann, eds. *Approaches to the Modern Japanese Novel*. Tokyo: Sophia University Press, 1976.

Yamanouchi, Hisaaki. *The Search for Authenticity in Modern Japanese Literature*. New York: Cambridge University Press, 1978.

Chinua Achebe

Born: Ogidi, Nigeria
November 16, 1930

The first African writer to win broad critical acclaim in Europe and America, Achebe has shaped world understanding of Africa and its literature.

Rocon/Enugu, Nigeria

Biography

Chinua Achebe (ah-CHAY-bay) was born in Ogidi, in the Eastern Region of Nigeria, on November 16, 1930, to Isaiah and Janet Achebe, who christened their son Albert Chinualumogu—the former name after Queen Victoria's beloved consort and the latter a powerful name in Igbo—suggesting that strong inner forces stand aligned to fight for him. Isaiah Achebe, a catechist for the Church Missionary Society, and his wife traveled through eastern Nigeria as evangelists before settling in Ogidi, Isaiah's ancestral Igbo village, five years after Chinua Achebe's birth. Growing up in Ogidi, Achebe had contact with both Christian and Igbo religious beliefs and customs, but he developed a special affinity for his pagan uncle and his family.

Achebe's first lessons were in Igbo at the church school in Ogidi, but he began studying English at age eight. An avid reader and outstanding student, fourteen-year-old Achebe entered Government College, a highly selective secondary school in Umuahia taught in English; many of his classmates went on to become prominent figures in Nigerian public life, including the poet Christopher Okigbo, who later helped Achebe found the Citadel Press and who died in the civil war. Upon graduation, Achebe accepted a Major Scholars medical scholarship to University College in Ibadan (an associate college of the University of London), a highly prestigious award resulting from his having attained the top African scores on the colonial examinations, but after one year he switched to English literature, forfeiting his scholarship but receiving financial assistance from his older brother John and other relatives.

Achebe and the Yoruban playwright Wole Soyinka, later Nigeria's best-known authors, were undergraduates together at University College, each publishing his first work as undergraduates. Achebe's first published fiction, "Polar Undergraduate," later collected in *Girls at War, and Other Stories* (1972), satirizes student behavior. In his third year he edited the *University Herald*. The short stories produced while in school include "The Old Order in Conflict with the New" and "Dead Man's Path." After graduation in 1953, he took a producing position for the Nigerian Broadcasting Corporation (NBC).

Achebe had sent his only copy of *Things Fall Apart* to a British typist, who set it aside without a glance, but his NBC superior Angela Beattie rescued it. *Things Fall Apart* was published in 1958 and won the Margaret Wrong Memorial Prize in 1959 for its contribution to African literature. If Achebe had never written anything else he would still stand as an acclaimed author because of the power and influence of that single volume, translated into fifty languages and selling more than eight million copies. In 1960, the year of Nigeria's independence, Achebe published *No Longer at Ease*, winner of the Nigerian National Trophy. He spent the remainder of 1960 and part of 1961 traveling through east Africa and interviewing other African writers. Back in Nigeria, he held a number of offices with the Nigerian Broadcasting Company, including talks director, controller, and director of the Voice of Nigeria in Lagos. He married Christie Chinwe Okoli, with whom he fathered two sons, Ikechukwu and Chidi, and two daughters, Chinelo and Nwando. His own children inspired his children's stories.

In 1962, Achebe became the founding editor of Heinemann's African Writers series, and in 1963, he traveled in the United States, Brazil, and Britain on a UNESCO (United Nations Educational, Social, and Cultural Organization) fellowship. Achebe published *Arrow of God* (1964), receiving the Jock Campbell Award from *New Statesman* in 1965 for his accomplishment. Publication of the prophetic novel *A Man of the People* (1966) was followed by successive military coups, massacres of Igbos, and the secession of Biafra in 1967. Forced to leave Lagos after the second coup, during the Nigerian civil war Achebe became a spokesperson for the Biafran cause in Europe and North America and served as a senior research fellow at the University of Nigeria in Nsukka, renamed the University of Biafra during the war.

After three years of bitter struggle, Biafra surrendered, and Achebe, more dedicated than ever to preserving Igbo culture, began editing *Okike: An African Journal of New Writing*. He published his literary response to the war in *Beware, Soul Brother, and Other Poems* (1971) and *Girls at War, and Other Stories*, winning the Commonwealth Poetry Prize in 1972 for *Beware, Soul Brother, and Other Poems*, published in the United States as *Christmas in Biafra, and Other Poems* (1973).

From 1972 to 1976, Achebe taught at the University of Massachusetts in Amherst, where his wife earned a doctorate, and at the University of Connecticut. After the 1976 assassination of Nigerian President Murtala Mohammed, for whom Achebe had great respect, the author returned to teach at the University of Nigeria at Nsukka. In 1979, Achebe was elected chairman of the Association of Nigerian Authors and received the Nigerian National Merit Award and the Order of the Federal Republic. In 1982, he and Obiora Udechukwu edited *Aka weta: Egwu aguluagu egwu edeluede* (1982; aka weta: an anthology of Igbo poetry).

Disillusioned by President Shehu Shagari's failure to fight the corruption impoverishing Nigeria and saddened by the death of Mallam Aminu Kano, the leader of the People's Redemption Party (PRP), Achebe served as deputy national president of the PRP in the election year of 1983. In a small pamphlet, *The Trouble with Nigeria* (1983), he presented his political prescription for improving Nigeria. After Shagari's reelection and removal from office by a subsequent military coup, Achebe once again concentrated his energies on artistic and cultural projects, editing the bilingual *Uwa ndi Igbo: A Journal of Igbo Life and Culture*. In 1986, he was appointed pro-vice chancellor of the State University of Anambra at Enugu.

Nigeria's Civil War and resultant political conflicts so horrified Achebe that he could not write long fiction. Believing that art must guide readers to examine moral issues and offer lessons to lead them to better lives, he feared whatever he said might be turned to the service of destruction, oppression, or evil. Finally, in 1987 he published his first novel in more than twenty years, *Anthills of the Savannah* (1987), and he returned to teach at the University of Massachusetts in Amherst (where he met author James Baldwin), the City College of New York, and Bard College. In 1988, he published a collection of essays titled *Hopes and Impediments*. In 1990, a serious car accident on the Lagos-Ibanan expressway and the lag time between injury and medical care left Achebe paralyzed from the waist down and confined to a wheelchair.

In 1992, Achebe, threatened with imprisonment, fled the repressive Nigerian regime to Europe, only to return to serve as president of the Ogidi town union, an honorary position recognizing his dedication to his ancestors' ancient stories. He then served as the Charles P. Stevenson Professor of Languages and Literature at Bard College for fifteen years. In the meantime, Biyi Bandele converted *Things Fall Apart* into a play, produced in 1997 by the Performance Studio Workshop of Nigeria and presented as part of the Kennedy Center's African Odyssey series the next year. In 1999, Achebe was appointed goodwill ambassador to the United Nations Population Fund (UNFPA), encouraging family planning and reproductive health worldwide. In *Home and Exile* (2000), Achebe evaluated the past seventy years of African literature, his lifetime. The same year, fellow Igbo, novelist, and critic Phanuel Egejuru collected tribute names for her authoritative biography *Chinua Achebe: Plain and Simple* (2001), in which other Africans praised Achebe as both "teacher" and "double eagle" in recognition of his bridging two worlds: Africa and the West.

In 2003, Kenyan Catholics tried to ban *A Man of the People* from their school curricula; in 2004,

Achebe rejected an award from the Nigerian government to protest its tyranny. Achebe won the 2007 Man Booker International Prize for fiction. In 2008, he was working on a short novel on ancient myths to be part of The Canongate Myth Series. That year also marked the fiftieth anniversary of the publication of *Things Fall Apart*, which was celebrated by conferences and tributes worldwide.

ANALYSIS

Achebe establishes a human context for understanding modern Nigerian history. *Things Fall Apart* describes the devastating first contacts between European and Igbo cultures at the beginning of the twentieth century and bends over backwards to demonstrate good and bad on both sides. The subsequent institutionalization of European religious and political structures is examined in *Arrow of God;* the uneasy years immediately preceding independence are explored in *No Longer at Ease*; the excitement and disappointment of Nigeria's First Republic are the subjects of *A Man of the People*; the suffering produced by the Nigerian civil war is the theme of *Girls at War, and Other Stories* and *Beware, Soul Brother, and Other Poems*; and the corrupt authoritarianism that has characterized Nigeria's Second Republic is the focus of *Beware, Soul Brother, and Other Poems* and *Anthills of the Savannah*. Indeed, the title of his commentary, *The Trouble with Nigeria*, identifies a concern central to his entire canon.

As a corrective to European literature's stereotypical portraits of Africans as unvaryingly backwards, Achebe demonstrates the value and viability of traditional Igbo culture, describes Nigerians as complex human beings with a strong sense of community and tolerance, and establishes the independence of African literature. In "The Role of a Writer in a New Nation," he identifies his first priority: to inform the world that "African peoples did not hear of culture for the first time from Europeans; that their societies were not mindless . . . that they had poetry and, above all, they had dignity." Achebe, however, does not idealize the precolonial past, for he knows that it could not have survived unaltered in a modern world; instead, he shows built-in systems for communities and individuals and explores continuities with the past that can coexist with modern society.

Achebe's conflicted protagonists, torn between self-realization and social responsibility, demonstrate the difficulty of attaining such a balance. The destructive pull of individual pride thwarts each character's movement toward communal acceptance. In *Things Fall Apart*, Okonkwo overcomes personal humiliation to win community respect, but his inflexible refusal to accommodate himself to the increasing influence of colonial government and Christianity alienates him from his clan and drives him to violence that necessitates personal sacrifice. In *Arrow of God*, the priest Ezeulu earnestly wishes to be a good religious leader, but his proud refusal to adapt religious dictates to the necessities of circumstance leads to Christian dominance in his village and to his own madness. In *No Longer at Ease*, the idealistic Obi self-righteously resists the corruption of government service, alienating himself from his fellow civil servants and the clan members who funded his education (Achebe's touch of self-deprecating autobiography); yet when his proud need to maintain an expensive lifestyle leads him to accept a bribe, his amateurish attempt results in his arrest. In *A Man of the People*, the cynical Odili, who collaborates in Nanga's political manipulation of rural people, learns to see the corrective value of traditional beliefs. *Anthills of the Savannah* offers the most hopeful view, with Beatrice showing that traditional values can exist in altered but viable forms in the present.

In his fiction, Achebe opposes interpersonal, political, cultural, and linguistic forms of authoritarianism. He associates inflexible refusal to recognize the validity of multiple viewpoints—the central flaw of his protagonists—with the cultural arrogance of colonial powers and the cynical greed of Nigerian officials. Stylistically, Achebe refutes this myopic authoritarianism through multiple perspectives and irony. In *Anthills of the Savannah*, he repeats the Igbo proverb, "Where something stands, there also something else will stand," to indicate his belief in the fluidity of perception, the duality of existence, and the adaptability of Igbo culture. He represents this fluidity in his fiction by mixing literary English, pidgin English, and a colloquial English that approximates the rhythms of Igbo speech; he also mixes Igbo proverbs, songs, and rituals with allusions to European literature and uses irony and unreliable narrators to question authoritarian voices. To create an open, nonauthoritarian view, Achebe balances one novel against another; thus, the naïvely idealistic Obi Okonkwo of *No Longer at Ease* is a tragicomic version of his grandfather, Okonkwo, in *Things Fall Apart*. Achebe's decision to write in English instead of his native Igbo broadened his work to include a worldwide audience but brought criticism that he was assisting in the destruction of Igbo culture. He, in turn, blamed the missionaries' mangled translations of the Bible for destroying the Igbo language, but he has since moved toward greater use of native languages by editing the Igbo poetry anthology *Aka Weta* and the bilingual journal *Uwa ndi Igbo.*

Achebe has been an active, visible public figure in Nigeria since the 1950's, and, not surprisingly, his writings parallel his personal experiences. His early sympathetic portrayals of traditional Igbo culture were, in part, gestures toward expiating his own guilt over the rare educational privileges that he enjoyed. His skillful satire of the abuse of power and language in books such as *A Man of the People* mocks his own involvement in the development of Nigeria's mass media. After the Nigerian civil war, in which Achebe and many other Igbo writers took an active part, his writings became more directly utilitarian and political. After teaching in the United States made him realize that the most widely taught book concerning Africa was Joseph Conrad's *Heart of Darkness* (1899, serial; 1902, book), Achebe became more sympathetic to African authors who renounced the use of colonial languages and more aware of the extent to which Americans and Europeans misunderstand and ignore Africa's problems.

THINGS FALL APART

First published: 1958
Type of work: Novel

A warrior opposing colonialism's threat to Igbo culture strikes back and must sacrifice himself and his reputation to save his village and achieve personal balance.

Achebe's title from William Butler Yeats's poem "The Second Coming" invokes an ironic, apocalyptic vision warning of a new order from Africa that will destroy the status quo; thus, the novel describes the European destruction of Igbo culture but suggests a potential future shift of power reinvigorating Africa, a theme in Achebe's later work *Home and Exile. Things Fall Apart* disproves white stereotypes of Igbo as primitive savages, amoral and unsophisticated, and asserts the viability of preconquest Igbo culture through the tragic story of Okonkwo and his village. A warrior determined to counter the reputation of his lazy imprudent father, Okonkwo wins community respect and titles for his hard work, public service, and martial courage. However, this hero, like William Shakespeare's Coriolanus, is flawed. His obsessive fear of repeating his father's failures drives him to extremes in a culture proud of its balance. Humorless and short-tempered, he beats his wife in the Week of Peace, alienates his son with reprimands, joins the ritual killing of a boy he considers a son just to appear manly, and accidentally shoots a youth, resulting in his seven-year banishment to his mother's village.

This period of separation distances him from the communal life of Umuofia, so while still ambitious after his return, he now appreciates the bonds of kinship and the comfort of a community speaking with one voice. Unfortunately, he fails to understand the inroads the British have made on his community. Christianity in particular divides families and undermines traditional systems of government, justice, and religion. His eldest son's conversion to Christianity separates Okonkwo from his lineage, and when another convert desecrates a traditional totem, Okonkwo leads the Umuofians in destroying the missionaries' church. Like Okonkwo, the Umuofians face separation from their past and a future requiring difficult compromises; yet Achebe carefully shows that the decentralized structure of Igbo society allows for such change.

Okonkwo, personally unwilling to adapt to cultural change and believing that his fellow Umuofians will wage war against the whites who have insulted their representatives, murders the district commissioner's messenger. However, the village understands that this act will bring retaliation, possibly the deaths of everyone in the village, as happened to neighboring Abame. At the end of the novel, Okonkwo proves his worth and restores balance to his life and to his village by committing a womanly act, suicide, that renounces everything he has stood for but protects his people. His friend, Obierta, calls Okonkwo the best man among them, for he has given up his place in the memories of his people so they will not suffer from his act. He is an exceptional individual whose final act both restores him to his clan and forever alienates him from it. Okonkwo's Christlike sacrifice confirms that Umuofia is a living culture capable of adapting to meet new challenges.

The central theme of all Achebe's novels is the tragedy created by the British contempt for African religion, law, culture, and people, yet Igbo accommodation to change remains a survival mechanism enabling Africans to endure untold hardships. In *Things Fall Apart*, Achebe effectively refutes European stereotypes of African culture, offering instead a complex, fluid portrait of Igbo culture as essentially democratic, pluralistic, tolerant, and community-centered. It is, however, a society whose acceptance of difference within its community assured dramatic future change after English hegemony.

No Longer at Ease

First published: 1960
Type of work: Novel

An idealistic young Nigerian bureaucrat, trapped between his traditional background and his European education, succumbs to the corrupting influences of government service.

Achebe's title *No Longer at Ease* from Yeats's "Sailing to Byzantium" suggests that like the wise men in Yeats's poem, Obi Okonkwo, a young civil servant in the colonial Nigerian government, and his nation are trapped between two eras. Like his grandfather Okonkwo in *Things Fall Apart*, who stands for the vanishing traditional African, Obi stands for the vanishing idealist in a world of compromise. Ironically, *No Longer at Ease* opens and

closes at Obi's bribery trial. The novel provides a retrospective look at Obi's progress from the remote village of Umuofia to an English university and then to a position with the Nigerian civil service in Lagos, where he finally succumbs to the prevalent practice of bribery and is caught. A diminished version of his grandfather, Obi is crushed by cultural forces beyond his control, but the pettiness and ineptitude of his crime make him a paradoxical tragicomic hero. His innocence makes him a criminal; his coveted education does not provide him with wisdom; and the support of his clanspeople increases his sense of loneliness.

Obi is the first from his village to receive a European education, his expenses paid by clan members hoping to enhance the status of their village and reap future economic dividends. However, idealistic romance and failure to manage his finances complicate Obi's life. He falls in love with a woman marked by a traditional, hereditary taboo that Obi rejects as primitive superstition, but his naïve determination to be thoroughly modern places him in direct conflict with family and clan. At first, he eschews the customary practice of accepting bribes, self-righteously viewing doing so as anachronistic behavior that the new generation of educated, idealistic civil servants will eradicate, but his obligation to repay the clan and his determination to maintain a lifestyle commensurate with his civil service position eventually lead him to accept payments. When he succumbs to custom, he handles the bribery so amateurishly that he is caught and convicted.

Although Obi has been shaped by the traditional Igbo culture of Umuofia, the Christianity of his father, the idealism of English literature, and the corrupt sophistication of Lagos, he is at ease nowhere. As a child, he dreamt of the sparkling lights of Lagos. In England, he writes pastoral visions of an idealized Nigeria. Disillusioned by the corruption of Lagos, he returns to his home village only to witness a truck driver attempting to bribe a policeman and to have his parents' reject his proposed marriage. Obi naïvely tries to maintain the idea of his own integrity as a detribalized, rational, thoroughly modern man, but his reintegration into Nigeria fails because he cannot assimilate successfully any of the competing cultures through which he passes. He finds it impossible to mediate the conflicting duties thrust upon him, and his steady progress in the novel is toward despair and withdrawal.

No Longer at Ease, set in Lagos on the verge of Nigeria's independence, depicts an urban jungle that combines the worst of European and African cultures. Centralization has led to inefficiency and corruption; traditional Igbo communalism has devolved to the narrow pursuit of advantage. Having learned the Western desire for material goods without having sufficient income to satisfy them, Obi, like the nation, must choose between corruption and bankruptcy.

HOME AND EXILE

First published: 2000
Type of work: Essays

Achebe surveys his life experiences as he defended Nigeria and Nigerians, countering imperialist assaults on that home with Nigerian perspectives, finding balance even in exile.

The title *Home and Exile* summarizes the essence of this work: Achebe's discovery of Igbo values and ways as his true home, despite years abroad, an exile paralleling the Igbo experiences with oppressive European literature undermining their sense of worth, defining them as primitive savages, and justifying European ways as superior. The book consists of three lectures delivered over a three-day period, December 9-11, 1998, at Harvard University: "My Home Under Imperial Fire," "The Empire Fights Back," and "Today, the Balance of Stories."

The first essay records Achebe's youthful discovery of Nigeria as his spiritual and intellectual home when his missionary family retired and returned to their ancestral home. Achebe developed a love of

Igbo ways and a deep-seated desire to attack denigrators. He rejects the word "tribe" as a racist misnomer, asserting that the Igbo are neither "primitive" nor bound by blood ties, with their language complex, including major and minor dialects, and their sociopolitical identity purposefully defined by disdain for the concept of a single ruler. He finds the term "nation" more appropriate for a loose federation of people with strong individual identities, loyalty to independent towns or ministates, a love of competition and controversy, and a marketing network for disseminating goods and news. He emphasizes the Igbo love of song, dance, proverbs, and storytelling and so deep-seated a tolerance of difference that they refuse to impose their religious beliefs even on outsiders seeking to join them. He depicts his formal education as Eurocentric but describes a landmark rebellion when, in 1952, a class of Nigerian university students rejected as absurd author Joyce Cary's derogatory racial stereotyping in *Mister Johnson* (1939). This rebellion led the young Achebe to scrutinize the connection between the slave trade and literature written to justify it and to recognize the appropriation of his homeland by imperialistic propaganda.

Achebe's second essay, "The Empire Fights Back," explores his outrage at racist depictions of his people and home, his decision to fight back in novels providing Nigerian perspectives, and his willingness to face considerable trouble to tell worthy stories. He contrasts the works of Joseph Conrad and Elspeth Huxley with F. J. Pedler's call for authentic African literary voices in *West Africa* (1951), and he deplores the mind-set that led British-educated Africans to mock Amos Tutuola's *The Palm-Wine Drinkard and His Dead Palm-Wine Tapster in the Dead's Town* (1952) for presenting an African perspective. For Achebe, the launching of Heinemann's African Writers Series marked the turning point in African literature, rejecting imperialist voices in favor of true Africans. He ends with Jomo Kenyatta's parable of British imperial practices, "The Gentlemen of the Jungle," to demonstrate African writers fighting back.

The final essay praises Salman Rushdie's description of postcolonial literature as "The Empire Writes Back," W. E. B. Du Bois's hopes for racial parity, and Ama Ata Aidoo's sympathetic tales of the afflicted poor, but it criticizes V. S. Naipaul's imperialist rejection of impoverished peoples and Rushdie's assertion that literature can exist apart from a writer's national roots. Achebe concludes that African literature has found its voice since the 1950's and that such literature finds its worth, not in a universal civilization, but in a writer's home. African writers long exiled from their heritage by literature justifying imperial conquest have found their literary home in Africa, whether they live there or in exile from it.

SUMMARY

A socially and politically committed storyteller and writer who has garnered worldwide critical acclaim, Chinua Achebe has, more than any other African author writing in English, redefined modern African literature and helped the world value African culture without ignoring the difficult problems postcolonial African nations face. For a lifetime, he has battled the corrosive effects of racism on individuals and on Africa as a whole. He writes about Africa for Africans, bridging three periods: from the colonial era of his birth, to the years of nationalist protest of his youth, to the modern age of Nigerian independence and the oppressive regimes that have dominated his country. His novels examine more than one hundred years of Igbo culture. *Things Fall Apart* will undoubtedly remain Achebe's best-known work, but his entire canon makes a consistent and central contribution to the world's literature.

Carl Brucker; updated by Gina Macdonald and Elizabeth Sanders

BIBLIOGRAPHY

By the Author

LONG FICTION:
Things Fall Apart, 1958
No Longer at Ease, 1960
Arrow of God, 1964
A Man of the People, 1966
Anthills of the Savannah, 1987

SHORT FICTION:
"Dead Men's Path," 1953
The Sacrificial Egg, and Other Stories, 1962
Girls at War, and Other Stories, 1972

POETRY:
Beware: Soul Brother, and Other Poems, 1971, 1972 (pb. in U.S. as *Christmas in Biafra, and Other Poems*, 1973)
Collected Poems, 2004

NONFICTION:
Morning Yet on Creation Day, 1975
The Trouble with Nigeria, 1983
Hopes and Impediments, 1988
Conversations with Chinua Achebe, 1997 (Bernth Lindfors, editor)
Home and Exile, 2000

CHILDREN'S LITERATURE:
Chike and the River, 1966
How the Leopard Got His Claws, 1972 (with John Iroaganachi)
The Drum, 1977
The Flute, 1977

EDITED TEXTS:

Don't Let Him Die: An Anthology of Memorial Poems for Christopher Okigbo, 1932-1967, 1978 (with Dubem Okafor)

Aka weta: Egwu aguluagu egwu edeluede, 1982 (with Obiora Udechukwu)

African Short Stories, 1985 (with C. L. Innes)

Beyond Hunger in Africa, 1990 (with others)

The Heinemann Book of Contemporary African Short Stories, 1992 (with Innes)

MISCELLANEOUS:

Another Africa, 1998 (poems and essay; photographs by Robert Lyons)

About the Author

Booker, M. Keith, and Simon Gikandi. *The Chinua Achebe Encyclopedia.* Westport, Conn.: Greenwood, 2003.

Egar, Emmanuel Edame. *The Rhetorical Implications of Chinua Achebe's "Things Fall Apart."* Lanham, Md.: University Press of America, 2000.

Egejuru, Phanuel Akubueze. *Chinua Achebe: Pure and Simple, an Oral Biography.* Stoke-on-Trent, England: Malthouse Press, 2001.

Emenyonu, Ernest N., ed. *Emerging Perspectives on Chinua Achebe.* Trenton, N.J.: Africa World Press, 2004.

Jaya Lakshmi, Rao V. *Culture and Anarchy in the Novels of Chinua Achebe.* Bareilly, India: Prakash Book Depot, 2003.

Mezu, Rose Ure. *Chinua Achebe: The Man and His Works.* London: Adonis and Abbey, 2006.

Ogede, Ode. *Achebe and the Politics of Representation: Form Against Itself, from Colonial Conquest and Occupation to Post-Independence Disillusionment.* Trenton, N.J.: African World Press, 2001.

Okpewho, Isidore, ed. *Chinua Achbebe's Things Fall Apart: A Casebook.* Oxford, England: Oxford University Press, 2003.

Yousaf, Nahem. *Chinua Achebe.* Tavistock, England: Northcote House, 2003.

DISCUSSION TOPICS

- Examine Chinua Achebe's ideas about conflict, violence, and war in at least two of his works. What do humans do to other humans, and why? Who or what do people blame for things going wrong? Provide examples to support your assertions.

- According to Achebe, the traditional African way of life fell apart and Africa is now a corrupt imitation of European systems, religions, and manners. What things "fell apart" with the coming of the Europeans? What valuable aspects of African culture have been lost?

- Examine the nature of Achebe's heroes. For example, what makes Okonkwo in *Things Fall Apart* or Ezeulu in *Arrow of God* tragic heroes? Are they heroes in the Western tradition?

- How does Achebe depict the role of women in Igbo culture? What is the significance of the proverb "Mother is supreme"? Consider how Okonkwo's attitudes toward women help bring about his fall or their invention of a new kind of storytelling in *Anthills of the Savannah*.

- Outline the structure of one of Achebe's novels or chapters. Is it loose or tight? What role does repetition play? Can topic ideas be readily identified or are they buried in the text? How does the structure relate to his message and/or goals?

- What parallels do you find between the fictional state of Kangan in *Anthills of the Savannah* and Idi Amin's Uganda? Why would Achebe create a fictional African state rather than write directly about Nigeria or Biafra?

- In stories like "Dead Man's Path," Achebe pits traditional ways and beliefs against European ways and attitudes. Provide examples of such conflicts from his works.

DOUGLAS ADAMS

Born: Cambridge, England
   March 11, 1952
Died: Santa Barbara, California
   May 11, 2001

Adams was a pioneer in both humor and science fiction and was among the first to combine the two genres, creating The Hitchhiker's Guide to the Galaxy *and other popular novels.*

BIOGRAPHY

Douglas Noel Adams was born in 1952 in Cambridge, England, where he spent much of his early life and his years of education. Adams's signature trait was unpredictability. He was master of the unexpected—when his life story trudged toward the usual university chapter, Adams set off on a hitchhiking trip through Europe that stimulated one of his most innovative ideas: a hitchhiker's guide to the galaxy.

The years at Cambridge University for Adams were centered not so much on studying English as on Footlights, the undergraduate comedy society that he shared with his lifelong comedic hero John Cleese, a member of the Monty Python comedy troupe. Like many Footlighters, Adams attained fame in the comedy world, contributing to episodes of *Monty Python's Flying Circus* and the science-fiction series *Dr. Who.* He was inspired by such popular icons as his literary favorites P. G. Wodehouse and Kurt Vonnegut and was influenced even more by the Beatles.

Adams's career took off with *The Hitchhiker's Guide to the Galaxy* (1979). The popular series started out as a radio program for the British Broadcasting Corporation (BBC) that aired from 1978 through 1980; he adapted the program as a book in 1979 and a television series in 1981, and it later was used as the basis of an animated film, a computer game, and a feature-length film. He extended the Hitchhiker's series with *The Restaurant at the End of the Universe* (1980); *Life, the Universe, and Everything* (1982); and *So Long, and Thanks for All the Fish* (1984). This popular success secured Adams's fame in the world of comedy and ushered him into the world of science fiction. Adams attended science-fiction conventions, campaigning for humor there at the same time that he promoted science fiction to humor fans.

Adams went in a new direction in his next novel *Dirk Gently's Holistic Detective Agency* (1987), the story of a private detective with a holistic approach to solving his cases; he followed it with a sequel, *The Long Dark Tea-Time of the Soul,* in 1988. He returned to the Hitchhiker's series in his final novel, *Mostly Harmless* (1992).

Adams married Jane Elizabeth Belson in 1991, and the couple had a daughter, Polly. An atheist, Adams was so opposed to the christening of his daughter that he invented his own naming ceremony. He placed his faith in science, not in religion. Science was his way of making sense of the universe: He tried to understand the universe better so he could better display it to his readers from his eye-opening perspective.

To the ongoing chagrin of his publishers, Adams rarely met a publication deadline. At one point, a frustrated publisher insisted that he end the sentence he was writing and send in a manuscript. The book was published, as was a sequel that tied the loose ends that the half sentence created.

In 2001, Adams was in Los Angeles to adapt *The Hitchhiker's Guide to the Galaxy* for a feature film. He suffered a heart attack and died in Santa Barbara, California, on May 11, 2001, at the age of forty-nine. Adams had produced some of the most innovative, most enjoyed, and—in their own way—most inspiring works to come out of twentieth century England.

ANALYSIS

Humor is the keystone of Douglas Adams's fiction. His sense of humor is decidedly understated, influenced by the deadpan Monty Python school of laughs. He has a knack for distilling something as impossibly complicated as the Ultimate Answer to the Universe into a two-digit number. He can take something as simple as a bath towel and instill it with such cosmic significance that readers may want to meditate on their linen closets. His style of humor relies on unexpected narrative turns delivered by means of witty twists of the English language. His linguistic deftness and narrative adroitness enable Adams to make readers regularly laugh out loud.

His innovative views of the universe allow readers to step back from the status quo and look at things from a different perspective. Both reader and protagonist are provoked into viewing life afresh on virtually every page of his novels through delightfully unnerving story lines that tend to make readers smile and the protagonist scratch his head wondering where he can find a good cup of tea.

Adams pokes fun at virtually everyone. He satirizes governments, bureaucracy, business, technology, philosophers, dictionaries, airports, politicians, bad poets, queues—anything in which he can place his cosmic comic barbs. He is an equal-opportunity satirizer, pointing out the flaws of almost everything while simultaneously dramatizing its unrealized potential.

Adams's fiction is replete with imagined technology—technology that pretends to improve life while actually complicating it. Characters in this fiction may find themselves battling some computer program or automated coffee maker to complete a simple task. Adams was a fan of cutting-edge technology who saw that newfangled gadgets could make life more difficult. The familiarity of that disillusionment may be why readers can easily relate to the many absurd situations that Adams's characters experience.

Religious disbelief shows up frequently in Adams's works in the form of philosophical questions. Characters constantly search for the meaning of life, always unsuccessfully. The nihilistic Adams depicts humankind's utter insignificance in the vast realms of the universe. His whimsical evidence for the existence of God tends to make the possibility of the divine disappear altogether. He negates not only God and humanity but the universe itself, describing the destruction of the cosmos as the "gnab gib," the opposite (and reverse spelling) of the "big bang," in which the universe was created.

Adams's novels tend to be episodic, following colorful characters around the universe as they battle illogic, gravity, and deadlines. His picturesque and picaresque characters grandly traverse time and space in interstellar slapstick adventures. He often features an Everyman character with whom readers can readily relate, a normal human being from Earth. This unlikely hero is thrust into extreme circumstances, forced to deal with crises ranging from zero gravity to galactic protocol to depressed robots. These Everyman heroes are not extremely intelligent, not particularly good-looking, not even skilled with automatic firearms; the typical Adams protagonist experiences his biggest thrill when walking to his mailbox.

Adams places his characters in outlandish plots. For example, the mailbox might explode at the moment the protagonist goes to open it or a character might find himself unsuspectingly teleported into a passing spaceship and a cascade of increasingly improbable events that render him confused and vulnerable. The predicaments of these characters make readers realize that they are not the only ones in the cosmos who are overwhelmed; readers share awkward moments with Adams's protagonists, who are subjected to situations that test their abilities to adapt.

THE HITCHHIKER'S GUIDE TO THE GALAXY

First published: 1979
Type of work: Novel

Arthur Dent, with his towel and his alien friend Ford Prefect, begins an intergalactic journey by hitchhiking off the soon-to-be-demolished planet Earth.

The Hitchhiker's Guide to the Galaxy is the first book of the five-volume series (which Adams humorously called a "trilogy") based on Adams's successful radio series of the same name. An immediate best seller, it has remained popular for more than a quarter century.

In a quiet suburb of London, Arthur Dent is minding his own business when his morning is interrupted by bulldozers and wrecking machines coming to destroy his house. The home, which blocks the path of a new bypass, is slated to be torn down. Things go from bad to worse when Arthur's friend, Ford Prefect, who has drunk too much at the nearest bar, enlightens Arthur about the imminent destruction of Earth. Ships from the Vogon Constructor Fleet surround the planet, commissioned to destroy it to make way for the new hyperspace express bypass, whose path Earth is blocking. Soon Arthur's house, along with the rest of the planet, is drifting through space in tiny particles of recently vaporized matter.

Fortunately for Arthur, Ford turns out to be an experienced intergalactic hitchhiker who manages to smuggle the two of them aboard a Vogon craft moments before the end of the Earth. As punishment for their hitchhiking, the Vogons submit the stowaways to the torture of listening to poetry— Vogon poetry is widely regarded as the universe's worst. When the hitchhikers miraculously survive this death sentence, the Vogons eject them into outer space to a more certain death by asphyxiation.

During the painful poetry reading, Zaphod Beeblebrox, president of the Imperial Galactic Government, steals a remarkable spacecraft powered by the new Infinite Improbability Drive. As he pilots the craft, the *Heart of Gold*, away from the intergalactic police, he improbably picks up Arthur and Ford exactly one second before their inevitable deaths, the first of many improbable things that regularly occur in the vicinity of the spaceship.

The hitchhikers are greeted by Zaphod and two other travelers, Marvin and Trillian. Trillian, formerly known as Tricia McMillan, met Arthur at a London party a few years before; Marvin is a chronically depressed robot. The group determine to band together to aid Zaphod's flight from the intergalactic police.

They travel to Magrathea, where customized planets are produced. Long ago, Magratheans con-

structed a massive computer planet in a quest to find the Ultimate Question to Life, the Universe, and Everything. The Ultimate Answer had already been discovered to be forty-two. That computer planet, the travelers realize, is none other than Arthur's own Earth. Unfortunately, the vast computer with its intricate organic program was destroyed by the bureaucratic blundering of the Vogons precisely five minutes before completing its ten-million-year calculation.

Arthur and Trillian carry enough of Earth within them to complete the crucial calculation. They are less than happy to contribute to that cause, however, as the calculation will damage their brains and make them unusable. After a near-fatal stay on Magrathea, the travelers escape the planet, heading off into the sunset toward the Restaurant at the End of the Universe.

Adams's uniquely humorous style contains creative descriptions of the universe and even such unlikely insights as glimpses into the thought processes of a sperm whale. The story is persistently interrupted and enriched by entries from *The Hitchhiker's Guide to the Galaxy* describing phenomena the characters have recently encountered or are about to experience. Readers learn about Vogons, poetry, towels, and much else. At first glance, it appears that these entries have little to do with the plot's development, but Adams manages to tie seemingly random and insignificant trivia into the story line.

The book sets itself up marvelously for a sequel, and Adams wrote four more novels in which Arthur, the commonplace English protagonist—still wearing his bathrobe, carrying his trusty towel, and driven by his unquenchable thirst for tea—quests for his lost planet through hilarious cosmic adventures.

THE RESTAURANT AT THE END OF THE UNIVERSE

First published: 1980
Type of work: Novel

The sequel to The Hitchhiker's Guide to the Galaxy *follows the hitchhikers to the end of the universe in quest of the meaning of life and good food.*

The Restaurant at the End of the Universe continues the story of Arthur Dent; Trillian, his sometime girlfriend; Zaphod Beeblebrox, president of the Imperial Galactic Government; Marvin the depressed robot; and Ford, his longtime hitchhiking companion. *The Heart of Gold* is speeding away from Magrathea, the adventurers having barely escaped there with their lives at the end of *The Hitchhiker's Guide to the Galaxy.*

Arthur inadvertently overloads the computer's systems by asking for a good cup of English tea. When the approaching Vogon ship, sent to kill Arthur and Trillian because of their ties with Earth, opens fire on the *Heart of Gold*, the computer is so focused on brewing a pot of tea that it cannot devote the needed resources to provide an adequate defense. The characters once again narrowly escape what appears to be certain death when Zaphod manages to summon his great-grandfather to bail them out.

As a result of that rescue, Zaphod and Marvin mysteriously disappear from the ship, finding themselves in the offices of *The Hitchhiker's Guide to the Galaxy,* the self-proclaimed repository of all knowledge. After Zaphod and Marvin make it past the existential elevator to find the office of Zarniwoop, Zaphod realizes why his great-grandfather sent him there—he was reminding Zaphod that he is in fact searching for the man who runs the universe.

Zaphod is transported to Frogstar World B, the most evil planet in the universe, and subjected to the Total Perspective Vortex. The Vortex reveals to its victims the entire scope of the universe and the excruciatingly small part that they play in it. It invariably destroys the viewer, demonstrating the high moral lesson that in order to survive as a sentient being one must not have too strong a sense of proportion. Yet Zaphod learns he is not the least but the most important thing in the universe because his universe was created especially for him by Zarniwoop. The two together continue the search, in the real universe, for the man who rules the universe.

Zaphod, Trillian, Arthur, and Ford end up, astonishingly, in Milliways, the Restaurant at the End of the Universe, an entertainment emporium that takes advantage of deep pockets and cataclysmic upheavals of matter. It and its counterpart, the Big Bang Burger Bar, use time travel to provide customers with the experience of the two biggest events in the history of the universe: its creation and its demise. After dinner and a brief brush with death, Zaphod and Trillian materialize back on the *Heart of Gold*, now piloted by Zarniwoop. They travel across space propelled by the ship's Infinite Probability Drive and land on the planet of the ruler of the universe. After a disappointing chat, they leave Zarniwoop behind to cope with the unimpressive ruler.

Arthur and Ford find themselves in a strange spaceship peopled with the unwanted exiled third of a distant planet's population. After crash-landing with the outcasts, they wander around for a while, meeting some creatures clearly in need of evolution's guiding hand. Arthur and Ford eventually recognize that they are on prehistoric Earth. The outcasts quickly create committees, subcommittees, documentaries, and management meetings which enable them to declare war on an uninhabited continent and declare tree leaves legal tender. Ford realizes that the prehistoric people are sadly dying off, leaving the crash-landed bureaucrats as the sole ancestors of the human race.

The book concludes with Zaphod and Trillian chatting purposelessly with the ruler of the universe, Arthur and Ford celebrating with humankind's ancestors at a management party, and Marvin missing and unaccounted for.

The Long Dark Tea-Time of the Soul

First published: 1988
Type of work: Novel

Dirk Gently, "holistic detective," is caught between Norse gods, an angry eagle, his murdered client, his annoyed girlfriend Kate, and a frighteningly dirty fridge.

The Long Dark Tea-Time of the Soul is a sequel to the original Dirk Gently novel *Dirk Gently's Holistic Detective Agency*. Gently makes his living as a "holistic" detective, basing his detective work on "the absolute interconnectedness" of all things. This leads to interesting investigative strategies. Gently rejects Sherlock Holmes's idea that whatever is left after ruling out all impossibilities must be the truth. Instead, Gently insists on not rejecting a possibility merely because of its complete impossibility. His faith in the impossible proves a remarkably successful detection strategy.

Kate Schechter is on her way to Norway to visit a friend. Kate gets delayed in line at the airport behind a large Norse-looking man who has no passport, credit card, or birth certificate. This disregard for red tape makes the bureaucratic check-in girl increasingly inflexible and rude. Kate ends up missing her flight and on her way out of the airport gets rocked by an explosion that causes the check-in girl to vanish mysteriously.

Meanwhile, Dirk Gently has just remembered an appointment. His morning to this point has featured luxurious sleeping, a protracted staring contest with his refrigerator, and wishing he had a rich client—a wish which finally reminds him of his appointment. He hurries, five hours late, to the client who has complained of death threats from a green man with a scythe. When Dirk at long last arrives at his client's house, he finds police cars surrounding the home and his client sitting in a chair, his severed head spinning on a record turntable. The green man with the scythe appears to have gotten to Dirk's client before Dirk did.

In the meantime, Kate visits an unusual medical institution, where she looks for the large Norse man who thwarted her plans for a holiday in Nor-

way. She meets a number of patients with strange ailments but cannot locate the man, whom she ultimately discovers to be Thor, the Norse god of thunder. On the way from the hospital, Kate's car is rear-ended by Dirk, who is following her because he is lost. Dirk gets lost so often he has devised a system in which he follows anyone who seems to know where he or she is going. Dirk maintains that this counterintuitive process usually gets him where he needs to be, though seldom where he thought he was going.

Dirk and Kate realize that their paths have led them both on a collision course with Thor. Kate drives home to find Thor waiting for her; Thor found her house because she had given him her address at the airport in an attempt to help him make his flight. She aids him again, removing floorboards embedded in his back from his father's recent punishment. They fly off together, clinging to Thor's thrown hammer, toward Valhalla, where Thor plans to confront his father about some vast, vague injustice.

Dirk makes it home to discover an angry eagle on his doorstep who seems to be trying to tell him something. When the eagle threatens him, Dirk escapes from the house on a quest for a cigarette, a pursuit which leads him eventually to follow a group of beggars through a secret passageway into Valhalla. There he meets the Draycotts, a couple who have drafted a contract which exchanges the gods' powers for cash. Odin, canny but sleepy

leader of the gods, signed the contract against the will of his son Thor, triggering the thunder god's angry reaction.

The book ends with the deaths of the Draycotts in a freak accident with a fighter jet, annulling their contract. Thor manages to straighten out most of the problems that he has created. Dirk, having experienced difficulties with a sofa impossibly stuck on his staircase and a saltcellar that cannot possibly work the way it does, returns home to his shiny new fridge.

SUMMARY

Douglas Adams's innovative narrative and inimitably warm humor earned him a place among the best-loved British authors. His science fiction may lack the usual rapid-fire action plot, but his novels are filled with creative descriptions, witty wordplay, and charming characters.

Steven C. Walker

BIBLIOGRAPHY

By the Author

LONG FICTION:
The Hitchhiker's Guide to the Galaxy, 1979
The Restaurant at the End of the Universe, 1980
Life, the Universe, and Everything, 1982
So Long, and Thanks for All the Fish, 1984
Dirk Gently's Holistic Detective Agency, 1987
The Long Dark Tea-Time of the Soul, 1988
Mostly Harmless, 1992

SHORT FICTION:
"A Christmas Fairly Story," 1986 (with Terry Jones)
"The Private Life of Genghis Khan," 1986
"Young Zaphod Plays It Safe," 1986

RADIO PLAYS:
The Hitchhiker's Guide to the Galaxy, 1978-1980
The Original Hitchhiker Radio Scripts, 1985 (pb. in England as *The Hitchhiker's Guide to the Galaxy: The Original Radio Scripts*, 1985)

TELEPLAYS:
Doctor Who, 1978-1980
The Hitchhiker's Guide to the Galaxy, 1981
Hyperland, 1990

NONFICTION:
The Meaning of Liff, 1983 (with John Lloyd)
Last Chance to See, 1990 (with Mark Carwardine)
The Deeper Meaning of Liff: A Dictionary of Things There Aren't Words for Yet—But There Ought to Be, 1990 (with Lloyd)

EDITED TEXT:
The Utterly, Utterly Merry Comic Relief Christmas Book, 1986 (with Peter Fincham)

MISCELLANEOUS:
The Salmon of Doubt: Hitchhiking the Galaxy One Last Time, 2002

DISCUSSION TOPICS

- Douglas Adams was among the first to combine the genres of science fiction and humor. What effects did this new combination have on the science-fiction genre? The humor genre?

- How do Adams's Everyman characters draw readers into the story?

- What does the immense popularity of the Hitchhiker's series suggest about the sort of books readers enjoy?

- What role does the persistent emphasis on food play in Adams's novels?

- What advantages and disadvantages of high-technology gadgets does Adams highlight?

- How does Dirk Gently's style of detective work differ from the detective work to which most readers are accustomed? What is the effect of this unusual approach to the genre?

- Marvin the paranoid android came into being around the same time as the droids of *Star Wars*. What besides paranoia separates him from his counterparts in the *Star Wars* films?

- Adams was a devout atheist, yet many of his books deal directly with deities. Why?

About the Author

Gaiman, Neil. *Don't Panic: Douglas Adams and "The Hitchhiker's Guide to the Galaxy."* New York: Titan Books, 2005.

Hanlon, Michael. *The Science of "The Hitchhiker's Guide to the Galaxy."* New York: Macmillan, 2005.

Simpson, M. J. *Hitchhiker: A Biography of Douglas Adams.* Boston: Justin Charles, 2003.

_____. *The Pocket Essential Hitch Hiker's Guide.* 2d ed. Chicago: Trafalgar Square, 2005.

Webb, Nick. *Wish You Were Here: The Official Biography of Douglas Adams.* New York: Ballantine Books, 2003.

Yeffeth, Glenn, ed. *The Anthology at the End of the Universe.* Dallas, Tex.: BenBella Books, 2004.

AESCHYLUS

Born: Eleusis, Greece
    525-524 B.C.E.
Died: Gela, Sicily (now in Italy)
    456-455 B.C.E.

The earliest of the three great tragedians of ancient Athens, Aeschylus wrote grandiose and highly religious trilogies in which all three plays dealt with a single legend.

Library of Congress

BIOGRAPHY

Throughout most of the ancient world, the city of Eleusis, fourteen miles northwest of Athens, was known primarily as the site of the Eleusinian Mysteries. Mysteries, in the religious sense, are sacred rites of initiation. The Eleusinian Mysteries honored the goddesses Demeter and Persephone, told the story of Persephone's abduction by Pluto, the god of the underworld, and offered their initiates a blessed afterlife. By the late sixth century B.C.E., the Eleusinian Mysteries were known in all parts of the Greek world, attracting worshipers both from Athens and from distant cities across the Aegean Sea. In 525-524 B.C.E., in this village filled with shrines, pilgrims, and the votive offerings of the faithful, there was born a playwright who was to reinterpret the ancient legends of his people from a profoundly religious perspective. He was the poet Aeschylus (EHS-kuh-luhs).

Aeschylus was a member of the Eupatridae, the ancient nobility that had once ruled Athens and all the cities of Attica. The Eupatridae were not a single family but rather a loose alliance of families, related by intermarriage, who shared an interest in preserving their wealth and aristocratic privileges. Aeschylus's father, Euphorion, had at least four sons: Cynegeirus, Ameinias, Euphorion the younger, and Aeschylus himself.

In 499 B.C.E., at the age of twenty-six, Aeschylus presented his first set of tragedies at the Festival of Dionysus (called the Great Dionysia) in Athens.

The titles of these early tragedies have not been preserved and do not appear to have been among the poet's most successful works. During the fifth century B.C.E., prizes were awarded to playwrights who, in the opinion of ten judges, composed the finest tragedies performed during that year's festival. Aeschylus did not win the tragedy award in 499, and, indeed, he would not receive this prize until he was already forty years old.

From that time onward, however, Aeschylus would be victorious in tragedy competitions twelve more times. His works were also frequently revived, and frequently successful, after his death. That was a singular honor since few Greek playwrights had their tragedies revived until much later.

At about the same time that Aeschylus first began writing plays, the Greek cities of Ionia (the west central coast of Turkey) rebelled against the Persians, who had ruled them since 546 B.C.E. The rebellion of the Ionians received support from Athens, and that prompted the Persians to launch an extended series of punitive invasions into Greece. These invasions are known collectively as the Persian Wars. After reconquering Ionia in 494 and unsuccessfully attempting a northern invasion of Greece in 492, the Persians landed a huge army at a bay off the plain of Marathon, only twenty-six miles from Athens itself, in the late summer of 490. The Battle of Marathon became a source of Athenian pride for more than a century. In this battle, a small group of Athenians and their Plataean allies, together outnumbered ten to one by the Persians, inflicted a humiliating defeat upon the enemy. The Spartans, arriving too late for the battle, were amazed at the extent of the Greek victory. A total of about 6,400 Persians were killed at the Battle of Marathon, while only 192 Athenians lost their lives.

One of the Athenians who died at the Battle of Marathon was Aeschylus's brother Cynegeirus. According to the Greek historian Herodotus, Cynegeirus was killed during the fierce fighting around the Persian ships. Aeschylus, too, fought at Marathon, though he survived to participate in other battles of the Persian Wars. One of these battles, at Salamis in 480 B.C.E., was later commemorated in Aeschylus's tragedy the *Persai* (472 B.C.E.; *The Persians*, 1777), the only surviving Greek tragedy to deal with a historical, rather than a mythological, event.

The trilogy that contained *The Persians* won the award for tragedy for its year. Sometime later, the poet Sophocles won his first competition against Aeschylus. In the number of his tragedy victories, Sophocles was to become the most successful tragic playwright of the fifth century. Nevertheless, in about 429 B.C.E., when Sophocles' masterpiece *Oidipous Tyrannos* (*Oedipus Tyrannus*, 1715) was first performed, Sophocles did not receive the first prize. That victory was awarded to Philocles, a nephew of Aeschylus, whose works have not survived.

An obscure passage of Aristotle's *Ethica Nichomachea* (335-323 B.C.E.; *Nicomachean Ethics*, 1797) states that Aeschylus defended himself against the charge of divulging the mysteries by saying that he did not know that these were secrets. Clement of Alexandria interpreted that to mean that Aeschylus had unintentionally written a passage in one of his tragedies that resembled a sacred hymn of the Eleusinian Mysteries. Moreover, Clement suggested that Aeschylus had defended himself from the charge of exposing these secrets by proving that he had never been initiated. Nevertheless, a passage in the *Batrachoi* (405 B.C.E.; *The Frogs*, 1780) by the comic poet Aristophanes does seem to imply that Aeschylus had participated in the sacred rites of his native town (lines 886-887). The meaning of Aristotle's remark thus remains unclear.

In the years before his death, Aeschylus made at least two, possibly three, trips to Sicily. For one of these trips, around 472 B.C.E., Aeschylus composed the tragedy *Aetnae*, honoring the foundation of the new city of Aetna by Hiero, the tyrant of Syracuse.

In 456-455, during the last of these journeys, Aeschylus died in the city of Gela on Sicily's southern coast. The legend that arose concerning the death of Aeschylus is bizarre and almost certainly the invention of a later comic author. According to this legend, Aeschylus died when he was struck on the head by a tortoise that an eagle had been carrying off as prey. The eagle, it is said, had been searching for a place to smash the tortoise's shell and had mistaken Aeschylus's bald head for a stone.

The Greek traveler Pausanias states that Aeschylus composed his own epitaph, which, remarkably, contains no mention of his tragedies. "Beneath this monument lies Aeschylus of Athens, the son of Euphorion, who died in wheat-bearing Gela. The grove at Marathon could speak of his famed courage as could the long-haired Persians who learned of it there." Aeschylus left behind a number of relatives who also went on to become successful tragedians. In addition to his nephew Philocles, Aeschylus's sons Euphorion (who won first prize at the tragic festival of 431 B.C.E.) and Euaeon were famous dramatists.

ANALYSIS

In Aristophanes' comedy *The Frogs* (lines 1019-1029), the poet Euripides challenges Aeschylus to explain what he did in his tragedies to make his audience more valiant and heroic. Aeschylus replies that he composed the *Hepta epi Thēbas* (467 B.C.E.; *Seven Against Thebes*, 1777), a play that filled everyone who saw it with a martial spirit. Aristophanes then goes on to say that Aeschylus's *The Persians* inspired young Athenians to imitate their elders' thirst for victory and contained a startling dramatic spectacle by bringing onstage the ghost of Darius, the dead king of the Persians.

These three elements—a spirit of heroism, a didactic tone, and lavish spectacle—were understood by Aeschylus's contemporaries to be the central features of his dramatic style. That style is already present in *The Persians*, the play that is considered to be the earliest of Aeschylus's seven extant tragedies. In *The Persians*, the Greeks' courageous defense of their homeland is coupled with a surprisingly sympathetic view of the Persians themselves. Moreover, while the Persians' defeat is presented in that play as due to the valor of the Greek warriors, Aeschylus attributes the Greek victory even more to the Persians' own hubris (excessive pride, over-confidence, and insolence). The didactic message of this play thus has meaning for the Greeks, as well as for their enemies: Pride can cause even a victorious army to be humbled; moderation is the safest path, even in success. That was a lesson that the Athenians would need to learn repeatedly throughout the fifth century B.C.E.

The lavish spectacle of Aeschylus's *The Persians* was due, in large part, to the magnificent costumes worn by the actors. In other plays, Aeschylus carried his interest in vivid spectacle even further. According to legend, at the first performance of the *Eumenides* (458 B.C.E.; English translation, 1777), pregnant women miscarried and children fainted at the horrifying appearance of the Furies. In the *Choēphoroi* (458 B.C.E.; *Libation Bearers*, 1777), the blood-drenched bodies of Aegisthus and Clytemnestra were displayed to the audience, and the robe in which Clytemnestra had entangled Agamemnon was unfurled in full view. These striking visual images, combined with the verbal imagery of Aeschylus's text, made these tragedies exceptionally vivid, at times even shocking, when they were first performed.

Aeschylus was also responsible for several important innovations in the staging and design of Greek tragedy. Born less than ten years after the victory of the tragic poet Thespis at the first Great Dionysia, Aeschylus invented many features that later ages would view as essential to Greek tragedy. Aristotle says in the *De poetica* (c. 334 B.C.E.-c. 323 B.C.E.; *Poetics*, 1705) that Aeschylus increased the number of actors from one to two, reduced the size of the chorus, and made dialogue prominent in his plays. Before Aeschylus's time, tragedy consisted of a single actor whose role was limited to exchanges with a large chorus. The introduction of a second actor permitted Aeschylus to explore different points of view, report new information from offstage, and create a more natural flow of dialogue. The character played by the second actor could question the protagonist about why a certain course of action was chosen. The second actor could also respond, either rationally or emotionally, to what the protagonist had said.

This questioning and interchange between the first and second actors was central to the dramatic purpose of Aeschylus. Unlike later playwrights such as Sophocles and Euripides, Aeschylus was interested in sweeping historical and religious forces more than in individual characters. This concern is also why Aeschylus preferred to write connected trilogies where a single theme or story was traced through all three plays. (The "trilogies" of Sophocles and Euripides were not trilogies at all in the modern sense. They were simply three plays sometimes performed on a single occasion.) In the *Oresteia* (458 B.C.E.; English translation, 1777), for example, Aeschylus traced the fulfillment of a curse through several generations of the same family. In the trilogy that contained the *Prometheus desmōtēs* (date unknown; *Prometheus Bound*, 1777), Aeschylus explored the nature of power and the development of justice among the gods.

Great theological questions, such as Why do people suffer? and How can a supremely good and supremely powerful deity permit evil in the world?, were never far from Aeschylus's mind. At times, the chorus deals with these issues explicitly as it comments upon the action of the play. At other times, the question is raised through the development of the plot itself.

Aeschylus's view is always panoramic, dealing with difficult questions and eschewing simple answers. While Euripides would later be criticized for his fascination with disreputable human impulses, Aeschylus could reinterpret even a base or primitive myth so as to give it a lofty religious and moral tone. In Aeschylus's treatment, for example, the slaying of Agamemnon and its consequences are transformed into an examination of retributive justice and its limits. In the *Seven Against Thebes*, the moral ambiguity of the encounter between Eteocles and Polyneices is eliminated: To Aeschylus, the defender of Thebes was right and the traitor to Thebes was wrong, and their situations were not at all comparable. As Aristophanes has Aeschylus say in *The Frogs* (lines 1053-1054, 1056), "It is the duty of the poet to hide the base, not to teach it or to display it in clear view. . . . Most of all, it is our duty to discuss what is noble." That is a value which may be seen in each of Aeschylus's plays.

Aeschylus's panoramic vision and his eagerness to address complex issues may also be seen in his frequent dramatic use of the "double bind." A double bind occurs when a character is doomed to failure no matter which alternative action is chosen. Nearly every Aeschylean tragedy presents at least one character who is caught in this type of situation. Thus, Orestes must either kill his mother or leave his father unavenged, Eteocles must either face his own brother in battle or doom Thebes by leaving one of its gates undefended, and Pelasgus in the *Hiketides* (463 B.C.E.?; *The Suppliants*, 1777) must either face war with the Egyptians or permit the Danaids to pollute his sanctuary with their suicide. In each of these cases, there is no simple solution, no solution at all that will avoid great suffering to the central characters. Yet the moral problems that interested Aeschylus were always ones in which this type of dilemma must be faced and somehow resolved.

The human characters of Aeschylus's plays seem entangled in forces far larger than themselves, in insoluble paradoxes, great curses, and divine plans that may take several generations to be understood. This grand design of Aeschylean tragedy has also affected the language of his plays. Aristophanes has Aeschylus say in *The Frogs* (lines 1059-1061) that, "the poet must choose words equal to his great thoughts and ideas. Godlike men should use more majestic words than ordinary men, just as their cloaks are more splendid than ours." As a result, the language used by Aeschylus is rich in compound words and difficult grammatical structures. For example, in the long opening chorus of the *Agamemnōn* (458 B.C.E.; *Agamemnon*, 1777), the two sons of Atreus are described as "twin-throned and twin-sceptered" (line 43), the expedition to recover Helen of Troy is termed "a woman-avenging war" (lines 225-226), and the gag that bound Iphigeneia before her sacrifice is called "the guardian of her fair-prowed mouth" (line 235). Similar examples may be found in any of Aeschylus's tragedies. These difficult, often ponderous terms help maintain the spirit of grandeur that the poet is trying to evoke and elevate his language over that of everyday speech.

SEVEN AGAINST THEBES

First produced: *Hepta epi Thēbas*, 467 B.C.E. (English translation, 1777)
Type of work: Play

A curse upon the ruling house of Thebes is fulfilled as the king must do battle with his own brother, who is one of seven generals attacking the city.

Seven Against Thebes was the third play in a 467 B.C.E. trilogy that also included the tragedies *Laius* and *Oedipus*, both of which are now lost. At its first performance, *Seven Against Thebes* would have provided a climax, summarizing themes that the poet had been developing through two previous tragedies. In this way, *Seven Against Thebes* would have been similar to the *Eumenides* (458 B.C.E.; English translation, 1777) in presenting the final results of a curse that had long afflicted a particular family.

The political situation of Athens in Aeschylus's own day had an important effect upon *Seven Against Thebes*. First, though the tragedy is set in Thebes and deals exclusively with Theban characters, neither the word "Thebes" nor "Thebans" appears anywhere in the tragedy. Aeschylus is careful always to replace these terms with the Homeric expressions "city of Cadmus" and "Cadmeans," recalling the name of the mythical founder of Thebes. Aeschylus did that because Thebes had gone over to the enemy in the Persian Wars. Direct reference to the city was thus likely to offend his audience. The recent end of the Persian 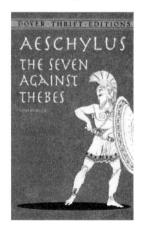 Wars also helps to explain why the chorus refers to the invading army as "foreign-tongued" (line 170, one of Aeschylus's characteristic compound adjectives), even though, according to legend, this army was composed of Argives and Thebans. Athens had recently emerged victorious over a "foreign-tongued" enemy, and the audience would naturally associate an invading army with alien speech.

The passions roused by the Persian Wars explain why Aeschylus sees the conflict between Eteocles and Polyneices as less morally ambiguous than did his successors. Both Sophocles, in the *Antigonē* (441 B.C.E.; *Antigone*, 1729), and Euripides, in the *Phoinissai* (409 B.C.E.; *The Phoenician Women*, 1781), presented the two brothers as each having right on their sides, at least to some degree. Yet Aeschylus had fought in a battle caused by the treason of Hippias, the exiled tyrant of Athens who had led the Persians to Marathon. Unlike Sophocles and Euripides, therefore, Aeschylus could not present treachery to one's native city as justifiable for any reason. That is why only Eteocles' point of view is presented in this play and the audience is shown only the tragedy of a warrior who dies defending his country.

Since the original audience's memories of the Persian Wars were still fresh, the issues addressed by the *Seven Against Thebes* would have been particularly interesting when the play was first performed. Those issues, and the sheer grandeur of Aeschylus's language and the costumes worn by his characters, would also have made the play seem less "static" than they do when it is read today. It is sometimes said that the central episode of this tragedy, in which each of the seven generals of the invading army is first described and then paired with a defender of the city, resembles the catalog passages of epic poetry rather than the tense drama of most Greek tragedy. Nevertheless, it should be remembered that there is tension in this scene as Eteocles misses one opportunity after another to avoid meeting his own brother in battle. It should also be remembered that Greek audiences, far more than later audiences, enjoyed vivid description for its own sake and would have delighted in Aeschylus's account of the armor and blazons of the seven enemy generals.

ORESTEIA

First produced: 458 B.C.E.; includes
   Agamemnōn (*Agamemnon*, 1777);
   Choēphoroi (*Libation Bearers*, 1777);
   Eumenides (English translation, 1777)

Type of work: Plays

As this trilogy begins, Agamemnon, king of Argos, is slain by his wife, Clytemnestra, after returning from the Trojan War; his son, Orestes, avenges the death by killing Clytemnestra and her lover, Aegisthus; haunted for this crime by the Furies, Orestes is freed when a new court is established at Athens.

The *Oresteia* is the only ancient Greek trilogy to survive. (Sophocles' Theban Trilogy consists of three plays that were actually written many years apart and never performed together during the poet's lifetime.) The three plays of the *Oresteia* are the *Agamemnon*, the *Libation Bearers*, and the *Eumenides* ("kindly ones" or "furies"). The *Proteus* (458 B.C.E.), the *Oresteia*'s satyr play (a humorous work traditionally performed at the end of a trilogy), has been lost; it is unclear whether the *Proteus* would have continued the plot of the *Oresteia* or, as is more likely, dealt with the encounter of Odysseus and Proteus described in the *Odyssey* (c. 725 B.C.E.; English translation, 1614).

A central motif of the *Oresteia* is the curse that has afflicted Agamemnon's family for several generations. Tantalus, Agamemnon's great-grandfather, had slaughtered his own son, Pelops, after divulging the secrets of the Olympian gods and stealing from them the nectar and ambrosia that conveyed immortality. Pelops, whom the gods later restored, betrayed and killed the charioteer, Myrtilus, by pushing him from a cliff. As Myrtilus fell to his death, he cursed Pelops and all of his descendants; that was the origin of the curse upon this household. Pelops's son, Atreus, butchered the children of his brother, Thyestes, and tricked Thyestes into eating the flesh of his own sons. When Thyestes learned what he unwittingly had done, he cursed Atreus and all of his children; the curse upon the house of Atreus was thus renewed. Atreus's son, Agamemnon, after whom the first play in this trilogy was named, sacrificed his own daughter, Iphigeneia, in order to obtain winds necessary to carry him to Troy. There, Agamemnon was responsible for the defeat of the Trojan army and the slaughter of many innocent victims.

This entire line of bloodshed, crime, and curse all devolves upon the single figure of Orestes, the son of Agamemnon who gives his name to the trilogy. Orestes must put an end to the curse, and he can do so only with the help of the gods. Moreover, Orestes stands at the end of another line, a line not of kinship this time but of vengeance or retributive justice. The Trojan War began when Paris, the son of the Trojan king Priam, abducted Helen, the wife of Agamemnon's brother, Menelaus. To avenge this crime, Agamemnon and Menelaus were responsible for the deaths of many innocent victims, including Agamemnon's daughter, Iphigeneia. To avenge her death, Agamemnon is killed by his wife, Clytemnestra, in the first play of the *Oresteia*. Orestes is then bound by duty and honor to avenge his father, but to do so would entail killing his mother. Caught in this "double bind," Orestes can escape only with the gods' help. To end the cycle of retribution, the gods Apollo and Athena must intervene and create a new institution, a court that for all future time will replace endless reprisals with divine justice.

Seen from one perspective, therefore, the *Oresteia* traces the development of law from the time when its enforcement rested with the family to the poet's own day, when the enforcement of law was overseen by the courts. The Areopagus, the court that Athena establishes in the *Eumenides*, was still operating in Aeschylus's lifetime. Though the court's charter had been restricted by the liberal statesman Ephialtes only four years before the *Oresteia* was first performed, the Areopagus still had jurisdiction in most murder trials, as Aeschylus suggests.

The development of the Athenian court is presented in the *Oresteia* as a necessary step in human progress. Without the court, justice would not be possible since law would be enforced according to the dictates of individual families, not the will of the city as a whole.

Aeschylus's religious perspective meant that the removal of the curse and the creation of the Athenian court were possible only through the intervention of the gods. Only a divine power, Aeschylus argues, has the perspective necessary to see larger issues at work. Ordinary mortals, living for only a single generation, are limited in terms of the experience upon which they can base their judgments. The gods, however, are detached from the passions that afflict the mortals in these plays. They can maintain a proper perspective, see "the big picture," and develop solutions that would never have occurred to the protagonists themselves. By writing connected trilogies such as the *Oresteia*, Aeschylus sought to convey some of this larger perspective to his audience, to encourage them to think, not merely in terms of their own time, but in terms of all of human history.

In order to provide some unity to sprawling trilogies such as the *Oresteia*, Aeschylus used repeated patterns of imagery that could remind the audience of earlier episodes. For example, in the opening scene of the *Agamemnon*, the image of light rising out of darkness is used repeatedly. The watchman is lying upon the roof of the palace at dawn, when a new light appears in the east. Rather than the rising sun, however, it is the beacon fire, arranged by Clytemnestra, which signals the end of the war at Troy. This "false dawn"—literally false, since the fire is man-made and not a natural light—creates a sense of foreboding that is soon fulfilled. The promise of a new dawn of peace goes unkept when Agamemnon, who survived ten years of fighting at Troy, is slain by his own wife upon his return home. This imagery of light and darkness occurs again at the very end of the trilogy when torches are lit for a procession guiding the Eumenides back to their subterranean home. The hope is that, this time, the "new dawn" really will bring peace to Argos and end the curse upon the house of Atreus. The Eumenides, addressed as the "children of night" (*Eumenides*, line 1034), are asked to bless all the earth and ensure that the long-awaited dawn of peace truly has arrived.

Another common source of imagery in the *Oresteia* is the imagery of blood. In Greek, as in English, the word "blood" (*haima*) has a number of different connotations: It may be used to symbolize the family ("bloodline," "blood relation"), violence ("bloodshed," "blood bath"), or miasma ("bloodstained," "bloodguilt"). The loss of blood may be seen as medicinal ("bloodletting") or violent ("blood spilling"). Because of these different impressions conveyed by the word "blood," Aeschylus uses this root repeatedly in describing the house of

Atreus, a family afflicted by violence and miasma, a family where those related by blood so frequently shed one another's blood.

Imagery of animals also appears in the *Oresteia,* with many different connotations. For example, in the *Agamemnon,* the attack upon Troy by Agamemnon and Menelaus is compared first to an attack of eagles shrieking for their lost young (lines 49-51), then to birds of prey brutally seizing a pregnant hare (lines 114-120). Similarly, Orestes in the *Libation Bearers* refers to himself and Electra as "the orphaned offspring of their father, the eagle" (line 247). These images are useful in that they associate Agamemnon with both the regal splendor of the eagle and this bird's ferocious savagery. Other animal imagery is also common in the *Oresteia:* The watchman lies upon the palace roof "dog-like" (*Agamemnon,* line 3); Helen of Troy is like a lion cub who causes grief for those who had nurtured it (*Agamemnon,* lines 716-736); Aegisthus is a "powerless lion who rolls in his master's bed" (*Agamemnon,* line 1224); Clytemnestra and Aegisthus are twin snakes who have been slain by a single stroke (*Libation Bearers,* line 1047); and the god Apollo contemptuously calls the Furies "a herd of goats who lack a herdsman" (*Eumenides,* line 196). In this way, Aeschylus uses imagery of animals both to reinforce the nature of his characters and, by repeating and developing certain images, to provide a sense of continuity throughout his extended trilogy.

PROMETHEUS BOUND

First produced: *Prometheus desmōtēs,* date unknown (English translation, 1777)
Type of work: Play

At the order of Zeus, the Titan Prometheus is bound to a rock in the Caucasus as punishment for aiding humankind.

Prometheus Bound was the first work in a trilogy that also included the plays *Prometheus Lyomenos* (*Prometheus Unbound*) and *Prometheus Pyrphoros* (*Prometheus the Fire-Bearer*), neither of which has survived. Since the final two dramas of the trilogy have been lost, it is difficult to determine Aeschylus's original intention for the work as a whole.

This problem is intensified since the date of the trilogy is unknown. A reference (lines 363-372) to the eruption of Mount Aetna in 479 suggests that

Prometheus Bound may date later than this event. Aside from that, however, scholars cannot agree whether the play was written early or late in Aeschylus's career or even whether it is a genuine work of Aeschylus.

The theme of *Prometheus Bound* is the conflict between force and justice. The supreme god Zeus has recently assumed control of the universe from the Titans and is ruling like a petty tyrant. He has bound Prometheus to a rock in a remote corner of the earth because Prometheus gave the gift of fire to humankind, a race whom Zeus had sought to destroy. To the original Athenian audience, which had expelled the tyrant Hippias only in 510 B.C.E., Aeschylus's references to tyranny in this play would have been topical. Moreover, it is surprising to find that these references are applied to the god Zeus, usually depicted in Aeschylean tragedy as the defender of justice and the patron of civil law.

The reason for the strange image of Zeus in this play was probably made clear in parts of the trilogy now lost. Justice, in Greek society, was frequently seen as a balance or a sense of proportion among conflicting demands. In the *Prometheus Bound,* Zeus, early in his reign, has not yet attained that balance. As the trilogy progressed, a sense of proportion must have been found between Zeus's excessive desire for order and Prometheus's extreme desire to benefit humankind. (Indeed, Prometheus is described as bestowing honors upon mortals "beyond what was just," at line 30. In the last line of the play, Prometheus states that Zeus has punished him "beyond what was just," line 1093.) Justice can only occur when there is a complete proportion of all things, including both discipline and mercy.

Like the *Seven Against Thebes, Prometheus Bound* has been criticized as being a "static" play. Indeed, once Prometheus has been bound to the rock in the opening moments of the tragedy, nothing "happens" on stage for the duration of the drama. Oceanos and his daughters arrive to give comfort to Prometheus. Hermes brings additional threats from Zeus. Beyond these, however, there is no movement in the tragedy. In the *Prometheus Bound*, this lack of movement intensifies the audience's sense of Prometheus's punishment. The drama becomes as motionless as the captive protagonist himself, and, even at the end of the tragedy, it is unclear how additional progress may be possible. The way in which Aeschylus solved this problem would only have been revealed in the next two plays of the trilogy.

SUMMARY

The tragedies of Aeschylus are dramas of incredible grandeur. Their language is intentionally elevated over the common speech of everyday life. Their focus is upon the great struggles of gods and heroes from the remote past. Their interpretation of Greek mythology presents sweeping historical or religious patterns rather than dwelling upon individual characters. Unlike Sophocles, who focused upon individual heroes in his dramas, or Euripides, who sought to bring even the gods down to the level of ordinary mortals, Aeschylus presented figures who were larger than life, figures who were entangled by forces even greater than themselves.

One of the sweeping historical patterns frequently encountered in Aeschylean tragedy is that of the "double bind." In this situation, characters find that they are doomed no matter what they do. In some cases, as in the *Seven Against Thebes*, the double bind arises because of a curse placed upon the hero's family. In other cases, such as in the *Oresteia*, the intervention of the gods is necessary in order to prevent the hero's destruction and to see that justice is restored to the world.

Jeffrey L. Buller

BIBLIOGRAPHY

By the Author

DRAMA:
Of the more than eighty known plays of Aeschylus, only seven tragedies survive in more or less complete form.
Persai, 472 B.C.E. (*The Persians*, 1777)
Prometheus desmōtēs, date unknown (*Prometheus Bound*, 1777)
Hepta epi Thēbas, 467 B.C.E. (*Seven Against Thebes*, 1777)
Hiketides, 463 B.C.E.? (*The Suppliants*, 1777)
Oresteia, 458 B.C.E. (English translation, 1777; includes *Agamemnōn* [*Agamemnon*], *Choēphoroi* [*Libation Bearers*], and *Eumenides*)

About the Author

Goward, Barbara. *Telling Tragedy: Narrative Technique in Aeschylus, Sophocles, and Euripides*. London: Duckworth, 2004.
Heath, John. *The Talking Greeks: Speech, Animals, and the Other in Homer, Aeschylus, and Plato*. New York: Cambridge University Press, 2005.
Herington, John. *Aeschylus*. New Haven, Conn.: Yale University Press, 1986.

DISCUSSION TOPICS

- What aspects of Aeschylus's background prepared him to be the first major tragic dramatist in ancient Athens?

- What sets *The Persians* apart from other Greek tragedies?

- Explain Aeschylus's contributions to the staging of tragedies.

- What does it mean to assert that Aeschylus's view was "panoramic"?

- Aeschylus's plays are probably performed less often for modern audiences than those of Sophocles and Euripides. Considering the merits of his work, what might account for this situation?

- Speculate: Why does only the *Oresteia* survive as an ancient Greek trilogy?

Hogan, James C. *A Commentary on the Complete Greek Tragedies: Aeschylus.* Chicago: University of Chicago Press, 1984.

Kuhns, Richard. *The House, the City, and the Judge: The Growth of Moral Awareness in the "Oresteia."* Indianapolis, Ind.: Bobbs-Merrill, 1962.

Lloyd, Michael, ed. *Aeschylus.* New York: Oxford University Press, 2007.

Podlecki, Anthony J. *The Political Background of Aeschylean Tragedy.* Ann Arbor: University of Michigan Press, 1966.

Spatz, Lois. *Aeschylus.* Boston: Twayne, 1982.

Taplan, Oliver. *The Stagecraft of Aeschylus.* Oxford, England: Clarendon Press, 1977.

SHMUEL YOSEF AGNON

© The Nobel Foundation

Born: Buczacz, Galicia, Austro-Hungarian Empire
(now Buchach, Ukraine)
July 17, 1888
Died: Rehovoth, Israel
February 17, 1970

Agnon's use of fiction contributed significantly to the development of Hebrew as a secular, literary language.

BIOGRAPHY

Shmuel Yosef Czaczkes was born in Buczacz, Galicia, then part of the Austro-Hungarian Empire. He was the eldest of five children born to Shalom Mordecai Halevi Czaczkes and Esther Farb-Hacohen. His Jewish roots remained part of him; his lessons in the Talmud, Jewish folklore, and other Judaica inform the body of his works. He began writing at the age of eight, published his first poem in 1903, and then began regularly publishing both poetry and prose in Cracow, Poland. In 1906 and 1907, his works in both Hebrew and Yiddish appeared in Galician periodicals.

He moved to Jaffa, in Palestine, in 1907, became a Jewish court secretary, and served on the Land of Israel Council. Although he held Zionist ideals, his affinity was for the older, established Jewish population rather than for the newer arrivals. He describes the Jaffa of the early twentieth century in *Shevu'at emunim* (1943; *Betrothed*, 1966). He adopted the surname Agnon (AHG-nahn), became established as a writer, and began to write only in Hebrew. Like many of his colleagues, Agnon had one foot in the spiritual world of the shtetls of Europe and one in the modern life evolving in Israel.

In 1913, Agnon moved to Germany and read widely in German, French, and Russian literature and philosophy. He remained in Germany until 1924, working as a tutor and an editor. In Berlin, Leipzig, Wiesbaden, and Hamburg, he became ac-

quainted with Jewish writers, scholars, and Zionists, among whom were Gershom Scholem, the scholar of Jewish mysticism, and Martin Buber, the theologian and philosopher in whose journal, *Der Jude*, Agnon was published. The publisher Salman Schocken pledged Agnon a stipend for life to enable him to pursue his literary career. Agnon married Esther Marx in 1919 and had two children, Emuna, a daughter, and Shalom Mordecai Hemdat, a son. In 1924, he returned to Jerusalem after their home was burned, destroying Agnon's library of about four thousand rare works and manuscripts as well as the only copy of a novel on the verge of publication. During this period, he had gained a wide readership for his short stories, which were published in three different collections in 1921.

Agnon remained in Jerusalem for the rest of his life. His literary reputation was firmly established by the beginning of the 1930's. The *Sefer hama'asim* (the book of deeds) was published in 1932; *Sipur pashut* (*A Simple Story*, 1985) was published in 1935. A collection of short stories, two nonfiction works, and a collection about writing, *Sefer, sofer, vesipur* (1938; book, writer, and story), were followed by a short-story collection, *Elu ve'elu* (these and those) in 1941. *Oreach nata lalun* (1939, 1950; *A Guest for the Night*, 1968), a semiautobiographical work, marks the manifestation of Agnon's tragic, epic perspective, in which the perceiving mind chronicles the desolation of a world. In 1945, he published *T'mol shilsom* (*Only Yesterday*, 2000), a novel marked by its time: World War II and the Holocaust. It is said to be his best novel, marking a new phase of modern Hebrew literature.

He published prolifically throughout his lifetime, with his works being reissued and translated frequently. In addition to imaginative literature, he published works on religious themes. He received the Israel Prize twice, in 1954 and 1958, and the Nobel Prize in Literature in 1966.

ANALYSIS

Agnon wrote from experience of a cultural world that was disappearing. It was the world of the European shtetl. Much of his writing deals with the conflict of one who lives in two worlds, one being the old world, a world of faith and miracles, and the other being the new world, a world of reason but also of alienation. His writings, which in publication dates alone span the first three-fourths of the twentieth century, tell the modern epic story of the Jewish people as they moved from their Eastern European shtetlach to Israel, from the empire of Franz Joseph to the Israel of David Ben-Gurion.

This major theme of Agnon's work—the ability of the individual rooted in a tradition to maintain that attachment in the modern world—clarified itself in most of his works. It is reflected in his many short stories and in his novels.

His narratives move seamlessly between the fantastic and the realistic. He also adapts images and stories from Jewish folklore and religious literature to serve as modern symbols. Throughout his works, there is a consciousness of the presence of Jewish tradition and teaching, and there is a display of that awareness. He is obviously well versed in the biblical, postbiblical, and medieval texts of Jewish law, lore, and literature, as well as of other Western texts. Agnon chose to write in Hebrew, but not in a purely modern idiom—rather in a more elevated diction, somewhat akin to medieval Jewish texts.

Agnon's use of allusion, especially allusion to the Old Testament Bible and other works of Judaica, is not straightforward. His allusions are for literary effect and are often playfully comic, ironic, or satiric. His settings are Buczacz, Galicia, Jaffa, Jerusalem, the state of Israel, and pre-World War II Germany. Agnon's protagonists are often cut off from a sense of community, and the experience of a spiritual void or an existential angst causes them to rely upon religion for substance and direction.

It is difficult to tell exactly what Agnon's attitude is toward his themes and characters. For example, one's understanding of *A Simple Story* depends upon one's understanding of Agnon's attitude toward the novel's protagonist, Hirshel Horovitz. Agnon's style makes an exact reading impossible. This purposeful ambiguity, however, creates richness and texture, and it allows irony to resonate on several levels.

While a few of Agnon's short stories can be enjoyed merely as tales, his art demands a more involved reading. For example, "Agunot" (1909; English translation, 1970), may be taken to contain the kernel of Agnon's metaphysics. Agnon took his surname from the word *aguna*, a married woman whose husband is not with her for one reason or another. The word's meaning, in a larger sense, refers to all those who cannot be with the person with whom they belong or in the place where they belong. They are the alienated. "Agunot" concerns a young woman who falls in love with a young man but who has been betrothed to another, who in turn is in love with yet another. These lovers are all alienated from one another by social forces; on one level, they represent the Jewish people, dispersed and alienated. All people, to one degree or another, are *agunot*.

In *Only Yesterday*, Agnon displays mastery of the surreal: In a world that has fallen apart, the narrative begins to come out of the mind of a dog. All dreams are not nightmares, however, and some vary from the bizarre event to the understandable working out of a real-life situation.

While Agnon provides a miraculous explanation for the events in his fiction, he at the same time gives a natural explanation. In *Hakhnasat kala* (1931; *The Bridal Canopy*, 1937), for example, Reb Yudel's wife, Frummet, and their daughters discover hidden treasure at the moment when the existence of their family's world depends upon finding the dowry. On one level, this is a miracle, but on another, explicable, for the treasure had been hidden by noblemen escaping in war.

Agnon's work, taken at once, is rather like an epic of a civilization about to disappear. He remains reverential toward the values of his ancestors, and it is perhaps this characteristic that separates him from many of his contemporaries. Whereas most of his works either completely satirize or completely romanticize shtetl life and values, and often present a vision of despair, Agnon implies that within alienation is some ultimate vision of hope, a vision usually grounded in traditional belief.

While Agnon takes a variety of stances toward his themes and his characters, ranging from the tender and nostalgic to the ironic and satiric, his oeuvre overall maintains that there is transcendent meaning for which the fragmented twentieth century consciousness searches. This meaning is not necessarily rooted in Eastern and Central Europe. The ideal of Jerusalem is ubiquitous in his work.

Agnon's use of the first-person narrator allows him to draw the reader into a relationship with his narrators with great immediacy. Characters lead the reader on their epic journey, personally showing the reader the ordered ways of the old country and the way into the twentieth century and modernity.

THE BRIDAL CANOPY

First published: *Hakhnasat kala,* 1931
    (English translation, 1937)
Type of work: Novel

Reb Yudel Nathanson has three daughters for whom he must find enough money for dowries. By a miracle, his family finds hidden treasure.

The Bridal Canopy, a major work in Hebrew literature, has been compared to Miguel de Cervantes's *Don Quixote de la Mancha* (1605, 1615). On the surface, Agnon's work seems a simple tale set in early nineteenth century Galicia. On another level, the story is not simple. It treats Agnon's all-but-simple themes: good and evil, loss of faith, marriage as the fulfillment of a divine command, divine providence, the centrality of the Torah, and the return to Israel. The surreal scenes often concern the separation of the Diaspora Jew from the Holy Land and from the Torah. On one level, the story is charming and naïve, like a folktale, but on another level, it critiques its own naïveté.

The Bridal Canopy is a comedy, with Nuta, a wagoner and Reb Yudel's traveling companion, playing the foil. It evolves through parody, the creation not of Agnon the nineteenth century Eastern European Hasid, but of Agnon the twentieth century Israeli writer. An observant Jew, Reb Yudel is re-

sponsible for marrying his daughters and finding their dowries, or "bringing them under the bridal canopy" (as the Hebrew title indicates). His wife Frummet moves him to action, and, with the counsel of the Rabbi of Apta, he sets out on a wagon journey to fulfill his obligations. This sets the picaresque plot in motion, with Reb Yudel, Nuta the wagoner, and talking horses telling stories.

The first part of the story ends as Yudel sends Nuta home. He plans to wait for God to send a bridegroom. The comic device of mistaken identity comes into play. Although he is poor, he is mistaken for a wealthy man. A match is made for his daughter with the son of a family as wealthy as they mistakenly think Reb Yudel to be. When the family is despairing that they will never come up with a dowry appropriate to this financially ill-matched engagement, a miracle happens. Reb Reveille, the rooster, in escaping from being served to the potential in-laws, leads Frummet and the daughters to a hidden treasure, enough to supply huge dowries for all three daughters. Filled with gratitude, Reb Yudel and his wife go to Israel. The devices of comedy inform the artist's gentle attitude.

A SIMPLE STORY

First published: *Sipur pashut,* 1935 (English
    translation, 1985)
Type of work: Novel

Triangles of unrequited love provide the irony in this romance, in which the forces of community win over those of romantic love.

Agnon's irony begins with the title of *A Simple Story.* Nothing in this simple story is as it seems, aesthetically or thematically. Like many of Agnon's works, it is set in a shtetl in Galicia during the first decade of the twentieth century. Bluma Nacht is orphaned and taken to Shisbush, where her aunt, Tsiril Horovitz, and her uncle, Baruch Meir Horovitz, take her in but require that she serve as their maid. Bluma is a romantic figure, an unconstrained spirit. Heartbreak complicates the plot when Hirshel Horovitz, Bluma's cousin and in spirit her direct opposite, falls in love with her. Socially awkward and especially inept at romance, Hirshel is railroaded into a marriage with Minnah Tzeimlich, someone more appropriate to his station. Even this triangle seems simple compared to what is revealed when Bluma leaves the Horovitz household and goes to work for Akavia Mazal, who had, earlier in life, also been kept from marrying his love for economic reasons as had, incidentally, Baruch Meir Horovitz and Bluma's mother, Mirel.

Just as Hirshel could not oppose his mother and the matchmaker, so he cannot assert control over anything else in his life. Like the other characters, he does not have the religious faith of the world of *The Bridal Canopy*. Things are done in certain ways merely because that is the way they are done. Empty ritual provides no meaning. His frustration is turned inward, and he descends into madness, as have others in his mother's family, purportedly as the result of a curse. Hirshel in his madness is unable to speak, instead crowing like a rooster and croaking like a frog. Just as Hirshel's psyche fragments, so does the society in which he lives. As Minnah's mother says, everyone's troubles (including madness) can be attributed to the fact that "belief has been weakened."

Married to Minnah, Hirshel longs for Bluma. Agnon's gift for haunting ambiguity is manifested in plot and theme. If this were, in fact, a simple story, the theme would be that the good of the individual is served by that individual's serving his or her society. It is not a simple story, however, and Agnon's is not a simple consciousness.

Hirshel does not descend into complete madness, nor does he possess the object of his obsession. He is cured by Dr. Langsam and takes his ap-

propriate place within his marriage and his society. Bluma, a sympathetic character, disappears from the narrative. Her story remains open-ended. The narrator says that the ensuing events of her life "would fill another book." The narrator seems to see the other characters as mediocre and plodding, but theirs is the world that remains intact. Ritual, whether meaningless or not, provides for tranquillity and stability.

A GUEST FOR THE NIGHT

First published: *Oreach nata lalun*, 1939, 1950 (English translation, 1968)
Type of work: Novel

Returning to visit his childhood home in Galicia, the narrator realizes that his authentic existence can only be lived in Israel.

Initially serialized (1938-1939) in the Tel Aviv newspaper *Ha-Arets*, *A Guest for the Night* is a first-person narration of the disappearing world of Galicia and of one individual's relationship to two places and two times: Shibush and Israel, before and after World War I. On one level an autobiography, the novel grew out of Agnon's brief visit in 1930 to Buczacz. Like Agnon, the narrator loses home and library and is separated from his family. The story moves beyond autobiography, however, as the narrator describes how World War I has all but ended the old way of life in Galicia. The artfully articulated characters reflect different aspects of the narrator's perception of his own situation.

He returns to visit Shibush on Yom Kippur. In contrast to what he expected, he finds himself a stranger. Shibush seems very quiet, as if spiritually deserted, bearing the evidence of the ruins of war and of the pogroms that followed. The people he meets are crippled physically and emotionally, including the narrator's companion, Daniel Bach, whose brother has recently been killed by Arabs near Jerusalem and who has himself seen a corpse, wrapped in a prayer shawl, blown up. In the postwar decay, the scenes in the synagogue are haunting: Because of the war, there are no prayer shawls, no adornment for the sacred scrolls. The entirety of the novel, however, is not so bleak.

Everyone is going to leave Shibush, so the narrator is given the key to the *bet midrash* (house of study and worship), the only place of wholeness and tranquillity for the narrator. He loses it, replaces it, and, when he uses it to close the *bet midrash* for the last time, gives the key to the first baby born in Shibush in four or five years. In Israel, the narrator discovers in his suitcase the lost key. A legend states that all Jewish houses of prayer and of study in the Diaspora will relocate themselves in Palestine. When the *bet midrash* of Shibush relocates, the narrator will be able to enter.

The narrator says to Hanokh, a wagoner, "without the power of imagination the world would not go on living." Ironically, the narrator's problem with Shibush is not that it is in decline or that it is ravaged by war, but that he came seeking the Shibush of his imagination—as it was when he was a child, and as it has been constructed in his remembrance. He dreams also the dream of redemption in the Holy Land. In a sense, the people in Galicia, those who remained and those who returned, stopped being able to imagine, and therefore stopped living, while those in the land of Israel had to imagine in order to survive.

SUMMARY

Shmuel Yosef Agnon's work tells the story of his protagonists, who are not only the Jewish people but also humanity in general. His works resonate with themes typical of the twentieth century: the search for meaning and truth, the breakdown of traditional values, alienation, and the necessity of hope for the future.

Donna Berliner

BIBLIOGRAPHY

By the Author

LONG FICTION:
Hakhnasat kala, 1931 (*The Bridal Canopy*, 1937)
Bi-levav yamim: Sipur agadah, 1935 (*In the Heart of the Seas: A Story of a Journey to the Land of Israel*, 1947)
Sipur pashut, 1935 (*A Simple Story*, 1985)
Oreach nata lalun, 1939 (reprint 1950; *A Guest for the Night*, 1968)
T'mol shilsom, 1945 (*Only Yesterday*, 2000)
Shirah, 1971 (*Shira*, 1989)
Bachanuto shel Mar Lublin, 1974

SHORT FICTION:
"Agunot," 1909 (English translation, 1970)
"Vehaya he'akov lemishor," 1912
Me'az ume'ata, 1931
Sipure ahavim, 1931
"Ha-mitpahat," 1932 ("The Kerchief," 1935)
Sefer hama'asim, 1932 (reprints 1941, 1951)
"Pat Shelema," 1933 ("A Whole Loaf," 1957)
Beshuva vanachat, 1935
Elu ve'elu, 1941
Shevu'at emunim, 1943 (*Betrothed*, 1966)
Ido ve'Enam, 1950 (*Edo and Enam*, 1966)
Samukh venir'e, 1951
Ad hena, 1952
Al kapot hamanul, 1953

DISCUSSION TOPICS

- What is the relationship between Hebrew and Yiddish, and what might be the reasons for Shmuel Yosef Agnon's composing in both languages early in his career?

- What is a shtetl and why was this kind of setting suitable for Agnon?

- What makes the key an important symbol in *A Guest for the Night*?

- Discuss the effects of unusual points of view in Agnon's fiction.

- How do Agnon's works illustrate the theme of going home?

Ha'esh veha'etsim, 1962
Two Tales, 1966 (includes *Betrothed* and *Edo and Enam*)
Selected Stories of S. Y. Agnon, 1970
Twenty-one Stories, 1970
Ir umelo'a, 1973
Lifnim min hachomah, 1975
Pitche dvarim, 1977
A Dwelling Place of My People: Sixteen Stories of the Chassidim, 1983
A Book That Was Lost, and Other Stories, 1995

POETRY:
Agnon's Alef Bet: Poems, 1998

NONFICTION:
Sefer, sofer, vesipur, 1938
Yamim nora'im, 1938 (*Days of Awe,* 1948)
Atem re'item, 1959 (*Present at Sinai: The Giving of the Law,* 1994)
Sifrehem shel tsadikim, 1961
Meatsmi el atsmi, 1976
Korot batenu, 1979

MISCELLANEOUS:
Kol sippurav shel Shmuel Yosef Agnon, 1931-1952 (11 volumes)
Kol sippurav shel Shmuel Yosef Agnon, 1953-1962 (8 volumes)

About the Author

Aberbach, David. *At the Handles of the Lock: Themes in the Fiction of S. Y. Agnon.* New York: Oxford University Press, 1984.

Band, Arnold J. *Nostalgia and Nightmare: A Study in the Fiction of S. Y. Agnon.* Berkeley: University of California Press, 1968.

_____. *Studies in Modern Jewish Literature.* Philadelphia: Jewish Publication Society, 2003.

Cutter, William, and David C. Jacobson, eds. *History and Literature: New Readings of Jewish Texts in Honor of Arnold J. Band.* Providence, R.I.: Program in Judaic Studies, Brown University, 2002.

Fisch, Harold. *S. Y. Agnon.* New York: Frederick Ungar, 1975.

Green, Sharon M. *Not a Simple Story: Love and Politics in a Modern Hebrew Novel.* Lanham, Md.: Lexington Books, 2001.

Hochman, Baruch. *The Fiction of S. Y. Agnon.* Ithaca, N.Y.: Cornell University Press, 1970.

Mintz, Alan L. *Translating Israel: Contemporary Hebrew Literature and Its Reception in America.* Syracuse, N.Y.: Syracuse University Press, 2001.

Anna Akhmatova

Born: Bol'shoy Fontan, near Odessa, Ukraine, Russia (now in Ukraine)
June 23, 1889
Died: Domodedovo, near Moscow, Soviet Union (now in Russia)
March 5, 1966

Twice nominated for the Nobel Prize in Literature, Akhmatova contributed significantly to twentieth century poetry in spite of constant censorship and threats to her existence by the Soviet regime.

Biography

Anna Akhmatova (ak-MAH-tuh-vah), the third child of Andrey and Inna Erazovna, was born Anna Andreyevna Gorenko on June 23, 1889, in Bol'shoy Fontan, Russia. Her mother and younger sister Irina suffered from tuberculosis; at four years of age Irina died from the deadly disease. Only a year older, Anna felt as if a great shadow covered her entire childhood as a result of the death of her younger sister.

Moving north eleven months after Anna's birth, the Gorenkos settled in Tsarskoye Selo, the czar's village, where Anna spent most of her childhood. The aspiring poet found little support from her father, who, when hearing of her poetry, asked her not to bring shame upon his name. Anna Gorenko therefore became Anna Akhmatova at the age of seventeen, taking the name of her maternal grandmother.

In early childhood, Akhmatova became ill with what was later diagnosed as smallpox. Near death, she ultimately recovered and was deaf for a limited time as the result of her illness. Following her recovery, she began to write poetry, forever linking her writing with her life-threatening illness.

At around the age of fourteen, Akhmatova met Nikolay Gumilyov, a young Russian poet, who fell madly in love with the thin young girl with large solemn eyes and long dark hair. Even after she left Tsarskoye Selo, following her parents' divorce, to finish her schooling in Kiev, he persistently courted the young poet. By 1910, following her first rejection of his marriage proposal and his subsequent suicide attempt, Akhmatova married Gumilyov near Kiev, with a honeymoon in Paris.

The young poets enjoyed a literary life, forming a poets' guild with others who were seriously writing poetry. In 1912, Akhmatova published her first collection of poetry, *Vecher* (evening). That year she also gave birth to her son Lev Nikolayevich. With the publication of her second collection, *Chetki* (1914; rosary), she became enormously popular. Tragedy followed closely behind. Her husband enlisted in the military and was sent to the front upon the outbreak of World War I. Soon after, her father died, and she was hospitalized briefly for tuberculosis.

Akhmatova, however, continued to write, meeting other prominent Russian poets as her popularity increased. In 1917, the Russian Revolution broke out and was closely followed by the Bolsheviks' seizing power. The Gumilyovs divorced and Akhmatova married Vladimir Shileiko, a historian of ancient Assyria and Babylonia. Russia's civil war and its terrorism created a climate of fear for many poets. The civil war ended in 1921, but civil unrest continued. In addition, Akhmatova suffered another loss when her former husband Gumilyov was executed for conspiracy against the new regime. She published three more collections during these difficult times, including *Belaya staya* (1917; white flock), *Podorozhnik* (1921; plantain), and *Anno Domini MCMXXI* (1922), and for her efforts was publicly denounced by poets politically aligned with the Soviet regime. In spite of advice from friends to flee Russia, she found herself bound to her country even though she was forced to suffer numerous hardships. With the solidification of Communist power by Joseph Stalin, Akhmatova was not allowed to publish and subsequently was expelled from the Soviet Writers' Union.

Residing with friends following her second divorce, she endured the frequent arrests of her son Lev, one of the many to fall victim to Stalin's purges of 1935 to 1938. Millions of people were sent to prisons for political infractions. Lev spent approximately seven years in prison, leaving his mother to agonize over his fate. Along with her son, friends of Akhmatova faced similar fates. The ban on publication of her work was briefly lifted in 1940. The book *Iz shesti knig* (1940; from six books) was withdrawn from sale and from libraries within the year.

Her health failing, Akhmatova suffered a heart attack in 1940. In the following years she contracted and recovered from typhus while giving poetry readings in hospitals. Despite these setbacks she published a much-censored collection, *Izbrannye stikhotvoreniia* (selected poems), in 1943. While in Moscow, she gave a poetry recital and was greeted with a standing ovation. Rather than feeling elated, she was fearful of political repercussions.

In Leningrad, she was followed by the Soviet police and her room was bugged. The Communist Party censured one magazine and closed another for publishing the works of Akhmatova and Mikhail Zoshchenko, another Russian poet. According to the decree banning their works, the poets were responsible for "poisoning the minds of Soviet youth." Following another arrest of her son, Akhmatova published a cycle of propagandist poems in 1950 in hopes of helping her son. He was not released until six years later, following the death of Stalin. During Nikita Khrushchev's leadership, Akhmatova's works were published but censored. She was allowed to travel to Europe to accept an Italian literary award and an honorary degree from Oxford University in England. After almost sixty years of writing poetry, she died on March 5, 1966, near Moscow.

ANALYSIS

The challenge of articulating in poetic form the human experience of young love, the pains of love, and the love of country is inherent in much of Akhmatova's poetry. Her love for the Russian people, as shown in her collections *Rekviem* (1963; *Requiem*, 1964) and *Poema bez geroya* (1960; *A Poem Without a Hero*, 1973), made her one of the most admired figures of modern Russia. Most of all, it is her resilient, individualistic spirit that all readers embrace. Whether in the romantic persona in *Belaya staya* or in the melancholy persona of *Chetki*, Akhmatova gave her voice to the Russian people during a tragic period in their history.

Akhmatova uses concrete imagery to convey the themes of passionate, young love in her first collections. Unlike the Russian Symbolists of the early twentieth century, she sought to describe the experience of love using concrete, natural images, not religious, imaginary ones. The Acmeist literary movement, of which the poet was a part, dramatically influenced Akhmatova's earlier works. The Acmeists insisted on clarity of expression. Akhmatova used objective, concrete things to convey strong emotions. For example, in one poem, the wind, given the human attribute of recklessness, conveys the poet's emotional state to the reader: "And we observe the rites of our bitter meetings,/ When suddenly the reckless wind/ Breaks off a sentence just begun."

In her later works, as Akhmatova faced the challenges of adulthood and as her country experienced the pains of World War I and a subsequent civil war, her poetry adopted a more mature voice, and her literary devices became infused with her individual style. From *Anno Domini MCMXXI*, the following illustrates her more experienced persona:

Seven days of love, seven terrible years of separation,
War, revolution, a devastated home,
Innocent blood on delicate hands,
Over the rosy temple a gray strand.

The images of love and death became linked in her poetic vision as they were in her experience.

By 1922, Akhmatova's political difficulties had become unrelenting and her poetry was banned from publication. Although she was officially denounced by the government, people continued to read her poetry, passing copies of her poems among themselves. In addition, Akhmatova continued to write, dramatizing her personal tragedies. Intensely personal, her poetic voice reveals itself without the objective distance of earlier poems. Her poetic voice resonates with the knowledge that she speaks for more than herself: "I somehow sense the groaning and the sorrows/ Of unrecognized, imprisoned voices."

In addition to articulating the agonized voice of her people, Akhmatova sought to capture the essence of the art of writing poetry. In one poem she writes: "it carves, it shifts, it weaves,/ And slips through my hands alive." The difficulties of writing, of holding on to the muse, become a source of inspiration.

Requiem announces the birth of a national poet, capable of giving voice to the horrors imposed on the Russian people by Stalin's regime. In the preface of the work, she greets a woman who, like her, is standing outside a Leningrad prison waiting to hear the fate of a loved one. The woman asks the poet: "Can you describe this?" The poet answers: "Yes, I can." Amanda Haight, who interviewed Akhmatova during the last few years of Akhmatova's life, describes the poet as experiencing a personal resurrection in the final poems of *Requiem*. Further, she characterizes the poet as accepting her place in life and in history, no matter what the price. Accepting her suffering as part of her fate, the poet began to take stock of the past. The poetic voice is intensely personal yet dramatically universal. Akhmatova uses biblical allusions to accentuate the universality of her suffering. For example, in the poem "Crucifixion," she describes the mother of Christ as the ultimate symbol of suffering. Ultimately, the brief epic describes the individual's experience as it represents a moment in the history of a nation. The poet gives voice to not only a personal but also a national tragedy:

> I remember them always and everywhere,
> And if they shut my tormented mouth,
>
> Through which a hundred million of my people cry,
> Let them remember me also. . . .

"Confusion"

First published: "Smyatnie," 1914 (collected in *The Complete Poems of Anna Akhmatova*, 1997)

Type of work: Poem

Describing a painful meeting between two former lovers, the poem dramatizes the melancholy acceptance of love forever lost.

"Confusion," included in Akhmatova's popular collection *Chetki*, captures the tone of the entire

work, which focuses on the meetings and separations of lovers and former lovers. The poet describes the painful meeting as draining, yet necessary, because it provides closure for the relationship that has left her hanging on during "Ten years of cries and trepidation." As she looks into her former lover's face, she does not see in him the intense emotion that she feels. She sees only the "simple civility" reflected in his kiss of her hand. At the conclusion of the poem, her soul is both "empty and serene."

The feeling of love's being both painful and exhilarating permeates every line. Concrete imagery and physical descriptions represent the intense emotion felt by the poet. The lines "a mist clouds my eyes" and "with a kiss you brushed my hand" characterize these literary devices. This use of concrete imagery is common throughout most of her earlier works. Also representative of the poet's craft is her dramatization of the moment. She sketches as if it were a painting in motion, the lyrical quality of her verse reflected in the lines: "And I can no longer fly,/ I who was winged from childhood."

Further exemplified in the poem is the poet's reliance on the narrative form to provide movement. In addition, the fluidity of the poem illustrates that confusion is as much a part of life as are love and loss. The realization of this is demonstrated by the persona's recognition that her soul is now serene for the first time in ten years after "all my sleepless nights." Out of her confusion she has found an inner peace that would not have come if she had not loved and lost.

Amanda Haight, Akhmatova's biographer, describes *Chetki* as representing a poet who is "beginning to know how to survive" lost love and abandonment. Haight concludes that finally poetry now plays a positive role in the poet's life, allowing her a sense of freedom and individuality. In addition, *Chetki* marked the beginning of Akhmatova's popularity as a poet and the maturation of her adult poetic voice.

Anna Akhmatova

"DARK DREAM"

First published: "Chernyy son," 1922 (collected in *The Complete Poems of Anna Akhmatova*, 1997)
Type of work: Poem

In six parts, the poem chronicles the suffocating bondage of the relationship between a husband and wife.

From the collection *Anno Domini MCMXXI*, the poem "Dark Dream" unifies two of Akhmatova's important themes: her strength and her individuality. Moreover, it laments not only a personal loss of love but also the conflict of ideal love with the realities of a husband and wife's relationship.

The poet laments the slow death of the marriage bond. Although it is on "the edge of the stage" she struggles to hold on to it despite its exacting cruelty: "You forbid singing and smiling// As long as we don't separate,/ Let everything else go!" The poet learns that the love is too painful; in part 3 she describes the love as blood, gushing "from my throat onto the bed." The fourth part is all coldness and numbness. The lover is beyond feeling pain, beyond feeling love or passion, as exemplified in the following: "If necessary—kill me// Everything your way: let it be!" The concluding part is a rebirth of the persona's strength as she tells her husband that she will not be submissive to him. "You're out of your mind," she chides, to think that she will submit to his will. Ultimately saying good-bye to her husband, she resolves that they are no longer bonded together, but she feels compassion for him "because you let this pilgrim into your home."

The poet anguishes over the death of her marriage and laments its passing in stages. By the end of the narrative, she has let go of a part of herself, a form of death, and given birth to the artist once more, who loves singing and freedom. Moreover, she is one who no longer will submit to the "hangman" and his "prison."

The poem ends with hope as the poet says good-bye to her husband and concludes that she now has peace and good fortune, as should he for having taken her in. The bitter tone of much of the poem is replaced with one of acceptance of the end of their relationship.

REQUIEM

First published: *Rekviem*, 1963 (English translation, 1964)
Type of work: Poem

A series of poems, in the form of a short epic, tells of a suffering mother who longs to know the fate of her imprisoned son.

Requiem, never published in the Soviet Union, describes an intensely personal and national struggle for survival. The preface, dedication, two epilogues, and the intervening series of poems combine to form a brief epic about the grieving mother of a prisoner and her fellow sufferers who stand in the prison lines of Leningrad. Although never acknowledged, the first-person-narrator "I" leaves little doubt of the directly autobiographical nature of the poem.

The preface, "Dedication," and "Prologue" provide the exposition for the work, establishing the historical scene and providing the introduction to the persona—a grieving mother longing to know the fate of her imprisoned son. In the preface the narrator answers, "Yes, I can," to a woman's inquiry about her ability to describe the awful terror of "where, unhappily, my people were." She identifies the cars of the secret police as the dreaded symbols of death and despair, as carrying people, including her son, away at dawn.

The literary devices of her previous works form a multilayered journey into a terrifying time in human history. Akhmatova uses concrete imagery and symbolism, both universal and biblical, to convey the significance of the story she has to tell. For example, when she addresses death, she uses a series of similes to dramatize the various forms it may take: "like a bandit," "like a typhus-germ," or "like a fairy tale of your own invention." (This last simile alludes to the imaginary crime that was often used to convict a political prisoner.) In addition, physical descriptions capture the terror of the time: "There I learned how faces fell apart/ How fear looks out from under the eyelids."

In addition to imagery and symbolism, she utilizes biblical allusions to dramatize the stages of the mother's suffering as they coincide with the stages of Mary's suffering for Christ. Christ was taken away, wrongly convicted, then crucified in front of his mother. The persona's son proceeds through the same steps. Moreover, as the poet becomes a symbol of Mary's suffering, so does she represent her people's suffering. *Requiem* speaks of not only one person, but a people, in torment.

Like an epic hero, the poet does not give in but lends courage to her people through her poetry: "I see, hear, touch/ all of you." She, essentially, becomes them. In the final lines of the poem, she wishes to become a bronze monument placed in front of the Leningrad prisons, where she waited with millions like her.

SUMMARY

Anna Akhmatova is one of the major literary figures of the twentieth century because of her lyrical artistry and universal themes. Her own personal struggle to maintain artistic integrity and independence in the face of death embodies the spirit of the artist. Amanda Haight, her biographer, describes Akhmatova as "the instrument of a higher power" who accepted her function as poet to describe "this drama that is life." With her death her work was completed, but the primary purpose for her life remains with readers forever in her poetry.

Cynthia S. Becerra

BIBLIOGRAPHY

By the Author

POETRY:
Vecher, 1912
Chetki, 1914
Belaya staya, 1917
Podorozhnik, 1921
Anno Domini MCMXXI, 1922
Iz shesti knig, 1940
Izbrannye stikhotvoreniia, 1943
Stikhotvoreniia, 1958
Poema bez geroya, 1960 (*A Poem Without a Hero,* 1973)
Rekviem, 1963 (*Requiem,* 1964)
Beg vremeni, 1965
Sochineniya, 1965-1983 (3 volumes)
Poems of A., 1973
Requiem, and Poem Without a Hero, 1976
Selected Poems, 1976
You Will Hear Thunder, 1976
Way of All the Earth, 1979
Anna Akhmatova: Poems, 1983
The Complete Poems of Anna Akhmatova, 1990 (2 volumes), updated and expanded 1997

NONFICTION:
O Pushkine: Stat'i i zametki, 1977

About the Author

Driver, Sam N. *Anna Akhmatova.* Boston: Twayne, 1972.
Feinstein, Elaine. *Anna of All the Russias: The Life of Anna Akhmatova.* London: Weidenfeld & Nicolson, 2005.

DISCUSSION TOPICS

- Anna Akhmatova's early illness helped her to become a poet. Did her preoccupation with illness needlessly limit her range of subject matter?

- Despite the horrors of her life under Soviet Communism, especially under the rule of Joseph Stalin, Akhmatova continued to live in the Soviet Union. Was this decision a mistake?

- How do you explain a person of such individualistic spirit being reconciled to the oppressiveness of the society in which she lived?

- Is Akhmatova's notion that confusion is a part of love true? Is it an unhappy truth?

- Investigate the word "requiem" and its appropriateness as the title of her poems that are considered to be a short epic.

- Was Akhmatova a hero as well as a great poet?

Haight, Amanda. *Anna Akhmatova: A Poetic Pilgrimage.* New York: Oxford University Press, 1976.

Harrington, Alexandra. *The Poetry of Anna Akhmatova: Living in Different Mirrors.* New York: Anthem Press, 2006.

Hingley, Ronald. *Nightingale Fever: Russian Poets in Revolution.* New York: Alfred A. Knopf, 1981.

Kalb, Judith E., and J. Alexander Ogden, eds. *Russian Writers of the Silver Age, 1890-1925.* Vol. 295 in *Dictionary of Literary Biography.* With the collaboration of I. G. Vishnevetsky. Detroit: Gale, 2004.

Nayman, Anatoly. *Remembering Anna Akhmatova.* New York: Henry Holt, 1991.

Sinyavski, Andrei. *For Freedom of Imagination.* New York: Henry Holt, 1971.

Wells, David N. *Anna Akhmatova: Her Poetry.* Washington, D.C.: Berg, 1996.

Ryūnosuke Akutagawa

Born: Tokyo, Japan
     March 1, 1892
Died: Tokyo, Japan
     July 24, 1927

Considered the father of the modern Japanese short story, Akutagawa was a superb stylist whose carefully composed tales explore the subtle shadings of human morality in the perennial battle between good and evil.

BIOGRAPHY

Ryūnosuke Akutagawa (ahk-ew-tah-gah-wah)— or Akutagawa Ryūnosuke, in the surname-first Japanese custom—was the pen name of Niihara Shinhara, who was born on March 1, 1892, in the Kyobashi district of Tokyo, Japan. Born into an educated family that once had a centuries-old tradition of service in the imperial court's tea ceremonies, he was the son of dairy owner Toshizo "Binzo" Shinhara. His mother, Fuku Niihara, became mentally ill soon after her son's birth; she died, insane, in 1902. His father, unable to provide for the infant, put his son into the care of a maternal uncle, Michiaki "Dosho" Akutagawa, from whom the future author's surname was derived. The author later adopted the familiar name of Ryūnosuke (dragon son), claiming he was born in the hour, month, day, and year of the dragon, according to the Chinese calendar.

A lonely child with few friends, Akutagawa became absorbed in classical Chinese literature and popular Japanese fiction, particularly the work of Japanese authors Mori Ōgai and Sōseki Natsume. Akutagawa also was an avid reader of Western fiction. Beginning in 1910, he attended First High School, where he cultivated friendships with classmates Kan Kikuchi, Yūzō Yamamoto, Kume Masao, and Tsuchiya Bunmei—all of whom would become well-respected writers in Japan.

In 1913, Akutagawa, who would prove to be a brilliant student, was admitted to Tokyo Imperial University, where he majored in English literature. He concentrated on such authors as Edgar Allan Poe, William Morris, Jonathan Swift, Robert Browning, and Ambrose Bierce, many of whom would influence his work. He began writing soon after entering the university, where he and some high school friends published a literary magazine, *Shinshicho* (new currents of thought), featuring translations of English-language poems and fiction, as well as original works. Akutagawa's first published writings in *Shinshicho* were his translations of works by William Butler Yeats and Anatole France. During his tenure at the university, Akutagawa proposed to a childhood sweetheart, Yayoi Yoshida. His adoptive parents, however, disapproved of his choice of mate, and the two did not marry.

Akutagawa published his first short story, "Rashō-mon," in 1915 (English translation, 1952) in the journal *Teikoku Bongaku* (imperial literature), where it was noticed and praised by Natsume, who became the budding author's mentor. Akutagawa also began publishing haiku poems under the pseudonym Gaki and wrote numerous essays. Akutagawa was highly productive during his university years and in the period immediately following, turning out some of his most memorable work from 1916 through 1918, including the short stories "Hana" (1916; "The Nose"), "Gesaku zanmai" (1917; "A Life Devoted to Gesaku"), "Kareno-shu" (1918; "O'er the Withered Moor"), "Jigokuhen" (1918; "Hell Screen"), and "Hokunin no shi" (1918; "The Death of a Christian").

After receiving his degree in 1916, Akutagawa taught English at the Naval Engineering College in Yokosuka from 1916 through 1917. In 1918, he married Fumiko Tsukamoto, to whom he had become engaged two years earlier. The couple had three sons: Hiroshi, born in 1920, who became an actor; Takashi, born in 1922, who was killed during World War II; and Yasushi, born in 1925, who became a composer.

Although he was invited to lecture at the universities of Kyōto and Tokyo, Akutagawa gave up teaching in 1919 to devote himself to full-time writing. While his fiction was based on tales from Japanese history, folklore, and mythology, it was told in modern language and reflected contemporary sensibilities. In 1921, in order to support his family better, Akutagawa traded his career in fiction for a stint as a foreign correspondent for an Ōsaka newspaper. Though he wrote one of his best-known stories, "Yabu no naka" (1922; "In a Grove," 1952), during this time, the reporting venture was a disaster. While traveling for several months in China and Russia on assignment, Akutagawa contracted a variety of ailments, from which he never fully recovered and which greatly affected his later work.

The last five years of Akutagawa's life and career were characterized by a decline into physical and mental illness, marked by frequent nervous breakdowns, alienation, and drug addiction. His writing during this final phase—evident in such works as "Haguruma" ("Cogwheels"), "Aru ahō no isshō" ("A Fool's Life"), and "Bungeiteki na, amari ni bungeiteki na" ("Literary, Much Too Literary"), all published in 1927—turned increasingly autobiographical, as he sank into depression and became obsessed with the idea that he had acquired the schizophrenia that had unhinged his mother. At the end of his life, Akutagawa experienced visual hallucinations, grew ever more uneasy about his mental state, and became determined to kill himself. He attempted suicide early in 1927 but did not go through with it. His second attempt was long contemplated, carefully planned, and prompted by a sense of anxiety regarding his future. He took an overdose of drugs, theorizing it was the least painful method of ending his life and the least upsetting to his family. This time he was successful, and Akutagawa died of an overdose of barbiturates at the age of thirty-five on July 24, 1927.

Akutagawa did not write any novels but wrote more than two hundred short stories, as well as novellas, poems, and essays, many of which were published posthumously. Akutagawa is Japan's most translated writer and is among its most controversial literary figures. Eight years after the author's suicide, Kan Kikuchi initiated the Akutagawa Prize in memory of his former high school friend. One of Japan's most highly regarded literary awards, the annual Akutagawa Prize is given to promising new writers.

ANALYSIS

Ryūnosuke Akutagawa's short stories have the quality of fine jewels created by a master gemologist. They are crafted with great care and attention to detail; they are multifaceted, glimmering from a variety of viewing angles; they have hidden depths of meaning that are revealed upon close scrutiny; and they have a polish that makes their brilliance linger in readers' memories. The subject matter of Akutagawa's body of work can be divided loosely into three groups.

His earliest phase is represented by such stories as "Rashōmon," which concerns self-interest for the sake of survival; "Imogayo" (1916; "Yam Gruel"), which deals with gluttony; and "The Nose," a study in vanity. In his early works, Akutagawa retold stories from Japanese history and legend in modern language and from a contemporary psychological perspective. These tales were intended to demonstrate humankind's eternal conflict between noble and base instincts, and they generally serve to ironically illuminate less savory motivations that lead to socially unacceptable forms of behavior.

In the second group of stories, Akutagawa's emphasis shifted to realism to examine the nature of art and art's effects on life. Stories such as "Hell Screen," in which a medieval painter sacrifices his daughter to death by immolation in order to capture her agony for art's sake, and "Seika no ichi" (1922; "The Garden"), in which a modern man sacrifices his own health to restore a dilapidated Japanese garden to its pristine splendor, are emblematic of this period.

The final group, characterized by stories like "Cogwheels," a harrowing hallucination, and "A Fool's Life," a series of vignettes that encapsulate the author's mental deterioration, consist of intimate personal documentation of the author's absorption with his descent into insanity, which culminated in his suicide.

Many of the stories Akutagawa wrote throughout his career were overt examinations of faith, such as "Hōkyōnin no shi" (1918; "The Martyr") or "Nankin no Kirisuto" (1920; "Christ in Nanking"). Other stories contain religious undertones or incorporate elements of superstition and the supernatural. An early opponent of the self-confessional naturalism that held sway in Japanese literature during the time he flourished, Akutagawa seamlessly blended aspects of Eastern and Western philosophical thought. A well-integrated product of his Asian heritage and his English-oriented education, Akutagawa simultaneously combined the stoicism and fatalism of the one culture with the exuberance and spontaneity of the other.

In his scores of stories based upon historical material, Akutagawa was especially interested in three distinct eras from Japan's past. Of primary interest is the Heian (meaning "peace" or "tranquillity") period, an era that stretched for nearly four hundred years, from 794 to1185. During this period, the Japanese capital was moved to Kyōto, such Chinese influences as Confucianism dominated, and the samurai class came to power. Equally important, art and literature rose to prominence in the Japanese imperial court. The world's first novel, Murasaki Shikibu's *Genji monogatari* (c. 1004; *The Tale of Genji*, 1925-1933), and Sei Shōnagon's court exposé *Makura no sōshi* (*The Pillow Book*) were written during the Heian period, as were the words to Japan's national anthem. Akutagawa's most widely recognized stories, "Rashōmon" and "In a Grove," are set in this historically significant age.

A second era of interest is the Edo period (1603-1868), particularly the late Tokugawa Shogunate (1853-1867). This was a time of great upheaval, when Japan struggled to move from an isolated feudal culture to a modern society in step with the Western world. Akutagawa's "The Assassination of a Culture" (1918) is one of his stories set in this period.

The third era of concentration is the time in which Akutagawa came of age, the Meiji period (1868-1912), when Japan began to modernize and become a world power, and the succeeding Taisho age (1912-1926). These periods were marked by many economic and societal reforms; Japan embraced Western technology and expertise that allowed the country to triumph in such military engagements as the Sino-Japanese War (1894-1895) and the Russo-Japanese War (1904-1905), to become a partner of the Allied effort in World War I, and ultimately to embark on an ill-fated expansionist program leading to utter defeat in World War II. An example of Akutagawa's stories set in this period is the humorous "Negi" (1919; "Green Onions"), in which a Japanese waitress believes she resembles an American silent film star and acts accordingly.

During any phase of Akutagawa's productivity and regardless of his focus, his stories exhibit distinctive stylistic and literary characteristics. Chief among these is Akutagawa's skill in the precise, economical selection of deceptively simple, unambiguous words that nonetheless allow for multiple interpretations of meaning—though such subtleties are frequently lost in translation. Other stylistic characteristics are his satirical, sometimes cynical, outlook; his fondness for such literary devices as symbolism and metaphor; and his tendency (except for his later first-person autobiographical material) to present even horrific or gruesome information from a detached, third-person reportorial viewpoint. Despite the typically downbeat subject matter, there is often a sly wit and always a keen intelligence at work that uplifts the tales from merely morbid studies of depravity, corruption, or immorality to timeless fiction. Akutagawa does not telegraph his intentions or provide handy morals in his stories but lets his readers decide what to make of his often disturbing fiction.

A constant experimenter in form and presentation, the versatile and prolific Akutagawa structured his stories in a wide variety of ways. His fiction features confessions told from multiple viewpoints, straightforward narration, pseudoscreenplays, dialogue-heavy tales, and interior monologue. Characterization is a particular Akutagawa strength: He presents a complete panoply of human types—the braggart, the coward, the glutton, the envious, the lustful, and the greedy—and imparts to each an individual spin that stamps him or her as an original character. A master craftsman in the often underappreciated short-story form, Akutagawa is the embodiment of Seneca's proverb *Vita brevis est, longa ars*, or "Life is short, art is long."

"RASHŌMON"

First published: 1915 (collected in
Rashomon, and Other Stories, 1952)
Type of work: Short story

*A discharged samurai's servant takes shelter
in Kyōto's Rashōmon Gate, where he discovers an
old woman stealing the hair from an abandoned
corpse to make a wig she will sell in order to buy
food.*

One of Akutagawa's best-known stories, "Rashōmon" tells of a nameless servant in Kyōto who has
been laid off by his samurai master after an economic decline in the Heian period. The servant
takes shelter from a rainstorm in the Rashōmon
Gate. Once a proud, multistoried structure decorated with crimson lacquer, the gate has fallen into
disrepair and now serves as a den for wild animals,
a hideout for thieves, and a dumping ground for
unclaimed corpses.

As the servant sits considering whether to starve
to death—an honorable course of action—or to
dishonorably survive by becoming a thief, he sees
movement on the steps above and creeps upward with his hand on his
sword. He finds an old
hag plucking the long,
black hair from the head
of the abandoned corpse
of a woman. Disturbed by
her ghoulish behavior,
the servant confronts the
hag. She claims she is
stealing the hair to con-
struct a wig she will sell
for food in order to sur-
vive. The hag asserts her
action is fitting because
while the dead woman was alive, she survived by
less than honorable means—cooking snake meat
for sale and passing it off as fish.

Caught up in the logic of this argument, the servant succumbs to his instinct for survival. He, too,
becomes a thief; he overpowers the hag, rips the
shabby clothing off her body, and leaves her alive
among the scattered corpses. Clutching his ill-
gotten booty that he will sell to live for yet another
day, he runs off into the night, leaving the hag to
fend for herself as best she can.

"IN A GROVE"

First published: "Yabu no naka," 1922
(collected in *Rashomon, and Other Stories*,
1952)
Type of work: Short story

*A number of individuals give conflicting
testimony to a high police commissioner regarding
a crime that occurred in a grove—the alleged
murder of a samurai and the rape of his wife.*

"In a Grove" (sometimes translated as "In a Bam-
boo Grove") gained worldwide renown for serving
as the basis for director Akira Kurosawa's film
Rashōmon (1950), which won an Academy Award
for Best Foreign Language Film. A Heian era morality tale that in message—what should be considered good or evil depends upon the circumstances—"In a Grove" echoes Akutagawa's earlier
story "Rashōmon." "In a Grove" was probably inspired by some or all of several sources. They include an early Japanese story, "The Tale of the
Bound Man Who Was Accompanying His Wife to
Tanba" (twelfth century), which deals with a man
forced to witness the rape of his wife; Ambrose
Bierce's short story "The Moonlit Road" (1893),
which concerns the use of a medium to obtain the
account of a dead woman regarding her murder;
and Robert Browning's long narrative poem *The
Ring and the Book* (1868-1869), which presents a
murder from twelve points of view.

It is to Akutagawa's credit that whatever his inspiration, he constructed a short fictional piece
uniquely his own. In the process, he devised a
clever, intriguing, and memorable mystery story,
which anticipates the modern law enforcement
precept of the unreliability of eyewitnesses.

The three-thousand-word story consists solely of
the verbal testimony of seven different individuals—a woodcutter, an itinerant Buddhist priest, a
policeman, an old woman, the confessed thief and
murderer (Tajomaru), the woman who was assaulted (Masago), and a dead man (Takehiko,
summoned through the assistance of a medium)—

regarding the supposed murder of a man, the alleged rape of his wife, and the presumed theft of their belongings. Each deposition, given in a distinctive voice that by its style helps identify the speaker, adds details to the previous account, which seems to clarify the sequence of events but actually serves to confuse the issue. Discrepancies and contradictions abound; several people admit to various crimes, and many pertinent questions remain unanswered. Since each individual brings a personal agenda to his or her report, has a particular perspective on events, notices different details, and has difficulty being objective, none of the statements can be fully trusted. Takehiko is certainly dead, and Tajomaru was definitely found in possession of stolen goods, but beyond those scant facts lurks a host of unknowns.

SUMMARY

In his short stories, Ryūnosuke Akutagawa explores the depths of human behavior, particularly in times of stress—a reflection of the tension that consumed him throughout his short but productive life. A brilliant, if neurotic, writer, Akutagawa built suspense through the use of believably flawed characters placed in plausible situations, whose actions are described in crisp, simple language layered with symbols that give an extra dimension to his prose. In much of his work, Akutagawa remained detached from his unflinching narratives as a counter to the self-indulgent naturalism that prevailed in Japanese literature during his heyday. The author's bleak perspective can be seen as an extension of his inner turmoil related to the growing conviction that he was sinking hopelessly into inherited insanity. Dark as they are, Akutagawa's stories illuminate by example the principle that human beings in every time and place are linked by identical motivations, common concerns, and inevitable fates.

Jack Ewing

BIBLIOGRAPHY

By the Author

SHORT FICTION:
Rashōmon, 1915 (*Rashomon, and Other Stories*, 1952, 1964)
"Yabu no naka," 1922 ("In a Grove," 1952)
Aru ahō no isshō, 1927 (*A Fool's Life*, 1971)
Kappa, 1927 (English translation, 1970)
Tales Grotesque and Curious, 1930
Jigokuhen, 1946 (*Hell Screen, and Other Stories*, 1948)
Japanese Short Stories, 1961
Exotic Japanese Stories: The Beautiful and the Grotesque, 1964
The Essential Akutagawa: "Rashōmon," "Hell Screen," "Cogwheels," "A Fool's Life," and Other Short Fiction, 1999

DISCUSSION TOPICS

- In Ryūnosuke Akutagawa's story "Rashōmon," there is a wealth of animal imagery, including a cricket, fox, crow, dog, cat, lizard, monkey, snake, fish, chicken, and bird of prey. What do these animals symbolize in the story?

- What is the significance of the "red, festering pimple" on the servant's cheek in "Rashōmon"?

- In "Rashōmon," Akutagawa seems to support the notion that survival takes precedence over honor. Do you agree or disagree with this point of view?

- In the story "In a Grove," what crimes were truly committed, what were the motivations for the crimes, and who is/are the primary suspect(s) for each crime?

- The individuals who give testimony in "In a Grove" often contradict one another. Compare their accounts, set up a timetable of events, and discuss the inconsistencies.

- Why do you think Akutagawa structured "In a Grove" as a series of verbal statements? Why did he select the particular individuals to give testimony?

- From their portrayals as characters in "Rashōmon" and "In a Grove," extrapolate Akutagawa's attitude toward women.

MISCELLANEOUS:
Akutagawa Ryūnosuke zenshū, 1995-1998 (24 volumes)

About the Author

Kato, Shuichi. "Akutagawa, Kawabata, and Taisho Fiction." In *The Modern Years*. Vol. 3 in *A History of Japanese Literature*. Tokyo: Kodansha International, 1979-1983.

Keene, Donald. *Dawn to the West*. New York: Columbia University Press, 1998.

Klein, Leonard S., ed. *Far Eastern Literature in the Twentieth Century: A Guide*. New York: Ungar, 1986.

Lewis, Arthur O., and Yoshinobu Hakutani, eds. *The World of Japanese Fiction*. New York: E. P. Dutton, 1973.

Morris, Ivan, ed. "Introduction to 'Autumn Mountains.'" In *Modern Japanese Stories: An Anthology*. Tokyo: Charles E. Tuttle, 1977.

Rimer, J. Thomas. *A Reader's Guide to Japanese Literature from the Eighth Century to the Present*. Tokyo: Kodansha International, 1988.

Ueda, Makoto. "Ryūnosuke Akutagawa." In *Modern Japanese Writers and the Nature of Literature*. Stanford, Calif.: Stanford University Press, 1976.

SHOLOM ALEICHEM

Born: Pereyaslav, Russia (now Pereyaslav-Khmelnitsky, Ukraine)
March 2, 1859
Died: New York, New York
May 13, 1916

Through his often comic stories, Aleichem depicted the difficulties confronting Eastern European Jews as they faced threats to their traditional way of life in the late nineteenth and early twentieth centuries.

Library of Congress

BIOGRAPHY

Sholom Aleichem (ah-LAY-kehm) was the pen name of the Russian Jewish writer Sholom (or Solomon) Rabinovich. He was born in the Ukrainian town of Pereyaslav, but the family soon moved to nearby Voronko, the model for the fictional town of Kasrilevke in his writings. For a dozen years the young Sholom lived a comfortable life as the son of a wealthy and respected merchant, Menachem Nahum Rabinovich. However, his father suffered a financial reversal when Sholom was not yet thirteen, and soon after that Sholom's mother died of cholera. His father remarried, and the sharp tongue of his new wife gave rise to Sholom's first literary production, a collection of his stepmother's Yiddish curses.

His next literary production was a Hebrew-language novel written while attending a Russian-language high school in Pereyaslav. After high school Sholom found a position as a tutor for the daughter of a wealthy Jewish landowner. He promptly fell in love with his pupil, and her father sent him away. He eventually found an administrative position in the town of Lubny and while employed there began writing articles in Hebrew for various periodicals on social and educational issues.

He and his former pupil, Olga, reunited and were married in 1883. Now reconciled to the match, Olga's father invited his new son-in-law

back to his estate and supported him while he devoted himself full time to writing. That same year he published his first story in Yiddish, "Tsvey Shteyner" ("Two Stones"), and adopted the name Sholom Aleichem, which in Hebrew means "peace unto you" and is a traditional Jewish greeting.

Aleichem's first literary success was with the story "Dos Messerl" ("The Penknife") in 1886, one of many stories he wrote about children, this one focusing on a young boy's guilt over stealing a penknife. He also produced several full-length romantic novels in this period, but they were not successful. More significant was his work editing an annual anthology of Yiddish writing.

When his father-in-law died in 1885, Aleichem inherited his wealth, but he lost all the money in a stock market crash in 1890. For the rest of his life, Aleichem had to struggle to support himself and his family through the income from his writings and lecture tours.

In 1892, Aleichem published the first of his Menachem-Mendl letters, a series that would continue throughout the decade. In 1894, partly inspired by a milkman he met, he began publishing his sketches about Tevye the Dairyman. He also wrote a series of stories set in the fictional town of Kasrilevke and a satire called *Der farkishnefter Shnayder* (1900; *The Bewitched Tailor,* 1960).

In 1905, after a failed revolution in Russia, anti-Jewish pogroms, or riots, broke out throughout the country. In the wake of these, Aleichem decided to leave Russia, traveling first to central Europe and then to New York City. He was well received wherever he went; by this time was considered the world's leading writer in Yiddish and sometimes referred to as the "Jewish Mark Twain." However, he could not support himself in New York and returned to Europe, settling in Geneva, Switzerland.

In 1908, he fell ill with tuberculosis, after which he spent much of his time in European sanatoriums. He was declared cured in 1913, and when World War I broke out he and his family again traveled to the United States. His two visits to the United States inspired him to write his sketches about Mottel, the cantor's son. In this period he also wrote a series called *Ayznban geshikhtes* (railroad stories), published in periodicals from 1902 through 1911 and included in the English translation, *Tevye the Dairyman and The Railroad Stories* (1987). He also wrote several more novels.

He fell ill again in New York while still working on his Mottel sketches, and he died there on May 13, 1916. Thousands came to pay their respects, and after his death his reputation grew among literary scholars. He also indirectly reached a larger, non-Jewish audience through the 1964 Broadway musical *Fiddler on the Roof*, based on his Tevye stories; the musical was later adapted for the screen.

ANALYSIS

Like Mark Twain, to whom he is often compared, Aleichem was both serious and comic. Beneath a comic veneer he addressed serious issues about the situation of the Jewish community in Eastern Europe at a time of transformation and crisis. In Aleichem's day the traditional Jewish shtetl, or small town, was breaking down in the face of the forces of modernization and because of anti-Jewish laws and pogroms. Some Russian Jews fled to the cities, even though they could not legally live there, hoping to make a living in the new world of modern commerce and finance. Others fell victim to the anti-Jewish rioters, others emigrated, primarily to the United States, and some remained in Eastern Europe, trying to balance tradition and modernization.

Aleichem explores all these responses to the pressures of modernization in his major works, expressing a complex set of attitudes despite his accessible, colloquial writing style. Writing in Yiddish, the language of the Eastern European Jews, rather than in Hebrew, the language of the Jewish elite, he seeks to explore the everyday experiences of ordinary Jews from a sympathetic viewpoint, even while reserving the right to stand back and sometimes laugh at them.

Not only does he write in Yiddish, but Aleichem also hands over the narration of his major works to ordinary people with very little pretense to learning, Tevye the Dairyman's frequent quotations from the Bible notwithstanding. Aleichem speaks to his readers through the voice of Tevye or through Mottel, a mere child, or through Menachem-Mendl, the naïve investor, and his wife, the uneducated Sheineh-Sheindl. At times he uses a gentle irony at the expense of these characters, revealing their lack of understanding of the situations in which they find themselves; for instance, neither Menachem-Mendl nor his wife truly understands the world of speculators and brokers in which Menachem-Mendl seeks to make a living. Aleichem, however, does not mock his characters but seeks to reveal the struggles they are undergoing as they deal with their various situations, all of which in a sense are the same situation: the fate of the Eastern European Jews at the end of the nineteenth century.

THE ADVENTURES OF MENACHEM-MENDL

First published: *Menakhem-Mendl*, 1895 (English translation, 1969)
Type of work: Short stories

Menachem-Mendl and his wife exchange letters in which he describes his foolish business projects and she keeps telling him to come home.

Originally published as independent pieces, the Menachem-Mendl letters were gathered into a collection published in 1895, at which point Sholom Aleichem revised and expanded the stories to form a coherent whole. In this final form they constitute an epistolary novel of sorts—a novel in which all of the narration is done through letters.

In his first letter, Menachem-Mendl writes from the city of Odessa to tell his wife, Sheineh-Sheindl, who lives in the small town of Kasrilevke, how well he is doing as a currency speculator. He exaggerates so much that the reader is immediately skeptical, as is his wife, who wants him to provide more details. Throughout these letters Sheineh-Sheindl will continually ask for more details of her husband's business ventures, while Menachem-Mendl will continually say he has no time to write.

Menachem-Mendl's reluctance to say more is perhaps part of his struggle for independence from the shtetl life in Kasrilevke. In the opinion of literary critic Dan Miron, Menachem-Mendl is trying to break free of traditional life. He has escaped to the city and is never going home, despite his wife's desire that he return. At the same time, he does keep writing her, suggesting that he cannot fully free himself; he wishes to maintain some contact with the traditional life he has left behind, even while seeking to throw himself into a more modern existence.

Part of the comedy, which is also tragic, derives from Menachem-Mendl's inability to fully understand the modern life in which he is trying to participate. Sheineh-Sheindl understands it even less, and there is humor in her misunderstanding his references to coffee shops (she thinks they are the names of women) and her confusion over what her husband is doing. She keeps wanting to know the size and weight of the currency and stocks he is investing in, as if they were solid objects.

Part of Aleichem's point is that these are not solid objects, but mere air, as Sheineh-Sheindl says at one point, and without anything solid beneath him, Menachem-Mendl perpetually falls. Thus, he eventually loses everything in his currency speculations and has to start again with nothing. He does, however, persist in starting over and over again, trying one business venture after another, moving from currency speculation to being a commodity broker, to discounting, to investing in real estate, forests, sugar mills, and mines, and to trying his luck as a writer, a marriage broker, and an insurance agent. Unfortunately, he has no luck at all, and though he is resolutely upbeat in the earlier letters, by the end he sometimes gives way to despair before deciding he should immigrate to the United States.

Another source of humor is the repeated contradiction between the flowery, conventional way both Menachem-Mendl and Sheineh-Sheindel begin their letters and the actual content that follows. Presumably they have learned the "proper"

way to start a letter, which for Sheineh-Sheindl always involves thanking God that everyone is in good health. This is usually followed, however, by her writing that she or the children are ill. She also invariably signs off as Menachem-Mendl's devoted wife, but this usually comes after a tirade against his foolishness and a demand that he end his speculations, stop ignoring his family, and come back to her. On the surface there is an attempt to maintain the forms of propriety and well-being, but underneath there is trouble and dissatisfaction.

Religion is notably absent from these letters. It is an absence brought to readers' attention early on, when Menachem-Mendl notes that trading goes on in Odessa until the time when evening prayers are said in Kasrilevke. Menachem-Mendl seems too busy with business to attend to prayers and religion; business, in fact, seems to be his new religion, as well as a way to break free from his traditions. Also notable is the fact that Menachem-Mendl's lodgings remind him of a jail. He is seeking freedom from the shtetl, but he seems to have found not freedom but a new sort of bondage, which includes perpetually avoiding the police, who might arrest him at any moment for living illegally in a city where Jews are forbidden to reside.

After his currency business fails, Menachem-Mendl moves to a new city, Yehupetz, a fictionalized version of Kiev. Sheineh-Sheindl becomes increasingly impatient, having expected him to return home after his first failure, and she begins to talk of her troubles at home. The author Hillel Halkin has suggested that Sheineh-Sheindl's inclusion of more news from home may indicate that she subconsciously realizes that the only communication and intimacy possible with her husband will be through these letters. Also, since the news from home is usually negative, involving illness, death, broken engagements, fires, and bankruptcies, the total effect is of failure everywhere: Menachem-Mendl is a failure in the big city, and in the small town nothing goes right.

TEVYE THE DAIRYMAN

First published: *Tevye der Milkhiger,* 1894–1914 (English translation, 1949 as *Tevye's Daughters;* also known as *Tevye the Dairyman*)
Type of work: Short stories

After a cheerful Tevye tells how he struck it rich in the dairy business, a sadder Tevye tells the stories of his daughters' marriages.

Like the collection of Menachem-Mendl's letters, the stories in *Tevye the Dairyman* were originally published separately and then collected and published in book form. The stories are all monologues, in which Tevye is supposedly addressing Sholom Aleichem himself, and in them Tevye presents himself as a folksy philosopher, frequently quoting the Bible and other religious texts, although his references are always connected to the concerns of everyday life.

The first Tevye episode is the sunniest, as indicated by its title, "Dos groyse Gevins" ("Tevye Strikes It Rich"; also translated as "The Jackpot"), in which an impoverished Tevye goes into the dairy business by pure happenstance. He offers a ride to two women lost in the forest and as a reward receives money and a cow. This almost magical encounter makes Tevye and his wife, Golde, happy, and when he speaks about it eight or nine years later, Tevye is able to be philosophical about his earlier poverty. It is all up to God, he says; the main thing is to work hard, have confidence, and leave things to God. Throughout the stories, Tevye talks about God in a familiar way; he even seems to be mocking Him at times, as when he says that in his days of poverty his family went hungry three times a day with God's help.

Still, in this first episode Tevye seems happy in his faith, something that will change in the later episodes, in which Tevye suffers tragedy after tragedy and begins to compare himself to the biblical Job. Like Job, he demands an explanation from God and also seems to lose his faith. However, in the earlier episodes he is still cheerful, even when he loses money through a foolish partnership with Menachem-Mendl. Man plans and God laughs, says Tevye, but not bitterly, more philosophically.

In the next episode Tevye has a chance to marry his eldest daughter, Tsaytl, to the town's wealthy butcher, Layzer Wolf, but Tsaytl wants to marry the poor tailor, Mottel Kamzoyl. At first Tevye is resistant, not just because Layzer Wolf has more money but also because the parents traditionally decide whom their children should marry. In the end, however, Tevye lets Tsaytl marry the tailor, and the result is more or less happy because she gets to marry the man she loves. The situation does, however, prompt Tevye to complain to God about the lack of justice in the world: Why should others be rich and he not? It also makes him wonder what the world is coming to when children make the decisions.

The next four episodes all concern marriages or proposed marriages that in some way undermine tradition. First there is Hodl, Tevye's second-oldest daughter, who wants to marry a revolutionary activist. Again, one of the issues is who decides, but there is also the clash between traditional ways and revolutionary ideas. Tevye again goes along, but this time the result is less happy; Hodl's new husband is arrested and sent to Siberia, and she follows him there.

In a heartbreaking episode, Tevye's daughter, Chava, falls in love with a non-Jewish boy, whom she wants to marry. This Tevye cannot accept. He has gone a certain distance in accommodating modern ways, but the traditional Jewish insistence on marrying within the Jewish faith is not something he is prepared to violate. When Chava insists upon marrying the Gentile, Tevye disowns her.

In the next episode, his daughter Shprintze falls in love with the son of a rich Jewish family. This pleases Golde, but Tevye is wary. People like money too much, he says, moving away from his earlier desire to be rich. He also thinks the rich family will oppose the match, and he is right. They spirit their son away, and Shprintze drowns herself in despair.

In the last marriage episode, Beilke, out of concern for her father, agrees to marry a rich man she does not love in order for her family to have some money. She marries the rich man, but instead of making Tevye happy, the marriage leaves him feeling that his daughter has sacrificed her own happiness. He now seems even more opposed to the pursuit of money; it just brings unhappiness.

In the final episode, a pogrom breaks out, forcing Tevye and others to flee, and though the pogrom is presented comically, it seems like a grim conclusion to an increasingly dark tale.

THE ADVENTURES OF MOTTEL, THE CANTOR'S SON

First published: *Mottel, Peyse dem Khazns,* 1907-1916 (English translation, 1953)
Type of work: Short stories

After the death of his father and the failure of various business ventures, Mottel, his family, and their friend Pinye set out for America.

The Adventures of Mottel, the Cantor's Son is another collection of Sholom Aleichem's stories. This time the stories are told by a young child, Mottel, whose father is dying. Despite this imminent death, or perhaps because of it, Mottel seems exuberantly happy. When his father dies and he becomes, according to the terminology of the shtetl, an orphan, he is even happier because it means everyone treats him nicely and he is excused from attending school. The critic Dan Miron suggests that the deeper reason for this happiness is that Mottel wishes to break free of the shtetl's restrictions, which are represented by his father. However, in the opinion of critics Frances Butwin and Joseph Butwin, Mottel's happiness is an Oedipal victory for the son over the father, avoiding the father-son conflict found in other stories by Aleichem.

Mottel spends as much time as he can outdoors, playing with a neighbor's calf or going fishing. He also steals fruit from a garden, which lands him in trouble. He has a nightmarish experience staying with an old man, who first tries to read him a book by the medieval scholar Moses Maimonides and then threatens to eat him, perhaps suggesting that looking back into the past may be dangerous.

Mottel mainly looks forward and wants to have adventures. He is thus quick to join his brother Elye in various business ventures, such as manufacturing soft drinks, producing ink, and working as exterminators. Elye, who has a book suggesting all these projects, is sometimes compared to Menachem-Mendl; like Menachem-Mendl, all Elye's projects come to nothing. Moreover, as Miron notes, all of Elye's projects involve poison; it is as if such business ventures are poisonous, at least if they remain connected to the Old World. Only when the family escapes to the New World do their business ventures begin to succeed. America, it seems, is the Promised Land, where everything will finally work out.

The family experiences difficulty in getting to America, including a brush with thieves and murderers at the Russian border. Once out of Russia they encounter further problems, most notably getting medical clearance to enter the United States. Mottel's mother, who is still attached to the shtetl they left behind, cries continually, and the others warn her that this will hurt her eyes so she will be unable to pass the medical examination. This turns out to be true; as Dan Miron says, this nostalgic attachment to the shtetl, manifested through tears, becomes a disease and an obstacle to emigrating. Thus, the family must find another way to free themselves from the Old World.

Meanwhile, Mottel develops a talent as a caricaturist and is always doodling, prompting his brother to slap him repeatedly, perhaps because drawing likenesses is a violation of Jewish tradition. Mottel is continually trying to break free of tradition and continually slapped down for it, but he remains cheerfully exuberant throughout, eagerly looking forward to the hustle and bustle he expects to find in New York.

Once the family arrives in America, Mottel celebrates it as a place for the underdog, while the family's friend Pinye praises its freedom and democracy and the opportunity it provides to get ahead economically. Some of the family members are reluctant to seize this opportunity because it involves beginning at the bottom as manual laborers, and they see such work as demeaning to the family of a deceased cantor. Pinye, however, pushes them forward and they get jobs, ignoring the hierarchical rules of the Old World. They also immerse themselves in American culture, from chewing gum to film houses to learning English.

Left unfinished when Aleichem died, the Mottel stories end with the family moving on from factory work to operating a street stand to planning to open their own store. They are also planning to move; moving, indeed, is what Mottel loves about America. Throughout the book he is a force for movement, action, and adventure, and for breaking free of old ways.

SUMMARY

In his short stories, Sholom Aleichem examines the life of Russian Jews, forced to live in the shtetls, from several different angles. Menachem-Mendl seeks to escape from traditional shtetl life by throwing himself into the pursuit of money, but this leads him nowhere. Menachem-Mendl's wife, Sheine-Sheindl, remains in the shtetl, demanding that Menachem-Mendl return. Her life seems to be one long litany of woes. In the Menachem-Mendl letters, therefore, Aleichem seems to suggest that neither staying in the shtetl nor rejecting it for a life spent pursuing wealth will offer happiness.

The sympathetically presented Tevye offers another approach to the problem. He tries to balance traditional shtetl life with the forces of modernity represented by his independent-minded daughters. This approach does not work either, ending in death, separation, and expulsion.

Then there is Mottel, who exuberantly flees to America, embracing freedom, democracy, and economic opportunity. Mottel, along with Pinye, reaches for more than just money in the manner of Menachem-Mendl; they seek a whole new way of life, and this approach seems to work. For Aleichem, it seems that the way out of the dilemma posed by the clash of tradition and modernity is to immigrate to America, where the Eastern European Jews can begin life anew.

Sheldon Goldfarb

BIBLIOGRAPHY

By the Author

SHORT FICTION:
Tevye der Milkhiger, 1894-1914 (*Tevye's Daughters*, 1949; also known as *Tevye the Dairyman*)
Menakhem-Mendl, 1895 (*The Adventures of Menachem-Mendl*, 1969)
Der farkishnefter Shnayder, 1900 (*The Bewitched Tailor*, 1960)
Mottel, Peyse dem Khazns, 1907-1916 (*The Adventures of Mottel, the Cantor's Son*, 1953)
Jewish Children, 1920
The Old Country, 1946
Inside Kasrilevke, 1948
Selected Stories of Sholom Aleichem, 1956
Stories and Satires, 1959
Old Country Tales, 1966
Some Laughter, Some Tears, 1968
Holiday Tales of Sholem Aleichem, 1979
The Best of Sholom Aleichem, 1979
Tevye the Dairyman and The Railroad Stories, 1987
The Further Adventures of Menachem-Mendl, 2001

LONG FICTION:
Natasha, 1884
Sender Blank und zayn Gezindl, 1888
Yosele Solovey, 1890 (*The Nightingale*, 1985)
Stempenyu, 1899 (English translation, 1913)
Blondzne Shtern, 1912 (*Wandering Star*, 1952)

DISCUSSION TOPICS

- Discuss Sholom Aleichem's presentation of the clash between tradition and modernity in the Jewish community.

- What is the role of religion in Aleichem's works?

- How does Aleichem portray America in his works?

- At the end of *Tevye the Dairyman*, Tevye asks God to explain the meaning of life. What answer, if any, does Aleichem provide to this question?

- How does Tevye's attitude toward money change, and why?

Marienbad, 1917 (English translation, 1982)
In Shturm, 1918 (*In the Storm*, 1984)
Blutiger Shpas, 1923 (*The Bloody Hoax*, 1991)

DRAMA:
A Doktor, pr. 1887 (*She Must Marry a Doctor*, 1916)
Yakenhoz, pr. 1894
Mazel Tov, pr. 1904
Tsuzeyt un Tsushpreyt, pr. 1905
Die Goldgreber, pr. 1907
Samuel Pasternak, pr. 1907
Stempenyu, pr. 1907
Agenten, pb. 1908
Az got Vil, Shist a Bezem, pb. 1908
Konig Pic, pb. 1910
Shver tsu zein a Yid, pb. 1914
Dos groyse Gevins, pb. 1915 (*The Jackpot*, 1989)
Menshen, pb. 1919
Der Get, pr. 1924
The World of Sholom Aleichem, pb. 1953
Fiddler on the Roof, pr. 1964

NONFICTION:
Fun'm yarid, 1916 (*The Great Fair: Scenes from My Childhood*, 1955)
Briefe von Scholem Aleichem und Menachem Mendl, 1921

About the Author

Butwin, Joseph, and Frances Butwin. *Sholom Aleichem*. Boston: Twayne, 1977.
Denman, Hugh. "Shalom Aleichem." *Encyclopaedia Judaica*. 2d ed. Detroit: Macmillan Reference USA, in association with Keter, 2007.
Frieden, Ken. *Classic Yiddish Fiction: Abramovitsh, Sholem Aleichem, and Peretz*. Albany: State University of New York Press, 1995.
Gittleman, Sol. *Sholom Aleichem: A Non-Critical Introduction*. The Hague, Netherlands: Mouton, 1974.
Halkin, Hillel. "Introduction." In *The Letters of Menakhem-Mendl and Sheyne-Sheyndl and Motl, the Cantor's Son*, by Sholem Aleichem. Translated by Hillel Halkin. New Haven, Conn.: Yale University Press, 2002.
_____. "Introduction." In *Tevye the Dairyman and The Railroad Stories*, by Sholem Aleichem. Translated by Hillel Halkin. New York: Schocken Books, 1987.
Miron, Dan. *The Image of the Shtetl, and Other Studies of Modern Jewish Imagination*. Syracuse, N.Y.: Syracuse University Press, 2000.

ISABEL ALLENDE

Born: Lima, Peru
August 2, 1942

Known for works about the social and political heritage of South America, Allende is the first woman Latin American novelist to receive international recognition.

© Miriam Berkley

BIOGRAPHY

Isabel Allende (ahl-YEHN-dee), daughter of Francisca Llona Barros and Tomás Allende and niece of former Chilean president Salvador Allende Gossens, was born in Lima, Peru, where her father was serving as a diplomat. When she was three years old, her parents divorced and her mother took her home to Santiago, Chile.

She spent her childhood in the home of her maternal grandparents Isabela and Augustín Llona. Along with her mother, who encouraged her storytelling, they greatly influenced her understanding of people and love of writing. Her grandmother, a spiritualist, believed the supernatural was an integral part of everyday living, and she routinely held séances and used tarot cards. Her grandfather, a conservative landowner, was a moody and domineering man. It was this couple and their home from which she drew material for her first novel, *La casa de los espíritus* (1982; *The House of the Spirits*, 1985). The household also included an uncle who filled the house with books, and as a child she read widely in the literatures of many countries. Though her contacts with her father ceased, she remained close to his family, especially to his brother Salvador Allende Gossens, a doctor and socialist politician.

Allende attended private schools in Santiago, and following her mother's remarriage to another diplomat she lived abroad. When she was fifteen, she returned home. A year later she left school to take a job as a secretary for the United Nations' Food and Agriculture Organization in Chile. Her work involved contacts with journalists, and it was not long before she began her journalism career.

For more than ten years, Allende's life and career proceeded smoothly. In 1963, she married an engineer, Miguel Frias, and they had two children: Paula and Nicolas. From 1967 through 1974 she served as writer and editor for the feminist magazine *Paula*. During this time she met the Chilean poet Pablo Neruda, who told her that her real talent lay in storytelling. From 1970 through 1975 she worked for television channels 7 and 13 in Santiago, where she acquired popularity by conducting interviews and hosting a comedy program. In the early 1970's, she also gained recognition for her involvement in making documentaries and for writing plays and stories for children. Her uncle, meanwhile, continued his political career, and in 1970, Salvador Allende Gossens became the first freely elected socialist president in Latin America.

Her life abruptly changed on September 11, 1973, when General Augusto Pinochet Ugarte led a military coup that led to the death of her uncle and overthrew his socialist government. "I think I have divided my life [into] before that day and after that day," Allende told *Publishers Weekly* interviewer Amanda Smith in 1985. "In that moment, I realized that everything was possible—that violence was a dimension that was always around you." Not believing that a dictatorship could last in Chile, Allende and her family remained there for more than a year. Her efforts to help the opposition, however, soon made life too dangerous for them, and in 1975, the family moved to Caracas, Venezuela.

Even though she was a known journalist in Chile, Allende did not find a journalism position, nor did she do much writing when she first moved to Caracas. From 1979 to 1982, she worked as a school administrator. In 1981, her grandfather in Chile told her that he was dying. To keep the past alive, she began a letter to him that evolved into *The House of the Spirits*.

She finished the book in 1982, but because Latin American editors were prejudiced against women writers and were used to reading shorter works, finding a publisher was difficult. Eventually a literary agent in Spain placed the work with a Barcelona publisher, and the book was published in 1982. In 1985, it appeared in English translation. The book was later made into a film in English. As this process evolved, Allende published a children's book, *La gorda de porcelana* (1984; *The Porcelain Fat Lady*, 1984).

Allende, fluent in English, left Venezuela in the spring of 1985 to teach for a semester at Montclair State College in New Jersey. Back in Caracas, her weekly column appeared in the newspaper *El Nacional*. Her second novel, *De amor y de sombra* (1984; *Of Love and Shadows*, 1987), also explores themes of political repression. Her third novel, *Eva Luna* (1987; English translation, 1988) follows a venerable literary form—the picaresque novel—in its exploration of redemptive love and resistance to political terror.

Following the publication of her third novel, she began work on a collection of stories that used the narrator of *Eva Luna* as a storyteller. In 1987 she was divorced. The next year she spent the fall semester as Gildersleeve Lecturer at the University of Virginia and the spring semester as a guest lecturer at Barnard College. In the spring of 1989 she taught creative writing at the University of California at Berkeley and that same year met Willie Gordon, a lawyer from California who admired her books. The two were married and settled in San Rafael, California. *Cuentos de Eva Luna* (1990; *The Stories of Eva Luna*, 1991) met with critical and popular acclaim equal to that of her earlier works. Allende's fourth novel, *El plan infinito* (1991; *The Infinite Plan*, 1993), charts the social upheavals not of Latin America but of the United States.

In 1992, her daughter Paula, who was born in 1963, died after a porphyria attack that sent her into a year-long coma. During that year, Allende wrote an autobiographical letter for Paula, which became the memoir entitled *Paula* (1994; English translation, 1995). Allende's official Web site calls this publication an autobiography, whereas the publisher labeled it a novel. In memory of Paula, on December 9, 1996, Allende founded the Isabel Allende Foundation, an institution that provides grants for programs working to advocate and maintain the basic rights of women.

In the last years of the twentieth century, Allende published the nonfiction work, *Afrodita: Cuentos, recetas, y otros afrodisiacos* (1997; *Afrodite: A Memoir of the Senses*, 1998); the critically acclaimed novel *Hija de la fortuna* (1999; *Daughter of Fortune*, 1999); and *Portrait sépia* (2000; *Portrait in Sepia*, 2001), a novel about the granddaughter of Eliza Sommers, the protagonist in *Daughter of Fortune*. Typical of Allende's fiction, both of these novels touch on the themes of political and social strife, self-discovery, and self-acceptance. In addition, she was awarded the Dorothy and Lillian Gish Prize in 1998 for contributing to the beauty of the world.

She subsequently published three novels for young adults: *Ciudad de las bestias* (2002; *City of Beasts*, 2002), *El reino del dragón de oro* (2003; *Kingdom of the Golden Dragon*, 2004), and *El bosque de los pigmeos* (2004; *Forest of the Pygmies*, 2005). Along with these books, she published *Mí país inventado* (2003; *My Invented Country: A Nostalgic Journey Through Chile*, 2003), a memoir that has similarities to the letter that she began writing for her grandfather, which was the inspiration for *The House of the Spirits*. She followed this with a retelling of the Zorro legend in the novel *Zorro* (2005; English translation, 2005) and *Inés del alma mía* (2006; *Inés of My Soul*, 2006), a work of historical fiction about Inés Suarez, a sixteenth century Chilean pioneer from Spain. Among several other international honors she has received throughout her career, Allende was named ambassador to the Hans Christian Andersen Foundation in 2004.

ANALYSIS

Since her appearance on the international literary scene, Allende has been known as a writer who blends Latin American political and social issues into compelling narratives that have popular appeal. However, limiting comments about her to that narrow scope neglects Allende's other literary talents. Not only does she have a tremendous story-telling ability; she is also adept at weaving many characters into plots that cover generations and at creating strong, memorable female characters. She is thoroughly proficient at adding the dimension of Magical Realism to her otherwise historically realistic novels. All these elements combine to illustrate her main theme: that to be human requires insight into injustice and recognition of the power of love.

Allende's female characters are at the heart of her novels and short stories. In *The House of the Spirits*, Alba, granddaughter of the domineering Esteban Trueba, suffers rape and torture at the hands of the military government. Through her courage, she is able to withstand the horrors. She is also helped by other strong women who are equally brutalized. In *Of Love and Shadows*, Irene risks death to escape from those who would kill her for her work with underprivileged classes. Her strength comes from interacting with poor women and seeing their strength. In *The Stories of Eva Luna*, Belisa Crepusculario makes her living selling words, strong messages that have power. In *Daughter of Fortune*, Eliza—the motherless daughter who is adopted by her wealthy English immigrant relatives—risks her life as a stowaway on a Dutch ship sailing from Valparaiso, Chile, to San Francisco; she also survives the brutal chaos of northern California during the 1849 gold rush in an attempt to reclaim a love that was forbidden in Valparaiso. Inés Suarez of *Inés of My Soul* is also a brave woman who is in search of a lover in a chaotic "new world" and finds her own strength and independence in the process. These women come from diverse backgrounds, but they all use their strength, creativity, and courage to resist oppression. Furthermore, these women embody the traits important to Latin American women and women everywhere who keep inspiration and hope alive.

Allende sets these characters into plots with many minor characters. One of her talents lies in skillfully weaving all of their stories together. *The House of the Spirits* and *The Infinite Plan* cover three generations and include the lives of at least fifteen characters. *Of Love and Shadows*, *Eva Luna*, and *Daughter of Fortune* have fewer characters but also focus on storytelling. In her works, something is always happening; there is always plot. The pages are rich with characters and events.

Allende's stories have an added dimension: Magical Realism, a literary technique in which the fantastic and the realistic are both present and described with equal equanimity. According to Allende, Magical Realism is a literary device or a way of seeing in which there is space for the invisible forces that move the world: dreams, legends, myths, emotion, passion, and history. She believes that this view of life is not unique to Latin American writers but instead belongs to the literatures of all developing countries where the sudden accelerations of change juxtapose the old and the new. According to Allende, Magical Realism is the capacity to see and to write about all dimensions of reality, not just the realistic.

In *The House of the Spirits*, the magic of Clara (modeled after Allende's grandmother) adds another dimension to one's understanding of the world. Clara has a remarkable clairvoyant ability, having known the spirit world since childhood. Spirits tap on tables or play Chopin on the piano in order to bring her messages about where to search for lost items. In *The Infinite Plan*, Allende includes fewer elements of Magical Realism, perhaps because it is set in a country that puts little faith in things that are not subject to analysis. In *Daughter of Fortune*, Magical Realism is displayed by the character Mama Fresia, who often mixes a sort of Santoria with unorthodox worship of the Catholic saints to cure or mollify mental and physical maladies and who takes the young Eliza to a fortune teller who predicts her fate and destiny: both will be consequences of her love.

This literary style amounts to a strong thematic statement on the limitations of reason and analysis. Magical Realism and spirituality allow Allende to emphasize her main theme, the power of love. She has said many times that she believes so strongly in the power of love, generosity, and justice that she is not bothered that some critics call her sentimental. Love empowers a person to overcome personal tragedy. Love also allows a person to see injustice and do something about it. At the end of *The House of the Spirits*, Alba's love helps Esteban Trueba realize that his politics destroyed his own family. In *The Infinite Plan*, Gregory, with the love of the woman who records his story, sees the injustice he is perpetrating upon his family and turns his efforts toward renewing himself. In *Daughter of Fortune*, the pursuit of love allows Eliza to understand her identity, establish personal freedom, and potentially end a cycle of denial and cognitive dissonance among her family members.

Allende has said that she writes to speak for those who have no political power. Her work is a record of her attempts to preserve the memories of Latin America, including the injustices, the hopes, and the women heroes about whom one rarely hears. Her writing is her commitment to her fellows, and an act of love. In her works, the personal becomes the political.

THE HOUSE OF THE SPIRITS

First published: *La casa de los espíritus,* 1982 (English translation, 1985)
Type of work: Novel

Memories of three generations reveal the turbulent personal, political, and social realities of Latin America.

In 1981, several years after Isabel Allende had fled her native Chile to settle in Caracas, Venezuela, her grandfather, with whom she had lived as a child, told her that he was nearing one hundred years old and was going to die. He reminded her of his belief that as long as people live in memories, they do not really die. To keep alive all the people and places she had to leave when exiled from Chile, Allende began a letter to him that recalled the past.

The letter was never sent, but instead became the manuscript for Allende's first and best-known novel, *The House of the Spirits.* In it, she re-creates her own past by interweaving the stories of three generations of the fictional Trueba family. Throughout the book, but especially in the early chapters, she uses the literary technique of Magical Realism, a blending of realistic and fantastic detail, which adds an emotionally resonant dimension to the characterizations and to the theme of self-discovery through love.

The story is told by Alba, granddaughter of the central character Esteban Trueba, as a way of coming to terms with the horrors of her life. Though many other characters appear, the plot focuses upon Esteban Trueba, who, as a young peasant,

sees the young and beautiful Rosa, daughter of a senator, in the street one day and vows he will marry her. Rosa possesses special spiritual qualities. Like her grandmother, she is able to make objects move, see into the future, and recall the dead. Nine years later Esteban has become rich, but because Rosa is dead, he marries her sister Clara and builds the magnificent house that becomes the house of the spirits and the setting for much of the novel.

Clara is the link with the spirit world and is the opposite of her domineering, possessive, willful husband. As he moves further and further into worldly events and pleasures, she retreats into a world of silence and spiritual insight. Their children grow in this weird atmosphere of the abstracted silent mother and the possessed father who alternates between  intense love and intense wrath. His rages reach their peak when he finds out that his daughter Blanca is pregnant.

It is through Alba, Blanca's daughter, that he finally gains some humanity. Alba's affair with a rebel leader results in her being taken prisoner and tortured and raped by the military government that her grandfather supports. In jail she records her family history from her grandmother's diaries. These memories enable her to transcend her suffering and to love Esteban, who has lived by exploiting others. When she is released and reconciled with her grandfather, he realizes the power of love and looks for a chance of fulfillment with her child, whose uncertain parentage (he is either the child of her lover, the rebel leader, or of brutality— the rapes she suffered in prison), represents a culmination of the family's history.

The plot structure of the book is circular. At the end, another generation of Truebas is to be born. It too will be tied to the past by memories, while facing a present full of violent social and political struggles. Throughout the many tragedies, the power of love will enable them, as it has their ancestors, to survive.

"AND OF CLAY ARE WE CREATED"

First published: "De barro estamos hechos," 1990 (collected in *The Stories of Eva Luna*, 1991)

Type of work: Short story

A television journalist finds his life changed by the death of a thirteen-year-old girl buried in debris from a volcanic eruption.

"And of Clay Are We Created," the last short story in Isabel Allende's collection *The Stories of Eva Luna*, is based upon a real event. Omayra Sanchez was a young victim of the 1985 earthquake in Colombia. The story is told by the heroine of Allende's third novel *Eva Luna*, whose lover, Rolf Carlé, is the main character. With a carefully crafted plot and delicate images, Allende illustrates the theme of self-discovery through love, the same theme that runs through all the stories in this volume.

The story's first line, "They discovered the girl's head protruding from the mudpit, eyes wide open, calling soundlessly," not only begins the action and sets the story but also establishes the image of the eyes and the theme of insight. The last sentence of the paragraph foreshadows the ending: "Rolf Carlé . . . never suspect[ed] that he would find a fragment of his past, lost thirty years before."

Rolf finds that past; the girl, Azucena, enables him to close the gap between his experiences and his feelings so he can confront it. Azucena is one of twenty thousand victims of a volcanic eruption that has wiped out an entire Latin American village. Arriving by helicopter, Rolf, a maker of television documentaries, finds himself first on the scene filming the volunteers trying to reach the girl, who is buried up to her neck in quicksandlike mud. Within minutes, the girl's plight is broadcast throughout the world.

Rolf remains by her side. Throughout the night he tells stories of his adventures as a newsman to keep up her courage. Miles away, the narrator, Eva Luna, watches television and feels the pain of both Azucena and Rolf. She tries to get a pump sent to the site, but her efforts are futile. She even tries to help Rolf through her "force of mind."

Later she watches the morning broadcast.

Things have degenerated, but Rolf, now near exhaustion, still tries to keep the girl's spirits up. More cameras and equipment arrive, and the worldwide focus on the young girl intensifies, making the scene so real to Eva that she envisions herself by their side using her love to help them endure the suffering.

On the second night, Rolf begins to talk of his life, speaking with an intensity like that of the volcano that has caused this tragedy. Beginning with the horrors of the concentration camps in Germany, he goes back even further to recall the abuse of his childhood by an evil father and his guilt over the fate of his retarded sister. As he finishes, he is in tears, ironically consoled by the dying Azucena.

In the morning, the president arrives and positions himself for the cameras beside the buried child. Rolf keeps his vigil throughout that day. Eva recalls the moment when, despite the president's promises of help, the two give up hope. The strength of her love enables her to empathize with them as they accept the things that cannot be changed. On the night of the third day, with the cameras focused upon her, the girl dies.

Returning to Eva, Rolf is a changed person. He has set aside his cameras. Now able to see things clearly, he needs time to heal the wounds in himself just as the mud will cover the holes in the earth. The story ends with a thematic connection to the beginning sentence.

THE INFINITE PLAN

First published: *El plan infinito*, 1991 (English translation, 1993)

Type of work: Novel

One man's search for love and self-esteem leads him through struggles symbolic of those facing a generation of Americans.

In Allende's fourth novel, she exchanges the Latin American setting and memorable heroines of the previous three books for an American setting and a male protagonist. *The Infinite Plan* tells the story of Gregory Reeves, son of an itinerant preacher. In it, Allende relies on realistic detail rather than elements of Magical Realism. She continues to use her skillful narrative techniques to interweave the lives of many characters who represent twentieth century American lifestyles.

Gregory, his mother, sister, and a family friend travel around the country in the 1940's with his father Charles, who tries to win converts to the infinite plan, his peculiar doctrine of destiny and salvation. When Charles becomes ill, the group settles in a Hispanic barrio of Los Angeles, where Gregory finds that life is even harder than on the road. As a white misfit, he suffers the pains of being an outsider as well as the usual pains of adolescence. These are somewhat eased by Pedro and Immaculada Morales, who become his surrogate parents, and by their daughter Carmen, who becomes a lifelong friend.

In addition to the Morales family, Gregory has other mentors. They help him cope as his family life deteriorates. His father dies, his mother withdraws into the world of the infinite plan, and his sister eats to avoid her problems. Gregory is initiated into sex by Olga and into the life of the mind by Cyrus, a communist elevator operator at the public library. These people, like others Gregory meets throughout the novel, are not developed in depth but represent an array of desires, fantasies, and stupidities.

Graduating from high school, Gregory leaves the barrio for Berkeley to begin his search for himself in earnest. There he enthusiastically encounters the 1960's hippie scene and begins another succession of adventures that represent a generation of Americans in their own social, political, and spiritual journeys. After a few years, the Berkeley scene leaves him empty and he ends up going to Vietnam to find himself as a man. Allende's description of the Vietnam War emphasizes its horrors and their effects on Gregory.

Gregory returns from Vietnam determined to become a rich lawyer and to embrace the yuppie ethic of success. These values also fail to bring him happiness or self-esteem. He marries twice; both marriages are disasters resulting in two neurotic children, one a daughter who becomes a drug-addicted prostitute and the other a hyperactive son. Throughout all this misfortune, Gregory continues to rely upon his childhood friend Carmen, who has since become a world-renowned jewelry designer and successful single mother, having adopted the son of her dead brother and a Vietnamese woman. At the end of the novel, Gregory begins to face the mess of his life rather than run away and, with a multicultural cast of characters, begins to pick up the pieces.

Gregory tells his story to an anonymous woman with whom, the reader assumes, he will form some relationship. The plot progresses by alternating between his and her point of view. Using this technique, Allende succeeds in exposing the reader to many of the social and political problems, and their solutions, of the late twentieth century United States. When Gregory is in his late forties, he realizes that there are no quick fixes.

DAUGHTER OF FORTUNE

First published: *Hija de la fortuna,* 1999
   (English translation, 1999)
Type of work: Novel

Prejudice and hypocrisy caused by an oppressive system of social stratification in nineteenth century Chile push a beloved daughter away from her family and toward self-knowledge and freedom.

Daughter of Fortune introduces readers to a young woman named Eliza Sommers, who, shortly after being born, was placed on the doorstep of Rose and Jeremy Sommers's home in Valparaiso, Chile. Even though Eliza was an orphan, Miss Rose brought her up as if she were her own daughter and assured her that she was of British blood, as were all the Sommerses. Rose and Jeremy were unmarried siblings who came to Valparaiso when Jeremy acquired a position as the director of the British Import and Export Company. Rose supported this claim of British heritage with a story about the day they found Eliza on the doorstep. According to Miss Rose, Eliza was found in a beautifully adorned basket beneath an intricately handwoven blanket that only wealthy people could afford. Eliza, who has a memory of magical proportions, remembers being found in a soapbox covered with a wool sweater that smelled of cigar and the sea. Mama Fresia, the Sommers's cook, Eliza's first friend, and her companion in the world of Magical Realism, verifies Eliza's version. However, Rose's version turns out to carry some validity as well.

It is not long before Eliza falls in love with Joaquin Andieta, a Hispanic clerk who works for Jeremy's company. Their love affair is filled with angst, secret meetings, and clandestine plans; this is because the social order places Hispanic people well below those of pure European ancestry, keeping them in destitute poverty and just above the native South Americans, who are not seen as people at all. Rose was grooming Eliza to marry a wealthy man of European descent; therefore, Eliza's relationship with Joaquin is taboo. Eliza, however, puts all of her faith in Joaquin, who seems to love his socialist ideals more than he loves her. He soon embezzles money from Jeremy's company and heads off to San Francisco, where he thinks he will make his fortune by finding gold during the 1849 gold rush.

Eliza follows him to California after meeting Tao Chien, the cook on her "Uncle" John Sommers's ship. Tao helps her stow away aboard a vessel on which he also serves as cook. After barely surviving this trip, Eliza takes the identity of a boy, more specifically Tao Chien's little brother, in order to survive in California. Her brave journey in California in search of Joaquin is the catalyst that forces the Sommers family to admit to hypocrisy, deception, and human weakness. It is one of many examples in Allende's fiction that illustrates how the power of love can unravel systematic injustice.

The major characters in Allende's novels often include a patrician family who hide secrets in order to maintain their status at the top of the social order. In this case, Jeremy and Rose's obsession with keeping up appearances in order to avoid being ostracized by their own kind causes a potential cycle of self-abuse and an eventual breakdown of the family. They set a standard for civilized behavior that is not achievable. Consequently, they place those standards upon Eliza, which drives her away. The secrets that Jeremy, Rose, and John Sommers hold could free Eliza from the guilt and pain that may cause her demise, but they selfishly hold on to their false sense of social status, even though Eliza is suffering and lost.

The women in Allende's fictional families often pay the greatest price for this hypocrisy. Even when raised by a wealthy family, the daughters are intended to be breeders. Many of Allende's female characters rise above this limitation, but they often have to separate themselves from mainstream society and their families to accomplish this, as does Eliza. This oppressive atmosphere is also negative for the most romantic male characters in Allende's novels. If they truly love a woman, they are caught in the trap of cognitive dissonance. Their cultural beliefs do not match their actions, which causes some male characters, such as Tao Chien, to function on the brink of nihilistic insanity. Allende shows time and time again that if one truly loves another, then systematic oppression by gender or race becomes a terrible mistake that could not only damage individuals and families, but also entire governments and nations.

SUMMARY

Isabel Allende has commented that when people lose their homeland and become detached from their past, memories become more important. Those memories of Chilean and Hispanic people and places are Allende's subjects. Her themes, the search for love and self-knowledge, are universal. Using rich plots interwoven with a kaleidoscope of characters, she examines the tumultuous social and political heritage of Latin America. Her Magical Realism produces a blend of the real and the supernatural that adds a fuller landscape to the worlds she creates. These qualities have made her one of the best-known writers of Latin America.

Louise M. Stone; updated by Troy Place

BIBLIOGRAPHY

By the Author

LONG FICTION:
La casa de los espíritus, 1982 (*The House of the Spirits*, 1985)
De amor y de sombra, 1984 (*Of Love and Shadows*, 1987)
Eva Luna, 1987 (English translation, 1988)
El plan infinito, 1991 (*The Infinite Plan*, 1993)
Hija de la fortuna, 1999 (*Daughter of Fortune*, 1999)
Portrait sépia, 2000 (*Portrait in Sepia*, 2001)
Zorro, 2005 (English translation, 2005)
Inés del alma mía, 2006 (*Inés of My Soul*, 2006)

SHORT FICTION:
Cuentos de Eva Luna, 1990 (*The Stories of Eva Luna*, 1991)

NONFICTION:
Civilice a su troglodita: Los impertinentes de Isabel Allende, 1974
Paula, 1994 (English translation, 1995)
Conversations with Isabel Allende, 1999
Mi país inventado, 2003 (*My Invented Country: A Nostalgic Journey Through Chile*, 2003)
La suma de las días, 2007 (*The Sum of Our Days*, 2008)

CHILDREN'S LITERATURE:
La gorda de porcelana, 1984 (*The Porcelain Fat Lady*, 1984)
Ciudad de las bestias, 2002 (*City of the Beasts*, 2002)
El reino del dragón de oro, 2003 (*Kingdom of the Golden Dragon*, 2004)
El bosque de los pigmeos, 2004 (*Forest of the Pygmies*, 2005)

MISCELLANEOUS:
Afrodita: Cuentos, recetas, y otros afrodisiacos, 1997 (*Aphrodite: A Memoir of the Senses*, 1998)

About the Author

Allende, Isabel. *Conversations with Isabel Allende.* Edited by John Rodden. Austin: University of Texas Press, 2004.

Carvalho, Susan. "The Craft of Emotion in Isabel Allende's *Paula*." *Studies in Twentieth Century Literature* 27 (Summer, 2003): 223-238.

DISCUSSION TOPICS

- Some characters in Isabel Allende's books value money and power over human dignity. What happens to these characters? Why?

- Define Magical Realism. Discuss examples of Magical Realism in any Allende novel.

- Define irony. Using any Allende novel, discuss practical examples of this literary technique.

- How does love change the characters in Allende's fiction? What does the pursuit of love make them do? What are the benefits and drawbacks of love in Allende's books?

- What causes political unrest in Allende's novels? Are the causes and effects of political problems in her stories similar to the causes and effects of political strife in reality?

- Allende has expressed her value of the Hebrew saying, "The story is truer than true." What does this mean? Does it have anything to do with justice, human potential, and the unseen and often unnoticed power of love?

- Can we learn anything about reality from a fictional tale? How so?

- What do women have to do to overcome oppression in Allende's books?

- How does the oppression of women negatively affect men in Allende's novels? It seems that there is often a "boomerang" effect.

- Most families in Allende's books have hurtful secrets. How does burying truth and shirking responsibility damage a family's offspring?

Correas de Zapata, Celia. *Isabel Allende: Life and Spirits.* Translated by Margaret Sayers Peden. Houston, Tex.: Arte Público Press, 2002.

Cox, Karen Castellucci. *Isabel Allende: A Critical Companion.* Westport, Conn.: Greenwood Press, 2003.

Frame, Scott Macdonald. "The Literal and the Literary: A Note on the Historical References in Isabel Allende's *La casa de los espíritus.*" *Studies in Twentieth Century Literature* 27 (Summer, 2003): 279-89.

Gough, Elizabeth. "Vision and Division: Voyeurism in the Works of Isabel Allende." *Journal of Modern Literature* 27 (Summer, 2004): 93-120.

Lindsay, Claire. *Locating Latin American Women Writers: Cristina Peri Rossi, Rosario Ferré, Albalucía Angel, and Isabel Allende.* New York: Peter Lang, 2003.

JORGE AMADO

Born: Ferradas, near Ilhéus, Bahia, Brazil
August 10, 1912
Died: Salvador, Bahia, Brazil
August 6, 2001

The author of numerous internationally famous novels, Amado became the representative of Brazilian literature.

BIOGRAPHY

Jorge Amado (uh-MAH-doo) was born on a cacao farm in the northeastern Brazilian state of Bahia. When Amado was a year old, his father was wounded in a murder attempt. A year later, a flood devastated the family farm and the Amados were forced to move to the town of Ilhéus. The family recovered from its financial losses and soon purchased a new farm, as well as a second home in Ilhéus. At age ten, Amado entered boarding school, where he was introduced to literature. His father denied his request to transfer to another boarding school, and Amado left school and wandered through Bahia before making his way to his paternal grandfather's home. Following a stay at another boarding school, where he immersed himself in literature, Amado worked, at age fifteen, as a reporter. He had already begun writing fiction. He joined a writers' group. His first novel, *O país do carnaval* (the land of carnival), was published in 1931, when Amado was nineteen.

Amado entered law school in 1931, and though he would eventually earn his degree, he was more interested in writing and things literary. Following the publication of his second and third short novels, Amado's first full-length novel, *Jubiabá* (English translation, 1984), appeared in 1935. It was an immediate success. Two other novels, including the award-winning *Mar morto* (1936; *Sea of Death*, 1984), followed quickly.

Amado was becoming known for the leftist nature of his novels and was imprisoned briefly by the Getúlio Vargas regime in 1936. Afterward, he embarked on a trip that took him all over Latin America and North America and during which he had

contact with numerous writers, artists, and social activists. He returned to Brazil the following year, only to be arrested once again and to see his books banned and burned publicly. Released soon thereafter, Amado remained in Brazil until 1941, when, as a result of the oppressive nature of the Vargas regime, he took up residence in Argentina. He returned to Brazil in 1942, was arrested again, and was released on the condition that he remain in Salvador, the capital of his native state of Bahia. In 1942, he published *Terras do sem fim* (*The Violent Land*, 1945). He separated from his wife Matilde, whom he had married in 1933 and with whom he had a daughter, in 1944, was elected vice president of the First Congress of Brazilian Writers in 1945, and married his second wife, Zélia Gettai, in the same year. When the Vargas regime fell in 1945, Amado was elected to the Chamber of Deputies as a Communist. The Communist Party in Brazil was outlawed in 1947, however, and Amado went into voluntary exile the following year, spending most of the next several years in Europe.

Amado's political activities and his travels had, except for relatively small exceptions, taken him out of the literary spotlight since 1946. He returned to the forefront of Brazilian fiction, however, in 1958, with the publication of *Gabriela, cravo e canela* (*Gabriela, Clove and Cinnamon*, 1962), an award-winning, best-selling novel that was shockingly different (humorous and sensual as opposed to dogmatic and heavy-handed) from his earlier works. *Gabriela, Clove and Cinnamon* marked the beginning of a new and more popular Amado.

The 1960's saw Amado's nomination for the Nobel Prize in Literature, his election to the Brazilian

Academy of Letters, the installation of a military dictatorship in Brazil, and the publication of several of the writer's most famous works, among them *A morte e a morte de Quincas Berro Dágua* (1961; *The Two Deaths of Quincas Wateryell*, 1965), which had actually first been published in 1959 but was now reissued in a volume with another short novel. *Dona Flor e seus dois maridos* (1966; *Dona Flor and Her Two Husbands*, 1969) is perhaps Amado's most internationally famous novel. *Tenda dos milagres* (1969; *Tent of Miracles*, 1971) also appeared in what for Amado was a prodigious decade.

In 1971, Amado traveled with his wife to North America, where he spent two months as a writer-in-residence at Pennsylvania State University. This decade also saw the publication of several of the author's important novels: *Tereza Batista cansada de guerra* (1972; *Tereza Batista: Home from the Wars*, 1975), *Tiêta do Agreste* (1977; *Tiêta, the Goat Girl*, 1979), and *Farda, fardão, camisola de dormir* (1979; *Pen, Sword, and Camisole*, 1985). A number of film versions of Amado's novels premiered during the 1970's, chief among them *Dona Flor and Her Two Husbands*.

Amado continued to write and travel in the 1980's and 1990's. His *Tocaia Grande: A face obscura* (*Showdown*, 1988) came out in 1984, a year prior to the return of civilian government to Brazil. The Jorge Amado Cultural Foundation was established in Salvador in 1987. Amado's twenty-second novel, *Capitán de altura*, was published in 2000, sixty-nine years after his first. He died of heart and lung failure on August 6, 2001, four days before his eighty-ninth birthday.

ANALYSIS

Jorge Amado was the most illustrious Brazilian novelist of the twentieth century. Within Brazil, Amado was seen as a national treasure, while abroad he was considered by many readers and critics to be almost the personification of contemporary Brazilian letters. Many of his novels have become classics of Brazilian literature; several have found an international audience. His novels have been made into films, and almost all of Amado's novels have been translated into numerous languages. Amado's novels, however, are not without controversy.

Amado's career can be divided into two basic phases: the pre-1958, or pre-*Gabriela, Clove and Cin-*namon phase, and the post-1958, or post-*Gabriela, Clove and Cinnamon* phase. In general, Amado's pre-1958 novels are gritty and proletarian. In these works, Amado chronicles the struggles of the downtrodden and oppressed, and he champions their causes. The author's sympathies, as reflected both in the description and the actions of his characters, are clearly on the side of the underdog. His rather one-dimensional, rebellious, proletarian heroes speak the language of the masses and show themselves to be more virtuous than their oppressors. Amado, through virtually every element of these frequently heavy-handed works, leaves no doubt as to the message he wishes to communicate.

This is not to say, however, that Amado's pre-1958 novels are not worthy of praise. The novels of this period have been lauded for how vividly they portray the Brazilian underclasses and for, in many cases, their inclusion and equally vivid depiction of Brazil's Afro-Brazilian culture (in *Jubiabá*, for example). Even with their heavily politicized content, some of these novels present love stories, or at least love subplots, the treatment of which borders on the lyrical. Virtually all the pre-1958 novels, from the best (the consensus choice being *The Violent Land*) to the weakest, show the aspect of Amado's fiction that most readers and critics alike consider to be the author's greatest strength. He is, quite simply, a master storyteller.

Had Amado quit writing prior to 1958, he would have been considered a major writer of the so-called novel of the Brazilian northeast and his fame within Brazil would have been assured. It is the works he published beginning in 1958, *Gabriela, Clove and Cinnamon* being the first of these, however, that won him international fame.

The Amado of *Gabriela, Clove and Cinnamon* and that of subsequent novels was in many ways a new Amado. The change was not one of political conviction but of approach. Amado's post-1958 novels continued to expose and denounce social injustice. The realism and proletarian directness of his earlier novels had been replaced, however, with irony, picaresque humor, parody, and satire. The new Amado still favored the lower classes, clearly, but his support of them and his antipathy toward the privileged classes no longer came across in heavy-handed fashion. Rather, there is an exaltation of the former and parody of the latter. Correspondingly, while the pre-1958 Amado novels are very serious works, the post-1958 Amado novels are frequently downright funny, with the upper classes almost always the butt of the joke. Amado's social message still gets through; it is merely conveyed in a more entertaining and an artistically subtler package.

The post-1958 novels are also frequently more sensual and freer in general with respect to social mores. In these novels, Amado celebrates the freedom to pursue a life unrestricted by bourgeois values. His colorful characters—from rum-swilling bums to sexually uninhibited young women to naked ghosts—with whom Amado consistently sympathizes, flout Brazil's proper and regulated middle- and upper-class society.

Amado's pre-1958 novels and his post-1958 novels do have more in common, however, than the author's sympathy for the downtrodden. One element found in both phases of Amado's career is his celebration of Afro-Brazilian culture, and, in fact, this element appears even stronger in the post-1958 Amado. Amado continues to be the master storyteller in his second phase; in fact, he appears to have only gotten better in this area.

Amado's works are not without controversy. He has been criticized for exploiting the misery of the lower classes and for romanticizing and even, in his second phase, idealizing and trivializing their lives. He has been criticized as well for promoting racial and cultural stereotypes, for bordering (in post-1958 works) on the pornographic, for demeaning women (this despite the fact that many of his strongest and wisest characters are women), for repeating episodes and characters, for stylistic sloppiness, for being technically uninnovative, for being superficial, and for being too popular. All of this combined has led several critics to decry the quality of Amado's works and to challenge his place in Brazilian literature. Despite the controversy surrounding his works, however, Amado remains one of the most widely read and most internationally famous Brazilian novelists.

GABRIELA, CLOVE AND CINNAMON

First published: *Gabriela, cravo e canela*, 1958 (English translation, 1962)
Type of work: Novel

The sensual love story of Gabriela and Nacib is set against the backdrop of a changing Brazil.

Gabriela is a beautiful, uneducated, young mulatto girl who, escaping the droughts in the Bahian backlands, walks into the town of Ilhéus in the 1920's in search of a better life. She is hired as a cook by Nacib Saad, the Syrian owner of a bar named Vesuvius, and her cooking skills and her beauty soon make the bar a major attraction. Nacib and Gabriela become lovers, and Nacib soon marries this girl of the cinnamon-colored skin who always smells of cloves. Nacib's attempts to make Gabriela a respectable, middle-class wife fail, however, and he soon finds the sexually free Gabriela in the bed of another. He does not kill her, however, as Brazilian tradition at the time suggests he do. He instead annuls the marriage and dismisses her as his cook at the bar. With the absence of Gabriela and her culinary delights, business at the bar quickly falls off, and Nacib, too, realizes that he still loves Gabriela. At the end of the novel, he has taken her back both as his cook and, this time, as his mistress.

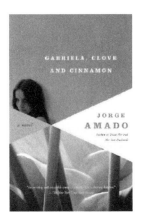

The story of Gabriela and Nacib is but the foreground of this novel. *Gabriela, Clove and Cinnamon* is, above all, about social, political, and attitudinal change in a small Brazilian town during the 1920's. Much of the novel centers on the efforts of a young, Rio de Janeiro-born businessman named Mundinho Falcão to bring social and economic progress and political reform to Ilhéus and the local old guard's efforts, including an assassination attempt on one of Falcão's supporters, to combat such changes. Change clearly wins in the novel, however, as Falcão's side wins in the local elections, and a powerful local planter, a colonel, whose murder of his unfaithful wife and her lover opens the novel, is sent to prison for his crime, something that would not have happened in the old Brazil. Even Nacib's annulment of his marriage with the unfaithful Gabriela, as opposed to his exercising his tradition-dictated right to kill her, reflects a new social attitude, an attitude that promotes a freer, less restricted society, the spirit of which is symbolized in the carefree, uninhibited Gabriela.

This novel marks the beginning of the second phase of Amado's career. Like its predecessors, it still conveys a social message, but it does so within the context of a sensual and always entertaining story that makes the message both more subtly presented and easier to take.

THE TWO DEATHS OF QUINCAS WATERYELL

First published: *A morte e a morte de Quincas Berro Dágua*, 1961 (English translation, 1965)

Type of work: Novel

A man dies and is visited by his drunken cronies. The group sets out for one more night on the town together.

The Two Deaths of Quincas Wateryell tells the story of Joaquim (or Quincas) Soares da Cunha, a respectable, middle-class man who left his nagging wife, his equally nagging daughter, his spineless son-in-law, and his job as a petty bureaucrat to become a rum-guzzling vagabond on the streets of Salvador, Bahia. His surname became Wateryell the day that he mistakenly drank water instead of his usual white rum and let out a yell of "Waaaaaaater!" that was heard for blocks. As the short novel opens, Quincas has died. His family is notified, as are his street cronies. The family, embarrassed that Quincas's death may open up questions among family and friends concerning his life since his leaving home, comes to sit with the body in Quincas's small room in the lower-class section

of Salvador. Quincas's street companions, four of the most colorful and comic characters to be found in Amado's works, come to pay their respects and spell the family in their vigil. Soon after Quincas's friends are alone with his body, they hear Quincas speak, prop him up in the casket, and begin to share drink with him. They soon decide that they should have one more night on the town together. Quincas and his friends head out to the streets and visit Quincas's girlfriend. They later stop in a bar, where Quincas starts a fight. They finally make their way to a friend's boat, where they get caught in a storm and Quincas, yelling out his last words, dives into the sea, dying as he always wished he would, at sea rather than on land. (Regarding the novel's title, this last death may even be Quincas's third death, his first one being a symbolic one when he left home, his second coming at the beginning of the story. How many deaths Quincas endures depends on one's interpretation of the story.)

Some readers consider this book to be Amado's masterpiece, both because of its entertaining story and because of the way in which it makes deliberate use of ambiguity. The work is a commentary on the importance of appearances and the materialism of the middle class, as opposed to the *joie de vivre* and fidelity of friendship of the lower classes. It is also a treatise on the nature of reality and the ability of language to capture (or deliberately avoid capturing) it. Virtually every aspect of the presentation of Quincas's story, told by a narrator who has pieced the story together from various witnesses, many of whom were drunk and anything but reliable, leaves open the question of what really happened to Quincas Wateryell once he expired alone in his room. A case can be made both for his temporary resurrection and for his body being dragged from the casket and down the street by his drunken friends, only to be flung into the sea as the storm tossed the boat about. Amado, through both his questionable narrator and his descriptions of Quincas's "actions," deliberately provides no concrete answers. In fact, Amado seems to go to considerable lengths to eliminate the possibility of definitive conclusions, which, of course, supports the theme of the ability (or lack thereof) of language to capture reality.

DONA FLOR AND HER TWO HUSBANDS

First published: *Dona Flor e seus dois maridos,*
  1966 (English translation, 1969)
Type of work: Novel

*A woman's unfaithful, gambling husband
dies and then returns, naked and visible only to
her, soon after she has married his exact opposite.*

The novel opens during Carnival in Salvador, Bahia. Dona Flor's first husband, Vadinho, has just died while dancing the samba in the streets, dressed as a woman. Dona Flor holds a wake and the popular Vadinho's numerous friends, including everyone from political heavyweights to prostitutes, come to pay their respects and reminisce about their carousing, sexually promiscuous, and gambling friend. Vadinho's funeral is even better attended than his wake. Afterward, however, the young, respectable Dona Flor is alone, her life empty. She deeply misses Vadinho, who, though he was unfaithful to her, came and went at all hours, and gambled away their money, was a passionate and spontaneous lover. Flashbacks tell of the couple's life together.

Dona Flor decides to move on with her life. She meets and marries, following a very proper courtship, Dr. Teodoro Madureira, a local pharmacist. He is everything Vadinho was not: faithful, respectable, formal. He is also not the lover that Vadinho was. This becomes apparent on the couple's honeymoon. Still, Dona Flor is happy because her life is stable, her place in society a respectable one. Dona Flor's stable, if rather boring, existence changes radically, however, when, on the night of her first wedding anniversary with Teodoro, she finds a naked Vadinho lying on the couple's bed, returned from the dead and visible only to Dona Flor. His only interest is in making love to Dona Flor. Dona Flor fights off Vadinho's advances and her own desires for some time, during which Vadinho visits his old friends (who, unlike Dona Flor, cannot see him) and makes considerable fun of Dona Flor's new husband. Afraid that she will no longer be able to resist her own urges to give in to Vadinho's advances, she asks that one of the Afro-Brazilian gods take Vadinho away, only to change her mind at the last minute. As the novel ends, Dona Flor, content to live with both Vadinho and Teodoro, walks down the street with her second husband on one arm and her first husband, still naked and visible only to her, on the other.

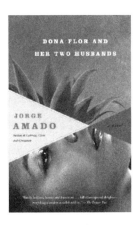

This comic and sensual novel shows the struggle between the respectable and passionate sides of Brazilian society and the difficulty a person, and particularly a woman, faces in fusing both sides in order to find happiness. *Dona Flor and Her Two Husbands* is another example of Amado's ability in his post-1958 phase to communicate a serious social message in an entertaining form.

SUMMARY

Through both hard-hitting social novels, in his pre-1958 phase, and humorous and sensual novels, in his post-1958 phase, Jorge Amado earned a reputation as a master storyteller whose sympathies always lie with Brazil's underclasses. His works won for him fame both within Brazil and without.

Keith H. Brower

BIBLIOGRAPHY

By the Author

LONG FICTION:
O país do carnaval, 1931
Cacáu, 1933
Suor, 1934
Jubiabá, 1935 (English translation, 1984)
Mar morto, 1936 (*Sea of Death,* 1984)
Capitães da areia, 1937 (*Captains of the Sand,* 1988)
Terras do sem fim, 1942 (*The Violent Land,* 1945)
São Jorge dos Ilhéus, 1944 (*The Golden Harvest,* 1992)
Seara vermelha, 1946
Os subterrâneos da liberdade, 1954 (includes *Agonia da noite, A luz no túnel,* and *Os ásperos tempos*)
Gabriela, cravo e canela, 1958 (*Gabriela, Clove and Cinnamon,* 1962)
Os velhos marinheiros, 1961 (includes *A morte e a morte de Quincas Berro Dágua* [*The Two Deaths of Quincas Wateryell,* 1965] and *A completa verdade sôbre as discutidas aventuras do Comandante Vasco Moscoso de Aragão, capitão de longo curso* [*Home Is the Sailor,* 1964])
Os pastores da noite, 1964 (*Shepherds of the Night,* 1967)
Dona Flor e seus dois maridos, 1966 (*Dona Flor and Her Two Husbands,* 1969)
Tenda dos milagres, 1969 (*Tent of Miracles,* 1971)
Tereza Batista cansada de guerra, 1972 (*Tereza Batista: Home from the Wars,* 1975)
Tiêta do Agreste, 1977 (*Tieta, the Goat Girl,* 1979)
Farda fardão, camisola de dormir, 1979 (*Pen, Sword, Camisole,* 1985)
Tocaia Grande: A face obscura, 1984 (*Showdown,* 1988)
O sumiço da santa: Una história de feitiçaria, 1988 (*The War of the Saints,* 1993)
A descoberta da América pelos Turcos, 1994
Capitán de altura, 2000

POETRY:
A estrada do mar, 1938

DRAMA:
O amor de Castro Alves, pb. 1947 (also known as *O amor do soldado*)

NONFICTION:
ABC de Castro Alves, 1941 (biography)
Vida de Luíz Carlos Prestes, 1942
O cavaleiro da esperança, 1945 (biography)
Guia das ruas e dos misterios da cidade do Salvador, 1945
Bahia de todos os santos, 1945 (travel sketch)
Homens e coisas do Partido Comunista, 1946
União Soviética e democracias populares, 1951

DISCUSSION TOPICS

- Jorge Amado celebrates Afro-Brazilian culture. What similarities are there between Afro-Brazilians and African Americans?

- Explain the basis for your judgment as to how many deaths Quincas suffered.

- Defend Amado against one of the following labels that have been applied to him: antifeminism, stylistic sloppiness, superficiality.

- What facts in Amado's life seem to have led to his leftist philosophy?

- Does the great rise in Amado's reputation during the 1960's owe more to changes in his writing or to changes in his society?

- Consider the features of Amado's later work that have led critics to call it more artistic.

O mundo da paz, 1951 (travel sketch)
Bahia boa terra Bahia, 1967
Bahia, 1971 (English translation, 1971)
O menino grapiúna, 1981
Navega ção de Cabotagem, 1992

CHILDREN'S LITERATURE:
O gato malhado e a andorinha sinhá: Uma historia de amor, 1976 (*The Swallow and the Tom Cat: A Love Story*, 1982)

About the Author

Brower, Keith H., Earl E. Fitz, and Enrique Martínez-Vidal, eds. *Jorge Amado: New Critical Essays.* New York: Routledge, 2001.

Chamberlain, Bobby J. *Jorge Amado.* Boston: Twayne, 1990.

Dinneen, Mark. "Change Versus Continuity: Popular Culture in the Novels of Jorge Amado." In *Fiction in the Portuguese-Speaking World: Essays in Memory of Alexandre Pinheiro Torres*, edited by Charles M. Kelley. Cardiff: University of Wales Press, 2000.

Ellison, Fred P. *Brazil's New Novel: Four Northeastern Masters.* Berkeley: University of California Press, 1954.

Fitz, Earl E. "Jorge Amado." In *Latin American Literature in the Twentieth Century: A Guide*, edited by Leonard S. Klein. New York: Frederick Ungar, 1986.

Lowe, Elizabeth. "The 'New' Jorge Amado." *Luso-Brazilian Review* 6, no. 2 (1969): 73-82.

McDowell, Edwin. "Jorge Amado Dies at 88: Brazil's Leading Novelist." *The New York Times*, August 7, 2001, p. B7.

Nunes, Maria Luísa. "Jorge Amado." In *Dictionary of Brazilian Literature*, edited by Irwin Stern. Westport, Conn.: Greenwood Press, 1988.

———. "The Preservation of African Culture in Brazilian Literature: The Novels of Jorge Amado." *Luso-Brazilian Review* 10, no. 1 (1973): 86-101.

YEHUDA AMICHAI

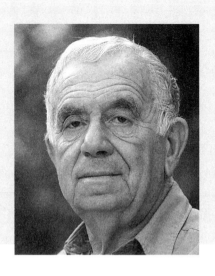

Born: Würzburg, Germany
May 3, 1924
Died: Jerusalem, Israel
September 22, 2000

Amichai's poetry, fiction, and drama chronicle the twentieth century Israeli experience as masterfully as do the works of any figure in Hebrew literature. As Israel's first major poet, Amichai explored—with a prescient authenticity and remarkable stylistic control—the triumphs and tragedies that have come to characterize a nation.

BIOGRAPHY

Yehuda Amichai (ah-mee-KI), deemed by countless critics and scholars to be Israel's master poet of the twentieth century, was born in Würzburg, Germany, in 1924. He immigrated with his family to Palestine in 1936, where they sought refuge from the persecution of the Nazis. Amichai was educated in provincial Hebrew schools and became a teacher in them after graduation. In World War II, Amichai served as a soldier with the British in Europe, an experience that provided inspiration for many of his writings. Shortly after the war, Amichai was once again called to military service, joining the fight for Israeli independence. Initially, he enlisted as a member of the Palmach (commando troops) of the Haganah, an underground Jewish militia. Later he saw active duty as an Israeli soldier, both on the Negev front and in the battle for Sinai, both major campaigns in the Arab-Israeli war of 1947-1948. Shortly thereafter, Amichai became an Israeli citizen.

Having grown up in a strict Orthodox Jewish household, Amichai obtained a solid background in Hebrew language, theology, and culture that strongly informs his writing. After completing military service, he embarked on a career as a writer, determined to contribute his distinctive voice to the fledgling Israeli literary movement. Even though his English was impeccable, he opted to write exclusively in Hebrew, a gesture of reverence to both Jewish faith and culture. Because of his

strong early ties—both intellectually and politically—to Great Britain, Amichai's early work shows the pronounced influence of the British metaphysical school. Many of his early poems pay homage to the elaborate metaphorical conceits and precise, ornate diction of seventeenth century English masters George Herbert and John Donne. However, his penchant for linguistic concision and emphasis on imagery in his poems clearly reflect the influence of English and American modernists such as W. H. Auden, William Carlos Williams, and Ezra Pound.

Despite his English-language influences, Amichai was first and foremost a Hebrew writer. By 1962 he had already published two volumes of poetry in Hebrew, *Akshav u-ve-yamim aherim* (1955; now and in other days) and *Ba-ginah ha-tsiburit* (1958; in the park), as well as a collection of short stories and a play. By the mid-1960's he was already enjoying the reputation among his contemporaries in Israel, to quote *The New York Times Magazine* critic Robert Alter, as "the country's leading poet." The English translation of his 1963 novel *Lo me-'akshav, lo mi-kan* appeared in 1968 as *Not of This Time, Not of This Place* and increased public knowledge of the Israeli writer in the United Kingdom and the United States. The novel chronicles the experiences of a former Israeli soldier who, after World War II, struggles with the question of whether to return to his native Germany or to remain in Jerusalem to build a new life. Because of the novel's poignant subject matter and provocative autobiographical elements, it was well received by critics in both the United States and the United Kingdom. By the end of the decade, Amichai's position as a key figure in contemporary Jewish literature was firmly established.

In addition to the English-language publication of *Not of This Time, Not of This Place*, 1968 also saw the appearance of Amichai's first major English-language poetry collection, *Selected Poems*, translated by Assia Gutman. Gutman, Harold Schimmel, and British poet Ted Hughes contributed translations of Amichai's work to his next English-language collection, *Selected Poems of Yehuda Amichai* (1971). Other English translations of Amichai's poetry include *Songs of Jerusalem and Myself* (1973), *Travels of a Latter-Day Benjamin of Tudela* (1976), and *Amen* (1977), the latter volume translated by Hughes. The two most definitive compilations—both published by Harper—are *The Selected Poetry of Yehuda Amichai* (1986) and *Yehuda Amichai: A Life of Poetry, 1948-1994* (1994).

Amichai's works also enjoy a prestigious international reputation. His poems have been translated into almost forty languages, including French, German, Swedish, Spanish, and Catalan. Critic Stephen Kessler has praised Amichai as "one of the planet's preeminent poets. . . . Jewish down to the bones, his humanity . . . broadly universal," while poet and essayist C. K. Williams noted in *The New Republic* in 2000 that Amichai's writings embody "the shrewdest and most solid of poetic intelligences." Preeminent American critic Edward Hirsch has likened Amichai's poetry to the works of seminal English Romanticist William Wordsworth, while also noting its stunning similarities to the works of key modernist William Carlos Williams. Hirsch has called *Travels of a Latter-Day Benjamin of Tudela* a "miniature Jewish version of Wordsworth's *The Prelude*" and described Amichai as "a representative man with unusual gifts who in telling his own story also relates the larger story of his people."

Patuah sagur patuah (1998; *Open Closed Open: Poems*, 2000) is generally regarded as Amichai's magnum opus. *Publishers Weekly* praised the book as one of the major poetic works of the decade, and in his obituary for Amichai, C. K. Williams eloquently reflected that:

To sojourn with Amichai in the vast, rugged, sympathetic domain of his imagination is to be given leave to linger in one of those privileged moments when we are in a confidential and confident engagement with our own spirits, when we know with certainty that such a process of imaginative self-investigation is proper and just.

ANALYSIS

Early in his literary career, Amichai decided to write exclusively in Hebrew. Although he could have just as easily chosen to write in English or German, Amichai's decision to compose in his native tongue may be described as no less than deliberate. The fact that much of his poetry deals with overtly political subject matter is reinforced by the awareness that its language of origin is Hebrew. Steeped as he was in the Western tradition, Amichai doubtlessly knew that to reach an audience outside of Israel his works would eventually have to be translated. However, it is clear that he opted nonetheless to write in Hebrew in order to make a statement. Amichai chose Hebrew not only because it was his first language but more important because an awareness of the choice adds legitimacy and urgency to the cause and plight of his people—the most prevalent theme in his work. Readers in other languages are forced to consider that they are approaching Amichai's delicate syntaxes and nuanced metaphorical conceits in translation, not in their intended language. To adequately explore the depths of Amichai's writings, readers must either learn Hebrew or at least place their wholehearted trust in a good translator—both of which draw increased attention to the language and to the cultural legacy with which it is inextricably entwined.

Amichai's works are characterized not only by a brazen and unapologetic sense of nationalism but also by an amazing gift for metaphor. Rich, allusive, and complex as they often are, Amichai's metaphors seek to immerse his reader in a universe of lush, profound, sometimes even elusive conceits. Imaginatively speaking, Amichai often asks much of his readers—but he gives them a great deal in return. One cannot step away from his poems in particular without thinking that their idea of what can be imagined, compared, or even contemplated has not been stretched to its limits by a reading experience that is both enriching and informative.

Stylistically, Amichai's poems are perhaps best described as economical if not minimalistic. Decidedly sparse and devoid of all but the most essential exposition, Amichai's poems rely instead on the originality and depth of his figurative language for their energy and focus. Just as likely to draw attention to the nature of readers' responsibilities to their community, nation, or world as they are to the state of their souls, Amichai's metaphors often seem to do the impossible—they simultaneously navigate the topographies both of state and of spirit.

Although noted for his terse, often enigmatic, lyric poems, Amichai showed his versatility by working in a broad variety of literary forms. Works like "Yerushalyim 5728" ("Jerusalem 1967") and *Travels of a Latter-Day Benjamin of Tuleda* reveal the more expansive and epic dimensions of his poetry, while his novel *Not of This Time, Not of This Place* displays Amichai's talent as a boldly polemical and stylistically innovative prose fiction writer. He also wrote a number of perceptive critical pieces for various magazines and journals, and his play *Masa'le-Ninveh* (pb. 1962, pr. 1964) was first produced in Israel in 1964. He translated a number of works from German into Hebrew, showing his prowess not only as a writer but as a gifted linguist as well.

"MY FATHER'S DEATH"

First published: "Mot Avi," 1955 (collected in *Yehuda Amichai: A Life of Poetry, 1948-1994*, 1994)

Type of work: Poem

Through the playful language of a child's nursery rhyme, a grieving son recounts his father's passing and describes his own attempts to deal with the aftermath of this profound loss.

Initially included in his first volume of poetry, *Akshav u-ve-yamim aherim*, the deftly concise but remarkably incisive poem "My Father's Death" deals with one of Amichai's most pervasive themes—the labyrinthine implications of death on the experi-

ence of life. The brilliant translation of the poem included by Benjamin and Barbara Harshav in their definitive retrospective, *Yehuda Amichai: A Life of Poetry: 1948-1994*, preserves the whimsical, childlike diction of the Hebrew version but also reveals a poem that is remarkably seasoned and deeply introspective.

Rhyme schemes are rare in Amichai's poetry, which, generally speaking, is pointedly modernistic in its avoidance of traditional poetic devices. However, "My Father's Death," although ominous in theme, employs a series of rhymes, such as "places/ spaces," "bow/ now," "soon/ moon," and "endeavor/ forever," that are more evocative of Mother Goose than of William Carlos Williams. Nonetheless, the effect is both stunning and appropriate; Amichai masterfully uses a child's language to disarm his readers of their adult defenses. He then proceeds to reinform those readers' reckoning of one of life's most tragic but inevitable experiences—the death of a father—in deft and startlingly perceptive terms. Of himself and his grownup siblings, all struggling to make sense of their father's passing, the speaker remarks "We went to call [our father's] God, to bow:/ May God come and help us now."

Although the language of the poem is remarkably childlike, its insights are the exclusive domain of the adult. Seeking to understand the profundity of the idea that an all-wise and all-knowing God has called his father away to Heaven, the speaker is utterly at a loss to express himself in adult terms. Instead he opts for a language that has never failed him, that of the heartbroken child. Of the God who has mysteriously taken his father, the speaker reflects "And God takes pains, is coming soon," and in both a profound and conciliatory attempt to comprehend God's omnipotence can say only that after returning to paradise God "hung His coat on the hook of the moon." By the final couplet of the poem, the speaker remains admittedly inept in his ability to adequately understand either his father's death or God's purpose in authoring it. Death, like life, is ultimately viewed as a miracle because of its oblique power and indisputable finality: "But our father, who went out on this endeavor—/ God will keep him there forever."

"OUT OF THREE OR FOUR PEOPLE IN A ROOM"

First published: "A-mach a triuir no ceathrar," 1958 (collected in *The Selected Poetry of Yehuda Amichai*, 1996)
Type of work: Poem

This early but significant poem offers a terse but perceptive meditation on war, indifference, and the sense of isolation with which all people must inevitably contend.

Although not blatantly political in focus, "Out of Three or Four People in a Room" is clearly informed by Amichai's experiences in war. Both of its stanzas open with the same refrain: "Out of three or four people in a room/ One always stands at the window." However, each stanza regards the figure of which it speaks, the "One," in unique but related terms.

In stanza one, the figure, here deliberately unnamed, gazes from a window on the ravages of a just-concluded battle. The figure witnesses "the evil among thorns/ And the fires on the hill," left only with an emptiness that appears to be the only tangible result of the carnage. He observes that before the battle "people . . . went out whole," only to return after the conflict "Like small change to their homes." Clearly, Amichai's metaphor expresses the ambiguity many Israelis felt in the wake of their "victory."

By stanza two, the poem's political imagery becomes even more blatant. No longer faceless, the poem's central figure takes on both a face and a gender. "His hair dark above his thoughts," the figure adopts the identity of a soldier, complete with "kit bag" and "rations." He seeks a reason for fighting, but, like his desperate and disillusioned cohort in the opening stanza, is ultimately left only with hollow epithets to console him.

"A PITY. WE WERE SUCH A GOOD INVENTION"

First published: 1967 (collected in *The Selected Poetry of Yehuda Amichai*, 1996)
Type of work: Poem

In this poem about the breakup of a marriage, the speaker attempts to reconcile himself with his ambivalence about the split. Although he acknowledges that the relationship's end was inevitable, he admits its value as a vital stage in his and his former spouse's emotional growth.

Lauded for its startling directness and austere language, "A Pity. We Were Such a Good Invention" in many ways epitomizes the stylistic tendencies for which Amichai's poetry is best known. Notably minimalistic, the original Hebrew version contains a mere eleven lines and thirty-five words. Benjamin and Barbara Harshav's English translation is only slightly more expansive at seventy-two words. Still, the poem contains a wealth of insight about the nature of human relationships.

A number of critics have noted the pronounced influence of the English metaphysical school, particularly of John Donne and George Herbert, in Amichai's poetry. Critic Edward Hirsch compares "A Pity. We Were Such a Good Invention" to the classic Donne works "The Good-Morrow" and "The Canonization," citing its incisive attempts at combining erotic, religious, and political imagery to characterize the nature of matrimony. For example, in the poem's remarkably imaginative central conceit, the speaker compares his betrothal to his wife to an amputation. The ensuing consummation of the marriage is likened to "An aeroplane made from a man and wife." The poem's closing lines beautifully describe the ambivalence of their tragic, brief union as a period in which they "hovered," albeit like a malfunctioning aircraft, "a little above the earth."

In the manner of Donne, Amichai chooses to draw original and enormously provocative comparisons between things that are seemingly unlike, such as marriage and amputation, divorce and airplane flight.

NOT OF THIS TIME, NOT OF THIS PLACE

First published: *Lo me-'akshav, lo mi-kan,*
1963 (English translation, 1968)
Type of work: Novel

An émigré from Germany to Palestine struggles with the question of whether to return to Germany or remain in Jerusalem in the aftermath of World War II.

The highly autobiographical novel *Not of This Time, Not of This Place* recounts the struggles of its protagonist, Joel, over the question of whether to return to his native Germany or to remain in Jerusalem, where he has found himself after the end of World War II. Jerusalem appeals to Joel because of the stimulation he derives from its exotic locale. A young archaeologist at the city's Hebrew University, Joel dreams of staying in Jerusalem because of the vague promise of discovering a new lover. Although he is married, he is only tentatively loyal to his wife and views the prospect of an illicit love affair as a chance to embark on a new life in a new country.

In contrast, the "old" aspects of Germany, with much of the nation reduced to ruin, offer Joel little incentive to return. However, there is one compelling reason to go back: Joel feels morally obligated to return to Germany and confront the former Nazis who murdered his close childhood friend. Another friend enigmatically suggests that Joel both remain in Israel and return to Germany. But how is he to live two lives at once, in two completely different countries?

At this point, the novel embarks on a brave stylistic experiment; it splits into two parallel but alternating narratives, one told in the third person and the other told in the first person. In the third-person narrative, Joel remains in Jerusalem and enters into an obsessive love affair with an American woman. Seeking to reinvent himself, Joel experiences a series of events that reveal new sides of himself. Ultimately, he realizes he can never completely shake off his past, but he does find that he can at least dim its memory by immersing himself in the quixotic landscapes Jerusalem offers. In the alternate first-person narrative, Joel returns to Ger-

many. In literal terms, he seeks understanding of and vengeance for his former friend's murder. Figuratively, he likewise seeks reconciliation with his nebulous but undeniable past.

Some reviewers have criticized the parallel narratives for being uneven, finding the Jerusalem passage more energetic and metaphorically lush than the episodes set in Germany. However, it is important to keep in mind that the novel's central purpose is to seamlessly merge style with substance. The Jerusalem narrative embodies hope, fancy, and the pursuit of a bigger and brighter future that can and sometimes does shelter people from their unresolved pasts. Naturally, such subject matter calls for the wistful, quixotic depictions that Amichai grants it. The German narrative, on the other hand, is driven by a different purpose. It tells the story of Joel's direct reconciliation with his ominous and unresolved past, one that must be related in more Spartan, less fanciful imagery and language. With commendable precision, Amichai seamlessly weaves the two narratives into a provocative and innovative whole.

"JERUSALEM 1967"

First published: "Yerushalyim 5728," 1967
(collected in *The Selected Poetry of Yehuda Amichai,* 1996)
Type of work: Poem

This twenty-two-section poem is a major meditation on Jerusalem, capital city of Israel, almost twenty years after statehood was won. It reflects upon the city's triumphs and follies in the wake of a generation of independence.

Perhaps the most unique characteristics of "Jerusalem 1967" are its length and figurative expansiveness. Known primarily for his distinctly concise lyric poems, here Amichai opens up and for once allows himself the space and abandon requisite of such a portentous subject. In a sense, Jerusalem serves both as the capital of Israel and the capital of the poem. Throughout its twenty-two thematically varied but stylistically cohesive sections, Amichai explores the countless notions—political, spiritual, and personal—that his adopted homeland

and its luminous capital have come to embody in the two decades that it has been the poet's home.

"Jerusalem 1967" does not attempt to define the city; Amichai never implies that such a feat is even possible. However, through a series of colorful vignettes he does attempt to evoke all of its vibrancy, complexity, and mystery. 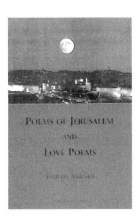 The opening stanzas of the poem describe Jerusalem as a place of refuge, its speaker exuberantly observing that "A person returning to Jerusalem feels that places/ That were painful no longer hurt." By the middle sections, Jerusalem is paradoxically transformed into a haven of moral ambiguity, a place of "children growing half in the ethics of their fathers/ And half in the teachings of war." In the concluding section of the poem the speaker is somehow able to reconcile himself to the fact that such an ancient and monolithic city cannot be summed up in a series of mere metaphors, no matter how bold or illustrative. Instead, all he

can conclude is that Jerusalem "is built on varied foundations/ Of restrained scream." It is indeed the city's restraint, its silence, its stoic and unflinching obstinacy that makes it the evasive totem of awe that "Jerusalem 1967" purports it to be.

SUMMARY

Several critics and scholars have lauded Yehuda Amichai as perhaps the most significant Hebrew poet of his, or maybe any, generation. His writings possess an unmistakable resonance and undeniable skill that have won him the adulation of readers throughout the world. In addition to scores of other accolades, Amichai won the prestigious Israel Prize in 1982 and was nominated for the Nobel Prize in Literature on multiple occasions. However, Amichai never received the Nobel Prize. Some have attributed this to the outspoken political nature of his work, suggesting that his ideology was perhaps too audacious to curry favor with the selection committee's more conservative members. However, even if one finds Amichai's politics too overt or dogmatic, it is difficult to dispute his compelling and exceptional poetic gifts. It is indisputable that Amichai is one of the key figures of twentieth century poetry.

Gregory D. Horn

BIBLIOGRAPHY

By the Author

POETRY:
Akshav u-ve-yamim aherim, 1955
Ba-ginah ha-tsiburit, 1958
Be-merhak shete tikvot, 1958
Shirim, 1948-1962, 1962
Akshav ba-ra'ash, 1968
Selected Poems, 1968
Selected Poems of Yehuda Amichai, 1971
Ve-lo 'al menat lizkor, 1971
Songs of Jerusalem and Myself, 1973
Me-ahore kol zel mistater osher gadol, 1974
Travels of a Latter-Day Benjamin of Tudela, 1976
Amen, 1977
Ha-zeman, 1978 (*Time,* 1979)
Shalyah gedolah, she-elot uteshuvot, 1980 (*Great Tranquility: Questions and Answers,* 1983)
Love Poems, 1981 (bilingual edition)
She'at ha-hessed, 1983

Me'adam ve-el adam tashav, 1985

The Selected Poetry of Yehuda Amichai, 1986, revised 1996

Travels, 1986 (bilingual edition)

Poems of Jerusalem: A Bilingual Edition, 1988

The Early Books of Yehuda Amichai, 1988

Even a Fist Was Once an Open Palm with Fingers, 1991

Nof galui 'enayim/ Open Eyed Land, 1992

Poems of Jerusalem and Love Poems: A Bilingual Edition, 1992

Yehuda Amichai: A Life of Poetry, 1948-1994, 1994

Akhziv, Kesaryah ve-ahavah ahat, 1996

Patuah sagur patuah, 1998 (*Open Closed Open: Poems*, 2000)

LONG FICTION:

Lo me-'akshav, lo mi-kan, 1963 (*Not of This Time, Not of This Place*, 1968)

Mi yitneni malon, 1972

SHORT FICTION:

Be-ruah ha-nora'ah ha-zot, 1961

The World Is a Room, and Other Stories, 1984

DRAMA:

No Man's Land, pr. 1962

Masa' le-Ninveh, pb. 1962, pr. 1964

RADIO PLAY:

Pa 'amonim ve-rakavot, 1968 (pr. as *Bells and Trains*, 1966)

DISCUSSION TOPICS

- Although many readers find Yehuda Amichai's poetry to be "political," is political ideology actually the central concern of his poetry? If so, does it enhance or detract from his appeal?

- In what ways do Amichai's life and works intersect? To what effect does he use his own experiences—as a soldier, scholar, writer, and believer—to add resonance and power to his writings?

- Do you find Amichai's preoccupation with brevity and conciseness to be positive or a negative feature of his poems?

- The narrative technique employed in Amichai's novel *Not of This Time, Not of This Place* is unconventional. Do you find it effective? Why or why not?

- Because Amichai wrote exclusively in Hebrew, his poems have presented problems for English translators. Compare the available English translations of his poems. How do the variations from one translation to the next affect your interpretation of Amichai's poems?

About the Author

Abramson, Glenda, ed. *The Experienced Soul: Studies in Amichai*. Boulder, Colo.: Westview Press, 1997.

_____. *The Writing of Yehuda Amichai: A Thematic Approach*. Albany: State University of New York Press, 1989.

Alter, Robert. *After the Tradition: Essays on Modern Jewish Writing*. New York: Dutton, 1969.

_____. "Israel's Master Poet." *The New York Times Magazine*, June 8, 1986, 40.

Cohen, Joseph. *Voices of Israel: Essays on and Interviews with Yehuda Amichai, A. B. Yehoshua, T. Carmi, Aharon Appelfeld, and Amos Oz*. Albany: State University of New York Press, 1990.

Hirsch, Edward. "In Language Torn from Sleep." *The New York Times Book Review*, August 3, 1986, pp. 14-15.

_____. "At the White Heat." In *How to Read a Poem: And Fall in Love with Poetry*. New York: Harcourt Brace, 1999.

Lapon-Kandelshein, Essi. *To Commemorate the Seventieth Birthday of Yehuda Amichai: A Bibliography of His Work in Translation*. Ramat Gan, Israel: Institute for the Translation of Hebrew Literature, 1994.

Publishers Weekly. Review of *Open Closed Open*, by Yehuda Amichai. (March 20, 2000): 71.

Williams, C. K. "Yehuda Amichai" (obituary). *The New Republic* (October 9, 2000): 28.

KINGSLEY AMIS

Born: London, England
April 16, 1922
Died: London England
October 22, 1995

One of England's most gifted and versatile contemporary writers, Amis distinguished himself as a poet and as an essayist but above all as a seriocomic novelist.

© Washington Post; reprinted by permission of
the D.C. Public Library

BIOGRAPHY

Kingsley William Amis (AY-mihs) was born in London on April 16, 1922. His father, William Robert, worked as a senior clerk in the export division of Colman's Mustard and fully expected his only child to enter commerce. His son's intention, however, was to be a writer—a poet, really—though it was not until the publication of his rollicking and irreverent first published novel, *Lucky Jim* (1954), that Amis received worldwide recognition, winning the W. Somerset Maugham Award in 1955. By Amis's own account, he had been writing since he was a child, but without notable success. To read his early poetry is an embarrassment for him, he has said; his first novel, "The Legacy," written while he attended St. John's College, Oxford, and rejected by fourteen publishers, was later abandoned altogether because it was boring, unfunny, and loaded with affectation. He also considered the novel derivative: He felt that he was writing someone else's book, while what he wanted to say needed a new story and a new style.

Several factors influenced Amis's development into a writer whose novels and style are unique and universally recognized. His comic proclivities were encouraged by his father—a man with "a talent for physical clowning and mimicry." Amis described himself as "undersized, law-abiding, timid," a child able to make himself popular by charm or clowning, who found that at school he could achieve much by exploiting his inherited powers of mimicry. That was true not only at the City of London School—where he specialized in the classics until he was sixteen, then switched to English—but also at Oxford, where he earned his B.A. (with honors) and M.A. degrees in English.

School friends testified to Amis's capacity for making others laugh. Philip Larkin's description of their first meeting in the introduction to his own novel *Jill* (1946, 1964), suggests that it was Amis's "genius for imaginative mimicry" that attracted him: "For the first time I felt myself in the presence of a talent greater than my own." The novelist John Wain recalled how, in the "literary group" to which both of them belonged, Amis was a "superb mimic" who relished differences of character and idiom. Later as a writer, like Charles Dickens, Amis sometimes acted out with his face and his body the appearances and the actions of his characters while creating them. More important, many of his fictional people would appear as fine mimics themselves, using masquerades, role playing, practical jokes, and faces of all kinds for sheer enjoyment, to cover up certain insecurities, or to defend themselves from boredom and other unpleasantness in their lives.

This period of "intensive joke swapping," as Larkin called it, continued when Amis entered the army in 1942. He became an officer, served in the Royal Signals, and landed in Normandy in June, 1944. After service in France, Belgium, and West Germany, he was demobilized in October, 1945.

He later recalled how he and a friend wrote part of a novel based on "malicious caricatures" of fellow officers. This period also was to provide material for stories such as "My Enemy's Enemy," "Court of Inquiry," and "I Spy Strangers"; its immediate effect, however, was to open his eyes to the world, to all sorts of strange people and strange ways of behaving.

Amis's status as an only child also added to his development as a writer, for at an early age he found himself seeking "self-entertainment." He read adventure stories, science fiction, and boys' comics. During these years, Amis also became interested in horror tales. After seeing the Boris Karloff version of *Frankenstein* (1931) and *The Mummy* (1932), Amis became interested in what might be called the minor genres for reasons of wonder, excitement, and "a liking for the strange, the possibly horrific." He became aware that the detective story, various tales of horror or terror, and the science-fiction story provided vehicles both for social satire and for investigation of human nature in a way not accessible to the mainstream novelist.

In view of his early tastes in reading, then, it is not surprising that Amis went on to write genre novels of his own. In *The Green Man* (1969), for example, he would turn the ghost story into an examination of dreaded death and all of its imagined horrors. In *The Riverside Villas Murder* (1973), he would use the detective story to explore how a child perceives the world: The detective analogy lies in the idea that the world of the senses is a series of clues, from which people try to piece together reality. In *The Alteration* (1976), he would use the counterfeit world of science fiction to dramatize a boy's attempt to comprehend the consequences of adulthood and of his possible failure even to experience that stage in the sexual sense. In these instances and others, Amis would use contemporary literary genres as a means of exploring a world both absurd and threatening.

Along with his natural comic gifts and his interest in genre fiction, Amis's development was affected by his initial exposure to an English tradition that resisted the modernist innovations influential in America and on the Continent. His dislike for experimental prose, for mystification, is attributable in part to the influence of one of his Oxford tutors, the Anglo-Saxon scholar Gavin

Bone, and to Amis's readings of certain eighteenth century novelists, whose ability to bring immense variety and plentitude to their work without reverting to obscurity or stylistic excess Amis found appealing.

Amis attributed his personal standards of morality to his readings in Charles Dickens, Henry Fielding, and Samuel Richardson and to the training in standard Protestant virtues that he received as a boy at home. Both of his parents were Baptists, but in protest against their own forceful religious indoctrination, their visits to church became less frequent as they grew older. Any reader of Amis's works—for example, *Russian Hide-and-Seek* (1980) and *The Old Devils* (1986), for which he won the Man Booker Fiction Prize—soon becomes aware that there is in his writings a clear repudiation of traditional Christian belief. Nevertheless, from his parents he received certain central moral convictions that crystallized a personal philosophy of life and art. Hard work, conscientiousness, obedience, loyalty, frugality, patience—these lessons and others were put forward and later found their way into his novels, all of which emphasize the necessity of good works and of trying to live a moral life in the natural—as opposed to the supernatural—world.

Amis was knighted in 1990. In August, 1995, he had a fall, which may have been the result of a stroke. He died in London on October 22, 1995.

ANALYSIS

Like most novelists, Amis was interested above all in human nature, and for most of his life he trained both eye and ear upon the exploration of that subject in all of its fascinating dimensions. From that exploration a primary theme emerged, one to which Amis himself referred when writing about G. K. Chesterton, whom he greatly admired, and Chesterton's novel *The Man Who Was Thursday* (1908). In that book, Amis sensed "a feeling that the world we see and hear and touch is a flimsy veil that only just manages to cover up a deeper and far more awful reality." It is a feeling that the reader encounters in Amis's work as well, for the assumption underlying his novels is that people live in a broken world. The ever-increasing erosion of traditional values, the breakdown of communication everywhere, the seeming absence of any spiritual reality, the impossibility of the existence of any heroic figures—these are some of the painful conclusions following an imaginative investigation into the world as seen by Amis.

These bleak realities are not, of course, new to the evolution of the novel. What distinguishes Amis is that he communicates what could be an otherwise overwhelmingly black vision in such an engaging, entertaining, and readable way. His wit, his sense of style, his devotion to language and its revelation of character, the range of emotions that he elicits from his reader, and the richness of his invention all compel respect and critical attention.

Although at times his vision is bleak, his novels rarely make for bleak reading. For always, beneath the entertainment and eighteenth and nineteenth century fictional techniques for which he is known, there runs a consistent moral judgment that advocates the virtues of hard work, responsibility, decency, faith, and love—an enduring, if beleaguered, value system that defends the English language, traditions, customs, and freedoms against all of their assorted enemies.

The first public manifestation of his moral vision appears in *Lucky Jim* (1954). From that point, its development is clear and consistent. In his early novels—*Lucky Jim*, *That Uncertain Feeling* (1955), and *I Like It Here* (1958)—his fictional world is filled with verbal jokes, amusing or disturbing role playing, and outrageous incidents. Detached from political causes and the progress of their own lives, the protagonists of these stories are part rebels, part victims, part clowns who seek to compromise with or to escape from such facts of life as boredom, hypocrisy, and ignorance. Although each novel carries a serious moral interest, the mishaps encountered and sometimes caused by its unlikely heroes generate laughter instead of tears, because the reader is led to believe that through all of this chaos there is an ordering of events that will ultimately bring security and happiness.

Beginning with *Take a Girl Like You* (1960), however, Amis's view of life grows increasingly pessimistic. Now the world is an opportunistic, self-centered one in which the heroine must fend for herself; life for this character is more serious, more precarious, and less jovial. In *One Fat Englishman*

(1963), *The Anti-Death League* (1966), and *I Want It Now* (1968), life is often an absurd game in which the characters are suffering, often lonely individuals, with little chance for leading the good life, a life free from anxieties, guilts, and doubts.

In his next four novels, Amis's characters live on a darkling plain in a nightmare world in which both young and old are victims of a predominating malevolent presence. *The Green Man* (1969), *Girl, 20* (1971), *The Riverside Villas Murder* (1973), and *Ending Up* (1974) are exemplars of Amis's increasing concern with the question of human depravity, the ambiguity of perfidy, and the existence of evil forces in a world that is driven supposedly by the forces of good.

The potency of evil, the destructiveness of guilt, the often uncertain quest for identity and peace of mind, the perils of old age—these are some of Amis's central philosophical concerns in *The Alteration* (1976), *Jake's Thing* (1978), and *Russian Hide-and-Seek* (1980). Amis once again finds a great many ways to convey the message that human beings suffer, life is difficult, and comic masks conceal great anguish. Only occasionally is this grim picture relieved by some sort of idealism, some unexpected attitude of unselfishness and tenderness. In these novels, the social fabric has given way completely, so that the old mores no longer apply and, indeed, have either been replaced by depraved ones or not replaced at all, leaving a moral vacuum.

Finally, in *Stanley and the Women* (1984), *The Old Devils* (1986), *Difficulties with Girls* (1988), and *The Folks That Live on the Hill* (1990), Amis moves away from the broad scope of a society plagued by trouble to examine instead the troubles plaguing one of that society's most fundamental institutions: marriage. His characters are not going to regain the old sense of security that their lives once held, and Amis does not pretend that they will. What success they manage to attain is always partial. What, in the absence of an informing faith or an all-consuming family life, could provide purpose for living? More simply, how is one to be useful? This is the problem that haunts Amis's characters, and it is a question, underlying all of his novels, that now comes to the forefront.

LUCKY JIM

First published: 1954
Type of work: Novel

In this satire on life in an English provincial university, a young lecturer lives a highly comic secret life of protest against the hypocrisy and pseudointellectualism of certain members of the British establishment.

Lucky Jim belongs to the genre of fiction known as the picaresque novel—with its episodic lurchings, its opportunistic hero, and its emphasis on satirizing various English character types. Although resourceful, the picaro is by tradition simple, a naïf who reveals, by his simplicity, the tattered moral fabric of a society based on pretension. It is Amis's great achievement in *Lucky Jim* that he has taken the ramshackle form of the traditional picaresque novel, centralized his moral theme (the firm value of being one's own person), and added the conventional plot element of lovers separated by evil forces.

To develop his moral stance in *Lucky Jim,* Amis divides his characters into two easily recognizable groups: generally praiseworthy figures, the ones who gain the greatest share of the reader's sympathy, and evil or at best worldly and corrupt characters who obstruct the fortunes of the good ones. Jim (the awkward outsider), Julius Gore-Urquhart (his benefactor or savior), and Christine Callaghan (the decent girl who accepts Jim despite his faults) are distinguished by moral honesty, personal sincerity, and a lack of pretense. Among the antagonists are Professor Welch (Jim's principal tormentor), Bertrand Welch (the defeated boaster), and the neurotic Margaret Peel (the thwarted "witch"), all of whom disguise their motives and present a false appearance. Gore-Urquhart functions as a mediator between common sense (Jim) and excess (the Welches), providing the norm by which to judge other frequently unstable personalities.

As the protagonist, Jim Dixon's character is established immediately with the description of his dual predicaments: He has a job that he does not want but for financial reasons is trying hard to keep, and he has become involved, without quite knowing why, with Margaret, a younger but better-established colleague. It becomes immediately apparent that academic life for Jim is little more than a running duel with his superior, a never-ending speculation as to whether he will be dropped at the term's end or continued on probation for another year.

The picaresque novel is commonly a novel of quest, and Jim's standby and salvation through his own journey is a strong sense of humor that enables him to make light of much very real distress and disaster. Although he hates the Welch family, he knows that deference to them is essential if he is to retain his job. In order to maintain self-respect, however, he resorts to a comic fantasy world in which he can express rage or loathing toward certain imbecilities of the social group that the Welch set represents. His rude faces and clever pranks serve a therapeutic function—a means by which Jim can express token resistance that will not seriously endanger his always-tenuous position.

Late in the novel, Jim is to deliver an important public lecture at the college honoring Welch. Once again, Jim is underwhelmed by the absurdity of the situation. He gets drunk, perfectly parodies Welch's mannerisms to the glee of some onlookers and the dismay of others, and passes out in front of the whole assemblage. The lecture could have been Jim's ticket to a secure future. Instead, it is somewhat less than Jim's shining hour.

Yet just when it seems that Jim's career is at its nadir, his horizons expand. He is offered a job as secretary to Christine's uncle, Julius Gore-Urquhart, a wealthy patron of the arts. When Christine breaks off with Bertrand, she and Jim are free to begin a new romance with the magical attractions of London before them. In the end, the novel affirms the importance of common decency over pretension, of honesty over duplicity, of good intentions over bad. Jim makes his own luck, it seems, through kindness, decency, and good humor in the face of great distress.

The imaginative core of the novel, then, is not the fact that Jim rebels or that he wins, but in the way that he rebels and wins. The ending is a satisfying conclusion to all the comic injustices that have occurred earlier. This happy ending is not contrived; it comes about naturally and can be explained in part as a convention of the novel, in part as the protagonist's wish-fulfillment, in part as his final nose-thumbing at the spiteful and malicious people whom Amis brings to life. The ending is based on the affirmation of a moral order, and as such it is both acceptable and laudable.

THE GREEN MAN

First published: 1969
Type of work: Novel

A seduction, an orgy, a homosexual parson, two exorcisms, and a monster are features of this powerful and moving parable of the limitations and dismay inherent in the human condition.

The Green Man is a medieval coaching inn at Fareham, Hertfordshire, and fifty-three-year-old Maurice Allington is its landlord. Plagued by anxiety, fears, depression, discontent, and an inner emptiness, Maurice seeks peace of mind under conditions that militate against it. His principal reaction to this unhappiness is to immerse himself in the mundane activities of life. There, the reader meets Maurice as a man on the run—from himself. Drink, women, and the tedious minutiae of the innkeeping business offer more satisfying— if only temporary—escapes. Add to this disquiet and revulsion the ever-growing urge toward self-destruction, and there begins to be felt in this novel a truly contemporary pulsebeat. Like the typical protagonist in the works of Albert Camus, Maurice emerges most convincingly as a complicated, self-divided, haunted man in a world that does not make sense.

Unlike Jim Dixon, Allington is given the unique opportunity to make sense of the world through supernatural intervention. The Green Man has its own special ghost, the wicked Dr. Thomas Underhill, who used his knowledge of the black arts for various evil deeds, including the conjuring of a powerful monster, the novel's other "green man," a creature of branches and twigs and leaves capable

of rending an ordinary man. Underhill's final triumph is to reveal his power beyond the grave in pursuit of Maurice and his daughter.

While other characters cannot believe in the ghost, the intensity of Maurice's belief invites the reader to suspend that disbelief. Amis eases his readers into an acceptance of the supernatural by means of a variety of elements: the common sense and worldly character of the narrator, the characterization of the guests, the skillful use of incidental details to create the air of reality. People eat, drink, argue, reconcile, read, share, and make love with little or no expectation that anything out of the ordinary will (or can) happen.

As the tension grows, so does Maurice; he passes through various stages of awakening to the truth of himself and another world. Underhill, as a doppelgänger, is evidence that evil is a real and active presence in the world and not just a concoction of the mind. His ghost is also a means by which Amis can credibly account for the forces that seek Maurice's destruction—all that afflicts, mystifies, and weighs on him.

The discovery of Underhill's power brings Maurice to a deeper consideration of the question of survival after death and prepares him for a conversation with still another supernatural agent, of quite a different kind from Underhill. Amis personifies God as a character in his own right, in the guise of a young man who expresses puzzlement and a certain degree of helplessness over the events unfolding in the world of his creation. Maurice's transformation from an alienated man to an unwitting hero who chooses to take on the responsibilities of an absentee God forms the dramatic core of the novel.

In his pursuit and eventual destruction of Underhill and the monster, Maurice gains self-knowledge. He begins to realize that his "affinity" to Underhill has taken many guises. Maurice has reduced people to mere objects, beings manipulated and controlled by a more powerful master, just as Underhill controlled his monster. For Underhill, further, sex and aggression and striving for immortality are all bound up together; it becomes clear, as Maurice struggles with the evil spirit, that the same holds true for him.

When the terrifying battle is finally over and the selfish Maurice has been softened by the closeness of disaster, he recognizes and responds for the first time to the love of his daughter, who agrees to look after him. Thus, the book is about moral education. Although the haunting was a terrifying experience, for Maurice it was also a rewarding one, for he has changed; he wants hereafter to be kind, not because social mores (in the shape of family and friends) tell him to do so, but because he has learned from facing his own potential for wickedness how destructive evil can be in any form. In exorcising Underhill and the monster, he has also exorcised the evil potential in his own character. The experience has ennobled him. He accepts the limitations of life and, most important, comes to an appreciation of what death has to offer—a permanent escape from himself.

JAKE'S THING

First published: 1978
Type of work: Novel

Jake Richardson holds a grudge against the world, a world of change and instability that is reflected on a personal level in his impotence.

In *Jake's Thing*, much more is going on with Jake Richardson than his loss of sexual control; the society in which he lives, the London and the Oxford of 1978, has also moved, subtly but surely, out of his range of understanding and/or desire, and Jake has responded by becoming bitter and cynical. A fifty-nine-year-old Oxford don, neither his career nor his other activities stimulate much interest in him, so that his desires—social, professional, emotional—have become as stultified as his sexual ones. Perhaps it is not coincidental that Jake's impotence comes at a time when Comyas College is debating the question of admitting women to its hallowed, previously all-male-inhabited halls. Jake, who is fighting for his psychic life on several fronts, inadvertently exposes his deep hostility to the project during a college meeting, where his colleagues had expected him to "speak for the ladies." At the end of his travail, and after nearly three hundred pages of unrelenting exposure to the incompetence and stupidity of professional therapists and the institutions that sustain them, Jake's desire for sex is gone, his dislike for women has intensified,

and he decides that he would just as soon remain impotent.

Like Jim Dixon, Jake Richardson is an academic misfit who likes to drink, has a keen eye for hypocrites and phoneys, writes articles that bore even himself, copes with ferocious inner monologues on his own prejudices and irrational likes and dislikes, has a rollicking sense of fun, plays practical jokes, enjoys puns and wordplay, and talks to himself in voices that parody types whom he has encountered in books, television, films, the army, and the academy. Like Jim, he suffers from the undesired attentions of a neurotic woman who stages a fake suicide attempt. Both characters manage to reconcile inner thoughts and outer statements in a public denunciation of a cause, delivered while they are drunk.

Many of the comic set pieces in *Jake's Thing* are reminiscent of some of the classic scenes in *Lucky Jim*, in that they serve to set the protagonist's role as an outsider to the contemporary world. That alienation often serves to parody the protagonist himself. Like Jim Dixon, Jake is caught in a snare of his own devising; his readiness to do battle with his foes and his gift for running into squabbles, fights, and embarrassments increases the chaos in a life that is already frustratingly out of control. Those frustrations are many, as they were for Jim, and signify the social and cultural impotence that Jake feels. The world around him is no longer to his liking, and everyday incidents painfully amplify that effect. Jake is no longer at home on his own turf, and that sense of foreignness compels him to withdraw further and further from the contemporary world. Jim's problems with his department chairman, with some of his students, and with a potential publisher for his essay on shipbuilding techniques are, of course, similar sources of frustration and outward signs that he is a man out of sync, immersed in the wrong culture for his personality.

In spite of the resemblances between the two novels, however, there is in fact a great conceptual jump from one to the other. Suffering from a general weariness, of which his loss of libido is but one indication, Jake has definite feelings about the modern world: He does not like it. There is no equivocation, no attempt to be "fair," to look at things from other angles as Jim was inclined to do. The world is going from bad to worse, changes that infuriate and baffle Jake. Included on his list of personal dislikes are airplanes, American tourists, psychologists, the working class, the young, strangers, sloppy language, wealthy Arabs, cocky youngsters, advertisements, telephones, architecture, cuisine—in other words, all facets of present-day England. Above all, he discovers that he despises women. His only real pleasure is in finding his expectations of dirt, decay, inefficiency, and boring and stupid behavior fulfilled. Amis's use of Jake's seething narration, his scathing internal commentary, and his sometimes vicious dialogue are instrumental in creating the universe of misogyny, prejudice, and dissatisfaction.

While *Lucky Jim* ends with a triumphant revelation to Jim of a new life, a new world, *Jake's Thing* ends with a closing down, a spurning of the world for which Jake feels at best indifferent—a retreat into TV dinners and TV films. By the end of the novel, Jake has arrived at a stage of rejecting everything. Evidence points to a deepening misanthropy in Jake as he agonizes over his spiritual isolation, vainly attempts to recover his interest in sex, and learns to come to terms with impotence and acedia, the deathlike condition of not caring. In the end, readers see in Jake a gesture of impotence, puzzlement, anger, and eventual retreat from the contemporary world. All of this gives the novel an overall mood of defeat and confusion far removed from the light comedy so much in evidence in *Lucky Jim*. Amis has come from the notion that one can choose to be happy (as in *Lucky Jim*) to the statement that there is no happiness possible in this world and one must accept powerlessness as a natural state.

THE OLD DEVILS

First published: 1986
Type of work: Novel

Through a microcosm of failed human relationships, Amis depicts the culmination of the decay of contemporary life.

The Old Devils tells of Alun Weaver, who has chosen to retire from his successful television career in London as a kind of "professional Welshman" and third-rate poet and return after thirty years with his beautiful wife, Rhiannon, to South Wales. The novel explores over a span of a few months the effect of this return on their circle of old friends from university days.

The old devils—a group of Welsh married couples all in their sixties and seventies—are retired. They do little else than reminisce about lost opportunities and a grander Wales and grumble about slipping dentures, dietary restrictions, and dwindling physical energies while drinking steadily, ignoring the large role alcohol has played in the mental, physical, and spiritual decay about which they complain. The men, however, are not alone in their reverence for the bottle. At the same time, their spouses gather elsewhere, ostensibly to drink coffee but more often to consume bottle after bottle of wine, to chain-smoke, and to pursue conversations about their marriages, sex, and assorted other topics in an atmosphere reeking of alcohol fumes and stale cigarettes.

The physical ill health these cronies worry about extends to the spiritual health of their marriages. With one major exception, the women in this novel are not only plain, hard, sharp, critical, or cross but also lack any reasonable relationships with their husbands that would make significant communication possible. Only Alun and Rhiannon, married for thirty-four years, seem still to have an appetite for life and love as well as drink, and most of their misunderstandings lead only to teasing, not to disaster. Yet their arrival arouses conflict among their old friends.

The conflict comes in part because their return revives memories of various youthful liaisons and indiscretions, and also because the egotistical Alun immediately sets out to re-woo the three women with whom he had affairs in the old days. Alun plays at adultery as if it were an idle pastime: His casual tone, however, is a poor disguise for the emptiness and pain felt by his objects of attention, or by his wife, Rhiannon, who tolerates his philandering, or by the husbands, who either suspect it or know of it yet are resigned to doing nothing about it. Near the end of the story, Alun chokes on his whiskey and water and falls forward, dead of a stroke. Given his reputation, it is not surprising to find that there is no sadness over his death—only surprise, and a thought or two that are quickly brushed aside by the others as a minor inconvenience.

The Old Devils is about more than an aging present; it is also very much about the past and its impingements upon everyone. Many of the characters in *The Old Devils* are carrying scars from bitterness and regret because of something that happened in their lives long ago, something they hide carefully from the world but on which their conscious attention is fixed. Past choices weigh heavily on all of them. These old devils are bedeviled by worries and fears of all kinds that deepen their uncertainty about life and increase their preoccupation with the past. Indeed, Amis points out that one of the reasons old people make so many journeys into the past is to satisfy themselves that it is still there. Yet when that, too, is gone, what is left? In this novel, what remains is only the sense of lost happiness not to be regained, only the awareness of the failure of love, only the present and its temporary consolations of drink, companionship, music, and any other diversions that might arise, only a blind groping toward some insubstantial future. Neither human nor spiritual comfort bolsters the sagging lives and flagging souls of the characters.

As in earlier novels, Amis finds in the everyday concerns of his ordinary folk a larger symbolic meaning, which carries beyond the characters to indict a whole country. In this story, unemployment is high, people lead purposeless lives, and the culture is dying. Buses are always late. Businesses suffer from staff shortages. There is an obvious absence of trade and enterprise, mines are closed, docks are dead. A local chapel has been deconsecrated and turned into an arts center; another has been converted into a two-screen pornographic theater, two extremes that underline the uselessness of the spiritual and its transformation from the divine into the mundane. Thus, the novel examines an often debilitating process of moral and spiritual decay, a lessening of these people as human beings as life goes on and how their hopes have dimmed along with their physical and mental powers.

SUMMARY

In all of his novels, Kingsley Amis tries to understand the truth about different kinds of human suffering and then passes it on to the reader without distortion, without sentimentality, without evasion, and without oversimplification. Underlying all Amis's novels is the hero's quest for happiness, for meaning, for a life of morality and common sense in an ever-darkening world. In thirty-six years, he moved from fundamentally decent people who choose to act in a manner that has at least some significance, to utterly depraved ghosts, to people young and old stripped of their humanity, impotent and mad. The objects of his humor have broadened and deepened over the years, too.

No one can deny Amis's great technical gifts. He has never forgotten that the traditional first aim of most writers has always been to please the reader. The popularity of his art, the impressive body of critical literature, the review attention and honors given him—all testify to his continuing hold on the popular imagination. He is a writer for difficult, changing times.

Dale Salwak

BIBLIOGRAPHY

By the Author

LONG FICTION:
Lucky Jim, 1954
That Uncertain Feeling, 1955
I Like It Here, 1958
Take a Girl Like You, 1960
One Fat Englishman, 1963
The Egyptologists, 1965 (with Robert Conquest)
The Anti-Death League, 1966
Colonel Sun: A James Bond Adventure, 1968 (as Robert Markham)
I Want It Now, 1968
The Green Man, 1969

Girl, 20, 1971
The Riverside Villas Murder, 1973
Ending Up, 1974
The Crime of the Century, 1975 (pb. in a newspaper series 1975; pb. in book form 1987)
The Alteration, 1976
Jake's Thing, 1978
Russian Hide-and-Seek, 1980
Stanley and the Women, 1984
The Old Devils, 1986
Difficulties with Girls, 1988
The Folks That Live on the Hill, 1990
The Russian Girl, 1992
You Can't Do Both, 1994
The Biographer's Moustache, 1995

SHORT FICTION:
My Enemy's Enemy, 1962
Collected Short Stories, 1980
We Are All Guilty, 1991
Mr. Barrett's Secret, and Other Stories, 1993

POETRY:
Bright November, 1947
A Frame of Mind, 1953
A Case of Samples: Poems, 1946-1956, 1956
The Evans Country, 1962
A Look Round the Estate: Poems, 1957-1967, 1967
Collected Poems: 1944-1979, 1979

NONFICTION:
New Maps of Hell: A Survey of Science Fiction, 1960
The James Bond Dossier, 1965 (with Ian Fleming)
What Became of Jane Austen? and Other Questions, 1970
On Drink, 1972
Tennyson, 1973
Rudyard Kipling and His World, 1975
An Arts Policy?, 1979
Everyday Drinking, 1983
How's Your Glass?, 1984
Memoirs, 1991
The King's English: A Guide to Modern Usage, 1997
The Letters of Kingsley Amis, 2000 (Zachary Leader, editor)

EDITED TEXTS:
Spectrum: A Science Fiction Anthology, 1961, 1962, 1963, 1965 (with Robert Conquest)
Harold's Years: Impressions from the "New Statesman" and the "Spectator," 1977
The Faber Popular Reciter, 1978
The New Oxford Book of Light Verse, 1978

DISCUSSION TOPICS

- As a boy, Kingsley Amis did much clowning. How does a knack for clowning help a writer?

- Amis was one of the British writers of the post-World War II era called "angry young men." Was he correct to reject that characterization, as he did?

- What makes *Lucky Jim* an affirmation of the moral order?

- What evidence do you see in favor of the suggestion that detective and horror stories can help a writer understand human nature?

- Consider the following: Like Charles Dickens, Amis is seen as a novelist whose works over the years grew less humorous and more pessimistic.

- How is one to be useful? Determine why an older writer, like Amis in his later years, should be concerned with this topic.

The Golden Age of Science Fiction, 1981
The Great British Songbook, 1986 (with James Cochrane)
The Amis Anthology, 1988
The Pleasure of Poetry: From His "Daily Mirror" Column, 1990
The Amis Story Anthology: A Personal Choice of Short Stories, 1992

About the Author

Bradford, Richard. *Kingsley Amis.* London: Edward Arnold, 1989.

Gardner, Philip. *Kingsley Amis.* Boston: Twayne, 1981.

Keulks, Gavin. *Father and Son: Kingsley Amis, Martin Amis, and the British Novel Since 1950.* Madison: University of Wisconsin Press, 2003.

Leader, Zachary. *The Life of Kingsley Amis.* New York: Pantheon, 2007.

McDermott, John. *Kingsley Amis: An English Moralist.* Basingstoke, England: Macmillan, 1989.

Ritchie, Harry. *Success Stories: Literature and the Media in England, 1950-1959.* London: Faber, 1988.

Salwak, Dale, ed. *Kingsley Amis: A Reference Guide.* Boston: G. K. Hall, 1978.

_____. *Kingsley Amis: In Life and Letters.* New York: St. Martin's Press, 1990.

_____. *Kingsley Amis: Modern Novelist.* London: Harvester Wheatsheaf, 1992.

MARTIN AMIS

Born: Oxford, England
August 25, 1949

Amis established himself as a master of satire by revealing the grotesque distortions of a world destroying itself with drugs, sex, crime, ethnic and religious hatred, and environmental destruction.

Cheryl A. Koralik

BIOGRAPHY

Martin Louis Amis (AY-mihs) was born on August 25, 1949, in Oxford, England. He is the son of Kingsley Amis, the famous novelist, and Hilary Amis, daughter of a shoe-manufacturing millionaire. These parents would soon plunge young Martin into a kind of nomadic existence as they moved from one place to another, an odyssey that would require him to attend no fewer than fourteen different schools and live in at least three different countries. This heterogeneous background, in fact, may well account for his uncanny ability to appreciate various cultures, classes, and occupations.

Martin Amis, along with his older brother Philip and younger sister Sally, spent his early childhood years in Swansea, southern Wales, where the elder Amis held a teaching position at Swansea University. While in Swansea, Kingsley Amis published his most famous novel, *Lucky Jim* (1954), and the instant success of that novel initiated a string of new teaching appointments, including a crucially important year (1959) in Princeton, New Jersey. During that year, the ten-year-old Martin began to acquire his lifelong fascination with the exuberance of American slang, as shown much later in his brilliantly comic masterpiece *Money: A Suicide Note* (1984), which is set in both New York and London.

In 1960, the Amis family settled once more in England, this time in Cambridge, but the family unity was shattered the next year, when Kingsley and Hilary Amis were divorced. Young Martin spent the next year, 1962, on the island of Majorca, Spain, in the company of his mother, sister, and brother. There he attended an international school with a wide variety of students. In 1963, he returned to England and briefly became a professional actor by landing a role in the film production of *A High Wind in Jamaica* (1965). During the next year, he attended school in London, where the primary focus of his life was social not academic, for he spent the bulk of his time investigating the lowlife of the city, not unlike the feckless ne'er-do-wells of his novel *London Fields* (1989).

Around 1965, possibly under the influence of his stepmother, the novelist Elizabeth Jane Howard, Amis began to read serious literature and prepare himself for a university career by attending a series of "crammers" or preparatory schools. In 1968, he was admitted to Exeter College, Oxford; in 1971, he received a B.A. with first-class honors in English.

Amis began his career as a man of letters in 1971, although at first he was operating strictly behind the scenes as a book reviewer for *The Observer* and as editorial assistant and fiction and poetry editor of the *Times Literary Supplement*. Simultaneously, public acclaim attached itself to his name after the appearance of *The Rachel Papers* (1973), a detailed and largely autobiographical work about the sexual exploits of a student named Charles Highway. Even though *The Rachel Papers* was Amis's first novel, it received unusually lavish praise from the demanding British reviewers and won the prestigious Maugham Award in 1974, exactly twenty years after his father had won the same award for *Lucky Jim*.

In 1975, Amis became the assistant literary editor of the *New Statesman*, a magazine with which he would remain closely associated after becoming a full-time writer for that publication. In 1975, Amis also wrote his second novel, the controversial *Dead Babies* (1975), which explores the effects of drugs in a communelike setting that is destroyed by horrifying violence. This gruesome and realistic treatment of drug-induced madness caused the second American publisher to change the title to *Dark Secrets* (1977).

Success (1978), Amis's third novel, continued his preoccupation with sexual excess, as well as with autobiographical elements. Certainly it can be no coincidence that the narrative plot of *Success* revolves around the lives of two brothers, Terry and Gregory Riding, and one sister, Ursula. The additional element of incest caused quite a few reviewers to find the book repugnant or brutish, even though it clearly deals with the larger theme of old and new money and of class warfare in Britain.

In 1980, Amis became embroiled in a strange and celebrated case of literary plagiarism when he discovered that the American essayist and novelist Jacob Epstein had plagiarized some fifty passages from *The Rachel Papers* while composing *Wild Oats* (1980). Epstein later conceded his guilt, but the exact number of passages used was never established to Amis's complete satisfaction. Nor was Amis completely pleased by the revised edition of *Wild Oats*, with all of the plagiarized passages excised. It is worth noting that Amis took no legal action against Epstein; his primary concern, as always, was his integrity as an author.

Amis's fourth novel, *Other People: A Mystery Story* (1981), bears a close resemblance to *Success* in its use of the doppelgänger or "double" motif, a pattern that has been underscored by scholars and critics of Amis's work. Instead of closely related brothers, *Other People* features the closely related sides or "halves" of a woman whose personality is split into two beings, one called Mary Lamb, the other Amy Hide.

Amis married Antonia Phillips, an American professor specializing in aesthetics, in 1984. That same year he published *Money*, an extravagant, witty, and linguistically inventive book that began to reveal the extent of his maturing talent. The hero, John Self, an alcoholic self-abuser, looms as an obese figure of comic pathos. Yet his story is also the story of the failure to make art, even bad art, in the form of a pornographic movie in a culture of pure greed. One of the "characters" in *Money* happens to be a young British novelist named Martin Amis.

After the publication of *Money*, Amis turned his attention to collecting and publishing various essays and occasional short stories he had written for periodicals and newspapers. *The Moronic Inferno and Other Visits to America* (1986) and *Einstein's Monsters* (1987) were the well-received results. *London Fields*, his biggest and most ambitious novel, somehow manages to combine journalistic precision with the kinds of literary invention that have made Amis a significant presence on the literary scene.

With the critical success and considerable sales of *London Fields* and given his charismatic status as England's enfant terrible of letters (although Amis by this time was in his forties), for the next decade Amis both endured and exploited his rock star status as a celebrity. Amis's private life, including several romantic breakups, reports of an illegitimate daughter, the death of his father in 1995, and a national fascination with the exorbitant advances he commanded, were all part of tabloid coverage. Despite such distraction during the decade, Amis completed his most technically daring and thematically provocative works. Early on there was his experimental tale of the Nazi Holocaust, *Time's Arrow; Or, The Nature of the Offense* (1991), which was short-listed for the Man Booker Prize. It was essentially a story told in reverse, as a doctor in an American hospital recounts his narrative life story backward, moving with inexorable horror toward his early life as a doctor in the concentration camps. *The Information* (1995) is a caustic insider's look at the dark underside of London's prestigious publishing scene, particularly the pettiness and envy of the contemporary writer, which centers on the midlife crisis of a once-promising novelist who cannot stomach the success enjoyed by a fellow writer whose talents he deems far below his own. Two other novels—*Night Train* (1997) and *Yellow Dog* (2003)—immersed the reader in Amis's characteristic night world of violence and mayhem, the first a police procedural about a mysterious suicide, and the second a bizarre Jekyll-and-Hyde tale of a perfect husband who after a blow on the head reverts to violence, lust, and anger.

Increasingly, Amis, who had published a steady stream of reviews and essays in a variety of prestigious journals and magazines and had collected them in several well-received volumes, turned to nonfiction. It was the 2000 publication of *Experience*, a nonlinear memoir of his difficult relationship with his father and of his own literary evolution, that garnered Amis considerable critical admiration, as well as the James Tait Black Memorial Prize for Biography and the National Book Critics Circle Award for Nonfiction. A subsequent work, however, embroiled Amis in contentious public debates. *Koba the Dread: Laughter and the Twenty Million* (2002), a kind of meditation on the evil of Joseph Stalin's reign of terror and its comparative neglect in historic memory against the far more widespread outrage expressed over Adolf Hitler, examined in part why Communism proved such an attractive ideology for leftist intellectuals in the early twentieth century, among them, of course, Amis's own father. Although historians took issue with Amis's liberal reading of Stalin's reign, that research led to Amis's triumphant return to fiction in *House of Meetings* (2006), a complex psychological study of two brothers in Moscow who both fall in love with the same Jewish girl on the eve of Stalin's pogrom.

After the September 11, 2001, terrorist attacks in the United States, Amis emerged as an outspoken commentator on the implications of the events. He was appalled by the actions, publishing broadsides and giving dozens of interviews that spelled out his opinions. He maintained that the attacks revealed the depth of the hatred the disenfranchised Islamic culture felt toward the United States, and that fanaticism could never be logically understood, that it was a death cult like Nazism, and that such toxic logic could only be fostered by the perverted thinking of organized religion. That argument, collected in essays published in *The Second Plane: September 11, Terror and Boredom* (2008), provoked widespread response and positioned Amis where he long wanted to be: at the center of an international firestorm of debate.

Amis continued to live in London and taught creative writing at the University of Manchester. He has evolved through being a hip bad-boy rock-star celebrity writer to establishing a significant position as the defining voice of British letters—audaciously experimental, relentlessly controversial, uncompromisingly Swiftian in his anger, and supremely a careful and deliberate wordsmith of extraordinary power.

ANALYSIS

On first reading Amis's books, the reader will probably hear echoes of many twentieth century novelists. One perceives the zany, scatological world of Philip Roth, the skewed universe of Truman Capote, the meditative voice of Saul Bellow, the complicated plot lines of Thomas Pynchon or Kurt Vonnegut, and the high-voltage linguistic displays of Tom Wolfe, Vladimir Nabokov, and Anthony Burgess. Yet even though Amis has written about many of these famous novelists (especially in *The Moronic Inferno and Other Visits to America*), he remains stylistically unique. There is a certain blending of choppy British street slang, complicated literary allusions, playful puns or witticisms, and outrageously irreverent names that collectively brand each piece of fiction as belonging only to Amis. To read Amis is to experience the literary equivalent of skydiving or deep-sea diving, where the most familiar objects become strange and surreal and where time itself slows down or speeds up in a fashion that is altogether unnerving.

Style ultimately means the way an author invents and manipulates language to suit his or her particular requirements. In Amis's satiric universe, the intent is always to poke fun at the colossal moral and social breakdown of the twentieth century. Like all good satirists, Amis is making the reader laugh at outrageous and illogical events that might otherwise be taken for granted. If Amis writes about sexual degradation, greed, trickery, and lying, he is not glorifying but denouncing these low points of human behavior. One of his favorite devices to evoke laughter is to create ridiculously appropriate—or inappropriate—names, as did the great British novelist Charles Dickens when he created such memorable figures as Pip, Scrooge, and Tiny Tim.

In *Money*, for example, a novel-length parable on greed and self-absorption, Amis gives these pecuniary names to certain appropriate characters: Buck Specie, Sterling Dun, Lira Cruzeiros, and Anna Mazuma. In this monetary madhouse, automobiles have a high visibility and high status value and so receive names such as Torpedo, Boomerang, Culprit, Alibi, Jefferson, Iago, Tigerfish, Autocrat, and Farrago. The hero, improbably named John Self, drives an ultraexpensive Fiasco, which is perpetually breaking down and requiring more and more expensive parts. John Self is engaged in hiring actors for his new film, and again the satiric creativity of Amis produces such actors' names as Nub Forkner, Butch Beausoleil, and Lorne Guyland. The technical crew is composed of Micky Obbs, Kevin Skuse, and Des Blackadder. All of these characters calm their nerves with the angelic tranquilizer Serafim. Amis actually makes a guest appearance in his own novel, and as the character "Martin Amis" reminds John Self near the end of the narrative, "Names are awfully important."

These unforgettable and oddly appropriate names are perhaps the most distinctive stylistic trait in all of Amis's novels: Charles Highway in *The Rachel Papers*, Terry Service in *Success*, Mary Lamb in *Other People*, and the gallery of characters in *London Fields*, including Guy Clinch, Nicola Six, Keith Talent, Lizzyboo, Marmaduke, Chick Purchase, and Trish Shirt, among others. Names are indeed important to Amis's artistry.

Closely akin to the making of names is the making of new words, or neologisms, and Amis delights in coining new terms or concocting hyphenated phrases in a manner that outdoes Tom Wolfe or Anthony Burgess. The antihero of *Money*, for example, crisscrosses the vast space over the Atlantic Ocean as he shuttles back and forth between London and New York, leaving behind a wake of "jetslime." In the latter portions of the narrative, this same peripatetic John Self begins to perceive the hollowness of his own existence and castigates himself for being no more than a "cyborg" or "skinjob."

When Amis is not inventing new words, he feels free to push every key on the linguistic keyboard, from technical, scholarly, academic, and literary English all the way down the scales to American and British slang. In all of his books, vulgar words abound, as do slang terms such as "yob" (lower-class person), "bim" (short for "bimbo," an unflattering term for a woman), "rug" (hair), and "snappers" (teeth). Amis delights in any kind of linguistic artifact, especially those that help to define a culture or a character. He is amused by the American tendency to misspell just about everything, to

use apostrophes with plural nouns ("light's" for "lights"), or to enclose nouns in unnecessary quotation marks.

This obsession with language allows Amis to develop memorable characters, like John Self and Keith Talent, because their personality is equivalent to the way they speak and write. This same preoccupation with language also facilitates the development of larger themes that organize the many strands of Amis's narrative designs. He tends to work with a small number of basic themes that he explores in different ways and at different levels of complexity in all of his novels.

The critic Karl Miller, in his important study *Doubles: Studies in Literary History* (1985), identified the principal theme in Amis's work as "doubling." Plot lines, characters, and situations always tend to be echoed in the universe according to Amis, such as the two brothers in *Success* or the characters "Martin Amis" and "Martina Twain" in *Money*. The two other major themes in Amis's work are planetary decay and the muselike woman. *The Moronic Inferno and Other Visits to America, Money*, and *London Fields* all presuppose a world on the brink of ecological disaster. In this world there is always a magnetic feminine presence, such as Selina Street or the inscrutable Nicola Six, whose blandishments and seductions literally keep the men moving through a world of smog, acquired immunodeficiency syndrome (AIDS), and gamma rays.

Amis's moral sensibility and his penchant for literary experimentation continued to contest for predominance in his work after *London Fields*. The works that defined Amis's emergence into his maturity—most notably *Time's Arrow, Experience, Koba the Dread, House of Meetings*, and *The Second Plane*—extended his early fascination with foregrounding literary concerns in narratives that examine difficult and thorny moral issues and sustain a tension between ethical commentary and formal experimentation. By taking on some of the most controversial and provocative subject matter available to a writer in the late twentieth century—many incendiary public issues, including religious fanaticism, corporate greed, humanity's taste for violence, the corruption of sexuality, and mass-scale ethnic cleansing, as well as far more personal concerns, including the ego of the writer, the evolution of the writer, and the influence of family and friends—

Amis continued to extend the range of traditional linear narration, inevitably posing in the minds of his harshest critics questions about the appropriateness of such literary experiments given the heft and gravitas of the issues. In addition, Amis developed into one of the finest and most careful prose stylists since George Orwell, the cadence and music of his prose always assuming a far more distinctive place than the moral and ethical outrage he investigates. Thus, Amis has emerged as a contested presence in British contemporary letters, admired for his precise and vital prose and his nervy formal inventiveness and both reviled and endorsed for his uncompromising moral views, a provocative sense of outrage, Swiftian in its dimensions, that has not subsided across nearly three decades of writing.

What has emerged, however, over Amis's works in the 1990's and after September 11, 2001, is a new and profound interest in the poignancy of extraordinarily ordinary lives, a sympathy that really had little place in the abrasive works before *Time's Arrow*. This sympathy is felt in the poignant descriptions of his own childhood in *Experience*; in the moving account of the doomed children in the concentration camps in *Time's Arrow*, and in the psychological complexities of the narrator in *House of Meetings*, sentenced to ten years in Stalin's labor camps, making his peace with his own violent past and coming to terms with his brother, a pacifist and poet. That interest in psychological depth and a Dostoyevskyan sense of the difficult ambiguities of moral behavior lend a level of complexity to Amis's later fiction.

MONEY

First published: 1984
Type of work: Novel

English film director John Self tries unsuccessfully to launch a pornographic film in New York and in the process goes bankrupt.

Money: A Suicide Note (and its successor, *London Fields*) allows Amis to introduce a new kind of character, the corrupt or profane artist figure. In *Money* the would-be artist is John Self; he is echoed in Lon-

don Fields by the figure of Keith Talent. Having made his mark by producing and directing pornographic commercials for British television, John Self, a rapacious and epically greedy human being, is approached by Fielding Goodney, a bisexual financier who volunteers to underwrite the full production costs of a new film to be made by Self in America. Goodney's proposal, of course, is an elaborate ruse, the first of many traps into which the obese Self will fall without any conscious deliberation.

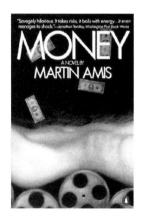

In reality, Goodney is using Self's credit line to finance the entire project in New York, just as Self's partners in a London advertising agency are essentially living off Self's earnings. In the end, his credit cards become useless, he is evicted from a New York hotel, and he flies back to London, where he is evicted again, this time from his flat. Even his beloved Fiasco, a car as unreliable as all the people in his life, finally falls apart and refuses to run.

Before this collapse occurs and before he fails even in his own suicide, the pill-popping, alcoholic Self takes the reader on a grotesque binge of transatlantic hopping, slumming in New York's topless clubs and striptease joints, drinking impossibly large amounts (in taverns, bars, hotel rooms, and airplanes), and eating innumerable greasy American hamburgers and hot dogs (his favorite foods). The embodiment of greed, Self "feeds" on everything; he is never satisfied. Ultimately, he feeds upon himself and engineers his own destruction. Amis seems to be saying that John is a Self that has no "self" outside alcohol, drugs, sex, and money. He is the consummate consumer, an Everyman for twentieth century New York and London.

New York and London are depicted as polluted cities on both the spiritual and physical planes, and if the smog and drugs are not enough to confuse Self, there are doubles everywhere. Fielding Goodney doubles as a transvestite who follows Self everywhere. London and New York are the double locales of the book, and even the Muse-woman is doubled, taking the forms of sluttish, conniving Selina Street and cultured, elegant Martina Twain. Street satisfies the grossest physical needs of Self, but she, too, is greedy. While living with Self, she somehow manages an affair with Ossie Twain, an undertaking that makes virtually everyone unhappy. Only "Martin Amis" and Martina Twain tell Self the truth, namely that his film *Good Money* is abominable, just like his life. The tenderest and funniest moments in *Money* occur when Martina tries to reform John by taking him to concerts and introducing him to the work of George Orwell. Yet since he is only half an artist, Self can never fully appreciate genuine art.

LONDON FIELDS

First published: 1989
Type of work: Novel

Nicola Six, an inscrutable temptress, involves three men in a complex scheme to make her suicide as artistic and destructive as possible.

Set in Margaret Thatcher's London, replete with smog, skinheads, and strange weather (the product of El Niño and other meteorological disturbances), *London Fields* is a grand novel that combines Amis's mature themes into a compelling synthesis that might be taken as a kind of parable for urban life. Artist figures abound, including Sam, the American narrator who occupies the flat of an absent British writer named Mark Asprey; Keith Talent, the con man and philanderer extraordinaire who treats dart throwing as high art; and the Muse-woman, Nicola Six, who believes she will be murdered on her thirty-fifth birthday, which will occur on November 6 (hence her name, Nicola Six). Nicola is a jaded, listless symbol of the kind of dead end to which glitzy, urban life inevitably leads. She is bored by everything, even by sex, which was once her forte, as documented in photographs once taken by Asprey and later discovered by Sam. Nicola doubles, triples, and quadruples herself in *London Fields*, adopting various disguises (social worker and groupie at a darts tournament) and playing different roles (demure virgin, schoolteacher, and whore), all the while manipulating

the three men who come into her life at the Black Cross pub: Talent, Guy Clinch, and Sam.

Nicola and Keith conspire to defraud Guy, a rich businessman who is snugly ensconced in a world of upper-class privilege with a wife named Hope, a sister-in-law named Lizzyboo, and an obnoxious baby boy named Marmaduke, a veritable demon of the playpen. Keith prides himself on being a "cheat," a petty criminal who steals directly and indirectly from everyone, even his wife, who faithfully tends their daughter while Keith conducts open affairs with Nicola and a string of women with names such as Deb-

bee, Trish, Analiese, Fran, Iqbala, and Petronella. Keith Talent is one of Amis's supreme fictional creations, a lewd but dazzling figure who tries to write a book on darts and keep a journal even though he can barely spell. As Martina Twain did with John Self, Nicola Six does with Keith Talent, teaching him how to read John Keats, the true artist of love and beauty. In the end, the only artistry Nicola experiences is that of Sam, who turns murderer and dispatches her in the front seat of his car on November 6, exactly as she predicted.

TIME'S ARROW

First published: 1991
Type of work: Novel

When Odilo Unverdorben, an American doctor going by the name Tod T. Friendly, dies, his soul journeys back to birth, in the process revisiting his experiences as an Auschwitz doctor.

To explore the moral horrors of the Nazi Holocaust in a way that would ultimately implicate the reader in a most unnerving immediacy, Amis devised an intricate narrative device in which the narrative is told in reverse, based on the scientific theory, one widely exercised in speculative fiction, that time actually moves backward. The narrative is concise, barely 150 pages, with Amis recognizing the difficulties and demands of such a narrative strategy. To tell the narrative, Amis creates a kind of talking soul that comes into existence at the moment when its host body, a retired German-American doctor in upstate New York named Tod T. Friendly, dies after a car accident. Within this narrative device, this soul acts as a witness-narrator (the voice can only watch and cannot interfere) as Dr. Friendly's body begins to reengage his life, although this time he lives it backward, moving with furious momentum back to his life as an intern in New York City. At first reading, of course, the reader puzzles (much as the narrator-witness) over the implications of Dr. Friendly's life: his struggle with alcohol, his dispassionate preoccupation with the human body, his inability to give himself emotionally to his numerous liaisons, and, most disturbing, his grim dreams about babies and children.

The narrator tunes into an inexplicable sense of some ghastly secret that pulls at the events, a secret offense; the book's subtitle, *The Nature of the Offense*, is taken from the agonized memoirs of concentration camp survivor and novelist Primo Levi. In deftly handling the intricacies of a reverse narrative, Amis maintains the narrative suspense by developing the sense of foreboding, the sense of imminent revelation, as the doctor boards a ship bound for Spain and from there makes his way through a series of hiding places, even as his German accent becomes more pronounced. In the harrowing sections where the doctor, now known as Odilo Unverdorben, participates in the ghastly experiments and mass killings at the Auschwitz concentration camp, the reverse narrative creates an unsettling experience. Dead bodies in the crematoria return to flesh and walk out of the gas chamber, and the narrative follows as the Jews grow fat in the camps and eventually board trains that take them home.

Here Amis risks diminishing the horrors of the concentration camps by deploying a gimmicky, narrative trick; indeed, Amis was criticized for placing narrative experimentation above history and at the expense of outrage. However, this narrative device occasions an interactive experience: The narrator-soul misses the point of the horror and delights in identifying with the doctor, given the apparent movement toward happiness. It is the readers who must understand the magnitude of the brutality that appears to be erased so casually: From the vantage point of a half century later, readers understand the savage irony of watching the doomed Jewish people depart the camps. Amis compels his readers to act as the narrative's conscience. As the life of Odilo Unverdorben (ironically German for "uncorrupted") continues its reverse path back to childhood, back to the arms of his own mother, and ultimately back to his own birth, readers understand the implications of the narrative device. Unverdorben is offered as that most terrifying figure of twentieth century history: a creature without a soul. Thus, the occasion of his death alone engenders a moral conscience that must helplessly watch the consequences of such inhumanity.

SUMMARY

Although surely one of the most cerebral and intellectually engaged writers of the fin de millennium and one its most compelling moral satirists, Martin Amis disdains didacticism in literature and rejects the so-called novel of ideas as a remedy for human behavior. He does not believe that literature can fix its culture. Rather, Amis is supremely a satirist who uses the technology of language, particularly the exquisitely turned phrase, the experimental narrative structure, and caustic irony, to expose with abrasive and uncompromising honesty the greed, cruelty, obsessions, and soullessness of late-century humanity.

Daniel L. Guillory; updated by Joseph Dewey

BIBLIOGRAPHY

By the Author

LONG FICTION:
The Rachel Papers, 1973
Dead Babies, 1975 (pb. in U.S. as *Dark Secrets*, 1977)
Success, 1978

Other People: A Mystery Story, 1981
Money: A Suicide Note, 1984
London Fields, 1989
Time's Arrow: Or, The Nature of the Offense, 1991
The Information, 1995
Night Train, 1997
Yellow Dog, 2003
House of Meetings, 2006

SHORT FICTION:
Einstein's Monsters, 1987
Heavy Water, and Other Stories, 1998

NONFICTION:
Invasion of the Space Invaders, 1982
The Moronic Inferno and Other Visits to America, 1986
Visiting Mrs. Nabokov and Other Excursions, 1993
Experience, 2000
The War Against Cliché: Essays and Reviews, 1971-2000, 2001
Koba the Dread: Laughter and the Twenty Million, 2002
The Second Plane: September 11, Terror and Boredom, 2008

MISCELLANEOUS:
Vintage Amis, 2004

About the Author

Dern, John A. *Martians, Monsters, and Madonnas: Fiction and Form in the World of Martin Amis.* New York: Peter Lang, 2000.
Diedrick, James. *Understanding Martin Amis.* 1995. Rev. ed. Columbia: University of South Carolina Press, 2004.
Keulks, Gavin. *Father and Son: Kingsley Amis, Martin Amis, and the British Novel Since 1950.* Madison: University of Wisconsin Press, 2003.
_____. *Martin Amis: Postmodernism and Beyond.* London: Palgrave Macmillan, 2006.
Miller, Karl. *Doubles: Studies in Literary History.* New York: Oxford University Press, 1985.
Morrison, Susan. "The Wit and the Fury of Martin Amis." *Rolling Stone,* May 17, 1990, 95-102.
Tredell, Nicolas, ed. *The Fiction of Martin Amis: A Reader's Guide to Essential Criticism.* London: Palgrave Macmillan, 2000.

DISCUSSION TOPICS

• Given Martin Amis's unforgiving and obvious contempt for his own culture's violence and greed, what is the value of his satire? Can satire fix social problems by raising awareness?

• Amis is often accused of lacking compassion, particularly in his creation of often stereotypical female characters and the lack of convincing love stories. How important is that sort of emotional argument to the work of serious fiction?

• Is it appropriate for a novelist to experiment with form and methods of telling a story when dealing with controversial issues such as terrorism and the Holocaust?

• Although Amis is a distinctly moralistic writer, he has contempt for organized religion. Trace the elements of his discontent with religion.

• How does the narrative technique of using character doubling, doppelgängers, and twins help Amis explore the complicated moral nature of the human soul?

• Amis's vision is distinctly urban. Assess his vision of the contemporary turn-of-the-century cosmopolitan scene.

• Does Amis's fascination with aberrant behavior, his graphic depictions of violence, his interest in drugs and decadent sex, and his use of obscene language detract from his moral vision or enforce it?

HANS CHRISTIAN ANDERSEN

Born: Odense, Denmark
April 2, 1805
Died: Rolighed, near Copenhagen, Denmark
August 4, 1875

Andersen is a world-renowned writer of more than 150 tales for children and adults.

BIOGRAPHY

Hans Christian Andersen was the only child of Hans Andersen, a poor cobbler, and his wife, Anne Marie, who was fifteen years her husband's senior. Hans was born only two months after the marriage of his parents. The couple was ill-matched in many ways. His father was somewhat educated and a free thinker, his mother almost illiterate and a superstitious believer. Both were loving parents, however, determined that their son should do better in life than they.

After his father's death, when Andersen was eleven, his mother became a washerwoman and sent the boy to work in a local cloth mill and then a tobacco plant. It seems that his work in both places consisted of entertaining the other workers by telling stories and improvising songs. His mother remarried after two years of widowhood, this time to a more successful shoemaker, and life improved materially for the boy.

From his earliest years the lonely child had played with his homemade puppet theater, devised little plays and poems, and dreamed of a career in the theater. With little money and no prospects, the gangling fourteen-year-old left Odense, Denmark, and set out for Copenhagen. In response to his mother's fears, he confidently replied, "I shall become famous; first you go through a cruel time, and then you become famous." As Andersen was fond of pointing out in later years, his youthful assessment was quite accurate.

Andersen's attempts to work in any capacity at Copenhagen's Royal Theater came to little, but he refused all advice to return to Odense and be apprenticed in some trade. Reduced almost to begging for enough money to stay alive, in 1822 he submitted a play, "Alfol," which persuaded Professor Rahbek, one of the theater's directors, that Andersen had talent, but needed an education. Rahbek then sent Andersen to Jonas Collin.

Collin was not only a director of the Royal Theater but also a powerful man in the government, one of the king's chief advisers. Persuaded by Collin, the theater directors agreed to pay for Andersen's education and support him until graduation. He was sent away to Slagelse Latin School, where he was shocked to be put into a class with boys half his age. In addition, the rector, Simon Meisling, an insensitive man, made his life in the classroom very unpleasant, and he was further upset by Mrs. Meisling's repeated attempts to seduce him.

The youth was very grateful to his patron, Collin, but at the same time, as Signe Toksvig points out in *The Life of Hans Christian Andersen* (1933), his pride made it difficult for him to ask for such things as replacements for worn-out clothing. All his effort at school culminated in his passing the university entrance examinations in only five years. During that time he went from serious self-castigation to self-adulation, in an almost manic-depressive cycle. These severe mood swings continued throughout most of his life. As Andersen put it in a letter to Collin: "I know I am much too childish; a smile only, a kind word, fills my soul with joy, and a cold look can awaken complete despair in me."

Returning to Copenhagen, relieved to be clear of the Meisling family, Andersen was taken into the Collin household, which provided a welcome contrast. He could then have entered the university but decided instead to pursue his career. He started with a simple piece, *Fodreise fra Holmens canal til Østpynten af Amager* (1829; a journey on foot from Holman's canal to the east point of Amager), which contained reveries of his past, images of a future in which airships would make world travel easier, and much stream-of-consciousness writing. It was a success.

At this time Andersen fell in love, for the first time, with Riborg Voigt, the sister of a friend. She became engaged to someone else before he declared himself. Riborg was the first of a number of women who might have provided what Andersen always said he wanted—a family life—but he remained a bachelor who sublimated his feelings by weaving them into his stories.

Andersen's relationship with Collin's daughter, Louise, began with the deserted lover confessing his feelings to the sympathetic young woman. It ended with his believing he was in love with Louise. She, however, loved and married someone else, so it was fortuitous that her father made a successful appeal to the king for a two-year travel grant for the budding author. He visited twenty-nine countries in Europe, keeping copious diaries, and coming home to publish a successful novel.

At the same time, in an attempt to earn additional money, he published his first four tales, augmented thereafter in annual volumes, totaling 168 tales by the time of his death. As his second novel, *O.T.* (1836; English translation, 1845), and translations of all of his work began to appear in Germany and Sweden, he felt slightly more secure financially. International copyright law left much to be desired, however, in matching his increasing fame with his royalties. Also, he still wanted to be seen as a renowned playwright, a desire fulfilled when his play *Mulatten* (pr. 1840; the mulatto) was well received at the Royal Theater in early 1840.

Although he was nervous about fire in strange places and always carried an escape rope with him, Andersen continued to travel widely, visiting many famous literary people, including his idols Charles Dickens and Sir Walter Scott. He received many honors and decorations in Denmark and other European countries, and his tales became the most widely translated literature in the world except for the Bible.

The final love of his life was the celebrated Swedish singer, Jenny Lind, but that romance also was not consummated. Always aware of his unusual appearance—he was very tall with long arms and big feet—Andersen was never completely certain that people looked beyond these ungainly aspects of his appearance to find him a fascinating person. He also never realized how his 70 pencil sketches, 250 ink drawings, and more than 1,500 unique paper cutouts would be collected as art after his demise.

The climax of Andersen's life came on December 6, 1867, when Odense made him an honorary citizen, amid great celebration. Schools were closed; there was a torchlight procession, and the whole city was illuminated in his honor.

The intimate friends of his last years were Moritz Melchior and his wife, Dorothea, who provided him with loving care to the end. He died of cancer of the liver at their estate, on the outskirts of Copenhagen, four months after his seventieth birthday.

ANALYSIS

Andersen is frequently mislabeled a gatherer of tales, like the Grimm brothers, or Asbjørnsen and Moe, Norwegian collectors of folktales, but he is quite different from these collectors, his contemporaries. Some of his early tales are based on traditional Danish stories that he had heard as a child, but he was a creative writer who added and altered characters, changed incidents, and above all, wrote in his completely unique style.

Furthermore, as his diaries show, many of the tales were based on his personal experiences. For example, in one of his best-known pieces, "Den grimme ælling" ("The Ugly Duckling"), Andersen is easy to identify as the duckling, the outsider, the different one who triumphs after hardships.

There are other flattering self-portraits. In "Svinedrengen" ("The Swineherd") he is a prince, spurned by the silly princess, and in "Den standhaftige tinsoldat" ("The Steadfast Tin Soldier") he is the loyal lover. There are also some negative self-views. In "Grantræet" ("The Little Fir Tree") the artist is always discontented; in

"Fyrtøiet" ("The Tinderbox") the fortune-hunter stops at nothing to gain his goal.

Since so much of Andersen's work is closely related to his life experiences, it is important to separate, to the extent possible, fact from the account Andersen gives in his autobiographies. For example, although he freely admits in his accounts of his life to his humble beginnings, he is loath to admit his fears of becoming mentally unbalanced like his paternal grandfather, or of being embarrassed, as a successful adult, by an unsolicited contact with his older half sister.

Possibly the greatest barrier to a complete understanding of his work is that he wrote in Danish, a language not familiar to many people. Often his stories were translated first into German, sometimes imperfectly, and then from German into English. Inaccurate translations were frequent. Mary Howitt, responsible for the first English version (1846) of his tales, committed elementary mechanical errors. Charles Boner elevated Andersen's language. Caroline Peachey embellished and bowdlerized the tales.

Another barrier to understanding is that some critics have incorrectly assumed that Andersen wrote only for children. His tales, however, were meant to appeal to readers of all ages. They are replete with colloquialisms, Danish puns, and irony. His conversational tone is a conscious stylistic device, not the result of careless composition.

Andersen does not point out a moral at the end of each tale, but rather allows the allegorical and ironic levels of the narrative to speak for themselves. This is also indicative of the tales' value as literature. There are, however, pure fairy tales, such as "Tommelise" ("Thumbelina"), in which animals and flowers are personified. There are science-fiction stories, such as "Om aartusinder" ("In a Thousand Years"), in which Andersen foretells air travel and concludes that "America's youth will visit old Europe, seeing it all in eight days" when they can fly. There are simple, realistic stories, such as "Vanddraaben" ("The Drop of Water"), in which Andersen likens the voracious organisms visible under a magnifying glass to the citizens of Copenhagen, who devour one another without reason.

Some of his tales, such as "Den lille pige med svovlstikkerne" ("The Little Match Girl"), "Hun duede ikke" ("She Was No Good"), and "Gart-neren go herskabet" ("The Gardener and the Lord and Lady") are critiques of the society of his time, in which a child could freeze to death on the street, a good woman could be exploited, then relegated to a pauper's grave, and an aristocratic couple could fail to appreciate the superior knowledge of their faithful gardener.

His themes frequently include a quest for fame and fortune, as in "The Tinderbox," or "Sommer-fuglen" ("The Butterfly"), in which the bachelor does not find a wife because he is indecisive about which flower he prefers. In some stories there is a philosophical quest—for example, a search for God, as in "Klokken" ("The Bell"), in which two young boys, a prince and a poor lad, are both called by the ringing of an unknown bell and the promise of revelation.

Sometimes Andersen writes of the triumph of the artist, as in "Sneglen og rosenhækken" ("The Snail and the Rose"), his answer to Søren Kierkegaard's critique of his novel *Kun en Spillemand* (1837; *Only a Fiddler*, 1845). Sometimes he writes about the defeat of the creative person, as in "Skyggen" ("The Shadow"), in which a crass imitation is venerated above the genuine. Some of the tales, such as "Lille Claus og store Claus" ("Little Claus and Big Claus") are quite violent (in a fairy-tale way), but more deeply frightening is the haunting "De røde sko" ("Red Shoes"), the story of a young girl who must keep dancing until she dies.

Andersen emphasizes familiar, homelike settings in most of his tales, even when on the surface it may seem otherwise. For example, in "Historien om en moder" ("The Story of a Mother") a woman searches for her missing child. The realm of the dead is described as a greenhouse, a familiar sight in Denmark. In the same way, Andersen's royal characters seem more domestic than regal, with the king opening the door of the castle in "Reisekammeraten" ("The Traveling Companion") and the queen making up the bed for a visitor in "Prindsessen paa ærten" ("The Princess and the Pea").

Much of Andersen's work is optimistic but almost as much is distinctly pessimistic—a dichotomy accurately representing Andersen himself. There is no doubt that knowledge of his life makes his writing more impressive. His stories and tales have long been cherished, however, by children and adults who do not have any special knowledge of the author. This signifies that at least the best of his work has the quality of universality that makes it stand the test of time.

"THE LITTLE MERMAID"

First published: "Den lille havfrue," 1837
(collected *The Complete Stories*, 2005)
Type of work: Short story

A beautiful mermaid falls in love with the prince she has rescued, but fails to win him and must die.

Andersen begins this tale with such a detailed description of the watery world, home of the sea king and his family, it becomes a very real setting. In his magnificent palace, the king, a widower, lives with his aging mother and his six mermaid daughters. Each princess has her own garden, planned with individuality, with the youngest princess wanting only rose-red flowers and a beautiful marble statue of a handsome boy, the remnant of a shipwreck.

The king and his mother have been to the surface many times, and the princesses are intrigued with their stories of the world above. As each mermaid becomes fifteen years old, she is allowed to go up and look around for herself, and each returns to tell the others what she has seen of cities, nature, and humans. These descriptions also are written very imaginatively, so that the reader may believe that one princess is frightened by a small dog, another floats on an iceberg, and a third plays with dolphins and whales. At last the youngest mermaid becomes fifteen and makes the journey to the surface.

She sees a three-masted ship, on which a party to celebrate a prince's sixteenth birthday is taking place. The little mermaid watches the handsome prince, whom she decides she loves. There is a severe storm; the ship is wrecked; the unconscious prince is left floating amid the rubble. The little mermaid manages to rescue him before returning to her undersea home but says nothing at first to her family about her experience.

Finally, she tells her sisters of her love, and they rise to the surface and show her his palace. She spends each evening gazing at her prince, although he is unaware of her. When she questions her grandmother about humans, she learns that they have a shorter life expectancy than sea people but that they do have eternal souls.

She then goes to an evil witch, who tells her how she can win the prince and acquire a soul. It is a hard bargain, because she must become mute. The sea witch cuts out her tongue. The mermaid drinks a magic potion that changes her tail to legs. If the prince marries her, she will acquire a soul. If he marries someone else, on that day she will turn to foam on the sea.

The prince becomes very fond of the little mermaid, but he does not think of her as his bride. He marries someone else. On the night of his wedding, the mermaid's sisters rise from the sea to save her. They have given all their hair to the witch in exchange for a knife that the little mermaid must drive into the heart of the prince as he sleeps. This she refuses to do. As she hurls herself into the dissolving foam, she is borne aloft by the daughters of the air, who explain to her that they earn their immortal souls by their good deeds, and she becomes one of them.

At the time of its publication, there was conjecture about the ending's being contrived, but in a letter, Andersen seems to indicate that he planned it from the beginning, having originally titled the story "Daughters of the Air." Andersen's feelings about religion may have made it difficult for him to condemn the loving mermaid with no possibility of acquiring an immortal soul. Andersen, who was not successful in love, perhaps identified with the little mermaid.

The famous bronze statue of the Little Mermaid by Edvard Eriksen was set up on the harbor promenade of Copenhagen in 1913.

"THE EMPEROR'S NEW CLOTHES"

First published: "Kejserens nye klaeder," 1837 (collected in *The Complete Stories*, 2005)
Type of work: Short story

An emperor is hoodwinked by two dishonest men who pretend they can weave magic cloth, seen only by the wise.

Based on a Spanish story from the fourteenth century, this tale was so cleverly altered by Andersen that it is still cited as an example of the foolish behavior of those in authority. He changed the Moorish king to an emperor. He reduced the number of swindlers from three to two. Most significantly, he changed the magic quality of the cloth so that those who could not see it were presumed either "unfit for their posts or hopelessly stupid."

The vain emperor spends his time and money on his only interest—his wardrobe. Along come two men who claim to be able to create a magic cloth. They are given money, silk, and gold thread without limit to complete this marvelous fabric. The fabric will be made into clothing for the emperor. The two men work on an empty loom, pretending to weave, while pocketing all the money and supplies.

Curious about the enterprise, the emperor first sends his honest prime minister to report on the progress, but when the old man sees nothing, he is afraid to tell the truth for fear it means he is unfit for his post or hopelessly stupid. The prime minister repeats to the sovereign what the swindlers tell him about the glorious design and wonderful colors of the cloth. Next, the emperor sends a second official with the same result.

At this point the emperor decides to see the fabric for himself, but both the emperor and the courtiers with him are afraid to say that they see nothing but an empty loom. When the day comes for the emperor to don the suit made from the nonexistent cloth, everyone pretends that it is real. The emperor heads a public procession in his underwear, with the crowd continuing the pretense.

Then, in innocence, a little child speaks: "But he hasn't anything on!" This fact is whispered from person to person; all the spectators shout the truth. The emperor says to himself: "I must go through with it, procession and all," and, drawing himself up still more proudly, he continues to walk with his chamberlains following—carrying the train that is not there.

It is only the child who has not yet become corrupted by the world who will tell what he or she sees. Another implicit moral lies in the emperor's knowing that he has been swindled, but refusing to acknowledge his error publicly.

"THE NIGHTINGALE"

First published: "Nattergalen," 1844 (collected in *The Complete Stories*, 2005)
Type of work: Short story

A Chinese emperor is given a bejeweled mechanical nightingale to replace a live one, but the real bird returns to save him from death.

The story begins as the Chinese emperor reads in a book about the best thing in his empire being a little nightingale that sings in a wood. He then demands that the bird be found, and after all the royal minions have failed, an assistant kitchen maid leads them to the bird.

The little nightingale is brought to the court, given a golden perch, and sings so beautifully that tears come to the eyes of the emperor. That is enough reward for the bird, who declines the gift of a golden slipper. The nightingale is put in a golden cage. Its daily walks are monitored by servants, and the bird believes that its freedom is gone.

The emperor of Japan sends a gift of a magnificent bejeweled mechanical nightingale to the Chinese court. A duet is arranged between the live bird and the mechanical one. The live nightingale is, after the failed duet, banished. The artificial bird, thought to be superior, is placed next to the emperor's bed. It plays the same song over and over, and in time, a wheel in its workings breaks. Even after repair, the bird can sing only once a year.

Five years pass, and the emperor is mortally ill. As the author puts it, "Death was sitting on his chest and had put on his gold crown and held in one hand the imperial gold sword, and in the other, his splendid banner." The emperor's good and wicked deeds come as troublesome images. A replacement emperor has been chosen. The emperor cries out to the mechanical bird to sing, but there is no one to wind it up.

The live nightingale returns to a branch outside the window and makes a bargain with Death—a song for the gold crown, a second for the gold sword, and a third for the splendid banner. As the bird sings about the quiet graveyard, Death's garden, watered by mourner's tears, Death drifts away in a cold white mist.

The emperor, fully recovered, understands when the nightingale tells him that he must fly free and "sing of good and evil which is kept hidden from you."

Written as both an allegory and a tribute to Jenny Lind, this tale is frequently cited as Andersen's best. It contains ironic references to the hierarchical social system; it has humorous touches; it speaks to the superiority of nature over mechanical, artificial copies of reality; and it appeals to all ages.

SUMMARY

A prolific artist, Hans Christian Andersen wrote diaries, letters, travel books, novels, plays, poems, and the tales on which his fame rests. His range was broad, not only in terms of the genres in which he worked but also in the variety of styles he employed. Hypersensitive, sometimes lonely and sad, he always sought approval and basked in the glow of any positive response, whether it came from friends, prominent literary figures, royalty, or the children to whom he read his tales aloud. He summarized his method of creating thus: "I seize an idea for older people—and then tell it to the young ones, while remembering that father and mother are listening and must have something to think about."

Edythe M. McGovern

BIBLIOGRAPHY

By the Author

SHORT FICTION:
Eventyr, 1835-1872 (*The Complete Andersen*, 1949; also *Fairy Tales*, 1950-1958; also *The Complete Fairy Tales and Stories*, 1974)
It's Perfectly True, and Other Stories, 1937
Andersen's Fairy Tales, 1946
Hans Andersen's Fairy Tales, 1953
The Complete Stories, 2005

LONG FICTION:
Improvisatoren, 1835 (2 volumes; *The Improvisatore*, 1845)
O. T., 1836 (English translation, 1845)
Kun en Spillemand, 1837 (*Only a Fiddler*, 1845)
De To Baronesser, 1848 (*The Two Baronesses*, 1848)
At være eller ikke være, 1857 (*To Be or Not to Be*, 1857)
Lykke-Peer, 1870 (*Lucky Peer*, 1871)

POETRY:
Digte, 1830

DRAMA:
Kjærlighed paa Nicolai Taarn: Elle, Hvad siger Parterret, pr. 1829
Agnete og havmanden, pr. 1833
Mulatten, pr. 1840

NONFICTION:

Fodreise fra Holmens Canal til Østpynten af Amager, 1829

Skyggebilleder af en reise til Harzen, det sachiske Schweitz, 1831 (*Rambles in the Romantic Regions of the Hartz Mountains, Saxon Switzerland etc.,* 1848)

Billebog uden billeder, 1840 (*Tales the Moon Can Tell,* 1855)

En digters bazar, 1842 (*A Poet's Bazaar,* 1846)

I Sverrig, 1851 (*In Sweden,* 1852)

Mit Livs Eventyr, 1855 (*The True Story of My Life,* 1847; also as *The Fairy Tale of My Life,* 1855)

I Spanien, 1863 (*In Spain,* 1864)

Et besøg i Portugal, 1866 (*A Visit to Portugal,* 1870)

Levnedsbogen, 1805-1831, 1926 (*Diaries of Hans Christian Andersen,* 1990)

MISCELLANEOUS:

The Collected Works of Hans Christian Andersen, 1870-1884 (10 volumes)

About the Author

Bloom, Harold, ed. *Hans Christian Andersen.* Philadelphia: Chelsea House, 2005.

Bredsdorff, Elias. *Hans Christian Andersen.* New York: Charles Scribner's Sons, 1975.

Godden, Rumer. *Hans Christian Andersen: A Great Life in Brief.* New York: Alfred A. Knopf, 1954.

Lurie, Alison. *Boys and Girls Forever: Children's Classics from Cinderella to Harry Potter.* New York: Penguin Books, 2003.

Spink, Reginald. *Hans Christian Andersen and His World.* New York: G. P. Putnam's Sons, 1972.

Stirling, Monica. *The Wild Swan: The Life and Times of Hans Christian Andersen.* New York: Harcourt Brace, 1965.

Wullshläger, Jackie. *Hans Christian Andersen: The Life of a Storyteller.* New York: Alfred A. Knopf, 2001.

Zipes, Jack. *Hans Christian Andersen: The Misunderstood Storyteller.* New York: Routledge, 2005.

DISCUSSION TOPICS

- How is Hans Christian Andersen's extreme emotional sensitivity reflected in "The Ugly Duckling"?

- In a letter to his mother, Andersen wrote: "First you go through a cruel time, and then you become famous." This process does not always work; what caused it to work with Andersen?

- How did Andersen take advantage of the nickname "the Swedish nightingale" of the famous singer Jenny Lind?

- What might be gained from reading more than one translation of an Andersen story?

- In injecting material for people of all ages into his stories for children, was Andersen like many writers today?

- What moral lessons do you see in Andersen's tales other than the ones pointed out at the end of his stories?

- Obtain and watch the 1952 film *Hans Christian Andersen.* Determine how closely this filmed version resembles the facts of his life.

© The Nobel Foundation

IVO ANDRIĆ

Born: Dolac, Bosnia, Austro-Hungarian Empire (now
    in Bosnia and Herzegovina)
    October 10, 1892
Died: Belgrade, Yugoslavia (now in Serbia and
    Montenegro)
    March 13, 1975

*In his short stories and novels, Andrić concentrates on the life of
the people of Bosnia, who have suffered long occupations by foreign powers and struggled for self-identification amid attempts
by those powers to assimilate them.*

BIOGRAPHY

Ivo Andrić (AHN-dreech) was born on October 10, 1892, in Dolac, a small town near Travnik in central Bosnia, at that time a part of the Austro-Hungarian Empire. Both of his parents were Catholics, which led to a long-standing controversy about whether he was a Serbian or a Croatian writer. After his father's death, his mother moved with Ivo to Višegrad, a town on the Drina River with its famous bridge built in the sixteenth century. Andrić attended elementary school in Višegrad, high school in Sarajevo, and universities in Zagreb, Vienna, and Krakow. As a student, he developed strong nationalistic feelings and joined Young Bosnia, a revolutionary movement the opposed the Austrian occupation of Bosnia. His political activism resulted in his being sentenced to a three-year term in prison, but he was released in 1917 because of poor health.

While in prison, he started his literary career by writing a book of prose poems, *Ex Ponto* (1918). Two years later, he published another book of prose poems, *Nemiri* (unrest). After World War I, Andrić entered the diplomatic service of the Kingdom of Yugoslavia. In 1923 he was a vice consul in Graz, but his position was endangered because he had not finished his graduate work at the University of Sarajevo. He enrolled at the University of Graz and received his doctorate after writing his dissertation in German, *Die Entwicklung des geistigen Lebens in Bosnien unter der Einwirkung der türkischen Herrschaft* (1924; *The Development of Spiritual Life in Bosnia Under the Influence of Turkish Rule*, 1990). He remained in diplomatic service in various capitals until 1941. Andrić continued to write during this time, primarily short stories, and was praised by many critics as the best Serbian short-story writer in the period between the two world wars.

At the beginning of World War II, Andrić was a Yugoslav ambassador in Germany. It was a very difficult position, for he had to represent his country against Adolf Hitler's aggressive policy, which eventually led to the German attack and occupation of Yugoslavia in April, 1941. Andrić resigned his position because the Yugoslav government had joined a military pact with Germany and the other Axis powers. He was sent back to Belgrade, where he spent the entire occupation, writing his major novels but refusing to join any side in the struggle between the Communist and nationalist forces for supremacy. After the war, Andrić accepted the new Communist regime, started publishing his novels, and participated in the literary life of the new Yugoslavia. He was honored as the best living Serbian writer and received numerous awards, culminating in the Nobel Prize in Literature in 1961.

Andrić continued to write, primarily short stories, brief novels, and essays. He was also working on the continuation of his Bosnian historical novels, which, unfortunately, remained unfinished. He died in Belgrade on March 13, 1975, hailed as the most important contemporary Serbian writer and the only southern Slav to win a Nobel Prize in Literature.

ANALYSIS

Ivo Andrić is considered to be the best Serbian writer of the twentieth century and not necessarily because he won a Nobel Prize. His books of prose poems, *Ex Ponto* and *Nemiri*, were not particularly impressive and he later refused to republish them. It was in the short story, however, that he excelled in his early career, becoming a leading short-story writer between the two world wars. In his stories he employed several themes that would reverberate throughout his writing career. Among them are characters who dwell on the distant past; characters displaying acute loneliness, who have difficulties reaching an understanding with others; the world as a reflection of the tragic elements in human existence; an immense capacity for suffering; the limited opportunities provided by his characters' surroundings, as in "Put Alije Djerzeleza" ("The Journey of Alija Djerzelez"); fear of life, as in "Prozor" ("The Window"); feelings of guilt, as in "Mila i Prelac" ("Mila and Prelac"), "Anikinavremena"("Anika's Times"), and "Smrt u Sinanovoj tekiji" ("Death in Sinan Tekke"); the divergence of two worlds in an individual, as in "Ćorkan i Švabica"("Ćorkan and a German Woman"); and hatred, sometimes reaching pathological proportions, as in "Mustafa Madjar" ("Mustapha Magyar") and "Pismo iz 1920" ("A Letter from 1920").

Andrić is not negating life, despite its shortcomings. For him, there is still hope in the struggle against evil and in life, and this is stronger than the forces that threaten to destroy life. One of the recurring metaphors Andrić uses to express this hope and optimism is a bridge connecting two opposites, as in the story "Most na Žepi" ("The Bridge on the Žepa") and especially in his novel *Na Drini ćuprija* (1945; *The Bridge on the Drina*, 1959). Thus, his short stories can be considered a preparation for his later, longer works, although his stories have their own intrinsic values, especially in their artistic qualities, such as the concision of style and purity of language.

The enforced quiet life during the German occupation, albeit stressful and dangerous, allowed Andrić to write his three novels, *The Bridge on the Drina*, *Travnička hronika* (*Bosnian Story*, 1958; better known as *Bosnian Chronicle*), and *Gospodjica* (*The Woman from Sarajevo*, 1965), all published in 1945. Although his short stories had touched upon many aspects of life in Bosnia, it was in *The Bridge on the Drina* that he gave them a full force. This novel established Andrić as a master of historical and semihistorical writing. The beautiful bridge over the Drina in Andrić's hometown, Višegrad, became one of the greatest symbols in all of Balkan literature.

The Bridge on the Drina covers life in Višegrad and its surroundings from the sixteenth century to World War I. It deals with various customs, most important of which is the "blood tribute," by which young Serbian children were taken to Turkey and raised as *janissaries,* or Turkish soldiers. One of these is Mehmed-Pasha Sokolovič, a vizier, or Turkish consul, who built the bridge in Višegrad as a tribute to his home country. From then on, the life of the people of Višegrad and other Bosnians centered around the bridge. The slave-labor peasants who were conscripted in the nearby villages resented the Turkish might represented by the bridge and were punished by the impaling of a peasant accused of sabotaging the bridge's construction. Andrić, however, saw the beautiful bridge as representing several symbols, the main one being a means of connecting separate halves, not only in a physical sense but also as linking various races, nationalities, and cultures. Everything that happened to the people of Višegrad had an echo on the bridge, where the people converged and commented on happenings around them.

Decades passed and things changed, at times drastically. Christians, Muslims, and Jews mingled more with one another. When the Turks gradually withdrew, the Austrians took over. Amid all the changes one thing remained constant—the bridge, which survived even the bombing in World War I. The new generation of Bosnians continued the tradition of gathering on the bridge, this time discussing the more important changes, such as the rise of Serbia to the east and the awakening of the young Bosnians facing the approaching conflagration. Yet, throughout these discussions, the bridge continued to stand in all its glory, reminding the inhabitants of the need for peace and togetherness. Thus the bridge, through its long life and seeming indestructibility, symbolizes the permanence of all life. The additional symbolism of the bridge can be seen its spanning of the two shores and as a thing of beauty humankind always strives to achieve. *The Bridge on the Drina* is a semihistorical novel written in a highly artistic manner and is a good source of general information about Bosnia, although not a substitute for a scholarly history.

Bosnian Chronicle is also a semihistorical novel, but it deals only with a short period of the Bosnian past, the first decade of the nineteenth century. However, as in many of his works, Andrić reaches for universal meanings, in this case examining the evils of foreign subjugation. The novel also expresses the author's visceral attachment to his origins, which lasted throughout his life.

The third novel, *The Woman from Sarajevo,* is artistically at a somewhat lower level than the other novels, but it is still an important achievement. The book tells the story of Rajka, a spinster who spends almost all of her life shunning relationships with men and worrying about money matters, traits she inherited from her father, who warned her about unscrupulous men. She once allowed herself to have a close relationship with a young man, but she was damaged by the experience. Her painful life leads to excessive egotism, selfishness, miserliness, an insensitivity to the needs of others, an absence of normal human drives, and, finally, an insecurity complex and persecution mania, ending in the ruin of herself and everyone with whom she is associated. Andrić shuns deeper philosophical or historical issues, concentrating on creating the character of Rajka, one of his best characterizations. The archetypal literary theme of miserliness, found in many other literatures, such as the works of Plautus and Molière, is handled somewhat differently by Andrić. Raja is the only miser who is a woman, and she still has some redeeming qualities, having been developed fully as an individual.

Of other works by Andrić, a novella or short novel *Prokleta avlija* (1954; *Devil's Yard*, 1962) deserves special attention. In a Turkish prison in Istanbul, the clash between a brutal warden and a young, freethinking scholar ends in the scholar's death. However, the scholar emerges as the moral victor of spirit over force. Again, the universal meaning employed here is that evil can be conquered, even within the walls of imprisonment.

Though life may be accursed and walled in, its creative forces emerge as much stronger than the adversities or the adversaries. This message may be considered as the most succinct philosophy of Andrić's works.

BOSNIAN CHRONICLE

First published: *Travnička hronika*, 1945 (English translation, 1958; also known as *Bosnian Story*)
Type of work: Novel

In the provincial Turkish capital in Bosnia at the beginning of the nineteenth century, the three consuls situated there—Turkish, French, and Austrian—carry on their duties amid the clash of cultures and diplomatic interplay.

According to some critics, *Bosnian Chronicle* is Ivo Andrić's best work. Although not as popular as *The Bridge on the Drina*, it contains many basic features of Andrić's writing. Perhaps for that reason, it was translated three times into English: as *Bosnian Story*, translated by Kenneth Johnstone in 1958, with a revised edition in 1979; as *Bosnian Chronicle*, translated by Joseph Hitrec in 1963; and as *The Days of the Consuls*, translated by Celia Hawkesworth and Bogdan Rakić in 1992. Andrić assiduously studied archives and other historical sources for this and his other major works, both complete and unfinished.

The events in the novel take place in the first decade of the nineteenth century, primarily in Travnik, a consular town in central Bosnia. Travnik, as well as most of Bosnia, was occupied by the Ottoman Empire following centuries of conquest of Balkan lands. The French had just occupied nearby Dalmatia and were concerned with the Turkish presence in Bosnia; the Austrians had always regarded neighboring Bosnia as a territory of their utmost concern. A combination of these three factors made a fertile ground for intrigues, in addition to executions of foreign policy matters of the three states extremely active in European affairs at the time. The consulate in Travnik was situated at the westernmost border of the Ottoman Empire and was the residence of a vizier. Since

France established its presence in the vicinity and the Turks were forced to retreat from Hungary, Travnik had acquired a significance beyond its strategic and political value.

Although the development of the novel's protagonists to a large degree was influenced by historical events, *Bosnian Chronicle* is more of a study of its characters than an historical novel. In the first decade of the nineteenth century, there were three Turkish consuls, or viziers, in Travnik, all three different in nature yet all conducting their duty for the advantage of the Ottoman Empire. Mehmed-Pasha, a former slave from Georgia, never forgets the state he serves with a friendly face and a smile, which makes it easier for other consuls to work with him. Ibrahim-Pasha is the opposite; he and his assistants and servants, a "museum of monsters," as the local people call them, make it difficult for him to work with the consuls. Ali-Pasha is the worst of the three. Efficient and merciless, he immediately executes all common criminals, believing that the Ottoman Empire must rule foreign territories with an iron fist.

The viziers are confronted by the French consul Daville, a well-educated and cultured man who writes classical poetry and admires Napoleon I. He has the difficult task of upholding the civility he is accustomed to in a primitive Balkan backwater. Needless to say, he often ends up on the short end in the struggle. To make matters worse, he is often shortchanged by the Austrian consul, von Mitterer, a cunning diplomat, who is interested primarily in taking advantage of the two adversaries' confrontations.

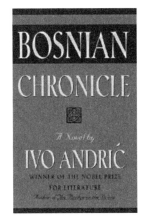

The demise of Napoleon I cuts short Daville's career, as well as the attempts of the French and Austrian consuls to bring some civilization to a primitive society. A mitigating force in this gloomy ambience is the role of women in the novel, especially Daville's wife. A deeply religious and emancipated woman, she helps her husband function in a manner corresponding to their upbringing.

There are several themes in *Bosnian Chronicle*. The difference between the East and the West is sharply pointed out. Fatalism, resignation, mistrust of foreigners and everything foreign, and disregard for the rights of individuals are contrasted by the comparatively enlightened world of France and Austria. The Westerners are mistrusted not only by their diplomatic opponents but also by the populace at large, which points to the way of life and thinking of the two worlds. Andrić does not treat this phenomenon as a matter of historical truth but as the personal experiences in the interplay of the main characters and the people at large. This makes *Bosnian Chronicle* not exactly a historical chronicle but rather a collection of human dramas and deep-seated conflicts. The important historical events at the beginning of the nineteenth century throw only a long shadow over the lives of the individual people of Bosnia.

Another theme found in the novel is the role of women. In addition to the aforementioned activity of Daville's wife, other female characters point to different kinds of women. Here Andrić compares the Asian women, who are little more than the objects of men's pleasure, to the Western women, who are more like partners to their men. In addition, *Bosnian Chronicle* also confirms the optimism expressed in many of Andrić's works that evil must be fought at all levels and a ray of hope is more than just that. The novel is thus raised to the level of universality, as is Andrić's wont.

As he does in in other works, Andrić uses this novel to express his own thoughts on life and history. His main idea is that, despite all the bleakness and backwardness, life throbs beneath the surface and human beings continue to strive toward a better life. Although it is difficult to say whether the bleakness and backwardness in this novel are caused by the Turkish rule of an iron fist or by the Westerners' lack of goodwill and pursuit of their own interests, human beings, even in such a backward state, can hope. Herein lies the universal meaning of *Bosnian Chronicle*.

SUMMARY

In describing life in Bosnia, Ivo Andrić transcends the real and the obvious and elevates the question of the meaning of human existence to the level of universality. Life as depicted by Andrić may be hard, bleak, and tortuous, but it is not Søren

Kierkegaard's "sickness unto death." One of the main messages from *The Bridge on the Drina* confirms Andrić's basic faith in the inviolability of life: "Life is an incomprehensible miracle because it is constantly being consumed and eroded and yet it lasts and stands firmly like the bridge on the Drina."

Vasa D. Mihailovich

BIBLIOGRAPHY

By the Author

LONG FICTION:
Gospodjica, 1945 (*The Woman from Sarajevo*, 1965)
Na Drini ćuprija, 1945 (*The Bridge on the Drina*, 1959)
Travnička hronika, 1945 (*Bosnian Story*, 1958; better known as *Bosnian Chronicle*)
Prokleta avlija, 1954 (novella; *Devil's Yard*, 1962)

SHORT FICTION:
Pripovetke, 1924, 1931, 1936
Nove pripovetke, 1948
Priča o vezirovom slonu, 1948 (*The Vizier's Elephant: Three Novellas*, 1962; includes *Priča o vezirovom slonu* [*The Vizier's Elephant*], *Anikina vremena* [*Anika's Times*], and *Zeko* [English translation])
Odabrane pripovetke, 1954, 1956
Panorama, 1958
The Pasha's Concubine, and Other Tales, 1968

POETRY:
Ex Ponto, 1918
Nemiri, 1920
Šta sanjam i šta mi se dogadja, 1976

NONFICTION:
Die Entwicklung des geistigen Lebens in Bosnien unter der Einwirkung der türkischen Herrschaft, 1924 (*The Development of Spiritual Life in Bosnia Under the Influence of Turkish Rule*, 1990)
Zapisi o Goji, 1961
Letters, 1984

MISCELLANEOUS:
Sabrana dela, 1963

About the Author

Butler, Thomas. "Reflections of Ottoman Rule in the Works of Petar Kočić, Ivo Andrić, and Meša Selimović." *Serbian Studies* 11 (1997): 66-75.
Ferguson, Alan. "Public and Private Worlds in *Travnik Chronicle*." *Modern Language Review* 70 (1975): 830-838.
Goy, E. D. "The Work of Ivo Andrić." *Slavonic and East European Review* 41 (1963): 301-326.
Hawkesworth, Celia. *Ivo Andrić: Bridge Between East and West*. London: Athlone Press, 1984.

DISCUSSION TOPICS

- What is the main theme in Ivo Andrić's novel *Bosnian Chronicle*? How does Andrić treat the conflict of foreign powers over Bosnia? Who seems to be victorious in that conflict?

- What is Andrić's view of religion as presented in *Bosnian Chronicle*?

- What are the symbolic meanings that can be perceived in Andrić's works?

- What are Andrić's views on history as extrapolated from his works?

- What do *Bosnian Chronicle* and *The Bridge on the Drina* have in common?

- Does Andrić view the Bosnians' quest for independence as viable?

Juričič, Želimir B. *The Man and the Artist: Essays on Ivo Andrić*. Lanham, Md.: University Press of America, 1986.

Kadič, Ante. "The French in *The Chronicle of Travnik*." *California Slavic Studies* 1 (1960): 134-169.

Mihailovich, Vasa D. "The Reception of the Works of Ivo Andrić in the English-Speaking World." *Southeastern Europe* 9 (1982): 41-52.

Vucinich, Wayne S., ed. *Ivo Andrić Revisited: The Bridge Still Stands*. Berkeley, Calif.: International and Area Studies Publications, 1995.

Wachtel, Andrew B. "Ivan Meštovič, Ivo Andrič, and the Synthetic Yugoslav Culture of the Interwar Period." In *Yugoslavism: Histories of a Failed Idea, 1918-1992*, edited by Dejan Djokič. London: Hurst, 2003.

GUILLAUME APOLLINAIRE

Born: Rome, Italy
    August 26, 1880
Died: Paris, France
    November 9, 1918

Perhaps the foremost French lyric poet of his generation, Apollinaire merged experimentation, tradition, and wild flights of imagination.

French Embassy Press & Information
Division, New York

BIOGRAPHY

Guillaume Albert Wladimir Alexandre Apollinaire (uh-pah-luh-NEHR) de Kostrowitzky was born August 26, 1880, in Rome, the firstborn, illegitimate child of an aristocratic Polish adventuress and an Italian army officer. Apollinaire would later profess total ignorance of his paternity, in part because it suited his artistic purposes to do so. Born Angelica Kostrowicka in 1858, the boy's mother adopted the French spelling, Kostrowitzky, when recording his birth. She addressed him as Wilhelm, nevertheless. A second son, Albert, who presumably shared the same father, was born in 1882.

Inclined toward exotic tastes and (possibly compulsive) gambling, Angelica no doubt seemed less than an ideal match for the boys' supposed father, Francesco Flugi d'Aspermont, who, in addition, was old enough to be her father. Francesco's family, led by his elder brother Don Romarino, a prominent Roman Catholic cleric, spared no effort to keep the couple apart, in time sending Francesco, by then nearly fifty, into apparent exile in the United States. Not long thereafter, Don Romarino saw fit to compensate Angelica by providing for the education of her sons, initially at a parochial school recently founded in Monaco, adjacent to the French Riviera. Thus did the future poet, of chiefly Italian ancestry (Angelica herself had an Italian mother), come to be schooled mainly in French, acquiring a strong sense of the French lyric tradition to complement his vivid imagination. In 1887, Angelica and her sons managed to survive a devastating earthquake that hit Monaco, spending several weeks in a rescue tent until suitable lodgings could be found. A number of Apollinaire's commentators have seen in the earthquake, and in the doomsday mentality that prevailed among the survivors, an early thematic source for Guillaume's often apocalyptic verse.

Following the closing of the Monaco school in 1896, the budding poet, known as Kostro to his classmates and friends, attended secondary classes, first in Cannes and later in Nice, but he abandoned his studies without receiving a diploma. His schooling, however, never interfered with his voracious reading, often in subjects never taught in class, nor with his first attempts at writing. It has been suggested that the d'Aspermont family might well have supported him in further studies, had he sought to pursue them, but frowned upon his chosen career as a writer. So too did Angelica, who clearly preferred her younger son Albert, who was sedate, even stodgy in manner, perhaps because she and Wilhelm were too much alike. In any case, he soon had to fend for himself, initially at the lower levels of journalism and ghostwriting, with other jobs thrown in to make ends meet. At one point, he took a job as a bank clerk, incidentally the chosen vocation of his brother Albert. In time, however, literary hackwork (including the writing of pornographic texts) would become his main occupation, allowing him access to the bohemian circles of Paris, where his family had settled at the beginning of the twentieth century. His personality, intense and outgoing, soon attracted a wide range of friends and associates in a literary and artistic adventure that would be talked about and written about long after.

Apollinaire's singular gift as a person, apart from his talents as poet and promoter, was that he was at once observant and dramatic, neither so self-absorbed that he was blind to his surroundings nor unable to communicate his observations and enthusiasms to an audience, large or small. It is thus hardly surprising that, like Charles Baudelaire before him, Apollinaire soon emerged both as poet and as art critic. Apollinaire appreciated the visual arts; in them he saw the immediacy for which poets always strive. Years after his death, Apollinaire's biographers and commentators were still arguing over just how much he actually knew about painting, but by then his work was long since done. With contagious enthusiasm, in recognition of kindred spirits, Apollinaire managed to showcase the artistic movement known as cubism, which included such tremendous talents as Georges Braque, Henri Matisse, and Pablo Picasso. Before the end of Apollinaire's short life, he also managed to introduce the word "surrealism," by itself a great contribution to the understanding of the human experience.

By the time he settled in Paris, calling himself Guillaume Apollinaire, the gregarious young writer had already begun writing striking, haunting poetry, often employing arresting references to history, religion, and the occult. A trip to Belgium with his mother, her current lover, and Albert in 1899 yielded brilliant, memorable images, as did his time spent in the Rhineland the following year as tutor to the daughter of the rich French widow of a German nobleman. Although by no means the first muse to inspire Guillaume's poetry, the girl's British governess, Annie Playden, became the best known of his early loves, immortalized in verses written both during and after what may or may not have been a full-fledged affair. It is known in any case that Apollinaire proposed to Playden while climbing a mountain, threatening to throw her over the side if she refused, and that Playden retracted her acceptance as soon as her feet were back on flat land. Years later, after World War II,

Playden expressed amazement when literary critics sought her out for interviews, supposedly quite unaware that the youth she had known had become a major French poet. The poems that Playden inspired nevertheless remain among the most innovative and memorable of those published in *Alcools: Poèmes 1898-1913* (1913; *Alcools: Poems, 1898-1913*, 1964). Apollinaire's next significant affair, at least in literary terms, was with the young painter Marie Laurencin, who, unlike Playden, shared her lover's artistic interests. Their often stormy relationship would last until the fall of 1912, generating many fine poems along the way. "Le Pont Mirabeau" ("Mirabeau Bridge"), written shortly after the breakup, is perhaps the best known and most frequently anthologized of all Apollinaire's poems. It is at once universal, ambiguous, and lyrical. The poem is a memorable addition to the poetic literature of lost love.

In 1911, in part because of a careless choice of friends and associates, Apollinaire, already famous as a champion and critic of the arts, was arrested and briefly incarcerated as a suspect in the theft of Leonardo da Vinci's *Mona Lisa* from the Louvre, a crime later found to be the work of some misguided Italian patriots. Although innocent of the charges brought against him, his detention at the infamous Santé prison in Paris hastened his rupture with Laurencin and brought forth a spate of despair and self-loathing duly recorded in his poetry. *Alcools* includes poems about these experiences. *Alcools* also contains the truly groundbreaking "Zone," among the most remarkable of modernist lyrics. The specter of having been accused of theft came back to haunt Apollinaire; he was suspected by some of his friends of having plagiarized "Zone" from Blaise Cendrars. By 1914, Apollinaire sensed that the long cultural party he had hosted was over.

When Apollinaire was thirty-four, World War I began. He was surely too old to be drafted, even had he been a French citizen. Although a native of Italy, he was in fact a stateless person, suspected by some of his detractors of being an Eastern European of Jewish ancestry despite his hereditary Roman Catholicism. He sought and eventually received citizenship in order to serve in the French army. Judging by the evidence of his actions, Apollinaire was aware that the world was changing and saw fit to take part. As he prepared for service, he found another mistress destined to be immortalized in his poetry. Louise de Coligny, an aristocrat drawn to Apollinaire by their shared sensuality, could not have cared less about his writing or his growing fame. If Annie Playden was simply unaware of his work, de Coligny was openly contemptuous of it. In addition, she often treated Apollinaire as her social inferior, which he was. Still, the poems addressed to "Lou," most not published until after World War II, are notable for their vivid imagery and sensual intensity. The affair with de Coligny was too turbulent to last for more than a few months, and before long Apollinaire was engaged to Madeleine Pagès, a young schoolteacher he had met on a train a year or two earlier and with whom he had corresponded. Mobilized on Easter Day, 1915, Apollinaire wrote to both women about his war experiences, his letters often interspersed with verse that was later published. In March, 1916, Apollinaire was sitting in a trench reading a magazine when a shard of shrapnel struck him in the head, piercing his helmet. Given the primitive state of brain surgery at the time, it is perhaps remarkable that he survived at all, although changes in his personality soon became painfully evident, as would changes in his looks later. The injury may have obliterated Pagès from his consciousness; he never wrote to her again, and in time he took up with the redheaded Jacqueline Kolb, whom he nicknamed "Ruby" and eventually married. It is to her that he wrote one of his finest late poems, "La Jolie Rousse" ("The Pretty Redhead"), the last poem in *Calligrammes* (1918; English translation, 1980). Having been disqualified from further military service, Apollinaire was as active in the artistic circles of Paris as his health would allow. In his weakened state, he fell victim to the international influenza epidemic of 1918, dying only two days before the end of World War I.

ANALYSIS

It might well be said of Guillaume Apollinaire that, had he never existed, he would have had to invent himself, as in many respects he did. Exploiting the "freedom" of being illegitimate (already a frequent theme in French literature), Apollinaire would proceed to explore his sense of self in a variety of poetic forms, exploring the fragmentation and reintegration of the self.

Although Apollinaire wrote plays and prose, it is as a poet that he made his strongest and most enduring literary statement. Uncertain of his nationality as well as of his paternity, Apollinaire was, in a sense, afloat in time and space, fatherless and free. Growing up in Mediterranean France, coming of age in the time of the first triumphs of modern technology, Apollinaire had a double fascination with applied science and with the mysteries of human identity; like his older contemporary Marcel Proust, Apollinaire seemed in many ways to anticipate, or even to predict, pending developments and discoveries in the field of psychology. His earliest writings show a vivid imagination fertilized by voracious reading in a wide variety of fields, some of them profane and obscene, most of them esoteric. Science fiction, offbeat prophecy, political theory, and occasional mysticism joined the teachings of the Roman Catholic church in Apollinaire's suggestible mind. Even his earliest poems, derivative of the Symbolist movement then in vogue, depict his experience as fragmented, distorted, and rearranged. Like those seen through a kaleidoscope, Apollinaire's images at first appear hard to decipher, yet with time and attention they yield both familiarity and beauty. Apollinaire's work, prose and verse, has been described as a letter to the world; it is intensely personal. Using creative distortion, he turned the mundane into the surreal.

Like Baudelaire before him, Apollinaire often sought, and found, beauty in the most unlikely places. Just as Baudelaire found in the rotting carcass of a dog an image for decomposed love, so would his successor as poet and art critic describe, in well-rhymed, unpunctuated quatrains, a grotesque banquet in which fragments of his own mind are served up, with the finest of sauces and preparations, to an assemblage of distinguished guests. The poem in question, "Le Palais" (in French, both "palace" and "palate"; English translation, "Palace"), derives also from the legend of Rosamond Clifford, alleged mistress of Henry II of England, who was married to Eleanor of Aquitaine. According to legend, Eleanor found the thread leading to Rosamond's secret castle and followed it to poison her. "Palace," denounced by some of Apollinaire's critics and admired by others, combines sex, violence, esoteric erudition, and lyrical beauty to evoke the poet's personal sense of fragmentation and self-loss. Supposedly inspired by

Apollinaire's often competitive friendship with his fellow poet Max Jacob, "Palace," although far from the best of Apollinaire's poems, is at once typical and transitional. Probably composed around 1902, it shows Apollinaire moving beyond Symbolism toward the new spirit that he soon claimed to share with the cubist painters.

As Apollinaire himself states in one of his last poems, "The Pretty Redhead," his entire career as a poet was about the conflict between order and adventure, between tradition and experimentation. Characteristically, even the tradition that he alternately sought and rejected—the French lyric tradition beginning with François Villon in the fifteenth century and ending with Paul Verlaine at the end of the nineteenth—was acquired rather than inherited, as was Apollinaire's French citizenship. Often, what appears to be experimentation turns out, upon examination, to be tradition in disguise. It is well known that the decision to omit punctuation from the poems in *Alcools* was made at the last minute, and that all but a few of the poems had originally been composed in more or less traditional form. The removal of punctuation provides more than the mere appearance of modernity; it frees the individual lines in order to permit a variety of interpretations. Nowhere is such freedom more evident than in the case of what has become his most famous poem, "Mirabeau Bridge," in which the lack of punctuation reinforces the effects of flowing water, time, and change. Even with traditional punctuation, "Mirabeau Bridge" would still be a remarkable lyric, in the tradition of Villon and Verlaine, but the absence of traditional "framing" frees it from the constraints of logic.

By the time *Alcools* was published, Apollinaire was already at work on the poems to be published in *Calligrammes*, some of which seem no more experimental than those in the earlier volume. Others, however, spread type over and around the page in visually arresting forms, often in frank imitation of drawing or painting, and it is those efforts that provided the volume with its title. Once again, however, the appearance of innovation is often no more than an appearance. Many of the verses, if rearranged on the page, turn out to be quite traditional in versification and rhyme scheme. For all of his interest in the plastic arts and in providing visually interesting poetry, Apollinaire never lost sight—or perhaps one should say hearing—of the lyric poet's primary vocation. Some of the poems may look strange but, when read aloud, they tend to sound quite right.

Although some of Apollinaire's wartime poems were published in *Calligrammes*, others, including many addressed to Louise de Coligny, were not published until after his death. They also are notable for their lyricism and typically vivid imagery. With a few notable exceptions, however, the poems released posthumously did little to enhance Apollinaire's reputation as a poet, which tended to fluctuate somewhat over the six decades between his death and the centennial of his birth in 1980. From 1950 to around 1965, there was much critical and historical interest in Apollinaire's life and work, with a number of significant books and articles to show for it. Yet by the time of Picasso's death in 1973 it seemed that Apollinaire's career, both as poet and as critic, had faded somewhat into the background. His reputation as a poet, although secure, fell somewhat short of what might have been predicted at the time of his death, when he appeared to be a herald of the future rather than the product, however self-invented, of his times.

ALCOOLS

First published: 1913 (English translation, 1964)
Type of work: Poetry

Apollinaire's first, and perhaps best, poetic statement, Alcools *includes verses written as early as 1898.*

Alcools, a book of poems, is notable for its lack of chronological order. The long poem that opens the volume, "Zone," was in fact one of the last composed before the book's publication. The title of the volume, although evocative of alcohol, in fact has more to do with distilled essences. An earlier working title, "Eau de Vie," suggests clear beverages, presumably alcoholic. Both titles also suggest something strong yet rare and fleeting.

By presenting his poems in apparently random rather than chronological order, Apollinaire was in fact making a statement, stressing product over process. He did not claim to have moved beyond his early work, but rather to be still present in it. Regardless of chronology, the poems differ widely in length, form, and content. Yet they are all of a piece. "Zone," in particular, is a remarkable piece of work, a de facto preface to the entire collection. Borrowing in part from cinematic technique, Apollinaire, in "Zone," frequently shifts viewpoints, alternately addressing himself in the first and second person, as if training a camera on himself. Recent inventions, such as cars and airplanes, figure prominently in "Zone"; yet the speaker seems to need no such transportation for his travels throughout Europe, from Paris to Prague to the Mediterranean.

Also included in *Alcools* are the "Rhenish" poems, composed during or just after Apollinaire's residence and travels in the Rhineland. Although technically stateless, the poet regards things German with the ironic detachment of a Frenchman, even as he shows some affinity for the German Romantic tradition. Some poems record overheard conversations, prefiguring later experiments to be published in *Calligrammes*. A Rhenish poem, "Schinderhannes," recalls with macabre humor the career of a German outlaw put to death a hundred years before the poet's German sojourn. The poems inspired by Annie Playden comprise a significant portion of *Alcools*, both in quality and in quantity; "La Chanson du mal-aimé" ("The Song of the Poorly Loved") is perhaps the most ambitious of the Annie poems, intensely lyric in assonance and rhythm, yet full of arcane references that have, over the years, demanded (and presumably repaid) close attention from critics. Anticipating both "Zone" and "Mirabeau Bridge," "The Song of the Poorly Loved" drifts on memories and sensory impressions, beginning on the streets of London where the speaker meets a street urchin who may well be Playden's double, or perhaps his own; thereafter he wanders back to Paris and his still-divided self. "L'Emigrant de Landor Road" ("The Emigrant from Landor Road"), likewise inspired by his rup-

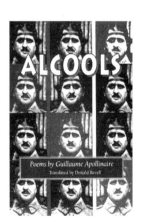

ture with Playden, contains a number of striking conceits and images.

The apparently random order of the poems in *Alcools* becomes clear only at the end, when "Vendémiaire" closes the collection that "Zone" may well have expressly been designed to open. "Vendémiaire" ("The Harvest Month"), designating the last drink before closing time and thus consistent with the title *Alcools*, may well have been written as early as 1909. It anticipates the disturbances that lay ahead in 1913. Allusions to recent Franco-German wars and wry political commentary about Paris as the center of France infuse Apollinaire's love song to his adopted city. The poem is prophetic of what was soon to follow. Ostensibly structured around a night of pub crawling in Paris, "The Harvest Month," like "Zone," declares and demonstrates the author's ambitions and talents, at once lyrical and thoughtful, striving toward, and sometimes reaching, poetic immortality. Some even finer verses and images occur in *Calligrammes*, which, however, is a less complete and satisfying collection than *Alcools*. The ironically titled "Merveille de la guerre" ("Wonder of War") applies Apollinaire's vivid imagery to the immediacy of combat, asserting also the poet's visionary mission. "Tristesse d'une étoile" ("Sorrow of a Star") uses arresting conceits in dealing with the poet's combat injury. "The Pretty Redhead," which fittingly closes *Calligrammes*, harks back to "Zone" in its sweep and technique, serving also as a fitting literary testament in honor of the poet's young bride. *Alcools* nevertheless remains Apollinaire's strongest poetic statement, best demonstrating the range and the scope of his singular talents.

SUMMARY

Often categorized as the first twentieth century French poet, Guillaume Apollinaire welcomed the new century with his arresting imagery and experimental verse forms, finding in the cubist and other modernist painters the visual counterpart to his own innovations. Ironically, the work of the painters Apollinaire promoted appears to have outlasted his own, which now appears less visionary than his contemporaries might have supposed. *Alcools*, nevertheless, contains a number of memorable, striking verses, frequently read and admired by later generations of poets.

David B. Parsell

BIBLIOGRAPHY

By the Author

POETRY:
Le Bestiaire, 1911 (*Bestiary*, 1978)
Alcools: Poèmes, 1898-1913, 1913 (*Alcools: Poems, 1898-1913*, 1964)
Calligrammes, 1918 (English translation, 1980)
Il y a, 1925
Le Guetteur mélancolique, 1952
Tendre comme le souvenir, 1952
Poèmes à Lou, 1955
Œuvres poétiques, 1956

LONG FICTION:
L'Enchanteur pourrissant, 1909
Le Poète assassiné, 1916 (*The Poet Assassinated*, 1923)

SHORT FICTION:
L'Hérésiarque et Cie., 1910 (*The Heresiarch and Co.*, 1965)

DRAMA:
Les Mamelles de Tirésias, pr. 1917, pb. 1918 (*The Breasts of Tiresias*, 1961)
Couleur du temps, pr. 1918, pb. 1920
Casanova, pb. 1952

NONFICTION:
Peintres cubistes: Méditations esthétiques, 1913 (*The Cubist Painters: Aesthetic Meditations*, 1944)
Chroniques d'art, 1902-1918, 1960 (*Apollinaire on Art: Essays and Reviews, 1902-1918*, 1972)

MISCELLANEOUS:
Œuvres complètes, 1966 (8 volumes)
Œuvres en prose, 1977 (Michel Décaudin, editor)

DISCUSSION TOPICS

- Was Guillaume Apollinaire's complicated early family life an advantage or disadvantage to him as a writer?

- Did Apollinaire have to have many love affairs to generate the love poems he wrote?

- What did Apollinaire mean by "surreal"?

- Consider whether Apollinaire's elimination of punctuation from the poems in *Alcools* is beneficial or an unnecessary distraction to the reader.

- What features of Apollinaire's poetry might be most likely to bring about a revitalization of his reputation?

About the Author

Bates, Scott. *Guillaume Apollinaire*. New York: Twayne, 1967.
Bohn, Willard. *Apollinaire and the International Avant-Garde*. Albany: State University of New York Press, 1997.
Davies, Margaret. *Apollinaire*. Edinburgh: Oliver & Boyd, 1964.
Hicken, Adrian. *Apollinaire, Cubism, and Orphism*. Burlington, Vt.: Ashgate, 2002.
Saul, Scott. "A Zone Is a Zone Is a Zone: The Repeated Unsettlement of Guillaume Apollinaire." In *Understanding French Poetry: Essays for a New Millennium*, edited and coauthored by Stamos Metzidakes. 2d ed. Birmingham, Ala.: Summa, 2001.
Shattuck, Roger. *The Banquet Years*. New York: Vintage Books, 1968.
Stamelman, Richard H. *The Drama of Self in Guillaume Apollinaire's "Alcools."* Chapel Hill: University of North Carolina Press, 1976.
Steegmuller, Francis. *Apollinaire: Poet Among the Painters*. New York: Farrar, Straus & Giroux, 1963.
Sweet, David LeHardy. *Savage Sight, Constructed Noise: Poetic Adaptations of Painterly Techniques in the French and American Avant-Gardes*. Chapel Hill: University of North Carolina Press, 2003.

AHARON APPELFELD

Born: Czernowitz, Bukovna, Romania (now
Chernovtsy, Ukraine)
February 16, 1932

*An escapee at age eleven from a Nazi detention camp, Appelfeld
made his way to Palestine and began to write books that chronicle
both the pre- and post-Holocaust periods.*

© Jerry Bauer

BIOGRAPHY

Aharon (also rendered "Aron") Appelfeld was
born on February 16, 1932, in Czernowitz, Romania, which is now Chernovtsy, Ukraine. During the
period between the two world wars, most of the
Jews in his birthplace were assimilated. The
Appelfeld family spoke German and made little effort to preserve their Jewish identity.

Czernowitz was overrun by German forces in
1939. Before long, the occupying intruders killed
Appelfeld's mother. The boy and his father, along
with other members of his family, soon were sent to
the Ukraine, where father and son were interned
separately in the Transnistria concentration camp.
The train on which the frightened, blond-haired
boy was taken to Transnistria was to become a pervasive symbol in Appelfeld's writing. Alone and too
young to understand the political implications of
his displacement, Appelfeld was sucked into the
forbidding freight car like a grain of wheat, a symbol that pervades his later writing, obviously reflecting the helplessness the boy felt at having his
life snatched away from him for reasons that he
failed to comprehend, a helpless object in the
hands of a malevolent government.

For the next three years, Appelfeld lived at the
whim of his captors in a setting in which people dis-
located solely on the basis of their ethnicity were
robbed of their dignity, their self-determination,
and, in many cases, their lives. The sensitive youth

saw how cheap life became in such situations. Yet
he thought deeply about how his people could
have come to such a pass in a country that was
seemingly civilized. Such musing became the basis
for his later writing about how European Jews, by
encouraging assimilation and by acceding without
protest to the growing inroads the government was
making upon them, probably were unwitting parties to their own destruction.

When Appelfeld escaped from Transnistria in
1943, he did not emerge into a welcoming society.
The Ukrainian peasants among whom he found
himself were as anti-Semitic as the Nazis who controlled the area. Appelfeld, however, used his
blond hair as a badge of Aryan lineage, albeit a misleading one. He took whatever work he could find,
sometimes as a farmer, sometimes as a shepherd.
His adult friends consisted mostly of thieves and
prostitutes. His younger friends were orphans enduring dislocations similar to his own, youths
whose lives were perpetually in danger.

When Germany surrendered in May, 1945,
Appelfeld was the youngest in a band of boys who
made their way to Italy, where he was again able to
pass as a Gentile. For a while, his group sought
sanctuary and was permitted to live in a Roman
Catholic church, where Appelfeld sang in the
choir.

Soon the boy, remembering his ethnicity, went
with his group of refugees to Naples, Italy, where
they came into contact with the Youth Aliya, a
group that urged Appelfeld and his companions to
go to Palestine, which was to become Israel in 1948.
In Palestine, Appelfeld spent mornings working in
the fields and afternoons studying Hebrew, which

he had to learn in order to succeed in his adopted country.

In 1948, he was conscripted into the Israeli army, in which he served until 1950, when he was deemed physically unfit for further service. He then passed his entrance examination for Hebrew University and was able to enroll there in 1950. He received both his bachelor's and master's degrees from Hebrew University, with a specialty in Hebrew literature.

After studying briefly in Zurich, Switzerland, and at the University of Oxford in England, Appelfeld returned to Israel to teach Hebrew literature at Ben Gurion University in the desert town of Beersheba. During the 1950's, he wrote prolifically, sending his poetry to an editor in Jerusalem, who, for three years, regularly rejected it. Appelfeld, however, refused to be discouraged and continued writing.

In 1960, Appelfeld married an Argentinean woman, Yehudit. Along with their two sons and one daughter, they eventually settled in Jerusalem. In the year Appelfeld married, his father emigrated to Israel but declined to recognize Appelfeld as his son.

Appelfeld's rise as an Israeli writer was becoming evident in the early 1960's, although his work had not yet been translated into English. In 1960, he won his first notable Israeli prize for poetry. Two years later, his first collection of short stories was published in Hebrew and, despite distribution problems, received favorable critical attention from a small but devoted cadre of readers.

He gained recognition from readers outside Israel when he won Israel's Bialik Prize in 1978 and the Israel Prize for Literature in 1983, by which time his *Badenheim, 'ir nofesh* (1975; *Badenheim 1939*, 1980), *Tor-ha-pela'ot* (1978; *The Age of Wonders*, 1981), and *Kutonet veha-pasim* (1983; *Tzili: The Story of a Life*, 1983) had appeared in English translation.

The air of doom that pervades much of Appelfeld's work stems from the horrors and uncertainties of his formative years, although he does not write directly about the Holocaust but rather about what preceded and followed it. He is passionately concerned with what can happen to a people if they allow their identities to be co-opted and their civil rights eroded. Appelfeld is prolific, having produced more than a dozen novels in Hebrew, several collections of his more than three hundred short stories, collections of essays, and a memoir, *Sipur hayim*, 1999 (*The Story of a Life*, 2004).

ANALYSIS

It has been said that most fiction is at its heart autobiographical. Appelfeld's work is almost wholly a retelling of his life story. The overriding concern in nearly everything he has written is the Holocaust, although he never writes in detail about it. Rather, it lurks as a constant presence, the more horrible because it is not broached directly or in detail. Much as the horrors in Greek tragedies occur offstage, so are Appelfeld's depictions of the horrors of the Holocaust left to his readers' imaginations. Anyone with a sense of history can fill in the grisly details that Appelfeld purposely omits.

Although he draws from the same factual base for most of his work, his writing is not boringly repetitive. He is able constantly to reshape images and details in fresh and novel ways. He is a master of restraint and verbal economy, exhibiting a minimalism that allows him to make his most salient points vividly and poignantly through understatement.

Appelfeld exhibits a consistently controlled objectivity about matters that are, in essence, highly subjective. He writes about the Holocaust by not writing about the Holocaust. He depends upon his readers' memories of its horrors to supply details too painful to relate overtly. He writes about what led to this cataclysm and about its aftermath or the gruesome events of this horrendous catastrophe that resulted in the deaths of some six million European Jews between 1939 and 1945.

Realizing that the dimensions of the Holocaust are so huge that they challenge the human imagination, Appelfeld elects to write around, rather than directly about, this historical event. He constantly searches for an answer to the recurrent question, "How could any such disaster have happened?"

He finds his answer in the major split he detects in Jewish society, one that surfaces in his stories. The rift lies between the intellectual Jews, who attached themselves to the mainstream culture of their societies by shedding most of the vestiges of their Judaic backgrounds and language, and the so-called *Ostjuden,* Jews from Eastern Europe, notably Poland, who were essentially philistines, merchants, and businessmen. They preserved Jewish traditions but were so bent on their remunerative business pursuits that they did not object to being excluded from the genteel and powerful social milieus of their countries. They traded exclusion for prosperous existences.

Both kinds of Jews were easily duped during the rise of Nazism in Germany and in Eastern Europe. The intellectuals wanted to be part of the mainstream culture, so they did not object when Nazism began to limit their freedoms. The *Ostjuden*, on the other hand, not wanting to jeopardize their financial security, overlooked the policies that gradually made them second-class citizens and, for the few who survived, stateless people.

The two classes of Jews that Appelfeld identifies have little use for each other, so the solidarity that might have been their salvation in the most critical time in their history was absent. It was into such an environment that Appelfeld was born. Among his earliest memories is one fundamental to *Badenheim 1939*, in which the Austrian resort being depicted is soon to be crowded with summer visitors. Dr. Pappenheim is to provide musical entertainment during the resort's high season. Appelfeld uses Trude, the Jewish wife of the local pharmacist, who is not Jewish, metaphorically. She is manic-depressive, driven to distraction by her perception of the sick world that surrounds her and that she fears threatens the welfare of her daughter. There is about this book an air reminiscent of the atmosphere with which Thomas Mann infused *Der Zauberberg* (1924; *The Magic Mountain*, 1927), although the implications of the disease that Trude senses in the environment are much broader than were those posed by Mann's novel.

In *Badenheim 1939*, one also finds persistent overtones of paranoia like those found in Franz Kafka's *Der Prozess* (1925; *The Trial*, 1937), a work with which Appelfeld acknowledges familiarity. In *Badenheim 1939*, the Sanitation Department erects fences and raises flags, steadily becoming an increasingly authoritarian factor in the lives of citizens, particularly of Jewish citizens. Against a backdrop of Rainer Maria Rilke's death poetry comes an announcement that all Jews must register with the Sanitation Department, presumably as a first step toward "sanitizing" the country of its Jewish citizens.

The intellectual Jews have disagreements with the *Ostjuden* about who has to register, while the Sanitation Department works covertly to collect dossiers on all the Jews in Badenheim. The department forbids entry into or exit from the town and quarantines the Jews who are within it. Appelfeld writes of the "orange shadow" that hangs over the town, a symbol that he uses frequently. Trude's delusions become realities as the Jews become a marked people. When trains arrive to relocate the captive Jews, Dr. Pappenheim speculates optimistically that they probably will not be taken too far because the boxcars in which they are to be transported are so filthy. The hapless Jews board the train, still thinking that their deportation to Poland is a transitional step, trying to minimize the import of what faces them.

Similar themes pervade most of Appelfeld's writing. He is obsessed with what the decadence of European Jews resulted in once Adolf Hitler came to power. Both groups of Jews about which he writes, the intellectual Jews and the *Ostjuden*, lapsed into decadence and sold out for their own gain. Both groups, in Appelfeld's view, felt an underlying self-hatred as Jews, ever alienated, ever shunned. In this self-hatred, fed by the dominant society, were the seeds of the destruction that was inflicted upon most Jews east of France from the late 1930's until the end of World War II.

Appelfeld writes of the dispossessed, the abandoned, those who hide, fearing for their lives, those who run from all that is dear to them because running is their only hope. He writes about dead mothers and unsympathetic fathers, about indifferent societies and vindictive institutions within those societies. Mostly, however, Appelfeld writes about complacence and the price it exacts in situations like that brought about by fascist rule in the decade between 1935 and 1945. He places some of the responsibility for the Holocaust squarely on the shoulders of a passive Jewish community that might possibly have saved itself had it rallied in a united way when the ethnic outrages of the period began.

TZILI

First published: *Kutonet veha-pasim,* 1983
   (English translation, 1983)
Type of work: Novel

Tzili, daughter of a Jewish family that tries to deny its Jewishness, sustains her tie with her historic past and survives the Holocaust.

In *Tzili: The Story of a Life,* Tzili Kraus is in some ways Appelfeld's female counterpart. As the story opens, she is the least favored of her parents' children because she, unlike her older siblings, is a poor student, something not to be encouraged in a Jewish-Austrian family with intellectual pretensions. The family, turning its back on its Jewish heritage, glories in its assimilation.

Tzili, a taciturn child, plays on the small plot behind her parents' shop, ignored by parents and siblings. She is abused because of her poor academic performance and is viewed as retarded. Her parents employ an old man to give their unpromising child lessons in Judaism, but she does poorly even in these lessons.

When it is apparent that fascists are about to enter their town, the Krauses leave, but Tzili stays behind to guard their property. She sleeps through the slaughter that ensues, covered by burlap in a remote shed. Now Tzili, on her own, must live by her wits. Part of what Appelfeld seeks to convey is that her inherent instinct for survival will serve her better than her family's intellectuality serves them. The family disappears, presumably victims of the Holocaust.

Appelfeld makes Tzili the symbol of a Judaism that survives through sheer pluck during a time of overwhelming difficulty. She consorts with prostitutes, works for peasants who physically abuse her, and struggles to hang onto what little hope there is. In time she links up with Mark, a forty-year-old who has left his wife and children in the concentration camp from which he escaped.

Like Appelfeld, Tzili looks Aryan and is relatively safe from identification as a Jew. She and Mark live by bartering, using some of his family's clothing as a trading medium for food. By the time Mark, now guilt ridden, defects, the fifteen-year-old Tzili is pregnant. She trades the clothing that

Mark has left behind for food. When this source of sustenance is exhausted, the pregnant Tzili finds work with peasants, some of whom beat her unmercifully.

With the armistice, Tzili joins a group of Jews freed from their concentration camps and goes south with them. She delivers her baby stillborn near Zagreb, but she survives—and with her survives the Judaism that nothing can extinguish. As the novel ends, Tzili and Linda, a woman who had earlier saved her life, are on a ship presumably heading for Palestine.

The theme of this story is survival in the broadest sense—the survival of one woman to symbolize the survival of the Jews and their philosophy. Tzili survives because she has not allied herself with the Jews who allowed assimilation or with the *Ostjuden* and their mercantile ambitions. Tzili lives because her instincts, her sheer intuition in time of crisis, serve her better than the artificial intellectuality of those who early shunned her and made her feel as though she was not part of her own family.

THE HEALER

First published: *Be-'et uve-'onah ahat,* 1985
   (English translation, 1990)
Type of work: Novel

Helga Katz, the daughter of a Jewish family in Vienna, suffers from an illness that leads the family to a healer in the Carpathian Mountains

In *The Healer,* the Katzes are bourgeois Jews who live in Vienna. When their daughter Helga begins to suffer from psychological problems, they seek help from every doctor available, but the treatment she receives brings no permanent improvement. Hearing of a healer in the Carpathian Mountains, the parents, Felix and Henrietta, decide they must take Helga there in a desperate attempt to restore her health. Their son Karl accompanies them when, in October, 1938, they take Helga to the Carpathians for six months of treatment.

The story's ironies are not inherent but are a product of what readers know about the history of the period. This is the last year Eastern Europe will be free from a fascist tyranny that will lead to the annihilation of most of the people involved in Appelfeld's story.

As the story develops, one realizes that the healer, the innkeeper, his Yiddish-speaking wife, and the Katzes themselves are marked for destruction. They perform their daily tasks, engage in their petty conflicts, fill their lives with small details that in the long run have little meaning. Hovering darkly above the entire narrative is the specter of what is soon to happen to Eastern Europe and to every Jew who lives there.

In this story, Appelfeld reiterates the notion of self-hatred that he is convinced helped lead to the downfall of European Jews during the Holocaust. This theme emerges in a discussion Henrietta has with the healer about Helga's name. Henrietta had wanted to name her daughter Tsirl, after the girl's grandmother, who was born in this rural region. She decided, however, that she could not give her daughter that name because of the ridicule that it would bring. Yet Henrietta, conditioned to the deceptions that Viennese society imposed upon its Jewish populace, does not rail stridently because she cannot give her daughter a Jewish name, saying merely that the name is "unusual" and would have caused people to laugh at the girl. In this exchange, Appelfeld clearly expresses the insidiousness of the Jews' overwhelming repression of their traditions and their acceptance of the conditions that would ultimately annihilate them.

KATERINA

First published: *Katerinah*, 1989 (English translation, 1992)
Type of work: Novel

A retrospective look at the growing anti-Semitism in Europe preceding the Holocaust from the point of view of Katerina, a seventy-nine-year-old Ruthenian peasant.

Seventy-nine-year-old Katerina, imprisoned for many years during the Holocaust, has returned to her Ruthenian origins in a fiercely anti-Semitic territory that has belonged intermittently to Romania, Moldavia, and Ukraine. When Katerina returns following the Holocaust, Ruthenia has been purged of nearly all its former Jewish population. A Gentile, Katerina has been imprisoned for murdering Karil, a fiercely anti-Semitic hoodlum who murdered her infant son, Benjamin, years earlier.

A social outcast, Katerina feels a greater affinity to Jews than to Gentiles. Her murdered son was fathered by Sammy, a fifty-year-old Jewish alcoholic.

Despite the anti-Semitism that causes people in Ruthenia to avoid any outward signs of being Jewish, Katerina seeks out a *mohel*, the Jewish dignitary who performs circumcisions as dictated by Mosaic law, to circumcise her son.

When Katerina goes back to Ruthenia after an absence of sixty-three years, she lives in a squalid hut on the property where she was born and where she lived during her early years. Katerina has been sheltered from the Holocaust by being imprisoned for the forty years that marked Adolf Hitler's rise and eventual collapse.

The only suggestion of what has been happening during this period are the boxcars filled with Jews that rattle past Katerina's prison on their way to concentration camps, the trains leading inevitably to places of doom. Some clothing and other items confiscated from the doomed Jews are eventually distributed to the prisoners, but the actual horrors of the Holocaust are never spelled out: Appelfeld depends upon the memories of his readers to supply the gruesome details of what happened to six million European Jews between 1939 and 1945.

In *Katerina*, Appelfeld creates parallel worlds, that of the prison where Katerina is incarcerated and that of the Holocaust from which she is removed by prison walls. Before Hitler's rise to power, Katerina was employed by Jews to look after their children. These children taught her to read Hebrew and to speak Yiddish. When she was incarcerated for killing Karil, she was abruptly removed from the society in which the Holocaust took place.

The Story of a Life

First published: *Sipur hayim*, 1999 (English translation, 2004)
Type of work: Nonfiction

A succinct, well-controlled memoir in which Appelfeld relates the course of his life over seven decades, one of which includes the Holocaust.

Until age seven or eight, Aharon Appelfeld led a privileged existence in the Ukraine, the only child of two doting parents. Suddenly his comfortable world was shattered. His mother was shot. He did not see her die, but he heard her screams as she was murdered by anti-Semites. Soon other members of his family also were annihilated. Finally the young boy and his father were forced to march for two months to a displacement camp, where they were held as prisoners. They marched in mud so deep that young children who were part of the march drowned in it.

The boy was separated from his father, but he was resourceful enough to escape after three years into the Eastern European forests that surrounded the camp. There, usually alone, sometimes with another escapee, he stayed until the end of the war, living as best he could. In the forest, he spent considerable time reflecting on the life he had once lived, especially the happy parts of it, memories of holidays with his parents and grandparents in the Carpathians. In this memoir, he captures many elements of his past life in a dreamlike way, perhaps the product of his musings during his time spent hiding out in the forest.

Because many of the events of his early life are too horrible to remember, Appelfeld represses them, but reading between the lines, one can glean some of the horrors that he has endured. He spent his early years lonely and threatened by forces of which he had reason to be terrified.

At war's end, the young man made his way to Palestine. He needed to learn Hebrew, a difficult task for him. His years of isolation had limited his ability to use language, and soon his use of German, his mother tongue, declined. He began to feel as though he had no language of his own, and with this feeling came a sense of his losing his identity. He also was learning to use language with the verbal economy for which his writing has received favorable notice.

Summary

With masterful restraint, Aharon Appelfeld works consistently to make his point: The Holocaust was as much attributable to Jewish passivity as it was to fascist activism. He presents the various faces of self-hatred that afflicted many European Jews during the rise of Nazism.

Jews of the period blinded themselves to such discomfiting indignities as forced registration with the authorities and mandatory relocations, which resulted in the deportation of millions of Jews to concentration camps. They refused to admit the realities that surrounded them, and by the time that they were conscious of the implications of these realities, it was too late for them to save themselves.

R. Baird Shuman

Bibliography

By the Author

LONG FICTION:
Ke' ishon ha-ayin, 1972
Badenheim, 'ir nofesh, 1975 (*Badenheim 1939*, 1980)
Tor-ha-pela'ot, 1978 (*The Age of Wonders*, 1981)
Kutonet veha-pasim, 1983 (*Tzili: The Story of a Life*, 1983)
Nesiga mislat, 1984 (*The Retreat*, 1984)
Be-'et uve'onah ahat, 1985 (*The Healer*, 1990)

To the Land of the Cattails, 1986 (also known as *To the Land of the Reeds*)
Al kol hapesha'im, 1987 (*For Every Sin*, 1989)
Bartfus ben ha-almavet, 1988 (*The Immortal Bartfuss*, 1988)
Katerinah, 1989 (*Katerina*, 1992)
Mesilat barzel, 1991 (*The Iron Tracks*, 1998)
Timyon, 1993 (*The Conversion*, 1998)
Unto the Soul, 1994
Layish, 1994
'Ad she-ya'aleh 'amud ha-shahar, 1995
Mikhreh ha-kerah, 1997
Kol asher ahavti, 1999 (*All Whom I Have Loved*, 2006)
Masa' el ha-horef, 2000
Polin erets yerukah, 2005 (*Poland, A Green Country*, 2005)
Pirhe ha-afelah, 2006 (*Blooms of Darkness*, 2006)

SHORT FICTION:
'Ashan, 1962
Ba-gai ha-poreh, 1963
Kefor 'al ha-arets, 1965
In the Wilderness: Stories, 1965
Be-komat ha-karka', 1968
Adne ha-nahar, 1971
Shanim ve-sha ot, 1975
Ke-me a edim, 1975

NONFICTION:
Masot be-guf rishon, 1979
What Is Jewish in Jewish Literature? A Symposium with Israeli Writers Aharon Appelfeld and Yoav Elstein, 1993
Beyond Despair: Three Lectures and a Conversation with Philip Roth, 1994
Sipur hayim, 1999 (*The Story of a Life*, 2004)
'Od ha-yom gadol: Yerushalayim, ha-zikaron veha-or, 2001 (*A Table for One: Under the Light of Jerusalem*, 2005)
Encounter with Aharon Appelfeld, 2003 (Michael Brown and Sara R. Horowitz, editors)

About the Author

Bernstein, Michael André. *Foregone Conclusions: Against Apocalyptic History*. Berkeley: University of California Press, 1994.

Blake, Patricia. Review of *Tzili: The Story of a Life*, by Aharon Appelfeld. *Time*, April 11, 1982, 97.

Brown, Michael, and Sara R. Horowitz, eds. *Encounter with Aharon Appelfeld*. Oakville, Ont.: Mosaic Press, 2003.

Budick, E. Miller. *Aharon Appelfeld's Fiction: Acknowledgment of the Holocaust*. Bloomington: Indiana University Press, 2005.

DISCUSSION TOPICS

- What essential differences exist between the intellectual Jews and the *Ostjuden* that Aharon Appelfeld depicts?

- Discuss specific instances of self-delusion that pervade Appelfeld's writing and that help to depict the position of Jews in a society that has turned against them.

- It has been said that people believe what they want to believe. Do you find instances in Appelfeld's writing that support this statement? Be specific.

- To what extent are Appelfeld's depictions of Jews objective? Subjective?

- Discuss the theme of dislocation as it applies to Appelfeld's fictional characters.

- How would you depict Appelfeld's attitude toward intellectuality?

- How specifically does Appelfeld's depiction of some of his characters that are used metaphorically relate to the broader context of Jewish society?

Coffin, Edna Amir. "Appelfeld's Exceptional Universe: Harmony out of Chaos." *Hebrew Studies* 24 (1983): 85-89.

Fuchs, Adi Japhet. *Appelfeld's Table*. Waltham, Mass.: National Center for Jewish Films, 2004. Videorecording.

Kalman, Ruthie. *Aron Apelfeld* [sic], *1959-2005*. Beersheba, Israel: Universitat Ben Guryon, 2005.

Roth, Philip. *Shop Talk: A Writer and His Colleagues and Their Work*. New York: Vintage International, 2002.

Shvarts, Yig'al. *Aharon Appelfeld: From Individual Lament to Tribal Eternity*. Hanover, N.H.: University of New England Press, 2001.

Wisse, Ruth R. "Aharon Appelfeld, Survivor." *Commentary* 76 (August, 1983): 73-76.

Yudkin, Leon I. "Appelfeld's Vision of the Past." In *Escape into Siege: A Survey of Israeli Literature Today*. Boston: Routledge & Kegan Paul, 1974.

LUCIUS APULEIUS

Born: Madauros, Byzacium (now near Mdaourouch, Algeria)
    c. 125 C.E.
Died: Possibly Carthage (now in Tunisia)
    After 170 C.E.

Apuleius wrote the novel Metamorphoses *and other works that reflect the major intellectual tendency in the Roman Empire of the second century C.E.: a desire for uncommon or even secret knowledge.*

BIOGRAPHY

Relatively little is known about the life of Lucius Apuleius (ap-yuh-LEE-yuhs). Since no ancient sources report "Lucius" as Apuleius's first name, it may be a guess by some Renaissance scholars, based on his use of it for the main character of *Metamorphoses* (second century C.E.; *The Golden Ass*, 1566). Aside from his place of birth, the earliest information known about him is that his father, a wealthy magistrate in Madauros, Byzacium (now near Mdaourouch, Algeria), left him a large inheritance, which Apuleius spent on education, including initiations into mystery religions, probably including those of the gods Dionysus and Isis. Even these details, along with almost all other biographical information, come from his own report of his trial, which is not the most reliable source. His defense, however, does demonstrate how he wished to be seen: a handsome, profoundly knowledgeable, aristocratic young philosopher, educated at Carthage and Athens and with legal experience in the courts of Rome.

Apuleius was tried for marrying the widow Aemilia Pudentilla, aged about forty, when he was presumably in his early thirties. Not only was this marriage unconventional for the time, but his wife's relatives charged that she was more than sixty years old and thus forbidden to wed by Roman law. He also was accused of marrying her for her money after bewitching her—a serious crime, punishable by death, if he were convicted. The best evidence that he won the case is that he circulated his defense, *Apologia* (158-159 C.E.; English translation, 1909), as proof of his rhetorical skills, something he could not have done if he had lost.

In his *Apologia*, Apuleius relates how he was traveling near Oea (now Tripoli, Libya), when he became ill and his former fellow student, Sicineus Pontianus, invited Apuleius to convalesce with him. Pontianus also suggested that Apuleius marry his (Pontianus's) mother, Pudentilla. Pontianus later became violently opposed to the match, although his will provides evidence that he eventually reconciled himself to it. The original accusation against Apuleius charged that he had murdered Pontianus, but that claim was dropped by the time of the trial.

Little is known of Apuleius's life after his trial. His works, *De mundo* (second century C.E.; concerning the world) and *De Platone et eius dogmate* (second century C.E.; concerning Platonic doctrine), mention a son named Faustinus, but whether this was a literal son and whether Pudentilla was the boy's mother are matters for speculation. By the nature of Apuleius's writings, he most probably was a lawyer and teacher in North Africa, active in literary, religious, and perhaps occult circles.

The lack of information makes it difficult to date his work, and scholars are particularly interested in determining when he composed his novel, *Metamorphoses*. That he does not refer to it in his *Apologia* may mean that the novel had not yet been written, since it would have been significant evidence of his interest in magic. If, however, his accusers were as barely literate as Apuleius makes them out to be, they might not have known about the novel. At the very least, then, the novel was not yet famous. Although its vigor and often scandalous subjects suggest a young author, its complexity could mean that he wrote it near the close of his career. Allusions in the *Florida* (second century C.E.; English translation, 1853), a collection of passages from his speeches, date the *Florida* to the late 160's or early 170's, and his description of his writings therein does not mention his having composed a novel. If his trial occurred between 158 and 159 C.E., if Faustinus was born thereafter and had grown old enough to be addressed in *De mundo* and *De Platone et eius dogmate* as a reader of those treatises, and if *Metamorphoses* was composed as the culmination of Apuleius's works, the author could not have died much before 170 C.E. During his lifetime, at least three cities erected statues in his honor.

In addition to the extant *Apologia, Florida, De Deo Socratis* (second century C.E.; *The God of Socrates,* 1852), *De Platone et eius dogmate, De mundo,* and *Metamorphoses,* Apuleius composed various lost works, including hymns in Greek and Latin to Aesculapius, god of medicine, as well as treatises on astronomy, astrology, and medicinal herbs. Apuleius lived at a time when medicine, science, religion, and magic were intertwined. Various other works, notably *Asclepius,* a treatise on hermetic philosophy and magic, have been ascribed to him.

After his death, Apuleius gained a reputation not only as a philosopher and novelist but also as a wizard. During his trial, he had refuted the charge that he was a wizard, while at the same time making numerous references to his knowledge of the occult. His accusers may have felt doubly uneasy: first, because they lost the case against him, and, second, that if they were correct in their allegations, Apuleius was not just a skilled speaker and writer but also an angry sorcerer.

ANALYSIS

Apuleius is now remembered as a rhetorician and author of a highly rhetorical novel, *Metamorphoses.* Typical of his writings, the novel's style overflows with literary embellishments, particularly archaic words and allusions, all displaying his uncommon education. His prose is rhythmically hypnotic, even to the occasional use of rhymes, so that it resembles the incantations of magicians.

The complexity of his style lends a basic ambiguity to the novel's tone. When he is at his best, as in the *Apologia,* the *Florida,* and the *Metamorphoses,* Apuleius's jokes manage to be simultaneously self-deprecating and boastful, as demonstrated in a

long and humorous passage defending how he brushes his teeth, an unconventional practice at the time. The *Metamorphoses* shifts between worldly cynicism and otherworldly idealism, as well as between playful pornography and serious preaching. Apuleius's actual attitudes thus remain hidden—appropriately, considering that his subject is the need for secrecy in magic and religion.

In the *Apologia,* he answers the charge that he possessed an implement of dark magic by saying that the object actually belonged to a mystery religion, and for this reason he is forbidden to reveal what it was. His emphasis on ironic masking and general concealment is typical of second century Latin literature; in this age, the tyranny of the Roman Empire often forced intellectuals to defensively hide or disguise their beliefs in allegories and other coded references.

Apuleius's early works trace the development of his duplicitous style and chart his literary development, which reached its most advanced state in the *Metamorphoses. De mundo* and *De Platone et eius dogmate,* both largely translation or paraphrase, mix Platonic concepts and other later ideas that are found in the *Metamorphoses.* More interestingly, the *Apologia* demonstrates his ability to write charming, first-person narration and his willingness to make fun of himself in small ways that win the readers' sympathies. For instance, his discussion of his erotic poems in *Apologia* shows courage and is similar to *Metamorphoses*'s first-person narrator, Lucius, who also admits his sexual embarrassments. By demonstrating the similarities of Apuleius's and Plato's love poems in *Apologia,* Apuleius implies that he simply follows a model for writing rather than creating poetry that discloses his private life. Similarly, conventional elements in the *Metamorphoses* cloak the autobiographical nature of the work.

Another parallel between the *Apologia* and the *Metamorphoses* is his attraction toward grotesque humor. In the accusations against Apuleius, for example, a slave and one of Apuleius's medical patients were allegedly bewitched into convulsions. In a flurry of puns, Apuleius claims the two men were epileptics; thus, keeping them from convulsing would have required him to perform magic. The *Metamorphoses* carries such nightmarish imagery further, with its sadistic violence and numerous transformations of humans into animals.

Like the *Metamorphoses*, the *Florida* evidences Apuleius's taste for the exotic, such as his description of a parrot from the Far East. Of all his works, however, *The God of Socrates* comes the closest to the *Metamorphoses*. The title, *The God of Socrates*, derives from Plato's having written that, from time to time, Socrates heard a voice dissuading him from various actions. Today, this might seem to mean that Socrates paid attention to his unconscious, but Apuleius makes it the pretext for discussing the idea that demons, the supposed source of this voice, were intermediate beings between people and gods. These demons included former human beings and lesser gods. Consequently, much of the supernatural cast of the *Metamorphoses*, including Cupid, Psyche, Isis, and Osiris, might be classified as demons.

Demons were the spirits particularly invoked by wizards. After discussing this supernatural world at length, Apuleius advocates an ethical life, so that people may become good demons, or lares, after their death; this passage of *The God of Socrates* is comparable to the immortality Lucius expects to attain at the close of the *Metamorphoses*. Since in psychological terms Apuleius's supernatural world represents the unconscious, *The God of Socrates*, and, even more, the *Metamorphoses*, have been favorites of psychologists, particularly those of the Jungian school, which considers gods and demons to be metaphors for deeply buried instincts, or "archetypes."

METAMORPHOSES

First published: Second century C.E.
(English translation as *The Golden Ass*, 1566)
Type of work: Novel

Desirous of learning magical secrets, Lucius seduces a servant girl into giving him one potion, but, unluckily, he receives another, which transforms him into a donkey until he can eat roses and return to human form.

In the fourth century, Saint Augustine called *Metamorphoses* "The Golden Ass," and since then this name has become better known than the book's actual title. The phrase "golden ass" may de-

rive from the golden, or esteemed, status the book achieved; it may also contrast the opposite connotations of "golden" and "ass," since the donkey had an ignominious reputation in Apuleius's time, being associated in the Egyptian religion with the evil god Seth, an enemy of the god Isis.

Typical of second century authors, Apuleius does not invent his basic plot but shows his education by taking it from a Greek work, probably one written by Lucian, who was rewriting a tale by Lucius of Patrae or an earlier Greek author. Consequently, Apuleius begins by depicting his character Lucius as a Greek, who apologizes for his unfamiliarity with Latin. Such an apology also allows Apuleius to excuse any foreign—in his case, African—idioms that might have found their way into his novel, but its intention most probably is to make the readers wonder at his highly rhetorical mastery of the language and to serve as a disguise for him. Near the end, however, his narrator Lucius describes himself as a "Maudauran," a reference to Apuleius's birthplace, as if Apuleius were revealing himself to be the narrator, but just briefly enough to leave readers wondering if the word, inappropriate to the character Lucius, might be a scribal error.

Even if, as Saint Augustine presumed, the protagonist Lucius were a self-portrait of the book's author, Apuleius still manages to distance himself from most of the book, which consists of stories told to Lucius. These stories serve as parallels for the main narrative, since, like it, the stories are tales of suffering that lead to knowledge about the supernatural. In a general way, then, they resemble what was known about the mystery religions of the time: These religions were institutions with harrowing initiations that allegedly brought their initiates enlightenment.

Metamorphoses begins with Lucius traveling to Thessaly, the land of his mother's family and an area famous for witchcraft. This introduces the pervasive theme of the novel—a connection of the feminine (particularly the maternal) and magic. Lucius hears a tale about a man named Socrates, who, like the philosopher Socrates, is rendered miserable by a shrewish woman, but in this case through her sorcery, which kills him when he reveals that she is an old witch. Although this story ought to frighten Lucius away from prying into magic, it incites his curiosity, as it may the readers'.

Thereafter, despite warnings, Lucius seduces Fotis, a servant of the witch Pamphile, to learn the witch's secrets. Lucius wishes to turn himself into an owl (symbolic of wisdom) but instead becomes a donkey (symbolic of ignorance), since he has stolen the witch's magic. Tantalizingly, several times during the narrative, Lucius comes in close contact with roses, the antidote needed to transform him back into his human form; roses were associated with the grace of various mother goddesses. Not until the novel's end, however, does he have an opportunity to eat roses and return to human form. Most of the other characters are punished by divinely powerful maternal figures, including the goddesses Isis, Venus, and Fortune, as well as by witches, who are said to control the heavens.

Captured by bandits, Lucius hears an old woman tell a tale to comfort the kidnapped girl Charite (grace). In the tale, Psyche (soul) is kidnapped by Cupid (the god of love), who was supposed to punish her for offending the goddess Venus, but Cupid instead falls in love with Psyche. Psyche has never actually seen Cupid, since the two met in a darkened room. At the instigation of her jealous sisters, Psyche breaks the taboo against seeing Cupid and takes a look at him. He flees and she pursues him, coming at last into the service of Venus, who requires Psyche to perform seemingly impossible tasks. With supernatural help, Psyche performs them, only to eventually fail because her curiosity causes her to look into a forbidden box. Cupid, however, obtains the help of the god Jupiter. Through this assistance, Psyche becomes immortal and gives birth to Voluptas (joy). The comforting import of this story about a miraculous rescue prefigures two later plot developments in the novel: Charite is saved by her lover and Lucius finds his salvation through Isis.

Before his salvation, Lucius encounters mortals at their worst; they torture him and one another in a series of sadistic escapades. Thus, the book is not just an initiation into heavenly secrets but also into terrifying and perversely sexual knowledge. Initiations into the mystery religions, however, tended to employ multifaceted imagery of the sexual and the terrifying, so the *Metamorphoses* has often been considered a glimpse into these. In addition, one of Lucius's first warnings against stealing knowledge was seeing a statue of Actaeon changed to a stag and killed by the disrobed goddess Diana for spying on her. Similarly, Psyche was punished for looking upon naked Cupid after he had forbidden her to do so. Apuleius repeatedly associates this theme of forbidden secrets with voyeurism and theft, sins that bring the perpetrators to the condition of animals, as with a thief slain while disguised as a bear.

If given freely, however, spiritual knowledge is restorative and healing. Without at first knowing to whom he should pray, Lucius prays, and Isis graciously appears, bringing deliverance and a direction for his life. In a procession of her worshippers, one of her priests enters, allows Lucius to eat roses, and explains how his former sufferings, due to blind Fortune, will now change to beatitude under the protection of Isis, described as a sighted Fortune. Once mystery initiations have taught religious secrets, Lucius's new awareness  will be reflected by the universe, under the guidance of Isis and her husband Osiris. Having partaken of this new understanding, symbolized by the roses, Lucius returns to human form and will neither behave like an animal, governed by base appetites, nor be treated like one. He becomes a priest, and, like Apuleius himself, a lawyer. In a dream, Osiris assures Lucius that despite rivals' envy of his learning and of his profound, new knowledge, he will be raised to legal success and the higher echelon of the priesthood.

Some scholars assume that this ending recruits readers into the worship of Isis and provides the best available glimpse of her mysteries. Others argue that it is satire, since its piety seems at odds with the preceding cynicism. At the conclusion, Lucius revels in a celibate life and a bald head—both ridiculous to average Roman readers. One of the initiatory priests is named Mithras, the god of different mysteries than Isis's. Is Mithras, who is Isis's priest, a humorous figure, or is he a hint that all the gods are ultimately Isis's servants? The book may be a joke and/or a profound paradox, encompassing both the ideal and grotesque aspects of life.

SUMMARY

Because in the second century, writing itself seemed magical to a largely illiterate public, Lucius Apuleius was one of the intellectuals playing with a situation that allowed the literate to serve as physicians, philosophers, counselors, and storytellers—roles for which the earliest models were medicine men and magicians. Particularly in *Metamorphoses,* this playfulness skillfully rouses his audience's desire for secret knowledge, even while showing how dangerous such a desire may be, thereby making reading all the more exciting. Especially as the earliest extant source for the story of Cupid and Psyche, *Metamorphoses* was a major influence on many later works, including Pedro Calderón de la Barca's play *Ni amor se libra de amor* (pb. 1664; love enslaved to love), Thomas Heywood's play *Love's Mistress* (pr. 1634, pb. 1636), Walter Pater's *Marius the Epicurian: His Sensations and Ideas* (1885), and C. S. Lewis's *Till We Have Faces: A Myth Retold* (1956).

James Whitlark

DISCUSSION TOPICS

- How does the story of "Cupid and Psyche" differ from some version of *Beauty and the Beast* or of the film *King Kong?*

- In *Metamorphoses,* what is Lucius Apuleius's attitude toward women?

- In *Metamorphoses,* what is Apuleius's attitude toward magic?

- Discuss religious allegory in *Metamorphoses.*

- Does Apuleius seem to be a sincere religious teacher, a con man, or some combination of the two?

- In *Metamorphoses,* what does Lucius learn?

- How does the dark humor in *Metamorphoses* fit into (or work against) its religious purpose?

BIBLIOGRAPHY

By the Author

LONG FICTION:
Metamorphoses, second century C.E. (*The Golden Ass,* 1566)

NONFICTION:
Apologia, 158-159 C.E. (English translation, 1909)
De Deo Socratis, second century C.E. (*The God of Socrates,* 1853)
De mundo, second century C.E.
De Platone et eius dogmate, second century C.E.
Florida, second century C.E. (English translation, 1853)

MISCELLANEOUS:
The Works of Apuleius, 1853
Apuleius: Rhetorical Works, 2002

About the Author
Accardo, Pasquale. *The Metamorphosis of Apuleius: Cupid and Psyche, Beauty and the Beast, King Kong.* Madison, N.J.: Fairleigh Dickinson University Press, 2002.
Finkelpearl, Ellen D. *Metamorphosis of Language in Apuleius: A Study of Allusion in the Novel.* Ann Arbor: University of Michigan Press, 1998.
Franz, Marie-Louise von. *"The Golden Ass" of Apuleius: The Liberation of the Feminine in Man.* Boston: Shambhala, 1992.
Gollnick, James. *The Religious Dreamworld of Apuleius' "Metamorphoses": Recovering a Forgotten Hermeneutic.* Waterloo, Ont.: Canadian Corporation for Studies in Religion, Wilfrid Laurier University Press, 1999.

Harrison, S. J. *Apuleius: A Latin Sophist.* Oxford, England: Oxford University Press, 2000.

Kahane, Ahuvia, and Andrew Laird, eds. *A Companion to the Prologue of Apuleius' "Metamorphoses."* Oxford, England: Oxford University Press, 2001.

Londey, David, and Carmen Johanson. *The Logic of Apuleius.* Philosphia Antiqua 47. New York: E. J. Brill, 1987.

Schlam, Carl C. *The Metamorphoses of Apuleius: On Making an Ass of Oneself.* Chapel Hill: University of North Carolina Press, 1992.

Tatum, James. *Apuleius and "The Golden Ass."* Ithaca, N.Y.: Cornell University Press, 1979.

ARISTOPHANES

Born: Athens, Greece
c. 450 B.C.E.
Died: Athens, Greece
c. 385 B.C.E.

As sole surviving examples of Athenian Old Comedy, the eleven complete plays by Aristophanes provide the best clue to the nature of literary comedy as it developed and reached fruition in the later fifth century B.C.E.

Library of Congress

BIOGRAPHY

Aristophanes (ar-uh-STAHF-uh-neez) was born in Athens, Greece, around 450 B.C.E., to parents Philippos and Zenodora. The date of Aristophanes' birth assumes he was at least nineteen years old when his first play, *Daitalēis* (banqueters), was produced in 427 B.C.E. by Kallistratos; he would have had to be that age to understand the requirements of the competition and to develop the requisite writing skill. That he was not yet old enough to have produced that play himself, a task assumed only in 424 B.C.E. with the production of *Hippēs* (*The Knights*, 1812) after several successful plays, would seem to vouch for the assumption. Admittedly, for reasons no longer clear, several other plays, aside from those written earliest and latest in his life, were produced by others: in 414, the *Ornithes* (*The Birds*, 1824), again produced by Kallistratos, and the nonpreserved *Amphiaraos*, produced by Philonides. Aristophanes was already bald, however, when the *Eirēnē* (*Peace*, 1837) was produced in 421 B.C.E. (line 771).

Though born in Athens, Aristophanes had lived in Aigina, where his family presumably acquired property after the Athenian seizing of that island in 431 B.C.E. He was of the tribe or greater "district" of Pandionis, one of ten such districts created by the Athenian politician Cleisthenes with the constitu-

tional reform of 508-507 B.C.E., and of the much older *deme*, the local or village "ward," of Kydathenaeus within the city. That was the same local ward of the famed politician Kleon, who receives considerable parody in *The Knights* and the *Sphēkes* (*The Wasps*, 1812) of 422 B.C.E. *Acharnēs* (*The Acharnians*, 1812) of 425 implies that subsequent to his earlier prizewinning play, the *Babylōioi* (Babylonians) of 426, Aristophanes has been prosecuted by Kleon for anti-Athenian propaganda. While that trial was unsuccessful at its legal level, Aristophanes' reputation as comic playwright was established, and in Kleon and the political structure of Athens, he had ample material for his buffoonery. That factor is particularly noteworthy considering the Peloponnesian War among the Greek city-states, especially Athens against Sparta, which dominated the historical epoch from 431 to 404 B.C.E.

Aristophanes was married, though his wife's name is not known. He had at least three sons, Araros, Nikostratos, and Philetairos, each of whom also wrote plays that were staged during the Middle Comedy era in the fourth century B.C.E. Aristophanes had produced a play named *Ploutos* in 408, though it is not the one that survives under that name. Rather the surviving *Ploutos* (*Plutus*, 1651), often considered the final example of Old Comedy, is a play staged in 388, though the occasion and achievement is not known; that play was produced by his son, Araros, who staged two other plays by his father, neither of which survive:the *Kōkalos* at the Greater Dionysia, and the *Aiolosikōn*, both of which were produced about 385. Aristophanes died in Athens sometime around 385 B.C.E.

ANALYSIS

Aristophanes' plays can be studied as sources for political or social history, as works of literature, and as dramatic works. In antiquity, Plato recommended them to Dionysius I, tyrant of Syracuse, when the latter wished to learn more about Athens; in the twentieth century, Viktor Ehrenberg employed them to write "a sociology of Old Attic Comedy." The distinction between the plays as literature and as drama rests upon the separation of poetic form from techniques of staging. Comic plays were usually produced only once: thereafter, they might be disregarded or studied as literature but were not "seen" again. The absence of staging instructions within the plays, as well as a frequent failure to differentiate the speakers clearly, meant that readers could become confused by the poetic content. It is no wonder that these masterpieces generated such an intensive study, since the comic poet was also a source of original and distinctive vocabulary needing clarification. The Greek biographer Plutarch, distinguishing the preferences of an elite, educated man from those of an ordinary, uneducated one, claims that Aristophanes suited the latter but not the former by virtue of "the vulgarity in speech," "the spectacle," and "the habits of a common laborer." The reader or student of Aristophanes must be prepared to enter a world filled with such material. Yet Plutarch's preferences also illustrate the changing tastes of another epoch and the lack of historical consideration for the development of comedy, as well as for the particular genius of Aristophanes.

In contrast to Plutarch, the observation made of Aristophanes by a fellow competitor speaks highly of his role. The Greek playwright Kratinos notes that "Aristophanes resembled Euripides in his concern for verbal precision and dexterity." The oldest manuscripts of Aristophanes date from the Byzantine empire of the tenth century C.E. An intensive study of the plays in the twelfth century noted his purity of language and quintessential example of the Attic dialect of the fifth century B.C.E. In spite of the changed environment of a Christianized Greek East, the coarseness of his humor is considered less a detriment than the positive value accorded to his opposition to war.

The obscenity charges against Aristophanes so frequently leveled by the literary critics of the nineteenth and early twentieth centuries are properly understood as reflections of changing societal tastes in different eras, as well as a failure to understand social history and satire, rather than actual indecency on the part of the comic poet. War and political machinations against people were the obscenities, not explicit sexual or scatological vocabulary; this truth is what Aristophanes knew. In his time the only thing forbidden in comedy was to resemble tragedy.

To understand specifics requires some attention to the history of comedy within Athenian life. The Greek philosopher Aristotle in his *De poetica* (c. 334-323 B.C.E.; *Poetics*, 1705), provides a short history of the poetic arts. According to Aristotle, the "more serious writers" of dramatic tragedy imitated illustrious events involving illustrious persons. The "lighter-minded" imitated the more ordinary events and persons. He qualifies this general point by specifying that comedy does not include the full range of "badness," but that to be "ridiculous" or to be made ridiculous points to a kind of deformity: "The explanations of laughter are errors and disgraces not accompanied by pain, or injury." Thus, for Aristotle, the comic mask, by which the characters in the play are identified and differentiated, is one of "deformity and distortion" within the proprieties required by the staging. Aristophanes was a master of the use of masks, though they also functioned to permit a rapid switch of character onstage as required by the limitation of three speaking actors.

While Aristotle could identify some of the development through which tragedy had passed, he wrongly concludes that "there are no early records of comedy, because it was not highly valued." Archaeological investigation has uncovered lists of the prizewinners within the history of the comedies. These lists evidence the connection of comedies to the history of festivals in the state and to the gods of the state. As Aristotle knew without exact chronological detail, "it was a long time before comic dramas were licensed by the magistrate; the early comedies were produced by amateurs." Yet he also knew that these productions were the outgrowth of phallic performances, which explains the perennial costuming within the plays.

From the remote past of the Greek world came

winemaking and celebrations of its accomplishment, associated with the god Dionysos. Specific developments are best understood within Athenian definitions. In the month Poseidion (December-January), following the picking of the grapes and their initial pressing, there was held the "Rural Dionysia." An explicit example from the Rural Dionysia, but slightly parodied, is preserved in *The Acharnians* (lines 237-279). In the next month, Gamelion (January-February), festivities (the "Lenaia") with phallic processions carrying the new wine shifted to the sanctuary within the city, where it was stored, and to the theater, where it was celebrated. Initially, "revelling songs" were part of the processions, from which evolved the more complex examples seen in the competitive series of comic plays, normally five except in some wartime years.

Festivities of the next month, Anthesterion (February-March), focused upon the tasting of the new wine and involved a great procession to the coastal marshes, where the god's arrival by ship, personified in the person of the king-archon, was dramatized. This event was followed in the month Elaphebolion (March-April) by further phallic processions from the walls of the city to a shrine and then back into Athens directly to the theater for the seasonal complex of plays (called "the City Dionysia" or the "Greater Dionysia"). This complex involved competitive trilogies of tragedies with a satyr play, plus another series of comedies. Remnants of the entering and exiting processionals, with their accompanying costumes, are embedded within examples of the surviving comedies.

Recovered inscriptional lists from the festivities and the City Dionysia provide a sequence as far back as 487 B.C.E., associating many details with the particular festival and giving the names of competitors, their plays, and the winners. For fifth century Old Comedy, at least 57 competitors have been identified, along with 374 lost play titles. Of the latter, thirty are ascribed to Aristophanes, in addition to the eleven plays that survive in their complete form.

The form of the comedy involves five elements, each with its own complexity: prologue, parodos (entrance of the chorus), episodic agon (formal "contest" or "debate"), parabasis (choral interlude), and exodos (final scene and exit). Insofar as comedy got beyond burlesque or slapstick, which

never completely disappeared, these elements constituted the structural integrity to which Aristotle gave the name "plot" and by which he evaluated the success of the poet.

Beyond these basic elements, Aristophanes employed a numerous variety of technically defined poetic meters and rhythms with brilliant skill. They are exceedingly difficult to reproduce in English, or in any other translation.

THE CLOUDS

First produced: *Nephelai*, 423 B.C.E. (English translation, 1708)
Type of work: Play

This play, a parody of the kind of intellectual development associated with Socrates, places such thinkers and their thoughts within the rarefied atmosphere of the "clouds."

The Clouds was staged at the City Dionysia of 423 B.C.E. and was awarded third place among the three competitors. Having taken first place with *The Acharnians* and *The Knights* at the Lenaia, respectively in the two preceding years (425 and 424), Aristophanes was very disappointed. The preserved text is a revision of the original as staged, building in a variety of ingredients reflecting his effort not only to revamp the failure but also to incorporate observations on that failure. Lines 521-525 make the point specifically: "I thought you were a bright audience, and that this was my most brilliant comedy, so I thought you should be the first to taste it. But I was repulsed, worsted by vulgar rivals, though I didn't deserve that."

Aristophanes takes as his theme the contrast between an older educational mode and the new interrogative style, associated with the name of Socrates. Apparently his first play, the *Daitalēis*, had already exploited a similar theme. *The Clouds* begins with a prologue (lines 1-262), which introduces the two principal characters, Strepsiades ("Twister"), worried by the debts accumulating because of the propensity for chariot racing of his long-haired son, Pheidippides ("Sparer of Horses," or "Horsey"). The idea occurs, with the assistance of "a student," to have the son enter the school

("Think-shop") next door, operated by Socrates, wherein by the logic of the sophists one should be able to learn how to talk so as to evade one's debts. When the son refuses to attend, lest his suntan be ruined, the father goes instead. He finds Socrates suspended in a basket from the roof, wherein rarefied thinking can be more appropriately done in the atmosphere of the clouds.

The parodos finally erupts with the entrance of the chorus of "clouds" singing and dancing (lines 263-509), following the incantations and chanted prayers of Socrates, to the alarm of Strepsiades. In brilliant repartee, the chorus is introduced as the goddesses, who, with wind, lightning, and thunder, patronize intellectual development. Yet the buffoonery that follows indicates that it is some weird intellect, for Socrates, in answer to questions about rain and thunder, assures Strepsiades that there is no Zeus but only clouds displaying analogies to the human bodily functions of passing water or gas. Strepsiades is convinced, and the parodos ends with his agreeing to become a student. A sequence of two parabases and two agon follow (lines 510-1452). The first parabasis (lines 510-626) provides the best evidence that the play in its present form has been rewritten; the second (lines 1113-1130) addresses the judges asking for the prize. Their function is typical, though they also serve as interludes between the episodic agon or scenes, and, whatever their present content, some similar kind of witty poetry addressed outside the play would have been present.

The first episode is the longer one (lines 627-1112). Strepsiades proves incompetent as a student, for he cannot memorize what is required but only wants to learn how to outwit creditors. Subsequent to his own dismissal, he forces Pheidippides to enroll under threat of expulsion from home. Included is the first agon (lines 889-1112), wherein Pheidippides is exposed to the debate between "Right" ("Just Logic") and "Wrong" ("Unjust Logic"), from which it is obvious that the argument of the latter will prevail.

The second episode is relatively short (lines 1131-1452). When Strepsiades learns the result of his son's education, though assured of its great success, he discovers that success means that his son now knows how to whip him. The second agon (lines 1321-1452) argues for the validity of that action, making reference, as the comic poets'

tended, to the tragic poets, the father preferring the older Aeschylus, characterizing older virtues, and the son siding with Euripides, whose newer notions are caricatured as immoralities. There are amusing anecdotes concerning child development in Strepsiades' argument to Pheidippides, but Strepsiades has been defeated by his own intentions.

The brief exodos (lines 1453-1510) involves Strepsiades getting revenge for his own sake by setting fire to the "Think-shop" next door.

THE WASPS

First produced: *Sphēkes*, 422 B.C.E. (English translation, 1812)
Type of work: Play

In the midst of war and without definitive leadership, a democracy can be pulled this way, then that, eliciting a lampooning of its very structure.

Having failed in 423 B.C.E. with his intellectual parody, *The Clouds*, Aristophanes returned to the more vulgar arena of politics. Considered to be the most perfectly structured of Aristophanes' plays, *The Wasps* took second prize at the Lenaia. It provides a complete pattern against which other plays can be measured.

The prologue (lines 1-229) begins on an early morning before the house of Philokleon ("Lover of Kleon") and his son Bdelykleon ("Hater of Kleon"), with two of their slaves, Sosias and Xanthias, discussing the peculiar illness of Philokleon, who has an obsession to serve daily on juries within the law courts—spelled out in a lengthy monologue (lines 85-135) by Xanthias—from which Bdelykleon is equally determined to prevent him. To get out of the house, Philokleon climbs the chimney pretending to be smoke, while Bdelykleon appears on the roof to stop him. The theme for the subsequent action is stated in lines 158-160: Philokleon fears the gods will punish him if any guilty defendant goes unpunished.

The arrival of the chorus in the parodos (lines 230-315), spectacularly costumed as "wasps" so that they may "buzz" around, over which are the garb of the jurors whose action often "stings," signals the beginning of the play's action. They are exclusively old men of Philokleon's generation.

The agon is twofold: In a scene interlayered with an irrelevant lyric that plays upon the nature of the wasp, the issue is defined (lines 316-525) by Philokleon and the leader of the chorus and formally debated (lines 526-727) by Philokleon and Bdelykleon before the chorus. Bdelykleon's argument prevails, convincing not only the chorus but also, intellectually if not emotionally, his father. The episode is extended (lines 728-1008), again with interlayered lyric, by dramatizing the agon, in a pretended domestic litigation intended to cure Philokleon of his illness by having him acquit a defendant. The context provides occasion to pan the actual politician Kleon, presumably in the audience.

The lengthy parabasis (lines 1009-1121), balanced between the leader and his chorus, and displaying the particular requirements of Attic lyric style with its highly technical linguistic components, serves to narrate the conflict that the playwright has had with his judges and audiences on previous occasions, upon which they have failed to understand him. Considerable insight into biographical matters emerges.

The play intentionally breaks down in the episodes that follow, for much buffoonery and satire occur. Philokleon warns of excessive drinking (lines 1122-1264), anticipating his own drunkenness, illustrated in the final scene (lines 1292-1449). In between comes the second parabasis (usually lines 1265-1291), wherein Aristophanes places in the mouth of the chorus leader, who is wearing a mask to represent the author, his bitter diatribe against Kleon for that earlier prosecution. Some translators prefer to switch this parabasis with the choral ode (lines 1450-1473) that would otherwise conclude these episodes, wherein Philokleon, apparently before his intoxication, could be envied for his change of character and his son praised for his wisdom. Others think that the intentional diabolical irony of Aristophanes would be best served by leaving the two sets of lines in their traditional places. Either way, the exodos (lines 1474-1537) is also a dance routine, with Philokleon executing a burlesque solo parodying those of various tragedies, including that of Euripides' *Kyklōps* (c. 421 B.C.E.; *Cyclops*, 1782).

THE BIRDS

First produced: *Ornithes*, 414 B.C.E. (English translation, 1824)
Type of work: Play

With the Peloponnesian War in an apparent mode of Athenian victory, occasion for complex fantasy seemed in order, and this genius of a spectacle resulted with its utopian "cloud-cuckoo-land."

The longest of the surviving comedies by Aristophanes is *The Birds*. It was entered at the City Dionysia, where it was awarded second prize. It is without a doubt Aristophanes' singular achievement of dramatic spectacle. The play's brilliantly plumaged chorus of birds appears to be based on a genuine knowledge of birds in their great variety, for beginning at line 268 Aristophanes introduces each different bird in the chorus, commenting upon its respective dress.

Peace had been the concern of the state in the preceding decade, and *Peace* had been the theme of Aristophanes' play that took second prize at the Greater Dionysia in 421 B.C.E. Yet peace had not come in the continuing war between Athens and Sparta. While *The Birds* was presented in a moment of impending success, for Athens it was merely a matter of months before the most disastrous events of the war. It is hard to be certain how perceptive the poet was, yet there is a haunting underlying mood.

The prologue (lines 1-259) begins with Athenian citizens Peisthetairos and Euelpides having abandoned the city, with its incessant penchant for litigation, earlier satirized in *The Wasps*, in search of some quieter country. Having been guided in their journey by birds, respectively a crow and a jackdaw, they call upon the mysterious Tereus, who, according to a tragedy by Sophocles, had been turned into a hoopoe, a multicolored bird with a large crest. After some explanatory conversation, Peisthetairos has the idea that the birds should build a city-state between heaven and earth, where they can intercept the sacrificial smoke of offerings made by humans to the gods, reestablishing the original supremacy of birds over both. The prologue ends with the hoopoe's song, full of marvelous plays upon birdcalls, summoning the other birds.

A long parodos follows (lines 260-450), wherein the chorus of birds enters upon the stage one by one, to be introduced, to be descriptively identified, and to receive comic association with leading personalities of the day. Since humans regularly eat birds, the initial reaction by the birds is hostility, but the hoopoe intervenes. The parodos concludes with the hoopoe's instruction to Peisthetairos to explain his idea to the birds.

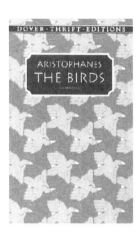

The agon (lines 451-675) provides the extended conversation involving the hoopoe and the chorus leader, a partridge, as the idea is expounded. The birds are gradually convinced. The establishment of the new land will require human assistance for structural details, but for the humans to participate in the construction enterprise it would be best if they grew wings. The agon ends with the hoopoe giving the humans a root to chew on that will produce wings, thereby preventing any threat that other birds might have against their former adversaries.

Parabases alternate with episodes. In the initial relatively brief parabasis (lines 676-800), the chorus of birds addresses the theater audience on the origin of birds and their value to humankind, concluding with an invitation to come live with them and an explanation of the advantage of having wings. The shorter first episode (lines 801-1057) brings back Peisthetairos and Euelpides, now with wings, of which they remain somewhat self-conscious. Yet it proceeds to the building of *Nephelo-kokky-gia* ("Cloud-cuckoo-land"), with Peisthetairos completely in charge. Both Euelpides and the hoopoe disappear from the play—a necessity of the limitation upon the number of speaking actors and of the large number of roles required in the two episodes. Various human personality types and bureaucratic functionaries appear looking for jobs in the new city-state, only to be driven off, with much good humor suggestive of the role that comedy

had in the parodying of the pompous nature of local government. The second parabasis (lines 1058-1117) sees the chorus of birds proclaiming its divinity, reflecting upon the carefree life it leads, but concluding with the appeal to the judges to award the prize to it.

A long second episode (lines 1118-1705) follows. After a description of the completed structures, it becomes evident that the Olympian gods are being warned of this new competition, and there follows, with plays upon the control of opposition within the democratic political process, the necessity to effect some kind of truce with the gods. Prometheus, the well-known opponent of Zeus, assists Peisthetairos in the negotiations; Poseidon, Herakles, and a Triballian god who speaks an unintelligible form of Greek represent the peace envoys from Olympus. When terms are finally established, preparations are made for the wedding of Peisthetairos to Basileia ("Miss Sovereignty"), Zeus's housekeeper, who together will reign over all from the palace of Zeus.

The exodos (lines 1706-1765) combines the wedding hymns, sung by the adoring chorus of birds, with the departure of the royal couple to assume their regnal place.

LYSISTRATA

First produced: *Lysistratē*, 411 B.C.E. (English translation, 1837)
Type of work: Play

As the Peloponnesian War relentlessly continued, Aristophanes toyed with the notion that the women, by withholding their sexual favors to their men, might elicit peace.

One of the shorter plays, *Lysistrata* appears to have been produced at the Lenaia, with no surviving indication of its achievement. The most outrageously notorious scenes in all drama could only have been staged in the Greek theater, with its base in the phallic-oriented festivals of the city-state cult.

The play also is famous for the role given to women, particularly noteworthy since there is no evidence for women attending Athenian theater, and since it entailed the somewhat comic difficulty of having men, already in their phallic-oriented costumes, play the roles of the women. Yet that same year, 411 B.C.E., Aristophanes appears to have submitted for the City Dionysia the *Thesmophoriazousai* (*Thesmophoriazusae*, 1837), another play with women as principal characters, and he returned to this theme several other times in subsequent plays.

The prologue (lines 1-253) introduces Lysistrata, an Athenian woman who seeks to achieve peace from prolonged warfare among the city-states, which the men have been unable or unwilling to accomplish. Her idea is to withhold all sexual relations from husbands or lovers until they agree to peace terms. In the opening scene,

she must first persuade diverse women, some of whose discourse provides marvelous examples of what else women of the time had within their duties, as well as upon their minds. The scene closes with the women convinced. In agreement, they seize the Akropolis, site of Athena's temple.

Aristophanes employs two half-choruses for this comedy, one of old men, the other of old women, to play off one another and as contrasts to the youthful feminine protagonists. The parodos (lines 254-386) involves their separate and successive entrances, first of men and then of women, each arriving to perform intended functions related to the war.

The episode (lines 387-466) begins with the abrupt entrance of the official magistrate, who learns first from the chorus of men and then from Lysistrata and her companions what is transpiring. That leads into the agon (lines 467-613) between Lysistrata and the magistrate, where the women's perspective upon war is made clear against the patriotic zeal of the government.

The parabasis (lines 614-705) juxtaposes in unusual fashion the two choruses against one another: the old men crying "tyranny," the old women responding "rights," even to advise the state. This interlude is designed to imply the passage of time, without which the subsequent episodes would be unintelligible.

In the first episode (lines 706-780), there is the threat to the movement by potentially disaffected women confronting their sex-starved men with permanent erection of their costumed phalluses. A choral interlude (lines 781-828) displays hatred of one another verbally and physically in the described actions. The second episode (lines 829-1013) magnifies the first with specific focus upon the married couple, Myrrine and her soldier-husband, Kinesias. As he, unsatisfied, exits, a herald from Athens's enemy, Sparta, arrives to report that the situation in his land goes badly in the same vein as in Athens. As a master of dialect, Aristophanes plays the two forms of Greek off each other; British translators have often relied on the ability to contrast English for the Athenians with a Scottish brogue for the Spartans.

A second parabasis (lines 1014-1042) allows the choruses to be reunited with considerable sentiment in the lyric, first separately and then together addressing the audience. Throughout the remaining episodes, interlayered with lyric (lines 1043-1246), the chorus continues to tease the audience, while ranking delegates from Sparta and Athens agree to peace. Lysistrata makes the speech of reconciliation (lines 1112-1157) in such nearly tragic style that it has been hard for many critics to reconcile her speech with the bawdiness of the play as a whole. Yet this is Aristophanes, perhaps at his best, suggesting to old enemies their more ancient common roots in Hellenism and their mutual obligations to one another.

The play ends with an exodos (lines 1247-1322) full of dancing revelry, yet with hymns of great beauty, even allowing the Spartan in his dialect to have the final song before all join in a four-line ode to Athena.

SUMMARY

Over a forty-year period, Aristophanes wrote at least forty plays whose titles are known, and in five instances he rewrote earlier plays. Of this number, only eleven plays survive in their complete form. Yet within these complete plays are some of the finest examples of Greek lyric, so that alongside his contemporary, the tragic poet Euripides, Aristophanes is remembered as a master of Attic poetry.

Clyde Curry Smith

BIBLIOGRAPHY

By the Author

DRAMA:

Aristophanes wrote at least forty plays whose titles are known; of this number, only eleven survive in their complete form, as follows:

Acharnēs, 425 B.C.E. (*The Acharnians*, 1812)

Hippēs, 424 B.C.E. (*The Knights*, 1812)

Nephelai, 423 B.C.E. (*The Clouds*, 1708)

Sphēkes, 422 B.C.E. (*The Wasps*, 1812)

Eirēnē, 421 B.C.E. (*Peace*, 1837)

Ornithes, 414 B.C.E. (*The Birds*, 1824)

Lysistratē, 411 B.C.E. (*Lysistrata*, 1837)

Thesmophoriazousai, 411 B.C.E. (*Thesmophoriazusae*, 1837)

Batrachoi, 405 B.C.E. (*The Frogs*, 1780)

Ekklesiazousai, 392 B.C.E.? (*Ecclesiazusae*, 1837)

Ploutos, 388 B.C.E. (*Plutus*, 1651)

About the Author

Bloom, Harold, ed. *Aristophanes*. Broomall, Pa.: Chelsea House, 2002.

Dearden, C. W. *The Stage of Aristophanes*. London: Athlone Press, 1976.

Dover, K. J. *Aristophanic Comedy*. Berkeley: University of California Press, 1972.

Harriott, Rosemary M. *Aristophanes: Poet and Dramatist*. Baltimore: Johns Hopkins University Press, 1986.

McLeish, K. *The Theatre of Aristophanes*. London: Thames & Hudson, 1980.

Pickard-Cambridge, Arthur W. *The Dramatic Festivals of Athens*. Reissued with supplements and corrections. Oxford, England: Clarendon Press, 1988.

Platter, Charles. *Aristophanes and the Carnival of Genres*. Baltimore: Johns Hopkins University Press, 2007.

Revermann, Martin. *Comic Business: Theatricality, Dramatic Technique, and Performance Contexts of Aristophanic Comedy*. New York: Oxford University Press, 2006.

Rothwell, Kenneth S., Jr. *Nature, Culture, and the Origins of Greek Comedy: A Study of Animal Choruses*. New York: Cambridge University Press, 2007.

Stone, Laura M. *Costume in Aristophanic Comedy*. New York: Ayer, 1981.

Ussher, R. G. *Aristophanes*. Oxford, England: Clarendon Press, 1979.

DISCUSSION TOPICS

- What do we need to know about comedy in Athenian life of Aristophanes' time to understand his plays?

- Plays in ancient Athens were performed competitively. According to modern critics, one of Aristophanes' best plays, *The Clouds*, did not win. How can we have a better idea of the value of a play than the people who originally saw it?

- One character in *The Clouds*, a rather foolish one, is the philosopher Socrates. To what extent could a playwright do a similar thing with a philosopher today?

- Consider the appropriateness of the title *The Wasps*.

- Aristophanes' plays were musical comedies, but we do not have the music. Can we properly judge his plays without knowing the music?

- Offer some possible reasons for the popularity of the play *Lysistrata* today.

ARISTOTLE

Born: Stagirus, Chalcidice, Greece
384 B.C.E.
Died: Chalcis, Euboea, Greece
322 B.C.E.

Known throughout the Middle Ages simply as "The Philosopher," Aristotle made significant contributions to a wide range of scientific, political, and philosophical topics.

Library of Congress

BIOGRAPHY

Aristotle (ar-uh-STAWT-uhl) was born in 384 B.C.E. in Stagirus, a small colonial town on the northern coast of the Aegean Sea, in Chalcidice, Greece. His father, Nicomachus, was a physician to the court of the Macedonian king Amyntas II. There is some speculation that being born into a physician's family led to Aristotle's later interest in biology, but that is at best only a partial account; both his parents died when he was quite young, and he was reared by an official in the Macedonian court.

At eighteen, Aristotle traveled south to Athens, where he became a member of Plato's Academy, where he spent the next twenty years. Many scholars have suggested that during these years in close association with Plato, Aristotle imbibed his master's otherworldly and idealistic philosophy and that Aristotle was only able to develop his own naturalistic and empirically based philosophy when he left the Academy after Plato's death. Other scholars have argued that when Aristotle arrived at the Academy, it was already a large and world-famous institution engaged in all forms of intellectual and scientific investigation. While scholars can be sure that Aristotle spent much time working on a wide range of intellectual topics during his twenty years at the Academy, it is uncertain who influenced him. When Plato died in 347 B.C.E., Aristotle left the Academy. He spent the next five or six years teaching and conducting biological research across the Aegean.

In 343 B.C.E., he received and accepted a request to return to Macedonia and tutor the young Alexander the Great. The relationship between the man who would be called simply "The Philosopher" throughout the Middle Ages and the future conqueror of the world was already an item for speculation when Plutarch wrote his profile of Alexander, which appears in *Bioi paralloi* (c. 105-115 C.E.; *Parallel Lives*, 1579), in the first century. Yet the political ambitions and ideals of the two men were so diverse that, whatever their personal feelings toward each other, it seems clear that Aristotle's three years of tutoring had little philosophical influence.

Once again he returned to Athens, and once again he was passed over when the presidency of the Academy became vacant. This time he opened a rival institution in the Lyceum, or gymnasium attached to the temple of Apollo Lyceus. Aristotle's reputation as a scholar was already sufficient to attract enough students and even some teachers from the Academy, so that the Lyceum became the second viable institution of scientific and philosophical research in the West.

With Alexander's death in 323 B.C.E., a brief but intense anti-Macedonian mood swept through Athens. Aristotle's Macedonian origins and connections were well known. Being an astute judge of human nature, Aristotle knew that his life was in danger. Not wanting Athens to "sin twice against philosophy"—a clear allusion to Athens's execution of Socrates on the same charges many years before—Aristotle withdrew to his native province. He died the following year, in 322 B.C.E., in Chalcis, Greece.

ANALYSIS

At the very heart of Aristotle's philosophy is the conviction that all things are teleologically ordered. There are two fundamentally different ways in which people explain events or things (understood in their broadest sense). Something is explained teleologically when its purpose or intention is made known. For example, a chair can be explained as an object made for sitting and a person's raised hand as an attempt to attract the teacher's attention. Alternately, something is explained causally when its physical antecedents are made known. For example, the crack in the brick wall can be explained as the result of a prior earthquake.

During the seventeenth and eighteenth centuries, there was a strong reaction against teleological explanations because it was believed that all real knowledge gives power and control over nature. Since teleological explanations of nature do not typically help to prevent or predict natural phenomena, they were deemed to be sterile, as was Aristotle's philosophy as a whole. This period's rejection of Aristotle, however, was based largely on a misreading of his works. Aristotle did not ignore physical causes. The majority of Aristotle's work deals with topics and issues that today are considered scientific. Moreover, Aristotle's scientific investigations reveal a great care and concern for thorough observations and the collection of empirical evidence before reaching any conclusions.

Though Aristotle himself never ignored or belittled the investigation of physical causes, his view of nature and the modern scientific view of nature are quite different. The tendency today is to follow the seventeenth century's view of science as primarily an attempt to control nature. Aristotle, instead, emphasized science's attempt to understand nature, and that, he steadfastly insisted, would include both kinds of explanations. In his work *De anima* (335-323 B.C.E.; *On the Soul*, 1812), Aristotle notes that some of his predecessors have tried to explain anger in terms of physical causes, while others have tried to explain it in terms of a person's intentions to seek retaliation. When asked whose explanation was better, Aristotle responded, "Is it not rather the one who combines both?"

According to Aristotle, an explanation is complete only if it has a place in a systematic and unified explanation of the whole of reality. The incredible range of topics on which Aristotle wrote is not simply the result of his wide interests. Rather, it is also the result of his conviction that all complete explanations must have their place in a systematic whole.

The goal of the special sciences—biology, physics, or astronomy, for example—for both Aristotle and modern scientists is to deduce an explanation of as many observations as possible from the fewest number of principles and causes as possible. Yet Aristotle would add that the scientist's work is not complete until those principles and causes are themselves explained. If the "first principles" of a discipline are simply assumed to be true, then the whole discipline is left hanging in midair.

Aristotle's method of justifying first principles begins with the notion of dialectic. Aristotle's principal works start with a discussion of what his predecessors have said on the topic being studied. While such a review would always include conflicting opinions, Aristotle believed that if conflicting opinions are forced to defend themselves against their opponent's objections, the result is typically a distinction that allows the two partial truths to be unified into a larger and more complete truth.

Though Aristotle was always seeking to find some truth in conflicting opinions, he was neither a skeptic nor a relativist with regard to scientific or moral knowledge. He was never reticent to point out his predecessors' mistakes, and he often was convinced that his arguments demonstrated where these predecessors made their mistakes in such a way that all rational people would agree. Aristotle's *Organon* (335-323 B.C.E.; English translation, 1812) contains the tools of such demonstrations and, as such, is the first systematic formulation of the principles of deductive and inductive logic. While contemporary logicians have increased the power and versatility of Aristotle's logic, his analysis of fallacious reasoning has never been shown to be in error.

METAPHYSICS

First published: *Metaphysica*, 335-323 B.C.E.
(English translation, 1801)
Type of work: Philosophy

This work is an analysis of what it means to exist and a determination of the kinds of things that actually exist.

Twentieth century philosophers have distinguished between descriptive metaphysics and revisionist metaphysics. Aristotle's metaphysics is clearly an attempt to describe, analyze, and justify the common beliefs about humanity and the world, not an attempt to persuade people to revise their prephilosophical views of the world in some radical fashion. Unless the revisionist metaphysics of Aristotle's contemporaries is understood, however, it is impossible to understand Aristotle's own accomplishment.

Previous philosophers, such as Heraclitus, argued that the only source of knowledge is that which is observed through one of the five senses, and since the testimony of the five senses reveals a continually changing world, it follows that absolutely nothing remains the same. A rock or a mountain may at first seem fairly stable, but close examination reveals that they, too, are continually being diminished by the winds and the rains. As Heraclitus said, it is impossible to step into the same river twice. Rocks and mountains may not change as quickly, but they change no less surely.

To be told that rivers, rocks, and mountains are continually changing appears to be relatively innocuous. Yet the logic of Heraclitus's argument makes it impossible to stop there. If the only source of knowledge is through the senses, then absolutely everything must be in a continual state of flux. A person who robs a bank, for example, can never be caught because whoever is charged with the crime is necessarily a different person than the one who actually committed it. Heraclitus's philosophical conclusions are clearly in radical opposition to the commonsense view of the world.

Other philosophers, such as Parmenides, argued for the exact opposite conclusion, namely, that all change is illusory. While Heraclitus appealed to empirical data, Parmenides appealed to reason. Consider everything that really exists in the entire universe precisely as it is at this particular instance, he believed. Whatever that "everything" is, it is by definition the Real, and anything else must therefore be unreal. Now if the Real were to change, it would become something that it is not, that is, it would become unreal. Yet the unreal does not exist. Thus, for anything to change is for it to become nonexistent. All change must therefore be unreal.

The radical opposition of Parmenides' philosophical conclusions are obvious from the start. What is not so obvious is exactly where his reasoning is mistaken. While the common people will be able to continue their daily tasks without ever addressing either Heraclitus or Parmenides' arguments, it would be inconsistent for Aristotle to insist that first principles must be dialectically justified and then simply ignore these revisionist arguments. Commonsense assumptions must be justified.

The three assumptions that Aristotle seeks to justify are, first, that things exist; second, that some things move and change; and finally, that the things in this universe that exist, move, and change are not totally unintelligible. The common element of all three beliefs is the notion of a "thing." What is a thing? Aristotle says that things have being (existence) and that a metaphysician's task is to make clear exactly what being is. In fact, he often defines the subject matter of metaphysics as the study of all things insofar as they exist.

Compare this definition with the definition of other disciplines. The subject matter of physics, says Aristotle, is things insofar as they are moving or changing objects. The subject matter of biology is things insofar as they are alive. The subject matter of ethics is things insofar as they are able to make rational choices between competing goods. One notices how the various subject matters of different disciplines constitute a hierarchical series from the particular to the general. Thus, a single person can be studied on at least three different levels. First, her or she can be studied by the moral philosopher as a "thing" capable of making rational choices. At a more general level, he or she can be studied by the biologist as a "thing" that is alive. At an even more general level, her or she can be studied by the physicist as a "thing" that moves.

The crucial metaphysical question for Aristotle

thus becomes the following: Is there any more general level at which one can study things than at the level of the physicist? Aristotle thinks that there is, namely, at the level at which things are studied simply insofar as they exist. This way of defining the different disciplines ensures that no important questions are begged. In particular, it leaves open the question of whether anything exists apart from space and time. One of the important conclusions in the *Metaphysics* is that such a being, the unmoved mover or God, does exist. Yet before addressing such interesting and difficult theological questions, Aristotle wisely directs his attention to the more mundane, but almost as difficult, question, What is a thing?

Aristotle begins by cataloging the ordinary sorts of things that exist in this universe. There is this particular rock, that particular tree, and his friend Theaetetus. The point of any catalog is to organize different things into classes where all members of a class share something in common. People do this sort of thing all the time. The very act of speaking constitutes a kind of ordering of objects into classes. To say, "Theaetetus is snub-nosed," is to place a particular individual into one class of things as opposed to a different class. This ability to speak, and hence, classify, is grounded in two basic facts.

First, there are two fundamentally different sorts of words—substantives and words that describe substantives. In Aristotle's terms, there are subjects and predicates. Certain words or phrases are always subjects, and others are always predicates. For example, it makes sense to say, "This tree is tall," but it makes no sense to say, "Tall is this tree" (unless this statement is understood simply as a poetic way of saying, "This tree is tall"). This fundamental fact of language leads to Aristotle's distinction between form and matter. In the above sentence, "this tree" refers to some matter that one can see, touch, and perhaps even smell, and "is tall" refers to the shape or form of the matter. Pure matter, however, is inconceivable. No matter what one tries to picture, it always has some shape or form. Therefore, considered by itself, matter is mere potentiality as opposed to actuality.

Can one, then, conceive of pure form? That is difficult, though nonetheless possible according to Aristotle. It is possible, for example, to conceive of a particular song's melody without actually hearing the song. In fact, Ludwig van Beethoven conceived

and composed his ninth symphony after he became totally deaf. In Aristotelian terms, he knew its form without ever experiencing its matter. Though Beethoven's is a special sort of case, it does help Aristotle make sense of God as pure form. In the vast majority of cases, though, Aristotle maintains that the matter and form of a thing always constitute a real unity and that they can only be separated conceptually.

People's ability to conceptually separate a thing's matter and form explains a second basic fact about language. A capacity with which all normal human beings are born is the ability to observe an incredible array of different sized, shaped, and colored objects and realize that they are all trees. Of course, the capacity to know that something is a tree presupposes much experience and instruction, but the fact remains—normal human beings are able to learn what makes an object a tree. Aristotle draws two conclusions from this fact. First, normal human beings are endowed with a capacity (*nous*) that enables them to abstract forms from matter. Second, nature is divided into natural kinds that humans discover and name when they abstract a thing's substantial form.

This last point leads to one final distinction— the difference between a thing's substantial form and what Aristotle calls its accidental form. A substantial form is that which makes a thing what it is. Change a thing's substantial form, and the thing becomes something else. Cut down an actual tree, and the mass of matter is no longer a tree but is potentially a house, firewood, or compost, which will eventually turn to dirt. Yet a tree can undergo many changes and still remain a tree. Prune a limb from a tree or pick its fruit and the accidental form of the tree changes. Yet the tree remains a tree.

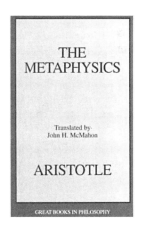

THE METAPHYSICS

Translated by
John H. McMahon

ARISTOTLE

GREAT BOOKS IN PHILOSOPHY

With these distinctions, Aristotle believes that he is able to justify commonsense beliefs about the world in the face of Heraclitus's arguments. While it is true that the five senses reveal that the accidental forms of things are continually changing, it is not true that a thing's substantial form is always changing. Thus, while there is a sense in which Heraclitus is correct, his failure to distinguish between matter and form, actuality and potentiality, and substantial forms and accidental forms invalidates his radical conclusion that everything is in a continual state of flux.

Having demonstrated that some things can remain the same, it remains for Aristotle to answer Parmenides and demonstrate how things can change. Aristotle begins by distinguishing two quite different uses of the verb "to be." To say, "The table is" (that is, "the table exists") says something quite different from saying, "The table is white." The former "is" asserts the existence of a thing; the latter "is" does not. "Whiteness" does not name a substantial form that itself exists; it only names an accidental form that cannot exist apart from actual things. While a table is actually white, it is also potentially red. Furthermore, if someone paints the table, and it becomes actually red, the table itself does not cease to exist while another table suddenly begins to exist. Parmenides' failure to distinguish between actuality and potentiality leads to his radical conclusion that nothing changes.

Aristotle is now in a position to analyze the commonsense notion of change by elucidating four ways that people use the word "cause." Consider, for a moment, a bronze statue. There are four different replies to the question of what makes that thing a statue: because it is made of bronze (material cause); because it is in the shape of a man (formal cause); because an artist shaped the matter the way that he did (efficient cause); or because an artist wanted to make a beautiful object (final cause). All four statements are true, yet no single one gives a complete explanation of the statue. According to Aristotle, any complete explanation of what a thing is, or why a thing changes, must mention all four kinds of causes.

The need for a final cause in all complete explanations has been the topic for much controversy, though there is no controversy that final causes play a central role in all Aristotle's thought. His ideas about causation are discussed in book 12 of the *Metaphysics*. Here, Aristotle repeatedly says that an infinite series of causes is impossible, but his words are somewhat misleading. He does not mean to assert that there is no infinite series of causes and

effects. In fact, he believes that the universe itself must be infinite. What Aristotle means by his claim is that if such an infinite series of causes exists without a first cause, then the series as a whole is itself unintelligible. In any series of causes, until the stopping point can be ascertained, one cannot really determine who or what is responsible for any member of the series. Yet since Aristotle believes that the universe always existed in some form, its first cause cannot exist at some point of time prior to all others. Instead, the first cause must be conceptually first.

Not all answers to the question, Who or what is responsible for the some particular thing or movement?, refer to something that exists temporarily prior to the thing or movement being explained. A large bowl of food will cause a hungry dog to run toward it. In such a case, it is sufficient, says Aristotle, that the cause (the bowl of food) and the effect (the dog's running) exist simultaneously; the cause does not have to exist before the effect. Similarly, Aristotle argues that God's existence as the most perfect of beings is the final cause or end of all motion, even though both God and the universe have always existed.

Furthermore, the fact that God moves the universe as a final cause, rather than as an efficient cause, explains why God Himself does not require a cause. In Aristotle's metaphysics, God is an unmoved mover. He is thus ultimately responsible for all movement and change in the universe without Himself moving. It makes no more sense to ask, "What moves God?" than it does to ask, "Why is a vacuum empty?"

NICOMACHEAN ETHICS

First published: *Ethica Nicomachea*, 335-323
  B.C.E. (English translation, 1797)
Type of work: Philosophy

Aristotle argues that happiness is the result of distinctly human activities performed well.

Aristotle believed that ethics was more a matter of character than of following rules. He was more concerned with what a person was than what he did. He realized that to a large extent a person's character is created by his actions. Yet making one's actions conform to rules was not the goal of morality. A person can obey all the rules of chess without being a very good chess player. So too, a person can follow all the rules of morality—never lie, steal, murder, or commit adultery—without being an especially good person.

The goal of morality, according to Aristotle, is human happiness. One of the questions that has received much attention from modern moral philosophers—Why be moral?—never arose for Aristotle because he simply assumed that achieving a stable and lasting happiness was everyone's goal.

Of course, Aristotle understood that there is a wide divergence of opinion among people as to what constitutes happiness—some say it is wealth, others say it is power or honor, still others say it is pleasure. People will only know which of these, or which mix of these, really leads to a life well lived, says Aristotle, by first determining the proper work or function of a person qua person.

The function of a carpenter is to build houses, and the function of an author is to write books. Given these distinct functions, it is not unreasonable to assume that a carpenter would feel frustrated if forced to write a book, and conversely, that an author would feel frustrated if forced to build a house. Each of these would rather be doing that which he or she is uniquely suited to do. Aristotle takes this argument one step further and argues that human beings are happiest when they are acting in accordance with their essential nature.

The essential nature of anything is the thing's work or function, that is, that which it does better than anything else. Observation reveals that humans are superior to all other animals in two areas, reasoning and social organization. Aristotle does not say that only humans are capable of reasoning. A dog can infer from his master's facial expression that he is about to be punished. Yet dogs cannot discover, or understand, what is common to all punishments because they cannot know (*nous*) the essence of punishment. Dogs may be able to communicate with a series of growls and barks, but they are not able to create a language that defines and categorizes things according to their essential natures.

Similarly, while dogs live in packs and exhibit a rudimentary social nature, that social structure is determined by instinct. This tendency is evident by the invariant nature of that organization within a single species. Human social organizations are voluntary, and thus, they exhibit a wide variety of political structures ranging from the monarchical to the democratic.

Aristotle now becomes more specific as to exactly how human beings flourish. Since they are by nature rational, humans have a need and desire for knowledge. Only when this natural desire is fulfilled can humans be truly happy. Second, the nature of a person as a social animal means that men and women have a natural need and desire for friends. The *Nicomachean Ethics* devotes a fifth of its chapters to the nature and value of friendship.

In Aristotle's philosophy, a human being's rational and social nature feed and nourish each other. Their rational capacities, for example, must be developed by good parents and teachers, and good parents and teachers are only found in well-ordered societies. Conversely, well-ordered societies presuppose knowledgeable citizens. Thus, knowledge and virtue go hand in hand.

Aristotle defines virtue as "the mean relative to us, a mean which is defined by a rational principle, such as a man of practical wisdom would use to determine it." He explains himself with an example. Consider, he says, the different caloric needs of a heavyweight boxer in training and of a teacher during spring break. What may be too few calories for the boxer may very well be too many for the teacher. There is no set number of calories that all people ought to ingest. Similarly, consider the virtue of liberality. What may be a stingy contribution to charity by a rich man may be an overly generous contribution by a person of moderate means with a family to support.

Yet Aristotle is not a moral relativist. He is not saying that, since people in different cultures have different beliefs about what is right or wrong, there are therefore no moral absolutes. There is nothing in Aristotle's ethic that makes mere difference of belief a morally relevant factor in the determination of the mean. A society that believes that wealth is largely the result of individual initiative might believe that contributing 2 percent of one's income to charity is a worthy goal. A different society that believes that wealth is largely a gift of nature might believe that giving only 2 percent of one's income to the less fortunate would be unthinkably tight. Though these two cultures have different beliefs, that in itself, Aristotle would say, is morally irrelevant in determining the morally proper mean.

While the caloric needs of different people vary, what those needs are is not determined by majority opinion, but by the nutritional expert. So too, the mean in moral matters is not determined by popular opinion. Rather, it is determined by a rational principle, and that rational principle is in turn determined by the man or woman of practical wisdom.

The healthy individual has a desire for exercise and proper food. Regardless of what others say, his judgment in these matters is correct because of the obvious effect of his wholesome practices on his own life. According to Aristotle, one ought to reason similarly in ethical matters. Just as people know a physically healthy person when they see one, they also know a happy person when they see one. Of course, when Aristotle says a person is happy, he is not referring to an emotional state of someone who wins the state lottery. Such a condition is the result of external conditions and not the result of voluntary action. Rather, when he speaks of the happy woman, he is speaking of the woman who is happy largely as a result of what she has herself done. Her happiness is stable because it "feeds on itself" in the same way that a winning college basketball team continues winning year after year because it is able to recruit the best high school players. Similarly, a happy person is one who succeeds in the worthy things that she sets out to do. When she does, she receives satisfaction, and this in turn encourages her to set out to accomplish other worthwhile goals. That causes the cycle to repeat. It is this sort of person that Aristotle says determines the "rational principle" in moral matters.

POETICS

First published: *De poetica*, c. 334-323 B.C.E. (English translation, 1705)
Type of work: Literary criticism

This is a work of theoretical and practical literary criticism, especially with regard to tragic drama.

Aristotle's *Poetics*, though short, has been widely influential outside philosophical circles. Yet it is doubtful that it can be fully appreciated outside Aristotle's philosophical system as a whole.

Central to all Aristotle's philosophy is the claim that nothing can be understood apart from its end or purpose (telos). Not surprisingly, the *Poetics* seeks to discover the end or purpose of all the poetic arts, and especially of tragic drama. Understood generally, the goal of poetry is to provide pleasure of a particular kind. The *Metaphysics* begins, "All men desire to know by nature," and the *Nicomachean Ethics* repeatedly says that the satisfaction of natural desires is the greatest source of lasting pleasure. The *Poetics* combines these two with the idea of imitation. All people by nature enjoy a good imitation (that is, a picture or drama) because they enjoy learning, and imitations help them to learn.

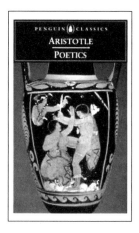

Of particular interest to Aristotle is the pleasure derived from tragic drama, namely, the kind of pleasure that comes from the purging or cleansing (catharsis) of the emotions of fear and pity. Though the emotions of fear and pity are not to be completely eliminated, excessive amounts of these emotions are not characteristic of a flourishing individual. Vicariously experiencing fear and pity in a good tragedy cleanses the soul of ill humors.

Though there are many elements of a good tragedy, the most important, according to Aristotle, is the plot. The centrality of plot once again follows from central doctrines of the *Metaphysics* and the *Nichomachean Ethics*. In the former, Aristotle argues that all knowledge is knowledge of universals; in the latter, he states that it is through their own proper activity that humans discover fulfillment.

For a plot to work, it must be both complete and coherent. That means that it must constitute a whole with a beginning, middle, and end, and that the sequence of events must exhibit some sort of necessity. A good dramatic plot is unlike history. History has no beginning, middle, and end, and thus it lacks completeness. Furthermore, it lacks coherence because many events in history happen by accident. In a good dramatic plot, however, everything happens for a reason. This difference makes tragedy philosophically more interesting than history. Tragedy focuses on universal causes and effects and thus provides a kind of knowledge that history, which largely comprises accidental happenings, cannot.

SUMMARY

Aristotle's philosophy is not flawless. Even his most vigorous contemporary defenders are quick to point out his errors—for example, his belief that some people are slaves by nature and that women are naturally inferior to men. Many people today would argue that such pronouncements, made with complete confidence at the time, prove that what is true for one person may not be true for someone else. Rather than being patronized by those who would excuse his errors by relativizing truth, however, Aristotle would much prefer simply to be refuted with good arguments and careful observations. These are much more central to his philosophy than any particular conclusions that he reached on any particular topic.

Ric S. Machuga

BIBLIOGRAPHY

By the Author

NONFICTION:
The works listed here date to Aristotle's Second Athenian Period (335-323 B.C.E.), except for *Zoology*, which is dated to the Middle Period (348-336 B.C.E.):
Analytica posterioria, n.d. (*Posterior Analytics*, 1812)
Analytica priora, n.d. (*Prior Analytics*, 1812)
Aporemata Homerika, n.d. (*Homeric Problems*, 1812)
Aristotelous peri geneseōs kai phthoras, n.d. (*Meteoroligica*, 1812)
De anima, n.d. (*On the Soul*, 1812)
De poetica, c. 334-323 B.C.E. (*Poetics*, 1705)
Ethica Nicomachea, n.d. (*Nicomachean Ethics*, 1797)
Metaphysica, n.d. (*Metaphysics*, 1801)
Organon, n.d. (English translation, 1812)
Physica, n.d. (*Physics*, 1812)
Politica, n.d. (*Politics*, 1598)
Technē rhetorikēs, n.d. (*Rhetoric*, 1686)
Tōn peri ta zōia historiōn, n.d. (*Zoology*, 1812)
Topica, n.d. (*Topics*, 1812)

About the Author
Ackrill, J. L. *Aristotle the Philosopher.* New York: Oxford University Press, 1981.

DISCUSSION TOPICS

- Aristotle was Plato's student. Is it surprising that he disagreed with Plato in so many ways?

- Aristotle believed that all things are teleologically ordered. Does it seem that we believe in teleological explanations today?

- Aristotle taught in a "gymnasium" called a "lyceum." What do these two nouns mean today? Do these institutions have anything important in common?

- Educated people today find fault with many of Aristotle's ideas. Why do they find a need to study this man nearly two and a half millennia after his time?

- Explain in your own words Aristotle's argument about what causes happiness.

- In Aristotle's *Poetics*, he considers that tragedy brings about the catharsis of the emotions of fear and pity. What makes "catharsis" an effective metaphor?

Adler, Mortimer J. *Aristotle for Everybody*. New York: Macmillan, 1978.

Barnes, Jonathan. *Aristotle*. New York: Oxford University Press, 1982.

Gerson, Lloyd P. *Aristotle and Other Platonists*. Ithaca, N.Y.: Cornell University Press, 2005.

Grene, Marjorie. *A Portrait of Aristotle*. Chicago: University of Chicago Press, 1963.

Konstan, David. *The Emotions of the Ancient Greeks: Studies in Aristotle and Classical Literature*. Toronto: University of Toronto Press, 2006.

Kraut, Richard. *Aristotle: Political Philosophy*. New York: Oxford University Press, 2002.

Shields, Christopher. *Aristotle*. New York: Routledge, 2007.

Veatch, Henry V. *Aristotle: A Contemporary Appreciation*. Bloomington: Indiana University Press, 1974.

MATTHEW ARNOLD

Born: Laleham, England
    December 24, 1822
Died: Dingle Bank, Liverpool, England
    April 15, 1888

Arnold is preceded only by Alfred, Lord Tennyson, and Robert Browning as an important poet of Victorian England. His critical essays, emphasizing the role of literature in the amelioration of society, had a profound influence on twentieth century literary criticism.

Library of Congress

BIOGRAPHY

Matthew Arnold was born in Laleham, England, on Christmas Eve, 1822, the second child and first son of Dr. Thomas and Mary Penrose Arnold. In December, 1827, Thomas Arnold was elected headmaster of Rugby School, where the family began residence in August, 1828. It was the beginning of an auspicious career for Thomas Arnold, who would distinguish himself as the foremost educational reformer of the English public school. In addition to a general enhancing of academic quality, Dr. Arnold's reforms for his new students specifically included the introduction of modern languages and mathematics into the center of the curriculum, the fostering of a higher moral tone, and the inculcation of a greater sense of social responsibility among the privileged Rugby students toward the lower classes of English society. Dr. Arnold's social and intellectual perspective had a pronounced influence on his son, who, although he did not begin studies at the school until 1837, lived at the center of the Rugby community.

Enrolled at Winchester School in August, 1836, for one year of preparatory study, Matthew Arnold subsequently entered Rugby in late summer of the following year. He was a desultory student, frequently late for class and poorly disciplined in his approach to his studies. It was an attitude that caused considerable concern for his parents, particularly his father, whose kindly but intimidating presence was clearly part of the problem. By 1840, his final year, Matthew had done much to redeem

himself. He won the school poetry prize for "Alaric at Rome" and was successful in competition for a coveted scholarship to Balliol College, Oxford.

At Oxford, Arnold deepened his friendship with the poet Arthur Hugh Clough, who had been a friend of the family and a student of Dr. Arnold at Rugby. They frequently disagreed on many of the leading issues of the day, but Clough, until his death in 1861, proved a steady and important influence. Their relationship is commemorated in Arnold's elegiac poem "Thyrsis," in which the poet reviews and reexamines the ideals, both spiritual and literary, that the two young men shared as Oxford undergraduates.

Although something of a dandy, much preoccupied with fashionable dress and demeanor in his undergraduate years, Arnold managed to take a second-class honors degree in 1844 and, a year earlier, to win the coveted Newdigate Prize for his poem "Cromwell." In the following year, he won a fellowship to Oriel College, Oxford, which at the time was the storm center of the Tractarian controversy—the celebrated Oxford Movement—led by John Henry Newman. Along with Clough and Thomas Arnold, Newman was the third contemporary figure to have an important effect on the direction of Matthew Arnold's thinking. Although Arnold was now a firm adherent to the theological liberalism of his father, he nonetheless approved of many of the more salient points of Newman's conservative position, particularly the need to intensify religious feeling and sincere spiritual conviction and to counteract ambiguous religious liberalism.

In 1846, Arnold traveled in France and Switzerland, and he returned to England the following year to settle into gentlemanly employment as private secretary to Henry Petty-Fitzmaurice, marquis of Lansdowne. It was an undemanding position, offering considerable time for writing new poems and editing others. Between 1849, when he published his first collection, titled *The Strayed Reveller, and Other Poems*, and 1855, the year that marked the appearance of *Poems, Second Series*, Arnold submitted to the world most of the poetry that he would write in his lifetime. In 1857, he was elected to the chair of professor of poetry at Oxford, a position that he held for the next ten years. His tenure at Oxford culminated in the publication of his final volume of verse, *New Poems* (1867), which contained the remarkable "Dover Beach." The position paid a small stipend and required only three lectures per year. Following a government appointment as inspector of schools in April, 1851, a position that he would hold simultaneously with the Oxford Poetry Chair, Arnold married Frances Lucy Wightman, daughter of Sir William Wightman, a judge of the Court of the Queen's Bench.

From the 1860's through the 1880's, Arnold's creative efforts shifted from poetry to prose. He concentrated on literary and social criticism and gave considerable attention to the improvement of public education in England. Much was to be learned, he believed, from a study of educational methods and procedures on the Continent. Toward this end, he toured in his official capacity the schools of France, Germany, and Switzerland and published his findings and observations in a series of essays: "The Popular Education of France"; "A French Eton"; and "Schools and Universities on the Continent." His literary criticism of the 1860's, particularly extended essays such as *On Translating Homer* (1861), *Essays in Criticism* (1865), and *On the Study of Celtic Literature* (1867), largely comprised lectures delivered at Oxford. *Culture and Anarchy*, his extended study of the ills of a materialistic, contemporary society, appeared in 1869. From October, 1883, until March, 1884, Arnold traveled in the United States and gave a series of lectures, which were published in 1885 under the title *Discourses in America*. In 1886, he made a second trip across the Atlantic to give additional lectures but returned to England that same spring, resigned his inspectorship, and effectively retired from public life. On April 15, 1888, Arnold died in Liverpool of a sudden heart attack. He was sixty-five.

ANALYSIS

Although great poetry should transcend the limits of time, Arnold's poetry must be read in the context of his turbulent age if it is to be understood fully. He is a post-Romantic coming into full conflict with the British empire at the height of its expansion and industrialization. The effects of this conflict comprise the themes of his poetry: spiritual stasis and enervation, humankind as an alien figure in the cosmos, the absence in the modern world of spiritual and intellectual values, values largely subsumed by industrial growth and materialism. Arnold's poetry, however, offers no solutions, nor is it particularly articulate on the exact nature of the dilemma. Among the English poets, his mentors were William Wordsworth and John Keats, both of whom influenced his style and aesthetic perspective. His best work, exemplified in poems such as "Dover Beach," "The Scholar-Gipsy," "Rugby Chapel," "Thyrsis," "The Buried Life," and "Stanzas from the Grande Chartreuse," is outwardly calm and lucid, containing the same sincerity, dignity, and restraint that characterized his Romantic predecessors. It also pursues the same elusive serenity. It is a pursuit inherently complicated by the resulting tension between the temporal or "real" world of distracting sensory phenomena and the transcendent realm of the ideal.

Three social factors in the "real" world were largely responsible for the intellectual and spiritual division that Arnold felt so keenly and expressed in his poetry. Charles Darwin's *On the Origin of Species by Means of Natural Selection* (1859) brought new, scientific knowledge to the forefront, all but eclipsing the established authority of traditional beliefs. The Oxford Tractarians, following the lead of Newman, sought to bring English Christianity back to a more universal, conservative view, away from the "broad church" liberalism that, for many, threatened to become the secular bulwark of British Protestantism. The "Chartist" reform movements of 1832 and 1867, with recurrent calls for the expansion of suffrage, entailed a broadening of democracy that, for many, threatened the traditional stability of government guided by aristocratic values. In literature, the long popular Romanticism of novels by writers such as Sir Walter Scott, who extolled chivalric heroism, legend, and tradition, was gradually forced to give way before the realism of Charles Dickens, William Makepeace Thackeray, George Eliot, and Anthony Trollope.

To all of this Arnold responded with a poetry of general lament for the divisions of modern life, for the sense of fragmentation that now pervaded the age. In "Stanzas from the Grand Chartreuse," Arnold describes himself as "Wandering between two worlds, one dead,/ The other powerless to be born." The "dead" world of innocence and natural joy was the freely received gift of nature, a world in which emotion and intellect remained counterpoised on either side of a spiritual fulcrum. "We had not lost our balance then," he has the title character say in "Empedocles on Etna," "nor grown/ Thought's slaves, and dead to every natural joy." The world into which the poet is "powerless to be born" is a world of serenity characterized by unity and order. Its genesis lies in the pursuit of "culture," which Arnold defines in *Culture and Anarchy* as "a study of perfection, harmonious and general perfection which consists in *becoming* something rather than *having* something." The optimistic quest for perfection is an objective with which Arnold deals extensively in his critical essays, but in his poetry he remains immersed in melancholy. What little hope there is for the future lies in a vaguely intuitive recognition of truth, which is stimulated by those elements of culture that awaken humankind and enrich the human condition.

In his prose, Arnold examines the issue of England's societal malaise in even greater detail. Having all but abandoned poetry after the 1850's, he devoted the last thirty years of his life to prose criticism. His essays addressed four general areas: education, religion, literature, and society. His writings on education dealt with contemporary issues and are of interest primarily to historians concerned with curricula in English and Continental schools of the nineteenth century. On religious issues, Arnold produced four books: *St. Paul and Protestantism, with an Introduction on Puritanism and the Church of England* (1870), *Literature and Dogma* (1873), *God and the Bible* (1875), and *Last Essays on Church and Religion* (1877). All are responses to the various religious controversies that swept through Great Britain in the latter half of the nineteenth century,

which were spurred in part by the ferment caused by the Oxford Movement and the evolution theories of Darwin.

Of much greater interest to posterity than Arnold's writings on education and religion have been his critical examinations of society. In *Culture and Anarchy* and *Friendship's Garland* (1871), he expresses his growing concern with the suspect values of a Victorian middle class. This middle class, which he termed "Philistines," was, in Arnold's view, puritanical, inflexible, and selfishly individualistic. In short, it was wholly unprepared to confront the problems inherent in the combination of a growing industrialism, an expanding population, and an increasing and clamorous call for widespread democracy. To transform society, it would be necessary to eliminate the classes that divide it, an objective to be achieved through universal education. Central to this universal education would be the promotion and encouragement of culture.

The pursuit of culture is understandably at the center of his literary criticism. Nowhere is this more apparent than in his *Essays in Criticism*. It is in the first essay, "The Function of Criticism at the Present Time," that Arnold offers most succinctly his critical manifesto. Criticism, as he defines it, is "a disinterested endeavor to learn and propagate the best that is known and thought in the world." It is this awareness, he further states—which the critic discerns and shares with the reader who pursues culture—that will nourish humanity "in growth toward perfection."

"DOVER BEACH"

First published: 1867 (collected in *New Poems*, 1867)
Type of work: Poem

As traditional beliefs are undermined by nineteenth century "progress," even the aesthetic verities of Love and Beauty are overwhelmed by doubt and despair.

"Dover Beach" is a brief, dramatic monologue generally recognized as Arnold's best—and most widely known—poem. It begins with an opening stanza that is indisputably one of the finest examples of lyric poetry in the English language. The topography of the nocturnal setting is a combination of hushed tranquillity and rich sensory detail. It is the world as it appears to the innocent eye gazing on nature: peaceful, harmonious, suffused with quiet joy. The beacon light on the coast of Calais, the moon on the calm evening waters of the channel, and the sweet scent of the night air all suggest a hushed and gentle world of silent beauty. The final line of the stanza, however, introduces a discordant note, as the perpetual movement of the waves suggests to the speaker not serenity but "the eternal note of sadness."

The melancholy strain induces in the second stanza an image in the mind of the speaker: Sopho-

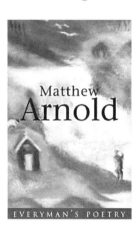

cles, the Greek tragedian, creator of *Oidipous Tyrannos* (c. 429 B.C.E.; *Oedipus Tyrannus,* 1715) and *Antigone* (441 B.C.E.; *Antigone,* 1729) standing in the darkness by the Aegean Sea more than two thousand years ago. The ancient master of tragedy hears in the eternal flux of the waves the same dark note, "the turbid ebb and flow/ Of human misery." Thus, the speaker, like Sophocles before him, perceives life as tragedy; suffering and misery are inextricable elements of existence. Beauty, joy, and calm are ephemeral and illusory. The speaker's pessimistic perspective on the human condition, expressed in stanzas two, three, and four, undercuts and effectively negates the positive, tranquil beauty of the opening stanza; the reality subsumes the misleading appearance. In the third stanza, Arnold introduces the metaphor of the "Sea of Faith," the once abundant tide in the affairs of humanity that has slowly withdrawn from the modern world. Darwinism and Tractarianism in Arnold's nineteenth century England brought science into full and successful conflict with religion. "Its melancholy, long withdrawing roar" suggested to Arnold the death throes of the Christian era. The Sophoclean tragic

awareness of fate and painful existence had for centuries been displaced by the pure and simple faith of the Christian era, a temporary compensation promising respite from an existence that is ultimately tragic.

The fourth and final stanza of "Dover Beach" is extremely pessimistic. Its grim view of reality, its negativity, its underlying desperate anguish are in marked contrast to the joy and innocent beauty of the first stanza. Love, the poet suggests, is the one final truth, the last fragile human resource. Yet here, as the world is swallowed by darkness, it promises only momentary solace, not joy or salvation for the world. The world, according to the speaker, "seems/ To lie before us like a land of dreams," offering at least an appearance that seems "So various, so beautiful, so new," but it is deceptive, a world of wishful thinking. It is shadow without substance, offering neither comfort nor consolation. In this harsh existence, there is "neither joy, nor love, nor light,/ Nor certitude, nor peace, nor help for pain."

Arnold closes the poem with the famous lines that suggest the very nadir of human existence; few poems have equaled its concise, sensitive note of poignant despair. Humanity stands on the brink of chaos, surrounded in encroaching darkness by destructive forces and unable to distinguish friend from foe. The concluding image of the night battle suggests quite clearly the mood of the times among those who shared Arnold's intellectual temperament, and it is one with which they were quite familiar. Thucydides' *Historia tou Peloponnesiacou polemou* (431-404 B.C.E.; *History of the Peloponnesian War,* 1550) describes the night battle of Epipolae between the Athenians and the Syracusans. Dr. Thomas Arnold, Matthew's father, had published a three-volume translation of Thucydides' text in 1835; it was a favorite text at Rugby. Another ancillary source was John Henry Newman, who, in 1843, published a sermon, "Faith and Reason, Contrasted as Habits of Mind," in which he alludes to the growing religious controversy of the time, describing it as "a sort of night battle, where each fights for himself, and friend and foe stand together."

"THE SCHOLAR-GIPSY"

First published: 1853 (collected in *Poems*, 1853)
Type of work: Poem

An Oxford student resists the increasingly materialistic emphasis of traditional university education, seeking instead inherent truths in the beauty of nature and in intellectual idealism.

For the central premise of "The Scholar-Gipsy," Arnold draws upon a legend of the area surrounding the university city of Oxford. The legend tells of a wandering scholar who rejects the material world of the academy to pursue a vague and idealistic objective. Arnold uses this story as a metaphor for his indictment of a world that is obsessed with materialism and individual advancement but is largely indifferent to culture and the pursuit of the ideal. In 1844, Arnold had purchased a copy of Joseph Glanvill's *The Vanity of Dogmatizing* (1661). Glanvill's book recounts the tale of an Oxford student who, with neither patron nor independent financial means, was forced to discontinue his studies and to make his way in the world. Increasing poverty leads him to join a band of roving gypsies, with whom he begins a new and very different education. From these vagabonds, who roam at will following rules and traditions that in no way answer to the world of "preferment," he discovers the power of the imagination stimulated by nature. Gradually he rejects the world of humanity and materialism. As the years become centuries, the increasingly mysterious scholar-gipsy continues his quest, a solitary figure always seen at a distance, carefully avoiding any contact with the corruption of modern civilization.

"The Scholar-Gipsy," with its bucolic setting, has many of the characteristics of the traditional pastoral elegy. These characteristics are clearly apparent in the first stanza. As, for example, John Milton does in "Lycidas" (1638), Arnold addresses the young poet, casting him in the role of the shepherd who has abandoned the "quest," the pursuit of the ideal, to go forth into the world of political change and turmoil. In 1848, Arnold's close friend, the poet Arthur Hugh Clough, left his post at Oxford in order to become more directly involved in the revolutionary social changes that were then restructuring all of European society. In the first stanza, the speaker calls upon the poet-shepherd to return, when the turmoil has settled, from leading the "sheep" of restless England. Return, he importunes the shepherd-poet, when "the fields are still,/ And the tired men and dogs all gone to rest." The speaker (Arnold) and his fellow poet will remain behind, in the natural setting, away from the din of the city. The third stanza is almost purely descriptive. It presents the speaker reclining amid the beauties of nature, which Arnold renders with true Keatsian sensuosity.

In the fourth through the seventh stanzas, Arnold relates the legend of the scholar-gipsy, drawn from "Glanvill's book." The secrets of the "gipsy-crew," the ultimate truth to be drawn from nature, remain elusive, the wandering scholar tells some former fellow students whom he encounters in the early days of his quest. When he has fully discovered that truth, he will impart it to the world; the skill to do that, however, "needs heaven-sent moments," divine or noumenal inspiration that lies beyond the knowledge and intellectual skills that one might develop at Oxford.

After the encounter with his former fellow students, the scholar-gipsy becomes a ghostly figure. He is occasionally sighted, but as one draws close he disappears, becoming, as the years pass, more an enduring illusion than a tangible reality. Gradually, only those who inhabit the country, those associated with the outdoors and the rural life beyond the civilization of cities, see the scholar-gipsy.

In stanzas 10 through 13, Arnold traces the scholar's gradual integration with nature through the passage of seasons. The country people who encounter him at different times and in different places throughout the year remark upon his "figure spare," his "dark vague eyes and soft abstracted air." The scholar, on his singular mission, has forsaken the world of humanity and is gradually fading from humanity into the countryside that he inhabits. He seeks an ultimate truth that lies somewhere beyond the confines of university walls and the politics of modern society.

The scholar-gipsy's quest is presumably the same pursuit of the ideal that was so much a part of Romantic poetry in the early nineteenth century. While John Keats and William Wordsworth had a very pronounced influence on Arnold, the influence of Percy Bysshe Shelley and Samuel Taylor Coleridge should not be discounted. An important common element among these early nineteenth century poets was the concept of the division between the real and the ideal, between the tangible world of sensory phenomena and the noumenal, "ideal" world. The Romantic poet seeks to transcend the distractions, the demands, the profound limitations of the world "enclosed by the senses five," as William Blake termed it. He or she seeks to encounter, through the powers of the imagination, the world of synthesis, harmony, unity, and ultimate truth in a world that is also beyond the limits of time and space. It is that transcendent condition, according to Wordsworth, when the poet is able to see "into the life of things," to perceive what Wordsworth calls "the hour/ Of Splendour in the grass, of glory in the flower." For the Romantics, the quest was continually interrupted by the demands of the material world. The poet inevitably plummets back to reality, falling, as Shelley said, "upon the thorns of life."

Arnold's pantheistic wandering scholar pursues the moment of Romantic inspiration and insight, waiting, as Arnold says in stanzas 12 and 18, for "the spark from heaven." In stanzas 15 through 17, Arnold praises the scholar-gipsy's single-mindedness, his pursuit of "*one* aim, *one* business, *one* desire." The legend has become the symbol for fidelity in the pursuit of a higher reality. The scholar-gipsy has not felt "the lapse of hours" but has become, like Keats's Grecian urn, "exempt from age."

In stanzas 20 through 23, Arnold characteristically gives full vent to his pessimistic view of the modern world. Life is "the long unhappy dream," one that individuals "wish . . . would end." Similar to the mood at the conclusion of "Dover Beach," this poem sees the mid-nineteenth century as a time when individuals "waive all claim to bliss, and try to bear." The aversion intensifies to the point where modern life is a contagious miasma, a veritable plague. The scholar-gipsy is right to avoid all social contact, to avoid "this strange disease of modern life/ With its sick hurry, its divided aims." He is warned to fly "our feverish contact," to save himself from the "infection of our mental strife." Not to heed this warning would mean that "thy glad perennial youth would fade,/ Fade, and grow old at last, and die like ours."

"The Scholar-Gipsy" effectively blends the Ro-

mantic sensibility of the late eighteenth and early nineteenth centuries with the Victorian reaction to the rapid growth of industrialism. It is one of Arnold's many poetic commentaries on a time when the "machinery" of the mind threatened the annihilation of both the soul and the artistically creative imagination.

CULTURE AND ANARCHY

First published: 1869
Type of work: Essays

As widespread democratic reform follows technological progress and a growing emphasis on materialism, Arnold addresses the potential danger in the loss of traditional cultural values.

Culture and Anarchy, Arnold's masterpiece of social criticism, was the direct result of the turbulence leading up to the second reform bill of 1867. The book comprises six essays, which were published serially in the *Cornhill Magazine* between 1867 and 1868 under the title "Anarchy and Authority." At the time that Arnold was preparing these essays, anarchy in English society was very much in ascendancy. From 1866 through 1868, there were a variety of social disturbances: riots in Trafalgar Square, Fenian and trade union demonstrations, anti-Catholic rallies, and suffrage protests in the industrial cities of Birmingham and Wolverhampton.

There was a rising tide of anarchy in England, and for Arnold it seemed that the entire country was in a general state of decline. Chief among the faults leading to this condition was an appalling smugness and insularity in the English character. As Arnold saw it, the typical English citizen was narrow and circumspect in the appreciation of the higher qualities and virtues of life. The cities in which he or she lived and worked expressed no beauty in their architecture; they were sprawling, industrial conglomerations. People were smug and cantankerous, loud in their assertions of individualism and personal liberty and adamant in their dislike of centralized authority, church or state. They were, however, obsequious in their respect for size and numbers in the burgeoning British empire and in their acquiescence to the "machinery" of its ever-expanding bureaucracies. Arnold's "typical" English citizen worshiped the materialism that generally determined societal values, but in religious matters he or she emphasized the "protest" in Protestantism and generally abhorred centralized spiritual authority. The English citizen was puritanical and inflexible.

The character of the Victorian middle class, in Arnold's view, was woefully inadequate to meet the problems it was currently facing, problems such as a rapidly increasing population, the unchecked rise of industrialism, and the continued spread of democracy. In addition to the middle class, which Arnold identified as "Philistines," there were two other classes to be considered: the aristocracy, identifed as the "Barbarians," and the lower classes, termed the "Populace." All in varying degrees were in need of culture, which Arnold defines as the pursuit "of our total perfection by means of getting to know, on all matters that most concern us, the best which has been thought and said in the world." Culture is the means by which to achieve the general amelioration of English society and the general improvement of English character.

Central to the universal apprehending of "culture" are two elements that Arnold terms "Sweetness and Light," the title of the first chapter of *Culture and Anarchy*. These terms, borrowed from Jonathan Swift's "The Battle of the Books," are rather vague and abstract, but they suggest an analogy to beauty and truth as they are used by Keats in "Ode on a Grecian Urn." "Sweetness," as Arnold uses it, is the apprehension and appreciation of beauty, the aesthetic dimension in human nature; "Light" is intelligence, brightened by open-mindedness, a full awareness of humankind's past, and a concomitant capacity to enjoy and appreciate the best works of art, literature, history, and philosophy. They are linked entities, aided in their development within the individual by curiosity and disinterestedness, the essential impartiality that dispels prejudice.

The successful infusing of Sweetness and Light into the individual and general character also requires a coalescence and a balance of two elements that are integral to the history of Western civilization. Arnold terms these elements "Hebraism and Hellenism," the title of chapter 4. Hebraism is the intellectual and spiritual heritage that is the basis of a Semitic and subsequently Judeo-Christian tradition. It is from the Hebraic influence that Western civilization derives a sense of duty, a work ethic, the value of self-control, and the importance of obedience to the will of God. This value of obedience is enforced by a strictness of conscience, a sense of imperfection rooted in a shared stigma of Original Sin. Hellenism, on the other hand, is an Indo-European rather than a Semitic heritage. Its worldview is largely the opposite of Hebraism. From Hellenism, humanity derives an open "philosophic" perspective, an ardor for thinking and knowing. It is characterized by a striving for an unclouded clarity of mind, an unimpeded play of thought among the questions of the universal order. It stresses a clear intelligence and a seeking to apprehend. In opposition to Hebraic strictness of conscience, Hellenism emphasizes a spontaneity of consciousness, a total intellectual and spiritual freedom in the pursuit of perfection. An inevitable collision, Arnold explains, occurred in the Renaissance, the period when Europe rediscovered Hellenic ideas and perspective. The result of this proximity and subsequent collision was the Hebraistic view that identified Hellenism with "moral indifference and lax rule of conduct." Hellenism, from the Hebraic perspective, was associated with a loss of spiritual balance, a weakening of moral fiber. The reaction solidified into Puritanism, bringing an end, in the seventeenth century, to the Renaissance in Europe.

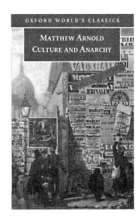

Arnold's leaning in *Culture and Anarchy* is clearly toward Hellenism and away from the dominance of Hebraism; but he recognizes that the path to perfection, the theme and purpose of the book, is to be found in a coalescence of the two, an extracting of the best of both elements. Neither Hebraism nor Hellenism is a law of human development, but each is a contribution. He advocates a reintroduction of Hellenism to counteract the static inflexibility of Puritan influence in the English character. What is needed is a Hebraic-Hellenic central authority, the establishment of the state as an organ of society's collective "best" self. This authority would be guided by Sweetness and Light and "right reason," Western civilization's Hellenic legacy. Such a central authority would check self-serving, solipsistic individualism, encourage culture, and eventually transform society.

It is important to recognize that Arnold does not offer *Culture and Anarchy* as an active blueprint for the reconstruction of society. He was, in the strictest sense of the word, apolitical. The book is intended as a spiritual awakening, but spiritual in a far broader context than a strict adherence to the "machinery" of organized religion. There is a better self that lies within collective humanity that Arnold urges his readers to rediscover. To avert anarchy, humankind must pursue culture, must keep as an essential objective the achieving of perfection. In such pursuit alone lies the eventual salvation of humanity and society.

SUMMARY

Matthew Arnold's poetry and prose criticism are devoted to the themes of spiritual stasis, the absence of intellectual values, and the general diminution of humankind in the face of growing materialism and expanding industrialism. Arnold was not a social scientist and made no pretense of offering practical solutions to real problems. His responses are high-minded at best, often vague and idealistic to a fault. In a world that is fragmented and divided among many creeds and material objectives, he laments both the loss of and the failure to reachieve a world of serenity characterized by unity, order, right reason, and culture. In addition to his accomplishments in poetry, Arnold's remarkable achievements lie in the standards set by his literary criticism and in his perceptive analysis of England's social malaise in the latter half of the nineteenth century.

Richard Keenan

BIBLIOGRAPHY

By the Author

POETRY:
The Strayed Reveller, and Other Poems, 1849
Empedocles on Etna, and Other Poems, 1852
Poems, 1853
Poems, Second Series, 1855
New Poems, 1867
Poems, Collected Edition, 1869
Poetical Works of Matthew Arnold, 1890

DRAMA:
Merope: A Tragedy, pb. 1858

NONFICTION:
Preface to Poems, 1853
On Translating Homer, 1861
Essays in Criticism, 1865
On the Study of Celtic Literature, 1867
Culture and Anarchy, 1869
St. Paul and Protestantism, with an Introduction on Puritanism and the Church of England, 1870
Friendship's Garland, 1871
Literature and Dogma, 1873
God and the Bible, 1875
Last Essays on Church and Religion, 1877
Discourses in America, 1885

DISCUSSION TOPICS

- Thomas Arnold, Matthew Arnold's father, was considered a fine schoolmaster. What might have caused the son to have so much trouble at Rugby School?

- Discuss the appropriateness of the phrase "eternal note of sadness" in "Dover Beach."

- What makes "Dover Beach" relevant today?

- Are there "scholar-gipsies" today? If so, who are they?

- Was Arnold too negative in his views of Victorian Englishmen in his *Culture and Anarchy*?

- Do Arnold's works show him to be an elitist? If so, is there any value in his elitism?

- Evaluate Arnold's statement that perfection is a matter of becoming, rather than having, something.

Civilization in the United States, 1888
Essays in Criticism, Second Series, 1888
The Complete Prose Works of Matthew Arnold, 1960-1976 (Robert Henry Super, editor)

MISCELLANEOUS:
The Works of Matthew Arnold, 1903-1904 (15 volumes)

About the Author

Faverty, Frederic E. *Matthew Arnold, the Ethnologist.* Evanston, Ill.: Northwestern University Press, 1951.
Grob, Alan. *A Longing Like Despair: Arnold's Poetry of Pessimism.* Newark: University of Delaware Press, 2002.
Hamilton, Ian. *A Gift Imprisoned: The Poetic Life of Matthew Arnold.* London: Bloomsbury, 1998.
Honan, Park. *Matthew Arnold: A Life.* Cambridge, Mass.: Harvard University Press, 1983.
Johnson, Wendell Stacy. *The Voices of Matthew Arnold: An Essay in Criticism.* New Haven, Conn.: Yale University Press, 1961.
McCarthy, Patrick J. *Matthew Arnold and the Three Classes.* New York: Columbia University Press, 1964.
Murray, Nicholas. *A Life of Matthew Arnold.* London: Hodder & Stoughton, 1996.
Pratt, Linda Ray. *Matthew Arnold Revisited.* New York: Twayne, 2000.
Raleigh, John Henry. *Matthew Arnold and American Culture.* Berkeley: University of California Press, 1957.
Trilling, Lionel. *Matthew Arnold.* New York: Columbia University Press, 1949.

MARGARET ATWOOD

Born: Ottawa, Ontario, Canada
November 18, 1939

Canadian writer Atwood, who has focused on political themes such as feminism, censorship, and human rights, has achieved an international reputation as a novelist and poet.

© Washington Post; reprinted by permission of
the D.C. Public Library

BIOGRAPHY

Margaret Eleanor Atwood was born in Ottawa, Ontario, on November 18, 1939, the daughter of Carl and Margaret Killam Atwood. In 1945, her father, who was an entomologist specializing in forest insects, moved the family to northern Ontario, the bush country that is featured in many of her works. Though the family returned a year later to Toronto, Atwood in later years would often visit the rural parts of Ontario and Quebec and spend a considerable amount of time at her country place. She attended high school in Toronto, and when she began writing at the age of sixteen, she had the encouragement of her high school teachers and one of her aunts. While attending Victoria College of the University of Toronto, she read Robert Graves's *The White Goddess: A Historical Grammar of Poetic Myth* (1948), which she claims "terrified" her because, while women are at the center of Graves's poetic theory, they are inspirations, not creators, and are alternately loving and destructive. This view of women writers did not daunt the aspiring writer, who has since helped to "correct" Graves's view and has focused much of her writing on women's issues and the themes of identity and empowerment.

After graduating from Victoria College in 1961, the same year that *Double Persephone* (1961), her first volume of poems, appeared, she attended Radcliffe College, receiving her M.A. degree in 1962. She has also done graduate work at Harvard University, but she remains resolutely Canadian, and the United States and its citizens are frequent targets in her writing. After her graduate work, she worked briefly as a cashier, waitress, market research writer, and screenwriter, and her work experiences have been transformed into her fiction. Atwood's work is often autobiographical. She also taught at Canadian universities during the 1960's and later in her career served as writer-in-residence at such diverse institutions as the University of Alabama, Macquarie University in Australia, and Cambridge University.

In the 1960's, Atwood primarily wrote poetry, although she did write an unpublished novel before *The Edible Woman* (1969) appeared. In *Double Persephone* and *The Circle Game* (1966), Atwood establishes the images and themes that characterize all of her poetry. She uses images of drowning, journeys, mirrors, and dreams to develop the contrast between life and art and between humanity's creation and nature. In *The Edible Woman*, Atwood develops the theme of gender politics by focusing on the plight of an engaged young woman threatened by her consuming fiancé, who wishes to fix and limit her role. Although gender pervades Atwood's poems, her novel provides an early statement about women's rights and has established her as a somewhat reluctant spokesperson for feminism.

In the 1970's, despite the publication of several volumes of verse, Atwood's most significant works were novels. *Surfacing* (1972) is widely regarded as one of her best novels and has been the subject of numerous critical studies. As a story of a woman who returns to the past to heal herself, the novel uses myth and psychology as it explores the issues of language, family, love, and survival—issues that also appear in her poems. *Lady Oracle* (1976) and *Life Before Man* (1979) also concern relationships, but they are notable for their humor, which is by turns satiric, parodic, wry, or broadly comic. Atwood's other prose achievement in the 1970's is her controversial *Survival: A Thematic Guide to Canadian Literature* (1972), a literary history of Canada that stresses the negative image of the victim in Canadian literature.

By the 1980's, Atwood's reputation was established; she had written several novels, more than a dozen volumes of poetry, a collection of short stories, and a literary history. In addition, she had written poems, received numerous prizes, and become active in the Canadian Civil Liberties Association. In short, she had become, for the non-Canadian reading public, the most notable contemporary Canadian writer. During the 1980's, she published several more volumes of poetry, but her literary reputation during this decade rests on her fiction, notably *Bodily Harm* (1981), *The Handmaid's Tale* (1985), and *Cat's Eye* (1988). While in *Bodily Harm* Atwood uses the *Surfacing* pattern of alienation and subsequent healing through a journey into a more primitive, natural state, *The Handmaid's Tale* is a radical break from the earlier novels. It is a dystopian science-fiction tale set in a future America, but it is also fiction that derives from Atwood's reading of contemporary totalitarian tendencies. With *Cat's Eye*, Atwood returns to her Canadian materials and themes as her painter-narrator journeys back to Toronto to rediscover herself. Some critics see the narrator as Atwood and regard the novel as her midlife assessment, a guide to her own work, and as one of her best novels.

Since 1980, Atwood has also published two major volumes of short fiction: *Bluebeard's Egg* (1983) and *Wilderness Tips* (1991). Her short stories, which resemble her novels in content and style, are themselves of such quality as to assure her a prominent place in Canadian literature. Atwood has become, however, more than a successful writer; she is a spokesperson for her causes and, as an editor, an arbiter of what constitutes good literature. In her work for PEN International and Amnesty International, she has vigorously opposed censorship, and, as an editor of volumes containing the "best" American and Canadian short stories, she

has shaped the standard of good writing. The many writing awards she has received attest to her literary reputation, and her Woman of the Year award from *Ms.* magazine (1986) reflects her political importance to the feminist cause. As editor, writer, critic, and political activist, she is without peer in North America. Her awards include the Governor-General's Award, Canada's highest literary honor, for *The Circle Game* in 1966; the Bess Hokin Prize for poetry in 1974; the Canadian Booksellers Association Award in 1977; and the Radcliffe Medal in 1980.

In 1993, the year she published *The Robber Bride*, she was named Chevalier dans l'Ordre des Arts et des Lettres by the French government. Her novel *Alias Grace* (1996), a fictionalized version of historical events, won the Giller Prize. Two years later she published another volume of poetry and received an honorary doctorate from Oxford University. Cambridge University (2001), Harvard University (2004), and the Université de la Sorbonne Nouvelle (2005) also awarded her honorary doctorates. Her *Oryx and Crake*, a dystopian novel about genetic engineering, was published in 2003. In 2004 she was honored at the University of Ottawa by having an international symposium, Margaret Atwood: The Open Eye, conducted on her work. *The Tent*, a collection of previously published poems, essays, and short pieces, plus her own accompanying drawings, appeared in 2006.

ANALYSIS

Although she has written poetry, short stories, screenplays, and novels, Atwood's work is remarkably consistent in content and theme. In spite of her international reputation, she remains resolutely Canadian in residence and in temperament. She has become more political and certainly is a writer of ideas, but, with the notable exceptions of *The Handmaid's Tale* and *Oryx and Crake*, she is not propagandistic and heavy-handed. Regardless of the genres in which she writes, Atwood is analytical, almost anatomical, in her dissection of characters and relationships. For the most part, hers is a landscape of the mind, although her writing is also rooted in geography, whether it be Toronto, the Canadian wilderness, or futuristic settings. In many ways, *Survival*, her literary criticism of Canadian literature, is a key not only to Canadian writers but also to Atwood herself. Much of her work is related to survival in an environment or relationship at once native and alien because, while ostensibly familiar, such contexts are also foreign to a character's sense of wholeness. For the most part, her characters live defensively, creating superficial, ordered lives that enable them to live in modern urban settings, but there is another, darker side that they repress. That darker, irrational self is associated with the wilderness, with nature, in an almost Emersonian sense.

In her novels, Atwood's protagonists are usually young women who have roots in the wilderness but who currently live in an arid urban (or suburban) environment characterized by materialism, consumerism, exploitation, and male chauvinism, all of which are seen as products of the United States. The landscapes, both literal and symbolic, of her novels shape the lives of her female characters, who are both women and products, objects in a society where everything is for sale. Ill at ease, uncomfortable, half-aware of their problems, they leave a society that ironically seems safe, despite the psychological and spiritual threats that it poses, for another environment, a more primitive and dangerous one; it is, nevertheless, a healing environment, because the journey, in Atwood's novels, is mythical, psychological, and literal. In *Surfacing*, the protagonist travels to a wilderness island; in *Bodily Harm*, she goes to the Caribbean. In both cases, the new environment seems alien or foreign, but in the new environments the characters confront the realities that they had repressed and emerge or "surface" as re-created people. The healing process is spiritual, usually related to a culture seen as more primitive. In *Surfacing*, the Native American culture aids the heroine.

Part of the healing process concerns regaining control of one's body and one's language. In *Edible Woman*, the protagonist sends her lover a woman-shaped cake as a substitute for herself; in *Surfacing*, the narrator uses her lover to replace the baby she had aborted; and in *The Handmaid's Tale*, Offred flees her role as breeder. In the novels, Atwood equates language with power, and the protagonist must articulate her feelings in gender-bound language. For example, in *Surfacing*, language erodes as the narrator returns to the primitive, irrational side of her nature. By "reporting" their experiences, her protagonists gain power and expose the ruling culture.

In her fiction, Atwood uses language as a poet would; she uses puns ("Offred" is "of Fred," but also "off red" with many meanings in *The Handmaid's Tale*), images (particularly water), and recurrent motifs. Moreover, she is aware, and hence suspicious, of the limits of language, of the problem of narration and voice. Her *Murder in the Dark: Short Fictions and Prose Poems* (1983) explores the issue of writing and the relationship between writer and reader (in 2002 she addressed the nature of writing in her *Negotiating with the Dead: A Writer on Writing*), but it also reflects the ease with which she moves from poetry to short fiction and blurs the distinction between the two genres. In fact, her short stories, as a group, are poetic in the way that she uses images and experiments with form to explore human relationships.

Atwood's poetry also concerns human relationships that are played out against geographical and psychological landscapes. Her early poetry volume *The Circle Game* establishes the garrison mentality of adults under emotional siege; they construct abstract patterns or maps that appropriate reality and keep others at a safe distance. The volume also develops the images of water and drowning suggestive of the descent into one's repressed self, of mirrors that entrap those more concerned with image than reality, and of violence that characterizes human relationships. In *Power Politics* (1971) she makes explicit the themes developed in *The Circle Game*; the myth of romantic love is exposed as a sham. Love is a power struggle in which partners victimize, exploit, and consume (as in *The Edible Woman*) each other. The "Circe/Mud" poems of *You Are Happy* (1974) reinforce the idea of exploited women, who are shaped, like clay, to suit their lovers.

The feminist politics of *Power Politics* and *You Are Happy* become more global in *Two-Headed Poems* (1978) and in *True Stories* (1981). In "Two-Headed Poems," Atwood uses two speakers to explore Canadian complicity in the "Americanization" process, and in *True Stories*, she attacks national "circle games" that enable Canadians to shield themselves from the harsh realities of international famine, violence, and terrorism. Atwood's poetry, like her fiction, has become increasingly political, but in neither form has she abandoned literature for propaganda. She remains committed to form and to experiments with narrative and language; she also has the ability, despite the seriousness of content, to use humor, ranging from puns to irony, to convey her vision of human relationships.

SURFACING

First published: 1972
Type of work: Novel

In her search for her missing father, the narrator retreats to the literal and psychological wilderness of northern Quebec, where she reexamines her life and symbolically re-creates herself.

Surfacing, Atwood's second novel, recapitulates many of the themes and images from both her poems and *The Edible Woman* (1969), her first novel. In both novels, for example, a young woman finally rebels against a technological society that would mold and shape her life and then experiences a psychological breakdown before emerging as a survivor with an integrated or whole personality. *Surfacing*, however, is a richer, denser novel because the journey that the unnamed narrator undertakes is literal, psychological, and mythical; the novel is further complicated by the unreliable narrator, who not only acknowledges fictionalizing her story but also must use the very rational language that she comes to distrust because it is the language of the Americanized culture that she rejects.

In the first part of the novel, the unnamed narrator (her lack of a name suggests a lack of real identity and implies that she does not belong in her culture) leaves the city and travels to the Canadian wilderness to find her missing father, who is perhaps dead. Her companions are David, a would-be cinematographer; Anna, his passive doll/girlfriend; and Joe, the narrator's shaggy lover and a frustrated potter. As they travel north, the narrator suggests that "either the three of them are in the wrong place or I am" and calls her "home ground" a "foreign country." When she later adds, "I don't know the way any more," it seems clear that she has become alienated from her parents (she also did not attend her mother's funeral) and from her past. She also is alienated from "them," the companions whom she comes to see as exploitive

"Americans" with the technology, pollution, and violence that slowly creep northward. As she narrates the story, she mentions her husband and a child, as well as a drowned brother. The brother, however, is not dead; he "surfaced," foreshadowing her own surfacing. The husband and child are also part of her fiction; she aborted the baby she conceived with her married lover, and that abortion, cutting her off from nature, still haunts her. She is an incomplete person, a point that Atwood makes by having her mention that Anna thought she was a twin; later, the narrator states, "I must have been all right then; but after that I'd allowed myself to be cut in two," obliquely referring to the abortion.

The narrator returns to the divided self at the beginning of part 2 and maintains that the language that divided the body and the head is "wrong," that she is "translating badly, a dialect problem." Atwood's concern with the limitations of language continues throughout the novel and reflects the growing distrust of the rational and the embracing of less conscious, more instructive modes of knowing. What the narrator comes to know is that David and Anna are in a mutually destructive relationship, which David attempts to capture on film, thereby defining Anna as object rather than person. The narrator, who had believed that she and David were similar in their lack of love, comes to understand that he is incapable of surfacing or becoming real: "He was infested, garbled, and I couldn't help him; it would take such time to heal, unearth him, scrape him down to where he was true." (This understanding occurs in part 3.) David is an exploiter, like the "Americans,"—ironically, real Canadians, who shot a heron "to prove they could do it," who wish to develop her father's island property, and who want to flood the area. In

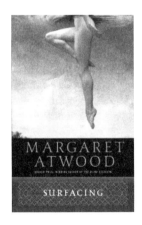

fact, part of David's problem is that, despite his clichéd attacks on the Americans, he has himself become "Americanized."

As time passes, the narrator discovers her father's drawings and her mother's scrapbook, two guides that lead her to the cliff where she hopes to find the Native American paintings and clues about her father's fate. When she dives, she finds instead "a dark oval trailing limbs," a vision that makes her confront the truth about her abortion. Since she describes the vision as a "chalice, an evil grail," the narrator's vision or epiphany becomes the answer, the end of the mythical quest or journey, although she cannot yet interpret it correctly. The vision, however, does radically alter her, setting her apart from her companions, who have "turned against the gods" and yet would persecute her for "heresy." "It was time for me to choose sides," she writes, but her choice is seen ironically as "inhuman." Part 2 concludes with her decision to immerse herself "in the other language," the language not associated with the dominant culture.

Part 3 of the novel begins with the narrator being impregnated by Joe, who has already been described as more "animal" than David or Anna and hence is the appropriate father foreshadowed in her childish picture of the moon-mother and horned man. While their union might reinforce the stereotypical gender roles that she has rejected, the narrator's description of their coupling is devoid of feeling; he is only a means of restoring the "two halves" separated by her complicity in the abortion: "I can feel my lost child surfacing within me, forgiving me." She then unwinds the film, symbolically denying David and Joe the power to capture their vision of reality and freeing Anna from her passive celluloid image, though Anna remains trapped in her compact, which shapes her appearance and life to the masculine will. The narrator hides when the others leave, turns the entrapping mirror to the wall, discards her wedding ring and clothes, leaves the cabin, and enters her parents' world. Language breaks down as she breaks "down" and then "through"; she sees both parents, who then return to nature, one as a jay, the other as a fish. When she wakes the next morning, the ghosts have been exorcised and she is free. At the end of the novel, she states that the most important thing is "to refuse to be a victim," but she must decide whether or not to go back with Joe. If she does, her description of him as "half-formed" implies that she, not he, will be the creator and shaper.

THE HANDMAID'S TALE

First published: 1985
Type of work: Novel

In a postnuclear war society governed by repressive, puritanical men, a young woman recounts on tape her survival and escape.

Set in the near future, a time just prior to the year 2000, *The Handmaid's Tale* is science fiction but also an indictment of the present, since Atwood's future is the reader's present. It is an atypical Atwood novel, her only novel not rooted in Canada and the only one to be so blatantly propagandistic. In it, she fulfills the promise of her narrator protagonist in *Lady Oracle* (1976): "I won't write any more Costume Gothics. . . . But maybe I'll try some science fiction." Atwood prefers the term "speculative fiction" because of the blending of future and present and maintains that all the events in the novel have a "corresponding reality, either in contemporary conditions or historical fact." Since the novel is set in Cambridge, Massachusetts, Atwood also indicts the American culture, which contains the "corresponding reality."

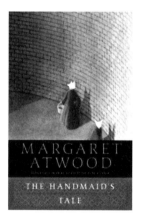

The novel begins with a quotation from the book of Genesis about a barren Rachel encouraging her husband Jacob to have children by her maid, Bilhah. In the aftermath of nuclear war, a new North American republic called Gilead (another biblical reference to fertility) attempts to correct a declining birthrate, caused by nuclear radiation and pollutants, by relegating fertile women to the role of Bilhah-like Handmaids, the breeders of society. (In fact, all Gilead women are assigned to one of eight roles, each distinguished by its own uniform.) In such a patriarchal society where religion, state, and military are combined, women's identities are controlled by men. Offred, the narrator, has lost her real name; she is "of Fred," in reference to the commander whom she services in a perverse, impersonal sexual coupling with his wife, Serena Joy, at the head of the bed. At the beginning of the novel, Offred recounts her training under the aunts—also a perverse parody of the training that nuns and sisters undergo; Offred's uniform, though red, resembles a nun's habit.

Despite her indoctrination, Offred chafes under the repressive regime, and, when her commander gives her access to his library, a male preserve—reading is dangerous for women—she becomes even more rebellious. She meets Moira, an old friend, at a brothel where the males circumvent their own repressive sexual roles and discovers that there is a revolutionary organization named Mayday, which suggests fertility and anarchy. Her rebellion is fueled by her illegal affair with Nick, the chauffeur, who restores her identity (she tells him her real name), liberates her sexually, and ultimately aids in her escape via the Underground Femaleroad, reflecting, through its parody of the slave underground railroad, the slavish position of women in Gilead.

Offred survives to tell her tale, not in traditional epistolary form but in tapes that have been edited by scholars in the year 2195. Atwood's account of the tapes, similar to traditional accounts about finding ancient manuscripts, is appended as "Historical Notes on *The Handmaid's Tale*" to the text of the novel, but, in suggesting that two centuries have not altered female/male relationships, the notes continue the novel's indictment of current culture. In keeping with utopian tradition, Atwood's site for the scholarly proceedings is the University of Denay, Nunavit (or the university of deny, none of it). Atwood's wry denial of the validity of the proceedings calls into question the male editing of female discourse; Professors Pieixoto and Wade have arranged "the blocks of speech in the order in which they appeared to go." Since Offred frequently alludes to the problem of articulating her feelings and experiences, the professors' presumptuous efforts are open to question.

While the proceedings are chaired by a woman, Professor Maryann Crescent Moon (perhaps a criticism of academic tokenism), the keynote speaker is a man, Professor Pieixoto, whose comments hardly represent an improvement over current male chauvinism. In his opening remarks, he alludes to "enjoying" Crescent Moon, "the Arctic

Chair." His further comments about the title of the book (the "tale"/"tail" being a deliberate pun by his male colleague) and his joke about the "Underground Frail-road" reveal the same chauvinistic condescension that characterizes current academic discourse. His unwillingness to pass moral judgments on the Gileadean society, because such judgments would be "culture-specific," reflects not scientific objectivity, which he already has violated by his editing, but his moral bankruptcy.

The Handmaid's Tale does survive, however, despite the male editing, as a "report" on the present/future; similarly, in *Bodily Harm*, the radicalized protagonist becomes a "subversive," who vows to "report" on the repressive society. The novel, like *Brave New World* (1932) and *Nineteen Eighty-Four* (1949), serves as an anatomy, an indictment, and a warning about current society. Among Atwood's targets are religious fanaticism, nuclear energy, environmental waste, and antifeminist practices. Like other utopian novels, however, *The Handmaid's Tale* is weakened by its political agenda, which creates one-dimensional characters and somewhat implausible events; the propaganda, however, also gives the novel its power, relevance, and appeal. Because of its popularity, it was adapted to film in 1990.

"THE CIRCLE GAME"

First published: 1964 (collected in *The Circle Game*, 1966)
Type of work: Poem

The speaker explores the emotional barriers that children and adults erect to remain separate and alienated.

The title poem of Atwood's *The Circle Game* (1966) develops the circle motif that pervades her poetry and represents the patterned, structured world that both controls and shelters individuals who seek and fear freedom from conformity. The seven-part poem juxtaposes the children's world and the adult world but suggests that childhood circle games, ostensibly so innocent, provide a training ground for the adult circle games that promote estrangement and emotional isolation. In the first part of the poem, the children play ring-around-a-rosy; but despite the surface appearance of unity, each child is separate, "singing, but not to each other," without joy in an unconscious "tranced moving." As they continue going in circles, their eyes are so "fixed on the empty moving spaces just in front of them" that they ignore nature with its grass, trees, and lake. For them, the "whole point" is simply "going round and round," a process without purpose or "point." In the second part, the couple plays its own circle games as the lover remains apart, emotionally isolated despite sharing a room and a bed with the speaker. Like the children, his attention is focused elsewhere, not on the immediate and the real, but on the people behind the walls. The bed is "losing its focus," as he is concerned with other "empty/ moving spaces" at a distance or with himself, "his own reflection." The speaker concludes that there is always "someone in the next room" that will enable him to erect barriers between them.

Part 3 moves from the isolation of part 1 to an abstract defensiveness that unconsciously enforces that isolation. The innocent sand castles on the beach are comprised of "trenches," "sand moats," and "a lake-enclosed island/ with no bridges," which the speaker sees as a "last attempt" to establish a "refuge human/ and secure from the reach/ of whatever walks along/ (sword hearted)/ these night beaches." Since the speaker has earlier equated "sword hearted" with the adult world, she implies that the adult world poses the real or imagined threat. Protection from "the reach" becomes the metaphor for the lover's unwillingness to have her "reach him" in part 4 (part 2 described her as "groping" for him). The lover's fortifications are more subtle verbal and nonverbal games ("the witticisms/ of touch") that enable him to keep her at a "certain distance" through the intellect that abstracts and depersonalizes reality. As the lover has been a "tracer of maps," which are themselves the abstraction of physical reality, he is now "tracing" her "like a country's boundary" in a perverse parody of John Donne's map imagery in his Metaphysical love poetry. For the lover, she becomes part of the map of the room, which is thus not real but abstract, and she is "here and yet not here," here only in the abstract as she is "transfixed/ by your eyes'! cold blue thumbtacks," an image that suggests distance, control, and violence.

The last three parts of the poem draw together

the children's world and that of the adults. In part 5, the speaker observes the contrast between the children's imaginative perception of violence (the guns and cannons of the fort/museum) and the adult perception of the domestication of that violence as the "elaborate defences" are shifted first to the glass cases of the museum and then, metaphorically, to their own relationship. The defenses become the "orphan game" of part 6, in which the lover prefers to be "alone" but is simultaneously attracted and repulsed by the family games in which parents "play" their roles. Metaphorically, he is on the outside looking in, observing but separated by the window barrier. In the last part of the poem, it is "summer again," itself a circle of the seasons, and the children's outside circle games are again mirrored by the adult's inside circle games. The earlier images—the "observations," the noises in the next room, the maps, the "obsolete fort"—resurface as the couple are neither "joined nor separate." The speaker, "a spineless woman in/ a cage of bones" (another image of entrapment), wants to break the circle, to erase the maps, to break the glass cases, to free herself from his "prisoning rhythms." The speaker recognizes and articulates the problem, but she cannot free herself of the circles.

"TWO-HEADED POEMS"

First published: 1978 (collected in *Two-Headed Poems*, 1978)
Type of work: Poem

Two speakers conduct a "duet" about the complex love-hate relationship between Canada and the United States.

The title poem of *Two-Headed Poems* is, according to the speaker, "not a debate/ but a duet/ with two deaf singers." In fact, the poem concerns the problems of being a Canadian neighbor to a world power whose corrupt values are expressed in the "duet." Like the Siamese twins, described as "joined head to head, and still alive," the United States and Canada are awkwardly joined: "The heads speak sometimes singly, sometimes/ together, sometimes alternately within a poem." At times, it is clear which country speaks, but not always, for the two countries do share, however reluctantly, some characteristics. The leaders of both countries are criticized, though the leader who "is a monster/ sewn from dead soldiers" is an American president of the Vietnam era, a recurrent motif in the poem. Yet Atwood is as concerned about language as she is with actions, the nonverbal gestures. One "head" asks, "Whose language/ is this anyway?" The corruption of Canadian English, itself a political act, stems from the passive nature of a people content to be Americanized, to shut down "the family business" that was "too small anyway/ to be, as they say, viable." The Canadians whose identity comes from "down there" in the United States are associated with "nouns," but they are also hostile (the candy hearts become "snipers") and impatient to act on their own:

> Our dreams though
> are of freedom, a hunger
> for verbs, a song
> which rises double, gliding beside us
> over all these rivers, borders,
> over ice and clouds.

The Canadian head calls for action to complete the sentence by combining with nouns, and the resultant language should not be a political statement, but a celebratory song, a "double" that transcends borders. The dreams of freedom are, however, only futile dreams, and the closing images are of being "mute" and of "two deaf singers." Communication between the two "heads" is, by definition, impossible, and Atwood clearly implies that the American/ Canadian coupling that impedes both countries is an aberration of nature.

ALIAS GRACE

First published: 1996
Type of work: Novel

Atwood creates a fictionalized account of the life of Grace Marks, a nineteenth century Canadian woman who was convicted of killing her employer and his mistress.

Atwood read about Grace Marks, the convicted murderess of her employer Thomas Kinnear and his mistress, Nancy Montgomery, in Susanna Moodie's *Life in the Clearings Versus the Bush* (1853), but she soon realized that Moodie's account was fictionalized. Grace added to the confusion by offering three different versions of the murder; James McDermott, who was hanged for his role in the murders, provided two more versions. Atwood had all this information, plus numerous newspaper accounts, when she wrote *Alias Grace*, to which she added prefatory materials and an "Author's Afterword." Despite the wealth of information, Grace's role in the murders remains, as Atwood put it, "an enigma."

Grace, the first-person narrator, tells two stories in the novel, one a stream-of-consciousness rendering of her thoughts and the other the story she tells Dr. Simon Jordan, a well-meaning psychologist who interviews Grace in prison. Aware of her situation, Grace tells Jordan what she thinks he wants to hear. Jordan, who dreams of establishing his own clinic, is bent on unlocking the "box" (the truth) but admits he does not have the key. He and Grace play a cat-and-mouse game, which she wins. A series of events leads Jordan into an affair with his landlady, who attempts to persuade him to help her murder her husband, who returns unexpectedly; this plot provides an ironic counterpart to the Kinnear and Montgomery murders. Jordan's reminiscences about the servant girls in his parents' home, and his fantasies about prostitutes indicate that he, not Grace, is obsessed with sex. After he rejects his landlady's plan, Jordan flees Canada, returns to his home in the United States, enlists in the Civil War, and then receives a head wound, which conveniently provides him with the amnesia that makes him forget his Canadian experiences.

In addition to the murders and the planned murder, the novel also recounts the sexual exploitation of a woman by a man. Mary Whitney, a friend and confidant of Grace's. Mary is seduced by a wealthy young man, whose parents are Mary's employers. He later rejects the pregnant Mary, whose subsequent death from a botched abortion is hushed up by her employers. Atwood's novel also includes marriages in addition to the one between Jordan and Faith Cartwright, a young woman chosen by Jordan's mother. Lydia, the prison governor's daughter, who has designs on Jordan, is married off to Reverend Verringer after Jordan's flight in order to preserve her reputation. Whether it is the exploitation of servant girls by their masters or the conventions of society that dictate the behavior of upper-class young women, women in this novel are not in charge of their lives.

In addition to the unreliable narrator, a staple of Atwood's fiction, *Alias Grace* contains other familiar elements, many of them gothic: murder, demonic possession, madness, secrets, supernatural elements (including hypnosis), and a fear of women and their power. Atwood uses the epistolary form (letters between Jordan and his dominating mother) and includes a ballad she wrote in a nineteenth century style. All of these elements are used to question not only the nature of truth but also the notion of colonial innocence in English Canada.

ORYX AND CRAKE

First published: 2003
Type of work: Novel

In a dystopian future of unlimited biotechnological progress, a young man and a laboratory-created "people" survive a global disease.

Oryx and Crake also uses an unreliable narrator, the Snowman (his real name was Jimmy), an outcast and survivor of a global disease created by his friend Crake. In this dystopian novel, Snowman recounts what led to the disaster and what is happening in the present. When the novel begins, Snowman is in the present, foraging for food and instructing the Crakers, "people" created by Crake. Crake and Jimmy were childhood friends with different interests: Jimmy was a "word person"; Crake was a "numbers person." Both lived with their parents in the Compound, a gated community of people who work for biotech corporations. After graduation, the friends drifted apart, Crake to the prestigious Watson-Crick Institute and Jimmy to the run-down Martha Graham Academy. The schools reflect the relative importance of the sciences (numbers) and the arts (words).

When they enter the job market, Crake works as a scientist for the biotech companies, and Jimmy becomes not a "wordsmith" but a "wordserf" in ad-

vertising. Eventually, Crake lures Jimmy to Watson-Crick, where Crake shows Jimmy the hybrid animals that the scientists are creating. Jimmy also learns that the scientists, who have cures for the known diseases, are creating new diseases and their cures to continue to make money. Crake's own department is ironically named Paradice, and its work involves creating populations with "ideal" characteristics, such as beauty and docility, because "several world leaders had expressed interest in that." The Crakers, as they come to be called, were programmed not to be racist, aggressive, sexually charged, or religious. Like other animals, they came into heat at regular intervals and urinated to mark their territory, but unlike other animals, they recycled their own excrement. Such "people" would therefore not experience the modern problems of "real" people.

Despite his aversion to modern problems, Crake falls in love, an emotion that leads to possessiveness and violence. Unfortunately, Jimmy is also in love with Oryx, a sexual waif he had seen on television when he was a child. She reappears as Crake's lover, after having been the victim of white slavery and pimps. Jimmy exhibits all the symptoms of romantic love: sleeplessness, jealousy (demanding information about Oryx's sexual past), and possessiveness. Oryx, however, is rooted in the present as the instructor of the Crakers. She also acts as a salesperson for the drugs that Crake's company is manufacturing. The drugs are programmed to cause instantaneous suffering and death, which occurs on a global scale. At Crake's instructions, Jimmy clears Paradice of all other personnel, which leaves him alone as an insulated, protected being. When Crake and Oryx appear at Paradice's door, Jimmy kills them.

Jimmy/Snowman, who believes that he is the sole "human" survivor of the disease Crake has unleashed (Crake had thoughtfully provided him with the antidote), carries on the instruction Oryx had begun. Because of his love/hate relationship with Crake, he provides the Crakers with a mythology that includes Crake as the Creator/God and Oryx as the Earth Mother. He pretends to correspond with Crake through a wristwatch with a blank face, suggesting that he and the Crakers are suspended in time. Eventually, he has to travel from the "pleeblands" back to Paradice to get supplies, but in the course of his journey he recalls past events and keeps uttering random words, almost as if his existence depended upon language. In the present, however, his journey is threatened by the hybrid animals that Crake created. When he returns from Paradice to the Crakers, he discovers that despite Crake's efforts, the Crakers are beginning to gain notions of ambition and hierarchy, notions that will lead to the problems Crake sought to prevent. Snowman also discovers that there are three other human survivors. Armed with a weapon, he tracks them down, but cannot decide what action to take, and the novel ends at "zero hour."

SUMMARY

As novelist, poet, literary critic, editor, and spokesperson for women's rights, Margaret Atwood is an international figure whose ideas and beliefs about consumerism, environmental damage, censorship, militarism, and gender politics pervade her writing. Though most of her work is set in Canada and reflects the survival theme that she claims is distinctly Canadian, her dissection of human relationships transcends national boundaries. She focuses on geographical and emotional landscapes in which her protagonists journey, usually to nature or to the wilderness, in order to shed civilization's influence, confront themselves, rediscover their true identities, and survive. Atwood's style, regardless of the genre, is poetic in that her delight in language is revealed through puns, metaphors, allusions, and ambiguous words and phrases that resonate with meaning. Though there is pessimism and despair in her work, there is also a wry sense of humor that is almost inevitably satiric.

Thomas L. Erskine

BIBLIOGRAPHY

By the Author

LONG FICTION:
The Edible Woman, 1969
Surfacing, 1972
Lady Oracle, 1976
Life Before Man, 1979
Bodily Harm, 1981
The Handmaid's Tale, 1985
Cat's Eye, 1988
The Robber Bride, 1993
Alias Grace, 1996
The Blind Assassin, 2000
Oryx and Crake, 2003
The Penelopiad: The Myth of Penelope and Odysseus, 2005

SHORT FICTION:
Dancing Girls, and Other Stories, 1977
Bluebeard's Egg, 1983
Murder in the Dark: Short Fictions and Prose Poems, 1983
Wilderness Tips, 1991
Good Bones, 1992 (pb. in U.S. as *Good Bones and Simple Murders*, 1994)
Moral Disorder, 2006

POETRY:
Double Persephone, 1961
The Circle Game, 1964 (single poem), 1966 (collection)
Talismans for Children, 1965
Kaleidoscopes Baroque: A Poem, 1965

Expeditions, 1966
Speeches for Dr. Frankenstein, 1966
The Animals in That Country, 1968
What Was in the Garden, 1969
Procedures for Underground, 1970
The Journals of Susanna Moodie, 1970
Power Politics, 1971
You Are Happy, 1974
Selected Poems, 1976
Two-Headed Poems, 1978
True Stories, 1981
Snake Poems, 1983
Interlunar, 1984
Selected Poems II: Poems Selected and New, 1976-1986,
    1987
Selected Poems, 1966-1984, 1990
Poems, 1965-1975, 1991
Poems, 1976-1989, 1992
Morning in the Burned House, 1995
Eating Fire: Selected Poems, 1965-1995, 1998
The Door, 2007

NONFICTION:
Survival: A Thematic Guide to Canadian Literature,
    1972
Second Words: Selected Critical Prose, 1982
*The CanLit Foodbook: From Pen to Palate, a Collection of
    Tasty Literary Fare*, 1987
Margaret Atwood: Conversations, 1990
Deux Sollicitudes: Entretiens, 1996 (with Victor-Lévy
    Beaulieu; *Two Solicitudes: Conversations*, 1998)
Negotiating with the Dead: A Writer on Writing, 2002
Moving Targets: Writing with Intent, 1982-2004, 2004
    (pb. in U.S. as *Writing with Intent: Essays, Reviews,
    Personal Prose, 1983-2005*, 2005)
*Waltzing Again: New and Selected Conversations with
    Margaret Atwood*, 2006 (with others; Earl G.
    Ingersoll, editor)

CHILDREN'S LITERATURE:
Up in the Tree, 1978
Anna's Pet, 1980 (with Joyce Barkhouse)
For the Birds, 1990
Princess Prunella and the Purple Peanut, 1995 (illustrated by Maryann Kowalski)
Rude Ramsay and the Roaring Radishes, 2004 (illustrated by Dusan Petricic)

EDITED TEXT:
The New Oxford Book of Canadian Verse in English, 1982

MISCELLANEOUS:
The Tent, 2006

DISCUSSION TOPICS

- Margaret Atwood's works always seem to involve a journey of some kind—literal, emotional, or both. What initiates the journeys, what impedes them, and how do the journeys end, if they do?

- Often in an effort to improve society, authorities resort to repressive measures. Discuss the motivations, expressed or covert, behind such efforts in Atwood's novels, especially *The Handmaid's Tale* and *Oryx and Crake*.

- Prisons, metaphorical and literal, play a large role in Atwood's works. Discuss the effect of both kinds of prisons on the characters in her works.

- Identity or the obfuscation of identity is a theme in many of Atwood's works, especially her novels. Not only do characters' names change, but they change with their names. Discuss Atwood's use of names and the problem of identifying just who some of her characters are. Why do you think Atwood uses this theme?

- Identify some positive or semipositive male characters in Atwood's fiction. What appear to be their flaws and what do their flaws disclose about the society and the nature of male/female relationships?

- Atwood uses unreliable narrators in many of her novels. To what purpose? How are the narrators related to the nature of truth in her novels?

About the Author

Bloom, Harold, ed. *Margaret Atwood.* New York: Chelsea House, 2000.

Bouson, J. Brooks. *Brutal Choreographies: Oppositional Strategies and Narrative Design in the Novels of Margaret Atwood.* Amherst: University of Massachusetts Press, 1993.

Cooke, Nathalie. *Margaret Atwood: A Biography.* Toronto: ECW Press, 1998.

_____. *Margaret Atwood: A Critical Companion.* Westport, Conn.: Greenwood, 2004.

Cuder, Pilar. *Margaret Atwood: A Beginner's Guide.* London: Hodder & Stoughton, 2003.

Grace, Sherrill E. *Violent Duality: A Study of Margaret Atwood.* Montreal: Véhicule Press, 1980.

Hengen, Shannon. *Margaret Atwood's Power: Mirrors, Reflections, and Images in Select Fiction and Poetry.* Toronto: Second Story Press, 1993.

Howells, Coral Ann, ed. *The Cambridge Companion to Margaret Atwood.* Cambridge, England: Cambridge University Press, 2006.

McCombs, Judith, ed. *Critical Essays on Margaret Atwood.* Boston: G. K. Hall, 1988.

Moss, John, and Tobi Kozakewich, eds. *Margaret Atwood: The Open Eye.* Ottawa, Ont.: University of Ottawa Press, 2006.

Neschik, Reingard, ed. *Margaret Atwood: Works and Impact.* Rochester, N.Y.: Camden House, 2000.

Rao, Eleonora. *Strategies for Identity: The Fiction of Margaret Atwood.* New York: Lang, 1993.

Reynolds, Margaret, and Jonathan Noakes. *Margaret Atwood: The Essential Guide.* London: Vintage, 2002.

Stein, Karen F. *Margaret Atwood.* New York: Twayne, 1999.

Sullivan, Rosemary. *The Red Shoes: Margaret Atwood Starting Out.* Toronto: HarperCollins, 1998.

Wilson, Sharon R. *Margaret Atwood's Fairy-Tale Sexual Politics.* Jackson: University of Mississippi Press, 1993.

W. H. AUDEN

Born: York, England
February 21, 1907
Died: Vienna, Austria
September 29, 1973

Auden's considerable body of work is remarkable for its uniqueness. He employed the poetic forms of a wealth of literary periods, and no other twentieth century poet so successfully blended, and stood apart from, prevailing modernist styles.

© Jill Krementz

BIOGRAPHY

Wystan Hugh Auden (AWD-ehn) was born on February 21, 1907, in York, England. He was the youngest son of George and Constance Auden. His father and mother belonged to a very distinct niche of early twentieth century Edwardian society—that of the politically liberal, scientific intelligensia. He came, nevertheless, from a very devout Anglo-Catholic home, and his early experiences with the Church would remain with him when he returned to it later in life. As a child, he was fascinated by the "magic" of Church of England rites, and this enchantment with the magical and the mystical also remained a lifelong characteristic. Auden's father was a distinguished physician and professor of medicine; his mother was a nurse. By all accounts, his family environment was loving, intelligent, clear-thinking—traits that were foremost in Auden as an adult. He received the standard schooling of an upper-middle-class male child in early twentieth century England. Beginning his education at St. Edmund's preparatory school at eight years of age, he attended Gresham's School at age thirteen.

At first, Auden intended to become a scientist, like his father. He was principally interested in both engineering and biology and planned to become a mining engineer. This career path was soon overtaken by another, however; while he was still at Gresham's, he began to write poetry. His first poem was published when he was seventeen. This early publication foreshadowed the fame that would come to him just a few years later while he was still in college. He entered Oxford in 1925 and very soon afterward had acquired a faithful clique. Those who knew him during his university years remember him as a rising star, someone who would clearly make a name for himself as a poet and thinker. A group of men who would later also be important poets formed around him—Stephen Spender, Cecil Day Lewis, and Louis MacNeice. Spender privately printed the first collection of Auden's poems in 1928, the year that Auden graduated from Oxford.

After graduation, he spend a year abroad, the traditional *Wanderjahr* of upper-class young Englishmen. When his parents asked in which European city he would like to spend his year, Auden surprisingly answered that he wanted to live in Berlin. Germany in the years of the Weimar Republic, before Adolf Hitler came to power, was an exciting place—stimulating, racy, intellectually bold. There, Auden became acquainted with the politically charged plays of Bertolt Brecht and the sexy, witty songs of the Berlin cabarets. He perfected his German during his year abroad, and throughout his life he would be influenced by German literature, both classical and modern.

When he returned to England, he became a schoolmaster, first at Larchfield Academy, in Scotland, then at Downs School, near Malvern, England. At the same time, however, his literary reputation was growing. His *Poems* appeared in 1930, firmly establishing his reputation as the most brilliant of England's younger generation of poets. Perhaps under the influence of Brecht, he had begun writing works that were broadly "dramatic." *Paid on Both Sides: A Charade* (pb. 1930, pr. 1931) reinforced the literary world's opinion of Auden as an important young writer.

Auden's adult life has frequently been divided into four segments, a division suggested by the poet himself in an introduction to his *Collected Shorter Poems, 1930-1944* (1950). The first segment runs from his undergraduate days through 1932, the second comprises the period from 1933 to 1938, and the third extends from 1939 to 1946; the fourth segment began in 1948. The first segment entails the period of his early fame—his notoriety as a brilliant, precocious undergraduate and the publication of his first important poems. This era of Auden's life might also be viewed as his "Freudian period"; in part, he viewed the work of this era as a kind of therapy, giving free play to fantasy and uncovering hidden impulses. Yet even this early poetry shows the social and political awareness that would infuse his poems throughout the 1930's.

By 1933, partly under the influence of Brecht and in reaction to the collapse of his beloved Weimar Republic, Auden became an outspoken critic of the political establishment—his life's second, political, segment. He became increasingly committed to left-wing causes and in 1937 journeyed to Spain as a stretcher-bearer in the struggle of the Loyalist Left against the forces of fascism. He also made use of theater as a way to gain wider public expression of his beliefs; he was a cofounder of the Group Theatre in 1932 and collaborated with Christopher Isherwood, a longtime friend, on several dramatic works. Moreover, he wrote film scripts for the General Post Office film unit, a government-sponsored creative effort that, among other subjects, frequently made films about working-class life in Britain.

Auden traveled widely during the 1930's, not only to Spain but also to Iceland (his family name, as "Audun," is mentioned in the Icelandic sagas), China, and the United States. His experience with the Spanish Loyalist armies had left him disillusioned with the Left, and his fame in England apparently meant little to him by this time. Thus, in 1939, he moved to the United States, marking the third period in his life story. Once again, he be

came a teacher—this time on the university level, as a member of the faculties of the New School for Social Research, the University of Michigan, and Swarthmore, Bennington, Bryn Mawr, and Barnard colleges. During the war years, Auden turned inward; he returned to the Anglo-Catholicism of his youth and wrote several long poems that explore his newly found meditative introspection. The last of these, *The Age of Anxiety* (1947), earned him the Pulitzer Prize in 1948.

During the last period of his life, from 1948 until his death in Vienna on September 29, 1973, Auden divided his time among the United States, Italy, and Austria. Eventually, in 1972, he established residence in Oxford, where he had earlier been named professor of poetry. He continued to write prolifically, although no long poems appeared after 1948. He published two volumes of prose, *The Dyer's Hand, and Other Essays* (1962) and *A Certain World* (1970), translations, and he collaborated on the librettos of several operas.

Many students of Auden's biography are struck by the series of enthusiasms that colored his life. Marxist, Freudian, Anglo-Catholic—a lover of Icelandic sagas, William Shakespeare, and Johann Wolfgang von Goethe—Auden continued until his last years to hold strong beliefs that are often central to his poetry. However, he was also a very private, introspective man. His love lyrics are among the twentieth century's most celebrated. His later Anglo-Catholicism revealed a powerful inward-turning element in his character, and his religious poems are obviously the result of much soul-searching.

ANALYSIS

Having come to fame early, Auden had the close attention of critics throughout his adult life, far longer than most poets. Being in the literary spotlight from young manhood clearly affected his own perspective on his work; in fact, in his later years, he rewrote, abandoned, and cannibalized many of his earlier poems because he felt this youthful work was "untrue." Essentially, he attempted to remake the outlines of his own body of poetry. Another effect of his early fame—or notoriety, as the case may be—was his fairly substantial audience (for a poet). Conscious of this loyal readership, he broadcast his political and social ideas throughout the 1930's. The effort was made in good conscience: He was only attempting to persuade his readers of what he felt was right. Yet perhaps in reaction, as the 1930's drew to an end, Auden withdrew from the spotlight. Having come to literary fame early, he tired of it; having spent nearly a decade fighting for a just society, he turned inward.

That is not to say that Auden's poetry lacked a strong streak of inward-turning from the outset. The early poems often have as their setting a wild, make-believe landscape concocted from a rich variety of sources: Icelandic sagas, Old English poetry, boys' adventure stories, and surreal fantasies that he had found in reading the Austrian neurologist Sigmund Freud. Throughout Auden's poetry, during all four literary states into which he divided his career, his work would have this same curious division between a highly personal mythology and the clear, logical setting forth of an argument. Many readers find the introspective level of Auden's poetry very obscure, although his poems are no more difficult than those of other twentieth century masters such as T. S. Eliot, Ezra Pound, or Wallace Stevens. Throughout his career, Auden was clearly fascinated by dreams and imaginative fantasies, and the drive to express this highly personal inner world contributes to his poetry's thorniness.

At the same time, Auden's poetry consistently presented to the world another outward face. Like any intelligent, sensitive young person, Auden lamented social and political injustice. In response, his work at this time is apocalyptic. The landscape portrayed in his early dramatic work *Paid on Both Sides* is a violent, confused one, populated by vindictive raiding parties armed with up-to-date weaponry and a medieval siege mentality. Critics at the time noted Auden's thorough familiarity with contemporary ideologies such as Marxism and capitalism, Freudianism, sexual freedom, and feminism. His youthful work attempts to employ these schools of thought to diagnose a diseased society, but, most scholars agree, the results are often confusing and amateurish. His short lyric poems, such as "Since You Are Going to Begin Today," remain his most lasting work of this period, a harbinger of the gifted lyric voice that he sustained throughout his career. The lyric poetry is open, candid, heartfelt, showing a young man alive to the world and to himself.

Actually, Auden was typical of many authors during the late 1920's and early 1930's, as writers moved from creating introspective works bound by personal symbolism toward socially committed poems, novels, and stories. The shift was natural: Adolf Hitler, Benito Mussolini, and Joseph Stalin had risen to power during this period, and the world was once again threatened by world war. Economically, too, the international community was entering a severe depression; while smaller nations continued to suffer poverty, the great powers also began to see widespread deprivation. Thus, it was natural for Auden, already politically aware, to strive, through poetry and drama, for a better world. He began consciously to aim his verse at a wide readership, chiefly through the poetic dramas staged by the Group Theatre. The 1930's saw the production of several Auden plays, of which the three most important—*The Dog Beneath the Skin: Or, Where Is Francis?* (pb. 1935, pr. 1936), *The Ascent of F6* (pb. 1936, pr. 1937), and *On the Frontier* (pb., pr. 1938)—were written with close friend Isherwood. Although spoken in verse, these plays were similar to the songs and skits of English music halls and German cabarets and sought to stir a large audience to action.

His poetry of the 1930's breathes fellow feeling, an eager love for humanity, and a conviction that universal harmony was not far away. Yet throughout the decade he continued to write personal poems, often love lyrics contemplating the brevity and fragility of emotions. A celebrated example is "As I Walked out One Evening," which uses the well-worn rhythms and phrases of popular love songs to picture love's uncertainty. Even a poem such as *Spain 1937* (1937), which offers a panorama of the people engaged in civil war, has an introspective side; at the same time as the speaker explores each person's social motivation, he also looks forward to a peaceful future where the participants may rediscover "romantic love." Although it would be inaccurate to say that Auden had been "embittered" by his experience in the Spanish Civil War, by 1939 he had, however, begun to express weariness with the state of the world. He had moved to the United States, and in "September 1, 1939," he sits in "one of the dives" on New York's Fifty-Second Street, watching as the "clever hopes expire/ Of a low dishonest decade." In "The Unknown Citizen," written a few months earlier, his tone is bitterly sarcastic as he describes the faceless, obedient automaton-citizen of the modern state.

In 1940, Auden to an extent put aside his political commitments and embraced religious and purely artistic ones. He returned to the Church of his boyhood, and his Christmas oratorio, *For the Time Being* (pb. 1944, pr. 1959), expresses this spiritual culmination. He also returned to his English literary roots through a careful study of William Shakespeare. The long poem *The Sea and the Mirror* (1944) explores the meaning of Shakespeare's *The Tempest* (pr. 1611, pb. 1623) as a parable of the artist and his creations. Finally, *The Age of Anxiety* investigates the psychic landscape of the postwar years, as Western culture struggled to recover from the traumas of the 1930's and 1940's. These later, longer poems are unquestionably difficult in language and theme, a far cry from the accessible, socially committed verse plays of the preceding decade.

By 1950, Auden was widely recognized as one of the two or three most important poets writing in English. Among his many other honors, he was awarded the Pulitzer Prize in 1948, the Bollingen Prize for Poetry in 1954, and the National Book Award in 1956. The poetry of his later years is brief, highly symbolic, but still recognizably his own—the old concerns with society are there, but filtered through an intensely personal lens. During the 1950's and 1960's, Auden also produced a number of translations from many literatures, including works by Johann Wolfgang von Goethe, Bertolt Brecht, St.-John Perse, and the young Russian poet Andrei Voznesensky.

SPAIN 1937

First published: 1937
Type of work: Poem

> *The Spanish Civil War signals the imminent collapse of the peacetime world—its art, learning, culture—and the ordinary lives of men and women.*

Spain 1937 tells a story that is partly autobiographical. As a sympathizer with the socially progressive forces of the Spanish Loyalists, Auden had gone to Spain to participate in the war as a stretcher-bearer. Once there, he witnessed the viciousness of civil conflict, not only between the opposing armies but also among the Loyalists themselves. He returned to England embittered with politics, especially the European variety, and would soon leave to establish residence in the United States.

Yet the tone of *Spain 1937* is generally elegiac—sad and wistful. In the poem's first six stanzas, Auden recalls the often-glorious history of this peninsular country, surveying its ocean-borne exploration of the world, its expansion of global trade, and its building of cathedrals. In the more recent past, he notes the more obvious "advances" in Hispanic civilization, the engineering of machines and the building of railroads. At the same time, he does not ignore Spain's darker past, such as the "trial of heretics" during the Inquisition. The distant past of discovery and religious feud and more recent signs of progress are erased, however, by the coming conflict: "But today the struggle" overtakes Spain. In stanzas 9 through 11, Auden suggests the causes of war, or at least the condition of the country as war begins. He pictures Spain's impoverished citizens in their "fireless lodgings" as they read the evening news and realize that they have nothing left to lose. Emboldened by the promises of Marxism, the poor invest their hope in the action of history and the forces of change. In response, the forces of reaction, the "military empires," "descend" on the fledgling progressive nation.

Yet Auden avoids portraying the Spanish Civil War as a simple struggle of good against evil. He foretells that this particular conflict will symbolize a greater horror to come. In stanzas 12 through 14, "life" answers the combatants, saying that it is their servant and it will shape itself to fill their desires, whatever these may be. Auden personifies the common life of the Spanish nation—and by implication the nations of the world—as a "bar-companion," willing to go along with anything. According to the personified life, the peoples of Europe propose the building of the "just city" in Spain, a free and equal commonwealth. Life, however, knows that the proposal is based on illusion, a kind of "suicide pact" born of romanticism. Nevertheless, it accepts the people's decision.

Driven by this romantic vision, people from all over flock to the civil war. In Spain itself, they "migrate" to the struggle like birds; in Europe, they rush to war on express trains; others farther away "float" over the oceans. All are drawn to Spain like moths to the flame, which Auden imagines as a giant "arid square" rather "crudely" slapped onto Europe. As people arrive to give their lives to the cause, to the ideology of Loyalist or Rebel, their bodies become the guarantees of their beliefs. Their emotions are now all channeled into warfare, and even their "moments of tenderness blossom/ As the ambulance and the sandbag."

Mirroring the poem's opening stanzas, the last seven stanzas also survey time—in this case, however, the future. Auden imagines the harmless, even slightly silly activities of humankind during peacetime: dog-breeding, bicycle races, or walks by the lake. This sort of "fun" is in desperate contrast to the present, where idealistic young people "explode like bombs" and pleasures are limited to badly rolled cigarettes and quick sex. The result is a debacle of which even the animals are ashamed: They look away from human evil. Meanwhile, the history that the poor hoped would redeem them may or may not turn in their favor. In any case, although history may lament those defeated in the war, it does not have God's power to pardon the evil that people do.

"AS I WALKED OUT ONE EVENING"

First published: 1940 (collected in *Another Time*, 1940)
Type of work: Poem

> *Telling his story in a ballad, the poet overhears a lover's song, which begins traditionally enough with vows of eternal fidelity but soon turns to stranger, less hopeful images.*

Most readers of "As I Walked out One Evening" will quickly notice something familiar about the rhythm of this poem: Auden has chosen to tell this apparently simple story in a simple, traditional poetic form, the ballad. The poem's rhythm and the rhyme strongly echo folk songs, and, in fact, the work's first line is a standard opening phrase in scores of variations on this old English and American love ballad. Yet right from the start, the poet suggests that this poem will not be as conventional

as one may think: As he takes his evening walk among the London crowds, the people seem like a field of wheat—a comparison not likely to be found in the ordinary folk song. In the poem's second stanza, though, the image is once again typical: The poet overhears a lover singing under a railway arch and reproduces the song for us.

In stanza 3, the first stanza of the repeated song, the lover makes the age-old lover's commitment: He (or perhaps she) will remain faithful for eternity, until the impossible comes to pass— "till China and Africa meet," until "the ocean/ Is folded and hung up to dry." Some of the images are whimsical and original; salmon "sing in the street" and the "seven stars go squawking/ like geese about the sky." These curious figures suggest that this lover is not like the usual ballad singer; he seems to have a quirky imagination. In any case, he is unafraid of time because he holds "the first love of the world" in his arms throughout the ages. The lover's song ends, and the poet hears the "whirring" of London's clocks, replying to the lover's grandiose claims about time. "You cannot conquer Time," the clocks warn the lover. The clocks describe a sinister Time, one that lurks in shadows and nightmares and carries cruel justice.

In stanza 8, the clocks portray life as it is actually lived; life, they say, is "leaked away" in worry and "headaches." Time's chief purpose, they stress, is to banish life's springtime pleasures, to disrupt the dance of love. It is better, they counsel, to "plunge your hands" in cold water and wake up to reality. The clocks, who know how time works better than the lover, say that the real image of eternity is the "glacier," whose presence is always near, as near, in fact, as the kitchen cabinets, where it "knocks on the cupboard" door. Real life is grim, the clocks say, and love is, as often as not, merely sex. Love is not a fairy tale. In actual day-to-day existence, the fairy-tale hero, Jack, is actually attracted to the cruel giant, and Jill is nothing more than a prostitute. Take a look in the mirror, the clocks advise the lover, and understand life's sadness.

Strangely, they say, "life remains a blessing," nonetheless, even though human beings eventually find it difficult to bless their existence. True redemption comes from loving one's disreputable neighbor, despite the neighbor's flaws, because both the lover and the neighbor are equally "crooked," equally wounded by time.

The last stanza is left to the poet to speak. By now it is very late, and the lovers have departed. Even the clocks have ceased their "chiming," and he perhaps feels as though time itself has finally stopped. Yet even so, the river continues to run beside him, reminding him of the impersonal passage of the hours.

"MUSÉE DES BEAUX ARTS"

First published: 1939, as "Palais des Beaux Arts" (collected in *Another Time*, 1940)
Type of work: Poem

A painting by an old master of the fall of Icarus sparks an appraisal of its theme by the poet-viewer: These painters knew all about life, especially the role of human suffering.

The much-anthologized "Musée des Beaux Arts," whose main subject is a painting by Bruegel, is itself a small "portrait," a tightly bound image of how people react to the suffering of others. The dramatic situation in the poem is easily imaginable: The poet is visiting an art gallery, the "musée" of the title, and has drawn to a halt in front of *Icarus* by the early Renaissance Flemish painter Pieter Bruegel (the Elder). The speaker has very likely just viewed a series of other paintings by old masters, in which traditional subjects, such as the Crucifixion or a saint's martyrdom, are prominent. *Icarus*, however, gives him pause: After he has studied it for a while, one may imagine, he reveals his thoughts.

Although the painting's theme is drawn from Greek mythology—the flight of Icarus too near the sun and his subsequent fall—the treatment is typical of Bruegel. This early modern painter delighted in the depiction of rural people in real-life settings; many of his works show peasants farming, going to market, or celebrating the harvest. Brue-gel's people are hardworking, not too pretty, and full of life. Renaissance painters, of course, devoted thousands of canvases to imagined scenes from Greek myths, like the one the Flemish artist has chosen for this picture. Ordinarily, however, a painter of this period would have placed Icarus in a restrained, "classical" setting, showing the noble tragedy implicit in the story. The myth relates how the inventor, Daedalus, and his son, Icarus, are imprisoned and escape using two sets of wings constructed by Daedalus of wax and feathers. Icarus, in his joy and pride, flies too near the sun, the wax melts, and he plunges into the sea. Thus, there is an irony implicit in Bruegel's painting; this grand, classical theme is placed in a humble, contemporary setting. Moreover, as Icarus falls into the sea in the background, everyone else continues going about his or her business.

The speaker finds great truth in this contrast between high tragedy and everyday life. As he contemplates the painting, he concludes that the old masters, Renaissance painters such as Bruegel, had a profound knowledge of human experience. The central fact of that experience, the masters show, is life's enormous variety: There are so many people in the world, feeling so many emotions and doing so many things, that moments of great significance pass by unnoticed. In another painting the speaker has seen, for example, the "aged" Magi "reverently, passionately [waiting] for the miraculous birth" of Christ. Yet at the very same time, children are playing nearby, oblivious to the impending Event. In another painting, a holy person is martyred in the foreground while a dog wanders in the background and a horse rubs against a tree.

Similarly, in *Icarus*, life continues while the young man drowns. The fall of Icarus takes place in the background—it is only one event in a very busy canvas. A peasant, for example, continues to plow his field, even though he may have heard Icarus's faint cry. The people on a "delicate" ship think that they may have seen something amazing—a "boy falling out of the sky"—but they are not sure, and, in any case, they have to be on their way. The point of the painting is not that people are cruel or even particularly indifferent. Rather, Bruegel, the speaker says, wants to show how suffering and death, which is understandably center stage in the life of the people to whom these things happen, are really merely trivial episodes in the greater scope of human existence. Is this how things must be? The speaker refrains from saying; his interest is not really in passing judgment on human conduct. Instead, he simply wishes to praise the unerring eye and wise judgment of masterful painters.

THE SEA AND THE MIRROR

First published: 1944
Type of work: Poem

The characters and situations from William Shakespeare's play The Tempest *are used to cast a new light on this drama's themes.*

Beginning where Shakespeare's play ends, *The Sea and the Mirror* exploits the ironic vein implicit in the drama. In the Shakespearean work, the magician Prospero is about to leave his exile on an island in the New World. The old man and his daughter, Miranda, had been cast adrift by his brother, Antonio, and left to die. The castaways reach an island inhabited by Ariel, a fairylike spirit, and Caliban, who is half human, half brute. Years later, King Alonso of Naples and his followers, including Antonio, are shipwrecked by Prospero's magic. His son, Ferdinand, falls in love with Miranda, Caliban plots with other followers to assassinate Prospero, and various other subplots arise. Yet Prospero is reconciled to his brother in the end; Ferdinand and Miranda are married; Ariel, who has been held captive, is freed; and Caliban is left "ruler" of the island.

It is at this point that Auden's long poem commences. The work begins with the play's stage manager addressing unnamed "critics." The manager points out that, although there are reasonable, scientific explanations for many human motives, only art can truly mirror the mystery of life. He suggests in the last stanza of the preface that Shakespeare was a supreme master of this truth.

In the poem's second section, Prospero bids good-bye to his spirit-servant, Ariel. His learning and the arts of magic now seem futile to him as he prepares to leave his solitude. He knows that he will soon return to "earth"; death is near. The aged magician reveals himself as something of a cynic, but he is critical of no one more than himself. He even

forgives the treachery of Antonio. He realizes that his own treatment of Caliban and Ariel, holding them as spiritual slaves, is unforgivable. Still, his mood is thoughtful and even mellow. Although he is happy that he is too old to feel the extremes of romantic love, he can view the love between Miranda and Ferdinand with equanimity.

In the second section, several of the "supporting cast" from the play speak soliloquies, beginning with Antonio. As the ship carrying them moves out to sea, he notes how contented everyone is—the result, he claims, of Prospero's spell. Yet he remains embittered and resists his brother's enchantment. Ferdinand's speech is to Miranda, his bride. He emphasizes his joy and their oneness. In the final italicized stanza—a device that will be repeated at the end of all the speeches to come—Ferdinand asserts his individuality to Prospero while contrasting his own identity with Antonio's. Stephano, the drama's drunken butler, declares his allegiance to his "belly," to things of the flesh. He concludes that his "nature" is "inert," and, like Ferdinand, he cannot know Antonio's kind of solitude. Gonzalo, the king's honest counselor, analyzes his own failure to understand the passions of the other characters. In his final stanza, he acknowledges that at least the power of the word, his "language," is "his own," even though he cannot understand the subtleties of Antonio's interior dialogue. King Alonso addresses his son, Ferdinand. He explains the pitfalls and complexities of rule. His individuality is in his worldly "em-

pire." Two sailors, the Master and the Boatswain, then describe their lives at sea, their homesickness and their simultaneous need to explore. Sebastian and Trinculo, two relatively minor characters, deliver similar speeches. The last short monologue is Miranda's. Prospero's daughter rejoices in her love for Ferdinand and her departure from her father's enchanted island.

Part 3, the poem's longest section, is an address by Caliban to the drama's audience. In Shakespeare's play, Caliban is virtually subhuman; in the world of this drama, he is clearly fitted to be a slave. Yet like many slaves, he revolts and tries to kill his master. Thus, the Shakespearan Caliban is crude, murderous, beastlike. In contrast, Auden's Caliban, as he reveals himself in this soliloquy, is erudite, subtle, even perhaps overly intellectual. He is also inexplicably modern; throughout his monologue are references to the twentieth century, such as fighter pilots or contemporary home furnishings. In fact, Caliban recalls Shakespeare's play as at once a distant part of his own life and a quaint, old-fashioned relic. Nevertheless, he draws the audience's attention to the parallels between his former situation and the modern world's grim conflicts; "whipping," slavery, and torture of the kind that he received at the hands of Prospero have not vanished. Instead, these things have become institutionalized and government sanctioned. Caliban's final message is grim: "There is nothing to say. There never has been."

The poem's final section, a postscript, is spoken by Ariel to Caliban. Now that Prospero, Miranda, and the other alien intruders have left their island, these two strange beings can reveal their true feelings. Ariel announces her love for Caliban and accepts him as he is; she loves him for his flaws, those same flaws that Prospero used as an excuse to enslave him. Now that the play's busy, complex characters are gone, presumably to continue with their mixed motives and subplots, Ariel and Caliban can return to a kind of motiveless paradise until their spirits are mixed in "one evaporating sigh."

SUMMARY

W. H. Auden's work in many ways contradicts the Romantic view that a poem should be an emotional outpouring, a sincere expression of pure subjectivity. Instead, he said, poetry is a "game of knowledge," a clear-eyed way of approaching objective truth.

In his own poems, this truth often adopted a moral or social guise. "Poetry," Auden wrote, "is a way of extending our knowledge of good and evil." Many of his poems are intended to help men and women make good moral choices, even though the way by which the poems do this is not always clear. Nevertheless, the body of Auden's poetry is exemplary for its vivid and strongly felt social conscience. His work also is marked by his fine ear and his instinct for rhythm, structure, and sound. This seamless joining of intelligence and verbal music signals that Auden is one of the master craftsmen of modern poetry.

John Steven Childs

BIBLIOGRAPHY

By the Author

POETRY:
Poems, 1930
The Orators, 1932
Look, Stranger!, 1936 (also known as *On This Island*, 1937)
Letters from Iceland, 1937 (with Louis MacNeice; poetry and prose)
Spain 1937, 1937
Journey to a War, 1939 (with Christopher Isherwood; poetry and prose)
Another Time, 1940
The Double Man, 1941 (also known as *New Year Letter*)
The Sea and the Mirror, 1944
For the Time Being, 1944
The Collected Poetry, 1945
The Age of Anxiety, 1947
Collected Shorter Poems, 1930-1944, 1950
Nones, 1951
The Shield of Achilles, 1955
Homage to Clio, 1960

About the House, 1965
Collected Shorter Poems, 1927-1957, 1966
Collected Longer Poems, 1968
City Without Walls, and Other Poems, 1969
Epistle to a Godson, and Other Poems, 1972
Thank You, Fog, 1974
Collected Poems, 1976 (Edward Mendelson, editor)
Sue, 1977
Selected Poems, 1979 (Mendelson, editor)
Juvenilia: Poems, 1922-1928, 1994 (Katherine Bucknell, editor)

DRAMA:
Paid on Both Sides: A Charade, pb. 1930, pr. 1931
The Dance of Death, pb. 1933, pr. 1934
The Dog Beneath the Skin: Or, Where Is Francis?, pb. 1935, pr. 1936 (with Christopher Isherwood)
The Ascent of F6, pb. 1936, pr. 1937 (with Isherwood)
On the Frontier, pr., pb. 1938 (with Isherwood)
Paul Bunyan, pr. 1941, pb. 1976 (libretto; music by Benjamin Britten)
For the Time Being, pb. 1944, pr. 1959 (oratorio; musical setting by Martin David Levy)
The Rake's Progress, pr., pb. 1951 (libretto; with Chester Kallman; music by Igor Stravinsky)
Delia: Or, A Masque of Night, pb. 1953 (libretto; with Kallman; not set to music)
Elegy for Young Lovers, pr., pb. 1961 (libretto; with Kallman; music by Hans Werner Henze)
The Bassarids, pr., pb. 1966 (libretto; with Kallman; music by Henze)
Love's Labour's Lost, pb. 1972, pr. 1973 (libretto; with Kallman; music by Nicolas Nabokov; adaptation of William Shakespeare's play)
The Entertainment of the Senses, pr. 1974 (libretto; with Kallman; music by John Gardiner)
Plays and Other Dramatic Writings by W. H. Auden, 1928-1938, pb. 1988
W. H. Auden and Chester Kallman: Libretti and Other Dramatic Writings by W. H. Auden, 1939-1973, pb. 1993

NONFICTION:
The Enchafèd Flood, 1950
The Dyer's Hand, and Other Essays, 1962
Selected Essays, 1964
Secondary Worlds, 1969
A Certain World, 1970
Forewords and Afterwords, 1973
Prose and Travel Books in Prose and Verse: Volume I, 1926-1938, 1996 (Edward Mendelson, editor)
Lectures on Shakespeare, 2000 (Arthur Kirsch, editor)
Prose and Travel Books in Prose and Verse: Volume II, 1939-1948, 2002 (Mendelson, editor)

EDITED TEXTS:
The Oxford Book of Light Verse, 1938
The Portable Greek Reader, 1948
Poets of the English Language, 1950 (with Norman Holmes Pearson; 5 volumes)
The Faber Book of Modern American Verse, 1956

DISCUSSION TOPICS

- Determine the characteristics of "anxiety" in the phrase W. H. Auden made famous in the title *The Age of Anxiety*.

- Are Auden's strongly asserted political beliefs and his tendency to inwardness contradictory?

- Show how "As I Walked out One Evening" is not a traditional love poem.

- Why did Auden, much more a student of German culture, focus his attention on Spain at the time of its civil war?

- With respect to "Musée des Beaux Arts," how would you answer the question: "Is this how things must be?"

- Explain whether *The Sea and the Mirror* is or is not an attempt to modernize William Shakespeare's *The Tempest* (pr. 1611, pb. 1623).

Selected Poems of Louis MacNeice, 1964
Nineteenth Century British Minor Poets, 1966
A Choice of Dryden's Verse, 1973

MISCELLANEOUS:

The English Auden: Poems, Essays, and Dramatic Writings, 1927-1939, 1977 (Edward Mendelson, editor)

About the Author

Blair, J. G. *The Poetic Art of W. H. Auden.* Princeton, N.J.: Princeton University Press, 1965.

Emig, Rainer. *W. H. Auden: Towards a Postmodern Poetics.* New York: St. Martin's Press, 1999.

Firchow, Peter Edgerly. *W. H. Auden: Contexts for Poetry.* Newark: University of Delaware Press, 2002.

Jarrell, Randall. *Randall Jarrell on W. H. Auden.* Edited by Stephen Burt with Hannah Brooks-Motl. New York: Columbia University Press, 2005.

Mendelson, Edward. *Later Auden.* New York: Farrar, Straus and Giroux, 1999.

Replogle, J. M. *Auden's Poetry.* Seattle: University of Washington Press, 1971.

Untermeyer, Louis. *Lives of the Poets.* New York: Simon & Schuster, 1959.

Wetzsteon, Rachel. *Influential Ghosts: A Study of Auden's Sources.* New York: Routledge, 2007.

Wright, G. T. W. *W. H. Auden.* New York: Twayne, 1969.

SAINT AUGUSTINE

Born: Thagaste, Numidia (now Souk Akras, Algeria)
      November 13, 354
Died: Hippo Regius, Numidia (now Bone, Algeria)
      August 28, 430

Augustine was one of the Fathers of the Church whose writings played an important role in explaining and developing the concepts of Western Christianity.

BIOGRAPHY

Saint Augustine's *Confessiones* (397-400; *Confessions*, 1620) describe his life to 387, the year he converted to Christianity. Born in a North African province of the Roman Empire, his name in Latin was Aurelius Augustinus. His father, Patricius, a farmer, local official, and a pagan, later converted to Christianity. His mother, Monica, a devout Christian, who was canonized a saint by the Roman Catholic Church, prayed and struggled for her son's conversion. She raised him as a Christian, but following the church practice of the day he was not baptized until adulthood. Augustine began his education in Thagaste, Numidia (now Souk Akras, Algeria), and when he was eleven or twelve, his parents sent him to school in nearby Madauros (now near Mdaourouch, Algeria).

In Madauros, Augustine studied classical languages and literature, as well as music, mathematics, and natural sciences. He rapidly gained eloquence in his native Latin, as well as Punic, a dialect of the ancient Phoenicians. The Roman poet Vergil made a lasting mark on his thought and expression. His immersion, both inside and outside the classroom, into pagan myth and literature, with all its moral and religious ambiguities, caused him to set aside his Christian upbringing, for a while becoming a pagan. He sought pleasure in lust, mischief, and notoriety for his indiscretions.

When Augustine returned to Thagaste in 370, his father Patricius wanted him to pursue rheto-ric—public speaking, the art of writing effective prose, and the study of grammar and logic. His father sent him to the great city of Carthage, near present-day Tunis, Tunisia, to complete his training to become a teacher. A businessman, Romanianus, assisted Patricius in financing Augustine's education in Carthage. At this time, Augustine met a Catholic woman who bore his child, Adeodatus, in 373; he lived with his son and common-law wife for nearly fourteen years.

In Carthage, Augustine studied rhetoric from 371 to 374. He adopted the teachings of Mani, a Persian who declared himself a prophet in 240. Mani taught a conflicting dualism of light and dark, good and evil, which was said to explain all facts, processes, and events. Augustine, trying to find an explanation for the problem of evil, thought Manicheanism a rational alternative to Christianity. Manicheanism accounted for evil by making God's power equal to the power of evil and by making God a material rather than a spiritual being. Augustine also was influenced in his quest for truth by reading Cicero, the Roman orator, statesman, and philosopher.

In 375, Augustine resumed teaching in Thagaste but the following year returned to Carthage. There, he started a school of rhetoric and renewed his association with the Manicheans, although doubting their teachings. In 382, he abandoned Manicheanism.

The next year, Augustine moved to Rome and later to Milan, where he became a professor of rhetoric. With much sorrow, he separated from his common-law wife. He studied the neo-Platonic philosophers Plotinus and Porphyry. Eventually, he learned of Ambrose, the bishop of Milan who would later attain sainthood. Ambrose's writings and sermons, as well as the conversion accounts of others, moved Augustine to rediscover Christianity. In 387, on Easter eve, he and his son were baptized by Ambrose. In 388, Augustine and his son returned to Africa, though his son died later that year.

In Thagaste, Augustine founded a lay monastery, an effort that led to the Rule of Augustine, the basis of several Augustinian religious orders. While visiting the neighboring port city of Hippo, he was called upon by its Catholics to be their priest, but he felt unworthy. He was ordained in 391 and consecrated a bishop in 395. As bishop of Hippo, Augustine defend Christianity from heresy and schism for forty years, formalizing fundamental Church doctrines. His comprehensive and detailed explanation of Christianity—the Gospel of faith, hope, and love—was unparalleled in his time. His constant and courageous actions on behalf of the Church earned him immense influence. He died in Hippo in 430, during a siege by Vandal armies.

Augustine was considered a saint by popular recognition before he was formally canonized by the Roman Catholic Church, instituted between 1000 and 1200. Within a year of his death, he was honored as a teacher by Pope Celestine I, the first of many popes to confer solemn tribute upon him. In 1298, he was proclaimed a doctor of the church, and his feast day is August 28.

ANALYSIS

Saint Augustine belongs to a group of ecclesiastical writers from the Patristic Age, called Fathers of the Church, who wrote from the end of the first century to the close of the eighth century C.E. Augustine's writings involve many spiritual and intellectual subjects and are written in many different forms; no one work conveys all of his views. His writings are theocentric or God-centered, often focusing on God's relation to human beings. For example, in accordance with Genesis 1:26, he asserts that each human being is made in the image of God; each person's equality, freedom, and dignity are bestowed by God and are thus inalienable.

Augustine assumes the existence of God as self-evident because it cannot be proven rationally. Life holds more than what can be shown with absolute certainty. Knowledge of God derives from faith, which, in turn, seeks understanding. Augustine declares that God is omnipotent and has the ability to do anything: God created all things out of nothing and is beyond all things. God exists from all eternity and is infinite. God, then, is outside the scope of all categories of thought, logic, language, number, or perception. In addition, God is all-knowing, all-powerful, all-holy, and all-worthy of full love, adoration, and obedience. God is also provident, guiding the course of history and the course of each individual's life.

The subject of God—a boundless, supernatural mystery—cannot even be glimpsed by the mind without the assent of the will and the heart and without the assistance of God's grace. Faith needs divine authority—the disclosure of Christ found in scripture as illuminated by the Holy Spirit. The vision of truth also requires the humility to learn and the diligence to strive and pray in the face of pain and sorrow. Humble faith attains what presumptuous knowledge cannot. One must possess the love that seeks, that reveals, and that brings confidence in what is revealed.

Augustine describes phases in the soul's enlightenment, echoing 1 Corinthians 13:12 and 2 Corinthians 12: 2-4. The soul will rise from knowledge obtained through the senses, to knowledge obtained through imagination, and to knowledge obtained through spiritual, intelligent intuition, a vision of the immaterial realm of God. The human mind can construct indirect analogies of this realm but cannot understand it by using temporal categories of time, space, and matter. The simplicity of God and the Trinity of Father, Son, and Holy Spirit are transcendent spiritual qualities. God's inner light allows the soul to recognize those qualities. The soul will know what it is seeing, and the knowing will transform the soul. As Augustine indicates in *Confessions*, the soul is the place for dialogue with God, where God's illumination occurs. He anticipates modern philosophers by making the inner life—the capacity to think, doubt, and believe—the starting point for knowledge.

Augustine writes that human beings cannot understand themselves other than through their relationship to God. They are a force directed toward God and will never find fulfillment until they turn to God. Although they have free will, human beings depend upon God, at once eternal and active. In *Confessions*, Augustine demonstrates these concepts through his own experience; in *De civitate Dei* (413-427; *The City of God*, 1610), he demonstrates these ideas through human history.

CONFESSIONS

First published: *Confessiones*, 397-400
    (English translation, 1620)
Type of work: Autobiography

Using literary devices in new ways, Augustine describes how the experiences of his own life led to the assured and transformative love of God.

Augustine wrote *Confessions* when he was in his mid-forties, after he had joined the Church. He writes openly about his experiences, undaunted by those who, remembering his past life, would challenge the sincerity of his convictions. He traces how the power of God's word can give victory over sin, closely following St. Paul's *Epistle to the Romans*.

In titling his book *Confessions*, which he intends to be plural, Augustine drew upon Latin words signifying more than the word "confession." For him, confession means the admission or confession of sin; the profession, demonstration, or conviction of faith; and the praise of God. It also implies the sense of agreement that results when the believer accepts what the Bible says about sin and salvation. Augustine's book registers confession, testimony, or witness in all of these ways.

In composing his *Confessions*, Augustine drew upon Roman and Greek literary forms, including the meditation, a personal and philosophical or spiritual reflection and self-examination, in the manner of the meditation written by Roman Emperor Marcus Aurelius. Augustine also drew upon the dialogues of the Greek philosopher Plato and the Roman dialogues of Cicero.

In addition, Augustine includes qualities of prayer as a direct expression of an individual's heart and mind to God, like David in the Psalms and Christ in the Gospels. He imparts a sense of spontaneous utterance or unstudied outpouring, moving from topic to topic and implying qualities of cross-examination. He depicts faith seeking un-

derstanding, with each having its own role, in harmony with the other. Augustine's address to God proclaims how his confusion and despair were altered into the very means by which he is to see himself clearly for the first time before God and how God's providence protected him.

Augustine puts readers in the position of hearing a soliloquy, a word he may have invented; it involves preestablished terms of conflict regarding characters and events associated with other times and places. Readers participate with Augustine in his questioning, there being no knowledge without it.

Moreover, in *Confessions* Augustine combines features of prose and verse. He uses poetic devices—simile, metaphor, rhythm, and literary vocabulary—to convey concentrated imaginative experience. Still, he writes with a quality of realism, of fidelity to fact, in a style close to everyday speech, as in a letter to a friend—in this instance, to God. As a prose poem, *Confessions* conveys a multitude of meanings, its language permeated by the language of the Bible.

Augustine's blend of literary forms, patterns of thought, feeling, and action, paganism and Christianity, resulted in a new literary category: the spiritual autobiography, an account of the individual's relation to God and how God's word, through Jesus Christ, becomes a living actuality in a believer's heart and mind. *Confessions* declared the importance of the individual soul and its relation to God. In addition, Augustine's book, the first ancient autobiography, includes the first detailed account of childhood. It also is one of the great documents in the study of memory and imagination.

Books 1 and 2 of *Confessions* concern Augustine's life prior to his arrival in Carthage. He describes his infancy and the recurring question of beginnings, his fascination with language, his boyhood, and his conflicting attitudes toward Christian and pagan wisdom and truth. He also describes his school days at Thagaste and Madauros, his adolescence, friendships, faults, and chaotic indirection.

Books 3, 4, and 5 recount his life in Carthage, his brief stay in Thagaste, his return to Carthage, and his years in Rome and Milan. While pursuing worldly ends, he leads the life of a seeker of truth, hoping to grasp it with the force of reason alone, endlessly curious. He studies theological and philosophical aspects of human free will and sin and ways in which the physical order of nature, the science of his day, reveals the spiritual order of God. Although the teachings of Plato and his contemporary followers, the neo-Platonists, have a strong impact on him, he is ultimately inspired by Ambrose's sermons to reconsider Christianity.

Books 6, 7, 8, and 9 focus on Augustine's life in Milan, his career goals, and his conflicts with physical desire. He struggles to understand how God, a spiritual entity who, while absolutely good, allows the existence of evil. He decides that evil has its origins in the weak will of human beings, owing to the Fall of Adam and Eve, which corrupted human ability to know or to will the good. He contemplates the necessity of divine grace through Christ as mediator between God and humankind. He feels his accumulating experience preparing him to understand how all things are from God, and, if not perverted by evil, will return to God. In July or August, 386, while in grief and agony, he hears a child's voice telling him to read scripture. At first he thinks he overhears children at play but concludes the command is divinely inspired and meant for him. He opens the Bible and reads the first words his eyes fall upon, Romans 13:13, and then a friend asks him to read the next verse. The light of conversion and conviction fills his soul, revealing the untold horizons of God. Later, through baptism, Augustine "puts . . . on the Lord Jesus Christ." He prepares to return to Africa. His mother, who has joined him in Milan, dies. He retells her life story and recounts their last conversation. His autobiography ends, having shown God's power and concern for him and for others.

In book 10, Augustine inquires into the nature of memory and self-awareness. He studies how the mind can transcend the sequence of time—past, present, and future—and how it can move in and out of these states in any order as desired, and thereby find evidence of God.

In books 11, 12, 13, Augustine explores the meaning of time, creation, and Genesis 1. He explains the simultaneous emergence of space, time, and matter; God's words bring immediate fulfillment, as well as sequential or interactive, cumulative development. God sustains creation as it embodies change, and though God himself remains changeless, creation moves toward its appointed end, as Augustine elaborates in *The City of God*. Augustine records his experiences in *Confessions* to help others find the path toward God and reach the goal, or at least find consolation, and readers for centuries have found both Christian faith and comfort in his book.

THE CITY OF GOD

First published: *De civitate Dei*, 413-427
(English translation, 1610)
Type of work: Nonfiction

Initially countering the pagan explanation for the decline of Rome, Augustine describes the drama of God's plan of salvation, the struggle of all people throughout history.

Augustine's *The City of God*, its title deriving from Psalms, as in 46:4 and 87:3, depicts a Christian world order guided by God's providence, as presented in the Bible. The Visigoth sacking of Rome on August 24, 410, one of the increasing number of attacks upon the Roman Empire, prompted many citizens, Christian and pagan, to account for these events. Augustine, now bishop of Hippo, was asked to explain. While the Roman Empire worshiped pagan gods, the empire grew to dominate the world; now, almost one hundred years after Emperor Constantine made Christianity the official religion in 312, the empire is failing.

In books 1 through 9, Augustine examines Roman polytheism. He indicates, for example, that Rome had suffered defeats long before the Christian era and had endured catastrophe. Pagan deities provided no protection then, even though Rome was believed to be partners with these gods. At one time, Romans demonstrated great human virtues, and God's providence allowed Rome to prosper, but its reward extended to the earthly realm and is subject to change. Moreover, Rome's transition from a republic to an empire resulted in declining moral standards and few checks upon its government. Emperors, assuming sacred status, undertook any manner of activity; even a Christian emperor could not dedicate the empire to Christ. That Rome attained an empire beyond its control resulted more from continual warfare and the quest for glory and renown than it did from the effort to improve the lives of its citizens. In addition, pagan deities, having their own areas of responsibility, could bring no stability or lasting happiness; they could only provide gratifications of the moment, empty gestures toward the unknown. Some of these pagan deities included local gods from the nations Rome had conquered, and the resulting mix of deities defied each others' morality and rationality.

Augustine explains that pagan deities, evil spirits, fallen angels, or mere glorified humans represented an attempt to imitate God. The once-official paganism of imperial Rome signified dangers. Roman emperors, along with their subjects, wanted flattery and comfort, not facts. As a whole, Romans did not understand that the coming of Christ marked the purpose toward which all creation draws. The Roman Empire could be a means of God calling all people—Romans, as well as Hebrews, Greeks, and barbarians—to Christ, whose kingdom, not of this world, demanded prior allegiance.

Augustine also indicates that worldly life affords no protection from evil, sorrow, and death. Still, adversity can hold treasures; what the world calls downfall and disaster often prove to be a blessing. God can bring good out of evil, though the loss is real.

In books 10 through 14, Augustine develops the Christian scheme of cosmic history and contrasts it with the alternative. He draws upon the account in Genesis of the Fall of Adam and Eve and the doctrine of Original Sin and Redemption. All human beings share in the sin of Adam and Eve and suffer the consequences: exile, pain, struggle, and death. Christ, however, triumphed when human beings were defenseless and brought salvation. Human beings are thus dependent upon divine grace; humankind's merits are God's gifts.

The Fall and the deeds of Christ gave rise to two cities: the Celestial City or the City of God, and the city of this world—the Earthly City or the city of the devil. Augustine uses the word "city" figuratively, referring to people of all times and places who do or do not love God as manifested in Christ. The conflict between these two cities is universal, which puts the situation in fifth century Rome within the context of eternity. The two cities offer opposing choices of the will, as with the fallen angels who sought to defy God. The love of God draws human beings outside and beyond themselves, upward toward eternal life; the love of the things of this world draws human beings inward and downward toward death.

Human beings define themselves through their commitments, and their commitments, as social beings, produce two distinctive cultures—one of God and the other of the devil. One culture lives by God's word; the unselfish love of God and of other people in God unites this culture. The other culture lives in contempt of God's word; selfish love, although self-defeating, unites this culture. The state or government reflects these contrasting commitments. Government can and should bring ideals of justice and peace into a sinful world, although life will seem to reward the wicked and punish the good.

Books 15 through 18 trace the temporal destinies of the two cities, their achievements, and how they intermingle and coexist. Augustine describes human life as a pilgrimage from the Earthly City to the Celestial City, a version of the theme of exile, wandering, and banishment. The faithful, exiled through the Fall of Adam and Eve from their true home with God, struggle to return. Spiritual priorities, driven by attachment to the goods of the Celestial City, must predominate over attachment to the goods of the Earthly City. Although living in both cities, the faithful must maintain a certain detachment from the Earthly City. If they persist, they will perceive the higher order of God and eventually enter the Celestial City; nothing can separate them from God's love. The saved, chosen from the City of God as it existed throughout time, are known to God only. Others, bound by the limits of the Earthly City, where all things end, will find no fulfillment; they duplicate the sin of the devil, rejecting God.

Books 19 through 22 describe the final destiny of the two cities and Christian teachings about death, judgment, heaven, and hell. At the end of the world, God will identify those who belong to the City of God and those who belong to the city of the devil. Their respective inhabitants will include both angels and the souls of human beings whose fates will be sealed eternally. Justice will reach from the deepest past to the farthest future. Christ will fulfill the purpose of creation—life in the City of God.

SUMMARY

Both Catholic and Protestant leaders have regarded Saint Augustine as an originator of the doctrinal traditions of Western Christianity. He put the Church on a spiritual footing that enabled it to survive the fall of the Roman Empire and to endure through the ages. In addition, the explanatory power of his philosophical, historical, and literary writings has had immeasurable consequences. For example, he developed a developed a literary tradition that includes such poets as Dante, Geoffrey Chaucer, and John Milton.

Timothy C. Miller

DISCUSSION TOPICS

- How does Saint Augustine describe God's word as a living actuality in the hearts and minds of believers?

- What do Augustine's *Confessions* and *City of God* indicate about the overall situation of human beings and their particular situations?

- How might those two works be explained as a process of vision—of spiritual, intellectual, and intuitive seeing?

- For Augustine, how does God speak in the events of history and in the personal lives of believers?

- How does Augustine provide multiple perspectives on human life, and how does he set it in the widest of all contexts?

- Describe Augustine's treatment of the theme of exile, of life as pilgrimage.

BIBLIOGRAPHY

By the Author

NONFICTION:
Contra academicos, 386 (*Against the Academics*, 1943)
De beata vita, 386 (*The Happy Life*, 1937)
De ordine, 386 (*On Order*, 1942)
Soliloquia, 386 (*Soliloquies*, 1888)
De immortalitate animae, 387 (*On the Immortality of the Soul*, 1937)
De magistro, 389 (*On the Teacher*, 1924)
De musica, 389 (*On Music*, 1947)
De vera religione, 391 (*Of True Religion*, 1959)
De sermone Domini in monte, 394 (*Commentary on the Lord's Sermon on the Mount*, 1875)
De doctrina Christiana, 396-397, 426 (books 1-3, 396-397; book 4, 426; *On Christian Doctrine*, 1875)
Confessiones, 397-400 (*Confessions*, 1620)
Annotationes in Job, 400
De Genesi ad litteram, 401-415 (*The Literal Meaning of Genesis*, 1982)
De civitate Dei, 413-427 (*The City of God*, 1610)
De Trinitate, c. 419 (*On the Trinity*, 1873)

About the Author
Battenhouse, Roy W. *A Companion to the Study of St. Augustine*. New York: Oxford University Press, 1955.
Brown, Peter. *Augustine of Hippo: A Biography*. New ed. Berkeley: University of California Press, 2000.
Chadwick, Henry. *Augustine*. Oxford, England: Oxford University Press, 1995.

Fitzgerald, Allan D., ed. *Augustine Through the Ages: An Encyclopedia.* Grand Rapids, Mich.: William B. Eerdmans, 1999.

Harrison, Carol. *Augustine: Christian Truth and Fractured Humanity.* Oxford, England: Oxford University Press, 2000.

Marrou, Henri. *St. Augustine and His Influence Through the Ages.* Translated by Patrick Hepburne-Scott. New York: Harper & Brothers, 1957.

Portalié, Eugenè. *A Guide to the Thought of Saint Augustine.* Translated by Ralph J. Bastian. Chicago: Henry Regnery, 1960.

Scott, T. Kermit. *Augustine: His Thought in Context.* New York: Paulist Press, 1995.

JANE AUSTEN

Born: Steventon, Hampshire, England
December 16, 1775
Died: Winchester, Hampshire, England
July 18, 1817

One of English literature's greatest writers, Austen captures the subtleties of human nature and social interaction with satiric wit and a precise, elegant style.

Library of Congress

BIOGRAPHY

Jane Austen (OWS-tuhn) was born on December 16, 1775, in the tiny village of Steventon, where her father, the Reverend George Austen, served as the town rector. Her mother, Cassandra Leigh Austen, was herself the daughter of a rector, and Jane was the seventh of the couple's eight children. An older brother, George, suffered from epilepsy and did not live with the family, and the couple's third son, Edward, was adopted by wealthy, childless relatives who took a strong interest in the boy throughout his childhood. The remaining six children, however, lived with their parents in the plain, comfortable village rectory.

George Austen was a scholarly man, and the household included a large library, from which Jane read extensively throughout her life. Much of the children's education took place under their father's tutelage, with two of Jane's brothers, James and Henry, both of whom attended the University of Oxford, assisting their father with the younger children's periods of schooling at home. Jane and her sister Cassandra received several years of formal education, first at private schools in Oxford and Southampton and later at the Abbey School in Reading.

The Austens were a lively, close-knit family. Literature was a shared family interest, and evenings in the rectory were often spent discussing works by the leading novelists of the day. Among Jane's favorite authors were Henry Fielding, Samuel Richardson, and Fanny Burney, and references to their work appear in both her letters and her own novels. Amateur theatricals were also a much-loved family pastime, and friends and neighbors were frequently recruited to participate in plays staged in the rectory barn. This interest, too, later found its way into Austen's work, most notably in *Mansfield Park* (1814). Indeed, family life itself is a frequent theme in Austen's work, and her heroines' relationships with parents and siblings are as fully developed as the romantic alliances on which their stories turn.

Jane's closest ties within her family were to her adored older sister, Cassandra. Three years apart in age and the only girls among the eight children, the two were close companions from childhood onward. Although Cassandra was engaged once, to a young man who died of yellow fever, and Jane entered into several brief romantic attachments, neither sister married, and the two lived together with their mother until Jane's death in 1817. Many of Austen's wittiest, most informal—and therefore most revealing—letters were written to Cassandra during their occasional separations, and it was Cassandra who most often had early glimpses of Jane's novels in progress. A less fortuitous result of the sisters' close bond, however, was Cassandra's decision following Jane's death to edit or destroy any of her sister's letters and papers that she feared might cast Jane in an unfavorable light. For Austen scholars, Cassandra's loyalty has been a source of much speculation and regret.

In 1801, George Austen retired as rector of Steventon and moved with his wife and two daughters to Bath, where he died in 1805. The family's years in this city were difficult ones; in addition to Mr. Austen's death, Mrs. Austen suffered a serious illness, and Jane herself is thought to have begun a romance with a man who died soon afterward. Following her husband's death, Mrs. Austen moved with her daughters to Southampton. In 1809, Jane's brother Edward, who had inherited the estates of the wealthy relatives who had adopted him years before, offered his mother and sisters a permanent residence at one of his properties, a house in the village of Chawton. It was there that Jane Austen would live until her death, from what is believed to have been Addison's disease, at the age of forty-one.

Austen's writing life is less easily chronicled. Inspired by her own love of reading, Austen began writing at the age of twelve. Now termed "the Juvenilia" by Austen scholars, three volumes of her early writings, dated between 1787 and 1793, remain in existence. Her first mature work, an epistolary novella titled *Lady Susan*, was written in 1794 or 1795 and published in 1871. Around that same time, she also began work on a second novel of letters, "Elinor and Marianne" (completed between 1795 and 1797), which she would rewrite two years later as *Sense and Sensibility* (1811). Between the two versions, Austen wrote a third epistolary novel, "First Impressions," which would later become *Pride and Prejudice* (1813). In 1798 or 1799, following the initial rewriting of "Elinor and Marianne," Austen began work on "Susan," which would later be retitled and published as *Northanger Abbey* (1818), her satire on gothic novels. Because of the frequent lapses in time between each novel's earliest drafts, completion, and eventual publication, the publication dates of Austen's work are no indication of when the books were actually written.

In 1803, two years after the move to Bath, "Susan" was sold to the publishers Crosby and Company for ten pounds. The book was never published, however, and Austen bought it back for the same amount six years later. Austen also began *The Watsons* (1871, fragment) in 1803, a novel she put aside and did not resume after her father's death two years later. In the difficult years following her father's death, Austen appears to have abandoned her writing entirely, resuming it only after 1809, when the family was at last settled at Chawton, where she embarked on a period of tremendous productivity.

Austen devoted the years between 1809 and 1811 to *Sense and Sensibility*, and in 1811 the book became her first published work. That same year, she began work on *Mansfield Park*, which continued throughout the next two years. The following year, 1812, Austen began extensive revisions on "First Impressions," abandoning its epistolary form for that of a traditional novel. The book was published in 1813 as *Pride and Prejudice*. *Mansfield Park* appeared the following year, shortly after Austen began work on *Emma*, which was published in 1815. Over the next two years, Austen wrote *Persuasion* (1818) and began work on *Sandition* (1925, fragment), which remained unfinished at the time of her death on July 18, 1817, in Winchester, England. Both *Persuasion* and *Northanger Abbey* were published posthumously in 1818.

ANALYSIS

In a letter written to her nephew several months before her death, Austen referred to her writing as "the little bit (two Inches wide) of Ivory on which I work with so fine a Brush," a description of her work that conveys its essence with remarkable precision. Austen is not a writer whose books are characterized by sweeping dramatic action unfolding against a vivid historical backdrop; nor are her novels treatises on social ills or controversial contemporary issues. Austen wrote instead about the world she knew—a world of country villages, of polite middle-class society, of family life, of love and courtship—and her books offer a portrait of life as it was lived by a small segment of English society at the end of the eighteenth and the beginning of the nineteenth centuries.

Yet so great is her talent and her insight into the complexities of human nature that the seeming simplicity of her books belies the universality of their perceptions. In turning her writer's gaze on the world around her, Austen reveals deeper truths that apply to the world at large. Her portraits of social interaction, while specific to a particular and very carefully delineated place and time, are nevertheless the result of timeless human characteristics. If one looks beneath the details of social manners and mores that abound in Austen's novels, what emerges is their author's clear-eyed grasp of the intricacies of human behavior.

What is also readily apparent is that human behavior was a source of great amusement to Austen.

Her novels are gentle satires, written with delicate irony and incisive wit. The famous opening lines of *Pride and Prejudice* capture her style at its best: "It is a truth universally acknowledged, that a single man in possession of a good fortune must be in want of a wife." Courtship and marriage are the subject of all six of Austen's completed novels, and she treats the topic with a skillful balance of humor and seriousness. The elaborate social ritual of courtship and the amount of time and energy expended on it by the parties involved provide Austen with an ideal target for her satirical portraits. Dances, carriage rides, and country walks are the settings for the romances that unfold in her books, and the individual's infinite capacity for misconceptions and self-delusions provide the books' dramatic structure. Her heroes and heroines misjudge each other, misunderstand each other, and mistake charm for substance and reserve for lack of feeling with a determination that seems likely to undermine their chances for happiness—until at last they find their way through the emotional mazes they have built for themselves and emerge with the proper mate.

Yet while Austen is happy to amuse her readers with her characters' foibles and missteps, she brings an underlying empathy to her creations as well. Her heroines are never figures of fun—that role is left to the stories' supporting characters—but are instead intelligent, sensitive, amiable young women who are eminently likable despite the flaws they may exhibit. It is human nature in all its complexity that fascinates Austen, and she is capable of providing her novels with interesting, well-developed central characters who are believable precisely because they are flawed. Her amusement is not scorn but rather a tolerant awareness of the qualities, both good and bad, that constitute the human character. It is this awareness that lends Austen's work its relevance and contributes to her stature in the hierarchy of English literature.

Also central to the high critical regard in which she is held is Austen's extraordinarily eloquent and graceful literary style. Austen's use of language is as sure and as precise as her character development; indeed, the two are inseparable. Whether she is depicting the selfish, greedy Mrs. John Dashwood in *Sense and Sensibility*, who says of a proposed yearly allowance for her widowed mother-in-law, "people always live forever when there is any annuity to be paid them," or characterizing Edmund Bertram's

pursuit of Fanny Price in *Mansfield Park* with the observation, "She was of course only too good for him; but as nobody minds having what is too good for them, he was very steadily earnest in the pursuit of the blessing," Austen sketches her characters and relates their stories with the elegance and wit that are the unmistakable hallmarks of her style.

Austen's work offers ample proof that, in the hands of a gifted writer, stories of ordinary lives filled with everyday events can transcend their outward simplicity and capture the intricacies of human nature. Austen's ironic portraits of the world she knew are both a revealing look at her own time and a perceptive examination of the workings of the human heart and mind.

SENSE AND SENSIBILITY

First published: 1811
Type of work: Novel

Two sisters, very different in nature, face obstacles as they find love.

Sense and Sensibility is a novel that is best understood within the context of the era in which it was written. Austen lived in that period of English history when eighteenth century rationalism was giving way to the increasing popularity of nineteenth century romanticism, as typified by William Wordsworth and the Romantic poets. The open embrace and deliberate cultivation of sensibility—deep feelings and passionate emotions—were perhaps a natural reaction to the admiration of reserve and practicality that had typified the preceding decades.

Austen's novel, her first published work, offers a portrait of two sisters, Elinor and Marianne Dashwood, who embody the two qualities set forth in the title. Elinor, the elder of the two, is intelligent, loving, and wise enough to see the potential folly in failing to temper emotion with good sense. Marianne, although sharing many of these qualities, lacks her sister's wisdom; she is, as Austen describes her, "everything but prudent."

Marianne's insistence on giving her emotions free rein leads her into an unhappy romance with the fortune-hunting Willoughby when she mistakes his false expressions of sentiment for love. Although Marianne's own excessive displays of emotion spring from genuine feeling, they blind her to the realization that less fervently expressed emotions may also be heartfelt and true. Waiting patiently throughout the book is the quiet, steadfast Colonel Brandon, a man of deep but reserved feelings who loves Marianne and whose true worth she comes to recognize only after she is forced by her failed romance with Willoughby to reassess her views.

Elinor remains her sister's mainstay throughout her unhappy first love, assisting her toward maturity with patience and tenderness. She, too, is in love, with her selfish sister-in-law's brother, Edward Ferrars. Both are restrained in their expressions of their feelings, Elinor out of modesty and a sense of

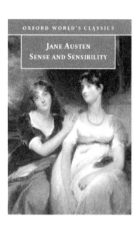

propriety and Edward because he is secretly and unhappily engaged to another woman favored by his snobbish mother. Yet adherence to principles of rational thought and good sense does not prevent Elinor from suffering greatly when she believes that her hopes of marrying Edward are impossible. Their eventual union is as happy and full of emotion as that of any two people in love.

Although her own sympathies are perhaps most closely aligned with those of Elinor, Austen writes with affection for both sisters and her message is one of compromise. She is careful to show that a balance of both heart and intellect is necessary for a full life—a blending of sense and sensibility that both Elinor and Marianne possess by the novel's close.

PRIDE AND PREJUDICE

First published: 1813
Type of work: Novel

A man and woman must reassess their first impressions of each other before they are able to find love.

Pride and Prejudice is the best known of Austen's six novels and ranks among her finest work. As in *Sense and Sensibility*, its story centers on two sisters, Jane and Elizabeth Bennet. Jane falls in love early in the book with the amiable, wealthy Charles Bingley. Bingley returns her sentiments but is temporarily persuaded to abandon the romance at the urging of his friend, Mr. Darcy, who does not detect love in Jane's discreet manner.

The book's true center, however, is the complex relationship between Elizabeth and Darcy. Both are intelligent and forthright, but their initial impressions blind them to the qualities in each other that will eventually form the basis for their love. Darcy is indeed proud and feels himself above the less refined country families in whose company he finds himself during his visit to Bingley. Elizabeth's mother, a vain, silly woman who is often a source of embarrassment to her daughter, is also an object of Darcy's scorn. When she overhears Darcy's assessment of her and her family, Elizabeth's own pride is wounded; she dismisses him as a proud, disagreeable man and is more than willing to believe the lies she is told about him by the charming, deceitful Wickham. For his part, Darcy's pride in his position and his family cause him at first to resist his attraction to Elizabeth and later to propose to her in a manner that she finds even more offensive than his initial hauteur.

Yet as time passes and their interest in each other continues, both Elizabeth and Darcy begin to see beyond their original judgments of the other's personality and character. Both possess a measure of pride and prejudice that must be overcome before they will fully understand one another, and Elizabeth's younger sister, Lydia, is unintentionally a catalyst for the change. Foolish and headstrong, Lydia runs away with Wickham, and it is only through Darcy's intervention that the two are married and the Bennet family is saved from disgrace.

Elizabeth has already learned the truth behind Wickham's slander toward Darcy, and Darcy's willingness to help her family despite her own stinging refusal of his proposal offers her a glimpse of the true nature of his character. Darcy, too, has changed, losing some of the stiffness and pride that accompanied his wealth and social standing.

The substantial emotional shift experienced by Darcy and Elizabeth is indicated by Mr. Bennet's reaction to the news of Darcy's second proposal: "'Lizzy,' said he, 'what are you doing? Are you out of your senses, to be accepting this man? Have you not always hated him?'" Mr. Bennet's reaction is understandable, given the disdain with which Elizabeth had expressed her initial reaction to Darcy. What her father has not been witness to—and the reader has—is Austen's gradual revelation of the qualities that Darcy and Elizabeth share and the manner in which each has come to appreciate these qualities in the other.

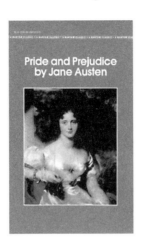

That theirs is a meeting of the mind and heart is clear, and those qualities that at last draw them to each other and impel them to overcome their early misunderstandings will form the basis for a strong and happy marriage.

MANSFIELD PARK

First published: 1814
Type of work: Novel

A timid young girl living with wealthy relations falls in love with her cousin.

There are several points that set *Mansfield Park* apart from the rest of Austen's work. Chief among them is Austen's depiction of her heroine, Fanny Price, a frail, quiet young woman who has none of the high spirits or wit of Elizabeth Bennet or Marianne Dashwood. Reared from the age of ten among wealthy relatives, Fanny is an unobtrusive presence in the household at Mansfield Park, useful and agreeable to everyone and steadfast in her secret affection for her cousin, Edmund Bertram.

Fanny's manner contrasts sharply with the livelier, sometimes careless behavior of her cousins and their friends. Only Edmund spends time with the gentle Fanny, although his own affections have been captivated by the sophisticated Mary Crawford. With Fanny's uncle, Sir Thomas Bertram, away on an extended stay in the West Indies, the cousins and their friends decide to put on an amateur theatrical production of a scandalous French play. Only Fanny refuses to participate, out of natural modesty and a certainty that her absent uncle would not approve. Sir Thomas returns unexpectedly and does not approve, much to his children's chagrin, but Fanny quickly falls from his favor when she refuses the proposal of Mary Crawford's brother, Henry, who had begun an unwelcome flirtation with her after Fanny's cousin Maria married another man.

Distressed by her uncle's disapproval, Fanny visits her parents and her eight brothers and sisters, only to discover that her years at Mansfield Park have left her unable to fit easily into her noisy, often vulgar family. She is summoned back by Sir Thomas when Maria leaves her husband for Henry Crawford and Maria's sister, Julia, elopes. Now fully appreciated by her uncle, Fanny comes into her own, winning the love of Edmund Bertram.

Because Austen's novels often adopt the tone of their heroines, *Mansfield Park* is a more somber, less satirical book than *Pride and Prejudice.* Fanny is a young woman who has been shaped by both her separation from her family and her awkward position as a poor relation in a wealthy household. Yet, it is her alienation from her cousins that has perhaps saved her from taking on their faults. They have been spoiled while she has been grateful; she has grown in sensitivity and moral strength while they have been indulged. In Austen's world, true worth is always recognized in the end, and Fanny's resistance to the more worldly pursuits of her cousins and their friends wins for her the love of her adored Edmund.

Fanny is also alone among Austen's heroines in her uncertainty as to her position in society. Catherine Moreland of *Northanger Abbey* may visit wealthy friends, but she enjoys a secure place in her own family, as do the Dashwood and Bennet sisters and Emma Woodhouse of *Emma*. Only Anne Elliot of *Persuasion*, unappreciated by her self-centered father and sister, somewhat approximates Fanny's experience. It is a situation that lends great poignancy to Fanny's experiences and one which Austen conveys with great feeling and perception.

Mansfield Park is perhaps the most controversial of Austen's novels. While some critics fault its author for abandoning the irony and elegant wit that characterize most of her work, others praise her for her willingness to undertake a variation on her usual themes. In Fanny Price, Austen has created a heroine who must engage the reader through her gentleness rather than her spirit, and Fanny does that with admirable success.

EMMA

First published: 1815
Type of work: Novel

A good-hearted but indulged young heiress misguidedly plays matchmaker for her friends.

The forces that shape the dramatic action in *Emma* are described by Austen in the book's opening paragraphs; they are the qualities possessed by Emma Woodhouse herself. In this novel, Austen turns her satiric talents to a portrait of a wealthy young woman with "a disposition to think a little too well of herself," who has yet to acquire the sensitivity to realize that the emotional lives of her companions are not toys for her own amusement.

With an adoring, widowed father and an indulgent companion, Emma has reached early adulthood secure in the belief that she knows what is best for those around her. When her companion marries, Emma replaces her with Harriet Smith, an impressionable young girl from a local school, and quickly decides that the girl's fiancé, a farmer, is beneath her. Persuading Harriet to break off the engagement, despite the misgivings of Emma's admiring friend, Mr. Knightley, Emma sets in motion a chain of romantic misunderstandings that will come close to ruining Harriet's chances for happiness. After playing with the romantic futures of several of her acquaintances, Emma at last recognizes the dangers of her interference and realizes that her own chance for happiness has existed within her grasp for some time in the person of Mr. Knightley.

Emma is one of Austen's best novels, with some critics holding it in higher regard than *Pride and Prejudice*. In Emma Woodhouse, Austen has created one of her most memorable heroines, a willful, headstrong, yet fundamentally well-intentioned young woman whose intelligence and energy need the tempering of experience before she can be judged truly mature. She gains this experience through her relationship with Harriet when her manipulations backfire and she finds that Harriet believes herself to be in love with Mr. Knightley. With the force of a revelation, the truth of what she has done comes to Emma, along with the realization that she loves Knightley herself. As Austen writes, "Her own conduct, as well as her own heart, was before her in the same few minutes." Seeing herself and her actions clearly for the first time, Emma is forced into difficult but necessary self-doubt and self-examination, a new but ultimately valuable experience for a young woman who has never before had cause to doubt her own judgment.

That Emma will learn from her mistakes is clear, and her happiness with Knightley, who has known and admired her since childhood, seems assured. *Emma* is Austen's commentary on how little anyone knows about the workings of another's heart and affections, and her heroine's painful lesson is evidence of her creator's wisdom.

SUMMARY

Although she completed only six novels, Jane Austen has retained a position of great critical acclaim among English novelists. A writer of great wit and elegance of style, she depicts her characters' strengths and weaknesses with tolerance and sympathy.

Finding, as she once noted in a letter to her niece, that "3 or 4 Families in a Country Village is the very thing to work on," Austen examines the world she knows with delicate irony and wry humor, revealing in the process a grasp of the subtleties of human nature that transcends her books' deceptively ordinary settings and events.

Janet Lorenz

BIBLIOGRAPHY

By the Author

LONG FICTION:
Sense and Sensibility, 1811
Pride and Prejudice, 1813
Mansfield Park, 1814
Emma, 1815
Northanger Abbey, 1818
Persuasion, 1818
Lady Susan, 1871 (novella)
The Watsons, 1871 (fragment)
Sanditon, 1925 (fragment), 1975 (completed by Anne Telscombe)

SHORT FICTION:
Minor Works, 1954 (volume 6 of the *Oxford Illustrated Jane Austen*; edited by R. W. Chapman)

NONFICTION:
Jane Austen's Letters to Her Sister Cassandra and Others, 1932 (R. W. Chapman, editor)

CHILDREN'S LITERATURE:
Catherine, 1818
Lesley Castle, 1922
Three Sisters, 1933

MISCELLANEOUS:
Love and Friendship, and Other Early Works, 1922

DISCUSSION TOPICS

• Explain how Jane Austen, working in a narrow social range and with limited experience of the world, could succeed so brilliantly as a novelist.

• Distinguish the main characteristics of her novels that differentiate them from the eighteenth century novels that made up a great deal of her literary background.

• How does Austen help her readers to become better readers?

• In *Sense and Sensibility*, Elinor develops sympathy for the incorrigible Willoughby. Determine whether or not that is a flaw in Elinor's personality.

• *Pride and Prejudice* begins with Mr. Bennet's problem of finding suitors for his five daughters. Explain Austen's avoidance of making his problem the theme of the novel.

• How does one explain the popularity of Austen's novels with filmmakers?

About the Author

Bloom, Harold, ed. *Jane Austen*. Philadelphia: Chelsea House, 2004.
Grey, J. David. *The Jane Austen Companion*. New York: Macmillan, 1986.
Jenkins, Elizabeth. *Jane Austen: A Biography*. London: Victor Gollancz, 1986.
Le Faye, Deirdre. *Jane Austen, the World of Her Novels*. New York: Abrams, 2002.
Nokes, David. *Jane Austen: A Life*. New York: Farrar, Straus and Giroux, 1998.
Tanner, Tony. *Jane Austen*. Cambridge, Mass.: Harvard University Press, 1986.
Teachman, Debra. *Student Companion to Jane Austen*. Westport, Conn.: Greenwood Press, 2000.
Todd, Janet. *The Cambridge Introduction to Jane Austen*. New York: Cambridge University Press, 2006.
Tomalin, Claire. *Jane Austen: A Life*. New York: Knopf, 1997.
Williams, Michael. *Jane Austen: Six Novels and Their Methods*. New York: St. Martin's Press, 1986.

ISAAC BABEL

Born: Odessa, Ukraine, Russian Empire (now in Ukraine)
July 13, 1894
Died: Butyrka prison, Moscow, Soviet Union (now in Russia)
January 27, 1940

Using simple, colloquial language, Babel captured a vision of two worlds—the Cossacks and the gangsters of Odessa—which would not long survive the Soviet regime.

BIOGRAPHY

Isaac Emmanuelovich Babel (BA-byihl) was born in the Moldavanka, the Jewish quarter of Odessa, then a part of the Russian Empire, on July 13, 1894. His parents Emmanuel and Fanya Babel were firmly middle class and not entirely comfortable with this lively cosmopolitan city full of foreigners and colorful gangsters. As a result, they moved to Nikolaev, about eighty miles up the coast, shortly after Isaac's birth. Ever the compulsive mythologizer, Babel would later conveniently forget this detail of his upbringing, just as he brushed over his father's prosperous agricultural machinery business and depicted him as a simple shopkeeper. To be fair to Babel, however, he was writing in the Soviet Union at a time when it was often expedient to soft-pedal bourgeois origins and emphasize one's closeness with the working people.

In any case, his family's modest wealth could not insulate them from the fact they were Jews in a virulently anti-Semitic society, where pogroms, or riots, broke out with alarming regularity. His granduncle was murdered during the pogrom of 1905, and Babel had to watch his own father kneel in supplication to a Cossack officer. However, that act of self-abasement did not spare the family business from a mob of looters or consequent financial ruin. Upon the family's return to Odessa in 1906, Isaac himself had to struggle to be admitted to the Russian-language commercial school, since the regular Russian-language high schools had a harsh quota limiting the number of Jewish students they would admit.

At this time, Babel's literary interests began to

flower, but not in the way one might have expected for a young man of his background. He had little interest in either Hebrew or Yiddish literature, instead preferring the great Russian writers of the era, including Leo Tolstoy and Anton Chekhov. He also developed a strong interest in Western literature, particularly French writers such as Guy du Maupassant and François Rabelais. In these authors, Babel found a vision and power in marked contrast to the resignation and frequent self-pity of his coreligionists' writings.

His literary yearnings led him to the imperial capital, St. Petersburg, where he lived in defiance of restrictions against Jewish settlement. Although this course of action exposed him to considerable hardship, it also put him in contact with writer Maxim Gorky, who enabled Babel to get his first stories published in 1917. The stories proved controversial enough to get Babel indicted for obscenity by the imperial government. However, the government was overthrown in the Russian Revolution, and as a result Babel was never tried for these charges.

Babel served in the army under the provisional government, and when the Bolsheviks took over he flung himself into work on behalf of the new government. He was attached to the *konarmiia*, or "mounted army," under Semyon Budyonny, the semilegendary Cossack fighter who would become a marshal of the Soviet Union. For a Jew to ride among Cossacks was somewhat akin to a fox running with hounds or a mouse playing with cats, so Babel adopted the revolutionary pseudonym of Kiril Lyutov to enable him to work as a war correspondent for the army newspaper, *Krasny Kav-*

alierist (Red Horseman), during the Russian Civil War and the subsequent war with Poland.

After the war, Babel spent a few years sorting out his experiences and finding the proper voice in which to put them down on paper. In 1923, he published his first sketches of events in the Polish campaign, which would later become the collection *Konarmiia* (1926; *Red Cavalry*, 1929). His frank portrayals of violence and cruelty earned him the enmity of Budyonny, who considered Babel to have libeled the troops.

The success of *Red Cavalry* emboldened him to follow it up with another book, *Odesskie rasskazy* (1931; *Tales of Odessa*, 1955), a collection of stories about his early life in that city's Jewish community. However, things were rapidly changing in the Soviet Union. The heady days of Vladimir Ilich Lenin's new economic policy were coming to a close. Lenin's death was followed by a quick and brutal power struggle, which brought Joseph Stalin to the forefront. Stalin progressively crushed all dissent and every breath of individuality in the arts.

In response, Babel almost ceased to publish altogether, and in 1934 he delivered a speech to the Writers' Congress, the trade union to which all writers in the Soviet Union were required to belong, in which he talked about developing a "genre of silence." He was permitted to travel abroad, where he experimented with writing in French, but as soon as he returned to the Soviet Union and the growing atmosphere of terror, his inspiration ran dry.

Babel also began to develop dangerous friendships. His marriage had failed, and he had an affair with Yevgenia Gladun, later to become the wife of Nikolai Yezhov, an up-and-coming member of the Soviet secret police, the Cheka or NKVD. He developed a working relationship with Genrikh Yagoda, the NKVD chief who became the first executor of Stalin's Great Terror, and wrote a fictionalized history of the Soviet secret police. After Yagoda was removed from his position for having been inadequately enthusiastic in pursuing Stalin's enemies and replaced by Nikolai Yezhov, Babel maintained his friendship with the Yezhovs. Even when it became obvious that Yezhov was losing Stalin's favor, Babel continued to visit.

In 1939, Yezhov was arrested, and not long afterward Babel received his own knock on the door. His manuscripts were confiscated, and many of them vanished forever, very likely destroyed by the secret police when they proved of no use in implicating further victims. Babel was held at secret police headquarters for some time before he was shot on the morning of January 27, 1940. Only after Stalin's death and subsequent denunciation by Nikita S. Khrushchev could Babel's writings once again be discussed freely in the Soviet Union, but even then the truth about his death was hidden by layers of secret police obfuscation. The true story of Babel's last days and death did not emerge until Mikhail Gorbachev's program of glasnost in the 1980's and the subsequent fall of the Soviet Union.

ANALYSIS

The famed Victorian English dandy and writer Oscar Wilde once said of his writing that he had spent an entire morning taking a comma out and the afternoon putting it back in. Isaac Babel showed much of the same meticulousness in his writing. Each of his sketches was a tiny work of brilliance, agonized over for days in order to produce a perfect image that would burn in the reader's mind. He once showed an interviewer a thick sheaf of paper which proved to be no fewer than twenty drafts of one of his stories, "Liubka Kazak" ("Lyubka the Cossack").

Babel's prose was far removed from any sort of Victorian ornateness. He preferred to employ a spare, even severe language that eschewed any excess. There was no room for extended description or explanation in his stories. Instead, Babel preferred to rely upon sharp, well-chosen images of the story's events in order to develop his characters' relationships and actions. As a result, the events and characters of his stories have considerable power to remain in a reader's mind long after the story is finished and the book is returned to the shelf. One cannot quickly forget the Cossack commander Savitsky or the Jewish gangster Benya Krik, men fairly bursting with energy, ready and willing to take what they want.

Babel's approach to the literary portrayal of violence has been one of the most controversial aspects of his writing. Unlike his prerevolutionary predecessors, Babel was unsparing in his portrayal of the darker side of human nature, particularly in the war-torn Poland of *Red Cavalry* but also among the seamy underside of Odessa. He dared to show these places in all their gritty reality, depicting rape, torture, and murder in a carefully chosen and spare prose that captures the lolling of a corpse's head as skillfully as it describes the light slanting down on the sacred art of a church located just behind the battle lines.

However, realistic portrayals of violence were not the only characteristic of Babel's writing that set him apart from previous authors and made him part of a new literary movement. He was also fascinated with the speech of the ordinary people, and he used rough colloquial language not only in the characters' dialogue but also in the narrative, capturing the distinct nature of his characters' points of view. Although this technique, known as *skaz* from the Russian word *skazit'*, meaning "to say," could easily have become an excuse for carelessness in a lesser writer, Babel adopted it with a sure and poetic mastery of tone. The reader can tell that Babel himself is quite aware of the strictures of standard literary Russian and is departing from them as a deliberate artistic choice, in a controlled fashion, to bring the reader closer to the ordinary people and the manner in which they actually speak.

RED CAVALRY

First published: *Konarmiia*, 1926 (English translation, 1929)
Type of work: Short stories

Babel depicts the battles between the Russian revolutionaries and the Poles with a raw energy and vividness.

Red Cavalry (or *Konarmiia* in Russian) is a collection of short stories firmly planted in the birth trauma of the Soviet Union. To the Russian reader of the 1920's, *Red Cavalry* had the sound of the new language of the new regime. The very word *konarmiia* was a coinage of the Russian Civil War, a joining of the Russian words for "horse" and "army," and was used to replace the old word for cavalry, with its associations of elite regiments staffed by aristocrats. However, the English translator did not attempt to capture that sense, instead choosing the more descriptive title *Red Cavalry*. Even in translation, however, *Red Cavalry* loses little of the raw energy of the original Russian.

This collection of short stories begins with a bang in "Perekhod cherez Zbruch" ("Crossing into Poland"), with the news that Novograd-Volynsk has been captured. The narrator describes how he crosses the Zbruch River, followed by an encounter with a Jewish family in the house where he is to be billeted for the night. Each of the stories follows a similar pattern, with the first-person narrator, Kiril Lyutov, having various encounters with the Cossacks and with the Poles and Jews in the territories through which the army rides. Almost all the encounters are violent, and each is vividly limned with strong, active words.

Although there is no obvious continuing between the chapters and each story can be read as a stand-alone tale or vignette, together the stories add up to a plot line that is more than the sum of its parts, making the book resemble a novel rather than merely a collection of unrelated short stories. The overall theme of the book is Lyutov's acclimation to life among the fierce and wild Cossack horsemen. Through rough and often bitter experience he learns to accept violence with an approximation of the casualness with which the Cossacks approach it. When he goes into battle with an unloaded weapon and his deception is discovered, the Cossacks curse him as a coward, venting their disgust at cowardly, bespectacled intellectuals in general. Yet at the same time they depend upon him to read them their unit newspaper and to write letters home to their families, for they are almost entirely illiterate. It is a curious and awkward symbiosis, but Lyutov begins to adapt, until in "Moi pervyi gus" ("My First Goose") he is able to appropriate and kill a gander he finds waddling about the barnyard of an old woman with whom he argued over recompense for quartering. For the first time he gains a measure of real respect from the Cossacks because he has proven himself capable of the same sort of unthinking violence they practice so casually. His experience also gives him new insight into the values of the Cossacks, as can be seen in the story of the death of Commander Trunov.

This fearless Cossack, knowing full well that he will die in taking on an enemy aircraft, hands over his boots so some other soldier can use them, since they still have plenty of wear in them.

Yet even in the final story, Lyutov remains a man apart, never able to see the world in the casual manner of the Cossacks, who view life as a green meadow upon which women and horses walk. In this final image, *Red Cavalry*, which is meant to be an unsparingly realistic portrayal of warfare, still retains some of the idealism of the Romantics, in particular the concept of the Noble Savage, whose naturalness has not been warped by civilization's hypocrisies.

TALES OF ODESSA

First published: *Odesskie rasskazy,* 1931
   (English translation, 1955)
Type of work: Short stories

Babel writes about life in the Jewish ghetto of Odessa, including tales featuring Benya Krik and other local gangsters.

Like *Red Calvary*, each story in *Tales of Odessa* can stand on its own, but together the stories create a whole that is more than the sum of its parts. However, in this collection the elements of violence, while still present, are less overwhelming than the wholesale destruction of the war-torn countryside during the Polish campaign of 1920. The cruelties of Odessa are smaller, more subtle, but they still have the power to destroy. At times, as can be seen in "Istoriia moei golubiatni" ("The Story of My Dovecote"), one of Babel's earlier stories that was not included in *Tales of Odessa*, they can erupt into an anti-Semitic pogrom different only in the scope and degree to which the perpetrators are sanctioned by the central government.

Jewishness and anti-Semitism are the major themes of *Tales of Odessa*. Although Babel wrote in Russian for a Russian audience, there is a deep thread of similarity between the *Tales of Odessa* and the body of Yiddish literature that was produced by Odessa's Jewish community in the years before the Russian Revolution, particularly the work of Sholom Aleichem, who wrote stories about the Jew-

ish community as both an enclosed society and a vulnerable group surrounded by hostile Gentiles. Babel, however, did not take quite the same indulgent attitude toward his coreligionists. His attitudes and mind-set had been reshaped by his experiences riding with the Cossacks, and as a result he was more willing to criticize the flaws and weaknesses of a Jewish society whose members often tried to survive by keeping its collective head down in the face of hostility.

Thus, his heroes are not meek and submissive Jews but the nearest approximation he could find to the Cossacks. Like those fierce horsemen, Benya Krik (literally, Benny the Shouter) and the gangsters of the Jewish ghetto are quick with their fists, fearless in the face of danger, and unwilling to allow anyone to place limitations on their freedom to experience life to the fullest. When the police try to raid their gathering during a wedding ceremony, they burn down the police station. Benya both fights and cons his way through life, using his fists or his glib tongue depending upon which can gain him the best advantage. However, there always is more than a little self-mocking in the humor of these stories, with Babel poking fun at the very concept of the grand, the epic.

Because *Tales of Odessa* was published after *Red Cavalry*, most critics generally assumed that the stories in *Tales of Odessa* were written after those in *Red Cavalry*, even though the stories in *Tales of Odessa* are in many ways weaker. As a result, there has been a sense that Babel somehow exhausted his creative capacities in writing *Red Cavalry*, and *Tales of Odessa* represented a diminishment of his ability. Since the fall of the Soviet Union, however, literary historians have been able to examine many of the obscure regional journals in which the Odessa stories originally appeared in 1922 and 1923, and thus have demonstrated that, far from representing a decline, the stories show the development of an author who was still working on perfecting the stories that would become *Red Cavalry*. Only with the success of that book did Babel go ahead and collect the earlier set of stories in *Tales of Odessa*.

SUMMARY

Isaac Babel's continual focus upon characters at once grim and colorful, combined with the peculiar way in which he died, served to make his writings a highly desirable "forbidden fruit" in the

Soviet Union for many decades. Even after his rehabilitation in the 1960's, the official editions of his works, carefully edited to remove references that were still politically problematic—such as an appearance by Leon Trotsky at the end of the segments that make up *Red Cavalry*—were printed in very small editions and thus nearly impossible to acquire if one did not have the appropriate connections. Even in the West, Babel remained largely unknown because many scholars felt awkward about approaching stories that were so unsparing in their portrayals of the cruelty of war.

Leigh Husband Kimmel

BIBLIOGRAPHY

By the Author

SHORT FICTION:
Rasskazy, 1925
Istoriia moei golubiatni, 1926
Konarmiia, 1926 (*Red Cavalry*, 1929)
Odesskie rasskazy, 1931 (*Tales of Odessa*, 1955)
Benya Krik, the Gangster, and Other Stories, 1948
The Collected Stories, 1955
Izbrannoe, 1957, 1966
Lyubka the Cossack, and Other Stories, 1963
You Must Know Everything: Stories, 1915-1937, 1969

DRAMA:
Zakat, pb. 1928 (*Sunset*, 1960; also known as *Sundown*)
Mariia, pb. 1935 (*Maria*, 1966)

SCREENPLAYS:
Benia Krik: Kinopovest', 1926 (*Benia Krik: A Film Novel*, 1935)
Bluzhdaiushchie zvezdy: Kinostsenarii, 1926

POETRY:
Morning in the Burned House, 1996

NONFICTION:
1920 Diary, 1995

MISCELLANEOUS:
Isaac Babel: The Lonely Years, 1925-1939, Unpublished Stories and Private Correspondence, 1964, 1995 (Nathalie Babel, editor; translated by Andrew R. MacAndrew)
The Complete Works of Isaac Babel, 2001 (Nathalie Babel, editor; translated by Peter Constantine)

About the Author

Bloom, Harold, ed. *Isaac Babel*. New York: Chelsea House, 1987.
Carden, Patricia. *The Art of Isaac Babel*. Ithaca, N.Y.: Cornell University Press, 1972.
Charyn, Jerome. *Savage Shorthand: The Life and Death of Isaac Babel*. New York: Random House, 2005.
Pirozhka, A. N. *At His Side: The Last Years of Isaac Babel*. Translated by Anne Frydman and Robert L. Busch. South Royalton, Vt.: Steerforth Press, 1996.

DISCUSSION TOPICS

- Did Isaac Babel's riding among the Cossacks of the Mounted Army and his close association with Nikolai Yezhov during the Great Purges reflect a persistent desire to toy with danger?

- How does Babel's portrayal of the Cossacks in *Red Cavalry* reflect the Romantic ideal of the Noble Savage?

- Although the Cossacks are the nominal heroes of the *Red Cavalry* stories, Babel's portrayal of the Polish Jews shows surprising elements of sympathy alongside negative images of filth and poverty. To what degree does this reflect Babel's own ambivalence about his origins?

- How are the Jewish gangsters of the *Tales of Odessa* similar to the Cossacks of *Red Cavalry*?

- How does Babel use humor in his portrayal of the gangsters in *Tales of Odessa* to mock concepts of heroism?

BERYL BAINBRIDGE

Born: Liverpool, England
November 21, 1933

English writer Bainbridge has achieved popular and critical acclaim on both sides of the Atlantic for her darkly funny and sometimes tragic novels featuring sharply drawn characters, often from the lower classes, who struggle with the ironies and disappointments of life.

BIOGRAPHY

Beryl Bainbridge was born on November 21, 1933, in Liverpool, England, during the depths of the Great Depression. She was raised in the town of Formby, not far from Liverpool. Her parents, Richard and Winifred Baines Bainbridge, encouraged Beryl and her older brother to read and write. The family, however, was not a happy one. Richard Bainbridge was prone to emotional instability and his violence colored Bainbridge's youth. Writing became a means of escape from her difficult home environment. At ten, she produced her first book, but she destroyed it. Her next literary work was called *Filthy Lucre: Or, The Tragedy of Andrew Ledwhistle and Richard Soleway*, completed when she was about thirteen but not published until 1986.

Bainbridge was expelled from school at age fourteen when she was discovered with a lewd note. Subsequently, at age sixteen and with her mother's encouragement, she joined the Liverpool Playhouse Company to study acting and work as assistant stage manager. She remained there until 1952; her experiences formed the basis of her later novel *An Awfully Big Adventure* (1989).

In 1954, Bainbridge married artist Austin Davies. The couple had two children, but the marriage ended in divorce in 1959. Throughout her marriage and thereafter, Bainbridge continued to write. In 1958, she completed a novel that would be published in 1972 as *Harriet Said*, the account of two girls who ultimately commit murder. After her divorce, she was briefly married again to writer Alan Sharp, by whom she had a third child. During this period, she also produced her third novel, *A Weekend with Claud*, published in 1967. In a pattern that she would follow in later life, Bainbridge radi-

cally revised this novel for republication in 1981, cutting the story to the bare bones and renaming it *A Weekend with Claude*. Likewise, *Another Part of the Wood* (1968) was revised and republished in 1979.

Bainbridge often used her own memories and family members as the basis for her books. *The Dressmaker* (1973; published in the United States as *The Secret Glass*, 1973) was based on her two aunts' experiences during World War II while living in Liverpool. In addition, *The Bottle Factory Outing* (1974) was based on her own employment at a bottling factory in the late 1960's. In this black comedy, one of the main characters is murdered at a picnic she has planned for the workers of a bottle factory, who ultimately throw her body into the ocean. While reviews of this novel were mixed, it garnered for Bainbridge her first Man Booker Prize nomination and won the *Guardian* Fiction Award in 1974. Bainbridge followed this novel with *Sweet William* (1975), *A Quiet Life* (1976), and *Injury Time* (1977), which won the Whitbread Award that year.

In 1978, Bainbridge briefly left the autobiographical subject matter of her earlier work and turned to history for her next endeavor. Her novel *Young Adolf* (1978) imaginatively recreated a visit to Liverpool by Adolf Hitler in 1910, demonstrating the events in his life that turned the young man into a psychopathic dictator bent on world domination. The work was well received, and in 1978 she was named a fellow of the Royal Society of Literature. She also began working on teleplays and screenplays of some of her earlier novels.

After the publication of the 1980 novel *Winter Garden*, Bainbridge made a series of documentaries for the British Broadcasting Corporation

(BBC) based on literary subjects before turning to a historical subject once again with *Watson's Apology* (1984). In this novel, she reimagined the life of writer John Selby Watson, who murdered his wife. Again, reviews were mixed. She followed the novel with a volume of short stories, *Mum and Mr. Armitage: Selected Stories of Beryl Bainbridge*, published in 1985.

In 1989, Bainbridge published one of her best-known and best-loved novels, *An Awfully Big Adventure*. For subject matter, she returned to her youthful experience of working as an assistant stage manager in Liverpool during the post-World War II years. She again created characters who need but are unable to give or receive love. *An Awfully Big Adventure* earned for Bainbridge yet another Man Booker Prize nomination in 1992. Bainbridge also attracted new readers for her work after the release of the 1995 film based on the novel.

Returning to her pattern of alternating autobiographical material with historical sources, Bainbridge based her 1991 novel, *The Birthday Boys*, on the ill-fated expedition of Antarctic explorer Robert Scott. Scott's journals, recovered after his death while attempting to reach the South Pole in 1912, were Bainbridge's primary sources, as were the memoirs of one of the survivors of the trip.

Over the next several years, Bainbridge occupied herself with a collection of newspaper columns published as *Something Happened Yesterday* in 1993 and with a second volume of short stories published in 1994. In 1996, Bainbridge turned to one of the biggest historical events of the twentieth century for her next novel: the sinking of the ocean liner *Titanic*. That novel, *Every Man for Himself*, was nominated for a Man Booker Prize and won the Whitbread Novel Award. Her 1998 novel, *Master Georgie*, a story set during the Crimean War, was yet another contender for the Man Booker Prize. Although it did not win that award, it was the winner of the W. H. Smith Literary Award and the James Tait Black Prize. Bainbridge's love of the theater reemerged during the late 1990's, when she began contributing a column to the monthly theater magazine *The Oldie*. A collection of those columns, *Front Row: Evenings at the Theatre, Pieces from "The Oldie,"* appeared in 2005. Meanwhile, Queen Elizabeth II recognized Bainbridge as a Dame of the British Empire in 2000 for her creative contributions to the United Kingdom.

According to Queeney (2001) once again found Bainbridge visiting a distant historical period. The novel traced the relationship between Samuel Johnson, the well-known dictionary writer, and Hester Thrale, the wife of a wealthy brewer. Bainbridge used the character of Queeney, Hester's eldest child, as the narrator, interspersing episodes with letters written by Queeney much later as a plot device.

The assassination of Robert F. Kennedy in 1968 served as the backdrop for Bainbridge's novel *The Girl in the Polka Dot Dress*, scheduled to be released in late 2009. Bainbridge took her title and subject matter from a small detail in the police report regarding the event: Several witnesses recalled having seen a young woman wearing a polka-dot dress who was nowhere to be found when the police arrived.

Bainbridge continued to live in England, where she was considered to be a national treasure. Her work has earned both critical and popular acclaim for more than forty years.

ANALYSIS

Bainbridge's novels, while all very different from one another in subject, share certain characteristics. Certainly, the setting is extremely important in each of the books; indeed, the setting becomes almost another character in many of the novels. For example, a number of the novels are set during World War II or immediately thereafter in Liverpool, England. Liverpool, a dirty, industrial city, was heavily bombed during the war, and its residents lived through extreme deprivation during this time. In Bainbridge's novels, the lower classes in particular have a difficult time putting food on the table and simply staying warm. In addition, there is a clear depiction of class-consciousness throughout all of the novels set in mid-twentieth century England. Likewise, Bainbridge's historical fictions also offer realistic and factual details about the times and places in which they are set.

Bainbridge's characters often share a need for intimate relationships. They are looking for love, but few can find even affection. In particular, Bainbridge's use of sexual scenes in her books borders on the disturbing. The encounters are never tender, but rather are often darkly humorous, violent, or simply sad. While body parts engage in intimate behavior, it is as if the hearts and minds of the characters are elsewhere. There is a callousness to human interaction in Bainbridge's novels that is at once heartbreaking and compelling.

Bainbridge's novels also display a dark humor. Amid the often macabre story lines, she inserts ironies that are funny in spite of their tragic consequences. For example, in *An Awfully Big Adventure*, Stella plays Tinker Bell in a production of J. M. Barrie's *Peter Pan* (pr. 1904, pb. 1928) by holding a flashlight. She hears of the death of a man she is having an affair with just as Peter asks the children in the audience to clap to bring Tinker Bell back to life. Stella drops the flashlight, in effect killing Tinker Bell, and traumatizes the children. Likewise, in *The Bottle Factory Outing*, it is ironically the character who has planned the outing who winds up murdered. The response of the rest of the characters to the death is both comic and dreadful.

Finally, from Bainbridge's early novel *Harriet Said* to her 2001 novel, *According to Queeney*, the writer has pushed the edges of narrative reliability. She does so in several ways. For one, she pares away all but the most essential details of her stories; in fact, there are times when critics have suggested that she has pared too much away, leading to ruptures in the narrative. Moreover, characters in the novels often see the same events in very different ways. The reader, then, is left in a place of indecision. In *The Birthday Boys*, for example, the same story is told by explorer Robert Scott and four members of his team. Of the five, who is the most reliable? Which version of the story is to be believed? The use of flashbacks as a structuring device also impacts narrative reliability. Characters who earlier participated in an event will later remember the event in different ways. Thus, which account should be trusted, the "present" interpretation or the flashback? Finally, Bainbridge often uses historical figures as fictional characters. Consequently, each reader will bring to the novel previous knowledge that will butt up against the fictional representation. In novels such as *Young Adolf*, Bainbridge attempts to create a past for one of the most infamous people in history, Adolf Hitler. That readers find some sympathy for the young Adolf is a tribute to Bainbridge's skill as a writer. It also demonstrates just how far a narrative can be stretched.

Few contemporary writers are as prolific as Bainbridge, and even fewer can claim the overwhelming critical and public acclaim. Eccentric, innovative, creative, funny, and disturbing, Bainbridge's work defies simple classification.

An Awfully Big Adventure

First published: 1989
Type of work: Novel

A strange, motherless teenager attempts to find her way amid the colorful characters of a local repertory theater staging Peter Pan *in 1950's Liverpool.*

An Awfully Big Adventure is one of Bainbridge's best-known novels. A film adaptation of the book, directed by Mike Newell and starring Alan Rickman, Hugh Grant, and Georgina Cates, was released in 1995. Bainbridge used her own experiences as a young assistant stage manager in a local Liverpool repertory theater as the backdrop for the story of Stella, a troubled teenager who affects each of the other members of the troupe without realizing it.

The setting of the novel is grim; lower-class life in Liverpool after World War II is depicted as gritty and hard. Stella lives with her uncle and her uncle's girlfriend, who do their best to care for the young woman who was abandoned by her wild mother some sixteen years earlier. Uncle Vernon wants to save Stella from the fate of so many young women who find themselves working in factories or restaurants when they leave school, and he calls in many favors to secure her a spot at a repertory theater.

The book opens by dropping readers into a scene that they will not understand until much later in the book. Clearly, something is very wrong; Meredith Potter, the troupe director, finds a girl in the props room, a girl who turns out to be the story's protagonist, Stella. After a brief but angry encounter, Stella runs from the theater, taking refuge in a phone booth outside.

The novel then flashes back to the story of Stella's first day at the theater and follows through chronologically until it returns to the opening scene. Because the reader knows from the opening pages that something dreadful will happen before the book ends, the entire story is told under a pall.

Each member of the company has his or her own secrets. Stella, who is by all accounts an odd young woman, has a knack for delivering knockout blows without even being aware of it through casual remarks or thoughtless actions. Moreover, each of the characters is in love with the wrong person. Stella, for example, has a crush on Meredith. Although the rest of company knows that he is a homosexual, Stella does not. When Meredith does not return her advances, she has an affair with O'Hara, an older, legendary actor. The affair is meaningless to her, but it has dire consequences for O'Hara, who recognizes in Stella, too late, a woman he loved some sixteen years earlier.

Indeed, the consequences of earlier choices flood the end of the novel. Not one of the characters escapes unscathed from the troupe's production of *Peter Pan*. In the final scene, Stella stands in the telephone booth, speaking to a recording of the time she calls "Mother."

ACCORDING TO QUEENEY

First published: 2001
Type of work: Novel

The later years of Dr. Samuel Johnson, the famed lexicographer and writer of the eighteenth century, and his relationship with the married Hester Thrale are narrated many years later by Hester's daughter Queeney.

Most contemporary readers know about Dr. Samuel Johnson through two works: Johnson's own *A Dictionary of the English Language: To Which Are Prefixed, a History of the Language, and an English Grammar* (1755) or James Boswell's *The Life of Samuel Johnson, LL.D* (1791). Johnson enjoyed fame and notoriety during his own lifetime and continues to be remembered as one of the most important writers of the eighteenth century. In *According to Queeney*, Bainbridge imaginatively re-creates Johnson's later years, when he was closely connected to Hester Thrale, the wife of a wealthy brewer.

Bainbridge structures the novel through two narrative voices. The first is a third-person authorial voice that details specific events in the lives of the characters. At the close of each section, a second narrative voice enters, that of Queeney, Hester Thrale's eldest child. These sections are in the form of letters written long after the described events. Queeney's interpretation of events is often at odds with the section the reader has just completed. As a result, it is difficult to construe "the truth" of the event. By so constructing her novel, Bainbridge both gives and takes away: Just as the reader settles into the story, the subsequent epistle undermines the narrative itself. Bainbridge thus calls into question the whole notion of historical truth. Rather, she seems to suggest, there are only interpretations.

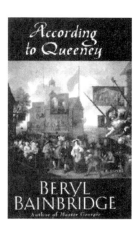

The Samuel Johnson who emerges from *According to Queeney* is one beset with emotional difficulties. He clearly suffers from obsessive-compulsive disorder, as well as mind-robbing depression. At the same time, he shows sympathy and love to young Queeney, something seriously lacking in her life.

Hester Thrale, a woman who bears some ten children, only to lose most of them, is also an enigma. Viewed through Queeney's eyes, she is a bitter, vicious woman, devoid of any maternal instinct. Readers, however, may find in her a fear of intimacy brought about by her loss of so many of her babies. Her problems with Queeney may stem not from loving her too little but from loving her too much.

The major parts of the novel trace the travels of Johnson and the Thrales across England and throughout Europe. By the end, Johnson has been abandoned by Hester, who has married a young Italian voice teacher after the death of her husband. Johnson dies without seeing her again.

SUMMARY

Whether she is writing about memories from her personal past or using historical events as the basis of her fiction, Beryl Bainbridge creates memorable characters and spot-on dialogue in her many novels. While some critics find her writing to be too spare, most acknowledge her deftness of plot and her skill in structuring highly inventive and creative works. Her novels often traverse the ground between comedy and tragedy. Often eccentric, always innovative, Bainbridge's novels call into question notions of history, truth, love, and fate.

Diane Andrews Henningfeld

BIBLIOGRAPHY

By the Author

LONG FICTION:

A Weekend with Claud, 1967 (revised 1981 as *A Weekend with Claude*)
Another Part of the Wood, 1968 (revised 1979)
Harriet Said, 1972
The Dressmaker, 1973 (pb. in U.S. as *The Secret Glass*, 1973)
The Bottle Factory Outing, 1974
Sweet William, 1975
A Quiet Life, 1976
Injury Time, 1977
Young Adolf, 1978
Winter Garden, 1980
Watson's Apology, 1984
Filthy Lucre: Or, The Tragedy of Andrew Ledwhistle and Richard Soleway, 1986
An Awfully Big Adventure, 1989
The Birthday Boys, 1991
Every Man for Himself, 1996
Master Georgie, 1998
According to Queeney, 2001

SHORT FICTION:

Mum and Mr. Armitage: Selected Stories of Beryl Bainbridge, 1985
Collected Stories, 1994

NONFICTION:

Something Happened Yesterday, 1993
Front Row: Evenings at the Theatre, Pieces from "The Oldie," 2005

About the Author

Baker, John F. "Total Immersion in the Past." *Publishers Weekly* 245, no. 45 (November 9, 1998): 52-53.
Gerrard, Nicci. "The Death of Tinkerbell." *New Statesman and Society,* January 5, 1990, 38-39.

DISCUSSION TOPICS

- What techniques does Beryl Bainbridge use to make her characters come alive for readers?

- What role does the setting play in each of Bainbridge's novels?

- What are some examples of irony in Bainbridge's novels, and how does she use irony as a plot device?

- What is black humor and how does it function in *An Awfully Big Adventure*?

- Bainbridge has written a series of historical novels, including events such as the Crimean War, the sinking of the *Titanic*, and the doomed Antarctic expedition of Robert Scott. What do her novels tell readers about the nature of history and the nature of narrating history?

- In *According to Queeney*, Bainbridge uses an innovative structure by having a section of straight narration concerning some event in Samuel Johnson's life, only to follow it by a letter from the adult Queeney that refers to the event. How do the letters undermine the flow of the narration? Do the letters clarify or complicate the picture the novels paints of Johnson?

- In *An Awfully Big Adventure*, how does Stella affect each of the other characters? What is the result for each of them of her presence in the troupe? Is Stella aware of the consequences of her actions and comments?

Jagodzinski, Cecile M. "Beryl Bainbridge." In *British Novelists Since 1960: Fourth Series*, edited by Merritt Moseley. Vol. 231 in *Dictionary of Literary Biography*. Detroit: Gale Group, 2000.

Lassner, Phyllis. "'Between the Gaps': Sex, Class, and Anarchy in the British Comic Novel of World War II." In *Look Who's Laughing: Gender and Comedy*, edited by Gail Finney. Langhorne, Pa.: Gordon and Breach, 1994.

———. "Fiction as Historical Critique: The Novels of Beryl Bainbridge." *Phoebe* 3, no. 2 (1991): 12-24.

Punter, David. "Beryl Bainbridge: The New Psychopathia." In *The Hidden Script: Writing and the Unconscious*. London: Routledge and Kegan Paul, 1985.

Rennison, Nick. *Contemporary British Novelists*. London: Routledge, 2005.

Wenno, Elisabeth. *Ironic Formula in the Novels of Beryl Bainbridge*. Goteborg, Sweden: Acta Universitatis Gothoburgen, 1993.

HONORÉ DE BALZAC

Born: Tours, France
May 20, 1799
Died: Paris, France
August 18, 1850

Balzac developed the novel into a superb instrument for the realistic depiction of contemporary life and created a gallery of characters that have become part of the mythology of French culture.

BIOGRAPHY

Honoré de Balzac (BOL-zak) was born in Tours, France, on May 20, 1799. His father, Bernard-François, was a government official of peasant origin. His mother, Anne-Charlotte-Laure Sallambier, from a family of similar background but higher status, was twenty-two years younger than her husband. Honoré, the first of their four children, felt closest to his sister Laure in his childhood and early youth. Educated at boarding schools, he was a voracious reader and showed an early interest in philosophy. In 1814, the Balzac family moved to Paris.

From 1816 to 1818, Balzac attended the Sorbonne, studying law and philosophy. He was apprenticed to a lawyer but resolved to pursue literature as his profession. For seventeen months between 1818 and 1820, supported by his parents, Balzac lived in a tiny garret in Paris and dedicated himself to learning the craft of writing. The first product of this apprenticeship was a five-act tragedy, *Cromwell* (wr. 1819-1820, pb. 1925), inspired by the neoclassical dramas of Pierre Corneille and Jean Racine. The verdict of both family and outsiders was unanimous: Balzac should give up writing. He left his garret and returned to his family but continued to write.

Balzac now experienced a second literary apprenticeship, producing numerous anonymous potboilers and writing popular fiction and self-improvement manuals in collaboration with pulp novelists and journalists. He did not, however, neglect the cultivation of more serious literary interests; even the potboilers show the growing influence upon Balzac of his great predecessors François Rabelais, Molière, and Jean-Jacques Rousseau, as well as the leading writers of the Romantic movement, whose early growth paralleled Balzac's lifetime. A watershed year for this movement was 1830, which saw revolutionary upheavals across Europe and the ascendance of such Romantic luminaries as Victor Hugo, Stendhal, George Sand, and Alfred de Vigny.

In 1824, Balzac's parents left Paris, and he was on his own again. He experienced a renewed interest in philosophy, meditated on politics and religion, and absorbed the new literary trend toward satirical and topical realism. Yet he still lacked recognition as a writer and was regarded as a man without a real career. His parents urged him to plunge into the world of business with their financial backing. Thus between 1825 and 1828, with ingenuity and enthusiasm but little patience for detail, Balzac pursued the commercial side of book production. All of his investments in publishing, bookselling, and printing went bankrupt. The experience, however, bore fruit in his understanding the economic forces of society, thus enriching his novels though not his bank account.

In 1828, Balzac rededicated himself to writing and at last had a modest success with the first novel to which he later signed his name, *Les Chouans* (1829; *The Chouans*, 1885). For the next nineteen years, Balzac wrote steadily and enjoyed a growing success, and by 1831, his self-confidence led him to add "de" to his name. By 1831, Balzac had the concept, put into effect later, of intertwining most of his works into *La Comédie humaine* (1829-1848; *The Comedy of Human Life*, 1885-1893, 1896; also known as *The Human Comedy*, 1895-1896, 1911).

The novels of this cycle that have become an integral part of French culture, their heroes and heroines seen as virtual archetypes, include *La Peau de chagrin* (1831; *The Wild Ass's Skin*, 1888), *Le Médecin de campagne* (1833; *The Country Doctor*, 1887), *Eugénie Grandet* (1833; English translation, 1859), *Le Père Goriot* (1834-1835; *Daddy Goriot*, 1860, also as *Père Goriot*), *La Cousine Bette* (1846; *Cousin Bette*, 1888), and *Le Cousin Pons* (1847; *Cousin Pons*, 1880).

Even more than most writers, the concrete and sensual Balzac felt that his talent was nourished by beautiful, exotic, and delicious things. His pursuit of social success showed a thirst for the sumptuous and aristocratic—not out of simple materialism but rather to satisfy an appetite for what he called the "Arabian nights" atmosphere of Parisian high life. Thus his extravagances outstripped his income, and debt was a constant goad both to produce more and to improve his social contacts. He was fortunate in his friends and protectors, above all Mme Laure de Berny, his most important woman friend.

Beginning in 1832, almost two years before actually meeting the Polish-born Countess Eveline-Constance-Victoire Hanska (née Rzewuska), Balzac conceived an idealized passion for her in the course of an exchange of letters that she had initiated. Their eventual meeting and liaison were complicated by the necessity that Balzac stay on good terms with Hanska's husband. When Hanska became a widow in 1847, the planned marriage with Balzac was postponed until Hanska's affairs could be put in order. Marrying a foreigner meant that Hanska had to transfer ownership of her huge estate at Wierzchownia, located in the Ukraine, to her daughter. That she was willing to do, as Hanska, like Balzac, greatly preferred Paris.

In 1848, numerous misfortunes struck at once. New revolutions flared across Europe. Apart from more serious destruction, the sale of books virtually ceased at the very moment when Balzac was most in need of money. Also at that time, Balzac's health, long abused, collapsed. His heart and di-

gestion were beyond repair. He enjoyed a few months of happiness on Hanska's estate, whose beauty he began to describe in unfinished notes called the "Lettre sur Kiev" (1847). Thereafter, his health rapidly declined. On March 14, 1850, Balzac and Hanska were married in Berdichev, Ukraine. With Balzac gravely ill, he and Hanska made an excruciatingly difficult journey back to Paris, where Balzac died days later on August 18, 1850.

ANALYSIS

The fullest expression of Balzac's vision is *The Human Comedy*. Although it comprises more than ninety novels and stories, it was never completed. Enough is in place, however, to allow one to grasp the outer limits and inner workings of a complete universe. As Napoleon I set out to conquer Europe—a parallel of which Balzac was well aware—Balzac set out to conquer the world that he envisioned by capturing it in words. Province by province and realm by realm, Balzac added to his universe of human types, occupations, and conditions.

The idea of using recurring characters—coming to the foreground in some works, receding to the background in others, thus creating an effect of multidimensional reality—came to Balzac spontaneously, indeed as an organic outgrowth of his work. Yet he found philosophical support for his method in the thinking of French naturalist Geoffroy Saint-Hilaire regarding the unity in diversity of all creation.

Balzac bases his compelling vision upon portraits of physically and psychologically convincing individuals. The reader is made to care enough about Balzac's individual characters to absorb even the most prosaic details of their occupations and, eventually, the workings of the social forces that buffet them.

One of Balzac's most moving characters is Père Goriot, in the novel of the same name. At first, Balzac reveals little more of him than that he is a retired pasta maker, a thoroughly prosaic profession. Before the story began, when Goriot had first moved to Mme Vauquer's boardinghouse, he was rotund and portly and wore a coat of cornflower blue. Then Goriot goes into a decline, which is depicted only through humble, concrete details. Both the reader and Goriot's fellow boarders are brought to an extreme pitch of suspense as Balzac withholds all explanation. At last, clues surface that suggest a hypothesis: A girl comes to visit Goriot, gliding into his room like a snake, with "not a speck of mud on her laced cashmere boots."

Balzac was one of the first great literary realists of the nineteenth century to discover that the most prosaic details of real life are themselves poetry. It requires an unobtrusive mastery and poetic inspiration to make such unlikely material as "laced cashmere boots" speak to the reader's emotions. Yet while Balzac could have created beauty with an unrelieved inventory of prosaic details, he does not limit himself in that way. His portraits of girls and young women shine with a luminous charm. In creating such portraits, which always have an element of the ideal, Balzac combines realistic detail with metaphor. His range of memorable characters includes the spiritual Eugénie Grandet and the worldly but noble Mme de Beauséant.

An important organizing element of Balzac's world, one which raises it to a higher aesthetic pitch than the real world it resembles, is contrast. The author shows wealth side by side with poverty, the ascetic beside the profligate, beauty beside ugliness, the ideal and the cynical, the urbane and the rustic, virtue and vice. Such contrasts abounded in his own life and in the city that he loved—Paris, the "ocean that no line can fathom," the world within a world. Just as no quality can exist without its opposite, proud Paris cannot exist without the provinces. Yet, paradoxically, the extremes can sometimes change places or masquerade in each other's raiment.

Balzac, who began his literary career by following the tragedies of Racine and Corneille, reached for a higher insight in *The Human Comedy*. If Dante's *La divina commedia* (c. 1320; *The Divine Comedy*, 1802) had provided a guide to Hell, Purgatory, and Heaven, then Balzac would write a no less comprehensive account of this world. To call it "comedy" was not a facile decision, though "tragicomedy" might have been more accurate; time and again, Balzac's heroes make great sacrifices that are unnecessary, unappreciated, misunderstood, or, worst of all, drive out of reach the very goal that they are seeking. The "human" side of Balzac's epic is in the universals of human nature that he reveals. In a world where the real and illusory are intertwined, simple human love endures as the great, and only nonillusory, value.

While Balzac's psychological insight is the foundation of his realism and enduring interest for the reader, his understanding of the political and economic workings of his society adds depth to the picture. Ideologically, Balzac was Roman Catholic, conservative, and at times an avowed monarchist. He was too keenly aware of the opportunism in human nature to put much faith in radical political ideology. He also expressed an almost visceral aversion to the "mud" in which the lower classes lived and with which his heroes dread being spattered. Yet in the heyday of Romantic contempt for the "Philistine" (in other words, everyone who was not an artist, from the humblest tradesmen to upper-class professionals), Balzac had a generous, democratic acceptance of so-called ordinary people. A human being, to Balzac, was by definition never ordinary, and the distinctions of class had no effect on the universal human dilemmas of how to live, whom to love, and what choices to make.

Despite his humanistic spirit, Balzac was acutely aware of the pervasive role of money throughout the French society of his day. It was a glue binding all together, from the lowest to the highest. Its power to corrupt provides the saddest, most pessimistic, and most ironic pages of *The Human Comedy*.

With Balzac, creative fiction comes of age, and the outer parameters of the realistic novel are clearly indicated even if Balzac did not live to fill them in completely. Later novelists who proudly acknowledged their debt to him include Fyodor Dostoevski, Henry James, and Balzac's compatriots Guy de Maupassant and Marcel Proust.

THE WILD ASS'S SKIN

First published: *La Peau de chagrin*, 1831 (English translation, 1888)
Type of work Novel

Balzac contrasts the exercise of will and calm wisdom, dissipation and asceticism, involvement in life with all its delights and pains and withdrawal.

Inspired by Balzac's contrasting ideas about the nature of the will and the expenditure of necessarily finite vital force, *The Wild Ass's Skin* is the first and probably the greatest of Balzac's "Philosophical Studies," a subdivision of *The Human Comedy.* Raphaël de Valentin has run out of money and decides to throw himself in the River Seine. Waiting for nightfall, he enters an old curiosity shop, where an old man offers him a magical wild ass's skin, *un peau de chagrin* (in French the latter word means both "shagreen," or wild ass's skin, and "grief" or "vexation"). The wishes of its possessor will be fulfilled but the skin will shrink in proportion to the number and strength of those wishes. When it has shrunk into nothing, its owner will die.

The old man has lived to a great age by avoiding desire and its turmoil; Raphaël declares that he wants to live to excess. Rushing from the shop, he falls in with friends who take him to an orgy. There he recounts at length to a fellow guest how years of contented denial and scholarly work in a garret were followed by the agony of his love for the heartless Countess Foedora, for whom he had squandered money earned by writing and gambling. The morning after the orgy, Raphaël learns that he has inherited the vast wealth he had wished for but sees that the skin has perceptibly shrunk. He realizes that he can do whatever he wants, but he wants now to do nothing and therefore husband his life.

He organizes a regime in which he is never obliged to express a wish. Cut off from almost all human contact, he effectively abdicates from life for the sake of going on living, constantly attempting the impossible task of repressing the slightest desire.

Raphaël again meets Pauline, the daughter of his former landlady, who had always loved him. Now she is rich and conforms to his idea of the perfect society lady. He is overwhelmed by her beauty and goodness, and he returns her feelings. There follow days of ecstasy. Sometimes Raphaël feels that love is worth its cost, but in fear he eventually flees Pauline. When she finds him he cannot control his desire, which causes the disappearance of the final remnant of the ass's skin and therefore his death.

EUGÉNIE GRANDET

First published: 1833 (English translation, 1859)
Type of work: Novel

The selfless goodness of Eugénie Grandet survives the harshness of her miserly father and the treachery of her lover, but her moral triumph is not accompanied by any hope of happiness.

Eugénie Grandet shows Balzac at his most idealistic. He presents three characters who are completely incorruptible in the face of the greed that surrounds them. Eugénie Grandet, her mother, and their servant Nanon all lead lives that are virtually monastic in their self-denial. Despite the fabulous wealth that has been accumulated by the shrewd and unscrupulous winemaker, Monsieur Grandet, his family lives in

a wretched house, under strict and despotic rules enforced by him.

While Grandet, a miser who doles out candles and sugar cubes one at a time, keeps his wife and daughter ignorant of their enormous fortune, the local townspeople are very well aware of it. Indeed, talk of Grandet's millions is the chief subject of gossip. While everyone in town is well aware that Grandet is a most unsavory character, he is regarded with awe and forgiven every trespass because of his millions of francs. As Eugénie turns twenty-three, her father assumes that he will marry her off to the candidate of his choosing. Two local figures vie for her hand, with no thought of anything but her father's money. As all the principals are gathered for Eugénie's birthday, an unanticipated guest arrives from Paris like a magnificent peacock descending on a barnyard.

The peacock is Eugénie's cousin Charles, the son of Old Grandet's younger brother. Young Charles is visiting the poor country cousins to humor his father, from whom he is bringing a letter to Old Grandet. Unbeknown to Charles, the letter contains news of his father's bankruptcy and intended suicide.

In the few days that the young man is allotted to mourn, before he is sent to "the Indies" to make his fortune, he and his cousin fall in love. The worldly Charles has loved before; but as Balzac describes this first love of Eugénie, it is as if she were truly seeing the world for the first time. Eugénie is constantly accompanied by the imagery of light. As light is the first thing that people love, asks Balzac, then is not love the very light of the heart?

In one of many plot ironies anticipating the stories of Guy de Maupassant, Eugénie gives Charles all of her gold coins, mainly gifts from her father. As a pledge of both his own and the money's return, Charles gives her a golden case with two exquisite portraits of his parents. Charles, however, uses Eugénie's money to pursue trade yielding the quickest profit, including traffic in slaves. He stays away for seven years, forgets all about her, and becomes utterly corrupt and cynical. Eugénie has to face a terrible day of reckoning when her father, who craves the sight of gold as if addicted to it, discovers that she has given all of her coins away. She refuses to tell her father anything.

The struggle of wills between father and daughter is as epical, in its own way, as any struggle in the House of Atreus (Balzac's analogy). Drama is created not by the object of contention but by the clash of principles. On Grandet's side, there is the individual's sense of absolute ownership, mastery, will, and desire. On Eugénie's side, there are moral and religious principles: fidelity, charity, pity, respect for family bonds, and love. Eugénie's mother, long ago reduced to psychological slavery by Grandet, is crushed by Grandet's harshness and suffers a decline that results in her death.

Grandet's obsession with self-enrichment and the physical possession of gold never flags. Balzac's ultimate miser differs significantly from Harpagon, Grandet's great seventeenth century French predecessor in *L'Avare* (pr. 1668, pb. 1669; *The Miser*, 1672) of Molière. Molière used his archetype to provoke ridicule and pity. Yet Grandet, who has his own sardonic sense of humor, dupes others to the very end and dies almost contentedly, with his millions intact. The contrast between Grandet and his daughter can be compared to that between Shylock and Portia in William Shakespeare's *The Merchant of Venice* (pr. c. 1596-1597, pb. 1600); it is

more stark than that between Molière's miser and his children.

PÈRE GORIOT

First published: *Le Père Goriot*, 1834-1835
    (English translation, 1860)
Type of work: Novel

A young provincial makes his choice to pursue the vanity of the world, while an old man sacrifices himself so that his two daughters may have a glittering life.

Père Goriot is a novel of beautifully balanced ironies. A young provincial, Eugène de Rastignac, comes to Paris and finds lodging in the same boardinghouse as a decrepit former pasta maker, Père Goriot. While the other lodgers make Goriot the butt of their jokes, Eugène feels an instinctive sympathy for him. Goriot, formerly wealthy, has inexplicably fallen upon hard times; for no visible reason, his fortune has melted away. He bears his humiliation with a seemingly imbecilic meekness. Another mysterious lodger, Vautrin, takes a liking to young Eugène and shocks him with a cynical offer to help him escape poverty. Vautrin eloquently states the philosophy that the ends always justify the means.

The setting is Balzac's Paris, a semimythic place that foreshadows the Paris of Charles Baudelaire's *Les Fleurs du mal* (1857, 1861, 1868; *Flowers of Evil*, 1931). The evil and the angelic live side by side and wrestle in this setting. Evil, with the unbridled power of money on its side, appears to have the upper hand. Eugène, from motives of wishing to help his family, especially his two sisters, decides to put aside the drudgery of his law studies and apprenticeship and take a shortcut to easy wealth. He persuades his mother, back home in the provinces, to sell her jewels and asks his sisters for their savings in order to outfit

him for his great adventure of storming high society. While only a poor relation, he wishes to exploit his family connection with the socially powerful Mme de Beauséant.

Meanwhile, it comes to light that Père Goriot has sacrificed all that he had, down to the last silver memento from his late wife, in order to keep his two spoiled daughters in a blaze of glory. In particular the elder daughter, Mme Anastasie de Restaud, has exploited Goriot in order to pay the bills run up by her young lover, Maxime des Trailles. She haughtily rejects Eugène, who tries to insinuate himself into her good graces, being himself irresistibly drawn to the luxury for which she has sold her father.

Goriot's only slightly less ruthless younger daughter, Delphine, then becomes the object of Eugène's relentless pursuit, initially in order to spite Anastasie and Maxime. Eugène, however, falls in love with Delphine. Like her adoring father, Eugène sees Delphine's total selfishness but is blinded by her goddesslike beauty and the need to feel that he pleases her. Rather than being able to make use of them, Eugène becomes as much the sisters' victim as their old father.

With no more left to give, Père Goriot, as pitiful as King Lear, is dying. He is barred from both his daughters' homes. In any event, they have been so profligate that they have not the wherewithal to help him. Yet so long as he is allowed simply to love them, Goriot experiences happiness. Eugène uses the last of the money that he has received from home to pay for Goriot's burial. Then he heads for the house of Delphine, still dreaming of his future conquest of society.

COUSIN BETTE

First published: *La Cousine Bette*, 1846
   (English translation, 1888)
Type of work: Novel

A hate-fueled poor relation plots against the family she sees as having slighted her, with the obsessive philandering of its head aiding her machinations.

A brilliant and vivid portrait of the Paris of Louis-Philippe, *Cousin Bette* is a portrait of hidden

rage and hatred directed against a prominent but vulnerable family. Hector Hulot has done well during Napoleon I's wars, proving himself an efficient chief transport officer and winning the beautiful and noble—if peasant—Adeline Fischer as his wife. Adeline and her sister, the jealous Lisbeth, thin, dark, and ugly, are taken by Hulot to the Paris of the Emperor Napoleon, where Bette, as she is called, nurses her hatred and resentment of her sister. Bette saves Wenceslas Steinbock, an expatriate Polish count and talented sculptor, from suicide. She forms an odd half-maternal relationship with him, and she responds with carefully concealed rage when Hulot's daughter, Hortense, wins the handsome Pole as husband. Bette then forms a pact with mercenary Valérie Marneffe, recently installed mistress of the aging Baron Hulot, against the Hulot family. If Valérie can be compared with Becky Sharp in English novelist William Makepeace Thackeray's *Vanity Fair* (1847-1848), then Bette is a portrait of venomous malice whose only parallel is William Shakespeare's Iago in *Othello, the Moor of Venice* (pr. 1604, pb. 1622, revised 1623). She sets out to destroy the family that has patronized and slighted her.

Like Père Goriot and Eugénie Grandet's father, Hulot is a monomaniac. His obsession is women, who are more important to him than even the necessities of life, his honor, and the happiness of his family. Valérie persuades him that he is the father of her child. Steinbock, now also Valérie's lover, is told he is the father, too, as are the rich retired businessman Célestin Crevel and Montès de Montéjanos, a Brazilian aristocrat and Valérie's first love. Hortense accidentally learns of her husband's infidelity, leaves him, and weeps with Adeline, to the secret joy of Bette.

Hulot asks his wife's uncle, Johann Fischer, to go to Algeria, now in the process of colonization by the French, and take grain from the Algerians in order to sell it to the French army at considerable profit. However, instead of sending Hulot the money he had anticipated, Fischer is obliged to ask for 200,000 francs to avert disgrace when the plot is discovered. Financially broken, asked to shoot himself by his superior in the War Department, and ostracized by his upright brother who dies of the disgrace, Hulot leaves his home to avoid creditors.

He hides himself in obscure quarters of Paris

and lives with a succession of working-class mistresses, occasionally accepting money from Bette, who keeps her knowledge of his whereabouts from Adeline. His wife, however, accidentally finds him in the course of her charitable work and the two are reconciled. Bette dies of a combination of tuberculosis and grief, mourned by all as the family's good angel.

The senescent baron, however, is soon pursuing the kitchen maid, whom he makes a baroness after Adeline dies of the shock of the discovery. Meanwhile, Valérie has been poisoned by the betrayed Montéjanos and Steinbock has returned to Hortense.

SUMMARY

Honoré de Balzac is an almost pure example of the creative impulse at work. Founded in the author's broad knowledge of society, his characters grow, interact, and pursue their trades as if they had a life of their own. Balzac acknowledged their autonomy, which he believed was limited only by the basic laws of his lifelike world. While a higher justice occasionally intervenes in Balzac's world, it is primarily human choices that determine the ironic course of the myriad individual lives in *The Human Comedy*.

D. Gosselin Nakeeb; updated by M. D. Allen

BIBLIOGRAPHY

By the Author

LONG FICTION:
La Comédie humaine, 1829-1848 (17 volumes; *The Comedy of Human Life*, 1885-1893, 1896 [40 volumes]; also as *The Human Comedy*, 1895-1896, 1911 [53 volumes]): Includes all titles listed below.
Les Chouans, 1829 (*The Chouans*, 1885)
Physiologie du mariage, 1829 (*The Physiology of Marriage*)
Gobseck, 1830 (English translation)
La Maison du chat-qui-pelote, 1830, 1869 (*At the Sign of the Cat and Racket*)
Le Chef-d'oeuvre inconnu, 1831 (*The Unknown Masterpiece*)
La Peau de chagrin, 1831 (*The Wild Ass's Skin*, 1888, also as *The Magic Skin* and as *The Fatal Skin*)
Sarrasine, 1831 (English translation)
Le Curé de Tours, 1832 (*The Vicar of Tours*)
Louis Lambert, 1832 (English translation)
Maître Cornélius, 1832 (English translation)
La Femme de trente ans, 1832-1842 (includes *Premières fautes*, 1832, 1842; *Souffrances inconnues*, 1834-1835; *À trente ans*, 1832, 1842; *Le Doigt de Dieu*, 1832, 1834-1835, 1842; *Les Deux Rencontres*, 1832, 1834-1835, 1842; and *La Vieillesse d'une mère coupable*, 1832, 1842)
Le Médecin de campagne 1833 (*The Country Doctor*, 1887)
Eugénie Grandet, 1833 (English translation, 1859)
La Recherche de l'absolu, 1834 (*Balthazar: Or, Science and Love*, 1859; also as *The Quest of the Absolute*)
Histoire des treize, 1834-1835 (*History of the Thirteen*; also as *The Thirteen*; includes *Ferragus, chef des dévorants*,

DISCUSSION TOPICS

- Discuss the monomania evidenced by some of Honoré de Balzac's most important characters: the miserliness of Old Grandet, the paternal love of Père Goriot, the hatred of Bette, and the erotomania of Baron Hulot.

- Balzac describes Père Goriot as a "Christ of paternity." How accurate or helpful is this characterization?

- One critic describes the loving Adeline Hulot as a "sublime sheep." Is her apparently infinite capacity for forgiveness admirable, or is it the reverse?

- Consider *Père Goriot* and *Cousin Bette* as portraits of Restoration Paris (1816-1830) and the Paris of Louis-Philippe (1830-1848). What forces dominate society in each case?

- Discuss *Eugénie Grandet*'s depiction of provincial France.

1834 [*Ferragus, Chief of the Devorants*; also as *The Mystery of the Rue Solymane*]; *La Duchesse de Langeais*, 1834 [*The Duchesse de Langeais*]; and *La Fille aus yeux d'or*, 1834-1835 [*The Girl with the Golden Eyes*])

Le Père Goriot, 1834-1835 (*Daddy Goriot*, 1860; also as *Père Goriot*)

Melmoth réconcilié, 1835 (*Melmoth Converted*)

Le Lys dans la vallée, 1836 (*The Lily in the Valley*)

Histoire de la grandeur et de la décadence de César Birotteau, 1837 (*History of the Grandeur and Downfall of César Birotteau*, 1860; also as *The Rise and Fall of César Birotteau*)

Illusions perdues, 1837-1843 (*Lost Illusions*)

Splendeurs et misères des courtisanes, 1838-1847, 1869 (*The Splendors and Miseries of Courtesans*; includes *Comment aiment les filles*, 1838, 1844 [*The Way That Girls Love*]; *À combien l'amour revient aux viellards*, 1844 [*How Much Love Costs Old Men*]; *Où mènent les mauvais chemins*, 1846 [*The End of Bad Roads*]; and *La Dernière incarnation de Vautrin*, 1847 [*The Last Incarnation of Vautrin*]])

Pierrette, 1840 (English translation)

Le Curé de village, 1841 (*The Country Parson*)

Mémoires de deux jeunes mariées, 1842 (*The Two Young Brides*)

Une Ténébreuse Affaire, 1842 (*The Gondreville Mystery*)

Ursule Mirouët, 1842 (English translation)

La Cousine Bette, 1846 (*Cousin Bette*, 1888)

Le Cousin Pons, 1847 (*Cousin Pons*, 1880)

SHORT FICTION:

Les Contes drolatiques, 1832-1837 (*Droll Stories*, 1874, 1891)

DRAMA:

Cromwell, wr. 1819-1820, pb. 1925

Vautrin, pr., pb. 1840 (English translation, 1901)

La Marâtre, pr., pb. 1848 (*The Stepmother*, 1901, 1958)

Le Faiseur, pr. 1849 (also as *Mercadet*; English translation, 1901)

The Dramatic Works, pb. 1901 (2 volumes; includes *Vautrin, The Stepmother, Mercadet, Quinola's Resources*, and *Pamela Giraud*)

NONFICTION:

Correspondance, 1819-1850, 1876 (*The Correspondence*, 1878)

Lettres à l'étrangère, 1899-1950

Letters to Madame Hanska, 1900 (translation of volume 1 of *Lettres à l'étrangère*)

About the Author

Bellos, David. *Balzac: "La Cousine Bette."* London: Grant and Cutler, 1980.

_____. *Honoré de Balzac: "Old Goriot."* Cambridge, England: Cambridge University Press, 1987.

Festa-McCormick, Diana. *Honoré de Balzac.* Boston: Twayne, 1979.

Hunt, Herbert J. *Honoré de Balzac: A Biography.* London: Athlone Press, 1957.

McGuire, James R. "The Feminine Conspiracy in Balzac's *La Cousine Bette.*" *Nineteenth-Century French Studies* 20, nos. 3/4 (Spring/Summer, 1992): 295-304.

Marceau, Félicien. *Balzac and His World.* New York: Orion Press, 1966.

Maurois, André. *Prometheus: The Life of Balzac.* New York: Harper and Row, 1966.

Oliver, E. J. *Honoré de Balzac.* New York: Macmillan, 1964.

Prendergast, Christopher. *Balzac in Fiction and Melodrama.* New York: Holmes & Meier, 1978.

Pritchett, V. S. *Balzac.* New York: Alfred A. Knopf, 1973.

Robb, Graham. *Balzac: A Biography.* London: Picador, 1994.

Rogers, Samuel. *Balzac and the Novel.* Madison: University of Wisconsin Press, 1953.

Saxton, Arnold. *Honoré de Balzac: "Eugenie Grandet."* Harmondsworth, England: Penguin Masterstudies, 1987.

Stowe, William W. *Balzac, James, and the Realistic Novel.* Princeton, N.J.: Princeton University Press, 1983.

JOHN BANVILLE

Born: Wexford, Ireland
December 8, 1945

Banville is considered one of Ireland's best contemporary writers for his philosophical novels that treat the lack of clarity in human perception and the inevitable alienation of the individual.

BIOGRAPHY

John Banville (BAN-vihl), who was born in Wexford, Ireland, is one of that country's most revered living writers. His father, Martin, worked in a garage, while his mother, Agnes, worked at home caring for Banville, his brother Vincent, and his sister Vonnie. He was educated by the Christian Brothers, who are known throughout Ireland as strict disciplinarians, and also attended St. Peter's College in Wexford. Banville decided to forgo a university education to avoid being dependent upon his family and worked instead as a computer operator for Ireland's national airline, Aer Lingus, a job that facilitated his desire to travel. He lived for a year in the United States in the late 1960's and met his wife, Janet Dunham, an American textile artist, in San Francisco. They married in 1969 and had two sons. Banville also had two daughters with Patricia Quinn, the former head of the Arts Council of Ireland.

After his return to Ireland in 1970, Banville accepted a job as a junior editor at the Irish Press. He published a short-story collection, *Long Lankin,* in 1970, and his first novel, the metaphysical *Nightspawn,* appeared the following year. His second novel, *Birchwood* (1973), a gothic fantasy about a diminished Irish family, has been compared to Charles Dickens's *Bleak House* (1852-1853).

Doctor Copernicus (1976), the first novel in what would become his scientific tetralogy, cast Banville into the international limelight. The series of novels deal with mathematics and astronomy as a means of perception. In the first novel, Nicolaus Copernicus, the sixteenth century Polish astronomer and first European to formulate the model of the solar system, is plagued with self-doubt, as is the astronomer in Banville's next historical novel, *Kep-*

ler (1981), which is based on the life and findings of Johannes Kepler, the seventeenth century German scientist who described planetary motion. The British mathematical genius Sir Isaac Newton, Banville's next scientific subject in the series, similarly deals with recurring self-doubt and the human imagination in *The Newton Letter* (1982). The final scientific novel, *Mefisto* (1986), is about a fictional mathematical prodigy, Gabriel Swan, who is engaged in a Faustian battle to save his soul. In this series, Banville equates this overwhelming self-doubt with the self-doubt experienced by writers.

In 1984, Banville was selected for membership in the highly prestigious Aosdána, an association of distinguished Irish artists who are entitled to a form of financial support from the Arts Council of Ireland, which allows them to work full time in their chosen field. Because memberships are limited, Banville resigned in 2000 to enable another artist to receive the stipend.

In 1989, Banville published the *The Book of Evidence,* the first book in a trilogy. This murder mystery gained him popular appeal as an author; it also was short-listed for Britain's prestigious Man Booker Prize and won Ireland's highly esteemed Guinness Peat Aviation Award. In the novel, protagonist Freddie Montgomery murders a Dublin servant named Josie Bell during an attempted art robbery. Banville followed this novel with *Ghosts* (1993), which once again features Montgomery, this time after his release from prison, when he is living on a desolated island and cataloging works of art. The third novel in Banville's trilogy, *Athena* (1995), has a protagonist named Morrow, who may actually be Montgomery in disguise.

In 1995, the Irish Press halted production and Banville lost his job. He accepted a position as a subeditor at the *Irish Times*. In 1998, he became the newspaper's literary editor, a position he held until the following year, when the newspaper was facing economic difficulties and offered Banville a financial settlement in returning for giving up his job.

In 1997, Banville published *The Untouchable* (1997). By entering the mind of protagonist Victor Maskell, a character based on real-life art curator turned spy Anthony Blunt, the novel examines self-abnegation and betrayal. In 2000, Banville turned to gothic suspense in *Eclipse* and continued this literary style in *Shroud* (2003). In the twenty-first century, Banville adopted the pseudonym Benjamin Black to write more mainstream mystery novels, using this name to publish *Christine Falls* (2006), a novel that received both critical and popular approval. Set in the dreary Roman Catholic Dublin of the 1950's, it relates how amateur sleuth Dr. Garret Quirke investigates the suspicious death of an unwed mother and the disappearance of her infant. Banville subsequently wrote two other mystery novels, *The Silver Swan* (2007) and *The Lemur* (2008), under the Benjamin Black pseudonym.

Banville has received numerous awards for his work, including the Allied Irish Banks Prize for *Birchwood*, a Macaulay Fellowship from the Irish Arts Council, the American-Irish Foundation Literary Award for *Birchwood* in 1976, the James Tait Black Memorial Prize for *Doctor Copernicus* in 1976, and the *Guardian* Prize for Fiction for *Kepler* in 1981. In 2005, he received the Man Booker Prize for his novel *The Sea* (2005).

ANALYSIS

A master of intricacy, Banville is highly regarded for his experimental, precise—some would say detached—prose style that has been described by critics as beautiful, lyric, innovative, original, haunting, dazzling, acute, clear-running, and flawlessly flowing. He often presents a series of interwoven narratives, instead of the more traditional chronological linear form, to unravel an intricate plot line that invariably has an unpredictable ending; for this reason, Banville has been compared to such illustrious Irish authors as Samuel Beckett and James Joyce. His plot structures are evocative of complex paintings wherein one must look beyond the surface time and time again to decipher the meaning. Indeed, many of Banville's characters are in some way connected with painting, a meta-

phor Banville uses as one of his numerous intertextual repetitions from novel to novel. For example, Freddie Montgomery in *The Book of Evidence* becomes an art thief obsessed with a seventeenth century Dutch painting, Victor Maskell in *The Untouchable* is an art curator, and Morrow in *Athena* is an art historian, as is Max Morden in *The Sea*.

Banville, whose novels thematically deal with deep personal loss, destructive love, and the excruciating psychic pain that accompanies freedom, has been called a postmodern writer for his play on words, his chronologically inconsistent narration, and his unnerving blurring of the truth. He insists that his writings have a greater chance of being fully understood if they are treated as a form of metafiction in the style of Beckett, the existentialist Irish author who haunts Banville's works. A master of irony, above all Banville is concerned with the relationship between fiction and reality. Although at times the reader can believe what Banville's first-person narrators are telling them, they are later jerked back into the reality that they are reading a work of fiction, and that the narrator is not only unreliable but quite possibly mad, or at least in a state of deep denial.

Like Beckett, Banville remains fluid in his evocative descriptions of landscapes and flows throughout a variety of settings and historical times that initially seem to be unrelated. As in the work of Beckett, everything is unpredictable and often what is passed off as narrative truth is distorted, or indeed a lie. One of the author's overarching concerns is the idea that despite readers' belief that everything they read is indeed real, they simultaneously understand that fiction is also "a parcel of lies." In this regard, readers learn quickly not to trust Banville because what he confides in his readers is not necessarily the truth, and the truth is something they may not learn until they turn the last page of the book.

Banville has often been compared to the novelist Vladimir Nabokov for his depiction of darkly introspective protagonists, similar to Humbert Humbert in Nabokov's *Lolita* (1955), who kidnaps his fourteen-year-old stepdaughter and inadvertently gets tangled up in a murder. Instead of being heroes, Banville's protagonists tend to be dark, brooding antiheroes who almost invariably appreciate art. For instance, in *The Book of Evidence*, Freddie Montgomery is a failed scientist without a conscience who abandons his wife and child in Greece and murders a woman simply because she got in his way. Max Morden in *The Sea*, whose name is reminiscent of the word "mordant," is caustic, conceited, and downright mean.

Banville's works are dense in literary and philosophical allusions, with the author paying particular homage to Marcel Proust, Joyce, Fyodor Dostoevski, and the philosopher Immanuel Kant. For example, in *The Book of Evidence*, Freddie Montgomery catalogs the things that bother him about prison, in particular the smell and the food. In this, Banville hails the French writer and philosopher Proust, who wrote about the interplay of meditation on the relationship between memory and imagination in *À la recherche du temps perdu* (1913-1927; (*Remembrance of Things Past*, 1922-1931, 1981). The restless wandering Freddie describes is evocative of Ulysses returning home to Ithaca, and, one removal from that allusion, Leopold Bloom's wandering around Dublin in Joyce's *Ulysses* (1922). The murder scene and Freddie's subsequent descent into madness are evocative of Dostoevski's *Prestupleniye i nakazaniye* (1866; (*Crime and Punishment*, 1886), in which Raskolnikov murders the old pawnbroker in a botched theft. Like William Shakespeare's character Lady Macbeth, Freddie scrubs and scrubs but cannot remove Josie Bell's blood. Freddie also remarks how he feels like a dangerous and unpredictable stranger, like the murderer in Robert Louis Stevenson's *The Strange Case of Dr. Jekyll and Mr. Hyde* (1886). Throughout *The Book of Evidence*, Banville also invokes philosopher Kant's "thing-in-itself" in his numerous references to Freddie's "other self."

THE BOOK OF EVIDENCE

First published: 1989
Type of work: Novel

This mystery novel examines the mind of a deranged drifter, who writes an account of the murder he committed and the mental consequences of his crime.

After abandoning his wife and son, thirty-eight-year-old Freddie Montgomery has returned to his native Dublin, committed a yet-to-be-revealed and heinous crime, and finds himself incarcerated, awaiting trial in a dark and dirty Dublin jail. The novel, which is partially based on an actual unsolved case of art thievery and murder in Britain, begins as Freddie, the first-person narrator, starts to write his confession, or his book of evidence. This beginning forces such questions as what crime did Montgomery commit, or indeed whether or not he actually committed a crime. What are his reasons for abandoning his family? Why did he return to Ireland? What happened to his career as a scientist? What is his purpose in writing this book of evidence? How did he come so far down in the world?

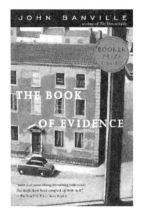

After a few moments spent in the company of his eerie, somnambulant voice, the reader begins to wonder whether or not Freddie Montgomery is even sane. As an antidote to uncertainty, Freddie believed that science would provide answers, only to find greater uncertainty. Since the story is revealed out of chronological order, in a sort of interior meditation before a flashback, the reader is forced to read the "evidence," as would a judge, bit by slow revealing bit.

Freddie writes of his travels to the United States to complete his scientific studies and how he meets Daphne, who accompanies him to Spain, where he falls in with a rough drug runner named Randolph. After ten years, he flees Spain and returns to Dublin. Upon his return, he gravitates to a notorious pub named Wally's, where he encounters an old friend, Charlie French, from whom he learns of his father's death. In need of money, Freddie wonders what happened to the paintings his father collected and is particularly concerned about a painting by Jan Vermeer. He makes his way to Coolgrange to see his mother, but he is not welcome. His mother realizes Freddie is only interested in selling the paintings. He is furious when he finds them missing.

During a visit to the estate of his friend, Anna Behren, Freddie spies the Vermeer painting, *Por-*

trait of a Woman with Gloves. He returns to the estate to steal the painting but bungles the theft, kills a female servant, and subsequently hides out in Charlie French's house, where the vision of the bloodied Josie Bell soon begins to haunt him. He questions how he came to be trapped inside a body not his own. Readers should keep in mind that Freddie is not trustworthy, and thus what he is writing in his book as evidence for his case cannot be trusted.

Visitors to Charlie's house more than likely inform the police of Freddie's whereabouts and he is sent off to jail. His lawyer wants him to plead guilty to manslaughter but Freddie is insistent that he must admit his guilt. His book of evidence then becomes a tool for redemption, a way for Freddie to expiate his soul. However, the final line of the novel, written in response to the police inspector's question about whether the content of the book is true, and Freddie's chilling response that all of it and none of it and "only shame," should be considered before the reader passes judgment.

In a subsequent Banville novel, *Ghosts,* Freddie reappears on a desolated island to welcome a shipwrecked community, in the style of William Shakespeare's *The Tempest* (pr. 1611, pb. 1623). In *Athena,* the reinvented Freddie has moved from scientist to art thief to an art historian named Morrow.

THE SEA

First published: 2005
Type of work: Novel

An aging man attempts to forget his present unpleasant circumstances by escaping into his past.

At the beginning of *The Sea,* first-person narrator Max Morden, an aging art historian, stands looking out to sea, which throughout the novel acts as an anchoring point between the past and the present. After losing his wife Anna to cancer, Max feels the compulsion to return to Ballyless, the site of an important childhood summer. It was in this seaside village that he first encountered the sophisticated Grace family and fell in love with both daughter and mother. The children, web-footed Myles and Chloe Grace, are psychically connected

twins. Their mother, Connie Grace, is beautiful, and their father, Carlo Grace, represents the god Bacchus—drunk, fat, all-seeing, and fully aware that the pubescent Max is smitten with his wife. The family travels with a teenage governess named Rose. Since Max's own home life is a shambles, he spends every minute he can with the fascinating family. Sandwiched in between his recollections of his distant past are Max's memories of a more recent event, the prolonged death of his wife Anna.

After fifty years, Max finds that the Grace's summerhouse, called the Cedars, has become a boardinghouse run by a Miss Vavasour. In an attempt to grapple with his memories and mourn his loss, he rents a room there. Despairing of ever finishing his monograph on the artist Pierre Bonnard, he has come to live among the rabble of his past, as he puts it, and ponder the idea that by devoting as much time as possible to recollection, he can perhaps live his life over. He drinks heavily.

Max soon realizes that the past is indeed not wholly what one remembers, the present is not entirely what one thinks, and the line between remembrance and creation is thin. Banville insists that memories are illusions. Like many of Banville's narrators, Max says that everything is something else, and he is correct. In time, Max realizes that his memories are mere perceptions and are recalled invariably in error. He recollects the first kiss he shared with Chloe; the surging sexual excitement when her mother opened her lap; the sad events surrounding the Graces when the twins drowned. He also understands that his life with his photographer wife Anna also was fraught with illusion.

In time, it becomes clear that Miss Vavasour is really the teenage governess Rose and that the affair Max imagined between Mr. Grace and Rose was really an affair between Mrs. Grace and Rose. For Max, everything in his life has been something else, which explains his failure, or perhaps his inability, to ever fully connect with another person.

SUMMARY

Considered among the best of Ireland's novelists, John Banville is highly regarded for his beautiful, precise, and lyrical prose style, his clever use of literary allusion, his dark humor, and his evocative philosophical ideas. His novels address deep personal loss, destructive familial love, the intense psychic pain that accompanies freedom, the illusionary aspect of human perception, and the inevitable isolation of the individual.

M. Casey Diana

BIBLIOGRAPHY

By the Author

LONG FICTION:
Nightspawn, 1971
Birchwood, 1973
Doctor Copernicus, 1976
Kepler, 1981
The Newton Letter, 1982 (novella)
Mefisto, 1986
The Book of Evidence, 1989
Ghosts, 1993
Athena, 1995
The Untouchable, 1997
Eclipse, 2000
Shroud, 2003
The Sea, 2005
Christine Falls, 2006 (as Benjamin Black)
The Silver Swan, 2007 (as Black)
The Lemur, 2008 (as Black)

SHORT FICTION:
Long Lankin, 1970, revised 1984

DRAMA:
The Broken Jug, pb. 1994 (adaptation of Heinrich von Kleist's *Der zerbrochene Krug*)
God's Gift, pb. 2000 (adaptation of Kleist's *Amphitryon*)

SCREENPLAYS:
Reflections, 1984 (adaptation of his *The Newton Letter*)
Birchwood, 1986 (adaptation of his novel)
The Last September, 1999 (adaptation of Elizabeth Bowen's novel)

TELEPLAY:
Seaview, 1994

NONFICTION:
Prague Pictures: Portraits of a City, 2003

DISCUSSION TOPICS

- As readers we are primed to believe everything the narrator tells us. Consider whether the first-person narrator in John Banville's *The Book of Evidence* is reliable. Can we believe his story?

- Banville's *The Book of Evidence* has been compared to Fyodor Dostoevski's *Prestupleniye i nakazaniye* (1866; *Crime and Punishment*, 1886). Compare Freddie Montgomery to Raskolnikov in their mental anguish, moral dilemma, and descent into madness following their crimes.

- How does self-doubt enter into the minds of narrator-protagonists Freddie Montgomery in *The Book of Evidence* and Max Morden in *The Sea?*

- Banville's first-person narrators have difficulty recollecting past events with precision. Discuss the idea of remembering versus creating.

- What, if any, are the similarities between Max Morden, the protagonist of *The Sea*, and Freddie Montgomery, the protagonist of *The Book of Evidence?*

- To what effect does Banville use literary and philosophical allusions?

John Banville

About the Author

Birkerts, Sven. "The Last Undiscovered Genius." *Esquire* 135, no. 1 (January, 2001): 50.

D'hoker, Elke. *Visions of Alterity: Representation in the Works of John Banville.* Amsterdam: Rodopi, 2004.

Fiorato, Sidia. *The Relationship Between Literature and Science in John Banville's Scientific Tetralogy.* Frankfurt am Main, Germany: Lang, 2007.

Hand, Derek. *John Banville: Exploring Fictions.* Dublin: Liffey Press, 2002.

Imhof, Rudiger. *John Banville: A Critical Introduction.* Dublin: Wolfhound Press, 1989.

Irish University Review: A Journal of Irish Studies, 36, no. 1 (June, 2006). Issue devoted to John Banville.

McMinn, Joseph. *John Banville, a Critical Study.* New York: Macmillan, 1991.

Julian Barnes

Born: Leicester, England
January 19, 1946

Barnes, described as a postmodernist with nineteenth century sensibilities, writes novels that use nontraditional forms to examine complex ideas.

© Miriam Berkley

Biography

Julian Barnes was born in Leicester, England, on January 19, 1946, to Albert and Kaye Barnes, who were French teachers and avid gardeners. He and his older brother Jonathan were raised in a very controlled environment, with no parental arguments, a mild interest in politics and none in religion, and a daily reading of *The Times* by their tight-lipped father. There were no spontaneous outbursts of any kind and few displays of affection. Childhood enthusiasms were sometimes doused by measured responses, and even efforts to gain approval for literary accomplishments in later years were stymied by terse acknowledgments.

Barnes initially attended schools in the Leicester area. When he was ten years old, the family moved to a London suburb and he won a scholarship to a private boys' school. For seven years, he took the forty-five-minute train ride into the city, spending his commuting time doing his homework. He went on to study French and Russian at the City of London School and then psychology and philosophy at Magdalen College, Oxford, earning his B.A., with honors, in 1968.

At the time of his graduation from Oxford, Barnes was undecided about a career path. Inherent restlessness led him to intersperse several jobs with additional studies in contract law, but he doubted that the legal profession would engage

him for long. In 1969, he accepted a job as a lexicographer for the supplement to the *Oxford English Dictionary*, a position he found both fascinating and tedious. He joked that as one of few males in a female-dominated office, he was often relegated to writing entries on sports references and on unpleasant or suggestive words. One of his greatest delights was in reading through earlier entries and finding humor in the work of fellow lexicographers. For example, the definition of "net" was "an expanse of holes held together with string."

After three years, he was tired of his job and ready for a change. He devoted his days to writing, accepting freelance assignments when the opportunities arose. In 1977, he became assistant literary editor and television critic for the *New Statesman*, serving in the latter capacity until 1981. From 1979 until 1981, he was deputy literary editor for *Sunday Times*, and from 1982 until 1986, he was a television critic for *The Observer.* In 1990, he was hired as the London correspondent for *The New Yorker* magazine, staying in that position until 1995. He married a highly successful literary agent, Pat Kavanagh, in 1979.

Barnes is reticent and guarded about the personal details of his life. He prefers to be judged on his work rather than on his personality or way of living. Comments from fellow writers and friends, however, give some idea of his personal life. Barnes conveys an image of a strong, silent man, private and reserved, but he sometimes becomes raucous during sporting events. He loves most forms of competition and is particularly avid about football. His college years were not particularly happy because of his shyness and unwillingness to join in the drunken rowdiness often expected of undergraduates. Domestic life, on the other hand, suits him well. He and his wife have created a home that resembles the orderliness of his childhood upbringing. While his wife and a gardener work on the flowers, he grows vegetables, often exotic ones. The couple entertain frequently, serving their guests favorite bottles from their wine cellar and asking that guest book signatures include sketched self-caricatures.

Barnes has received awards for his short and long fiction, as well as journalism. In the same year that he won the Somerset Maugham Prize for *Metroland* (1980), he also produced the first of four crime novels under the pseudonym Dan Kavanagh that chronicle the exploits of a slightly sleazy, marginally racist, bisexual detective named Duffy. While not ashamed of this genre, Barnes confessed that the character of Duffy comes from a darker side of his brain and that he changed location and used a different typewriter when working on those books.

His second novel written under his own name, *Before She Met Me* (1982), met with some success. It was the third novel, however, that launched him on a long and distinguished career as one of England's major contemporary novelists. *Flaubert's Parrot*, published in 1984, was short-listed for the Man Booker Prize and won the Geoffrey Faber Memorial Prize. Additionally, Barnes had the honor of becoming the first English writer to win the Prix Médicis, a French literary award. He went on to receive the E. M. Forster Award from the American Academy of Arts and Letters in 1986, the Prix Gutenberg in 1987, the Premio Grinzane Cavour in 1988, the Prix Fémina for *Talking It Over* (1991) in 1992, and the Shakespeare Prize from the Alfred Toepfer Foundation in Hamburg, Germany, in 1993. In 1995, France honored him as an Officier de l'Ordre des Arts et Lettres. His novels *England, England* (1998) and *Arthur and George* (2005) were short-listed for the Man Booker Prize, and *Talking It Over* and *Metroland* were adapted for film. Barnes even has a cookbook, *The Pedant in the Kitchen* (2003), to his credit.

ANALYSIS

Julian Barnes has said that he writes fiction "to tell beautiful, exact, and well-constructed lies which enclose hard and shimmering truths," adding that "some people don't like finding ideas in a novel" and have reacted "as if they've found a toothpick in a sandwich." He likes to leave his plots open and unresolved. His reputation for writing outside the bounds of tradition has earned him the label of being a postmodernist with nineteenth century sensibilities. He likes to experiment, seeing how much he can get away with before losing the thread of his story or the interest of his readers. The plot is always central but is often at the center of a web that includes many of the great social dilemmas, such as fidelity and infidelity, originality and imitation, reason and nonreason, art and life, and the past and the present. His books always question the reliability of memory and of historical truths purportedly gleaned from a past that is irretrievable. In Barnes's opinion, even autobiography is not much more than fiction, given its reliance on imperfect memory.

He explores opposites, believing that very little can be taken as true considering the constraints of what people are able to learn. Some things may be known, but what about the details that are not included—the small fish that escape the net of research? History is no less amorphous than memory. Even an "objective" historian selects parts of the past, and history, as well as memory, is always changing. Barnes hopes to bring about an awareness of the past as past, as irretrievable, and an acceptance of how ideas about the past have molded the present, which is the only reality, the only truth.

Barnes's novels cover a broad spectrum, from tales of escape and obsessions to weighty contemplations on the nature of art, death, religion, politics, and ethics. He views each new work as a separate entity, with its own characteristics and intent. He has said that at the start of any work, a writer has to be convinced that the enterprise is a departure for both the author and for the genre in general. He claims not to be overly concerned with wide acceptance or readership, though he appreciates being understood, having readers "get" him. Sometimes reading his works is a struggle, as they often encompass literary criticism, history, and psychology, in addition to telling a story. While it is possible to pinpoint certain themes in his works, Barnes resists the notion of having produced an oeuvre, joking that to be said to have one would mean that he is dead. He just writes one book after another. He rejects attempts on the part of critics to see what his books have in common.

Still, careful analysis yields some similar threads: obsession, in all its forms, love, infidelity, jealousy, the vagaries of the human heart, passions, inconsistencies, betrayal, and a search for authenticity in art and love and for constants in human relationships. He is often linguistically playful, experimenting with nontraditional narrative.

Many of his characters are driven by a need to seek answers to questions that might best be left unasked, to delve into the past, or to resolve real or imagined problems. Many of them are annoying, self-serving, unlikable. Barnes allows readers to be alone with his characters, to interact and roam freely through the narrative and then make up their own minds. He likes to stay out of the picture, tries to avoid mediating, and may not even have a narrator introduce a character. He keeps an authorial distance throughout.

Flaubert's Parrot

First published: 1984
Type of work: Novel

A widowed, retired doctor yields to an obsession with Gustave Flaubert, in part to draw close to the French writer but in actuality to escape confronting his own personal failures.

Barnes's first novel of note, *Flaubert's Parrot*, is a fictional biography of Gustave Flaubert, but only in the sense that it exposes the reader to some aspects of the French writer's personality and achievements. Barnes has likened his approach to the uncovering of an ancient tomb, where random holes are tunneled into the earth covering in an attempt to get a sense of the tomb before excavating and unsealing it. Barnes feels that such an approach might give the reader greater insight into the subject of the biography than a more traditional technique.

In large part, this novel follows the thoughts of the main character, Geoffrey Braithwaite, as he embarks on his mission to uncover the life of the esteemed Flaubert, attempting to separate fact from fiction, sometimes interpreting his findings to fit his own needs. Just as the human mind wanders, so does the narrative, with Braithwaite ruminating

about the problems inherent in writing biography, imagining arguments with Flaubert's critics, recalling rumors and innuendo about his subject, creating a few of his own scenarios, and gathering research materials, as well as telling the novel's story.

The book is a prime example of a story holding together seemingly disparate elements. It is divided into fifteen chapters, each a separate entity, but each shedding some light on either Flaubert or Braithwaite. It combines reality and fantasy, the natures of literary criticism and historical research, weighty ideas concerning the amorphousness of memory, and the impossibility of ever creating true history, all with an undercurrent of the main character's desperation as he attempts to explain his wife's faithlessness and suicide.

The first chapter sets up the premise of the novel, introducing Braithwaite, a doctor and amateur Flaubert scholar, who goes to France in search of the stuffed parrot that Flaubert was purported to have perched on his desk as a source of inspiration, his own personal muse, while writing "Un Coeur simple" ("A Simple Heart"). Braithwaite hopes that this talisman will bring him closer to the man who has figured heavily in his life, but to his dismay he learns of multiple "authentic" parrots. Still he perseveres in his mission.

Chapter 2 is a kind of free fall into the very nature of biography, or rather into the process of gathering and thinking about biographical materials. It has three chronologies, the first detailing Flaubert's triumphs, the second giving an account of his failures and disappointments, and the third listing the author's metaphorical references in his books. In another chapter, Braithwaite takes on literary critics who sometimes treasure small inconsistencies or mistakes in a work and create more furor than is warranted. He is particularly annoyed with one critic who faults Flaubert for changing Madame Bovary's eye color at least three times, not taking into consideration the impact of mood or temperament on eye intensity and shade.

Subsequent chapters deal with a mistress's accounting of her affair with Flaubert, an imagined train ride with the author, and the effects of the obscenity charges against him for writing *Madame Bovary* (1857; English translation, 1886). There are also two chapters on Braithwaite, one entitled "Dictionary of Accepted Ideas," and another in which he finally fulfills his awkward and hesitant promises to let the reader in on his full story. He acknowledges that in following his obsession, he may have been avoiding thinking about his wife, her many infidelities, and her suicide. The last chapter is an impossibly convoluted and all-encompassing final examination on Flaubert, his times, and prevailing philosophies, to be administered to students and collected at the end of three hours. Thus, Barnes ends the book with a last laugh.

ENGLAND, ENGLAND

First published: 1999
Type of work: Novel

An entrepreneur who wants to have one last stab at everlasting fame creates a virtual England, a kind of Disneyland where replicas of all the tourist attractions are featured in close proximity, in a pristine setting, to make the British experience much nicer for tourists.

Another well-received novel, this one more traditional than *Flaubert's Parrot, England, England* deals with the themes of what is authentic, what is unreal or a replica, what the nature of "Englishness" might be, and with the idea that anything can become a commodity, even history. It is an angry satire in three distinct parts. The opening and closing segments deal with Martha Cochran, first as a young girl of promise and later as a beaten-down, tired, disillusioned woman returned through a fablelike set of circumstances to preindustrial England.

The middle section depicts Martha when she is an ambitious manager, working for Sir Jack Pitman, a billionaire who is making one last bid for immortality, having already gained everything he needed in life. He is counting on adding to his fortunes to sate his need for power and wealth. He

purchases the Isle of Wight and constructs a theme park, a regional Disneyland that has all the major and cultural attractions of England: Buckingham Palace in half-scale, Robin Hood confined to a single forest (his bad deeds taking a backseat to his good ones), a double-decker bus, a black cab, warm beer, Anne Hathaway's cottage, Devonshire cream teas, the Manchester United soccer team, the white cliffs of Dover, and the Battle of Britain reenacted at regular intervals. Visitors can go to the Tower of London and stop for shopping and lunch at Harrod's department store on the top floor.

The park makes inconvenient locales more convenient, with no wasted money, no long-distance travel, no ill-kempt people, streets, or buildings to offend the affluent traveler. It is a place where actors are much gentler than their real counterparts. The featured lunch with Samuel Johnson is scrapped when the actor who depicts Johnson proves to be too closely modeled after the original in a certain boorishness of personality. He smells, has poor table manners, is depressing, irritable, asthmatic, makes fun of participants' homelands, and sulks.

In constructing this England, the architects need to deconstruct. Pitman's intent is to create a past that is more palatable to modern tastes by making everything more pleasant, conveniently located, easier to experience. He believes that replicas become more real than the actual thing. People are happy as long as they are never subjected to something they do not already know. The park is more in tune with the conventions of the day, having a well-balanced ethnicity, no gender bias, and no offensive inhabitants. In other words, the replica becomes the real, the preferred history. This is history remade; simulacra takes the place of reality and copies supplant originals.

SUMMARY

Julian Barnes's writing is precise, playful, always intelligent, always presenting opposites, and always intended to present readers with ideas rather than answers. He attempts to stay outside of the picture—an absent observer of his characters' interplay. He finds this distance essential to his stated goal of having his readers identify with and assume a one-on-one relationship with his characters. He has said there is a thin membrane between the reader and his characters, and he hopes with each new work to make that separation thinner.

In being both traditional and very much outside the norm, Barnes is difficult to classify and has gained respect as an intellectual, a commander of language, an artist with astute vision of life's absurdities, and an original. He is derivative of no one, least of all himself.

Gay Pitman Zieger

BIBLIOGRAPHY

By the Author

LONG FICTION:
Metroland, 1980
Duffy, 1980 (as Dan Kavanagh)
Fiddle City, 1981 (as Kavanagh)
Before She Met Me, 1982
Flaubert's Parrot, 1984
Putting the Boot In, 1985 (as Kavanagh)
Staring at the Sun, 1986
Going to the Dogs, 1987 (as Kavanagh)
A History of the World in 10-1/2 Chapters, 1989
Talking It Over, 1991
The Porcupine, 1992 (novella)
England, England, 1998
Love, etc., 2000
Arthur and George, 2005

SHORT FICTION:
Cross Channel, 1996
The Lemon Table, 2004

NONFICTION:
Letters from London, 1995 (essays)
Something to Declare: Essays on France, 2002
The Pedant in the Kitchen, 2003
Nothing to Be Frightened Of, 2008

TRANSLATION:
In the Land of Pain, 2002 (of Alphonse Daudet)

DISCUSSION TOPICS

- Julian Barnes wants readers to become involved with his characters. What methods does he use to break down the gap between readers and the book they are reading?

- Barnes attempts to maintain authorial distance in his works. What is his reason for doing this?

- Support the claim that Barnes is a postmodernist with his heart in the nineteenth century.

- What effect does Barnes aim to achieve in his nontraditional approach to fiction?

- Barnes is an intellectual, a novelist of ideas. In what ways do his books show his proclivity toward dealing with real problems?

- Barnes deals with opposites, with the two sides to every story. What impact does he hope this duality will have on his readers? What response is he hoping for?

About the Author

Birkerts, Sven. "Julian Barnes (1946-)." In *British Writers*, Supplement IV, edited by George Stade and Carol Howard. New York: Charles Scribner's Sons, 1997.

Guignery, Vanessa. *The Fiction of Julian Barnes: A Reader's Guide to Essential Criticism*. New York: Palgrave Macmillan, 2006.

Moseley, Merritt. *Understanding Julian Barnes*. Columbia: University of South Carolina Press, 1997.

Nunning, Vera. "The Invention of Cultural Traditions: The Construction and Deconstruction of Englishness and Authenticity in Julian Barnes' *England, England*." *Anglia* 119 (2001): 58-76.

Pateman, Matthew. *Julian Barnes: Writers and Their Work*. Tavistock, Devon, England: Northcote House, in association with the British Council, 2002.

Rubinson, Gregory J. *The Fiction of Rushdie, Barnes, Winterson, and Carter: Breaking Cultural and Literary Boundaries in the Work of Four Postmodernists*. Jefferson, N.C.: McFarland, 2005.

CHARLES BAUDELAIRE

Born: Paris, France
April 9, 1821
Died: Paris, France
August 31, 1867

Baudelaire's innovative use of poetic imagery in Flowers of Evil *laid the stylistic groundwork for the Symbolist poets, while his prose poems expanded the form of poetry.*

BIOGRAPHY

Charles-Pierre Baudelaire (bohd-LEHR) was born on April 9, 1821, in Paris, France. His father, François Baudelaire, was thirty-four years older than his mother, Caroline Dufayis. Born in 1759, François was ordained a priest prior to the French Revolution but was compelled to renounce his clerical order in 1793, the year of the most intense persecution of the clergy. François was already sixty years old at the time of his marriage to Caroline and he died in 1827 when their only child, Charles, was not yet six years old. The poet's father left him a heritage of Catholic faith that may have influenced both the moral preoccupations and the choice of imagery in Charles's later work and a financial inheritance that would come into Charles's control when he turned twenty-one. This money guaranteed the poet minimal subsistence in his adult years but became the source of a bitter dispute between him and his family.

After a year during which she devoted herself largely to her son, Caroline remarried in 1828. Her husband, Jacques Aupick, was very successful in his military career, rising eventually to the rank of general, but had virtually nothing in common with Charles, who resented Aupick's relationship with Caroline. Perhaps in rebellion against the authoritarian Aupick household, Baudelaire led an increasingly bohemian lifestyle in Paris. He had won prizes for his studies at the Collège Louis-le-Grand but was dismissed from it on disciplinary grounds. After earning his *baccalauréat*, he was supposed to study law but turned instead to the various temptations of Paris.

Fearing that when Baudelaire came into his inheritance in 1842 he would quickly squander it, his family sought to separate him from his Parisian companions. In May, 1841, he was forced to embark from Bordeaux on a voyage that would keep him out of France until the following February. The ship aboard which Baudelaire took passage was bound for India, but after a particularly rough rounding of the Cape of Good Hope, he abandoned it at the island of Mauritius in the Indian Ocean. After two months on this island and the neighboring Reunion, Baudelaire found passage on a ship returning to France. While this trip had been involuntary and Baudelaire returned from it as soon as possible, the exotic, tropical images he had encountered would play a central role in his subsequent poetry.

Back in France, Baudelaire justified his family's fears. During the two years following his coming-of-age, he spent much of the money that his father had left him and contracted numerous debts. To protect him from absolute poverty, his family instituted a legal procedure to have him effectively declared a minor and incapable of handling his own financial affairs. While this arrangement did preserve for Baudelaire a modest income from his remaining funds, he greatly resented this curtailment of his freedom. His correspondence for many years is filled with bitterness toward the lawyers administering his estate and pleas to his mother for additional money.

Soon after his return from his travels, Baudelaire began a lengthy affair with Jeanne Duval, a onetime actress of mulatto Caribbean origins, whose exotic appearance may have reminded him of his memories of Africa. Given his mother's ardent opposition to this relationship, there was no question of Baudelaire marrying Jeanne. They stayed together for a number of years, but even after their eventual separation, Baudelaire sent money to Jeanne when his meager resources permitted it. Duval survived Baudelaire. The last record of her comes from a friend of Baudelaire's, who recorded seeing her on a Paris street in 1870, obviously suffering from poverty and ill health. She was probably crippled by the same venereal disease that Baudelaire had contracted even before his departure for India.

How much of Baudelaire's physical suffering came from his syphilis and how much from the unhealthy conditions in which he lived is impossible to determine. Indeed, the two causes were linked because, unlike his contemporary, the novelist Gustave Flaubert, who suffered from the same illness but had numerous medical contacts, Baudelaire was never able to afford treatment for his disease. The chief form of his suffering, documented in his letters, concerned digestive complaints. His diet, however, was never healthy and often simply inadequate.

Living on what he regarded as a pittance from his inheritance and only occasional income from his writings, Baudelaire could afford no more than a series of rooms in residential hotels. He moved often, at one point six times in the course of barely a month, to avoid his creditors. In addition, Paris at that time lacked central heating, and there was often no money for firewood. Baudelaire wrote of one three-day period during a particularly cold December, when he spent the entire three days in bed as the only means of warming himself. Restaurants would extend only limited credit, and he had no other access to food. Even when he had money for food, however, much of it went to buy wine or opium.

Given the circumstances of his life, Baudelaire's ill health is understandable. What has amazed his readers is that, amid this stress and discomfort, he was able to produce a literary work that stands as a

milestone in modern literature. His poetry was not initially accepted. While a number of individual poems had been welcome in periodicals, the first collected edition, *Les Fleurs du mal* (1857, 1861, 1868; *Flowers of Evil*, 1931), was suppressed in 1857 when a famous lawsuit attacked its immorality. Eventually, all but six of its poems reached the public in a second edition of 1861, together with a large number of new works that have made the second edition the standard version now generally reprinted with the censured poems as an appendix.

Baudelaire yearned for acceptance as a poet, but during the height of his poetic productivity, he was read as an art critic for his commentaries on the annual Salons, the art exhibitions. When he died in Paris on August 31, 1867, at the age of only forty-six, his fame and influence were just beginning.

ANALYSIS

In terms of the evolution of literary style, Baudelaire was very much a man of his time, but his time was one of transition. The Romantic poets of the generation before him had taken the essential first steps to free poetic expression from neoclassical constraints. Victor Hugo declared in his 1829 preface to *Les Orientales* (1829; *Les Orientales: Or, Eastern Lyrics*, 1879) that "the poet is free." Hugo linked poetic expression to political liberty, a public dimension of the poet's role that Baudelaire would not follow, but he also adopted the varied poetic forms and wide range of nature images that would provide Baudelaire with the building blocks of his own style. Later, Symbolist poets such as Stéphane Mallarmé would in turn draw on Baudelaire's work to create a more complex and abstract poetic style. Later still, after Sigmund Freud transformed the view of the human mind, psychologists would explore subjective resonances of the images that Baudelaire had raised to the role of symbols. Baudelaire provided the link between two very distinct forms of expression.

The concept of "symbol," as it was to evolve in the works of the Symbolist poets, differs greatly from the allegorical use of an image to represent one, specific, other idea. Allegory has been a rich form of expresson since even before Christian tradition began to posit a link between bread and wine (the objects) and the body and blood of Christ (the idea represented). With the effusive nature description of the Romantic poets, quantities of images multiplied, but their applications remained simple. Alphonse de Lamartine's poem "Le Lac" ("The Lake") repeatedly invoked nature through lists of images—"Oh lake! mute rocks! grottoes! shadowy forest!"—but these objects represented only their own role in the scene that he described.

With his sonnet "Correspondances" ("Correspondences"), Baudelaire defined a new way of seeing objects in nature. The poem opens with the assertion that a voice within nature speaks: "Nature is a temple where living pillars/ Sometimes let forth confused words." Although the description of nature as a temple posits some form of religious revelation, the "confused words" that issue forth from it are not at once intelligible. They are symbols that must be interpreted: "Man passes through forests of symbols."

The reader is left to wonder how to interpret the mysterious symbols, but in these lines Baudelaire has provided a key. The image of the forest joins the "living pillars" of the first line to clarify that the living trees of the forest provide the pillars of nature's temple. Images that share a physical resemblance, trees and pillars, fuse to form a new concept, that of the place of worship displaced to the outdoors. The "correspondences" of the poem lie in the ways that various things resemble one another. The poet, who can perceive these affinities, can understand the mysterious unity of nature: "Like long echoes that fuse in the distance/ Into a dark, deep unity." The first similarity noted in the poem, that of trees and pillars, is based on their visually observed forms. Now, Baudelaire changes to a fusion of sounds as the echoes merge, and the sestet of his sonnet finds affinities in perfumes. This appeal to diverse senses characterizes Baudelaire's verse, where perfumes, especially, play a major role.

The most important function of the senses, however, lies in their interrelationships: "Perfumes, colors and sounds answer each other." The verb "to answer," with its implication of spoken language, recalls the "confused words" through which nature originally communicated. In the sense in which "response" implies exchange between participants, however, the verb posits a similarity between the messages of the senses. Thus, with "there are

perfumes as fresh as the flesh of children/ Sweet as oboes, green as fields," the perfumes are in turn likened to the texture of children's skin, the sound of oboes, and the color of fields. For Baudelaire, the perception of these messages of the senses, messages "containing the expansion of infinite things," allows the poet to understand mysteries hidden to the casual observer.

The role of the poet at this point is crucial. Baudelaire shared with many of his contemporaries the concept of the poet as a person of uncommon insight, whose perceptions went far beyond those of the masses. Attaining this vision, however, resulted from painful experience. Baudelaire's version of this suffering closely parallels the Fall of Man, as the poet, led astray from the beauties of the world largely by temptations associated with women, discovers that he has lost his transcendent vision.

A second sonnet much later in *Flowers of Evil*, "Obsession," returns to the images of "Correspondences" but in a much more negative context. The temple of nature remains, but it terrifies the poet: "Great woods, you terrify me like cathedrals." Conscious of his fallen state, the poet now flees those elements in nature that offer meaning: "How you would please me, oh Night, without these stars/ Whose light speaks a known language." The language of the stars testifies to what he has lost. Another sonnet documenting the poet's recognition of his fall places the reason for it clearly on his own debauchery. In "L'Aube spirituelle" ("Spiritual Dawn"), the enlightenment of his spirit corresponds to dawn awakening a reveler: "When in the house of debauchery the white and crimson dawn/ Enters together with the gnawing Ideal." The memory of the Ideal torments him, because it has now become "the unreachable azure."

The contrast between the spiritual ideal and fallen man parallels the radiant imagery that Baudelaire adopted from his trip of 1841 set against the depression of his life in Paris. Opposing images contrast the two ideas: "The sun has blackened the flame of the candles" (from "Spiritual Dawn"), but the dynamic element is the interaction between the two. The sun of the Ideal serves to darken the candles that light the debauchery.

"THE TRIP"

First published: "Le Voyage," 1861
    (collected in *The Flowers of Evil*, 2006)
Type of work: Poem

After retracing the frustration of the journey of his life, the poet posits the ultimate new beginning in the departure of death.

Baudelaire wrote "The Trip" in 1859, and in 1861 he added this poem to the second edition of *Les Fleurs du mal;* he found in it the ideal poem with which to conclude this work. The overall structure of *Flowers of Evil* is loosely autobiographical, beginning with the birth of the poet in the initial "Bénédiction" ("Benediction") and progressing through the emotional; the work also addresses the spiritual experiences of his life. "The Trip" begins again with the poet's childhood and serves as a final summary of the work before it offers a new, concluding hope.

The initial image is that of the child who can travel only in his imagination: "For the child who loves maps and engravings/ The universe satisfies his vast appetite." Yet immediately, the voice of the poet's experience intrudes to declare that this naïve enjoyment surpasses the reality of actual travel: "Oh how big the world is in lamplight/ How small the world is in the eyes of memory." The contrast of the vast and narrow perceptions of the world coincides with Baudelaire's dual vision. The poet perceives the vastness, while the fallen man sees the world close in around him.

The first section of the poem narrates a joyful departure: "One morning we leave, our minds enflamed." While the experience seems quite comfortable, the travelers find their will lulled to sleep: "Rocking our infinite nature on the finite seas." The physical limits of the ocean are contrasted this time with the unlimited potential of the human soul, lulled into unconsciousness. Baudelaire's choice of the verb "to rock" recalls his prefatory poem to *Flowers of Evil,* "Au Lecteur" ("To the Reader"), where the devil rocks the human soul before seducing it down to hell. As if this analogy were not warning enough, the following quatrain introduces the image of Circe, the seductress who sought to lure Ulysses to his doom in Homer's *Odys-*

sey (c. 725 B.C.E.; English translation, 1614). In "The Trip," however, Circe represents the danger inherent in all women, as men are "drowned in the eyes of a woman/ Tyrannical Circe with her dangerous perfumes."

A technique basic to Baudelaire's symbolism involves the progressive refinement of the definition of his central images as the same object or idea is repeated in varied contexts. In this final poem of his collection, much of the vocabulary has already acquired multiple connotations through previous usage. Thus, the woman's eyes and dangerous perfumes have become negative in the sense of contributing to the poet's seduction but remain positive in the appeal of their beauty. Such ambiguities caused the confusion that led the poet to lose sight of his ideal.

The travelers recognize the danger inherent in Circe, and "so as not to be changed into beasts, they become drunk/ On space and light and burning skies." To avoid the woman's domination, the "being changed to beasts" that threatened Ulysses and his crew, they become drunk. Yet this drunkenness, too, has been predefined in Baudelaire's lexicon as a source of danger. Already in "Benediction" the child-poet "disinherited becomes drunk on sunlight" as he enters the hazardous world, and the clustering of images of sun and drunkenness has been in several poems linked to dangers. Thus, while "The Trip" recapitulates to some extent the life of the poet, it draws on the poems that have gone before to give very precise definitions to its terms.

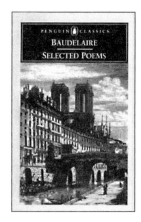

The central segment of the poem narrates the voyage, first, in part 2, still in Baudelaire's voice, and then in parts 3 through in a dialogue between the naïve child and the experienced travelers. In response to the child's repeated questions, the travelers finally declare that all that they have seen has been "the boring spectacle of immortal sin." Again, the language carries multiple meanings. While sin, especially oft-repeated, may indeed be boring, "Boredom" was also the name of the monster who, in "To the Reader," seduced men into losing their souls. Parts 7 and 8 return to the poet's own voice, providing in these two final sections a symmetry with the two opening sections of the poem. Baudelaire's conclusion concerns that "bitter knowledge that is gained from travel," and he compares the long frustration of travel to the story of the Wandering Jew. After relying on his own symbol vocabulary in the earlier parts of the poem, Baudelaire now expresses himself through traditional myth.

His last scene, paralleling the earlier use of Circe, is that of the Lotus Eaters, another of the perils that faced Ulysses. Their song invites the poet once again, "Come to get drunk," but he recognizes the danger: "By the familiar accent we recognize the specter." This ghost is that of the seductive woman: "Swim toward your Electra! / Says the woman whose knees we used to kiss."

The voyage ends with the poet seemingly alone, though he still speaks in a plural "we" that potentially incorporates all humankind. In the final section, composed of only two quatrains, the poet invites death: "Oh Death, old captain, it is time! raise the anchor! / This country bores us, oh Death! Let us set sail!" The maritime imagery redefines death. It will be a departure like any other, and as such it is nothing to be feared.

The vocabulary continues to draw on Baudelaire's previous usage, where sea voyages have been numerous and "boredom" has acquired multiple associations. Similarly, the next lines draw on the contrasts of light and darkness that have characterized Baudelaire's dual view of the world—"If the sky and the sea are as black as ink, / Our hearts, you know, are filled with light"—and his call for poison in the last quatrain repeats another recurring motif. This repetition of the familiar seems to reassure the reader that there is nothing new in this latest voyage.

"BY ASSOCIATION"

First published: "Parfum exotique," 1857
(collected in *The Flowers of Evil*, 2006)
Type of work: Poem

A woman's perfume inspires the poet to see a vision of an earthly paradise.

"By Association" details one of the many forms of departure that tempted Baudelaire throughout *Flowers of Evil* prior to his ultimate departure in "The Trip." The poem was published in the 1857 edition of *Flowers of Evil*, as well as in the 1861 edition, where it was situated between two other poems, "Hymne à la Beauté" ("Hymn to Beauty") and "La Chevelure" ("The Head of Hair"), on the general subject of the beauty of women. "By Association" also exemplifies Baudelaire's technique of developing both ideas and imagery through a sequence of related poems.

"Hymn to Beauty" addresses beauty in general, though clearly in female form, and reflects the dualism that Baudelaire recognized in this subject. The opening lines, "Do you come from deep heaven or from the abyss/ Oh Beauty?" recognize the danger of woman. Yet by the end of the poem, the poet willingly takes whatever risk that he must: What does it matter, if you—velvet-eyed fairy/ Rhythm, perfume, light, my only queen—you make the universe less ugly and time less heavy?" The attributes that Baudelaire ascribes to the woman reflect her duality. The allusions to "rhythm, perfume, light" recall the multiple sensory stimuli that contributed to the poet's vision in "Correspondences." Yet the reference to her eyes, the instruments by which women often overpower the poet elsewhere in *Flowers of Evil*, alludes to her potential dominance and links this poem to the one that is to follow.

"By Association" begins with the poet's eyes closed, in contrast to those of the woman, which are presumably open: "When with closed eyes on a warm autumn evening/ I breathe the odor of your warming breast." The poet's closed eyes imply that he is abandoning himself to the sensations provided by the perfume, sensations that still evoke, as they had in "Correspondences," a visionary experience: "I see stretched out before me happy shores/

Dazzled by the fires of a monotone sun." The vision, drawing on the suggestion of "exotique" in the title of the sonnet, conjures a setting frequent in Baudelaire's imagery. The "shores" suggest a sea voyage, while the dazzling sun suggests a tropical destination.

Dangers lurk even in this idyllic landscape. The sun described as "monotone" recalls Baudelaire's negative "boredom," and the second quatrain describing "a lazy island" anticipates the Lotus Eaters of "The Trip." The island is also inhabited by "women whose eyes astonish by their frankness." Yet the poet does not take warning from the power expressed in the women's eyes. The sestet describes an earthly paradise to which he is "guided by your perfume." In describing this paradise, Baudelaire briefly abandons the contradictory images that have rendered many of his visions ambiguous: "While the perfume of the green tamarind trees/ That circulates through the air and widens my nostrils/ Combines in my soul with the song of the sailors." The fusion of perfume and music returns to the experience of "Correspondences." This imaginative departure inspired by the woman continues in the following poem, "The Head of Hair," where the perfume of her hair carries the poet as far as "languorous Asia and burning Africa." Yet in the following, untitled poem "I adore you as the vault of night," the danger of passion reappears, as Baudelaire realizes that his experiences with the woman "separate my arms from the blue immensity."

Baudelaire's linking of themes and development of ideas from poem to poem through *Flowers of Evil* invites the reader to approach the work as a unit, both for the story that it traces of the poet's life and for the progressive development that it makes possible for his slowly evolving symbols.

"THE SWAN"

First published: "Le Cygne," 1861 (collected in *The Flowers of Evil*, 2006)
Type of work: Poem

Images of exile cause the poet to meditate on his own solitude.

In "The Swan," a poem appearing much later in *Flowers of Evil* than "By Association," Baudelaire's perspective has considerably evolved. Numerous disappointing experiences with women and other distractions have persuaded him that what he has lost through his dissipation has been of more lasting importance than what he has enjoyed. He now finds himself removed from his once-clear vision of his ideal.

The imagery of "The Swan" functions on two levels of complexity. The surface meaning remains deceptively simple. Baudelaire enumerates several examples of exile—Victor Hugo, Andromache, and the swan—and proposes them as simple analogies for his own separation from "old Paris." Hugo's name appears only in the dedication, but it would have been sufficient to remind the readers of Baudelaire's time that Hugo was in exile on the island of Guernsey. Andromache appears in the poem as she was after the fall of Troy, widowed and captive in a strange land: "Andromache, I think of you! This little river/ Poor, sad mirror where once shone/ The immense majesty of your widow's pain." The sad mirror of the river reflects not only Andromache's present suffering but also her former, happier life. The analogy of the river with the Seine, by which Baudelaire stands, "Suddenly fertilized" his "fertile memory," and he regrets, as he walks by the place du Carrousel near the Louvre, that the city of Paris is changing around him. As he passes a place where "animals were once sold," he meets "a swan that had escaped from its cage."

With the appearance of the swan, the complexity of the imagery changes. The bird suffers superficially because, in strange surroundings not adapted to its needs, it cannot find water to drink: "Rubbing the dry pavement with his webbed feet/ On the rough ground dragged his white plumage/ By a dry gutter the beast open[ed] his beak." Yet the wings dragging on the pavement convey the degree to which this animal is out of place in its surroundings. Baudelaire imagines the emotions of the swan, "his heart filled with the beautiful lake of his birth." The water that he needs is not merely what is necessary to drink but that of his homeland. The swan thus becomes the "strange and fateful myth" that figures Baudelaire himself. Yet Baudelaire remains in his native Paris. The nature of his exile becomes clear only through suggestions begun with the exotic webbed feet and "beautiful lake of his birth" of the swan that suggest the more tropical climates emblematic of Baudelaire's ideal.

Baudelaire sees himself like "the man in Ovid," an allusion to Ovid's distinction that man looks toward heaven and animals toward earth. Yet he looks at "the ironic and cruelly blue sky," cruel because it now mocks the poet's futile aspiration. In the second part of the poem, Baudelaire repeats this revelation, detailing the suffering of each creature in exile and adding the image of the Negress: "I think of the skinny and consumptive Negress/ Tramping in the mud, and seeking, with haggard looks/ The absent coconut trees of proud Africa." The plight of the woman, perhaps inspired by the example of Jeanne Duval, reinforces the haunting presence of tropical nature contrasted at the end of the poem with "the forest where my Spirit is exiled."

"A VOYAGE TO CYTHERA"

First published: "Un Voyage à Cythère," 1861 (collected in *The Flowers of Evil*, 2006)

Type of work: Poem

A traveler sees on the island of Cythera an emblem of his own fate.

"A Voyage to Cythera" shows the full evolution of the motif of departure in Baudelaire's work. In earlier poems, the poet shared the innocence exemplified by the child at the opening of "The Trip." Thus, in "By Association" he saw no reason not to abandon himself to the imagined departure inspired by the woman's perfume. "The Swan" reflects his recognition of separation from the ideal, but in a context of sadness rather than despair. The

images of death in "A Voyage to Cythera" finally document the extent of the poet's fall.

Baudelaire borrowed the circumstances of this poem from a story that Gérard de Nerval had told of his own visit to Greece in his *Voyage en Orient* (1851; *Journey to the Orient*, 1972). The poem opens with the familiar scene of a happy sea voyage: "My heart, like a bird, fluttered joyfully/ And soared freely around the rigging." The joyful bird representing the poet's heart recalls the use of the same image in "Elévation" ("Elevation"), a poem at the beginning of *Flowers of Evil*, and serves to show from what heights the poet has fallen. Immediately, the imagery of this joyous scene suggests the fall: "The ship rocked under a cloudless sky/ Like an angel drunk on radiant sunlight." The negative implication appears, not in the literal meanings of the words, but in special nuances that Baudelaire has attached to them. The rolling ship echoes the rocking action by which "Boredom" rocked humanity's will, and the drunken angel recalls the angel of "Benediction" who observed the child's drunkenness.

When the island of Cythera, once sacred to Venus, becomes visible to the travelers, it is devoid of its former charms, "proud ghost of the antique Venus." Baudelaire recalls the island's past, "Where the sighs of adoring hearts/ Roll like incense on a rose garden," and the perfume recalls Baudelaire's own seduction. Like Baudelaire, the island has changed. On its banks now stands a gibbet, upon which hangs the body of a man already being devoured by beasts of prey. Faced with this grotesque image, Baudelaire recognizes in it the emblem of his own condition: "On your island, oh Venus! I found standing/ Only a symbolic gibbet where hung my own image." His spiritual death was linked to women, even as this man's death was to the island that represented love. In his fallen state, the poet can only reach out to God: "Oh Lord! give me the strength and courage/ To contemplate my heart and body without distaste." The strength for which he prays may indeed provide the courage with which he will face death in his ultimate departure in "The Trip."

SUMMARY

Charles Baudelaire's personal evolution paralleled the evolution of his language. He came to recognize within his own life the signs of his spiritual fall, and the reader learns to attach special nuances to his often-repeated images. These evocative emblems finally become complex literary symbols. Baudelaire's major achievement lay in part in the creation of this symbol vocabulary through which each object may convey much more than simply its own identity.

The corollary to Baudelaire's symbol system was to become as important as the symbol itself. He persuaded his readers to analyze meaning in a new way, a process that would become fundamental to modern poetry.

Dorothy M. Betz

BIBLIOGRAPHY

By the Author

POETRY:

Les Fleurs du mal, 1857, 1861, 1868 (*Flowers of Evil*, 1931)
Les Épaves, 1866
Petits Poèmes en prose, 1869 (also known as *Le Spleen de Paris*; *Poems in Prose*, 1905, also known as *Paris Spleen*, 1869, 1947)
Complete Poems, 2002

LONG FICTION:
La Fanfarlo, 1847

NONFICTION:
Les Paradis artificiels, 1860 (partial translation as *Artificial Paradises: On Hashish and Wine as a Means of Expanding Individuality*, 1971; also as *Artificial Paradises*, 1996)
Curiosités esthétiques, 1868
L'Art romantique, 1868
Mon cœur mis à nu, 1887 (*My Heart Laid Bare*, 1950)
The Letters of Baudelaire, 1927
My Heart Laid Bare, and Other Prose Writings, 1951
Baudelaire on Poe, 1952
The Mirror of Art, 1955
Intimate Journals, 1957
The Painter of Modern Life, and Other Essays, 1964
Beaudelaire as Literary Critic: Selected Essays, 1964
Art in Paris, 1845-1862: Salons and Other Exhibitions, 1965

TRANSLATIONS:
Histoires extraordinaires, 1856 (of Edgar Allan Poe's short stories)
Nouvelles Histoires extraordinaires, 1857 (of Poe's short stories)
Aventures d'Arthur Gordon Pym, 1858 (of Poe's novel)
Histoires grotesques et sérieuses, 1864 (of Poe's tales)
Eureka, 1864 (of Poe's poem)

MISCELLANEOUS:
Œuvres complètes, 1868-1870, 1961

DISCUSSION TOPICS

- Consider the aptness of Charles Baudelaire's metaphor "forests of symbols."

- Baudelaire was very interested in the work of Edgar Allan Poe. Which seems more important to Baudelaire, Poe's musicality or his own use of symbols?

- How evil are Baudelaire's *Flowers of Evil*?

- How does a symbol differ from an allegorical image?

- The idea that nature is a temple is often found in the work of early nineteenth century poets. Distinguish Baudelaire's natural temple from those of American poets such as William Cullen Bryant and Ralph Waldo Emerson.

About the Author

Benjamin, Walter. *The Writer on Modern Life: Essays on Charles Baudelaire*. Translated by Howard Eiland et al., edited by Michael W. Jennings. Cambridge, Mass.: Harvard University Press, 2006.

Bloom, Harold, ed. *Charles Baudelaire*. New York: Chelsea House, 1987.

Carter, A. E. *Charles Baudelaire*. Boston: Twayne, 1977.

Evans, David. *Rhythm, Illusion, and the Poetic Idea: Baudelaire, Rimbaud, Mallarmé*. Amsterdam: Rodopi, 2004.

Hemmings, E. W. J. *Baudelaire the Damned: A Biography*. New York: Charles Scribner's Sons, 1982.

McLees, Ainslie Armstrong. *Baudelaire's "Argot Plastique": Poetic Caricature and Modernism*. Athens: University of Georgia Press, 1989.

Richardson, Joann. *Baudelaire*. New York: St. Martin's Press, 1994.

Sanyal, Debarati. *The Violence of Modernity: Baudelaire, Irony, and the Politics of Form*. Baltimore: Johns Hopkins University Press, 2006.

Sartre, Jean-Paul. *Baudelaire*. Translated by Martin Turnell. London: Hamish Hamilton, 1964.

Ward Jouve, Nicole. *Baudelaire: A Fire to Conquer Darkness*. New York: St. Martin's Press, 1980.

SIMONE DE BEAUVOIR

Born: Paris, France
January 9, 1908
Died: Paris, France
April 14, 1986

De Beauvoir was one of the twentieth century's most influential women, widely admired by feminists for her pioneering work, The Second Sex. *She also was a distinguished essayist and memoirist.*

Archive Photos

BIOGRAPHY

Simone de Beauvoir (duh boh-VWAHR) was born to an illustrious family that fell on financial hard times, with her father failing in a succession of business ventures. She grew up an awkward, bookish, and compulsively diligent adolescent. As a young woman she rebelled against both her mother's devoutly Catholic faith and bourgeois morality in general. At the Sorbonne she became a star student in philosophy and literature. Attending lectures at the École Normale Supérieure, she met Jean-Paul Sartre, with whom she formed a relationship that lasted until his death in 1980.

De Beauvoir and Sartre became not only lovers but also firm friends and literary, philosophic, and political partners. They initially decided on a "two-year lease" for their liaison, then renewed it for their lives. Each was free to take other lovers, but de Beauvoir availed herself sparingly of that privilege. Not so Sartre, for whom every woman was fair game. From the mid-1930's to the ends of their lives, de Beauvoir and Sartre were leaders of a changing group of students, friends, and lovers—a chosen rather than genetic family.

Through the 1940's and 1950's, existentialism was the most vital intellectual current in France, and Sartre and de Beauvoir were its chief proponents. She invariably went over his writing with him, arguing and clarifying ideas. In his appearances around the world she was nearly always beside him, even in his later years, when they had moved somewhat apart emotionally and totally apart physically. Despite the frequent brilliance of her own writing, Parisian wits would call her La Grande Sartreuse. It may be argued that she derived her intellectual identity and self-esteem largely from their association, which established them as intellectual icons.

De Beauvoir's own production as a writer was prodigious. She published several novels, a play, philosophical texts, several volumes of memoirs, collections of essays, travel diaries, numerous periodical articles, and many introductions to books by others. Her novels are unimaginative and based on her own experiences; her philosophical works are provocative but sometimes lack originality; her accounts of her travels show the marks of haste and superficial knowledge of the countries visited; her self-exploratory series of autobiographies, however, are often eloquent and moving, as are her books on Sartre's declining years, *La Cérémonie des adieux* (1981; *Adieux: A Farewell to Sartre*, 1984), on the onset of old age, *La Vieillesse* (1970; *The Coming of Age*, 1972), and on her mother's death, *Tout compte fait* (1972; *All Said and Done*, 1974). Her crowning achievement is her treatise on the oppression of women, *Le Deuxième Sexe* (1949; *The Second Sex*, 1953).

De Beauvoir wrote *The Second Sex* during her celebrated though intermittent affair with the American novelist Nelson Algren, her one great amorous passion. They met in 1947, when she was on a long visit to the United States and while Sartre was conducting an intense involvement with a woman whom de Beauvoir detested. For several years de Beauvoir and Algren exchanged transatlantic visits. Yet Algren felt himself an alien in Paris, and de Beauvoir could not conceive of residing permanently in Chicago. Finally, fidelity to her primary relationship with Sartre won. After her breakup with Algren, she embittered him by describing their intimacy in her novel *Les Mandarins* (1954; *The Mandarins*, 1956), which she dedicated to him.

In 1952, after de Beauvoir and Algren had renounced their romance, she began a long liaison with Claude Lanzmann, seventeen years her junior, an ambitious journalist who later became a distinguished film director. Their bond, never as strong as that between her and Algren, survived as a friendship, with Lanzmann making the funeral arrangements after de Beauvoir's death.

In 1965, Sartre decided to adopt a young Algerian student, Arlette Elkaïm, without first having consulted de Beauvoir. The adoption conferred French citizenship on Elkaïm, making her immune to deportation, and made her the executor of his literary estate. De Beauvoir was enraged and humiliated. After Sartre's death, she and Elkaïm fought bitterly. Elkaïm once sent a letter to a journal in which she disparaged de Beauvoir's relationship with Sartre. The two women engaged in publishing duels over Sartre's notebooks (edited by Elkaïm) and his letters to de Beauvoir (issued by de Beauvoir).

De Beauvoir devoted the years after Sartre's death largely to traveling with her closest woman friend, Sylvie le Bon, and to writing a generous memoir of the last decade of Sartre's life. On March 20, 1986, she was hospitalized, suffering from cirrhosis of the liver, pulmonary edema, and pneumonia. On April 14, she died, one day short of six years after Sartre's death.

ANALYSIS

France has a long tradition of women writers, such as Madame de La Fayette, Madame de Staël, George Sand, Colette, and Marguerite Duras. Simone de Beauvoir's work is perhaps most like that of Staël and Sand in terms of her preference for a large readership among her contemporaries and of her admission to the literary canon. De Beauvoir considered herself not to be a woman writer but a writer who happened to be a woman. She never sought to develop a particularly feminine language and was more influenced by Émile Zola and Ernest Hemingway than by Colette or Virginia Woolf. Indeed, she defined herself largely by her differences from bourgeois women: She insisted on not becoming a wife, mother, homemaker, or follower of fashion.

Yet de Beauvoir wrote on, and did political work for, women's issues. She showed that a woman could perform with distinction in the areas of philosophy and political theory, fields traditionally dominated by men. She insisted that women should become linked to their work, just as men always had been. In her fiction, from *L'Invitée* (1943; *She Came to Stay*, 1949) through *Les Belles images* (1966; English translation, 1968), she dramatized situations in which women deny their freedom to be their authentic selves, using their sex as an excuse and distorting their sense of themselves in relation to husbands and lovers. While *Les Belles Images* and *La Femme rompue* (1967; *The Woman Destroyed*, 1969) have female protagonists, her early work includes central characters of both sexes, and in her long and ambitious novel *The Mandarins*, the four most important characters are three men and one woman.

In *The Second Sex*, de Beauvoir used existential notions of people's need to establish their freedom in a purposeless, absurd universe to encourage women to resign themselves no longer to the role of the weaker and inferior person in relation to a man. She sought to show that false myths concerning women's nature had been created by both men and women. This book has acquired landmark status, inspiring women's movements throughout the world and making de Beauvoir one of the symbolic leaders of contemporary feminism. In this book and in many other essays and interviews, she tirelessly addressed issues of concern to women, advocating equality with men and total sexual freedom. When she visited Egypt in 1967, de Beauvoir criticized the Egyptian government's failure to put into practice the sexual equality decreed by its constitution. When in Israel, she noted that Israeli women had equal responsibilities during the nation's wars but were largely relegated to lower-paying, menial jobs in peacetime. She did not hesitate to incur displeasure among her compatriots by hailing the humiliating French defeat by the North Vietnamese at Dien Bien Phu, which ended France's role as a power in Indochina.

She asserted over and over again that her goal was to strip away the hypocrisies, prejudices, lies, and mystifications that prevented people from perceiving the truth. She sought to contribute to the intellectual and ethical elevation of humanity.

THE SECOND SEX

First published: *Le Deuxième Sexe*, 1949
   (English translation, 1953)
Type of work: Treatise

In a massive treatise, de Beauvoir describes women's historic victimization and advances feminist theories to establish women's equality with men.

The text is divided into two parts. In part 1, the more academic section, de Beauvoir discusses instances of women being oppressed throughout history, from early nomadic societies until the surprisingly late grant of suffrage in France in 1947. She draws impressively from a wide range of disciplines, including biology, psychology, sociology, anthropology, literature, and, of course, history. She attempts to assess women's biological and historical circumstances and the myths by which these have been explained, denied, or distorted. She recognizes that men have been able to maintain dominant roles in virtually all cultures because women have resigned themselves to, instead of rebelling against, their assigned subordinate status.

The Second Sex has two major premises. First, that man, considering himself as the essential being, or subject, has treated woman as the unessential being, or object. The second, more controversial premise, is that much of woman's psychological self is socially constructed, with very few physiologically rooted feminine qualities or values. De Beauvoir denies the existence of a feminine temperament or nature—to her, all notions of femininity are artificial concepts. In one of her most telling aphorisms she declares, "One is not born a woman; rather, one becomes one."

De Beauvoir derives her chief postulates from Sartre's philosophic work, *L'Être et le néant* (1943;

Being and Nothingness, 1947). In existentialist fashion, she argues that women are the sum of their actions. To be sure, a woman's situation is partly determined by menstruation and childbearing. She becomes human, rather than a "mere animal," to the extent that she transcends her biological characteristics and assumes her liberty in a social context.

In part 2, de Beauvoir undertakes a sociological and psychological survey of women in the midtwentieth century, concentrating on France and the United States. She analyzes the roles women widely adopt, seeing many of these roles (wife, mother, prostitute) as images that men have imposed on women. She deplores most marriages as demeaning to women, enslaving them in childrearing and housekeeping tasks. Prostitution is a state of female enslavement. Only "kept" women—mistresses—have occasionally asserted free choices.

De Beauvoir describes her vision of a free woman who will find emancipation through meaningful work, thereby gaining equal standing with men. Economic freedom is, for de Beauvoir, the key to woman's emancipation. Unless a woman can

affirm her freedom by doing constructive work, she lives only marginally. The total liberation of women will come about, de Beauvoir insists, only with the establishment of an authentically socialist society as conceived by Karl Marx, since capitalism prevents proletarian women from finding satisfaction in their labor.

The Second Sex has received considerable negative criticism for its bias against marriage and motherhood, its Marxism, its rejection of psychoanalysis, and its oversimplifications based on careless use of data. The study has nevertheless proved to be an inspirational text for countless women throughout the world and may well be the most powerful argument for women's rights to have appeared in the twentieth century.

THE MANDARINS

First published: *Les Mandarins,* 1954
    (English translation, 1956)
Type of work: Novel

This panoramic novel tells of a small group of leftist French intellectuals trying to remake their country between 1944 and 1950.

This long, intricate novel, for which de Beauvoir received the prestigious Goncourt Prize in 1954, was her favorite. The book is part autobiography, part social and political history, and part love story. It is in many respects autobiographical, with the psychiatrist Anne Dubreuilh standing in for de Beauvoir. Anne has been married for twenty years to an older man, Robert (Sartre), an author who has assumed the role of a good, dependable friend. Anne also has a passionate affair with an American writer, Lewis Brogan (Nelson Algren). She has a troubled relationship with an adult daughter, Nadine, a composite of two of Sartre's young mistresses. Then there are the journalist Henri Perron (Albert Camus) and a dislikably truculent writer, Scriassine (Arthur Koestler).

The novel's complicated plot covers a wide range of personal and ideological issues and is too dense with events for a detailed summary. It begins by dramatizing the rapturous joy with which French intellectuals welcomed the liberation of Paris in 1944. Robert, Henri, and Anne soon become conscious of the political complexities of the postwar situation, and their ardent hopes of a better world are shattered in the next six years. Friendships that flourished during the German Occupation founder on ideological and personal recriminations as the Cold War begins to dominate European politics. Perron, editor of a liberal newspaper, hopes to remain unattached to any political party. Yet Robert Dubreuilh has founded an existentialist-revolutionary party and seeks the support of Perron's paper for his organization.

As the clear-cut choices of wartime give way to the ambiguous options of peacetime, several of the leading personages are drawn into dilemmas in which a simple ethic of right or wrong no longer holds valid. Perron, for example, perjures himself in court to save a woman of whom he is enamored from being exposed as the former mistress of a Nazi officer—even though Perron is a Resistance hero. Robert Dubreuilh and Perron hold long conversations during which the formerly close friends find themselves increasingly polarized (as Sartre and Camus did), separated by Perron's militant anti-Stalinism and Dubreuilh's adherence to left-wing solidarity. Political power eludes these friends as they find themselves on the edge of social events instead of at their hub. Clearly the title, *The Mandarins,* can only be taken ironically.

Interwoven into the work's stories are several liaisons, of which the one between Anne Dubreuilh and Lewis Brogan is the most important. Based on the de Beauvoir-Algren attachment, it is not factually rendered. After Anne's affair with Lewis ends, she falls into deep depression and almost commits suicide. Through Anne's travails de Beauvoir seeks to depict a woman's problems of personal responsibility—to her husband, daughter, lover, profession, and self. These problems translate the intellectual and political difficulties of the male characters into emotional terms.

The novel falls short of its grand design because de Beauvoir lacks sufficient imaginative intensity and command of dialogue, tone, and style to enable her to transform her ideas into convincing art. Yet her high intelligence and breadth of historical perspective deserve praise.

THE PRIME OF LIFE

First published: *La Force de l'âge,* 1960
    (English translation, 1962)
Type of work: Memoir

This intellectual memoir describes de Beauvoir's life from 1929 to 1944.

This is the second installment of de Beauvoir's autobiographical series. It begins on a note of relief at her emancipation from her rigidly conservative family and ends on an even higher note of joy at France's deliverance from German Occupation. Dominating the work is de Beauvoir's friendship and alliance with Jean-Paul Sartre.

In July, 1929, she was a philosophy student at France's most distinguished university, the École

Normale Supérieure, when she met Sartre, a fellow student, while preparing for comprehensive orals. By the fall they had begun a friendship that was to become a lifelong union. They agreed that, while theirs was an "essential" love, it should not be allowed to degenerate into constraint or mere habit; nor should their partnership prevent them from experiencing contingent affairs with others. By the mid-to-late 1930's they had become the core couple, while teaching philosophy in Paris, of a group they termed "the Family." This was a social network of current and former students, friends, and lovers. It took the place of marriage and children for de Beauvoir and Sartre.

The 1930's were extremely active for de Beauvoir. She read voraciously in literature as well as philosophy and frequented, usually with Sartre, theaters, cinemas, art galleries, cafés, jazz clubs, and many lively, long-lasting parties. Often to the urban Sartre's discomfort, she loved to hike and climb rocks, touring most European countries. As World War II approached and then engulfed her, Sartre, and their friends, she and Sartre abandoned their apolitical individualism. Nazi atrocities convinced them, by mid-1939, that they needed to commit themselves to political action and social concerns. After some largely unsuccessful Resistance work, however, they decided to concentrate on their writing and made their literary reputations during the German Occupation. With the Allies' entry into Paris in the summer of 1944, de Beauvoir ends her book by expressing an ardent appetite for further challenges that the world may offer her.

At its best, *The Prime of Life* is a hymn to individual freedom and to the importance of the intellectual life. The dominant note of de Beauvoir's book is her uncompromising honesty about herself. She reveals her many extraordinary virtues: a splendid mind, acute sensitivity, high moral principles and conduct, courage, and a zest for virtually all experiences. She also displays her flaws: a lack of humor, wit, or tolerance, a tendency to intellectualize all behavior, and an inclination to sermonize. The book is an admirable testimony to crucial stages in the life of a great woman.

SUMMARY

As great as Simone de Beauvoir's writing is, her life was her prime achievement. Apart from the importance of *The Second Sex*, her documentary and philosophical writings have no lasting value and her fiction is unimaginative, limited by its direct confinement to her own milieu. De Beauvoir's memoirs, however, are a permanent addition to the literature of autobiography. They have considerable value as accounts of the intellectual, artistic, social, and political life of her time. They have even greater value, however, as establishing her personal myth as a woman who took bold risks to find a path for the free and full use of her life.

Gerhard Brand

BIBLIOGRAPHY

By the Author

NONFICTION:
Pyrrhus et Cinéas, 1944
Pour une morale de l'ambiguïté, 1947 (*The Ethics of Ambiguity*, 1948)
L'Existentialisme et la sagesse des nations, 1948
L'Amérique au jour le jour, 1948 (travel sketch; *America Day by Day*, 1953)
Le Deuxième Sexe, 1949 (*The Second Sex*, 1953)
Privilèges, 1955 (partial translation "Must We Burn Sade?," 1953)
La Longue Marche, 1957 (travel sketch; *The Long March*, 1958)
Mémoires d'une jeune fille rangée, 1958 (4 volumes; *Memoirs of a Dutiful Daughter*, 1959)
La Force de l'âge, 1960 (memoir; *The Prime of Life*, 1962)
La Force des choses, 1963 (memoir; *Force of Circumstance*, 1964)
Une Mort très douce, 1964 (*A Very Easy Death*, 1966)
La Vieillesse, 1970 (*The Coming of Age*, 1972)

Tout compte fait, 1972 (memoir; *All Said and Done*, 1974)

La Cérémonie des adieux, 1981 (*Adieux: A Farewell to Sartre*, 1984)

Lettres à Sartre, 1990 (2 volumes; Sylvie Le Bon de Beauvoir, editor; *Letters to Sartre*, 1992)

Lettres à Nelson Algren: Un Amour transatlantique, 1947-1964, 1997 (Sylvie Le Bon de Beauvoir, editor; *A Transatlantic Love Affair*, 1998; also pb. as *Beloved Chicago Man: Letters to Nelson Algren, 1947-1964*, 1999)

Philosophical Writings, 2004 (Margaret A. Simons, editor)

LONG FICTION:

L'Invitée, 1943 (*She Came to Stay*, 1949)

Le Sang des autres, 1945 (*The Blood of Others*, 1948)

Tous les hommes sont mortels, 1946 (*All Men Are Mortal*, 1955)

Les Mandarins, 1954 (*The Mandarins*, 1956)

Les Belles Images, 1966 (English translation, 1968)

SHORT FICTION:

La Femme rompue, 1967 (*The Woman Destroyed*, 1968)

Quand prime le spirituel, 1979 (*When Things of the Spirit Come First: Five Early Tales*, 1982)

DRAMA:

Les Bouches inutiles, pb. 1945

EDITED TEXT:

Lettres au Castor et à quelques autres, 1983 (2 volumes; vol. 1, *Witness to My Life: The Letters of Jean-Paul Sartre to Simone de Beauvoir, 1926-1939*, 1992; vol. 2, *Quiet Moments in a War: The Letters of Jean-Paul Sartre to Simone de Beauvoir, 1940-1963*, 1993)

DISCUSSION TOPICS

- What aspects of Simone de Beauvoir's work stand apart from her relationship to Jean-Paul Sartre?

- Did de Beauvoir learn more from men or from other women? Explain your conclusion.

- Is de Beauvoir correct in her belief that the self is "socially constructed"? If she is correct, does not that view reduce the realm of qualities that might be called "feminine"?

- De Beauvoir was essentially more of a philosopher or social critic than a literary person. Support or challenge this statement.

- Did de Beauvoir write too much? Could she have been more successful as a deliberate and painstaking artist?

About the Author

Bair, Deirdre. *Simone de Beauvoir: A Biography*. New York: Summit Books, 1990.

Card, Claudia, ed. *The Cambridge Companion to Simone de Beauvoir*. New York: Cambridge University Press, 2003.

Leighton, Jean. *Simone de Beauvoir on Woman*. Madison, N.J.: Fairleigh Dickinson University Press, 1975.

Marks, Elaine, ed. *Critical Essays on Simone de Beauvoir*. Boston: G. K. Hall, 1987.

_____. *Simone de Beauvoir: Encounters with Death*. New Brunswick, N.J.: Rutgers University Press, 1973.

Rowley, Hazel. *Tête-à-Tête: Simone de Beauvoir and Jean-Paul Sartre*. New York: HarperCollins, 2005.

Sandford, Stella. *How to Read Beauvoir*. New York: W. W. Norton, 2007.

Simons, Margaret A., ed. *The Philosophy of Simone de Beauvoir: Critical Essays*. Bloomington: Indiana University Press, 2006.

Winegarten, Renée. *Simone de Beauvoir: A Critical View*. Oxford, England: Berg, 1988.

SAMUEL BECKETT

© The Nobel Foundation

Born: Foxrock, near Dublin, Ireland
April 13, 1906
Died: Paris, France
December 22, 1989

Writing in both English and French, Beckett emerged during his forties as a master of both drama and fiction, his bleak vision of humanity often offset by the beauty of his prose.

BIOGRAPHY

In 1906, Good Friday happened to fall on the thirteenth day of April, bringing religion and superstition into rare conjunction. Samuel Beckett, whose writings contain more than their share of both, favored that date when citing his birth, although several of his biographers and commentators suggest a more likely birthdate later in the spring, citing a midsummer baptismal certificate as evidence. In any event, Samuel Barclay Beckett was born in the "comfortable" Foxrock district of Dublin sometime during the first half of 1906, the second son of William Beckett, who had prospered as an estimator of construction costs, and the former Mary Roe. William Beckett, born in Ireland of French Huguenot stock, thus bequeathed to his sons a mixed heritage that Samuel would often return in kind through his works, resulting in perplexity on both sides of the Channel.

Privately educated at Earlsfort House School, Portora Royal School, and Trinity College, Dublin, in keeping with his Protestant background, Samuel Beckett emerged during adolescence as a skilled student athlete, showing talent also in those academic areas that happened to interest him. It was not until his years at Trinity, however, that he truly distinguished himself as a student, having discovered French literature and thought under the tutelage of Trinity's Professor Thomas Rudmose-Brown. Graduating first in his class of 1927, apparently destined to succeed Rudmose-Brown at Trinity, Beckett received an exchange fellowship for 1928 to 1930 at the prestigious École Normale Supérieure in Paris. Before leaving for Paris, Beckett taught briefly at a boys' boarding school in Belfast, finding teaching a bore but not yet prepared to abandon his plans for an academic career. During the summer of 1928, Beckett visited relatives then vacationing in Germany, falling briefly and somewhat disastrously in love with his first cousin Peggy Sinclair, who, destined to die young of tuberculosis, would figure prominently in such later Beckett works as *Krapp's Last Tape* (pr., pb. 1958).

Already acquainted with most of the serious artists and writers then living in Dublin, who accepted him as their equal, Beckett lost little time developing similar acquaintances upon his arrival in Paris, helped by the friendship and connections of the writer Thomas McGreevy, the Trinity Fellow whom he had technically been appointed to replace. Mingling freely among French and expatriate writers, Beckett soon joined the circle of would-be writers surrounding Paris's most famous Irish expatriate of the period, James Joyce, who was then putting the finishing touches on the "work in progress" soon to be known as *Finnegans Wake* (1939). Although the exact extent and depth of Beckett's involvement in Joyce's life and career remain in dispute among both men's various commentators, it is clear in any case that the older writer, Joyce, influenced and inspired the younger one, Beckett; it is a matter of record, also, that Beckett was the object of a postadolescent crush on the part of Joyce's emotionally disturbed daughter Lucia, one year younger than Beckett. During the course of his two-year fellowship, involving minimal teaching duties, Beckett tried his hand at both poetry and prose, attracting the attention of several publishers and "little magazines" then serving English-speaking expatriates in Paris. By 1930, he had a contract from Hours Press to prepare a brief monograph on the Parisian novelist Marcel Proust, who, then as later, ranked with Joyce as a master of the modernist novel; significantly, Beckett's study of Proust would often be reprinted over six decades to follow, of interest to students of Beckett as well as to students of Proust.

Returning as planned to Trinity College after his fellowship ran its course, Beckett soon decided once and for all that teaching did not agree with him, claiming both that his students (mostly female) knew nothing and that he himself knew even less. While returning to the Continent in a sort of panic, he sent in a letter of resignation from Germany, thus sparing his mentors the unpleasant task of firing him for inattentive or, at best, eccentric teaching. Following the death of his father in 1933, Beckett moved to London, where he may or may not have undergone psychoanalysis, living on the proceeds of a share in his father's estate while working on the manuscript of *Murphy* (1938), his first completed novel. Beckett then traveled the British Isles and the Continent for two years in search of a publisher for the novel, finally finding one in 1937, the year that he settled permanently in France.

Barely surviving on commissions from writing and small portions of the family heritage sent to him from Dublin, Beckett soon blended in among the artists and writers then at work in Paris, and by late 1937 he had begun an amatory affair with the American heiress and art dealer Peggy Guggenheim. Early in 1938, Beckett, returning to his lodgings late at night, was accosted and stabbed by a local hoodlum whom he recognized on sight and who apparently was out to beg, borrow, or steal money that Beckett denied having on his person. The stabbing might well have proved fatal: Beckett spent weeks in the hospital, his lungs permanently damaged and susceptible to illness; only his thick, old overcoat had prevented the blade from reaching his heart. His rescuer on the scene was the musician Suzanne Deschevaux-Dumesnil, who applied first aid and arranged for his transportation to the Hôpital Broussais, where she later visited him. Before long, Suzanne, like Peggy Guggenheim some seven years Beckett's senior, would displace Guggenheim as the writer's companion of choice and would remain in that position for life, eventually becoming the first and only Mrs. Samuel Beckett.

Visiting his relatives in Ireland when war broke out on the Continent in 1939, Beckett returned home in haste to Paris out of loyalty to French and Jewish friends, a recent trip to Germany having confirmed his worst suspicions about Nazism. By late 1940, he was actively engaged in espionage activities with the French Resistance, working not for the French, as he later made clear, but against Adolf Hitler and all that he stood for. For the rest of his life, Beckett would remain resolutely apolitical, tending to downplay his Resistance activity as simple "Boy Scout stuff," keeping secret even from his closest friends the Croix de Guerre awarded to him in 1945 on the basis of his Resistance activities.

Late in the summer of 1942, after several close calls, Beckett and Suzanne (who by then was a Resistant herself) learned that their room had been infiltrated and that arrest was imminent. Little more than one step ahead of their pursuers, the two fled Paris with only the clothes on their backs, eventually finding their way to the small southern town of Roussillon, where they would wait for the war to end and where Beckett, facing enforced idleness, would write the novel later published as *Watt* (1953). After the war, Beckett returned to Ireland to check on his aging mother and other relatives, only to run into problems reentering France as a resident alien. In time, he found a workable solution, attaching himself as interpreter-storekeeper to an Irish Red Cross unit dispatched to the bombed-out city of St. Lô in Normandy. After several months of service, Beckett found his way back to his old apartment in Paris, where he soon embarked upon the most productive phase of his literary career. With Suzanne to look after his daily needs and, in general, to protect his privacy, Beckett soon produced the three novels known as *The Trilogy*, starting with *Molloy* in 1951 (English translation, 1955). By that time, Beckett had already written *En attendant Godot* (pb. 1952, pr. 1953; *Waiting for Godot*, 1954), which would bring him worldwide recognition almost immediately after its first performances early in 1953. From that point, Beckett lived and wrote as a rather reluctant celebrity, finding even his lesser works received with enthusiasm by scholars and critics. Awarded the Nobel Prize in Literature in 1969, Beckett died shortly before Christmas, on December 22, 1989, in Paris, having left instructions in his will that news of his death not be released until a week or so thereafter.

ANALYSIS

"I can't go on, I'll go on." Those last words of *L'Innommable* (1953; *The Unnamable*, 1958), the final volume of *The Trilogy*, tend to summarize the author's mature output both in prose fiction and in drama, in which human life and aspirations are reduced to bare essentials; in the short novel *Comment c'est* (1961; *How It Is*, 1964), two characters, presumably the last remnant of the human species, crawl toward each other through mud, subsisting on a diet of canned sardines left behind by a now-vanished civilization. In the memorable *"Fin de partie," suivi de "Acte sans paroles"* (pr., pb. 1957; *Endgame: A Play in One Act; Followed by Act Without Words: A Mime for One Player*, 1958), a Beckettian mime tries all possible human options, including suicide, only to end in apathy, waiting—for what? It is perhaps no accident that Beckett's creative "breakthrough" came in midlife with the first performances (in Paris) of *Waiting for Godot*, a visible illustration, three-dimensional when staged, of the "waiting" that, in Beckett's developing vision, was characteristic of all human life. Is all of humanity, as one of his characters would later say in *Endgame*, waiting for "it," meaning life, to end? If not, then what is humankind awaiting?

Born with the verbal instincts of the traditional Irish poet, Beckett defined himself early in life as a writer and apprenticed himself to James Joyce, arguably the outstanding Irish writer of his own time or any other and a leading exponent of high modernism. Unfortunately, Beckett's early work remains not only hopelessly derivative of Joyce but also quite immature in its convoluted jokes, puns, and mannerisms. Indeed, it was not until after World War II, when Beckett began writing originally in French, that he would discover and assert a truly original talent that would forever distance him from Joyce's direct influence.

When asked, the normally reticent, even taci-turn Beckett would give various cryptic explanations for his choice of writing idiom, perhaps the best-remembered of which is that it was easier for him to write "without style" in French. At the very least, the works composed originally in French are notably spare and deceptively simple, refreshingly free of the mannerisms that had marred Beckett's early works in English. Significantly, the new spareness of style would carry over into Beckett's own English versions of his works, as well as into those few later efforts, most notably *Krapp's Last Tape*, composed originally in English. Arguably, the evolution of Beckett's mature style had as much to do with his wartime experiences as with his change of language. *Waiting for Godot*, although set at no specific time, was assumed by many early commentators to be taking place in France during the Nazi occupation; indeed, the moral and psychological landscape of his late work suggests the "ground zero" of a world laid waste by postatomic war.

At once simple and complex, Beckett's plays and novels of the 1950's attracted many would-be interpreters; by the time Beckett won the Nobel Prize in Literature in 1969, his work had spawned a major academic industry, with dozens of books and articles already in print and dozens more to follow. Not infrequently, the various readings of Beckett tended to contradict one another; Beckett himself, maintaining a nearly reclusive silence that may or may not have been a pose, refused most requests to discuss or to explain his work, allowing critics of all persuasions to interpret his texts however they chose. By his middle sixties, Beckett, renowned as the creator of antiheroes for the stage, had himself become an anticelebrity of sorts, rarely seen, heard, or photographed yet assured that even the slightest of his new publications would attract enthusiastic attention. By the time of his death at eighty-three, only twenty years after he had received the Nobel Prize, Beckett's work and the legend generated by his reputation had become inextricably fused, making it more difficult than ever to separate, as his character Krapp had said, "the grain from the husks."

Although Beckett had written and published several volumes of prose fiction before the publication and performance of *Waiting for Godot*, it is doubtful that his "novels" would have drawn much attention, critical or otherwise, were it not for the runaway success of that first completed play; the subsequent successes of *Endgame* and *Krapp's Last Tape* would prove that *Waiting for Godot* was no fluke. Readers and spectators attracted to Beckett by his plays would then begin to discover his prose, in which the form of "the novel" is repeatedly questioned and tested. To be sure, most of the themes and concerns common to Beckett's plays are also to be found in his fiction, albeit in more concentrated, less readily accessible form: The narrator(s) of *The Trilogy*, for example, can be seen as one or more of the stage tramps in stationary pose, quite literally composing himself/themselves offstage, facing only a blank sheet of paper. Fortunately or unfortunately, the physical demands of the stage would force Beckett to be somewhat less cryptic in his dramatic efforts than in his fiction, and his plays continue to attract a somewhat wider audience.

In theater and fiction alike, Beckett stresses the essential solitude of humankind, whose efforts to discern meaning in life vacillate between pathos and bathos, often approaching a kind of grim humor. Most of Beckett's characters, whether on the stage or on the page, tend to share their creator's intense, even perverse preoccupation with mathematics and measurement, a concern that many commentators have traced back to Beckett's close study, during his fellowship years in Paris, of the life and career of the philosopher-scientist René Descartes and of Descartes's Belgian disciple Arnold Geulincx. The urge to count and to measure, leading as it does toward science and technology, may be seen as one of humankind's earliest and most abiding responses to the apparent chaos of the human condition, an effort to establish order. Hugh Kenner, in the first of his reliable studies of Beckett's work, isolated the theme and symbol of the "Cartesian centaur"—a man on a bicycle—as central to nearly all the author's basic texts. The bicycle, combining humankind's upright stance with the invention of the wheel, yet subject to frequent breakdowns and flat tires, shows both the ingenuity and the limitations experienced by Beckett's most memorable characters.

Even with technology (as represented by the bicycle), Beckett's human figures remain thwarted in their hopes and desires, more often carrying or pushing the bicycle than using it for extended locomotion as originally planned. In *Krapp's Last Tape*, the two wheels of a bicycle become the two reels of an early tape recorder, on which the striving but failed writer known only as Krapp had attempted to extend his mental locomotion, keeping track of time—and memory——through technology. Inevitably, he fails, falling back on the unreliable human memory that he abandoned years before. "What's to say?" he wonders aloud, preparing a "fresh" tape. "Not a squeak." Yet he keeps speaking, or squeaking, into a machine that has already failed him and will surely do so again.

WAITING FOR GODOT

First produced: *En attendant Godot*, 1953 (first published, 1952; English translation, 1954)
Type of work: Play

Two tramps wait by the roadside for someone who never appears, meeting instead a peculiar "master" and his equally strange "slave."

Arguably, *Waiting for Godot* provides an optimum point of entry not only into Beckett's enigmatic body of mature work but also into the antirational theater that emerged on the European continent during the decade following World War II, permanently altering the expectations of spectators (and playwrights) all over the world. In Beckett's first performed and published play, as in contemporary (but quite different) plays by Eugène Ionesco, Arthur Adamov, Max Frisch, and Friedrich Dürrenmatt, plot is all but discarded as a necessary element of drama, the tension residing instead in metaphysical concerns and in interaction (or noninteraction) among the characters.

The play is set on a desolate roadside, requiring little in the way of scenery. Two aging tramps, Vladimir (Didi) and Estragon (Gogo), reminiscent of the film comics Laurel and Hardy gone to seed, exchange desultory conversation as they wait for the arrival of a man called Godot, who in fact never appears. Vladimir, like Laurel, is spare of build; Estragon, like Oliver Hardy, considerably stouter. "Nothing to be done," says Estragon in the play's first line, which in fact summarizes all the ensuing dialogue and action, although Estragon, at that moment, refers only to the act of taking off his shoes. Beckett's lines, even when translated into

English from the original French, tend thus to send ambivalent messages and meanings that continue to reverberate long after the curtain falls. Like most of Beckett's marginal characters in both plays and fiction, Didi and Gogo, as they address each other with childlike nicknames, have obviously known far better days; both are well educated, as their dialogue soon makes clear, yet education proves to be of little help in their current predicament.

Shot through with philosophical speculations and learned references to Holy Scripture, the prolonged interchanges between the two tramps have prompted many commentators to find in the play religious overtones that may or may not have been intended; more to the point, it seems, is the simple act of waiting, and the basically human instinct to talk (or keep busy or both) in order to stave off boredom.

Divided into two approximately equal acts, the action of *Waiting for Godot* twice relieves Vladimir and Estragon of boredom through encounters with two additional characters, the arrogant, autocratic Pozzo and his mute (or at least tongue-tied) manservant Lucky, attached to Pozzo's body with a rope. Pozzo, like Estragon, is portly of build; Lucky, like Vladimir, is almost painfully thin. All four of the main characters are well past middle age, with ailments and impediments to suit. Pozzo, a caricature of the self-important rich man, will have lost his sight between his first and second encounters with the tramps; Lucky, although mute, will suddenly deliver himself, toward the end of act 1, of a learned but incomprehensible monologue that, for later generations of spectators, would recall the printouts of an ill-programmed computer gone berserk.

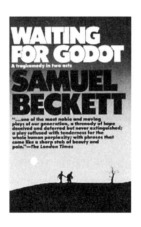

Apparently unexpected and quite unpredictable, *Waiting for Godot* would soon achieve landmark status in the history of Western drama, drawing upon the familiar (stock characters from silent film or British music hall, bowler-hatted and stiff-gaited), yet leading toward unexplored territory, in concept as well as in location. Still contemplating suicide, as they have more than once in the past, Vladimir and Estragon decide to leave because Godot has yet to show himself. As the curtain falls, however, they are both still in place, waiting.

ENDGAME

First produced: *Fin de partie*, 1957 (first published, 1957; English translation, 1958)
Type of work: Play

Four characters wait for the end of the world in an isolated room that resembles the inside of the human skull.

If *Waiting for Godot* recalls France during the Nazi occupation, where people waited in desolate spots for others who might or might not appear, *Endgame* recalls a bizarre bomb shelter in the wake of Hiroshima and worse disasters, or perhaps the post-Freudian human skull. In the center, at his own request, sits Hamm, a ham-actor or failed Hamlet, often confusing himself with King Lear, now blind and immobile, confined to a makeshift wheelchair that more closely resembles a throne mounted on casters. Downstage, contained in trash cans, are Hamm's parents Nagg and Nell, left legless after a tandem-bicycle accident years earlier in the Ardennes. The only character left standing is Cloy, who suffers from an ailment that keeps him from sitting down and who may or may not be Hamm's son.

In many ways, Hamm recalls Pozzo of *Waiting for Godot*. Used to the exercise of power, turning blindness to his own advantage as he spins his dreams and memories into delusions of grandeur, Hamm rules his shrinking domain with the endless "mind games" alluded to in the play's title, drawn from the game of chess. "Me to play," says Hamm in the first line of the English version, delivered after nearly five minutes of illuminated stage business on the part of Cloy. Using his own French original, Beckett might better have translated the line as "It's *my* turn, now," to be delivered in a childish, churlish tone.

Throughout the action of *Endgame*, Hamm does

indeed take his turn, doing most of the talking and insisting on a "turn" around the room, in his chair pushed by Cloy, after which he must return "to the center." A seemingly endless monologue, interrupted only by the nagging of his father, Nagg, recalls or imagines a time when Hamm, like Pozzo, was truly in control, sufficiently rich and influential to control far more than the space to which his questionable influence is now limited. There are no more bicycle wheels, indeed no more bicycles, a luxury that Hamm never afforded Cloy as a boy. "The light is sunk," planted seeds will never sprout, and Hamm is looking at "the end" even as Cloy jauntily seeks to make "an exit."

Even more self-conscious of the stage than *Waiting for Godot, Endgame* is still—for good or for ill—considered by many of Beckett's commentators to be his finest play, perhaps more satisfying for actors than for spectators. Technology, although much in evidence—the makeshift wheelchair, an invisi-

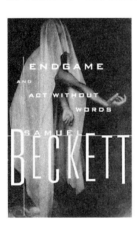

ble telephone long past usefulness, the defunct bicycles, a key-wound alarm clock that still rings loud enough "to wake the dead" but not the deaf—offers no exit or salvation to those held captive in the "end game," perhaps the game eternally played inside one's own skull. At the end of the play, with Hamm having staged his own death—but perhaps having really died—and his parents presumed dead, Cloy, bags in hand, moves downstage as if to make good on his threat or promise. Like Vladimir and Estragon, however, he remains poised but, as the curtain falls, still does not move. Where, indeed, would he go?

KRAPP'S LAST TAPE

First produced: 1958 (first published, 1958)
Type of work: Play

A failed, aging writer replays a "memoir" taped thirty years earlier, finding neither the truth nor the beauty for which he had aimed.

No doubt the best known of Beckett's mature efforts written originally in English, *Krapp's Last Tape* carries his theatrical experiment one step further, reducing the cast of characters to a single human actor, supplemented by a tape recorder playing back the same voice at a much earlier age, with references to still earlier recordings. Going well beyond the usual dramatic monologue, the interaction of the aging Krapp with his former self (or selves) raises *Krapp's Last Tape* to the dimension of full-scale theater.

Set "in the future"—tape recorders being relatively new at the time of the play's composition—*Krapp's Last Tape* presents the title character under the strong, merciless light of his workspace, light demanded by his increasingly poor eyesight. Light and shadow, sight and blindness figure prominently in Beckett's attempt to examine, and possibly correct, Marcel Proust's often-misinterpreted concept of "involuntary memory." Krapp has apparently intended to surprise himself with memories kept "fresh" on tape, but there are few surprises to be found. Krapp, like Proust, is a writer by choice, albeit a most unsuccessful one whose major publication has only sold seventeen copies, "to free circulating libraries beyond the seas." He is also, like Hamm and Pozzo, something of a poseur whose carefully phrased speeches, here recorded solely for his own benefit, ring hollow when heard across the gulf of time.

Like Vladimir and Estragon, Krapp is rather clownish in appearance and dress, prone to a variety of ailments no doubt inflicted by his lifestyle. A heavy drinker who interrupts the tape more than once to take a nip offstage, Krapp is also hopelessly addicted to bananas, despite chronic constipation. While onstage, Krapp eats at least two bananas and starts to eat more, stuffing them absently into his pockets as he prepares to leave the room. Both scatological and sexual in their symbolism, the bananas serve also to generate much interesting stage "business," as does the nearsighted Krapp's continual fumbling with keys, locks, reels of tape, and ledgers, Even when he can read his own writing in the ledger where he has cataloged his tapes, the cryptic notations make little or no sense to him. Choosing spool five from box three, Krapp must play the tape through in order to make sense of such references as the "black ball" and the "dark nurse." It soon becomes clear, though, that he has chosen that particular tape because of the final notation, "farewell to love."

Recorded some thirty years earlier on the occasion of his thirty-ninth birthday, the tape that occupies Krapp's attention on the evening in question itself refers back to even earlier tapes that the younger Krapp played just before recording his latest message to himself. His taped "journals," an evident attempt to subvert the fallibility of human memory through the "wonders" of modern technology, prove even more fallible than his own failing memory, which holds fast to a narrated love scene involving himself and a girl in a boat, no doubt the "farewell to love." Increasingly drunk and dispirited, Krapp will keep replaying that portion of the tape, fast-forwarding past sequences in which his thirty-nine-year-old self proudly holds forth on his literary ambitions and career. Clearly, the girl in the boat soon fell victim to those same ambitions, abandoned in favor of Krapp's "vocation." During the course of the play, however, Krapp becomes painfully aware that he has managed to save neither career nor memories, and that love has managed to pass him by, if only because he sidestepped it at the time. In his French version of the play, *La Dernière Bande*, Beckett substitutes a sexual allusion—implying arousal—for the scatological one implicit in the English title. Both elements are foregrounded in the play itself, leaving little doubt that Krapp has selfishly, if unconsciously, chosen the excremental over the erotic, and in old age has little choice but to lie in the bed that he has prepared for himself. Abandoning his attempt to record a fresh tape, the old man replays the love "scene" again, gazing blankly toward the audience as the tape continues, in silence.

Despite its unorthodox form, *Krapp's Last Tape* remains among the more explicit and accessible of Beckett's works, yet somewhat more complex than it appears at first glance or hearing. In this work, more than in any other, Beckett seriously questions the interrelationship of life and art, wondering aloud if art is worth the candle, or the ultimately blinding light above Krapp's table, described on his earlier tape as "a great improvement" that makes him feel "less alone. In a way."

THE TRILOGY

First published: *Molloy,* 1951 (English translation, 1955); *Malone meurt,* 1951 (*Malone Dies,* 1956); *L'Innommable,* 1953 (*The Unnamable,* 1958)
Type of work: Novels

A narrative consciousness writes itself into— and out of—existence, calling into serious question the convention of the "novel" as known to the reader of the 1950's.

"I am in my mother's room. It is I who live there now. I don't know how I got there." The narrative voice first known as Molloy calls himself into existence with such utterances and tries to sustain the reader's interest as he describes his observation of two possible pursuers noted only as A and C (Abel and Cain, perhaps). He directs his faltering moves back toward his elderly mother, with whom he can communicate only with knuckle-blows to the head, one number for yes, another for no, yet another for "money." "Composing" himself as he writes, or speaks, Molloy recalls a ritual of sucking pebbles, careful to rotate each of the small rocks through the pockets of his seedy overcoat so as not to suck the same one twice in one day. On another occasion, Molloy pulls from his pocket a miniature sawhorse in silver or silverplate with no recollection of its intended function as a knife-rest at formal dinners in a long-gone bourgeois society.

Riding with increasing difficulty on a bicycle possibly less functional than himself, Molloy runs down a small dog belonging to a woman known only as Lousse, who then detains him for reasons unspecified. Not long thereafter, the narrative viewpoint shifts to that of a certain Jacques Moran, whose fruitless search for Molloy will constitute the second half of the novel. Like Pozzo and Hamm, Moran is authoritative, even cruel, treating his adolescent son much as Pozzo treats his slave, Lucky. Just as Pozzo loses his sight between the acts of *Waiting for Godot*, so, too, will Moran lose his mobility and equilibrium during the course of his search, in effect becoming Molloy, or Molloy's double, carried about on the handlebars of the bicycle that Molloy once rode. The final sentence of Moran's narrative neatly negates the first, and incidentally all that has passed between.

"Malone is what I am called now," says the narrator at the start of *Malone Dies*, implying soon thereafter that the various Murphys, Molloys, and Morans were creatures of his own imagination, brought to life, abandoned, or killed at will. Like Hamm, the octogenarian Malone is a compulsive storyteller, calling to life a father and son known as Saposcat (Sapo for short), later to be known as Macmann. Alone in a room save for the creatures of his own devising, the invalid Malone dreams of poling his bed down a circular staircase as one would pole a raft downriver; regretting his eventual inability to record his own death, Malone contents himself with "killing off" characters in his endless narrative, meanwhile dropping hints that he might actually have committed murder at an earlier stage of his life. Malone presumably dies as his recorded monologue trails off into nothingness; yet in *The Unnamable* the narrative continues, presumably delivered by a legless man confined to a jar, just as Nagg is confined to a trash can in *Endgame*. The narrator may or may not be called Mahood, or perhaps Mahood is yet another "fictional" creature summoned into existence in order to be discarded at will. The narrative runs on and on as if self-driven, almost without punctuation, proceeding toward—and perhaps beyond—the outer limits of the fictional form.

SUMMARY

Although first expressed in the experimental fiction that he continued to write until his death, Samuel Beckett's lyrical pessimism found its strongest and most memorable expression in his plays, which represent both a landmark and a turning point in the history of world drama. Notable for their accessibility despite an apparent complexity, *Waiting for Godot*, *Endgame*, and *Krapp's Last Tape* remain in the worldwide dramatic repertory decades after they were first performed, challenging actors and audiences alike with their haunted, haunting humanity.

David B. Parsell

BIBLIOGRAPHY

By the Author

DRAMA:
En attendant Godot, pb. 1952, pr. 1953 (*Waiting for Godot*, 1954)
"Fin de partie," suivi de "Acte sans paroles," pr., pb. 1957 (music by John Beckett; *"Endgame: A Play in One Act," Followed by "Act Without Words: A Mime for One Player,"* 1958)
Krapp's Last Tape, pr., pb. 1958
Act Without Words II, pr., pb. 1960 (one-act mime)
Happy Days, pr., pb. 1961
Play, pr., pb. 1963 (English translation, 1964)
Come and Go: Dramaticule, pr., pb. 1965 (one scene; English translation, 1967)
Not I, pr. 1972, pb. 1973
Ends and Odds, pb. 1976
That Time, pr., pb. 1976
Footfalls, pr., pb. 1976
A Piece of Monologue, pr., pb. 1979
Rockaby, pr., pb. 1981
Ohio Impromptu, pr., pb. 1981
Catastrophe, pr. 1982, pb. 1983
Company, pr. 1983

Collected Shorter Plays, pb. 1984
Complete Dramatic Works, pb. 1986
Eleutheria, pb. 1995

TELEPLAYS:
Eh Joe, 1966 (*Dis Joe*, 1967)
Tryst, 1976
Shades, 1977
Quad, 1981

RADIO PLAYS:
All That Fall, 1957, revised 1968
Embers, pr., pb. 1959
Words and Music, pr., pb. 1962 (music by John
    Beckett)
Cascando, 1963 (music by Marcel Mihalovici)

SCREENPLAY:
Film, 1965

LONG FICTION:
Murphy, 1938
Molloy, 1951 (English translation, 1955; with
    Malone Dies and *The Unnamable* known as *The
    Trilogy*)
Malone meurt, 1951 (*Malone Dies*, 1956)
L'Innommable, 1953 (*The Unnamable*, 1958)
Watt, 1953
Comment c'est, 1961 (*How It Is*, 1964)
Mercier et Camier, 1970 (*Mercier and Camier*, 1974)
Le Dépeupleur, 1971 (*The Lost Ones*, 1972)
Company, 1980
Mal vu mal dit, 1981 (*Ill Seen Ill Said*, 1981)
Worstward Ho, 1983

SHORT FICTION:
More Pricks than Kicks, 1934
Nouvelles et textes pour rien, 1955 (*Stories and Texts for
    Nothing*, 1967)
No's Knife: Collected Shorter Prose, 1947-1966, 1967
First Love, and Other Shorts, 1974
Pour finir encore et autres foirades, 1976 (*Fizzles*, 1976; also known as *For to Yet Again*, 1976)
Four Novellas, 1977 (also known as *The Expelled, and Other Novellas*, 1980)
Collected Short Prose, 1991

POETRY:
Whoroscope, 1930
Echo's Bones and Other Precipitates, 1935
Poems in English, 1961
Collected Poems in English and French, 1977

NONFICTION:
Proust, 1931

DISCUSSION TOPICS

- What might be the reasons for Samuel Beckett's dismissing his anti-Nazi activities as "Boy Scout stuff"?

- Is *Waiting for Godot* political? Explain the basis of your conclusion.

- The word "endgame" is taken from chess but pertains to the stage of a game before a decision is actually reached. What implications does this word have as the title of Beckett's play?

- To what extent are Beckett's puns and jokes important in his mature novels and plays?

- English is considered a large and resourceful language, but Beckett often wrote in French. What characteristics of English seem to be contrary to his writing habits?

- In *Molloy*, there is a scene about sucking pebbles. Does it have reference to the story of Demosthenes, who thereby developed his oratorical powers, or is it about a man trying to solve a problem of rotation, or is it something else entirely?

- Does James Joyce's influence continue to pervade Beckett's mature work, or has he by this time succeeded in overcoming that influence?

TRANSLATION:
An Anthology of Mexican Poetry, 1958 (Octavio Paz, editor)

MISCELLANEOUS:
I Can't Go On, I'll Go On: A Selection from Samuel Beckett's Work, 1976 (Richard Seaver, editor)

About the Author
Alvarez, Alfred. *Samuel Beckett.* 2d ed. London: Fontana, 1992.
Barry, Elizabeth. *Beckett and Authority: The Uses of Cliché.* New York: Palgrave Macmillan, 2006.
Ben-Zvi, Linda. *Samuel Beckett.* Boston: Twayne, 1986.
Cohn, Ruby. *Just Play: Beckett's Theater.* Princeton, N.J.: Princeton University Press, 1980.
Cronin, Anthony. *Samuel Beckett: The Last Modernist.* New York: HarperCollins, 1997.
Fletcher, John. *About Beckett: The Playwright and the Work.* London: Faber & Faber, 2003.
Kenner, Hugh. *A Reader's Guide to Samuel Beckett.* New York: Farrar, Straus & Giroux, 1973.
_____. *Samuel Beckett: A Critical Study.* New York: Evergreen Press, 1961.
McDonald, Rónán. *The Cambridge Introduction to Samuel Beckett.* New York: Cambridge University Press, 2006.
Mercier, Vivian. *Beckett/Beckett.* New York: Oxford University Press, 1977.

Brendan Behan

Born: Dublin, Ireland
  February 9, 1923
Died: Dublin, Ireland
  March 20, 1964

Behan brilliantly combined humor and pathos in his plays and autobiographical novel.

BIOGRAPHY

Brendan Behan (BEE-uhn) was born in Dublin, Ireland, on February 9, 1923, to Kathleen Kearney and Stephen Behan. He was the oldest child of that marriage, but Kathleen, widowed by her first husband, had older children. Behan claimed his background was the slums of Dublin, but that, like so much he related, was a half-truth. His mother had grown up relatively poor but came from a musical and literary family; her brother wrote the Irish national anthem and was the stage manager at Dublin's Abbey Theatre. Behan's father spoke both French and Latin and read to his children from the works of Charles Dickens, Émile Zola, John Galsworthy, and Guy de Maupassant. Behan's grandmother, Granny English, was a particular influence, not always for the best: With her knowledge, Behan was sipping porter and whiskey by the age of eight.

Another influence on the young Behan was the Irish Republican Army (IRA). His father was in prison during the Irish Civil War when Behan was born, and the family was committed to the dream of a unified Irish republic. When Behan was a boy Ireland was neither unified nor a republic. Caught up in the romantic aura of violence associated with the outlawed IRA, he joined its youth organization as a boy and later became an IRA courier. In 1939, he was arrested in Liverpool, England, in possession of bomb-making materials. He was not on an approved IRA mission, and his actions were amateurish at best. Only sixteen, he served less than two years, from February, 1940, to December, 1941, in the Borstal, or juvenile reformatory prison. His incarceration eventually became the subject of his autobiography, *Borstal Boy* (1958).

Returning to Dublin, Behan was again soon in jail, this time for shooting at a policeman during a political demonstration. Sentenced to fourteen years, he served in various prisons, where he acquired material he later used in his first successful play, *The Quare Fellow* (pr. 1954, pb. 1956). Popular among the other inmates for his wit and singing ability, Behan began writing. "The Experiences of a Borstal Boy," a short article, was published in 1942. He also mastered the Irish language; several of his works were first written in Irish. He was released from prison at the end of 1946.

Behan quickly became involved in Dublin's postwar literary scene, where he drank, talked, laughed, argued, and fought with other writers and artists. A fictional portrait of Behan is found in J. P. Donleavey's *The Ginger Man* (1955, 1965) as the character Barney Berry. Behan was also attracted by a different world—the Gaelic west—one that exerted its influence on J. M. Synge, among others. Behan's troubles with the authorities continued. In 1947, he spent four months in jail in Manchester, England, and the following year was arrested in Dublin for assaulting a policeman. In subsequent years he was arrested numerous times, but for violence committed while drunk rather than for political acts.

The late 1940's found Behan in Paris. He began to think of himself as a serious writer, something difficult in the pub-centered, drink-and-talk atmosphere of Dublin. During the following decade Behan turned out a significant body of work—radio and stage plays, a newspaper column, and his major prose piece, *Borstal Boy*, published in 1958. *The Quare Fellow* was first produced at Dublin's small Pike Theatre in 1954, becoming a major success in London in 1956. *An Giall*, written in Irish and later in English as *The Hostage* (pr., pb. 1958), was produced in 1958. Unfortunately, the fame and fortune that resulted from his successes as a writer contributed to Behan's early death by alcoholism. Although he remained a relatively disciplined writer for a few years after his marriage to Beatrice Salkeld, his propensity for alcohol continued. His public appearances were notorious and popular in Dublin, London, New York, and elsewhere. Behan played the role of the drunken, badboy writer all too well. His final literary works, such as *Brendan Behan's Island: An Irish Sketch-Book* (1962), *Brendan Behan's New York* (1964), and *Confessions of an Irish Rebel* (1965), are relatively minor pieces. He died in March, 1964, at the age of forty-one. Thousands lined the streets of Dublin for the funeral cortege, a ceremony orchestrated by the IRA.

ANALYSIS

The militant republicanism that he inherited from his family and the years of imprisonment both in England and Ireland are the influences most apparent in Behan's writings. If Behan had not been sent to the juvenile reformatory after his arrest in Liverpool, there would have been no autobiographical *Borstal Boy*. It was in Ireland's prisons where he first began *The Quare Fellow*, which tells of the last few hours before the subject, the quare fellow, is to be hanged. *The Hostage*, Behan's other major drama, relates the saga of an English soldier kidnapped by the Irish Republican Army.

Early political commitments and years in prison made Behan more than merely a bitter reporter of his experiences. Anger is a major aspect of his writing. He is antiestablishment, as might be predicted, but not anti-English. His attitudes were far from knee-jerk Anglophobia; Dickens was one of his favorite authors, and his years in the Borstal exposed him to the sum of human types, from cruel authoritarianism to friendly camaraderie among his fellow prisoners, most of whom were English. Behan was a Catholic, steeped in that tradition, but a chief villain in *Borstal Boy* is a Catholic prison priest who excommunicates Behan for his IRA membership, thus sundering him from the sacraments and consolations of his church. In Behan's last major play, *The Hostage*, the least sympathetic character is the pompous and arrogant IRA officer in charge of the kidnapped English soldier. Behan's political ideology may be summed up in the following statement in the introduction to the program of *The Hostage*: "I respect kindness to human beings first of all, and kindness to animals. I don't respect the law; I have a total irreverence for anything connected with society except that which makes the roads safer, the beer stronger, the food cheaper, and old men and old women warmer in the winter, and happier in the summer."

Although Behan's plays were first produced in Dublin, he had greater success and recognition in London. His English fame coincided with the time of the "angry young men" such as John Osborne and his *Look Back in Anger* (pr. 1956, pb. 1957), and critics often categorized Behan as belonging to that theatrical movement. Behan's anger was not the same as Osborne's. Behan's writings, even the most serious, are generally imbued with humor—sometimes slapstick, sometimes satiric, usually both. He once claimed that he would laugh at a funeral as long as it was not his own. Generally his humor, no matter how broad, had a sharp point, and poignancy and desperation underscored it. In *The Quare Fellow* two inmates are to be hanged, convicted of murder. One has chopped up his brother; the other has killed his wife with a silver-headed cane. The latter is reprieved; the former, the quare fellow, is not. Behan's implication that wife-killing, especially with a silver-headed cane, is acceptable suggests something about both the value society gives women and the importance of class differences.

Although humor suffuses Behan's writings, his characters are inevitably trapped in desperate situations (prisons, for example) from which there is no easy escape. *Borstal Boy* is one of the great works of prison literature, and the account of his arrest and life in prison portrays a closed and brutal world. In *The Quare Fellow* it is not only the prisoners who are captives but also their guards and prison authorities. There is no formal prison in *The Hostage* but the setting is a brothel, which is another type of prison, not only for the British soldier but also for his IRA guards and the other inhabitants of the brothel, both sellers and buyers. Even history can be a prison. The Monsewer, the owner of the house, is an old Irish revolutionary, who has become a prisoner of his own biography and Ireland's past. In Behan's short story "The Confirmation Suit," a young boy is forced to don a suit for his confirmation made by a Miss McCann. The suit, however, has narrow lapels and large buttons, but in spite of his shame the boy is constrained to wear it to his first communion. There is no escape.

In Behan's world, nevertheless, there is always the possibility of freedom. After the boy's mother tells Miss McCann that he hates the suit, the boy discovers Miss McCann with head bowed, shaking with tears. Following her death, as an act of contrition he willingly wears the despised suit to her funeral. It is an act of homage to Miss McCann, but also a liberation of himself. In *The Hostage* the British soldier is accidentally killed when the Irish authorities storm the brothel in an attempt to free him. Even death, however, sometimes has no dominion. At the end of the play the soldier rises and sings.

THE QUARE FELLOW

First produced: 1954 (first published, 1956)
Type of work: Play

The Quare Fellow is the story of prisoners and guards in an Irish prison on the eve of the execution of a murderer, the title figure.

The Quare Fellow was Behan's first major theatrical success, originally playing in Dublin's Pike Theatre in 1954 and then produced by Joan Littlewood in London in 1956. It opens in a prison on the eve of an execution, shortly after one condemned prisoner, who murdered his wife, has been pardoned, but not the other. "Quare fellow," in the setting of the play, is the colloquial term for someone under the death sentence. The quare fellow of the title has been sentenced to die for murdering his brother with a meat cleaver. The play ends the following morning with the execution. Although the quare fellow, or rather his imminent execution, is the centerpiece of the play, the play is not about him. There is no question that he is guilty, and there is never any expectation he will be reprieved. He is not a likable figure, and there is no sympathy for him even from his fellow convicts—except for the fact that he is to be executed. The quare fellow never appears and utters no words.

The play relates not the effect of the execution upon the person to be "topped," or hanged, but the effect upon all the others—prisoners, guards, the hangman—involved in the event.

As a drama it is straightforward, with little to surprise the reader or audience; there is no doubt that the quare fellow will be hanged in the morning. Behan's brilliant dialogue—in part the result of his many years in prison—and his ready gallows humor propel the play despite the lack of plot. Behan's antiestablishment attitude focuses upon Holy Healey, the elegantly dressed prison visitor. Healey notes at one point that since condemned prisoners have access to a priest they will "die holier deaths than if they had finished their natural span." The warder responds that "We can't advertise 'Commit a murder and die a happy death,' sir. We'd have them all at it. They take religion very seriously in this country." Another prisoner wishes to get in touch with a friend who might post bail. The response is "Get a pail and bail yourself out." The events of the execution are told to the audience by one of the prisoners, in the terms of a horse race, with puns and verbal play relaying the step-by-step process of a hanging. Afterward, the prisoners bury the quare fellow, and although his last letters are supposed to be tossed into the grave instead of sent to his family, the prisoners take them—to be sold to one of the Sunday papers. Nothing is sacred, not even death.

BORSTAL BOY

First published: 1958
Type of work: Autobiography

A sixteen-year-old Irish boy is charged with political terrorism and is sentenced to a Borstal, an English reformatory.

In 1939, Behan was discovered in Liverpool with bomb-making materials and arrested as an IRA terrorist. Sixteen years old, he was treated as a juvenile and sentenced to three years in a Borstal. *Borstal Boy* is the autobiography that resulted from his experience. It belongs both to the genre of prison literature and to the long history of Irish-English relations, or animosities. It is also a coming-of-age story, similar to Mark Twain's *Adventures of Huckleberry Finn* (1884) and J. D. Salinger's *The Catcher in the Rye* (1951). Additionally, it is a great comic work. Finally, as a work reflecting prison life it bears comparison with *The Quare Fellow.*

The dialogue and use of dialect in both are superb, although the longer scope of *Borstal Boy* allows for greater digression, sometimes too much. The book, particularly the latter part, is often episodic. Behan, associated with the IRA and in possession of explosives when he was arrested, nevertheless quickly developed friendly relations with most of his guards and the other authorities as well as his fellow prisoners. Undoubtedly that was a result of Behan's exuberant personality, but it also says something about Behan's awareness of, and sympathy for, the universality of human experience. He was able to separate the English as a people from the policy of their government toward Ireland, which he deplored. In fact, young Behan, the urban Dubliner, often identified more with London cockneys and working-class boys from Liverpool than he did with rural Irishmen.

Behan experienced pain, fear, and brutality, particularly before he arrived at the Borstal, but what remains in the reader's memory is the humor. Behan could make himself the butt of this humor: On one occasion he was sentenced to solitary confinement for twenty-four hours, restricted to bread and water. During that short period he noted that if a warder had requested that he sing "God Save the King" in exchange for a piece of roast, he, an IRA terrorist, would have immediately complied.

The Borstal to which Behan was sent was organized more like an English public school than a punitive jail (if the distinction is not too fine). The boys had work assignments, but often considerable freedom. During the summer Behan and his "chinas"—best friends—were able to sneak away to the nearby seashore. More than anything else what made the Borstal bearable were the friendships that developed among the boys. On occasion relations were

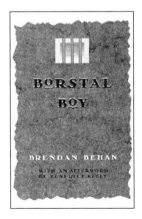

more intimate than simple friendship. In *Borstal Boy* Behan generally only alludes to the subject of homosexuality; in some of his other writings he was more explicit. As a result of the book's language, which was profane but realistic, because of the book's attitude toward the priest who denied Behan the sacraments, and possibly because of the homosexual allusions, *Borstal Boy*, critically acclaimed in the United Kingdom and the United States, was banned in Ireland. Many other Irish writers' works were banned as well. Perhaps Behan thought that the banning put him in good company.

THE HOSTAGE

First produced: 1958 (first published, 1958)
Type of work: Play

An English soldier is captured and held hostage in a brothel in reprisal for the imminent execution of an Irish rebel by the British.

The critics were enthusiastic about Behan's *The Hostage*, though they found it difficult to describe. On its surface, the story appears to be serious drama. A young English soldier, Leslie Williams, is kidnapped by the IRA on the eve of the execution of an Irish terrorist by the British. If the latter is executed, Williams will be murdered in retaliation. The setting is a brothel in Dublin. *The Hostage* is also a comedy of slapstick and satire as well as a musical production, with references to topical events.

The play is populated by the bawdy, the fanatical, the cynical, the corrupt, and the insane. The latter, the Monsewer (Monsieur), owns the building and was a republican patriot back in the glory days of Easter 1916. The house is run by Pat, also of the old IRA, who lost his enthusiasm for the cause. There are prostitutes—straight and gay—and assorted clients, as well as a minor civil servant who turns out to be a secret agent for the Irish police. Into this mélange Leslie is brought by the IRA, led by a fanatical officer. Even the house, like so many of the characters, has seen better days; the former luxurious mansion has become a whorehouse.

The English soldier and the Irish servant, Teresa, the play's two innocents, fall in love. They are both orphans, without family ties to the history that has led to the perversions—political, mental, and sexual—of the other characters. In *The Hostage*, the antiestablishment Behan takes on all orthodoxies. It is a typically Irish play in its concentration upon the tyranny of history. In Behan's hands, however, there is more farce in the grim story than there is tragedy. Song and slapstick are more prevalent than sorrow and tears, and although Leslie gets killed, it is not because of ruthless reprisal by the IRA but because he is accidentally caught in a comedic crossfire when the police arrive.

At the end of the play, however, first Leslie and then the rest of the cast sing, "O death, where is thy sting-ling-a-ling,/ Or grave its victory." Does Leslie represent the heroic figures of Irish myth, or is Behan suggesting that, like Christ, he has died for others' sins and risen again? Or is Behan mocking the realism of traditional theater? That is what makes *The Hostage* so fascinating: The theme is serious, or perhaps not; the ending is dramatic, yet farcical.

SUMMARY

Brendan Behan is an important writer but is not among Ireland's greatest authors. His major works are only three: *The Quare Fellow*, *Borstal Boy*, and *The Hostage*. He also wrote some excellent poetry in Irish and several fine short stories. His other writings are, for the most part, ephemeral. The major works, for all their brilliance, are not fully crafted. The years of disciplined writing were too few; his serious work ended several years before his early death in 1964. Nevertheless, to produce three near-masterpieces is a notable legacy.

Eugene Larson

BIBLIOGRAPHY

By the Author

DRAMA:
Gretna Green, pr. 1947
The Quare Fellow, pr. 1954, pb. 1956 (translation and revision of his Gaelic play "Casadh Súgáin Eile," wr. 1946)
The Big House, pr. 1957 (radio play), pr. 1958 (staged), pb. 1961
The Hostage, pr., pb. 1958 (translation and revision of *An Giall*)
An Giall, pr. 1958, pb. 1981 (in Gaelic)
Richard's Cork Leg, pr. 1972, pb. 1973 (begun 1960, completed posthumously by Alan Simpson, 1964)
The Complete Plays, pb. 1978

RADIO PLAYS:
A Garden Party, 1952
Moving Out, 1952

LONG FICTION:
The Scarperer, 1964 (1953 serialized, as by Emmet Street)
The Dubbalin Man, 1997 (serialized 1954-1956)

SHORT FICTION:
After the Wake, 1981

DISCUSSION TOPICS

- Like several other Irish writers, Brendan Behan seemed to contemplate Ireland best when he was away from it. What might be the reasons for being away in order to capture the essence of one's homeland?

- Is Behan's introduction to *The Hostage*, in which he writes about not respecting the law and "irreverence" to society, simply irresponsible or useful to his literary art?

- Behan liked to express his dislike of the English, but offer indications of his fiction that reflect tolerance toward the English.

- Explain how Behan's ironical wit counteracts his apparently outrageous ideas, such as the belief that wife-killing is acceptable.

- What are the paradoxes, the apparent contradictions, in Behan's depiction of prison life?

NONFICTION:
Borstal Boy, 1958 (autobiography)
Brendan Behan's Island: An Irish Sketch-Book, 1962
Hold Your Hour and Have Another, 1963
Brendan Behan's New York, 1964
Confessions of an Irish Rebel, 1965
The Letters of Brendan Behan, 1992 (E. K. Mikhail, editor)

MISCELLANEOUS:
Poems and Stories, 1978
Poems and a Play in Irish, 1981 (includes the play *An Giall*)

About the Author

Behan, Beatrice, Des Hickey, and Gus Smith. *My Life with Brendan.* Los Angeles: Nash, 1974.

Behan, Brendan. *Brendan Behan: Interviews and Recollections.* Edited by E. H. Mikhail. 2 vols. London: Gill & Macmillan, 1982.

Boyle, Ted E. *Brendan Behan.* New York: Twayne, 1969.

Brannigan, John. *Brendan Behan: Cultural Nationalism and the Revisionist Writer.* Dublin: Four Courts, 2002.

Bull, John. *British and Irish Dramatists Since World War II, Second Series.* Vol. 233 in *Dictionary of Literary Biography.* Detroit: Gale Group, 2001.

Mikhail, E. H., ed. *The Art of Brendan Behan.* New York: Barnes & Noble Books, 1979.

O'Connor, Ulick. *Brendan.* Englewood Cliffs, N.J.: Prentice-Hall, 1971.

O'Sullivan, Michael. *Brendan Behan: A Life.* Dublin: Blackwater Press, 1997.

APHRA BEHN

Born: Kent, England
  July 10, 1640 (baptized)
Died: London, England
  April 16, 1689

Behn, England's first professional woman writer, produced popular Restoration dramas and made noteworthy contributions to the development of prose fiction.

BIOGRAPHY

Concerning the family background and early life of Aphra Behn (bayn), virtually nothing is known with certainty. The sparse information that exists is usually contradictory. A parish register in the town of Wye shows that a baby named Aphara Amis was baptized in that town, in the county of Kent, England, on July 10, 1640. It is likely that she was born in the same year and in the same county, and Aphara Amis probably became Aphra Behn. While her literary works show that she was widely read, with a knowledge of several languages, nothing is known about her education. Early in life, she traveled to Surinam (modern Guyana), where she remained for a few months; the trip left an enduring impression and provided materials for her prose fiction and drama. She married a Dutch merchant engaged in business in London, a man who seems to have dropped out of her life by 1665. Scholars have suggested that he perished during the London plague of 1665.

In July, 1666, during the Anglo-Dutch War, she was sent to Antwerp, Belgium as an intelligence agent, a position she held until the end of December, 1666. Using the code name "Astrea," she posted numerous letters to her superiors in London, providing information she had gleaned about Dutch intentions and pleading for more money to meet her mounting expenses. The letters suggest that, like many agents of King Charles II, she was left to fend for herself. In one letter she reported that the Dutch had devised a plan to send warships up the Thames and attack the English navy. This account was ignored as too improbable. As a consequence, England experienced its most humiliating naval defeat in history. On June 13, 1667, Dutch warships sailed up the Thames River, cut the chain protecting the English fleet, destroyed several warships, and towed away the *Royal Charles*, the English flagship.

After Behn returned to London in 1667, she was imprisoned for debt, despite repeated appeals for relief to King Charles II, whom she had faithfully served. Presumably she eventually did receive support from Lord Arlington, the cabinet member in charge of intelligence, or his agent Thomas Killigrew (1612-1683), himself a dramatist, for she was released after a few months.

After her return to London, she turned to writing plays as a means of earning a living. Beginning with *The Forced Marriage: Or, The Jealous Bridegroom* (pr. 1670, pb. 1671), she wrote more than fifteen plays, of which many were highly successful. As a writer for the Duke's Company, she created dramas that were performed by the most talented actors and actresses of the time, including Anthony Leigh, James Nokes, Charles Hart, Elizabeth Barry, and Anne Bracegirdle. Following her success on the stage, Behn turned to prose narrative, translation, and poetry, producing several prose titles well-known in their time. Through her writings, she involved herself in the political controversies of the day, siding with the Tory cause in support of the Stuart monarchy. Plays such as *The Roundheads: Or,*

The Good Old Cause (pr. 1681, pb. 1682) included satire of the king's Whig opponents.

The life of an author during the Restoration was precarious unless revenues from the writings could be supplemented by generous and reliable patrons. Indications are that Behn endured periods of financial hardship throughout her life, and her health and fortune declined as the Stuart monarchy approached its demise. Unswerving loyalty to two Stuart kings did not assure even her safety; she was imprisoned in 1682 for satire directed against the Duke of Monmouth, King Charles's illegitimate son. In failing health, she found it necessary to continue working just to provide the necessities of life. She died April 16, 1689, and was buried in the cloisters of Westminster Abbey.

ANALYSIS

For an author whose career lasted less than twenty years, Aphra Behn was exceptionally prolific. Her canon contains at least seventeen dramas, and perhaps as many as twenty-one attributions are included. It also includes numerous occasional and lyric poems, fourteen titles in prose fiction, and a handful of translations. She launched her literary career with drama, a natural beginning for an aspiring writer of her time since the theater provided more secure financial rewards than publication. Her plays are exceptionally varied, including tragicomedies, comedies of wit and intrigue, and political satires. Like many authors of her time, she drew upon previous dramatists for plots and characters. For her portrayal of character, conflict, and setting, she is particularly indebted to earlier Jacobean dramatists, such as Francis Beaumont and John Fletcher, Thomas Middleton, Richard Brome, and John Marston. In addition to earlier plays, her sources include Spanish and French novellas and, for one drama, *The Widow Ranter: Or, The History of Bacon of Virginia* (pr. 1689, pb. 1690), a contemporary account of the Virginia colony.

Although her plots are often complex, she is noted for sprightly action and for colloquial, witty dialogue. These qualities appealed to her audience and led to theater revivals of some of her dramas well into the eighteenth century. A recurring theme is young love overcoming obstacles imposed by the lovers' society and elders. A related theme is the necessity for women to make their own choices in marriage.

In addition to drama, she wrote numerous works of prose fiction, ranging in length from short story to novel. Most of these were written late in her career, after 1684. Though normally classified as novels, the longer works are not true novels but rather antecedents of the genre. Her narrative technique includes numerous details to ensure a realistic effect. Frequently the narrator assures the reader that he or she has witnessed the events firsthand, lending a touch of realism. Yet the works lack the psychological realism of true novels, and coincidence is too frequent and too substantive for the settings that Behn creates. The sources are often French and Spanish romances, though many depend on English settings or contemporary events.

Her longest prose work, *Love Letters Between a Nobleman and His Sister* (1683-1687), is a roman à clef based upon a scandalous contemporary romance between a nobleman and his sister-in-law. Written in three parts, it enjoyed popular success despite a length of 200,000 words. Its significance lies in Behn's early use of the epistolary narrative technique, foreshadowing the eighteenth century novels of Samuel Richardson.

Romantic love, the dominant theme of Behn's fiction, often reaches heroic proportions. Stories such as "The Unfortunate Happy Lady" (c. 1697) and the novel *The Adventure of the Black Lady* (1698) depict success in love as a combination of forgiveness, intense passion, and endangered but inviolate virtue. This tendency to develop the theme of heroic love reaches its height in her best-known prose work, *Oroonoko: Or, The History of the Royal Slave* (1688), a narrative featuring an exotic setting and a hero who embodies love and honor. Even in a novel featuring the femme fatale like *The Fair Jilt: Or, The History of Prince Tarquin and Miranda* (1688), love is uncritical and entirely forgiving.

Among her poems, Behn wrote numerous lyrics, occasional verses, panegyrics, songs, prologues, epilogues, and a few satires. In her elegy on Edmund Waller, a poet prized for his polished verses, she professes that she learned the art of English poetry from studying his poems. The acknowledgment is noteworthy, for her heroic couplets reflect the idiomatic fluency and smoothness that one associates with Waller's poetry. She achieves the limpid diction and polish that marked the style of the best writings of her times though her poems lack the insouciant tone and sharp-edged satire of witty writing at its best. Her love poems often invoke the idyllic setting of the pastoral mode, and her finest love poetry achieves an effect that is simple, rhythmic, and eloquent. Two of her best-known lyrics, "Love Arm'd" and "Song" ("'Tis not your saying that you love"), are on the theme of unrequited love, perhaps a result of her ill-fated affair with John Hoyle, a London rake. The final stanza of "Song" illustrates the stylistic purity and earnest tone that the poems achieve:

> But if I fail your heart to move,
> And 'tis not yours to give;
> I cannot, wonnot cease to love,
> But I will cease to live.

Among her occasional poems are numerous prologues and epilogues that were published with her plays. Like other poems of this type, they appeal to the audience for approval or at least indulgence. These prologues and epilogues are written in heroic couplets, the dominant verse form of the age.

By 1680, Behn had begun working as a translator, producing poetry and prose of popular works. Her translations are from Latin and French, and the diversity suggests that she turned to translation not because she found the works congenial, but because she needed to supplement her income. By modern standards, her translations take excessive liberties with the originals, but her practice accorded well with the theory of translation put forth by John Dryden, the dominant literary figure of her time. His theory accepted paraphrase and alterations to accommodate the tastes and understanding of the audience.

THE ROVER: OR, THE BANISHED CAVALIERS

First produced: Part I, 1677 (first published, 1677)
Type of work: Play

In Naples, exiled English cavaliers seek pleasure and find suitable marriage partners.

Willmore, the Rover, arrives in Naples where he meets his fellow exiles Blunt, Frederick, and Belvile. They begin rather aimless adventures in quest of pleasure. Although Willmore is an example of the appealing, energetic Restoration hero of wit, it is the women characters who, indirectly, control the action. Hellena, destined by her father for a convent, wishes another kind of life and is willing to venture into the carnival setting to seek it. Once she has seen Willmore, she decides to make him her husband, even if she must pursue him in disguise. In order to thwart his affair with Angellica, an aged former mistress of a Spanish general, she disguises herself as a page. Her sister Florinda has been promised, against her will, to Antonio. Florinda has been in love with Belvile since he saved her life and that of her brother Don Pedro during a battle. Despite numerous mishaps and mistakes that endanger her, she manages to win Belvile in the end. Both women achieve marriages that will assure financial independence and compatibility and will not require excessive emotional commitment.

Not all pleasure seeking, however, achieves its ends. Behn implies that the persons must possess some attractive qualities and panache. Blunt, crudely direct in his hedonism, finds himself deceived and robbed by a courtesan. He represents the naïve country squire of Restoration comedy, who becomes the butt of farcical humor. On the other hand, Willmore's excesses—drunkenness, brawling, and promiscuity—are redeemed by his wit, savoir faire, and overall good nature.

The drama possesses an abundance of humor, sprightly wit, and farcical adventures. Although the celebration of loyalty may have been its greatest appeal for the Restoration audience, the drama is also noteworthy for its portrayal of strong-willed heroines who choose their own future and act to bring it about. The sequel, *The Rovers: Or, The Banished Cavaliers, Part II* (pr., pb. 1681) is generally regarded as inferior to the first part, although it is noteworthy for its use of two figures from commedia dell'arte: Harlequin and Scaramouche.

THE FAIR JILT: OR, THE HISTORY OF PRINCE TARQUIN AND MIRANDA

First published: 1688
Type of work: Novel

Miranda, a beautiful but amoral femme fatale, leads admirers into crime and destruction, but love and forgiveness restore most of the losses.

The Fair Jilt introduces the beautiful femme fatale Miranda, whose unconcerned and unrestrained pursuit of romance and pleasure jeopardizes the lives of others. The narrative divides into two loosely intertwined parts, one involving the heroine's love for an exiled German prince, Henrick, and a second involving her marriage to Tarquin, the only son of a wealthy Dutch merchant. Miranda, joint heiress with her younger sister to a large fortune, enters an Antwerp convent following the death of her parents, though she has no intention of making permanent vows.

In retaliation for Miranda's numerous shallow flirtations, the God of Love imposes upon her a deep, genuine love for a young Franciscan friar, who is devoted to his vocation and his vow of chastity. After learning that he is a German prince named Henrick (complete with a tragic past), Miranda begins pursuing him through letters and calculated meetings, offering herself and her inheritance and imploring him to elope with her. He steadfastly refuses all of her advances. Unable to comprehend that he would refuse her because of his religious devotion, she accuses him of rape and sees him sentenced to death, a sentence commuted to life imprisonment after some of her letters to him have been released.

In the second episode, she meets and marries the young Tarquin, whose love for her exceeds anything she feels for him. Having inherited her fortune and having become guardian for her sister's portion, she lives with Tarquin on a lavish scale in Antwerp, freely spending her sister Alcidiana's portion while discouraging would-be suitors. When Alcidiana asserts her independence and demands her inheritance, Miranda induces a page to murder her, but the effort at poisoning fails. The page is apprehended, tried, and hanged, while Miranda

herself is judicially humiliated by being forced to stand at the foot of the gallows. Still undeterred, she later persuades her devoted husband to shoot Alcidiana as she enters the theater. The bullet passes harmlessly through her garments, but Tarquin is apprehended and condemned to death. Miranda is sent to the prison where the princely friar is incarcerated. Upon release, the friar pleads for Miranda's freedom, and Tarquin is spared when the executioner wounds instead of kills him. After his recovery, Tarquin joins Miranda in Holland, where, having lost all Miranda's fortune, they are supported by the wealth of his father.

Behn portrays Miranda as an example of role reversal in love. Bent on dominance and self-assertiveness, she moves from tyrannizing over the friar to tyrannizing over her sister. Yet even she can be rescued from her excesses, and the book suggests that she has lived in quiet retirement with Tarquin until his death.

The story also admirably depicts Behn's concept of love as totally self-sacrificing and forgiving. Smitten by her beauty and charm, the other characters are putty in Miranda's hands. Yet willingness to forgive means that the worst evils can be remedied. Tarquin harbors no lasting resentment for the calamities she has brought upon him, and Prince Henrick, despite his two years' imprisonment on a false charge, is eager to beg mercy on her behalf. The limited suffering in the denouement, however, depends upon extravagant improbabilities and astounding coincidence. Despite a wealth of concrete detail and authorial testimony, the story lacks genuine realism, although realism was not a standard for judging long fiction in Behn's time.

OROONOKO: OR, THE HISTORY OF THE ROYAL SLAVE

First published: 1688
Type of work: Novel

Oroonoko, a heroic African prince, dies in an attempt to free himself and others from slavery.

Oroonoko: Or, The History of the Royal Slave, Behn's most significant novel, resembles *The Fair Jilt* in that she attempts to achieve verisimilitude by first-person commentary and an abundance of concrete detail. She asserts at the outset that the story is factual and claims to have known the characters and witnessed much of the action. She injects numerous details to enhance the realism, foreshadowing the narrative technique of Daniel Defoe and Jonathan Swift. She describes, for example, South American creatures such as the armadillo and the anaconda, and her account of the indigenous tribes idealizes their primitive and simple lives in the wilderness.

The narrative has two distinct parts. The first, set in the African country Coramantien, introduces the young prince Oroonoko, grandson of the country's aged king. Oroonoko is a Restoration love-and-honor hero, capable of intense passions. In love, Oroonoko knows no half measures, for Behn embraces the assumption of heroic love that great love implies a great soul. A man of natural nobility, he is not a primitive, but a well-educated, charismatic youth who can read Latin and French and speak English. He achieves rapport with all types of people, including the natives of the New World.

Trouble in his native land begins when he falls in love with Imoinda, the beautiful daughter of a general who has sacrificed his own life in battle to save Oroonoko's. After Oroonoko has secretly married Imoinda, his aged grandfather, king of Coramantien, decides to make her his wife and summons her to the palace. Deprived of his wife for months, Oroonoko conspires with friends at court to arrange a clandestine meeting. When the king discovers this, he decides to sell Imoinda into slavery because of the betrayal and tells Oroonoko that she has been put to death. The king refrains from taking action against Oroonoko because he is too powerful and too valuable.

Oroonoko, reminiscent of Achilles, withdraws from his role of military leader, depressed over his loss, until an attacking force endangers the country. He throws himself into the conflict and leads the king's forces to victory. Shortly thereafter, he is enslaved by a treacherous English captain, who lures him and his companions aboard a slave ship under pretext of holding a celebration. During the voyage across the Atlantic, the captain shows himself capable of other treachery and duplicity.

Oroonoko is sent to the English colony Surinam and assigned to a plantation supervised by Trefry, an educated Englishman. When he reaches the plantation, Oroonoko discovers to his amazed delight that Imoinda is living on the same plantation. The two are reunited and live in happiness together for a time. When Oroonoko learns that Imoinda will bear his child, he decides not to permit the child to be born into bondage. A natural leader, he persuades other slaves and their families to flee with him by night into the jungle. A militia pursues and either captures or kills most of the unarmed slaves. Last to be captured are Oroonoko and Imoinda. Their captors vacillate about their punishment. Trefry is inclined to be merciful, but Byam, a cruel master, is unforgiving and punitive. When Oroonoko realizes that he will have to endure further punishment, he kills Imoinda and afterward is captured in a paroxysm of grief. He recovers from his own attempted suicide and stoically endures slow death by dismemberment at the hands of his captors.

Oroonoko: Or, The History of the Royal Slave remains significant in the development of the novel for its narrator persona and for its use of concrete details to enhance realism. The narrator assures the reader that all the account is true and claims periodically to have encountered Oroonoko personally at specified points in the action. The abundant details are highly specific, though sometimes inaccurate, as when Behn attributes a length of thirty-six yards to an anaconda or describes tigers in Surinam.

Thematically the work touches on values that are typical of Behn's fiction, including the right of women to select their spouses, opposition to slavery, and condemnation of the slave trade. The work also includes a celebration of the primitive, though this celebration is qualified. The indigenous people of Surinam are admirably adjusted to life in their environment, but they are not so adaptable as the highly educated protagonist. Above all, the novel is an account of the hero who upholds the ideals of civilization among Europeans who are, for the most part, evil.

SUMMARY

Aphra Behn was the first woman in the history of English literature to earn her living as a writer. Behn's plays reflect the exuberant spirit of Restoration drama and succeeded with audiences of her time; some were regularly performed into the eighteenth century. Her primary significance to literary history, however, lies in her prose fiction. She is an important figure in the transition from the prose romances of the Renaissance to the modern novel. Her narrative art assures her interest to literary historians, and her humanitarian themes endow her works with lasting relevance.

Stanley Archer

DISCUSSION TOPICS

- How do Aphra Behn's dramas differ from representative Restoration plays?

- What traits of Behn's fiction anticipate eighteenth century English novels?

- What does Behn's experience as a spy contribute to her writings?

- It cannot be established whether Behn visited South America. How convincing of such a visit are the details in *Oroonoko*?

- Support the assertion that Behn was an extraordinary woman.

- What significance do you see in Behn's frequent habit of giving two titles to her works?

BIBLIOGRAPHY

By the Author

DRAMA:
The Forced Marriage: Or, The Jealous Bridegroom, pr. 1670, pb. 1671
The Amorous Prince: Or, The Curious Husband, pr., pb. 1671
The Dutch Lover, pr., pb. 1673
Abdelazer: Or, The Moor's Revenge, pr. 1676, pb. 1677
The Town Fop: Or, Sir Timothy Tawdry, pr. 1676, pb. 1677
The Rover: Or, The Banished Cavaliers, Part I, pr., pb. 1677
Sir Patient Fancy, pr., pb. 1678
The Feigned Courtesans: Or, A Night's Intrigue, pr., pb. 1679
The Young King: Or, The Mistake, pr. 1679, pb. 1683
The Rover: Or, The Banished Cavaliers, Part II, pr., pb. 1681
The Roundheads: Or, The Good Old Cause, pr. 1681, pb. 1682
The City Heiress: Or, Sir Timothy Treat-All, pr., pb. 1682
The Lucky Chance: Or, An Alderman's Bargain, pr. 1686, pb. 1687
The Emperor of the Moon, pr., pb. 1687
The Widow Ranter: Or, The History of Bacon of Virginia, pr. 1689, pb. 1690
The Younger Brother: Or, The Amorous Jilt, pr., pb. 1696

LONG FICTION:
Love Letters Between a Nobleman and His Sister, 1683-1687 (3 volumes)
Agnes de Castro, 1688
Oroonoko: Or, The History of the Royal Slave, 1688
The Fair Jilt: Or, The History of Prince Tarquin and Miranda, 1688
The History of the Nun: Or, The Fair Vow-Breaker, 1689
The Lucky Mistake, 1689
The Nun: Or, The Perjured Beauty, 1697

Aphra Behn

The Adventure of the Black Lady, 1698
The Wandering Beauty, 1698

POETRY:

Poems upon Several Occasions, with A Voyage to the Island of Love, 1684 (including adaptation of Abbé Paul Tallemant's *Le Voyage de l'sle d'mour*)
Miscellany: Being a Collection of Poems by Several Hands, 1685 (includes works by others)

TRANSLATIONS:

Aesop's Fables, 1687 (with Francis Barlow)
Of Trees, 1689 (of book 6 of Abraham Cowley's *Sex libri plantarum*)

MISCELLANEOUS:

La Montre: Or, The Lover's Watch, 1686 (prose and poetry)
The Case for the Watch, 1686 (prose and poetry)
Lycidus: Or, The Lover in Fashion, 1688 (prose and poetry; includes works by others)
The Lady's Looking-Glass, to Dress Herself By: Or, The Art of Charming, 1697 (prose and poetry)
The Works of Aphra Behn, 1915, 1967 (6 volumes; Montague Summers, editor)

About the Author

Aughertson, Kate. *Aphra Behn: The Comedies*. New York: Palgrave Macmillan, 2003.

Chalmers, Hero. *Royalist Women Writers, 1650-1689*. New York: Oxford University Press, 2004.

Hughes, Derek. *The Theater of Aphra Behn*. New York: Palgrave, 2001.

Hughes, Derek, and Janet Todd, eds. *The Cambridge Companion to Aphra Behn*. New York: Cambridge University Press, 2004.

Hunter, Heidi, ed. *Rereading Aphra Behn: History, Theory, and Criticism*. Charlottesville: University Press of Virginia, 1993.

Link, Frederick M. *Aphra Behn*. New York: Twayne, 1968.

Sackville-West, Victoria. *Aphra Behn: The Incomparable Astrea*. New York: Viking Press, 1928.

Todd, Janet. *The Secret Life of Aphra Behn*. New Brunswick, N.J.: Rutgers University Press, 1997.

_____, ed. *Aphra Behn*. New York: St. Martin's Press, 1999.

_____. *Aphra Behn Studies*. New York: Cambridge University Press, 1996.

Woodcock, George. *Aphra Behn: The English Sappho*. Montreal: Black Rose Books, 1989.

ARNOLD BENNETT

Born: Shelton, near Hanley, Staffordshire, England
May 27, 1867
Died: London, England
March 27, 1931

Bennett's reputation rests upon his novels of "the Five Towns," a re-creation of the Staffordshire of his youth, as well as on his later, intensely realistic portrayals of English life.

BIOGRAPHY

Enoch Arnold Bennett was born in Shelton, near Hanley, Staffordshire, on May 27, 1867, the son of Enoch and Sarah Ann Longson Bennett. The eldest of nine children, Bennett descended from a long line of Methodists whom he portrayed in his novels *Anna of the Five Towns* (1902) and *Clayhanger* (1910). His father, after working long days as a master potter, draper, and pawnbroker and spending his nights studying the law, qualified as a solicitor at the age of thirty-four, when Arnold was nine. The wealth of precise notation about such occupations in Bennett's novels seems to stem from his early years. He was also fortunate enough to observe the interaction of different social classes as his family's status steadily improved under the sway of his father's autocratic direction (depicted in *Clayhanger*) and his mother's pliable consent.

Bennett attended local schools, but his father determined that his son should be a clerk, and thus he had to forgo the opportunity of a college education. Almost immediately, Bennett resolved to get out of this clerkship, chafing at the life of the "Pottery towns," the filth and provincialism he delineates in *The Old Wives' Tale* (1908) and in other novels.

Bennett's first literary efforts were gossipy notes that appeared in the *Staffordshire Sentinel* while he was educating himself by reading English, French, and Russian authors. He eventually began a job as a clerk with a firm of lawyers in London, where he escaped forever the towns of his youth.

The sometimes gloomy and temperamental Bennett did not like the law, and to supplement his poor pay he turned to secondhand bookselling, which he put to good use in his evocation of Henry Earlforward in *Riceyman Steps* (1923). Soon he established a circle of friends, organizing musical evenings in which he would sing without a trace of the stammer he could not otherwise control. Honing his schoolboy French, he began to consort with artists, musicians, and writers and to publish stories in prestigious London literary magazines. He found his first novel, *A Man from the North* (1898), an agony to write and a commercial failure.

Enoch Bennett's purchase of shares in a periodical, *Woman*, provided Arnold with an assistant editorship, and under the pseudonym "Barbara" he published weekly reviews. As "Marjorie," he supplied gossip and advice in "Answers to Correspondents," later crediting this assignment as contributing to his knowledge of women's apparel, housekeeping, and their most intimate thoughts. Advancing to the position of editor, Bennett managed also to write reviews for other important journals and to thrust himself into the fads of his age: cycling and painting watercolors.

Perhaps because of his experience with so many different sorts of newspapers and journals, Bennett quickly showed his mastery of both serious and superficial literature, producing in the same year (1902) *Anna of the Five Towns*, one of his best novels, and *The Grand Babylon Hotel*, a slight but enjoyable comic thriller, published in the United States as *T. Racksole and Daughter*. The latter formed part of a series of novels that did nothing to enhance Bennett's literary stature, but they enabled him to earn enough money to satisfy his long-held ambition of living in Paris, where he moved in 1903.

Paris was the center of Bennett's literary universe, where he could commune with fellow writers and openly address subjects—particularly sex—that were prohibited in London. There was also the *demimonde* of Paris, the world of the theater and of women who were much freer in their sexual habits than those he had known in England. A young American woman rejected his marriage proposal, but in 1907 he married Marguerite Soulié, a proprietor of a dress shop who was previously connected with the theater. The early years of the marriage in Paris may have been Bennett's happiest, for it is where he conceived and wrote most of his masterpiece, *The Old Wives' Tale*, drawing quite directly on his experience of provincial England and cosmopolitan France.

Bennett continued his prodigious output into the next decade. He published short fiction: *The Grim Smile of the Five Towns* (1907); novels: *Clayhanger, The Card* (1911; published in the United States as *Denry the Audacious*, 1911), and *The Price of Love* (1914); plays: *Milestones: A Play in Three Acts* (pr., pb. 1912) and *The Great Adventure: A Play of Fantasia in Four Sets* (pr. 1912); nonfiction: *The Human Machine* (1908) and *Mental Efficiency, and Other Hints to Men and Women* (1911); and criticism: *Books and Persons: Being Comments on a Past Epoch* (1908-1911). As he drove himself relentlessly, his income increased and his health deteriorated. He experienced sleeplessness, exhaustion, and intermittent depression. After bouts of gastroenteritis, Bennett would dose himself with various pills and nerve tonics. Yet he had an enviable reputation as a sweet-tempered and generous man, which is somewhat belied by his later relations with his wife, from whom he separated in 1921.

During World War I, Bennett worked hard and without pay at a five-day-a-week schedule in the Ministry of Information, later basing an important novel, *Lord Raingo* (1926), on his experience. Continuing to write journalism, novels, and other books that would swell his total output to more than eighty titles, Bennett was lionized, feted, and offered titles he refused—always careful to remember his social roots, eschewing snobbery, and taking a line sympathetic to working men and women.

Toward the end of his career, he was often re-garded as a relic. His reputation in eclipse after coming under the heavy literary guns of Virginia Woolf and Rebecca West, Bennett died on March 27, 1931, in London, a prosperous writer mourned even by his severest critics, who noted the power of his kind and sympathetic personality and art.

ANALYSIS

Bennett's highest literary ambition was to become the English Flaubert. Profoundly influenced by Gustave Flaubert's novel *Madame Bovary* (1857; English translation,1886), Bennett set out to record a faithful, intensely accurate, and scrupulously realized account of English provincial life in the second half of the nineteenth century and the early twentieth century. Flaubert had shown that the single most important factor in literature was the writer's imagination, his ability to plumb the milieu and the minds of his characters. Rendering their worlds in meticulous detail, creating the canvas of human nature, would yield a godlike mastery of social reality and individuality and issue into an art that could stand by itself.

Flaubert's appeal to Bennett is obvious, for here was a man who wanted to transcend his place in the dirty pottery towns of the north of England, who in his early years had to bow to the authority of his strong-willed father. To create his own world for himself and to project that world into literature seemed to him to be the noblest and most exciting goal he could conceive.

The key to Bennett's success lay in his efforts to amass a densely organized and detailed view of social reality. In his best work he set a geographical boundary to his fiction, the territory of the five towns in Staffordshire—Tunstall, Burslem, Hanley, Stoke-on-Trent, and Longton—that he called in his fiction Turnhill, Bursley, Banbridge, Knype, and Longshaw. Within these environs, Bennett could map and plot and analyze human character and society with virtually exhaustive completeness. Thus in a "Five Towns" novel he could describe in riveting detail the transportation network, the items in the shops, the dress of men and women, the character and quality of their furniture, the local politics, the announcements and gossip in the newspapers, and the seemingly glacial, reluctant emergence of these provincial places into the modern world.

If Bennett found his first novel painful to write,

it is not difficult to see why. His novels are stocked with a profusion of data about social mores and material culture that are almost anthropological in their completeness. When Bennett describes the interior of a home, there is no doubt that he has fully imagined these features and must have found the creation of them arduous. The discipline of a mind capable of such extraordinary specificity, however, produced a magnificent storehouse of imagined environments that Bennett could quickly call upon, for he wrote his greatest and one of his longest works, *The Old Wives' Tale*, in less than a year.

Although Bennett's prodigious output varies in quality, even his least accomplished novels, plays, and criticism reflect his incredible inventory of subjects, which he would recycle throughout his long career. Thus *The Grand Babylon Hotel* initiated his writing about hotels, a characteristic that would appear regularly throughout his fiction. A miser appears in *Anna of the Five Towns* and then is given definitive treatment in *Riceyman Steps*. His women tend to split between the homelike and the unruly—Constance and Sophia in *The Old Wives' Tale*, Alice Challice and Hilda Lessways in *Buried Alive* (1908). Knowing Paris almost as well as his Five Towns, he turned to it in *The Old Wives' Tale, The Pretty Lady* (1918), and *Lilian* (1922).

Bennett's understanding of human nature is founded on the strong material basis of his fiction. His characters' minds and hearts are as plentifully filled as his houses, shops, and streets. A character's mind in Bennett's imagination has as much of a geography as does the locality in which he or she resides. For example, Constance in the *The Old Wives' Tale* has a mind like the draper's shop in which she was reared. She is dull, used to the dirt in the square that invades her household, and positively panicked by her sister Sophia's proposal that they live abroad. Constance has outfitted her life to suit the narrow confines of her provincial setting and knows that the strength and interest she can muster depends upon her devotion to local values.

THE OLD WIVES' TALE

First published: 1908
Type of work: Novel

Two sisters, Constance and Sophia Baines, choose opposite ways of life, accepting and rejecting their provincial roots, and reunite in their difficult, yet happy, last years.

The Old Wives' Tale is generally considered to be Benett's masterpiece. It captures both the provincial and cosmopolitan worlds that were the basis of both his life and his fiction. In this work, Bennett attained an exquisite balance between his two homes, England and France, and between his romantic and realistic sides that are mirrored in the lives of his two heroines, Constance and Sophia.

Constance and Sophia are the daughters of a well-known draper in Bursley. Constance finds it no trouble at all to accustom herself to the drab atmosphere of the shop, to obey her mother in every respect, and to wait upon her invalid father. The beautiful Sophia dreads commerce and is bored by it, preferring a career as a teacher, which her parents strictly forbid her to pursue. Of a romantic disposition, Sophia is quickly taken with Gerald Scales, a traveling salesman who persuades her to elope with him.

Book 1 of the novel is finely balanced between Constance and Sophia, so that the claims of the family and the desires of the individual are both given their due. The characters of Sophia and Constance come to the fore in a hilarious scene involving Samuel Povey, the chief assistant of the shop, who has fallen into a stupor induced by the drug he has taken to deaden the pain of an aching tooth. As his mouth drops open, Sophia deftly inserts a pair of pliers, extracting what she deems to be the offending tooth, only to discover that she has pulled the wrong one. Naturally, Constance is shocked by her sister's boldness, for she cannot imagine taking such liberties or behaving so recklessly. She can be neither as assertive nor as certain as her sister.

Book 2 is devoted to Constance's life, her marriage to Samuel Povey, the birth of her darling son, her management of the shop after the death of her parents, and her retirement to the rooms above the shop when she is bought out by a female assistant and her new husband, the family's dour attorney, Mr. Critchlow. Sophia largely disappears as a character, with Constance receiving only a few postcards that tell her that Sophia is still alive. It is to Bennett's credit that he manages to make Constance an interesting character when her personality is so clearly drab in comparison with her sister's. Bennett is successful because he is so well informed about the details of Constance's life and can show her inner feelings, making what would appear trivial matters to an outside observer important events in Constance's inner life. Bennett demonstrates how Constance makes her marriage and her career in the shop successful, so that within her limitations she performs admirably and heroically. At the same time, the intermittent mentions of Sophia whet the curiosity. What has she made of her life?

Book 3 shifts to Sophia, showing that Gerald Scales never meant to marry her. A spoiled young man with an inheritance, he planned only to make sport with Sophia, but her stolid refusal to have an affair with Scales forces him to marry her. Yet the marriage is a failure, a fact that Sophia prudently acknowledges when she takes advantage of her husband by stealing several hundred pounds to set aside for the day he leaves her.

After recovering from a serious illness occasioned by Gerald's departure, Sophia finds that she is a Baines after all; that is, she has a gift for business, setting herself up with a pension and gaining a reputation as an industrious, no-nonsense proprietor. She rejects various male suitors, saving both her money and her energy for business, paying little attention to the Paris to which her husband has taken her and in which she expects to remain, having given up all thoughts of contacting her family.

At fifty, life changes for Sophia when she is recognized by a family friend who is visiting Paris. Contact is initiated by Constance, who overwhelms Sophia with her sweetness. Sophia is impressed and gratified by her sister's generosity and her complete lack of criticism. Constance, in short, wel-

comes her sister home, and Bennett shrewdly conveys the way in which each must adjust to the habits of the other, sharing the Baines propensity for efficient household management but remaining divided on their views of the best way of spending their remaining years.

Book 4, titled "What Life Is," sums up what the novel is ultimately about: how the sisters come to terms with their mortality and measure the way they have lived. Constance dies, appropriately enough, by exhausting herself in a long walk to the polling booth to vote against the referendum that would unite the five towns and put an end to the provincial life she has treasured. Sophia dies at the shock of seeing her presumably dead husband, who has finally returned home in penury, a feeble old man whose presence floods her with memories of her youth, of her wayward romantic feelings that have given way to a much safer, if narrower, life.

RICEYMAN STEPS

First published: 1923
Type of work: Novel

Henry Earlforward, proprietor of a secondhand bookshop, gradually allows his miserly habits to overwhelm his life, causing the death of himself and his wife.

Riceyman Steps is a bleak novel about a miser. It is a tribute to Bennett's art that the novel is both enjoyable and moving. There is something about knowing a character so well that there is no human fault that cannot be sympathetically understood, if not condoned. So it is with Henry Earlforward, a neat, mild, and fastidious man. When he marries Elsie Sprickett, an equally fastidious and shrewd shop owner, he defeats her efforts to behave more generously and to spend more on life, and though she rails at him, she loves him, softening to his tender voice and his obvious devotion to her.

Bennett contrives a plot and a setting that mercilessly bear down upon the characters yet give them full play to express their individuality. They are not merely the victims of circumstances, but they are also not quite strong enough to alter their lifelong habits and prejudices. There is no area of life, for example, that Henry does not submit to his austere notions of economy. When Elsie attempts to surprise him by having his shop and home cleaned on their honeymoon day (they have agreed it is to be only one day), he insists on cutting the honeymoon short, not wanting to spend more money on what he sees as the extravagance of dinner and a motion-picture show. When they return home and he discovers the vacuum cleaners, he interviews one of the workers, asking him what they do with the dirt. Does it have a market value? Henry wants to know.

Henry denies himself and his wife food, trying to live without heat and light in his home as he does in his business. His mind measures virtually every act by what it costs, so that eventually he turns his own body into an emaciated version of his parsimonious temperament. Where he lives, Riceyman Steps, is but the external manifestation of Henry's reluctance to live a full, expended life. It is a neglected part of London that has not kept pace with the present and has little to recommend itself in the way of culture. Having inherited the book business from a relative, T. T. Riceyman, Henry becomes known by the place he inhabits: He is Riceyman, the human representation of the square, and the twenty Riceyman steps that mark the limit of his enterprise.

Neglecting himself and his wife, Henry does not see the signs of their physical deterioration. He will not spend money on a doctor, attributing his increasing pain to indigestion and his wife's ill health

to needless worry when in fact he is suffering from cancer and she will eventually die following an operation.

Riceyman Steps is perhaps Bennett's final word on the extremity of a certain kind of provincial mind that so starves itself that it cannot recognize the approaching death of the mind and the body. Yet Henry, like so many of Bennett's provincial characters, is likable, for he has an inner harmony, a fullness within the context of his own limitations, such as his full, almost sensual lips—a surprising feature in such a deprived figure.

SUMMARY

For all of his criticism of the provincial character, Arnold Bennett's fondness for figures such as Constance Baines and Henry Earlforward is apparent, for they are presented in loving detail and often exhibit a stalwart, dependable integrity that he much admires. They also represent the power of the past, of the status quo, and of the masses of people who content themselves with life as it is. Though Bennett himself did not choose to live a conventional life, he understood and sympathized with those who made such decisions, because he realized that there were certain compensations for them—chiefly, a sense of comfort and security that his more flamboyant and romantic characters could not achieve.

Carl Rollyson

BIBLIOGRAPHY

By the Author

LONG FICTION:
A Man from the North, 1898
The Grand Babylon Hotel, 1902 (pb. in U.S. as *T. Racksole and Daughter*)
Anna of the Five Towns, 1902
Leonora, 1903
The Gates of Wrath, 1903
A Great Man, 1904
Teresa of Watling Street, 1904
Sacred and Profane Love, 1905 (pb. in U.S. as *The Book of Carlotta*)
Hugo, 1906
Whom God Hath Joined, 1906
The Sinews of War, 1906 (with Eden Phillpotts; pb. in U.S. as *Doubloons*)
The Ghost, 1907

The City of Pleasure, 1907
The Old Wives' Tale, 1908
Buried Alive, 1908
The Statue, 1908 (with Phillpotts)
The Glimpse, 1909
Helen with the High Hand, 1910
Clayhanger, 1910
The Card, 1911 (pb. in U.S. as *Denry the Audacious*)
Hilda Lessways, 1911
The Regent, 1913 (pb. in U.S. as *The Old Adam*)
The Price of Love, 1914
These Twain, 1915
The Lion's Share, 1916
The Roll-Call, 1918
The Pretty Lady, 1918
Lilian, 1922
Mr. Prohack, 1922
Riceyman Steps, 1923
Elsie and the Child, 1924
Lord Raingo, 1926
The Strange Vanguard, 1928 (pb. in U.S. as *The Vanguard*, 1927)
Accident, 1928
Piccadilly, 1929
Imperial Palace, 1930
Venus Rising from the Sea, 1931

SHORT FICTION:
The Loot of Cities, 1905
Tales of the Five Towns, 1905
The Grim Smile of the Five Towns, 1907
The Matador of the Five Towns, 1912
The Woman Who Stole Everything, 1927
Selected Tales, 1928
The Night Visitor, 1931

DRAMA:
Polite Farces for the Drawing-Room, pb. 1899
Cupid and Commonsense, pr. 1908
What the Public Wants, pr., pb. 1909
The Honeymoon: A Comedy in Three Acts, pr., pb. 1911
Milestones: A Play in Three Acts, pr., pb. 1912 (with Edward Knoblock)
The Great Adventure: A Play of Fantasia in Four Sets, pr. 1912
The Title, pr., pb. 1918
Judith, pr., pb. 1919
Sacred and Profane Love, pr., pb. 1919
Body and Soul, pr., pb. 1922
The Love Match, pr., pb. 1922
Don Juan, pb. 1923
London Life, pr., pb. 1924 (with Knoblock)
Mr. Prohack, pr., pb. 1927 (with Knoblock)

DISCUSSION TOPICS

- Virginia Woolf, a great novelist, wrote that Arnold Bennett's novels leave the reader with "a feeling of incompleteness and dissatisfaction." Is she correct?

- What enables Bennett to write so well about provincial towns, like the one depicted in *The Old Wives' Tale?*

- Did Bennett write too many books, or does his work exemplify the value of ceaseless work to improve a writer's chances of succeeding some of the time? Explain your response.

- Consider the wisdom of Bennett's restricting his settings to five towns in one English shire.

- In *Riceyman Steps*, what traits of the miser make him likable?

Flora, pr. 1927
The Return Journey, pr., pb. 1928

NONFICTION:
Journalism for Women, 1898
Fame and Fiction, 1901
The Truth About an Author, 1903
How to Become an Author, 1903
Things That Interested Me, 1906
Things Which Have Interested Me, 1907, 1908
The Human Machine, 1908
Books and Persons: Being Comments on a Past Epoch, 1908-1911
Literary Taste, 1909
Mental Efficiency, and Other Hints to Men and Women, 1911
Those United States, 1912 (pb. in U.S. as *Your United States*)
Paris Nights, 1913
The Author's Craft, 1914
From the Log of the Velsa, 1914
Over There, 1915
Things That Have Interested Me, 1921, 1923, 1926
Selected Essays, 1926
Mediterranean Scenes, 1928
The Savour of Life, 1928
The Journals of Arnold Bennett, 1929, 1930, 1932-1933

About the Author

Barker, Dudley. *Writer by Trade: A View of Arnold Bennett*. London: Allen & Unwin, 1966.

Broomfield, Olga. *Arnold Bennett*. Boston, Twayne, 1984.

Drabble, Margaret. *Arnold Bennett: A Biography*. New York: Alfred A. Knopf, 1974.

Squillace, Robert. "Arnold Bennett's Other Selves." In *Marketing the Author: Authorial Personae, Narrative Selves, and Self-Fashioning, 1880-1930*, edited by Marysa Demoor. New York: Palgrave Macmillan, 2004.

_____. *Modernism, Modernity, and Arnold Bennett*. Lewisburg, Pa.: Bucknell University Press, 1997.

Swinnerton, Frank. *Arnold Bennett*. London: Longman, 1950.

_____. *Arnold Bennett: A Last Word*. Garden City, N.Y.: Doubleday, 1978.

Wright, Walter E. *Arnold Bennett: Romantic Realist*. Lincoln: University of Nebraska Press, 1971.

Young, Kenneth. *Arnold Bennett*. Harlow, Essex, England: The Longman Group, 1975.

THOMAS BERNHARD

Born: Heerlen, the Netherlands
February 9, 1931
Died: Gmunden, Austria
February 12, 1989

Bernhard's postmodernist fiction, formally bearing close resemblance to the interior monologues of Marcel Proust and Samuel Beckett, reveals the tortured souls and minds of his self-absorbed protagonists and narrators, striving in vain and often fatally for perfection in a world indifferent and even hostile to their artistic and intellectual ideals.

Courtesy, Teos

BIOGRAPHY

Thomas Bernhard (BEHRN-hahrt) was born Nicolaas Thomas Bernhard, the illegitimate son of Hertha Bernhard and Alois Zuckerstätter. When he was young, his father walked out on him and his mother. Bernhard never forgave his father for this desertion, nor could he forgive his mother for constantly blaming him for her misfortunes. Hertha Bernhard had to move from one menial job to another, even after she remarried in 1936. The only stability in the young boy's life was provided by his maternal grandfather, a writer, who took over his early education by taking him on long walks and holding forth on his own favorite writers and philosophers, among them Arthur Schopenhauer and Friedrich Nietzsche, which surely contributed to Bernhard's own existential pessimism in his later years.

Formal education was a traumatic experience for the young boy, as he attended a school formerly run by the Nazi government that was taken over by the Catholic Church after World War II. Bernhard claimed the transition was so smooth that he did not notice any difference between the two authoritarian regimes. At the age of sixteen, he apprenticed himself to a grocer in a blighted area of Salzburg, Austria. Much of Bernhard's dramatic and narrative work exhibits his hatred and contempt for the Catholic Church and for Austria's denial of its unconquered Nazi past.

The young man's dreams of becoming a singer were brought to an abrupt halt when he was diagnosed with a serious lung disease that brought him to the brink of death and forced him to spend considerable time in hospitals and sanatoriums. Bernhard's novels abound with characters who are obsessed with real or imagined illnesses, and the imagery of disease informs his view of Austrian society and the human condition in general. Against all odds, Bernhard survived to complete his studies in music and performing arts in Vienna and Salzburg in 1956.

After publishing four little-noticed volumes of poetry, the appearance of his first novel, *Frost* (1963; English translation, 2006), catapulted Bernhard to literary fame. The work already shows most of Bernhard's main thematic and stylistic traits; however, instead of the interior monologue form of his later novels, *Frost* is an epistolary novel. His notion of a congenital disease that affects Austrian society and the image of the cold that gradually increases and deadens human relationships is reminiscent of the apocalyptic novels of Samuel Beckett. His subsequent novels, including *Verstörung* (1967; *Gargoyles*, 1970); *Das Kalkwerk* (1970; *The Lime Works*, 1973); his acknowledged masterpiece, *Korrektur* (1975; *Correction*, 1979); and *Auslöschung: Ein Zerfall* (1986; *Extinction*, 1995), repeat with minor variations the dominant themes first contained in *Frost*.

With his reputation as one of Austria's foremost novelists of the twentieth century firmly established, Bernhard began a second and concurrent career as a playwright in the 1970's, starting with *Ein Fest für Boris* (pr., pb. 1970; *A Party for Boris*, 1990) and ending with *Heldenplatz* (pr., pb. 1988), which created an artistic scandal and a political uproar in Austria.

The recipient of many literary prizes, Bernhard had a love-hate relationship with his country that led him to offend many leading Austrian politicians, fellow writers, artists, and interviewers. This ambivalent attitude was evident when Bernhard's will was made public after his clandestine burial in Vienna on February 16, 1989, four days after his death. The will stipulated that nothing he had written, including any papers or documents that might be found, could be published or performed within the borders of Austria while the legal copyrights were in force. The executors of his will, primarily his half siblings, controversially lifted this ban after ten years, resulting in the performance of some hitherto unperformed plays under the direction of his longtime collaborator and friend Claus Peymann.

ANALYSIS

Thomas Bernhard's syntactically difficult prose can be made accessible to the reader by reference to his life, particularly his early years, and thus by a careful reading of his collected memoirs, *Gathering Evidence* (1985), the English translation of five German-language autobiographies published from 1975 until 1982. His illegitimate birth, the fact that he never knew his biological father, his strained relationship with his mother, his apparently ambiguous relationship with his stepsister, and particularly the chronic lung ailments that brought him to the brink of early death and dogged him all his life—all these would serve to explain the bleak outlook on life of his narrators and protagonists. His early acquaintance with the works of Schopenhauer and Nietzsche, as well as his negative experiences with the Catholic religion and the Austrian bureaucracy, particularly the national health system and its iniquities, could offer an ample explanation for the curmudgeonly alter egos in his novels. Most of Bernhard's protagonists are obsessed hypochondriacs, trying to isolate themselves in pursuit of unobtainable ideals, and blaming women, politicians, the unsupportive cultural and intellectual climate

of their homeland, and other imaginary distractions for their inability to act.

Such a biographical approach can yield much insight into Bernhard and his work, but it will be only of superficial and limited usefulness. Bernhard's prose has its sources in a venerable literary tradition, which it simultaneously rejects and refines. In many ways, Bernhard's novels are literary illustrations of his personal debates with artists and philosophers, past and present. Besides Schopenhauer and Nietzsche, there are intertextual references to Martin Heidegger, Ludwig Wittgenstein, Fyodor Dostoevski, Samuel Beckett, and French existentialist philosophers, as well as to many German and Austrian authors that prove Bernhard to be much less the self-created genius he pretended to be.

While some of Bernhard's early novels use the more traditional form of the epistolary novel and the fictional diary, his mature works are modeled on the irascible and lonely monologists of Beckett's novels and the hypochondriac ranter of Dostoevski's *Zapiski iz podpolya* (1864; *Notes from the Underworld*, 1913; better known as *Notes from the Underground*). At the end of most of Bernhard's novels, the narrators, after an uninterrupted and often frantic monologue in which they try to explain and justify themselves, fall silent or listen to music, since language is not adequate for expressing their thoughts. This confirms and illustrates the linguistic philosophy of Wittgenstein and his famous dictum that whereof one cannot speak, thereof one must be silent.

Bernhard believes that music is the medium which can rise above the limitations of verbal communication. Several critics have pointed out that Bernhard's novels, in particular *Der Untergeher* (1983; *The Loser*, 1991), are not constructed according to traditional principles of novelistic plot structure but follow the formal parameters of contrapuntal musical compositions, principally that of the fugue. Johann Sebastian Bach's *Goldberg Variations* (1741) have been shown to serve as the formal basis for *The Loser*, Bernhard's novel about pianist Glenn Gould.

Considering this structural principle, it is no surprise that Bernhard's mature novels are all repetitions and variations of the same themes. An eccentric loner, a man of high social standing, education, and intellect but always afflicted by a real or imaginary disease, is engaged in a project that will produce a perfect masterpiece. This project can be literary, critical, architectural, or musical; in every instance, the protagonists-narrators find themselves incapable of completing the project because they are hindered by their environment, frequently by a sister they accuse of being intrusive and interfering. The main reason for their procrastination, however, appears to be their subconscious awareness that their project will not live up to their own lofty expectations of perfection, even if they did complete it, but completion is impossible since it cannot be complete unless it is perfect. This desperate paradox leads some of the protagonists to suicide; others, facing the same dilemma they observe and describe in their friends, finally come to the realization that such perfection is not possible, but that human existence is made meaningful by persevering in the attempt to attain perfection, even though it is inevitably doomed.

In addition to this fundamental existential anguish that pervades Bernhard's novels, there is the more obvious and sometimes shrill dissatisfaction with the cultural and political state of affairs in the author's native country, Austria. The author never missed an occasion—even when the Austrian government awarded him prestigious and lucrative prizes and stipends—to revile his countrymen for their unwillingness to face their fascist past, their political opportunism, their adherence to outmoded social and artistic models, and their disdain and lack of support for contemporary art that questions their petite bourgeois tastes. Bernhard's dyspeptic narrators become virtual mouthpieces for his criticism of Austria and its political and cultural institutions. In some cases, his characters' diatribes against leading politicians and fellow artists were so transparent that legal action was taken against him and attempts were made to prevent the performance of one of his plays.

Bernhard was quickly recognized as one of the leading prose writers of the twentieth century by fellow writers and critics; despite their complexity, his novels found a wide readership in Europe. Readers in England and the United States were somewhat more reluctant to accept him, but the increasing praise of his prose by British and American critics has increased the readership in these countries, and excellent translations of almost all his prose works are now readily available. His compatriot, Elfriede Jelinek, who won the Nobel Prize in Literature in 2004, compellingly argues that all future German and Austrian novelists will have to measure themselves against the high standards set by Thomas Bernhard.

CONCRETE

First published: *Beton*, 1982 (English translation, 1984)
Type of work: Novel

An ailing would-be musicologist once more fails to start his study of the composer Felix Mendelssohn and relives a troubling experience from his past on the island of Mallorca.

Like all of Thomas Bernhard's mature novels, *Concrete* is written as one long paragraph representing a continuous interior monologue. In this novel, the monologue is in the form of a manuscript perused by an anonymous narrator, possibly after the death of the manuscript's author, Rudolph. The unnamed narrator is noticeable only by brief editorial references, such as "writes Rudolph," or "so Rudolph," which appear mainly at the beginning and the very end of the novel.

At the outset, Rudolph, who fancies himself a musicologist, once again attempts to start his magnum opus, a study of the composer Felix Mendelssohn, as he has done several times for the past ten years without ever writing a line. Convinced that he has only a few more years to live because he suffers from sarcoidosis, a usually nonfatal lung disease, he is determined to start writing. He attributes his inability to begin to the constant interruptions of his sister, whom he depicts as an anti-intellectual but apparently very successful business woman. Further excuses for his procrastination are the adverse cultural conditions in Austria, his health, and the climate, but the reader senses that the very completion of his project would deprive him of any reason to continue living—the completion of his life's work would also be the end of his life.

After a long rant about these obstacles that takes up two-thirds of the novel, Rudolph decides to follow his sister's advice to go to Mallorca for a change of scenery. However, shortly after arriving there, he remembers a young German woman, Anna Härdtl, whom he had met by chance in the same place two years before. At that time, Anna told him that her husband had just fallen from their hotel balcony, either by accident or by committing suicide due to the failure of their business, for which he had no talent. Rudolph had helped Anna find her husband's grave, which turned out to be in a huge concrete bunker he shared with a woman who was a total stranger. The self-absorbed Rudolph had left Mallorca and the young woman behind and returned to Austria. Now, two years later, Rudolph is seized by curiosity and possibly feelings of guilt. He revisits the grave site and discovers that Anna is now buried in the same concrete grave bunker as her husband. He finds out that Anna has committed suicide, news that leaves him in a state of extreme anxiety at the end of the novel.

Concrete—the title is obviously taken from the concrete grave that becomes Anna Härdtl's final resting place—is Bernhard's most accessible novel. The protagonist, a self-absorbed intellectual wracked with doubt and self-loathing, incapable of decisive action, is the prototypical Bernhard "hero." His long monologue, written to explain and to justify himself, is full of contempt for practical people who are capable of acting, if only in a sphere the narrator finds vulgar, but at the same time he envies people like his sister and Anna who actively take charge of their lives, even when that means committing suicide. The reader is left to ponder whether Rudolph's most recent epiphany will lead him to also act decisively, but it is more likely that his extreme state of anxiety will lead only to further excuses and procrastination.

CORRECTION

First published: *Korrektur*, 1975 (English translation, 1979)
Type of work: Novel

An anonymous narrator sorts through the posthumous papers and manuscripts his friend Roithamer left after killing himself and tries to find an explanation for the suicide.

Most critics consider *Correction* to be Thomas Bernhard's masterpiece. On the surface, the novel is very similar to *Concrete* and *The Loser*; indeed, one could call the three novels a trilogy on the dangers of striving for perfection. Whereas the other two are long interior monologues presented as one single paragraph, *Correction* is divided into two sections with individual headings. The first section is entitled "Hoeller's Garret," while the second part is called "Sifting and Sorting" and is noticeably different from the first part in style and content.

In the first section, the narrator—an intellectual afflicted with a lung disease—moves into the garret of a friend's house (the name Hoeller strongly evokes the German word *Hölle*, meaning "hell") to take charge of the papers of his longtime friend Roithamer, who has recently committed suicide. A note found on his body requested the narrator to become the executor and editor of his papers, especially of three versions of an essay that tries to explain the reasons for Roithamer's failed utopian plan to construct a cone-shaped building in the middle of a forest, intended as the perfect abode for his beloved sister. In some unexplained way, however, the building led to the death of his sister shortly after he installed her there, and Roithamer then hanged himself in a nearby forest clearing.

The title of the novel is taken from the corrections Roithamer has made to the essay, with each correction an attempt at condensation and reduction in order to clarify his concept of the conical building. The essay was written in the same garret where the narrator reads it, and this location leads the narrator to recall a stream of memories of his and Roithhaimer's common past, during which the reader discovers that the two men's backgrounds are remarkably similar.

In the second section, which deals with the narrator's sifting and sorting through Roithamer's papers, the original narrative voice increasingly disappears and the section is an apparently random perusal of the large number of Roithamer's papers the narrator has spilled out in the garret. For the most part, the dead man is allowed to speak from his papers without any attempt at editing or interpreting, although it is clear from the last phrases quoted from the papers that Roithamer had realized that he had pursued an impossible goal: trying to achieve perfection. By this single-minded quest he has killed his sister and set himself up for disappointment and despair, leading him inexorably to the clearing where he hanged himself.

Critics have commented extensively on the similarities between Roithamer and the philosopher Ludwig Wittgenstein, including a strong attachment to their sisters, the construction of eccentric houses, suicidal tendencies, and a growing despair in the power of language to adequately express complex ideas. The narrator begins to see how much he and Roithamer are alike and grows increasingly fearful that an interpretive understanding of Roithamer's papers might push him to the same fate. Therefore, he allows Roithamer to speak for himself through his papers, which he scans without any editorial plan. This seemingly unscholarly lack of method is the narrator's salvation. He has grasped that the process of sifting and sorting itself is healthy and productive, and the futile attempt at perfect understanding and expression is impossible, even with an infinite number of "corrections," and inevitably leads to "the clearing."

THE LOSER

First published: *Der Untergeher,* 1983
   (English translation, 1991)
Type of work: Novel

A concert pianist turned philosopher and writer has come to sift through the papers of his friend Wertheimer, who has recently committed suicide, and he reflects on the impact their former friend, piano virtuoso Glenn Gould, has had on their lives.

Written almost twenty years after *Correction, The Loser* strikingly resembles the earlier novel in both form and content. Whereas *Correction* deals with a character representing the philosopher Ludwig Wittgenstein and his pessimistic language philosophy, *The Loser* focuses on a highly mythologized Glenn Gould—some of his biographical data are intentionally wrong—and his quest for the perfect piano performance of Johann Sebastian Bach's *Goldberg Variations.*

Like most of Bernhard's novels, *The Loser* is a one-paragraph interior monologue. In this novel's monologue, the narrator is moved to reflect back thirty years, when he, Wertheimer, and Gould were

studying to become concert pianists in Salzburg. As in Bernhard's previous novels, all three main characters are afflicted by a lung disease and prone to self-absorption and self-doubt. Wertheimer has recently killed himself, and the narrator, who has been making little progress on his presumed magnum opus, a study entitled *About Glenn Gould,* has come to take charge of Wertheimer's papers, which would presumably shed light on the reasons for his suicide. Almost the entire stream-of-consciousness monologue is delivered during the brief time the narrator waits in a country inn near Wertheimer's house for the innkeeper to show him to his room.

The narrator conjectures that Wertheimer's suicide is tied in some way to the recent death of Gould. Both the narrator and Wertheimer had given up piano playing when they were confronted with the fact that they would always be second-rate compared to Gould. However, Wertheimer sought to become and to be Gould, thus "losing" his own identity. The German title of the novel cleverly hints at this misguided ideal; an *Untergeher* is a person who sinks or submerges himself, and the word also connotes "decline." Wertheimer's "loss" is that he cannot stand being himself but tries in vain to lose or submerge himself in Gould, who very perceptively gave him his nickname, The Loser, thirty years ago.

Wertheimer has not been able to overcome his disappointment for thirty years, in contrast to the narrator, who has turned his energies away from trying to become Gould and now merely tries to describe Gould's genius, an almost equally impossible task which nevertheless keeps him from despairing like Wertheimer.

In *The Loser,* Bernhard's diseased intellectual protagonist has been split into three variations of the same type. There is Gould, who realizes the impossibility of the perfect concert piano performance and turns to the recording studio and its technological possibilities to achieve the impossible; the narrator, who realizes his limitations early and turns his energies to the equally impossible quest of describing Gould's genius; and Wertheimer, who destroys himself by stubbornly refusing to live within his limitations, and in his attempt to achieve his ideal of becoming someone else, loses, or annihilates, himself. It is inevitable, therefore, that the narrator discovers that Wertheimer has burned all his papers after one last grotesque attempt at becoming Gould before killing himself. The narrator is left speechless, listening to Gould's famous recording of the *Goldberg Variations.*

SUMMARY

Thomas Bernhard is one of the most original postmodernist writers in the German language. His novels, written in the form of long monologues, portray disaffected and alienated intellectuals trying to come to terms with their increasing isolation in anti-intellectual, materialistic societies. While their harangues appear to be mostly directed against their social, political, and cultural environments, they frequently reveal their disappointment and frustration about their inability to achieve unrealistically high goals and the failure to find a common ground with their surroundings.

Bernhard, himself an iconoclastic loner, appeared to project much of himself into his narrator-protagonists, but it is also clear that he was not trying to make them antiestablishment heroes. His own fraught relationship with Austria was as schizophrenic as that of his protagonists: he loathed his native country for its past, its small-mindedness, and its conservatism, but he loved it enough to continue living there and to point out its flaws, realizing he could not expect any gratitude in return.

Franz G. Blaha

BIBLIOGRAPHY

By the Author

LONG FICTION:
Frost, 1963 (English translation, 2006)
Verstörung, 1967 (*Gargoyles*, 1970)
Das Kalkwerk, 1970 (*The Lime Works*, 1973)
Korrektur, 1975 (*Correction*, 1979)
Ja, 1978 (*Yes*, 1991)
Die Billigesser, 1980 (*The Cheap-Eaters*, 1990)
Beton, 1982 (*Concrete*, 1984)
Der Untergeher, 1983 (*The Loser*, 1991)
Holzfällen: Eine Erregung, 1984 (*Woodcutters*, 1987; also as *Cutting Timber: An Imitation*, 1988)
Alte Meister, 1985 (*Old Masters*, 1989)
Auslöschung: Ein Zerfall, 1986 (*Extinction*, 1995)
In der Höhe: Rettungsversuch, Unsinn, 1989 (*On the Mountain: Rescue Attempt, Nonsense*, 1991)

SHORT FICTION:
Amras, 1964 (English translation, 2003)
Prosa, 1967
Ungenach, 1968
An der Baumgrenze: Erzählungen, 1969
Ereignisse, 1969
Watten: Ein Nachlass, 1969 (*Playing Watten*, 2003)
Gehen, 1971 (*Walking*, 2003)
Midland in Stilfs: Drei Erzählungen, 1971
Der Stimmenimitator, 1978 (*The Voice Imitator*, 1997)
Three Novellas, 2003 (includes *Amras*, *Playing Watten*, and *Walking*)

POETRY:

Auf der Erde und in der Hölle, 1957

In hora mortis, 1957 (English translation, 2006)

Unter dem Eisen des Mondes, 1958

Die Irren-die Häftlinge, 1962

Contemporary German Poetry, 1964 (includes selections of his poetry in English translation)

DRAMA:

Der Rosen der Einöde, pb. 1959 (libretto)

Ein Fest für Boris, pr., pb. 1970 (*A Party for Boris*, 1990)

Der Ignorant und der Wahnsinnige, pr., pb. 1972

Die Jagdgesellschaft, pr., pb. 1974

Die Macht der Gewohnheit, pr., pb. 1974 (*The Force of Habit*, 1976)

Der Präsident, pr., pb. 1975 (*The President*, 1982)

Die Berühmten, pr., pb. 1976

Minetti: Ein Porträt des Künstlers als alter Mann, pr. 1976, pb. 1977

Immanuel Kant, pr., pb. 1978

Der Weltverbesserer, pb. 1979, pr. 1980 (*The World-Fixer*, 2005)

Vor dem Ruhestand, pb. 1979, pr. 1980 (*Eve of Retirement*, 1982)

Über allen Gipfeln ist Ruh: Ein deutscher Dichtertag um 1980, pb. 1981 (*Over All the Mountain Tops*, 2004)

Am Ziel, pr., pb. 1981

Der Schein trügt, pb. 1983, pr. 1984 (*Appearances Are Deceiving*, 1983)

Der Theatermacher, pb. 1984, pr. 1986 (*Histrionics*, 1990)

Ritter, Dene, Voss, pb. 1984, pr. 1986 (English translation, 1990)

Elisabeth II, pb. 1987, pr. 1989

Heldenplatz, pr., pb. 1988

Histrionics: Three Plays, pb. 1990

SCREENPLAY:

Der Italiener, 1971

NONFICTION:

Die Ursache: Eine Andeutung, 1975 (*An Indication of the Cause*, 1985)

Der Keller: Eine Entziehung, 1976 (*The Cellar: An Escape*, 1985)

Der Atem: Eine Entscheidung, 1978 (*Breath: A Decision*, 1985)

Die Kälte: Eine Isolation, 1981 (*In the Cold*, 1985)

Ein Kind, 1982 (*A Child*, 1985)

Wittgensteins Neffe: Eine Freundschaft, 1982 (*Wittgenstein's Nephew: A Friendship*, 1986)

Gathering Evidence, 1985 (English translation of the five autobiographical works *An Indication of the Cause, The Cellar: An Escape, Breath: A Decision, In the Cold*, and *A Child*)

DISCUSSION TOPICS

• Almost all of Thomas Bernhard's protagonists are afflicted by one disease or another. Is this merely a reflection of Bernhard's own lifelong bouts with illness, or does disease function as a metaphor in his novels?

• Most of Bernhard's novels are one-paragraph interior monologues by often eccentric characters. How reliable are these narrators? Can we take everything they say as fact?

• Bernhard has been called a "misogynist," or a hater of women. Is there evidence for that in his novels? Is there another possible explanation for the absence of female narrators in his novels?

• Most Americans associate Austria with images from the Hollywood film *The Sound of Music* (1965). Contrast and compare these images to Bernhard's portrait of Austria.

• In his novels, Bernhard frequently presents famous artists and thinkers, among them Glenn Gould and Ludwig Wittgenstein, but he falsifies easily verifiable biographical facts about them. Assuming that this is intentional, what might be his purpose?

• Some critics have discovered signs of comedy in Bernhard's novels. Can you find incidents or passages that would support this claim?

About the Author

Chambers, Helen. "Thomas Bernhard." In *After the Death of Literature*. Edited by Keith Bullivant. Oxford, England: Berg, 1989.

Dowden, Stephen D. "Thomas Bernhard." In *Dictionary of Literary Biography*. Vol. 85. Detroit: Gale Research, 1989.

_____. *Understanding Thomas Bernhard*. Columbia: University of South Carolina Press, 1991.

Honegger, Gitta. *Thomas Bernhard: The Making of an Austrian*. New Haven, Conn.: Yale University Press, 2001.

Long, Jonathan James. *The Novels of Thomas Bernhard: Form and Its Function*. Rochester, N.Y.: Camden House, 2001.

Modern Austria Literature 21 (1988). Issue devoted to Thomas Bernhard.

Olson, Michael P. "Misogynist Exposed? The Sister's Role in Thomas Bernhard's *Beton* and *Der Untergeher*." *New German Review* 3 (1987): 30-40.

John Betjeman

Born: London, England
     August 28, 1906
Died: Trebetherick, Cornwall, England
     May 19, 1984

Dedicated to making poetry accessible to, and understood by, the general reading public, Betjeman, with his indelible portraits of English towns, villages, and people, is a significant, modern literary voice.

Biography

Born in London, England, on August 28, 1906, John Betjeman (BEHCH-uh-muhn) was the only child of Mabel Bessie Dawson and Ernest Betjeman, a prominent businessman of Dutch ancestry and supplier of fine furnishings for exclusive shops. Betjeman's early years, especially those of his childhood, are recounted in his verse autobiography, *Summoned by Bells* (1960). Growing up in the North London Edwardian suburbs, Betjeman became painfully aware of class differences, the seemingly small but inexorable distinctions of income and status. He developed, even at an early age, a profound sensitivity to subtle forms of snobbery. Betjeman's family relations were somewhat strained, even perverse. His father, from whom the author later became estranged, figured into his poetry as a formidable reminder of his son's inadequacies, not only because the younger Betjeman did not enjoy hunting and fishing, as his father did, but also because he refused to continue in the family business. Betjeman's guilt for disappointing his parent was obsessive, extending to his imagining that he also had disappointed his father's employees.

Feeling the magnetic draw of poetry, Betjeman recognized even as an adolescent that his future lay in verse: "I knew as soon as I could read and write/ That I must be a poet" (*Summoned by Bells*). The young poet attended preparatory school at Highgate, London; his teacher there, T. S. Eliot, was a profound force in modern poetry. To Eliot, the young Betjeman would bind and submit his first poetic attempts in a volume titled "The Best of Betjeman." Eliot never commented, however, upon the schoolboy's verses. At Marlborough public school, which Betjeman entered in 1920, bullies teased and terrorized the youngster. One of Betjeman's classmates mocked his poem about a city church, thus humiliating the already sensitive and lonely adolescent. This experience traumatized the fifteen-year-old and contributed to his antipathy toward abusive criticism.

In 1925, Betjeman entered Magdalen College, Oxford, with plans of earning a degree in English, but, to his father's disappointment and to his own dismay, his irresolute lifestyle prohibited him from attaining academic success: "For, while we ate Virginia hams,/ Contemporaries passed exams" (*Summoned by Bells*). However, most of Betjeman's memories of Oxford were pleasant. There, he developed many friendships, most notably with Evelyn Waugh, who later became one of England's most prodigious novelists. Betjeman's talents did not go unnoticed at Oxford. C. W. Bowra, a renowned scholar, applauded Betjeman's verse, as well as his knowledge of architecture. Despite Bowra's admiration and affection, Betjeman was not showered with accolades at Oxford. Having neglected his studies, Betjeman won the distaste of his tutor, C. S. Lewis, a distinguished critic and author whom the poet later satirized in some of his poems. Failing repeated attempts to pass a simple qualifying exam, Betjeman was forced at last to leave Oxford. Stunned and saddened by his failure, the poet left college disillusioned, having fallen short of his dream of becoming a university don: "Reading old poets in the library,/ Attending chapel in an M.A. gown/ And sipping vintage port by candlelight" (*Summoned by Bells*). Despite his aversion to sports, Betjeman obtained, and held for a short time, a teaching post at Heddon Court School, in Barnet, Hertfordshire, a post secured, ironically, under the auspices of his mastery of cricket.

The 1930's saw Betjeman's popularity increase as he gained visibility and recognition. In 1931, the poet published his first book of poetry, *Mount Zion: Or, In Touch with the Infinite*, whose poems contained many of his major themes and revealed his interest in topography. That same year, Betjeman became assistant editor of the *Architectural Review*, a position that granted him exposure to many of England's prominent architects and architectural historians of the day. Betjeman left his position in 1933 and began editing a series of topographical guides to Britain. To her mother's chagrin, Penelope Chetwode, daughter of Field Marshal Sir Philip Chetwode, the commander in chief of India, accepted Betjeman's proposal of marriage in 1933. The couple had two children, Paul and Candida. In a few short years, Betjeman's second volume of verse, *Continual Dew: A Little Book of Bourgeois Verse* (1937), with its light and whimsical tone, appeared and immediately enjoyed success. Betjeman, however, wanted to be regarded as a serious poet, not merely a popular one, though the ambiguity of some of his best images and the complexity of his tone lay buried beneath his copious iambics. Nonetheless, the public flocked to buy his unpretentious verse. Not since Lord Byron and Alfred, Lord Tennyson had a poet been so embraced by the masses.

When World War II broke out, Betjeman's penchant for writing found various forms of expression. He served as a press attaché in Dublin for the United Kingdom Press, he functioned as a broadcaster for the British Broadcasting Corporation (BBC) in 1943, and he worked in the books department of the British Council from 1944 to 1946. These years saw the publication of *Old Lights for New Chancels: Verses Topographical and Amatory* (1940), as well as a new collection of poems, *New Bats in Old Belfries* (1945). Partly because of his enormous success as a writer of books on topology and architecture, such as *Ghastly Good Taste: Or, A Depressing Story of the Rise and Fall of English Architecture* (1933), *An Oxford University Chest* (1938), *Antiquarian Prejudice* (1939), and *English Cities and Small Towns* (1943), Betjeman's widespread reputation as a poet seemed almost overshadowed by his prose. Indeed, he had become a spokesperson for the preservation of

English architecture, especially Victorian architecture. When the war ended, Betjeman resumed his journalistic career, extending it to the increasingly popular medium of television, at which he won further notoriety.

The poetry of Betjeman's last forty years, though more overtly pessimistic than his previous work, reiterates many of the author's earlier themes, as exemplified in his volume *A Few Late Chrysanthemums* (1954). His continued acclaim, however, as a poet, broadcaster, and critic of modernity gained him widespread recognition, precipitating his being knighted in 1969 and appointed poet laureate in 1972, a position that he held until his death on May 19, 1984, in Cornwall, England.

ANALYSIS

In contrast to the erudite and often enigmatic verse of many of his contemporaries, Betjeman's poetry seems simple and natural. It lacks the features of fragmentation and austere intellectualism that typify much modern poetry, although Betjeman does recurrently embrace the common twentieth century themes of alienation and guilt. Eschewing obscurity, Betjeman embraces a conversational style, replete with narrative elements, and utilizes traditional meter and rhyme, though occasionally he employs metrical variations or substitutions. He borrows his forms especially from his nineteenth century predecessors. Because his verse is so natural, in fact, most critics fail to notice his penchant for ambiguity, evident in some of his better poems, such as "The Arrest of Oscar Wilde at the Cadogan Hotel," in *Mount Zion*, or "On a Portrait of a Deaf Man," in *Old Lights for New Chancels*. Betjeman's major themes underscore the defects of modernity, with its disregard for the aesthetic and its disrespect for the environment. They also highlight the author's spiritual doubt, his obsession with class, with guilt, and with death, as well as divulge his affinity for topography.

The verses of *Mount Zion* demonstrate the young author's interest in topography, especially English suburbia, with such memorable sketches as "Croydon" and Oakleigh Park of "The Outer Suburbs," with its "blackened blocks" and stained-glass windows. Betjeman's verse fuses reds and greens, oranges and blacks on his canvas of neighborhood sidewalks, churches, railways, and trams. *Mount*

Zion also reveals Betjeman's genius for mild satire and for humor, perhaps most noticeable in "The 'Varsity Students' Rag."

Though Betjeman figures as a significant modern poetic force, his exceptional prose writings are also a hallmark of his enormous productivity: works on England's cities and towns, churches and architecture, even a book on his friend, abstract painter John Piper. These prose works, like Betjeman's poetry, are marked by their readability and friendly, intimate tone.

Most of what is known of Betjeman's childhood, through his stay at Oxford until the beginning of his first teaching position, is captured in his blank-verse autobiography, *Summoned by Bells*. This work, written toward the middle of Betjeman's career, not only demonstrates the poet's proclivity for detail but also reiterates many of his earlier themes and preoccupations. Sharing some similarities with the confessional poets of the mid-twentieth century, Betjeman's verse in this volume is surprisingly candid, revealing the poet's fears and embarrassments, his defeats, as well as his victories.

Many of Betjeman's later volumes of verse, notably *A Few Late Chrysanthemums*, *High and Low* (1966), and *A Nip in the Air* (1974), deal, in part, with the present impinging upon the past and the results of that friction. Edwardian drawing rooms are replaced by abstruse monstrosities. Thus, Betjeman often establishes a series of antitheses, not only of artificial cities, belted in concrete, but also of artificial people, who, in the name of progress, awkwardly tread on the beautiful and the sacred, in flagrant abandon. The poet frequently illustrates this abrasive combination humorously, as in "Inexpensive Progress," from *High and Low*:

> Encase your legs in nylons,
> Bestride your hills with pylons
>   O age without a soul;
> Away with gentle willows
> And all the elmy billows
>   That through your valleys roll.

Betjeman likens the industrialized present's encroachment upon the landscape of the past to the human body, stripped of the gentle curves that signal its beauty, inevitably resulting in barrenness and ugliness. In the above passage, Betjeman shows his keen faculty even for spacing of the lines:

The indentations of the third and sixth lines imitate the once-rolling hills and gentle breezes that soon will vanish. Emphasizing the passing of a lifestyle that is continuously eroding, the poet's images of modern impatience and disregard are typically characteristic of his verse, perhaps best epitomized in the picture of the "Executive," from *A Nip in the Air*: "I've a scarlet Aston-Martin—and does she go? She flies!/ Pedestrians and dogs and cats—we mark them down for slaughter./ I also own a speed-boat which has never touched the water." In this light social satire, the poet plays with the ambiguous image of the speedboat, whose acceleration seemingly allows it to defy gravity. Simultaneously, the image speaks of the artificiality of an age whose leaders relish acquiring material goods for the sake of appearance, rather than for their intrinsic value or usefulness; the boat, after all, "has never touched the water."

Though the verdict on Betjeman's importance as a poet is still yet to be determined—he has spawned no imitators—his artistry has been appreciated by a generation of readers and poets alike. Poets such as England's Philip Larkin have lauded his verse, whereas his critics have complained of its sentimentality. Perhaps his greatest tribute has been the English poet W. H. Auden's dedication to him in *The Age of Anxiety* (1947), a verse dialogue reflecting man's isolation.

"ON A PORTRAIT OF A DEAF MAN"

First published: 1940 (collected in *Old Lights for New Chancels: Verses Topographical and Amatory,* 1940)
Type of work: Poem

The poem wryly contrasts the reality of death's putrefaction with a dead man's lifelong exuberance.

"On a Portrait of a Deaf Man," written in ballad stanza form (four-line stanzas of alternating iambic tetrameter and iambic trimeter, rhyming *abcb*) and published in *Old Lights for New Chancels: Verses Topographical and Amatory* (1940), exemplifies Betjeman at his best. Approaching the theme of death through images of the five senses, the persona juxtaposes the dead man's past vitality and productivity with his present idleness and deterioration, "his finger-bones/ Stick[ing] through his finger-ends." The poet blithely blends understatement, ambiguity, and paradox, revealing death, the eternal silencer, as the ultimate sign of "deafness":

> And when he could not hear me speak
> He smiled and looked so wise
> That now I do not like to think
> Of maggots in his eyes.

The comic, yet tragic, portrait of the man may be that of Betjeman's own father, whom he once described as "deaf" in *Summoned by Bells.*

Pointing out the dead man's peculiarities, including his fondness for "potatoes in their skin," "old City dining-rooms," the smell of the Cornish air after a rain, and even his penchant for knowing "the name of ev'ry bird," the poet wryly juxtaposes images of life's activity with death's passivity. The allusion to the man's preference for potatoes is more complex than might initially appear. Betjeman's father reportedly got angry if his potatoes were not cooked until tender. Ironically, now the man has become, metaphorically, a sort of "potato" in his "skin," the mush of his decaying body only loosely encompassed by his exterior layer of skin: "But now his mouth is wide to let/ The London clay come in." Betjeman's

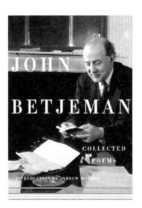

fusion of the macabre with the comic seems a bit perverse, yet frightfully funny, nonetheless. The image of humanity in this vegetative state bears some kinship to Andrew Marvell's lady in "To His Coy Mistress" (1681), whose virginity ultimately will be violated by worms in the grave.

Betjeman wants his reader to appreciate the incongruity of humanity's seeming importance with its final insignificance. Though the tone of the poem, on the surface, appears light and humorous, it is not without seriousness. The reader comes to realize, paradoxically, that the dead man, who appeared so vivid and alive, was "deaf" even in life, having failed to "hear" the voice of the persona and the "song" of the bird.

SUMMONED BY BELLS

First published: 1960
Type of work: Poem

In this autobiographical verse, spanning Betjeman's youth up to and including his leaving Oxford and securing a teaching position, the poet recollects his experiences.

Summoned by Bells, a blank verse autobiography, recollects Betjeman's childhood, marred by the abusive treatment of a nursery maid, Maud, who instilled in him the dread of damnation, more terrifying than any fiery rhetoric from any preacher's pulpit. It was she who preached to him about hell, rubbed his face in his own messes, and punished him for his tardiness: "'You're late for dinner, John.' I feel again/ That awful feeling, fear confused with thrill,/ As I would be unbuttoned, bent across/ Her starchy apron." Surprisingly, Betjeman's choice of meter, unrhymed iambic pentameter, heightens, rather than diminishes, the tension of the scene. The regular iambic rhythm with which the nurse delivers her matter-of-fact remark exposes her inflexibility. Maud's influence on Betjeman's themes of guilt and fear of death should not be overlooked.

Though the abusive relationship with Betjeman's nurse is easily discernible, more complex is the mental torment that the author suffered as a result of his relationship with his father. The poet admits that he could never please his "dear deaf father," especially after refusing his request to continue the family business: "Partly it is guilt:/ 'Following in Father's footsteps' was the theme/ Of all my early childhood." With each glance, Betjeman's father's eyes accused his son of failure. Even to his dying day, the elder Betjeman had a gaze that seemed to assail the poet, smarting like stinging nettles. Not surprisingly, Betjeman recounts his childhood years as being lonely. His remembrances include lost loves, childhood betrayal, insensitive remarks of a teacher who called him "common," and childhood bullies at his various schools. Trapped and beaten by two "enemies" at Highgate Junior School, then hurled into the bushes, the adolescent Betjeman emerged from the attack humiliated.

> There in the holly bush they threw me down,
> Pulled off my shorts, and laughed and ran away;
> And, as I struggled up, I saw grey brick,
> The cemetery railings and the tombs.

The reader need not be a psychologist to understand from this episode Betjeman's interconnected associations of fear, pain, and death; yet the poet's stance in relaying this experience appears neutral, that of an unbiased observer.

It would be incorrect to assume that *Summoned by Bells* contains merely embarrassing or tragic accounts of Betjeman's early life. For the most part, the book is a kaleidoscope of colorful topographical portraits of English landscapes and seasides, of city and country dwellings, and of the English people. Nor does Betjeman's volume lack good nature or compassion. When, as a child, the author fabricated an excuse to avoid fighting a fellow schoolboy, pleading that he had "news from home" that his "Mater was ill," his would-be combatant, Percival Mandeville, gingerly clasped him on the shoulder comfortingly and said, "All right, old chap. Of course I understand." This touching account, revealing the ease and spontaneity with which young boys may reverse their adversarial positions and exhibit signs of friendship, is one of the most memorable portraits of *Summoned by Bells*. The book is not without humor, either. In describing his mother's complaints about her tooth pain, Betjeman presents Mrs. Betjeman comically, as she charges that her infection is "just the same" as Mrs. Bent's, who "nearly died" of the disease, though the other lady's infection was "not, of course, so bad" as Betjeman's mother's own ailment.

SUMMARY

Ironically, John Betjeman's local color, his greatest strength, is the aspect of his poetry most often criticized: His lyrics are decidedly English, not universal. Whether he explores the mystery of faith, satirizes the imperfections of himself, his family, or the middle classes, or whether he nostalgically describes the countryside of Cornwall or a bath at Marlborough, Betjeman exhibits his wry compassion and demonstrates his facility for strict observation. Betjeman, the deliberate traditionalist, presents a discerning, not myopic, view of the world, his world, England. Indeed, his triumph lies in his partisanship.

Linda Rohrer Paige

BIBLIOGRAPHY

By the Author

POETRY:
Mount Zion: Or, In Touch with the Infinite, 1931
Continual Dew: A Little Book of Bourgeois Verse, 1937
Old Lights for New Chancels: Verses Topographical and Amatory, 1940
New Bats in Old Belfries, 1945
Slick but Not Streamlined, 1947 (W. H. Auden, editor)
Selected Poems, 1948 (John Sparrow, editor)
A Few Late Chrysanthemums, 1954
Poems in the Porch, 1954
Collected Poems, 1958 (third edition as *John Betjeman's Collected Poems*, 1970)
Summoned by Bells, 1960
High and Low, 1966
A Nip in the Air, 1974
Ten Late Chrysanthemums, 1975
Uncollected Poems, 1982

NONFICTION:

Ghastly Good Taste: Or, A Depressing Story of the Rise and Fall of English Architecture, 1933

An Oxford University Chest, 1938

Antiquarian Prejudice, 1939

Vintage London, 1942

English Cities and Small Towns, 1943

John Piper, 1944

First and Last Loves, 1952

The English Town in the Last Hundred Years, 1956

Collins' Guide to English Parish Churches, 1958

English Churches, 1964 (with B. F. L. Clarke)

Betjeman's Cornwall, 1984

John Betjeman: Letters, 1994-1995 (2 volumes)

John Betjeman: Coming Home, 1997

EDITED TEXTS:

English, Scottish and Welsh Landscape, 1944 (with Geoffrey Taylor)

English Love Poems, 1957 (with Taylor)

Altar and Pew: Church of England Verses, 1959

A Wealth of Poetry, 1963 (with Winifred Hudley)

DISCUSSION TOPICS

- List several obstacles to his career that John Betjeman overcame.

- What is meant by the term "copious iambics" as a means of describing Betjeman's poetry? Why might this form of poetry tend to curtail the effect of his verse?

- Explain the value of topography to a poet like Betjeman.

- By what means does Betjeman generate interest in his subject in "On a Portrait of a Deaf Man"?

- Comment on the suggestiveness of the title of the autobiographical poem *Summoned by Bells*.

- What is the theme of *Summoned by Bells*?

About the Author

Brooke, Jocelyn. *Ronald Firbank and John Betjeman*. New York: Longmans, Green, 1962.

Gibson, Walker. "Summoned by Bells." *Poetry* 97 (1961): 390-391.

Hillier, Bevis. *Betjeman: The Bonus of Laughter*. London: Murray, 2004.

_____. *John Betjeman: New Fame, New Love*. London: Murray, 2003.

_____. *Young Betjeman*. London: Murray, 1988.

Stapleton, Margaret L. *Sir John Betjeman: A Bibliography of Writings by and About Him*. Metuchen, N.J.: Scarecrow Press, 1974.

Wilson, A. N. *Betjeman: A Life*. New York: Farrar, Straus and Giroux, 2006.

MARIE-CLAIRE BLAIS

Born: Quebec City, Quebec, Canada
October 5, 1939

Only nineteen when she published the first of more than twenty novels, Blais is one of the most prolific and important French Canadian authors.

Courtesy, Overlook Press

BIOGRAPHY

Marie-Claire Blais (blay) was born on October 5, 1939, in Quebec City, Quebec, Canada, the first of five children of Fernando and Veronique Notin Blais. She began writing at the age of ten, an obsession that was discouraged both at home and at school. As the oldest child in a large working-class family, she was burdened by the need to help her family financially. She began her secondary education at a Catholic convent school but left at the age of fifteen, at her parents' request, to attend a secretarial school. From the age of fifteen to age eighteen, Blais worked as a stenographer for many different employers. Writing, though, was her passion and solace, and she continued to work in the evenings at her parents' home, which was always crowded and noisy. At nineteen, Blais moved to a rented room in Quebec City. She studied French literature at the Université Laval, reading Honoré de Balzac, Marcel Proust, Jean Genet, and the Surrealists and Symbolists, such as Arthur Rimbaud. She also made the acquaintance of Jeanne Lapointe and Père Georges-Henri Lévesque, both of whom would be instrumental to the success of her literary career.

Lévesque was impressed with Blais's early stories and urged her to continue writing. Blais completed *La Belle bête* (1959; *Mad Shadows*, 1960), and through Lévesque's influence and belief in her

promise as a writer, Blais's controversial novel was published in Canada. Because she was so young at the time of her first success, Blais was considered something of a precocious schoolgirl. *Mad Shadows* elicited both admiration and outrage in Quebec. A nightmarish fable, the violent emotions of envy and hatred and the consequences of the failure of maternal love are vividly dark and poetic. *Tête blanche* (1960; English translation, 1961) is another story embracing the theme of a childhood of isolation and despair, told in rich, poetic language.

Blais received a fellowship from the Conseil des Arts du Canada in 1960 and spent the following year in Paris, where she continued her education through literature and film. In 1962, she returned to Quebec and completed *Le Jour est noir* (1962; English translation published in *The Day Is Dark and Three Travelers: Two Novellas*, 1967). In 1963, with the support of the highly respected American critic Edmund Wilson, she was awarded the first of two Guggenheim Fellowships, which allowed her to move to Cambridge, Massachusetts, where she lived and wrote for several years. While in Massachusetts, Blais wrote *Les Voyageurs sacrés* (1966; English translation published in *The Day Is Dark and Three Travelers: Two Novellas*), an attempt to combine music, poetry, and sculpture. *L'Insoumise* (1966; *The Fugitive*, 1978) chronicles the disintegration of a family; *David Sterne* (1967; English translation, 1973), influenced by her feelings about the Vietnam War, is a cry against violence. Neglected by critics, these novels reflect the troubled decade of the 1960's, a time when Blais's vision moved from the tormented inner world to the outside political and social realm.

In Cambridge, Blais met the painter Mary Meigs.

A deep friendship developed, and Blais moved to Wellfleet, Massachusetts, to form a community with Meigs, who was living with her companion Barbara Deming. Meigs's lifestyle and work were to have a profound effect on Blais; at the refuge in Wellfleet, she produced *Une Saison dans la vie d'Emmanuel* (1965; *A Season in the Life of Emmanuel*, 1966). Translated into thirteen languages, it established her international reputation and was considered her most original and important work. It is a bleak, often humorous story about the lives of damaged children in church-dominated, impoverished, rural Quebec, and in 1966 Blais was awarded both the Canadian Prix-France Quebec and the French Prix Médicis for *A Season in the Life of Emmanuel*.

She received critical acclaim again in 1969, when she won her first Governor-General's Literary Award and *Livres et Auteurs Canadiens* magazine's Best Book Award for *Manuscrits de Pauline Archange* (1968; *The Manuscripts of Pauline Archange*, 1970). During the same year, she published her play *L'Exécution* (pb. 1968; *The Execution*, 1976).

Deeply troubled by the Vietnam War, Blais and Meigs moved to France in 1971, where they lived for four years. Dividing her time between Montreal and Paris, Blais explored homosexual love as a literary theme. In *Le Loup* (1972; *The Wolf*, 1974), she explores love and cruelty in her young male characters' homosexual relationships. She returned to the theme of homosexual love with *Les Nuits de l'underground* (1978; *Nights in the Underground*, 1979), in which she explores the sacred, self-liberating aspects of lesbian love.

During the 1970's, Blais's themes shift focus again, from the inner world of emotions and the suffering of individuals to the conflicts of national identity, long a struggle in provincial Quebec. While in France, she wrote *Un Joualonais, sa joualonie* (1973; *St. Lawrence Blues*, 1974); it is written in *joual*, Montreal's French street slang. She continued to explore these political themes in *Une Liaison parisienne* (1975; *A Literary Affair*, 1979). *Le Sourd dans la ville* (1979; *Deaf to the City*, 1980) earned Blais a second Governor-General's Literary Award. Part poetry, part prose, it is another study of anguish and of art as a means of salvation. Continuing to move her vision outward and to combine poetry and prose, Blais produced *Visions d'Anna: Ou, Le vertige* (1982; *Anna's World*, 1985). Another dark vision of the modern world, *Pierre, la guerre du printemps quatre-vingt-un*, appeared in 1984 (*Pierre*, 1993). Blais's work centers on the complexity and inherent pain of human life as she searches for a vision of the ideal, exposing the harshness of the reality that she has lived and observed. Blais was awarded the Prix David in 1982 in recognition of the major contribution she has made to the literature of Quebec.

In 1989, Blais published *L'Ange de la solitude* (*Angel of Solitude*, 1993), in which she portrayed lesbian love. Then in 1995, she published *Soifs* (*These Festive Nights*, 1997), for which she received another Governor-General's Award. This novel was the first work in her trilogy, which also includes *Dans le foudre et la lumière* (2001; *Thunder and Light*, 2001) and *Augustino et le chœur de la destruction* (2005; *Augustino and the Choir of Destruction*, 2007).

Blais was chosen Cambridge International Woman of the Year (1995-1996) for her contributions to literature and creative writing. In 1997, she was the recipient of the American Biographical Institute Decree of International Letters for Cultural Achievement. In 1999, she received the Prix d'Italie, in 2000 the W. O. Mitchell Literary Prize, and in 2002 the Prix Prince Pierre de Monaco. In addition to her fictional works, she has published *Parcours d'un écrivain: Notes américaines* (1993; *American Notebooks: A Writer's Journey*, 1996) and her autobiography *Des Rencontres humaines* (2002). Blais continues to be recognized as one of Canada's most significant and talented writers and as a writer of international importance.

ANALYSIS

The power of Blais's early fiction lies in her thematic obsession with the forces of evil and the suffering of children. Blais treats her characters with tenderness in their solitude, and they find, as she did in her own life, that art is the only escape from madness and death. Her writing has been characterized as bold and inventive, but her vision is profoundly bleak. Her work is in the tradition of the existentialists, who explore the consequences of psychological abandonment and abuse of the young as the crucible in which evil is created.

Her characters' capacity for evil and cruelty, and particularly the pathological relationships between mothers and children, shocked critics in the late 1950's. Although it was less of a sensation elsewhere, *Mad Shadows*, Blais's first book, created a furor of both admiration and outrage in Quebec because of its macabre and violent story. The theme of both *The Day Is Dark* and a novella, *La Fin d'une enfance* (1961), is the suffering and powerlessness of children trapped in emotional and spiritual isolation, even when surrounded by family and dominated by the cult of religious authority. The overbearing influence of religion, always negative and suffocating, is perceptible in the lives of all Blais's characters; the awakenings of adolescent sexuality, sensuality, and curiosity are the beginnings of an irrevocable "fall from grace." Poor families, however devout, are overburdened with many children and live in depravity, lovelessness, and intellectual and creative starvation.

Her subsequent novels, especially *A Season in the Life of Emmanuel*, have been described as "typically Canadian" in their evocation of rural poverty and hopelessness, of the harsh northern winters, and in the sense of dislocation in a country populated by a defeated people. Her passionate, poetic voice is original in its relentlessly realistic exposure of a repressed, dispirited, and intellectually deprived underclass.

Although her first work was dismissed by many American critics as the exaggerated fantasy of an adolescent author, it was regarded as a great phenomenon in France. Edmund Wilson was responsible for bringing Blais to the American literary audience. The most ardent and outspoken of her American supporters, Wilson included Blais in his study *O Canada: An American's Notes on Canadian Culture* (1965):

> Mlle Blais is a true "phenomenon"; she may possibly be a genius. At the age of twenty-four, she has produced four remarkable books of a passionate and poetic force that, as far as my reading goes, is not otherwise to be found in French Canadian fiction.

Wilson wrote the foreword for *A Season in the Life of Emmanuel*, a disjointed, often humorous story with a constantly changing point of view about the material and emotional poverty of a large, Catholic, lower-class, Quebec farm family. All the children are devastated by the evil in the adult world. Their innocence is betrayed by predatory priests, and they are brutalized by their family and crushed by the dreary lives to which they are resigned.

Blais was disappointed when many reviewers of this novel focused on its bleakness and the depravity of its characters, missing its ironic humor. She treats her characters with tenderness as they struggle, some with great vitality and creativity, against the wretchedness of their lives. Her style is greatly influenced by the French Surrealists and Symbolists and was regarded as a great phenomenon by the French critics.

Deeply affected by the political climate in the United States during the Vietnam War, Blais found it troubling that people could not see or take action against the clear dangers arising in the world's social conflicts and ecological disasters or the destruction of the earth. In the 1970's, Blais's landscapes changed from those of an undefined time and place to a world inhabited by real people who are struggling to find their vision in contemporary society. Her art is a prophetic cry for sanity and peace in a violent world.

During her time in France, Blais wrote two books exploring and celebrating homosexual love. *The Wolf* is a study of cruelty and love in male relationships, and *Nights in the Underground* concerns the sacred and self-liberating aspects of lesbian relationships. Blais drew her characters from life in the gay bars and the streets of Montreal and Paris. They live for love and sex and talk about both without inhibition or shame, celebrating this freedom in otherwise unhappy lives.

Moving further from the gothic inner world of *Mad Shadows* and some of her earlier works, Blais addressed the condition of Quebec as a "colony" of France and the need for a separate French Canadian national identity in *St. Lawrence Blues*. Written entirely in *joual*, a form of French street slang, *St. Lawrence Blues* is a satiric novel about an illegitimate orphan's life among outcasts in Montreal's down-and-out working class. Dedicated to the memory of Wilson, it was regarded by American critics as her best work to date when the English translation was published in 1974. Quebec critics were less impressed and were especially hostile toward her use of a literary form of *joual* as an expression of "nationalist pride."

Deaf to the City is an observation of travelers and exiles suffering yet surviving through art. It is another experiment with language, written as a long paragraph in wild poetry and prose. Blais again fused these two styles in *Anna's World* in the drugged, suicidal torment of a young woman living in an uninhabitable world. Blais's vision of the world as a truly terrifying and desperate place is also the subject of *Pierre*, which was critically acclaimed.

In her trilogy consisting of *These Festive Nights*, *Thunder and Light*, and *Augustino and the Choir of Destruction*, Blais once again explores themes addressed in her earlier novels. Children damaged by lack of their mother's love, the effects of overwhelming poverty, homosexual love, the anguish of living, and art as escape all appear in the novels. However, she also treats new themes, including lack of justice and capital punishment, the plight of women and nature, and animals as images of innocence and joy, as well as materialism as an escapist measure. The trilogy attests to Blais's ability to create prose embodied with a poetic force that transforms it into a song.

MAD SHADOWS

First published: *La Belle bête*, 1959 (English translation, 1960)
Type of work: Novel

A surreal tale of tortured relationships between a mother obsessed with her son's beauty and the unattractive daughter doomed by envy and the shallow nature of her mother's love.

Mad Shadows, Blais's first published work, created considerable controversy in Quebec. Many Canadian critics disliked it intensely; others thought it was astonishingly original and brilliant. Set in an unidentified time and place, the story begins on a train, as a young girl watches strangers become captivated by her brother's beauty. The grotesque, erotic pleasure that the mother takes in her son's physical beauty is matched only by her indifference toward her daughter, and it sets the tone for the tortured relationships that develop. In *Mad Shadows*, Blais explores what will become a theme in much of her later work: the creation of evil and the suffering of children caused by the failure of maternal love.

The world that Blais's characters inhabit is dark and loveless. The first critics and readers were shocked by the utter depravity of the relationships

between the mother, her lover, and her children and the starkness of the young author's vision. Yet the power of her vision and poetic style were undeniable; she was awarded the Prix de la Langue Française from L'Académie Française for *Mad Shadows* in 1961.

The mother, Louise, an attractive, vain widow, adores and spoils her simple-minded son, Patrice, a reflection of herself. Dimly aware of his own beauty, Patrice seeks his unformed self in every mirrored surface, pond, and window. His sister, Isabelle-Marie, is not beautiful; wounded by her mother's indifference, her feelings of envy toward her brother begin to overwhelm her. Louise is afflicted by a lesion on her face, a cancerous growth symbolic of the malignancy of her soul. She meets Lanz, an elegant, declining dandy, who becomes her lover; her attentions and affection now go to him, and Patrice, abandoned, rides his horse in a frenzy of jealousy, killing Lanz. In death, Lanz's shallowness is revealed as his wig and false beard disintegrate around him. Even so, Louise feels little rancor toward her son, the "beautiful beast."

Among Blais's recurring themes is the end of innocence and the fall from grace inherent in sexual awakening. For her characters, all consequences of love are tragic; in *Mad Shadows*, there is a sense that human beings are doomed at the moment of awareness and that happiness is illusory. For a short time, miraculously, Isabelle-Marie finds happiness in the love of a young blind man, Michael. Sight, symbolic of truth, would not allow the illusion of love to survive in Blais's nightmarish world; fearing rejection, Isabelle-Marie deceives Michael into believing that she is beautiful. They marry and have a daughter, Anne, and for a time enjoy a kind of simple happiness. When his sight suddenly returns, Michael discovers his wife's deception. Unable to hide his anger, he cruelly abandons Isabelle-Marie and their child, and, in misery, they return to Louise's farm.

Driven by her rejection and envy, Isabelle-Marie disfigures her brother by pushing his face into a pot of boiling water. No longer a beautiful object, Patrice is rejected by his mother and sent to an asylum, proving the shallowness of her love. Seeing his grotesque face in a lake's surface, Patrice is horrified and drowns in his own reflection. His suffering gives Isabelle-Marie some satisfaction, but even this does not bring her peace. *Mad Shadows* ends in a final act of suicidal despair, as Isabelle-Marie sets her mother's farm on fire and waits to throw herself under a train, leaving her young daughter to wander alone on the tracks.

A SEASON IN THE LIFE OF EMMANUEL

First published: *Une Saison dans la vie d'Emmanuel,* 1965 (English translation, 1966)

Type of work: Novel

Newborn Emmanuel, the sixteenth child of an impoverished Quebec farmer, is witness to the suffering of his siblings and the ways in which each rebels against fate.

A Season in the Life of Emmanuel was declared by critics to have been both "written by the devil" and among the best French Canadian novels. Blais moves her character from an earlier imaginary, gothic world into the recognizable world of French Canadian culture. The story takes place during the first year in the life of Emmanuel, the sixteenth child of a materially and emotionally impoverished farm family. Bleak, disturbing, and full of biting humor, this depiction of Quebec's church-dominated lower-class life is considered Blais's masterwork.

Blais begins the story with a constantly changing point of view, as the mother of this brood of children, some called only by their birth order number, gives birth to Emmanuel and then returns to work in the fields. The strongest influence in the lives of the children is their grandmother, the rigid and traditional caretaker of their futures. The mother has no name, no presence in the book, though her absence and failure are clearly felt as she moves through life exhausted and resigned to her wretched state. Maternal failure is a theme common to Blais's work, which often presents a world where children are limited and defined by their emotional and physical deprivation.

The main character in this novel is not Emmanuel but four of the older children. It is through his eyes that one sees their suffering, and none escapes the evil in the world. Heloise, believing that the sensuality that she experiences in adolescence is a religious calling, goes first to a convent, then to a brothel. Two of Heloise's brothers are sentenced to life in a reformatory, where they are molested by predatory priests and then made to suffer the stupefying life of factory work, accepting the inevitability of their fate. Jean-Le-Maigre, the most alive and creative of the brood, ends his short life in a sanatorium; his journal is the only evidence of his existence, as his death, like his life, becomes nothing more than another family burden.

Obsessed with death, the repression of children, and the perversion of religious authority, Blais's vision is one of stifled lives and the responses of suffering children, suffering sometimes with great joy and grace to the constant evil that they encounter in the adult world. Her realistic style fascinated French critics in particular. Playing with language, often with ironic and biting humor, she renders both depravity and grace with naturalistic detail, which is especially poignant in the emotional expression of the suffering of fragile children.  For many of Blais's characters, as in her own life, language and the act of writing are symbolic paths to salvation, forestalling spiritual death and madness. The humorous and touching autobiographical writings of Emmanuel's brother Jean-Le-Maigre are part of the structure of the book. Dying of consumption, his poems express his vitality and symbolize his rebellion against fate.

THESE FESTIVE NIGHTS

First published: *Soifs*, 1995 (English translation, 1997)
Type of work: Novel

Characters from different socioeconomic classes participate in a three-day-and-night celebration while trying to escape from and come to terms with the human condition.

In *These Festive Nights*, Blais combines the technique of stream of consciousness with an omniscient narrator, permitting her to take the reader from the mind of one character to another in a continuous flow of thought and language. She uses repetitive images and descriptions of the characters to make the shifts without interruption to her text or confusion for the reader. Long sentences, often multiple pages in length, broken only by commas, reinforce the ceaseless flow of the work.

The novel depicts a disparate set of characters, all of whom are in some way interconnected, yet all living very different lives socially, economically, and intellectually. There are the wealthy, well-educated (Renata, Claude Mère, and Melanie, Daniel, and their children Samuel, Vincent, and Augustino); the intellectuals and artists (Jacques, Charles, Fréderic, Jean-Mathieu, Caroline, Suzanne, and Adrien); the ill or dying (Renata, Vincent, Jacques, Fréderic, and Jean-Mathieu); the aging (Mère, Renata, Charles, Fréderic, Adrien, Suzanne, Caroline, and Jean-Mathieu); the refugees (Julio, Eduardo, Jenny, and Marie-Sylvie and her brother); the poor African Americans (Pastor Jeremy, Mama, Carlos, Le Toqué, Venus, and Uncle Cornelius); and the homosexuals (Jacques, Tanjou, Luc, and Paul). The characters portray variants of the human condition, all tainted by suffering and death, and attempt to escape, to find happiness or at least peace in life.

The novel is structured on the juxtaposition of opposites. The setting of the story is an island in the Gulf of Mexico. Surrounded by the sea, it is a natural paradise filled with beautiful plants, birds, animals, and pleasant weather. However, danger, death, and suffering are ever present. The sea provides beauty and pleasure but can kill. The en-closed estate of Daniel and Melanie assures safety from predators within its confines, but just outside the estate, hooded figures prowl and hiss. The life of Samuel, who has everything material, contrasts sharply with the life of the impoverished Carlos. However, both suffer from a lack of true affection from either father or mother. For his parents, Samuel is "something" to be exhibited; Carlos's parents view him as no good.

Illness, old age, death, and impending death play significant roles in the novel. Characters are haunted by images of death: families lost at sea, war atrocities, bombings, mutilations, hangings, and executions in the electric chair and by lethal injection. Both Jacques, who is dying from acquired immunodeficiency syndrome (AIDS), and Fréderic, incapacitated by old age, can no longer care for themselves. Fréderic and Mère have memory loss.

Through the characters of Mère and Renata, Blais examines the particular problems confronting women in a patriarchal society. Both Mère and Renata have experienced rejection by their husbands because they no longer possessed the attractiveness of youth. Renata speaks of herself as a vagabond, running away from fate. For her, injustice will always be a woman's fate, and a woman will always be seen as guilty for causing her own misery. Mère is obsessed with the need for women to become leaders, to change the world.

The novel ends with Mère listening to Venus and Samuel singing "O may my joy endure."

THUNDER AND LIGHT

First published: *Dans la foudre et la lumière*, 2001 (English translation, 2001)
Type of work: Novel

The sequel to These Festive Nights, *the novel probes deeper into the torments of the human condition and the difficulty of escaping it.*

In *Thunder and Light*, Blais continues the stories of many of the characters that she introduced in *These Festive Nights*, but here she concentrates more on what actually happens to the characters than on what they are thinking. She also adds characters drawn from or based upon actual events recorded in news reports.

The novel begins with Carlos running with his dog Polly. Carlos is determined to get even with Lazaro, an Egyptian immigrant who used to be his friend. Carlos intends to frighten him with an unloaded gun, but as fate will have it the gun is loaded and Carlos shoots Lazaro in the knee. He becomes what Pastor Jeremy and Mama always said he would—a no-good and a criminal.

Through the characters of Lazaro and Caroline's companion Charly, Blais addresses the problem of the ever-recurring cycle of violence in the world. Lazaro swears to have revenge for Carlos's act. His mother unsuccessfully tells him he must forgive Carlos, otherwise all of her actions have been pointless. His mother had rebelled against the unjust religious law that permitted her Muslim husband to confine and beat her. Lazaro, however, refuses to listen and rejects his mother. He was born Muslim and male and his heritage calls for vengeance. Charly, a Jamaican descendant of slaves, voices the same desire for revenge based on heritage. Carlos's sister Venus is also victimized by the circumstances of her birth. Venus had escaped a life of poverty by marrying a rich drug dealer, Captain Williams, but the captain has been killed and she now finds herself at the mercy of the captain's estate manager, Richard, who has her trapped in the house.

In this novel, Blais deals at length with the impossibility of eliminating suffering and anguish from human life. She juxtaposes characters who try to relieve suffering and characters who escape from it in art, creativity, and beauty. Asoka is a monk who every day witnesses the anguish and death of innocent people, especially children, as he ministers to the victims of war, while his brother Ari devotes himself to sculpting. Caroline, a photographer, has always photographed only beautiful people and objects. She refuses to record images of the victims of violence, war, and starvation, in con-

trast to the photojournalists, who with their photographs stamp these images into the minds of their readers.

The memorial service for Jean-Mathieu returns to the problem of mortality and God in a suffering world. Caroline muses on the death of her friend, on the exile of each person from the sensual world, and on the sense of loss and absence that comes to each individual.

Blais returns to the stream-of-consciousness technique she employed in *These Festive Nights* in her analysis of the impossibility of justice in the world and the cruelty of capital punishment. Tormented by the willingness of most judges to pronounce the death penalty, Renata thinks of nothing else as she prepares for a conference on the topic.

SUMMARY

Marie-Claire Blais has said that life for her would be unbearable without the solace of writing. The characters in her novels suffer so deeply that escape is possible only through death of the body or through salvation in the language of art. Her love of language and experimentation with form and style are a unique expression of her passionate, poetic vision of the suffering in a bleak and terrifying world.

The sum of Blais's work is a complex expression of the subjects that obsess her. Sometimes with the cold eye of a realist, often with ironic humor and great compassion, she writes in an unmistakable voice, in pursuit of the intangible.

Margaret Parks; updated by Shawncey Webb

BIBLIOGRAPHY

By the Author

LONG FICTION:
La Belle bête, 1959 (*Mad Shadows*, 1960)
Tête blanche, 1960 (English translation, 1961)
La Fin d'une enfance, 1961 (novella)
Le Jour est noir, 1962 (English translation in *The Day Is Dark and Three Travelers: Two Novellas*, 1967)
Une Saison dans la vie d'Emmanuel, 1965 (*A Season in the Life of Emmanuel*, 1966)
L'Insoumise, 1966 (*The Fugitive*, 1978)
Les Voyageurs sacrés, 1966 (English translation in *The Day Is Dark and Three Travelers: Two Novellas*, 1967)
David Sterne, 1967 (English translation, 1973)
Manuscrits de Pauline Archange, 1968 (*The Manuscripts of Pauline Archange*, 1970)
Le Loup, 1972 (*The Wolf*, 1974)
Un Joualonais, sa joualonie, 1973 (*St. Lawrence Blues*, 1974)
Une Liaison parisienne, 1975 (*A Literary Affair*, 1979)
Les Nuits de l'underground, 1978 (*Nights in the Underground*, 1979)
Le Sourd dans la ville, 1979 (*Deaf to the City*, 1980)
Visions d'Anna: Ou, Le Vertige, 1982 (*Anna's World*, 1985)
Pierre, la guerre du printemps quatre-vingt-un, 1984 (*Pierre*, 1993)
L'Ange de la solitude, 1989 (*The Angel of Solitude*, 1993)
"L'Exile" suivi de "Les Voyageurs sacres," 1992 (*"The Exile" and "The Sacred Travellers,"* 2000)
Soifs, 1995 (*These Festive Nights*, 1997)
Dans la foudre et la lumière, 2001 (*Thunder and Light*, 2001)
Augustino et le chœur de la destruction, 2005 (*Augustino and the Choir of Destruction*, 2007)

DRAMA:
L'Exécution, pb. 1968 (*The Execution*, 1976)
Sommeil d'hiver, pb. 1984 (*Wintersleep*, 1998)
L'Île, pb. 1988 (*The Island*, 1991)
Parcours d'un écrivain: Notes Américaines, 1993 (*American Notebooks: A Writer's Journey*, 1996)
Des Recontres humaines, 2002

About the Author

Dufault, Roseanna Lewis. *Acting Mothers: The Maternal Role in Recent Novels by Marie-Claire Blais and Anne Hébert*. Ada: Ohio Northern University, 1997.
Gould, Karen L. "Geographies of Death and Dreams in Marie-Claire's *Soifs*." *Quebec Studies* 25 (Spring, 1998): 9-14.

DISCUSSION TOPICS

- What role do political and social themes, such as poverty, discrimination, and racism, play in Marie-Claire Blais's work?
- How does Blais use repeated images in her work to reinforce continuity?
- How does Blais depict animals in her novels and what do they represent?
- How does Blais address the problem of God in a suffering world?
- Compare and contrast the lives of Samuel and Carlos in *These Festive Nights*.
- Discuss the mother-child relationship in Blais's novels.
- Blais uses vernacular in her dialogue, unique punctuation, and Surrealist images in her works. What is their affect on the reader's experience of reading?

Green, Mary Jean. *Marie-Claire Blais*. New York: Twayne, 1995.

Green, Mary Jean, et al., eds. "The Past Our Mother: Marie-Claire Blais and the Question of Women in the Quebec Canon." In *Postcolonial Subjects: Francophone Women Writers*. Minneapolis: University of Minnesota Press, 1996.

McPherson, Karen S. *Archaeologies of an Uncertain Future: Recent Generations of Canadian Women Writing*. Montreal: McGill-Queen's University Press, 2006.

Meigs, Mary. *Lily Briscoe: A Self-Portrait*. Vancouver, B.C.: Talonbooks, 1981.

Stratford, Philip. *Marie-Claire Blais*. Toronto: Forum House, 1971.

WILLIAM BLAKE

Born: London, England
November 28, 1757
Died: London, England
August 12, 1827

Blake's unique work combines poetry and painting in a compelling vision of humanity attaining its most blissful, creative, and enlightened condition. His work exemplifies the goals of the English Romantic movement.

BIOGRAPHY

William Blake was born on November 28, 1757, in London, the second of five children of James Blake, a hosier, and his wife, Catherine Blake. Blake was schooled at home until he was about eleven, after which he was sent to a drawing school, where he studied until 1772. He was then apprenticed for seven years to James Basire, a well-known engraver. In 1779, Blake began to study at the Royal Academy and also did commercial engravings for the bookseller Joseph Johnson. In 1782, Blake married Catherine Boucher, the illiterate daughter of a market gardener. Blake taught her to read and write, and eventually she helped him color his designs.

Blake had been writing poetry since the age of twelve, and by the early 1780's he was beginning to acquire a reputation among his friends as a poet and painter. Two friends, John Flaxman and the Reverend A. S. Mathew, paid the expenses for the publication of Blake's first volume, *Poetical Sketches*, in 1783. The following year, Blake wrote "An Island in the Moon," a satire on contemporary ways of thinking, but it was never published.

Three years later, Blake suffered a major blow when his younger brother Robert, to whom Blake was devoted, died of consumption at the age of nineteen. Blake, who from his childhood had revealed a capacity for visionary experience, said that, at the moment of death, he saw his brother's spirit ascending, clapping its hands for joy. Blake felt that Robert's spirit remained with him throughout his life. Indeed, it was Robert, Blake claimed, who gave him the idea for an original method of engraving, in which he etched poems and illustrations together on a copper plate, then printed them and colored them by hand.

His first experiments in this new method of illuminated printing were in the form of three tractates, in two versions, titled *There Is No Natural Religion* (1788) and *All Religions Are One* (1788). About this time, Blake first came under the influence of Emanuel Swedenborg, a Swedish scientist turned mystic philosopher. Blake attended the first General Conference of the Swedenborgians' New Jerusalem Church in London in April, 1789.

In the same year, Blake published his first masterpieces in illuminated printing, *The Book of Thel* (1789) and *Songs of Innocence* (1789). The latter celebrates a childlike state of spontaneity and joy, in which the divine world interpenetrates the natural world. The following year, 1790, Blake began work on his great satire *The Marriage of Heaven and Hell* (1790), which is at once a spiritual testament and a revolutionary political manifesto in support of the French Revolution.

Throughout the 1790's, Blake continued working as a commercial engraver, as well as completing artistic commissions from his patron, the civil servant Thomas Butts. For the most part, Blake saw this work as daily drudgery, undertaken solely to provide for his few worldly needs; his real interests lay in giving form to his own creative vision, which he did in a stream of illuminated books: *Visions of the Daughters of Albion* (1793), *America: A Prophecy* (1793), *Songs of Innocence and of Experience* (1794), *Europe: A Prophecy* (1794), *The [First] Book of Urizen* (1794), *The Song of Los* (1795), *The Book of Los* (1795), and *The Book of Ahania* (1795). In 1797, he commenced an ambitious long poem, *Vala: Or, The Four Zoas* (wr. 1795-1804, pb. 1963), which he kept revising over a ten-year period, retitling it *The Four Zoas* but eventually abandoning it unfinished. Few people, if any, in Blake's time understood these obscure books, and they attracted almost no buyers. This lack of public recognition set a pattern for the remainder of Blake's life. His one-man exhibition of sixteen of his paintings in 1809 and 1810 was a complete failure. Although he was embittered by his inability to find an audience, he did not allow his disappointment to weaken his dedication to his art.

Blake spent all of his life in London, except for the period from 1800 to 1803, when he lived at Felpham, a village on the Sussex coast in southern England. There, he was under the patronage of William Hayley, a minor poet who was also, in his time, a well-respected man of letters. Hayley provided Blake with some hack work, but Blake resented his patronizing attitude and eventually the two men quarreled. Blake's stay at Felpham is also notable for an incident in which Blake evicted a drunken soldier from his cottage garden. The soldier then accused him of uttering threats against the king. Blake was charged with sedition, tried, and acquitted in 1804. Blake had returned to London the previous year, 1803, and, in addition to working on some watercolors for one client and some designs for Hayley's *A Series of Ballads* (1802), he began work on his two lengthy masterpieces, *Milton: A Poem* (1804-1808) and *Jerusalem: The Emanation of the Giant Albion* (1804-1820). These were years of increasing obscurity for Blake, although in the last period of his life he gathered around him an admiring group of young painters, who recognized his genius. Blake's last great works were his engravings in *Illustrations of the Book of Job* (1825) and his *Illustrations of Dante* (1827), on which he was still working at his death on August 12, 1827, in London.

ANALYSIS

Blake stated his poetic and philosophical principles early in his career and never wavered from them, although there were some changes of emphasis as his work developed. He formed his imaginative world in opposition to the prevailing materialist philosophy, which he saw embodied in three English thinkers: Francis Bacon, John Locke, and Isaac Newton. Bacon was one of the founders of modern experimental science, but Blake detested this method of acquiring knowledge because it relied solely on objective criteria and encouraged the principle of doubt. In "Auguries of Innocence," Blake points out that this is not the way that the rest of the universe functions:

> He who Doubts from what he sees
> Will ne'er Believe do what you Please
> If the Sun and Moon should doubt
> Theyd immediately Go out.

In Locke, the philosopher who exerted an extremely powerful influence on eighteenth century thought, Blake found another opponent. In *An Essay Concerning Human Understanding* (1690), Locke argued against the belief that there are in the human mind "innate ideas," universal truths stamped on the mind at birth. For Locke, the mind was a *tabula rasa*, a blank tablet. Knowledge was gained only through sense experience and the mind's reflection on the data provided by the senses. Locke's views were anathema to Blake, for whom the first principle of knowing was not through the senses but through the mind. The mind is not a *tabula rasa;* it is fullness itself, the Divine Imagination, the eternal container of the permanent realities of existence. As Blake put it when he annotated the *Discourses* (1769-1791) of Sir Joshua Reynolds, president of the Royal Academy, who attempted to apply Lockean principles to art: "Reynolds Thinks that Man Learns all that he knows. I say on the Contrary that Man Brings All that he has or can have Into the World with him. Man is Born Like a Garden ready Planted and Sown. This World is too poor to produce one Seed."

For Blake, it is the mind that shapes the way that one perceives the object. He called this seeing through, not with, the eye. Different minds see in different ways:

> The Sun's Light when he unfolds it
> Depends on the Organ that beholds it.

This is a key idea in Blake, and he repeats it again and again. For Blake, the more imagination that is applied to the act of perception, the more true the perception will be. The world of sense, by itself, is illusory. Only the imagination, the formative power of the mind, can penetrate beyond surface appearances to the divine nature of existence, which permeates this "Vegetable Glass of Nature" and is also the true nature of the human self.

That was Blake's answer to the third member of his unholy trinity, Newton, the great seventeenth century scientist who not only discovered gravity but also synthesized many other contemporary theories into a grand system that appeared to explain all the laws that governed the physical universe. The problem with Newton's philosophy of nature, from Blake's point of view, was that it made the universe into a vast and impersonal machine that had no vital connection with human consciousness. By creating a split between subject and object, it had left humans alone and isolated in a universe over which they had no control. Against this dehumanizing tendency of natural philosophy, Blake opposed a universe in which joy, delight, and bliss are the essential constituents of both the human and nonhuman world. In his poem "Europe," for example, in answer to the poet's question, "what is the material world, and is it dead?" a fairy sings, "I'll chew you all alive/ The world, when every particle of dust breathes forth its joy." In such a universe humanity is not subject to an impersonal, mechanical order, presided over by a God who sits in judgment on it beyond the skies. On the contrary, when humanity exercises its imaginative powers to the full it becomes the Divine Humanity, the creator of a visionary time and space that reveals rather than obscures the eternal, immaterial essence of life. The universe becomes as close to humankind as its own heartbeat, as precious to it as its own blood.

Armed with this vision, Blake set himself the task of waging war on ignorance, on everything that he believed diminished or obscured the Divine Humanity. He developed a complex mythology, pieced together not only from his own visionary experiences but from a wide variety of sources. In addition to the Bible and the works of John Milton, which were a constant inspiration to him, he delved deeply into the Western esoteric tradition, including Neoplatonism, Hermeticism, Kabbalah,

and individual mystical thinkers such as Swedenborg and the seventeenth century German seer Jacob Boehme. However, Blake was never a slave to the thoughts of others; whatever he borrowed from his sources was put through the crucible of his own imaginative power and transformed into a vision that was uniquely his own.

AMERICA: A PROPHECY

First published: 1793
Type of work: Poem

This poem celebrates the American Revolution, which is seen as a victory over British tyranny and the birth of a new age of freedom for humanity.

America: A Prophecy was Blake's first attempt to present historical and contemporary events in mythological form so as to draw out their universal significance. The preludium introduces two mythological characters, the "shadowy daughter of Urthona," who is nature in an unfruitful time, and Orc, who embodies both the life-giving return of spring and the liberating, revolutionary energy that is about to be unleashed in the world through the American Revolution. Since Orc's birth fourteen years previously, the shadowy female has been bringing food to him. Throughout this period Orc has been chained to a rock, although his spirit soars and can be seen in the forms of eagle, lion, whale, and serpent.

Having reached the age of sexual maturity, Orc breaks free of his chains and seizes and ravishes the shadowy female. She erupts in joy, exclaiming that she recognizes him—Orc stimulates the periodic renewal of earth's procreative power—and declares him to be the image of God that "dwells in darkness of Africa" (perhaps an allusion to Swedenborg's belief that the Africans understood God better than the Europeans). The shadowy female then says she sees the spirit of Orc at work in America, Canada, Mexico, and Peru—places that had seen recent outbreaks of rebellion against established authority.

The poem itself begins on Plate 3. As war-clouds, fires, and tempests gather, some of the leading

American rebels—including George Washington, Tom Paine, and Benjamin Franklin—gather together. Washington makes a speech warning of the dangers the colonists face, and as he finishes, King George III and the British government—referred to as the Guardian Prince of Albion, or Albion's Angel (Albion is the ancient name of England)—appear to the rebels as a fiery dragon rising up from England. However, this apparition is countered by the appearance of Orc over the Atlantic Ocean. In Plate 6, in one of the most impressive passages in all of Blake's work, Orc announces the imminent outburst of freedom at all levels: political, spiritual, and cosmic.

Albion's Angel responds by denouncing Orc as a "Lover of wild rebellion, and transgressor of God's law." Orc replies that he is the "fiery joy" of life itself, which Urizen (the fallen god of reason in Blake's mythology and similar in function to the God of the Old Testament) imprisoned at the proclamation of the Ten Commandments. Now these commandments are to be abrogated.

In Plate 9, Albion attempts to rally support from his "Thirteen angels" (the colonial governors), but they refuse to respond to his call. "Boston's Angel" makes a speech in which he refuses to continue obeying an unjust system. In Plate 13, war breaks out and the British suffer defeats. Albion's Angel responds to these reversals by dispatching a deadly plague to America, but driven by the flames and fiery winds of Orc, the plague recoils upon the sender. The effects on England are devastating. Soldiers desert, rulers sicken, and priests are overthrown. In Plate 16, Urizen weeps as he beholds his world crumbling. For twelve years he manages to restrain the energies of Orc, until Orc breaks free once more in the French Revolution. The thrones of Spain and Italy shake; the restrictive moral law is burnt up by Orc's fires and a new age begins.

THE [FIRST] BOOK OF URIZEN

First published: 1794
Type of work: Poem

This work is a myth of Creation and the Fall as a result of the limiting activity of the rational intellect, embodied in the figure of Urizen.

The [First] Book of Urizen is an unorthodox version of the Creation and the Fall, written to satirize the traditional accounts in Genesis and John Milton's *Paradise Lost* (1667, 1674). In *The [First] Book of Urizen*, the creator, Urizen, is neither all-powerful nor benevolent; his creation is not "good" as in Genesis, but flawed from the beginning. As a product solely of the unenlightened rational intellect, his world is incomplete. Cut off from the creative power of the imagination, which is personified in the poem by Los, Urizen can only create a world full of suffering and death.

The [First] Book of Urizen begins with a preludium, in which Blake gladly accepts the call of the Eternals to dictate their story. The poem is then divided, like Genesis, into chapter and verse. Chapter 1 describes Urizen's activity in wholly negative terms. He is "unknown, unprolific," and "unseen"; he broods introspectively; he is "self-clos'd" and a "self-contemplating shadow." That is exactly the withdrawn, abstract type of mental activity that, in Blake's view, was responsible for many of the ills that he saw in contemporary society. By retreating into a void within himself, Urizen is beginning to close himself off from the primal joy of existence.

In chapter 2, it transpires that Urizen's activity is taking place before the creation of the world, before the existence of death, and before there are any material restrictions placed around the fiery delights of eternal existence. Urizen now reveals himself as the lawgiver, the Jehovah of the Old Testament, whom Blake associated with tyranny. Because Urizen cannot enjoy the free-flowing and joyful clash of opposite values in eternity, he attempts to create for himself "a joy without pain,/ . . . a solid without fluctuation." To his eyes, the Eternals live in "unquenchable burnings," when in fact these are the fires of the creative imagination as it constantly fulfills its desires. Failing to understand this, Urizen tries to fight with the fire and sets himself up as lord over all the other faculties. With his laws of "One command, one joy, one desire," he attempts to impose a false unity on the infinite diversity of existence. For Blake, this is the sign of a tyrant.

Throughout the poem, the Eternals are horrified by Urizen's self-defeating actions, which open up a series of separations between Urizen and eternity: "Sund'ring, dark'ning, thund'ring,"/ Rent away with a terrible clash,/ Eternity roll'd wide apart." As Urizen is forced out of (or expels himself from) eternity, he undergoes a gradual process of materialization. In a parody of the seven days of creation in Genesis, Urizen acquires a material body, which is also the material world. His awareness of eternal life vanishes. Horrified at what is taking place, Los, the creative imagination, watches the process, throws nets around Urizen, and binds him with chains to stop him from descending even further into the darkness of ignorance. In his later work, Blake regarded creation as an act of mercy because it put a limit to the Fall and so allowed the possibility of redemption.

In this poem, however, the emphasis is entirely on the pervasive negative consequences of Urizen's acts, which also affect Los, Urizen's counterpart in eternity. Los forgets his true creative function and allows himself to feel pity for Urizen, which in Blake's work is usually a negative emotion ("For pity divides the soul"). Los, like Urizen, is now a divided being, and the female portion of himself (which Blake calls the emanation) now takes on an independent life, separate from him. This first female form is named Enitharmon. The Eternals, who are androgynous beings, are appalled at this division into sexes, which is yet another sign of the Fall—an idea that Blake borrowed from his spiritual mentor, the German mystic Jacob Boehme.

In chapter 6, Los and Enitharmon give birth to a child, Orc, who elsewhere in Blake's work symbolizes revolutionary, redemptive energy. Los becomes jealous of Orc, and in an act that suggests at once the Crucifixion of Christ, the binding of Isaac by Abraham, and the chaining of Prometheus, Los and Enitharmon chain Orc to a mountain.

In the next chapter, Urizen explores his grim new world, trying to understand it by dividing and measuring, which is all that the rational intellect, cut off from the unifying power of the imagination,

can do. Urizen can only discover "portions of life." Nothing is whole or healthy, and Urizen sickens at the sight of it. As he traverses the cities of earth, he curses his creation and realizes that no being can keep his "iron laws one moment." A net stretches out behind him, born from the sorrow in his soul. Everything in creation is trapped by this net, which is named the net of religion. This image expresses Blake's dislike of conventional religion, based on moral laws and human reason alone. As Urizen's religion spreads across the earth, human beings find their senses, which in eternity are expansive— humans are able to perceive delight in everything— narrowing and shrinking, until, like everyone else in this poem, they "forgot their eternal life."

MILTON: A POEM

First published: 1804-1808
Type of work: Poem

In this epic poem, Blake corrects the errors of his predecessor, John Milton, and assumes the Miltonic mantle of poet and prophet of England.

In *Milton: A Poem*, Blake continues the argument with Milton that he had begun in *The Marriage of Heaven and Hell* (1790). In that book, Blake had identified the Christ of *Paradise Lost* (1667, 1674) with the restrictive values of reason and conventional morality, and Milton's Satan, whom Christ casts out, with the passionate energies of humankind, which to Blake were the sources of creativity. Blake thought that, although Milton was a great poet, he had put himself in service of a bad theology, and this had divided him against himself. In *Milton: A Poem*, which was written more than one hundred years after Milton's death, Milton is in heaven but unhappy. He decides to return to earth to redeem his errors and be reunited with his "sixfold emanation," the feminine aspect of himself, which is still wandering in torment in the earthly sphere. Historically, the emanation represents Milton's three wives and three daughters; symbolically, they are the aspects of his creative imagination that he repudiated in his earthly life.

Milton's decision to return to earth is prompted by his hearing of the Bard's Song, a key passage that occupies Plates 3 to 13 of this forty-three-plate, two-book poem. It is based on an episode in Blake's life, when he was living at Felpham under the patronage of William Hayley. Hayley urged Blake to pay more attention to earning a living, to put his artistic talents in the service of the commonsense world of "good taste." Blake thought that Hayley was a spiritual enemy who was trying to deflect him from his true artistic and prophetic path. In *Milton: A Poem*, Blake creates a cosmic allegory out of the conflict between them. Hayley becomes Satan; Blake is Palamabron, one of the sons of Los, the imagination. When the quarrel is brought out into the open, Hayley/Satan, whose crime is to assume a role that is not his own, reveals the tyrannical and arrogant self that hides behind his surface appearance of benevolence. He is the enemy of true poetic inspiration.

When Milton hears the Bard's Song, he recognizes himself in Hayley/Satan and resolves to return to earth, to cast off this false selfhood in an act of "self-annihilation." He passes through the different levels of Blake's cosmology, from Eden, the highest realm of imaginative activity, to Beulah, a feminine, sexual paradise, to the abyss of Ulro, the material world. There, in Plate 19, he encounters Urizen, the personification of the unenlightened rational intellect, who attempts to freeze Milton's brain. As they struggle with each other, Milton works like a sculptor, creating new flesh on the bones of Urizen; the shaping, enlivening vision of the artist strives to impart life to the Urizenic death principle.

A crucial moment now follows: The spirit of the descending Milton, like a falling star, enters Blake's left foot one day as he binds on his sandals. Blake becomes aware that in this tremendous instant,

Los, the imagination, has also entered and taken possession of him, and he knows that he is ready to fulfill his destiny as the poet-prophet of England, the seer whose task it is to awaken his country to the reality of the divine, and fully human, life. Much of the remainder of the first book of the poem is devoted to a transfigured vision of the time and space world, seen as the creative work of Los, whose task is accomplished in the single, eternal moment of poetic inspiration.

In book 2 of *Milton: A Poem* a female character named Ololon descends from Beulah to Ulro. It later transpires that she is Milton's emanation. She descends to Blake's cottage in Felpham, and he perceives her as a young girl. Ololon's sudden appearance in what Blake calls the Mundane Shell (the physical world) is another crucial moment in the poem. Like Blake's union with Milton and Los in book 1, it occurs in a timeless moment of mystical illumination, which Blake associates with the song of the lark and the odor of wild thyme. In this moment of heightened perception, eternity streams into time, and the effect is so powerful that it cancels out all the mistakes and perversions of the entire span of Christian history. A new era is at hand.

All the remaining events of the poem take place in this one instant. Milton, still continuing his descent into the physical world, appears in Blake's garden as the Covering Cherub, a symbol derived from the Bible that, in Blake's mythology, signifies the final manifestation of all the errors of the Christian churches. The Covering Cherub is closely linked with Satan the selfhood, who also now appears; the inspired Milton, who is hidden within the Covering Cherub, recognizes the false selves to which he formerly surrendered. In a great speech in Plates 40-41, he casts them off in an act of self-annihilation, giving his allegiance solely to the truth of poetic inspiration. Hearing Milton's speech, Ololon is cleansed also, and in a purified form she is able to unite with Milton. The poem ends on a note of apocalyptic hope for the reawakening of the entire humanity.

"THE TYGER"

First published: 1794 (collected in *Songs of Innocence and of Experience*, 1794)
Type of work: Poem

In awe, wonder, and puzzlement, the speaker asks a series of questions about the nature of the being who could create such a fearsome beast.

"The Tyger," from *Songs of Innocence and of Experience* (1794), is probably Blake's most famous poem. Its artful simplicity and pounding repetitions make a strong impression when the poem is read aloud. The meaning of "The Tyger," however, is not so easy to ascertain, and it has provoked a wide range of interpretations. The poem consists of six quatrains, each of which asks at least one question about the nature of the tiger's creator. None of the questions are answered. The central question of the whole poem appears in the fifth quatrain, "Did he who made the Lamb make thee?" This question recalls the poem "The Lamb," from the same collection, in which the question, "Little Lamb, who made thee?" is answered clearly. The lamb is made by Christ and is an obvious symbol of the mild and gentle aspects of Creation, which are easy to associate with a God of love. However, what about the more fearsome, destructive aspects of Creation, symbolized by the tiger? Do they proceed from the same God? Under what circumstances? Is the tiger only a product of the Fall of humankind? Or are there, perhaps, two Gods?

Crucial to interpretation are the first two lines of the fifth quatrain: "When the stars threw down their spears,/ And water'd heaven with their tears." This event appears to take place, from the evidence of the following line ("Did he smile his work to see?"), at the moment of the tiger's creation. It may be a reference to the fall of the rebel angels in Milton's *Paradise Lost*: "they astonished all resistance lost,/ All courage; down their idle weapons dropped." In Christian tradition, the stars are said to be the tears of the fallen angels. In *The Four Zoas*, Blake uses a phrase almost identical to the one in "The Tyger" in the context of Urizen's account of the Fall: "The stars threw down their spears and fled naked away/ We fell." In Blake's mythology, the immediate result of the Fall was the creation of the physical world. This cluster of associations sug-

gests that the tiger is a product only of the Fall, a suggestion that is strengthened by the phrase "forests of the night" in the first quatrain, which symbolizes Blake's fallen world of Experience.

Yet this does not seem to provide the whole answer to the riddle of the poem. The fire that burns brightly, if destructively, in the state of Experience is still the divine fire, the stupendous creative energy that can frame the "fearful symmetry" of the tiger. In the fallen world, however, it cannot be fully appreciated for what it is. In quatrain 3, for example, the awestruck speaker lapses into incoherence as he tries to fathom the mystery of the fierce aspect of Creation. As Blake puts it in one of the proverbs in *The Marriage of Heaven and Hell*, "The roaring of lions, the howling of wolves, the raging of the stormy sea, and the destructive sword, are portions of eternity, too great for the eye of man." The speaker in "The Tyger" cannot understand that, if there is a lamb, there must also be a tiger; opposites are necessary for the full manifestation of divine creativity.

Yet another possibility is that Blake was drawing on the teachings of the Gnostics, who flourished in the early years of the Christian era. For the Gnostics, the created world was a dark prison; it was not created by the true God but by an inferior power, the demiurge, who was often likened to the God of the Old Testament. If Blake indeed had this in mind—and elsewhere in his work he expresses a very similar view—the answer to the poem's central question, "Did he who made the Lamb make thee?" would be "no." The tiger would then be associated with the Old Testament God of fire and judgment, not the New Testament God of love, embodied in Christ.

SUMMARY

Ignored in his own time, William Blake came into his own in the twentieth century, and his status as one of the six greatest English Romantic poets is unlikely to be challenged. His intense spiritual vision, embodied alike in simple lyrics and complex prophetic books, amounts to a manifesto of the art, psychology, philosophy, and religion of human enlightenment. Creating his own mythology of the Creation, Fall, and Redemption of humankind, Blake offers a vision of the "Human Form Divine" that transcends the conventional wisdom regarding the nature of the human condition.

Bryan Aubrey

BIBLIOGRAPHY

By the Author

POETRY:
Poetical Sketches, 1783
All Religions Are One, 1788
There Is No Natural Religion, 1788
The Book of Thel, 1789
Songs of Innocence, 1789
The Marriage of Heaven and Hell, 1790
The French Revolution, wr. 1791, pb. 1913
Visions of the Daughters of Albion, 1793
America: A Prophecy, 1793
Europe: A Prophecy, 1794
The [First] Book of Urizen, 1794
Songs of Innocence and of Experience, 1794
The Song of Los, 1795
The Book of Los, 1795
The Book of Ahania, 1795
Vala: Or, The Four Zoas, wr. 1795-1804, pb. 1963
    (better known as *The Four Zoas*)
Milton: A Poem, 1804-1808
Jerusalem: The Emanation of the Giant Albion, 1804-1820
The Poems of William Blake, 1971

ILLUSTRATIONS AND ENGRAVINGS:
The Complaint and the Consolation: Or, Night Thoughts, by Edward Young, 1797
Blair's Grave, 1808
The Prologue and Characters of Chaucer's Pilgrims, 1812
The Pastorals of Virgil, 1821
Illustrations of the Book of Job, 1825
Illustrations of Dante, 1827

LONG FICTION:
An Island in the Moon, wr. c. 1784, pb. 1987
To the Public: Prospectus, 1793

NONFICTION:
A Descriptive Catalogue, 1809

About the Author
Ackroyd, Peter. *Blake*. New York: Knopf, 1995.
Bloom, Harold. *Blake's Apocalypse: A Study in Poetic Argument*. Garden City, N.Y.: Doubleday, 1965.
_____, ed. *English Romantic Poets*. Philadelphia: Chelsea House, 2004.

DISCUSSION TOPICS

- Show how central William Blake's visual artistry is to his success as a poet.

- What is the relationship between Blake's *Songs of Innocence* and *Songs of Experience*?

- Given the power and the simple language of some of his best poems, how does one explain Blake's difficulty in finding an audience?

- What is the basis of Blake's rejection of such notable English thinkers as Francis Bacon, John Locke, and Isaac Newton?

- What qualities of *America: A Prophecy* would have attracted Americans in Blake's time? What aspects of the poem do you think they would not have appreciated?

- Why do you suppose Blake found it necessary to "correct" John Milton a century after his death?

- Why, in "The Tyger," should symmetry be called "fearful"?

- Blake is sometimes called a mystic. What is mystical about him?

Clarke, Steve, and Jason Whittaker, eds. *Blake, Modernity, and Popular Culture.* New York: Palgrave Macmillan, 2007.

Damon, S. Foster. *A Blake Dictionary: The Ideas and Symbols of William Blake.* 1965. Rev. ed. Hanover, N.H.: University Press of New England, 1988.

Erdman, David V. *Blake, Prophet Against Empire: A Poet's Interpretation of the History of His Own Times.* 3d ed. Princeton, N.J.: Princeton University Press, 1977.

Frye, Northrop. *Fearful Symmetry: A Study of William Blake.* Princeton, N.J.: Princeton University Press, 1947.

Hagstrum, Jean. *William Blake: Poet and Painter.* Chicago: University of Chicago Press, 1964.

Larrissy, Edward. *Blake and Modern Literature.* New York: Palgrave Macmillan, 2006.

GIOVANNI BOCCACCIO

Born: Florence or Certaldo (now in Italy)
June or July, 1313
Died: Certaldo (now in Italy)
December 21, 1375

Although an erudite Latin humanist, Boccaccio is known primarily for The Decameron, *which reflects the medieval world, influenced such writers as Geoffrey Chaucer, and was a precursor of Renaissance thought.*

BIOGRAPHY

Giovanni Boccaccio (boh-KAH-cheeoh) was born in June or July of 1313 in Florence or Certaldo (now in Italy), the illegitimate son of Florentine merchant Boccaccio di Chellino. The identity of his mother is uncertain. He spent his early childhood in Florence, but in 1327 he moved with his father to Naples, where he studied banking, trade, and canon law. Boccaccio eventually abandoned his pursuit of a vocation in commerce and law for a literary life.

The years spent in Naples were crucial to Boccaccio's social, intellectual, and literary development. Because of his father's connections with the aristocracy of Naples, Boccaccio enjoyed the carefree and privileged lifestyle of the court of King Robert of Anjou. There, his passion for poetry and his superior aptitude in literature, both classic and medieval, flourished and formed the basis of his literary works. It was there that he began his early original poetry, which evidences a gift for narration: *Il filocolo* (c. 1336; *Labor of Love*, 1566), *Il filostrato* (c. 1335; *The Filostrato*, 1873), *Teseida* (1340-1341; *The Book of Theseus*, 1974).

In this body of work, Boccaccio introduces a female character, Fiammetta, whose charms are extolled throughout his early poetry. His first encounter with her is described in *Labor of Love*, where the poet sees her for the first time on Easter Sunday in the Franciscan Church of San Lorenzo in Naples. It is notable that the manner in which this encounter is described is consistent with Italian poet Dante's description of Beatrice, and is also remarkably similar to the reported meeting of Boccaccio's revered idol, Petrarch, and his beloved Laura.

During this period, Boccaccio encountered a man who would influence his life and his work considerably. While studying the law, he met Cino da Pistoia, a prestigious lawyer of the time, who was also a friend of Dante, author of *La divina commedia* (c. 1320; *The Divine Comedy*, 1802). Cino da Pistoia was a poet in his own right and a disciple of *il stil nuovo*, the "sweet new style," a school of poetry in the Tuscan idiom. Cino da Pistoia became a link to Dante, and through him Boccaccio acquired an appreciation for poetry in the vernacular. Similiarly, Boccaccio made the acquaintance of Dionigi da Borgo san Sepolcro, who had close ties with the Italian poet Petrarch. Petrarch was to become something of a mentor to Boccaccio, and his influence is evident throughout his works. During this time, Boccaccio was also surrounded by scholars who inspired a reverence for classical literature and a fascination with Greek culture, which would influence many of his future literary works. This appreciation of the classics would become one of the salient characteristics of the imminent Humanist movement.

Boccaccio's years in Naples were his happiest, and it was against his will that he returned to Florence in 1341 because of his father's financial difficulties. During the first years in Florence, Boccaccio sought work and contact with the northern aristocracy, while continuing to write more mature literary works such as *Il ninfale fiesolano* (1344-1346; *The Nymph of Fiesole*, 1597), and the *Elegia di Madonna Fiammetta* (1343-1344; *Amorous Fiammetta*, 1587, better known as *The Elegy of Lady Fiammetta*), which reflected cultural and spiritual situations of the era.

In 1348, Boccaccio was in Florence when it was struck by the Black Death, an event that inspired the writing of *Decameron: O, Prencipe Galetto* (1349-1351; *The Decameron*, 1620). His father, stepmother, and many friends died during this horrifying episode, and Boccaccio offers a vivid description of this deadly plague in the introduction to the work. The bulk of his writing on *The Decameron*, considered his masterpiece, was completed in the years during which Boccaccio was compelled to remain in Florence to administer his father's estate.

In 1350, Boccaccio finally had the opportunity to cultivate a deep, long-standing personal friendship with his most revered contemporary literary figure, Petrarch. When Boccaccio learned that Petrarch was expected to visit Florence, he arranged to welcome the poet to the city personally. A strong personal bond developed between the two men, which lasted until Petrarch's death in 1374. It has been said that, in his later years, Boccaccio questioned the validity of *The Decameron* and that it was Petrarch who persuaded him not to destroy the manuscript.

The last twenty years of Boccaccio's life are characterized by profound introspection, reflection on moral values, and his spiritual evolution. He shared with Petrarch the belief in the spiritual value of poetry and classical literature as being the highest expression of human civilization. During these years, Boccaccio composed his most erudite Latin treatises, which earned him fame as one of the great scholarly Humanists of the fourteenth century: *De mulieribus claris* (c. 1361-1375; *Concerning Famous Women*, 1943), *Genealogia deorum gentilium* (c. 1350-1375; genealogies of the Gentile gods), and *De casibus virorum illustrium* (1355-1374; *The Fall of Princes*, 1431-1438).

Following the political downfall and consequent exile of some of his most powerful friends in Florence in 1360, Boccaccio spent most of the last thirteen years of his life on his farm in Certaldo. He made two return visits to Naples and several trips to see Petrarch. After his last trip to Naples in the autumn of 1370, Boccaccio returned home to recopy and revise *The Decameron*. At the invitation of the city of Florence, he also gave public lectures on *The Divine Comedy*. He retired to Certaldo in 1374, where he died after a long illness on December 21, 1375.

ANALYSIS

An appreciation of the numerous and varied works of Boccaccio must begin with an understanding of the historical and cultural milieu in which they were conceived. Boccaccio was an innovative artist whose development as a writer sprang from a solid foundation on traditional medieval rhetoric and classical models. Evidence of medieval philosophy and literary devices, as well as those of ancient classical writers, pervades all of his works. Boccaccio was also engaged, however, in a new endeavor: the development of an Italian literary language comparably suitable for literary purposes, as Latin had been. Although vernacular Italian had been developed and used in the poetry of such authors as Dante and Petrarch, Boccaccio was the first Italian writer to employ the models of past classical traditions and style to develop a rich vernacular prose for fiction. This singular achievement, coupled with his masterful development of the narrative, places him among the greatest of Italian writers. His remarkable skill in characterization and his unparalleled status as a consummate raconteur influenced writers throughout the world.

A summary glance at the works of Boccaccio tempts the novice to categorize his literary efforts simply into three distinct phases. His first works, both poetry and prose, clearly reflect the conventional medieval treatment of the subject of idealistic courtly love. Characteristic emphasis on rhetorical eloquence, the heavy use of allegory and theological symbolism, and the ever-present influence of Dante as well as classic Greek writers are common threads throughout the writings preceding *The Decameron*.

At least superficially, *The Decameron* itself seems to stand out among the works of Boccaccio as an anomaly. This period in his life as a writer is markedly distinct from any other. In his later years, scholarship replaced creativity in the author, and the object of his efforts was to service the needs of those devoted to erudition. *The Decameron*, however, was neither the exposition of ideals of a romantic young poet nor work written for the consumption of scholars. Rather, it served, by the author's own admission, as a diversion for the new flowering class of the bourgeois public, particularly women. It is a unified collection of tales, many comic, some rather bawdy, written strictly to delight from the perspective of an open-minded realist, with winking tolerance of the flaws of human nature that motivate the actions of his various colorful protagonists.

An adequate analysis of Boccaccio's works must also address the fruits of his labor in an integrated manner. Numerous stylistic, thematic, and structural traits unique to the times and the author himself appear throughout his youthful works as well as his most advanced literary endeavors. The influence of Dante, Petrarch, and other poets who claimed allegiance to *il stil nuovo* (the sweet new style), a popular style of poetry of the time, is evident in the majority of Boccaccio's works, as well as the use of "tertiary rhyme," a rhyming device popularized by Dante. Also borrowed from these poets were the conventional themes of courtly love, the dedication to a particular lady and her heavenly beauty, and the ennobling power of love.

Perhaps the most significant Dantean influence in the works of Boccaccio is the use of allegory, whether under the guise of fictitious narrative, portraying a moral (*Amorous Fiammetta* and *The Decameron*), or as a representation of the refining effects of sensual love (*The Filostrato, The Book of Theseus*, and *The Decameron*). Erotic allegory and the use of history as allegory were also characteristic of Boccaccio's early works.

Boccaccio, like his colleagues, inherited and utilized the thematic resources of Old French ballads and traditions, as evidenced by *Labor of Love, The Filostrato*, and *The Decameron*, with their themes of star-crossed lovers confronting adversity in the form of social or class distinctions and consequent disapproval.

Although Boccaccio incorporated into his writings the vast legacy of literary forms and devices provided by his predecessors, he fashioned these elements into a new style, a new perspective, and created an art form that was to become uniquely his own. Boccaccio's greatest distinction lies in his vivid narrative style and strategy in his prose fiction.

It is first evidenced in embryonic form in *Labor of Love*, which is considered a plot model for *The Decameron*.

It is notable that, in both works, the author himself intrudes to explain his purpose in writing the book: to please the fair sex. *Labor of Love*, like *The Decameron*, begins with a group of characters who escape unpleasant reality by fleeing to a world of fantasy. The stories are told within a certain structure. As in *The Decameron*, there is a presiding officer to order and control the episodic events and certain problematic questions to be addressed and established at the outset.

The technique of writing a narrative that contains within it many narratives is characteristic of Boccaccio. It is present in *The Decameron* and *Labor of Love*; hints of it had also appeared in such earlier works as *The Nymph of Fiesole* and the *L'amorosa visione* (1342-1343; English translation, 1986). Numerous dominant themes and motifs so richly portrayed in *The Decameron* were cultivated in his earlier writings. The pathetic, abandoned, or scorned lover is one such figure; it inhabits *The Decameron* but was introduced in such early works as *The Filostrato, Amorous Fiammetta*, and *L'amorosa visione*. The theme of adultery is present throughout Boccaccio's writings, without necessarily a moral judgment.

The Decameron, however, views such things from a totally new perspective for the Middle Ages: a perspective that shrugs at human indecencies and failings and portrays them in a comic light. It is this unique, delightful perspective that has prompted literary critics to compare *The Decameron* to Dante's *The Divine Comedy*.

THE DECAMERON

First published: *Decameron: O, Prencipe Galetto*, 1349-1351 (English translation, 1620)
Type of work: Novel

Ten young people escape the city of Florence together during the Black Death and amuse each other by telling stories.

Contemporary Florence, during the terrible Black Plague, is the setting chosen by Boccaccio for

The Decameron, which historians generally agree was written between 1349 and 1351. A desire to escape the horrors of the city prompts a group of ten young people (seven women and three men) to retreat to a country villa. There, they amuse themselves by telling each other stories.

The structure of *The Decameron* begins with a frame. The author addresses his readers, whom he presumes to be women, in his prologue, declaring his intent. He offers *The Decameron* as a pleasant distraction to those tormented lovers whose woes are more difficult to endure. He then apologizes to the "charming ladies" for the book's unpleasant but necessary beginning. A graphic description in real-

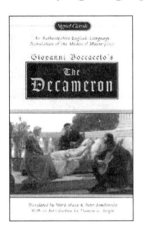

istic detail of the devastation of the plague in the city of Florence follows. The device of the frame was used by Boccaccio in earlier works, but on a smaller scale, as in *Labor of Love*. The frame in *The Decameron* provides a specific location and date to the story, while offering a realistic and reasonable explanation for such a collection of unchaperoned young people in a remote place. It further serves to unify what would otherwise be a loose collection of seemingly unrelated tales. The frame characters are the ten narrators, each endowed with intelligence, breeding, charm, and some distinguishing feature. Once settled in their country villa, it is proposed that each of the ten preside as queen or king for one day, choose a topic for that particular day, and invite everyone to recount an appropriate tale: thus, the significance of ten by ten, or one hundred stories, which explains the title and also satisfies medieval numerology.

The first day is ruled by Pampinea, the oldest, who assumes throughout the book a somewhat mature, motherly stance. There is no appointed topic of the day, but many of the stories told represent the tenor of the book as a whole. The tale of the debauched and irreverent Ciappelletto, who confesses falsely on his deathbed with such seemingly deep contrition to sins so minor as to render him a saint in the perception of those around him, is one

of the most famous stories in *The Decameron*. Vice and virtue intertwine in the work as in life, and Boccaccio chooses to begin with a symbol of ultimate evil.

Filomena rules the second day, and her theme is those who overcome adverse fortune to their advantage. Representative is the story of Andreuccio, a simple-minded horse trader from Perugia, whose misfortunes in the city of Naples teach him to sharpen his wits—an apt lesson for any merchant.

The third day, under the reign of Neifile, is dominated by stories of lust, although the proposed theme is the successes of people who seek to achieve through their own efforts. The use of ingenuity and guile to achieve seduction is common to most of the stories of the day, and members of the clergy are not spared as protagonists in this collection of characters.

The theme of the fourth day, ruled by Filostrata, is in striking contrast to its predecessor. The theme of unhappy loves is designated, and the stories that follow are, for the most part, of a pathetic, if not tragic, nature. One example is the story of Ghismonda, who eloquently defends her love of a man of low breeding to her disapproving father by stating that his is the only true nobility, one of character. Ghismonda ultimately kills herself after her father has the lover's heart cut out and sent to her in a goblet.

The fifth day is ruled by Fiammetta, who calls for stories of lovers whose trials have ended happily. The most moving story is that told by Fiammetta herself: the tale of Ser Federigo and his beloved falcon, which he ultimately sacrifices to please his lady. The focus in this episode is utmost chivalry, a reminder of the traditions dominating contemporary literature, and perhaps a personal comment on nobler times.

The theme for the sixth day, announced by Elissa, is the use of clever retort as a means of avoiding danger or embarrassment. The witty Filippa, who avoids the death penalty for adultery by eliciting an admission from her husband that he was never denied her charms and by exclaiming that she should not be punished for donating her leftovers to others, is exemplary.

The seventh, eighth, and ninth days, ruled by Dioneo, Lauretta, and Emilia, are devoted to tricksters: women who try to fool their husbands or men who play tricks on others. Human astuteness is praised, even if the emphasis seems to be on the comic. Many of the tales concern the Bruno-Buffalmaco pranksters, who never tire of victimizing their simple-minded companion, Calandrino, who is even duped at one point into thinking that he is pregnant.

The stories of the tenth day, according to Panfilo, are to be of those who acted liberally or magnanimously, in love or other matters. The theme on the tenth day is to treat only those actions motivated by generosity or lofty ideas. The last story is that of Griselda, who appears as a symbol of womanly virtue, of humility and goodness, and who thereby offers a poignant contrast to the very first tale and the figure of Ser Ciappelletto.

Viewing *The Decameron* as a whole, it is not surprising that critics have referred to it as "The Human Comedy" while comparing it to Dante's masterpiece. Human nature is examined and reexamined throughout, from the tragic to the comic, from noble to base, but always with a tolerance that is the force behind the comic spirit that only Boccaccio could create.

SUMMARY

Although influenced by past literary traditions and the classics, Giovanni Boccaccio developed a style and language uniquely his own in the area of prose fiction. A review of his earlier works reveals his gradual development toward the skilled use of vernacular Italian in narrative prose form. His masterpiece, *The Decameron*, was written at the pinnacle of his career as a literary artist, displaying without restraint his refined gifts for narration and rich characterization. *The Decameron* not only was an innovation in Italian literature but also became a fertile source of reference for authors throughout the world for centuries to come.

Victor A. Santi

BIBLIOGRAPHY

By the Author

SHORT FICTION:
Decameron: O, Prencipe Galetto, 1349-1351 (*The Decameron,* 1620)

POETRY:
Rime, c. 1330-1340
La caccia di Diana, c. 1334
Il filostrato, c. 1335 (*The Filostrato,* 1873)
Il filocolo, c. 1336 (*Labor of Love,* 1566)
Teseida, 1340-1341 (*The Book of Theseus,* 1974)
Il ninfale d'Ameto, 1341-1342 (also known as *Commedia delle ninfe*)
L'amorosa visione, 1342-1343 (English translation, 1986)
Elegia di Madonna Fiammetta, 1343-1344 (*Amorous Fiammetta,* 1587, better known as *The Elegy of Lady Fiammetta*)
Il ninfale fiesolano, 1344-1346 (*The Nymph of Fiesole,* 1597)
Buccolicum carmen, c. 1351-1366 (*Boccaccio's Olympia,* 1913)

NONFICTION:
Genealogia deorum gentilium, c. 1350-1375
Trattatello in laude di Dante, 1351, 1360, 1373 (*Life of Dante,* 1898)

DISCUSSION TOPICS

- Many of the great Italian writers and artists of medieval and Renaissance times were essentially men of Florence. How did Giovanni Boccaccio, a native Florentine, profit from his life in Naples?

- In what way did the combination of literary works by Dante and Petrarch influence Boccaccio?

- What was Boccaccio's contribution to Italian vernacular literature?

- Investigate the differences between Dante's and Boccaccio's use of allegory.

- Does there appear to be any plan involved in the succession of themes in the ten sections of *The Decameron*?

Corbaccio, c. 1355 (*The Corbaccio*, 1975)

De montibus, silvis, fontibus lacubus, fluminubus, stagnis seu paludibus, et de nominbus maris, c. 1355-1374

De casibus virorum illustrium, 1355-1374 (*The Fall of Princes*, 1431-1438)

De mulieribus claris, c. 1361-1375 (*Concerning Famous Women*, 1943)

Esposizioni sopra la Commedia di Dante, 1373-1374

About the Author

Bergin, Thomas G. *Boccaccio*. New York: Viking Press, 1981.

Branca, Vittore. *Boccaccio: The Man and His Works*. Translated by Richard Monges. New York: New York University Press, 1976.

Dombroski, Robert S., ed. *Critical Perspectives on "The Decameron."* New York: Barnes & Noble Books, 1977.

Edwards, Robert R. *Chaucer and Boccaccio: Antiquity and Modernity*. New York: Palgrave, 2002.

Forni, Pier Massimo. *Adventures in Speech: Rhetoric and Narration in Boccaccio's "Decameron."* Philadelphia: University of Pennsylvania Press, 1996.

Franklin, Margaret. *Boccaccio's Heroines: Power and Virtue in Renaissance Society*. Burlington, Vt.: Ashgate, 2006.

Hollander, Robert. *Boccaccio's Ten Venuses*. New York: Columbia University Press, 1977.

Kuhns, Richard. *"Decameron" and the Philosophy of Storytelling: Author as Midwife and Pimp*. New York: Columbia University Press, 2005.

Migiel, Marilyn. *A Rhetoric of "The Decameron."* Toronto: University of Toronto Press, 2003.

ROBERTO BOLAÑO

Born: Santiago, Chile
    April 28, 1953
Died: Barcelona, Spain
    July 15, 2003

Although his career was brief, Bolaño breathed new life into Hispano-American literature with novels, often epic in scope, that portrayed the equivocal relation of literature to life.

BIOGRAPHY

Roberto Bolaño (boh-LAHN-yoh) Ávalos was born on April 28, 1953, in Santiago, Chile. His father was a truck driver and amateur boxer, his mother a mathematics teacher. Although dyslexic and nearsighted, Bolaño was an enthusiastic reader as a child. The family lived in a series of small cities in south central Chile before moving to Mexico City in 1968.

Bolaño thrived in the Mexican capital, reading voraciously and eclectically, and he dropped out of school to immerse himself in the political and literary culture. He was especially devoted to poetry. Very much in the spirit of the hippie era, Bolaño grew his hair long and had a permanently hungry look. He joined the Trotskyite faction of Mexican communism and traveled to El Salvador to take part in the leftist movements there. In 1973, he returned to Chile to support the socialist government of President Salvador Allende. Not long afterward, General Augusto Pinochet Ugarte staged a coup, and Bolaño worked as a courier in the resistance to the military regime. He was arrested and spent eight days in jail as a political prisoner.

In 1974, Bolaño was again in Mexico City. There, with his friend Mario Santiago, he formed a reactionary literary movement, Infrarealism, influenced by Dadaism and the French Surrealist poet André Breton. Intent upon disrupting the staid establishment poetry of such figures as Octavio Paz (who won the 1990 Nobel Prize in Literature), Bolaño and Santiago soon became notorious for disrupting poetry readings by shouting out their own poetry from the audience. His first book of poetry was published in 1976, entitled *Reinventar el*

amor (reinventing love), and a similar volume appeared shortly afterward.

Infrarealism, however, proved short-lived, and a failed romance moved Bolaño to leave Mexico in 1977. After a year traveling through France, Spain, and North Africa, he lived for a while in Barcelona. He worked as an itinerant laborer in a variety of jobs, such as salesman, night watchman, dock worker, and grape picker, and continued to write poetry. He was also struggling with heroine addiction. He overcame it and in 1982 married Carolina Lopez, a Catalonian. He finally settled in the resort town of Blanes on the Catalonian coast and in 1984 published his first novel, *Consejos de un discípulo de Morrison a un fanático de Joyce* (advice of a disciple of Morrison to a Joyce fanatic), written with Antoni García Porta.

In 1990, he and his wife had a son, Lautaro, and later a daughter, Alexandra. To earn a living for his family, which he called his "only motherland," Bolaño concentrated on writing fiction. Able to devote himself to writing for long periods, he was prolific. By 1996, he was publishing at least one novel every year, as well as poems, essays, and newspaper columns.

It was the publication of *Los detectives salvajes* in 1998 that made him a sensation among Hispanic readers, as did its 2007 translation, *The Savage Detectives*, for English readers. In 1999, the novel earned him the Rómulo Gallegos Prize, the Spanish equivalent of the Pulitzer Prize, as well as the Herralde Prize the same year. He also won the Municipal Prize of Santiago for an earlier novel, *Llamadas telefónicas* (1997; phone calls). He published three volumes of poetry, and his nonfiction is collected in *El gaucho insufrible* (2000; the insufferable gaucho) and *Entre paréntesis: Ensayos, artículos, y discursos, 1998-2003* (2004; in parentheses: essays, articles, and discourses, 1998-2003).

Widely considered a major new writer, Bolaño remained a maverick, outspoken and often caustic. He disaffected mainstream writers, ridiculing, for instance, the Colombian Nobel laureate Gabriel García Márquez and the Chilean writer Isabel Allende. Nevertheless, his reputation steadily grew. At the same time, his health declined. Aware that he was dying, he rushed to complete a series of five interrelated narratives in order to ensure financial security for his family. He died on July 15, 2003, in a Barcelona hospital while awaiting a liver transplant. A year later these last fictional works, edited by his literary executor, were published as a single book, cryptically titled *2666* (2004; English translation, 2008), more than 1,100 pages long. It was an immediate success, hailed by some critics as the most important book in a generation.

ANALYSIS

Roberto Bolaño was a writer's writer. Literature was his subject matter. The fictions that people make out of their own lives constitute his primary theme, and the dangers of those fictions, especially as manifest in obsession, ambition, and self-deception, provide the narrative suspense of his plots. Moreover, he readily displays his debt to his favorite authors: Chilean writer Nicanor Parra, Argentine writers Jorge Luis Borges and Julio Cortázar, American writer Thomas Pynchon, and Irish writer James Joyce. Scores more are mentioned in his works, as well as literary movements, aesthetics, contests, prizes, and films. Each novel opens a panorama on modern literature, and many novels are interrelated.

Bolaño himself frequently appears as a character in his fiction, named directly or as "B" or as his alter ego, Arturo Belano. In fact, he draws much of his material from his own experience and that of people he knew. *The Savage Detectives*, for instance, borrows from his times with his friend Santiago, so much so that its second section is practically a roman à clef. This foundation in actual history helps give his fiction its exuberant immediacy and restlessness. Nearly all characters live wandering existences, and the hint is that those who settle down lose the vitality that sets them apart, for better

or worse. Many fictional characters also appear in more than one of Bolaño's novels, and passages in some novels give rise to later novels, as is the case with *Estrella distante* (1996; *Distant Star*, 2004), which expands on the ending of *La literatura Nazi en América* (1996; *Nazi Literature in the Americas*, 2008).

Bolaño makes use of several genres, mixing them, so that his narratives emerge from literary conventions but are not bound by them. Detectives and the pursuit of a mystery are central to his plots, either actual detectives like Romero in *Nazi Literature in the Americas*, amateur detectives like Belano and Lima, or scholars like those in the first section of *2666*. There are also scenes appropriate to satire, crime thrillers, romantic comedy, and the coming-of-age novel. Many stories are told by first-person narrators. This technique intensifies the immediacy of the narratives, but additionally Bolaño creates a prismatic effect in such novels as *The Savage Detectives* by using dozens of narrators, so that a story is not so much told as pieced together from every possible viewpoint.

Neither the intense literariness of the novels nor their manipulation of popular genres are ends in themselves. Quite to the contrary, Bolaño undermines conventions and foils the expectations of genre. His protagonists end up antiheroes, usually near death or left in fear and doubt at a novel's end. The effect is to remove literature from its usual status as an artifact, an entertainment created by satisfying typical plot and character patterns, and to impel readers to see the characters not as simply literary creations but as possible lives. In other words, when a fiction is not conventional, it seems more individual and lifelike. His innovation appears most strikingly in his refusal to offer neat resolutions for the conflicts that power his narratives, leaving unclear, for example, the fate of central characters or the truth about a mystery. This is a crucial quality to Bolaño's work, which Spanish critic Ignacio Echeverria termed the "poetics of inconclusivness." Much of previous Western literature, especially that of Latin America, has been criticized for becoming moribund because writers are content to satisfy the generic norms for closure or are obsessed with the aesthetics of aging literary movements. Bolaño makes a departure. Because he does, his stories appeal more to readers' knowledge of life rather than to their understanding of literary traditions.

Accordingly, Bolaño's fiction expresses human relationships and thereby reflects society, particularly politics. Having himself lived through political turmoil, he investigates the mechanics of moral failure and competition for power under the guise of ideology. To one of his translators, Chris Andrews, Bolaño's novels are an anatomy of social evil. Andrews distinguishes "four faces" of turpitude among Bolaño's characters: dictators, because they seek superiority; administrators, because they are concerned only with their own advancement within a system; accomplices (those who simply go along with events), because fear governs them; and sociopaths, because they care only for themselves. In a complementary approach, critic Siddhartha Deb argues that Bolaño's novels break down the distinctions between the past and the present, the imagination and experience, and the conscious and subconscious. Above all, Bolaño possesses a superior power among experimental writers to involve readers in the chancy, vital world of his stories.

THE SAVAGE DETECTIVES

First published: *Los detectives salvajes*, 1998
(English translation, 2007)
Type of work: Novel

An avant-garde movement in Mexico colors the lives of a disparate group of poets, revealing the symbiosis between society and literature.

The Savage Detectives recounts the history of avant-garde poets from 1975 in Mexico City until 1996 in Africa. Their literary movement, visceral realism, begins with a mischievous revolutionary fervor but later spins apart through jealousy, murder, flight, despair, insanity, and, in a very few cases, self-discovery. Although the underlying plotline is straightforward, the narrative structure and multiple points of view belong uniquely to this novel. It is divided into three sections that present the story out of chronological order.

"Mexicans Lost in Mexico" concerns the last two months of 1975 and takes place wholly in Mexico City. It is told through the diary entries of Juan García Madero, a seventeen-year-old whose ambi-

tion is to study literature and become a poet. He encounters two older poets, Arturo Belano and Ulysses Lima. Belano and Lima are *poètes maudits*, the founders of visceral realism, which is defined mostly by its vigorous opposition to mainstream Mexican literature. They gather about them a variety of younger poets, painters, and dancers, publish magazines, organize or invade poetry readings, and migrate from one dive to another in endless discussion. To finance their literary work they peddle marijuana. By chance, the pair discovers that a previous poet also used the term visceral realism to describe a literary movement. This poet is Cesárea Tinajero, a shadowy figure from the 1920's known for a single published poem. Belano and Lima decide to track her down.

Meanwhile, García Madero helps rescue a young prostitute, Lupe, from her pimp. As the section draws to a close, the pimp threatens violence if Lupe is not returned to him. With the timely help of Belano and Lima, García Madero and Lupe barely escape a shootout. The four flee Mexico City, heading for Sonora and the last known location of Tinajero

The long middle section, "The Savage Detectives," leaps forward in time. Belano and Lima have fled to Europe; no mention of García Madero or Lupe occurs until the last pages. The section comprises a series of testimonies about Lima and Belano told by former visceral realists and some others whom the pair interviewed about Tinajero. Although there is much humor (often bitterly ironical), sex, emotional and situational drama, literary and political quarreling, and historical anecdotes, the tone of these testimonies is curiously flat, as if they are legal depositions. With occasional exceptions they are presented in chronological order from 1976 until 1996. As each person tells a story, the reader gradually accumulates information about Belano and Lima. The reader learns that something bad has happened to them, and they live like lost souls, bouncing from one place to another in Nicaragua, France, Spain, Austria, and Israel. Lima eventually turns up in Mexico City again, years later, a broken man. Belano continues to write, makes a modest living for himself in Barcelona, marries, has a son, divorces, falls desperately sick with pancreatitis, and slides into despair. Knowing that he is dying, he goes to Africa as a correspondent, hoping to be killed in action. He is last seen near Monrovia, Liberia, trying to evade a rebel army.

"The Sonora Desert" reverts to García Madero's diary, which records the events of the first six weeks of 1976. Belano, Lima, Lupe, and García Madero speed north in a borrowed car, pursued by Lupe's pimp and his henchman. Searching throughout Sonora, Belano and Lima at last succeed in their detective work: They find Tinajero working as a washerwoman in a border town of down-and-out killers. Although her life has been a long decline into poverty, she has filled notebooks with her writing. Just as the four fugitives contact her, the pimp finally catches up. In a scene that bursts from tranquility into violence, Belano and Lima kill their pursuers with Tinajero's help, and she is killed in the process. In a cuttingly ironical twist, they never have a chance to talk to her about visceral realism. The four fugitives then split up. The final pages concern García Madero and Lupe, who have become lovers. He finds Tinajero's notebooks and reads them. Although he does not describe their contents in his diary, he refers to them as if they are a disappointment. He is forced to see beyond his ambition to become a poet, and the future looks as bleak as the desert that he and Lupe continue to roam.

Like García Madero, the antitype of Belano, Belano himself comes to recognize that the frame of his literary interest—visceral realism or any literary program—affords too narrow a perspective on what is really visceral in a person's experience. As a character remarks about one seriocomic episode, "It gave us a glimpse of ourselves in our common humanity. It wasn't proof of our idle guilt but a sign of our miraculous and pointless innocence." That is the real savagery of *The Savage Detectives*.

BY NIGHT IN CHILE

First published: *Nocturno de Chile*, 2000
   (English translation, 2003)
Type of work: Novella

On his death bed, a priest and literary critic seeks to justify his life, a life that is emblematic of Chile.

By Night in Chile opens with Father Sebastián Urrutia Lacroix, a celebrated literary critic and poet, on his deathbed confessing to the reader that although once at peace with himself, he no longer is. He is tormented by accusations from a mysterious "wizened youth" and struggles to justify his life. What follows, printed in a single paragraph, is a turbulent montage of images, anecdotes, stories, allegories, laments, and delusions.

Who the wizened youth is and the exact nature of his accusations provide the tension. There are hints of illicit sexuality, beginning with Urrutia's own father, who is remembered only in shadowy, phallic imagery, yet sex is but one of several diversionary leitmotifs. Urrutia enters the seminary at age thirteen, against his father's will, and soon after graduation in the late 1950's decides to become a literary figure. He allies himself to Chile's preeminent literary critic, who writes under the pen name Farewell. The mentor is indeed an old-fashioned

example of the Western literati, effete, independently wealthy, and sterile. Through Farewell, young Father Urrutia socializes with the cultural elite, meeting such luminaries as poet Pablo Neruda and eventually becoming a prominent critic and university professor himself.

However, as he seeks to foster Chilean literature in the patronizingly European mode of his mentor, Urrutia himself is suborned by politics. A conservative, he joins Opus Dei and is recruited by a Mr. Raef (fear) and Mr. Etah (hate) on a secret mission to save the great churches of Europe from deterioration. There follows black comedy, variously hilarious, touching, and outraging, as Father Urrutia travels through Europe and discovers that the greatest danger to the physical church is from the excrement of pigeons and doves, traditional symbols of peace.

Father Urrutia returns to Chile in time to witness the coup by General Augusto Pinochet Ugarte and the subsequent rule by a military junta. Again, Mr. Raef and Mr. Etah recruit him on a secret mission, this time to lecture the ruling generals on the fundamentals of Marxism, so that they better understand the mentality of their enemies. Another episode of dark comedy ensues as the generals behave like teenagers.

Meanwhile, Father Urrutia has to cease publishing his own poetry because he discovers, to his own horror, that themes of desolation, heresy, and despair irrepressibly emerge. At this point in his recollections, Father Urrutia comes to recognize that like many of his literary compatriots, his appreciation of Chile's underlying culture is selective, often precious, and self-deceiving. It is the Catholic Church and the voracious, militant conservatism of people such as Pinochet Ugarte that represents the real motive force in society. "Is it *always* possible for a man to know what is good and what is bad?" he asks piteously, understanding at last that the answer is no and that he, like other intellectuals, has let himself be used, out of vanity, by those in power for the maintenance of power. Two final recognitions come, both devastating to the priest: that "what we call literature" is simply a means to avoid a collapse into barbarity and that his mocking nemesis, the wizened youth, is his own conscience.

NAZI LITERATURE IN THE AMERICAS

First published: *La literatura Nazi en América*, 1996 (English translation, 2008)
Type of work: Novel

A faux biographical encyclopedia, this novel satirizes fascist literature, whose violent milieu entangles the central character, the author himself.

Nazi Literature in the Americas has the appearance of a biographical encyclopedia. The entries, varying in length from half a page to nearly thirty pages, discuss writers from throughout the two continents and from early in the twentieth century to as late as 2029, with Argentina receiving the most attention (eight entries) and the United States placing second (seven entries). There are writers of nearly all genres. Through most of the book the tone is detached, judicious, and scholarly. Gradually, however, as the author discusses thirty-one authors with fascist sensibilities under thirteen headings, it becomes clear to the reader that he is far from detached and that his purpose is ridicule. Moreover, he becomes involved in their world despite himself.

The headings provide a major clue to the author's attitude. The first is benign, "The Mendiluce Clan," about a wealthy poet and essayist who becomes a friend of Adolf Hitler, and, along with her daughter and son, are doyens of nationalistic, conservative literature in Argentina. As the book progresses, the headings turn increasingly sinister, for instance, "Poètes Maudits," "The Aryan Brotherhood," "The Infamous Ramírez Hoffman," and finally the "Epilogue for Monsters," which lists secondary writers, publishing houses, and books. The writers themselves, despite their varying styles and genres, reflect a reactionary vision of utopia, using such jingoist jargon as "golden age," "new order," "American awakening," "will," "new dawn," "rebirth of the nation," "resurrection," and "the absolute." Their underlying yearning is for autocracy based, variously, on race, creed, ideology, or class.

While espousing "family values" and other standards of conduct, few of the writers practice what they preach. Herein lies the book's mordant humor. These writers are violent (soccer thugs, mercenaries, torturers, and murderers), sexually promiscuous and deviant, sometimes ignorant, and treacherous. As the author comments about one writer, "Real life can sometimes bear an unsettling resemblance to nightmares." About Max Mirabilis, a writer who plagiarizes and lies shamelessly, the author observes that he learned two methods to achieve what he wanted—through violence and through literature, "which is a surreptitious form of violence, a passport of respectability, and can, in certain young and sensitive nations, disguise the social climber's origins." A coward, Mirabilis chooses literature. Others are lunatics, such as the Chilean Pedro González Carrera, who reports having been visited by "Merovingian extraterrestrials" and admires the Italian dictator Benito Mussolini.

The last writer is a figure of horror. A Chilean, Carlos Ramírez Hoffman is an air force pilot who creates poetic skywriting over Santiago. He is also a member of a death squad, murders a series of people, tortures others, then disappears. At this point the author, Bolaño, enters the novel as a character. Abel Romero, a private investigator on the trail of Ramírez Hoffman, asks for Bolaño's help. Together they track him down, but Bolaño begs Romero not to kill Ramírez Hoffman: "He can't hurt anyone now, I said. But I didn't really believe it. Of course he could. We all could. I'll be right back, said Romero." The ending insists that literature, even literature written by the lunatic fringe, has a way of turning personal.

SUMMARY

Toward the end of the twentieth century critics began to recognize in Roberto Bolaño a writer of force and invention beyond any other in Spanish-language literature. He is regularly called a genius, a trailblazer, the premier novelist of his generation, and a writer for the new era. Although his roots in the last century's Latin American literature are pronounced, Bolaño had no interest in imitating the Magical Realism of such writers as García Márquez or the nationalism of the "boom" of the 1960's. Because of that, Bolaño's work is refreshing, and it became a central influence in Latin American literature.

Nevertheless, to call Bolaño a Latin American writer, however much the continent flavors his fiction, is misleading. Much of his work takes place in the United States, Europe, or Africa. It is more accurate to consider his Latin Americanism as the impetus for his vagabond-like explorations of experience than as a regional or racial mentality. As another of his translators, Natasha Wimmer, notes in her preface to *The Savage Detectives*, Bolaño's appeal has been broad because he was not really from any one place, although he had ties to Chile, Mexico, and Spain; instead, he wrote postnationalist fiction. It is appropriate to an era when the status of nations is changing in the globalization of culture.

Roger Smith

BIBLIOGRAPHY

By the Author

LONG FICTION:
Consejos de un discípulo de Morrison a un fanático de Joyce, 1984 (with Antoni García Porta)
La pista de hielo, 1993
La senda de los elefantes, 1993 (also known as *Monsieur Pain*, 1999)
La literatura Nazi en América, 1996 (*Nazi Literature in the Americas*, 2008)
Estrella distante, 1996 (*Distant Star*, 2004)
Los detectives salvajes, 1998 (*The Savage Detectives*, 2007)
Amuleto, 1999 (*Amulet*, 2006)
Nocturno de Chile, 2000 (*By Night in Chile*, 2003)
Una novelita lumpen, 2002
2666, 2004 (English translation, 2008)

Roberto Bolaño

SHORT FICTION:
Llamadas telefónicas, 1997
Putas asesinas, 2001
El gaucho insufrible, 2003 (short stories and essays)
Last Evenings on Earth, 2006
El secreto del mal, 2007

POETRY:
Reinventar al amor, 1976
Muchachos desnudos bajo el arcoiris de fuego, 1979
Fragmentos de la universidad desconocida, 1993
Los perros románticos: Poemas, 1980-1998, 2000
Tres, 2000

NONFICTION:
Entre paréntesis: Ensayos, artículos, y discursos, 1998-2003 , 2004

About the Author

Andrews, Chris. "Varieties of Evil." *Meanjin* 66 (September, 2007): 200-206.

Corral, Will H. "Portrait of the Writer as a Noble Savage." *World Literature Today* 80 (November/December, 2006): 4-8

Deb, Siddhartha. "The Wandering Years: Roberto Bolaño's Nomadic Fiction." *Harper's Magazine* 314 (April, 2007): 99-106.

Ocasio, Rafael. *Literature of Latin America.* Westport, Conn.: Greenwood Press, 2004.

Zalewski, Daniel. "Vagabonds: Roberto Bolaño and His Fractured Masterpiece." *The New Yorker* 83 (March 26, 2007): 82-88.

DISCUSSION TOPICS

- Define "visceral realism" in *The Savage Detectives.* Is it a literary movement, a way of life, a fraud, an affectation, or a mixture of these?

- Roberto Bolaño's novels frequently have a central mystery or shadowy character that appears to motivate the plot, but they are never themselves completely elucidated. Why?

- Bolaño employs multiple points of view and narrative voices in some of his novels. Discuss how this technique builds suspense in *The Savage Detectives.* Does it lead to a resolution?

- Is Father Urrutia's attitude toward literature in *By Night in Chile* similar to Bolaño's?

- What details in *Nazi Literature in the Americas* suggest that it is fiction instead of a reference work? Discuss their effect, such as humor, satire, and political or literary critique, among others.

HEINRICH BÖLL

Born: Cologne, Germany
    December 21, 1917
Died: Merten, West Germany (now in Germany)
    July 16, 1985

A Nobel laureate in literature, Böll was known worldwide as the conscience of postwar Germany, attacking evils and advocating the humane through his speeches, essays, short stories, and novels.

© The Nobel Foundation

BIOGRAPHY

Heinrich Theodor Böll (buhl) was born December 21, 1917, in Cologne, Germany, to Victor and Marie Hermanns Böll, solidly middle-class, liberal Catholics from old Rhineland families. Böll's native region, the time of his birth, his parents' class, and their moral and religious convictions all were strong influences on his character and works. Although his parents suffered from the inflation of the 1920's and the Depression of the 1930's, so that Böll sometimes identified his background as middle-class, other times as proletarian, the Bölls provided their children with security, understanding, and freedom but did not hide social problems from them. Devout but independent-minded Catholics, the elder Bölls taught their children the tenets of Christian love but never forced formal practices on them. Consequently, young Böll realized the injustice when many of his proletarian friends could not attend *Gymnasium* (college preparatory school) with him.

An adolescent in the 1930's when Adolf Hitler rose to power, Böll never embraced Nazi teachings or activities, mainly because of the influence of his family. After *Gymnasium*, Böll worked in a bookstore, where he read such proscribed thinkers as Karl Marx and Sigmund Freud, until he was conscripted for compulsory labor in 1938 and 1939.

Later in 1939, shortly after entering the University of Cologne (with difficulty, since he was not a Nazi Party member), he was drafted into the army. Always opposed to war and Nazism, Böll suffered wounds three times; he deserted, forged passes, and devised his capture by Americans. He witnessed atrocities of Hitlerism but also enough incidents of compassion to reject the doctrine of collective guilt.

Returning to a bombed-out Cologne in November, 1945, Böll reentered the university to acquire a ration card, worked in the family carpentry shop and, later, for the city, and wrote; but his wife, Annemarie Cech, an English teacher whom he had married in 1942, virtually supported the family. A voracious reader, Böll had written six novels before the war. In 1947, he began publishing stories in periodicals. Two of these stories, about the difficulties of the postwar years, led Middelhauve, a publisher of technical books, to contract for Böll's fiction. In 1949, Middelhauve published the novella *Der Zug war pünktlich* (*The Train Was on Time*, 1956) and in 1950, *Wanderer, kommst du nach Spa . . .* (*Traveller, If You Come to Spa*, 1956), short stories about wartime and postwar dreams of a better world.

In 1951, *Wo warst du, Adam?* (*Adam, Where Art Thou?*, 1955), a novel about the absurdity of war, established Böll with critics. The same year, Gruppe 47, a prominent coterie of writers who met to read, criticize, and encourage one another's work, awarded its annual prize to Böll's humorous story "Die schwarzen Schafe" ("The Black Sheep"). In 1952, with a new publisher, Kiepenheuer and

Witsch, and a new novel about postwar poverty, hypocrisy, and bigotry, *Und sagte kein einziges Wort* (1953; *Acquainted with the Night*, 1954), Böll achieved financial and popular success. Throughout the 1950's, he produced a steady stream of novels, stories, radio plays, essays, humor, satire, and the pleasant *Irisches Tagebuch* (1957; *Irish Journal*, 1967), an account of his visits to Ireland, which he admired for its genuine Catholicism and its antimaterialism. These works won a steady stream of literary prizes.

Billard um halbzehn (1959; *Billiards at Half-Past Nine*, 1961) and the 1963 best seller *Ansichten eines Clowns* (*The Clown*, 1965) contrast the evil, materialistic, institutional, opportunistic "buffaloes" with the persecuted, sensitive "lambs." *The Clown* shows the influence of American novelist J. D. Salinger, whose *The Catcher in the Rye* (1951) Böll had translated in 1962. In the 1960's, Böll was also active in public life. His *Brief an einen jungen Katholiken* (1961; letter to a young Catholic) criticizes the position of the Church in Nazi and postwar Germany. In four lectures given at the University of Frankfurt in 1963 and 1964 and published in 1966, Böll identifies love, language, and commitment as defining human qualities and advocates an "aesthetic of the humane." In 1968, having witnessed the invasion of Czechoslovakia while visiting writers in Prague, Böll protested Soviet policies. In 1969, he campaigned for Willy Brandt and the Social Democrats against the authoritarian government of Konrad Adenauer's Christian Democrats.

Elected president of PEN, an international association of writers, in 1971, Böll in this position aided a number of Soviet dissidents, among them the novelist Aleksandr Solzhenitsyn. In 1972, the Swedish Academy gave Böll the Nobel Prize in Literature, citing especially *Gruppenbild mit Dame* (1971; *Group Portrait with Lady*, 1973), a recapitulation of the social and moral criticism that had filled his earlier works.

Although in poor health, Böll remained active in the 1970's and 1980's. His advocacy of due process for the terrorist Baaden-Meinhoff gang, which had been tried and condemned in the press, initiated a long controversy between Böll and the establishment. Böll's novels *Die verlorene Ehre der Katharina Blum: Oder, Wie Gewalt entstehen und wohin sie führen kann* (1974; *The Lost Honor of Katharina Blum: Or, How Violence Develops and Where It Can*

Lead, 1975) and *Fürsorgliche Belagerung* (1979; *The Safety Net*, 1982) depict, respectively, the "public violence" of journalistic slander and the horrors of both terrorism and systematic protection. In 1981, Böll joined the Bonn peace demonstration, a last straw, perhaps, that made Christian Democrats oppose making the social critic, but not the "great writer," an honorary citizen of Cologne. Böll responded that the two were one.

Böll died in Merten, West Germany, on July 16, 1985. *Frauen vor Flusslandschaft* (1985; *Women in a River Landscape*, 1988), about life in West Germany's capital, was published the next month.

ANALYSIS

In an interview given in 1976, Böll remarked: "There are authors whose immediate impulse to write is political. Mine was not." Indeed, he asserted, perhaps denying the salutary effects of didactic literature, perhaps denying the effects of circumstances on character, "I am of the conviction that what comes to one from outside does not change one very much. . . . Everything history throws at one's feet, war, peace, Nazis, communists, the bourgeois, is really secondary." Nevertheless, sociopolitical criticism, even satire, plays a primary part in his writings—so much so that Böll-scholar Robert Conrad warns critics against denying that Böll's work is "motivated by the challenge to gain aesthetic control over the experience of Nazi Germany, postwar guilt, and the inadequacies of West German democracy." Moreover, at the end of *The Lost Honor of Katharina Blum*, Böll's narrator affirms, though ironically: "Art still has a social function."

Böll's art indeed has a social function. In the early war story *Traveller, If You Come to Spa*, Böll discredits classical education that encourages war by emphasizing the martial: A mutilated soldier evacuated to his old *Gymnasium*, now a field hospital, observes the schoolroom ornaments—statues of a hoplite, Julius Caesar, Frederick the Great—and a war memorial. *Acquainted with the Night* shows the inequities in the currency revaluation and the Economic Miracle: A middle-aged husband working full-time cannot earn a decent living for his family. *Das Brot der frühen Jahre* (1955; *The Bread of Our Early Years*, 1957), shows another side: An up-and-coming young employee, whose former poverty has made him acquisitive, at last rejects the capitalist system, its excess profits, and its callousness, which is manifested in his fiancé, the boss's daughter. *Haus ohne Hüter* (1954; *Tomorrow and Yesterday,* 1957) shows poverty almost naturalistically determining the choices of one war widow, whereas another lives in inherited wealth not redistributed in the postwar democracy. *The Clown* castigates the cooperative establishment—the government, economic system, and Church—which lacks concern for the little people. *Group Portrait with Lady* criticizes the Communist Party for failure to live by its principles and Christian Democratic capitalism for its very tenets: profit, private ownership, self-interest, the exploitation of natural and human resources. The novel offers an alternative: direct antiexploitation action, rejection of excess profit taking, moderate work, and informal socialism. Böll's last book, about corruption in the Bonn government, "the only state we have," is certainly political.

Böll also said that he considered writing primarily a craft, but some critics have found his diction flat and his narration neither craftsmanlike nor inspired. Most, however, have recognized that Böll, like Günter Grass and other contemporaries, solved the problem of writing with a language that Nazi usage had made depraved and untruthful, by using elementary diction and syntax to reflect elemental or indifferent conditions, by playing ironically on Nazi perversions of the language, and by "bring[ing] something from a foreign terrain" into German by translating foreign literature. Böll has proven able to use diction and syntax to create many individual voices in his complex and sophisticated narrative structures.

In Böll's style and structure, critic J. H. Reid has found a number of the "marks of modernism": the disappearance of the "'omniscient,' commenting narrator" and his assumed audience; the reduction of chronological plot; "a tendency to spatialize . . . through montage, leitmotifs, and the reduction of narrated time." In *Acquainted with the Night,* for example, the husband and wife narrate alternate chapters, apparently as interior monologues with no communication between the two or with the reader. Though the narration of *Tomorrow and Yesterday* and *Billiards at Half-Past Nine* is in the third person, the narrator is rarely apparent; both novels are told from multiple viewpoints of unreliable characters, in two cases those of confused adolescents. In *Billiards at Half-Past Nine,* the account of three generations of a German middle-class family is refracted in the characters' memories in the course of ten hours. One character's daily billiard playing serves as a leitmotif; his random creation of geometric patterns by rolling the balls over the table symbolizes the apparently random structure of the novel. (Böll, of course, had to plan the structure carefully; he often did so with complex spatial color graphs.)

These practices create an autonomous aesthetic structure detached from literary traditions and, in many modern novels, an autonomous subjective world detached from the external world. In *The Clown,* for instance, the world is presented exclusively as Hans Schnier understands it. Yet, in *The Clown,* as in most of Böll's works, the real world and real time are the objects of the narrator's perceptions, and Böll's social criticism seldom gets lost in the narrator's psyche.

In his later works, Böll employs numerous postmodern (or premodern) techniques, as in *Entfernung von der Truppe* (1964; *Absent Without Leave,* 1965). Commentator Hans Magnus Enzenberger has enunciated the duty of the postmodern writer to take direct action or to document the struggles of the oppressed; Böll did both.

THE CLOWN

First published: *Ansichten eines Clowns,* 1963
   (English translation, 1965)
Type of work: Novel

> *In postwar Germany, a professional clown condemns materialism, opportunism, hypocrisy, and the Church and society's subordination of people to regulations.*

Although both its artistry and its themes have drawn contradictory evaluations, *The Clown* artfully reveals the perceptions of the title character, Hans Schnier. Hans's past-tense narration of three crucial hours creates the immediacy of stream of consciousness, punctuated with telephone conversations that trigger Hans's opinionated memories of his childhood in World War II and his life as an outsider in the postwar period.

Returning to his Bonn apartment, drunken, failed, and penniless after an injury on stage, Hans, the scion of the "brown-coal Schniers," who has separated himself from his wealthy family and their values, grieves that his companion, Marie Derkam, the Catholic daughter of an old socialist, has left him after seven years to marry Heribert Züpfner, a Catholic lay functionary. Hans telephones his family and Marie's circle of Catholics to seek money and news of Marie. In conversations with the Catholic officials, Hans espouses the spiritual and sensual marriage in which the lovers "offer each other the sacrament" and rejects the validity of legal and ecclesiastical marriage if it lacks reciprocal grace. Denying the virtue of Hans's relationship with Marie, the Catholics defend submission to "abstract principles of order" and reveal that Marie and Züpfner are honeymooning in Rome.

A call to Hans's socially prominent mother, a nationalist racist who in 1945 urged a last stand of children against the "Jewish Yankee" but now directs the Societies for the Reconciliation of Racial Differences, points up the hypocrisy of many rehabilitated Nazis in postwar Germany—as do Hans's recollections of Herbert Kalick, his Hitler Youth leader who has been decorated for popularizing democracy among the youth of postwar Germany. Hans cannot forget or forgive Kalick's responsibility for the death of a little orphan boy. Nor can Hans forgive his mother's sending her adolescent daughter, Henrietta, to death on antiaircraft patrol in the last days of the war.

Informed that Hans is in Bonn, his father, the industrialist whose fine looks and manner have made him a television spokesman for German economic renewal, visits the apartment and offers to support Hans if he will train with a "famous" mime recommended by a "famous" critic. Hans rejects his father's philistinism and his reverence for "money in the abstract." Although he remembers gratefully his father's having saved two women from execution in 1945, Hans rebuffs the old capitalist who accommodates himself to whatever political and social authority is current.

In other telephone conversations and memories, Hans condemns a popular preacher, Somerwild, and through him the Church, for pseudointellectualism, sophistry, and worldly self-aggrandizement. His brother, Leo, a seminarian, resists breaking curfew to bring Hans companionship and money—further evidence of legalism's inhibiting the Church's mission of consolation and charity. In reverie Hans foresees a stultifying conventional middle-class life for Marie and Züpfner.

A call from his agent and meditations on his profession, especially his memory of having refused to play satires on the West German democracy in East Germany, reveal Hans to be an artist in the tradition of the German cabaret clown: an entertainer whose satire reveals society to itself. After the three hours' traffic that passes in his mind, Hans, integrity intact but completely isolated from both groups and individuals, returns in cracked white face to the train station. There, still looking for a few coins and Marie, he sings a ballad of Catholic politics in Bonn with small hope that his performance may yet make church and state see itself. Yet if Marie, he says, sees him like this and remains with Züpfner, then she is dead and they are divorced. Institutional religion will have killed reciprocal love.

GROUP PORTRAIT WITH LADY

First published: *Gruppenbild mit Dame*, 1971 (English translation, 1973)
Type of work: Novel

An investigator researches the life of a naïve, sensual, generous woman who survives the vicissitudes of German history from 1922 to 1970.

Group Portrait with Lady, the comprehensive novel that earned for Böll the Nobel Prize, is written as the report of an investigator, identified only as the Author ("Au."), on the lady, Helene Marie ("Leni") Gruyten Pfeiffer, forty-eight in 1970, who has lived in but not with the Third Reich, the occupation, and the growth of the Federal Republic in Cologne. Au.'s informants and others whose lives touch Leni's constitute the 125-member group in the portrait. Although Au. professes to be an absolutely objective seeker of facts, he appears instead to be an advocate of Leni as a contemporary humanist saint, an alternate to the ambition-driven heroes of "Christian" capitalism.

Although the first half of the book recounts

Leni's life chronologically from 1938 to 1945, it is distractingly composed of short testimonies from the informants and the longer analytic commentary of Au. Named "Most German girl" in her elementary school for her blondness, Leni, mystically sensual but not cerebral, leaves convent school in 1938 at sixteen to work for her father, a building contractor. In 1940, when her brother and her sweetheart, Cousin Edward, are executed for selling an antitank gun to the Danes in reaction to serving in Hitler's army, Leni grieves terribly. Yet the next year she marries Alois Pfeiffer, a crude soldier whose lewd dancing she has mistaken for sensual love. When he dies in battle, she does not grieve but renews her association with the sensual, mystical Jewish nun from her convent school, Sister Rahel. In 1942, Sister Rahel dies of malnutrition; Leni's father is imprisoned for defrauding the government and distributing wealth by means of a dummy company, and all of his property, except Leni's house, is confiscated. Making an easy transition from middle class to proletarian, Leni in 1943 takes the job that she will hold for twenty-seven years. Indifferent to social class, race, or nationality, Leni makes wreaths in a microcosm: Pelzer, the nursery owner, is an opportunist forgivable because of terrible memories of childhood poverty; Leni's fellow workers include Nazis, neutrals, a disguised Jew, a Communist, and a Russian prisoner of war.

The structural and thematic center of *Group Portrait with Lady* recounts the love of Leni and Boris, the joyful Germanophile Russian prisoner. It begins with Leni's spontaneous act of humanity: On his first day in captivity, she offers Boris a cup of her precious coffee. The ecstasy of their first touch, hand on hand, illustrates spiritual sensuality. Their lovemaking in the cemetery during air raids demonstrates the power of life in the face of death; their fidelity, the true marriage that occurs when the lovers offer each other the sacrament.

With the birth of Boris and Leni's son, Lev, during the Allies' nine-hour raid on Cologne, the mode of narration changes. Au. records fluent accounts of 1945 in the words and voices of the informants: Boris in German uniform is captured by the Allies and dies in Lorraine; Leni, a natural commu-

nist who instinctively shrinks "from every form of profit-thinking," wants to join the Communist Party, but the institution cannot understand her.

Having sold her house for a pittance to Otto Hoyser, her father's old bookkeeper, Leni from 1945 to 1970 rents an apartment in it and sublets rooms to old acquaintances and foreign "guest workers," each according to his needs, and charges each even less than his ability to pay. When the Hoysers try to evict Leni in the name of progress, a committee sends a blockade of garbage trucks to delay the evacuation until the eviction order can be reversed. A model of classless solidarity, the committee includes a music critic, civil servants, a small-business owner, German and foreign laborers, and Au. himself.

Although in the span of the book Leni and members of the group portrayed have suffered dictatorship and war, and capitalism and evil have often triumphed, Au.'s report ends as a saint's life should: with a miracle. Leni's lodgers are secure. Leni herself is pregnant by a Moslem guest worker. Her brilliant son Lev, a garbage collector who practices "deliberate underachievement" to combat capitalism's excesses of ambitious overachievement, will soon join her. Even Au. has found happiness with a former nun. At least temporarily, "that which society has declared garbage" has triumphed over capitalistic exploitation.

SUMMARY

Although Heinrich Böll insisted that his characters were "compositions," not psychological creations, they have psychological reality. Hans, the reification of the clown metaphor, is actually an opinionated, sensitive, sentimental, narcissistic, nonintellectual man. Leni, an archetype, is real in generosity, sensuality, and will. "As an author," said Böll, "only two themes interest me: love and religion." With a dichotomous cast of "compositions," the evil self-servers and the persecuted pure, a contemporary sociopolitical setting, and a repertory of symbols, Böll condemned the sin of exploitation wherever it occurred and preached a religion of love made manifest in forbearance, generosity, and grace.

Pat Ingle Gillis

BIBLIOGRAPHY

By the Author

LONG FICTION:

Der Zug war pünktlich, 1949 (*The Train Was on Time*, 1956)

Wo warst du, Adam?, 1951 (*Adam, Where Art Thou?*, 1955)

Nicht nur zur Weihnachtszeit, 1952

Und sagte kein einziges Wort, 1953 (*Acquainted with the Night*, 1954)

Haus ohne Hüter, 1954 (*Tomorrow and Yesterday*, 1957)

Das Brot der frühen Jahre, 1955 (*The Bread of Our Early Years*, 1957)

Billard um halbzehn, 1959 (*Billiards at Half-Past Nine*, 1961)

Ansichten eines Clowns, 1963 (*The Clown*, 1965)

Ende einer Dienstfahrt, 1966 (*End of a Mission*, 1967)

Gruppenbild mit Dame, 1971 (*Group Portrait with Lady*, 1973)

Die verlorene Ehre der Katharina Blum: Oder, Wie Gewalt entstehen und wohin sie führen kann, 1974 (*The Lost Honor of Katharina Blum: Or, How Violence Develops and Where It Can Lead*, 1975)

Fürsorgliche Belagerung, 1979 (*The Safety Net*, 1982)

Der Vermächtnis, 1982 (*A Soldier's Legacy*, 1985)

Frauen vor Flusslandschaft, 1985 (*Women in a River Landscape*, 1988)

Der Engel Schwieg, wr. 1950, pb. 1992 (*The Silent Angel*, 1994)

Kreuz ohne liebe, 2003

SHORT FICTION:

Wanderer, kommst du nach Spa . . . , 1950 (*Traveller, If You Come to Spa*, 1956)

So ward Abend und Morgen, 1955

Unberechenbare Gäste, 1956

Doktor Murkes gesammeltes Schweigen und andere Satiren, 1958

Der Fahnhof von Zimpren, 1959

Erzählungen, Hörspiele, Aufsätze, 1961

Entfernung von der Truppe, 1964 (*Absent Without Leave*, 1965)

Eighteen Stories, 1966

Absent Without Leave, and Other Stories, 1967

Children Are Civilians Too, 1970

Die Verwundung und andere frühe Erzählungen, 1983 (*The Casualty*, 1986)

Veränderungen in Staech: Erzählungen, 1962-1980, 1984

The Stories of Heinrich Böll, 1986

DISCUSSION TOPICS

- How did the course of German history affect the early life and early career of Heinrich Böll?

- To what extent was it impossible for Böll to evade politically motivated literature?

- Consider the possibilities of Böll's writing that are beneficial to American writers who are themselves antagonistic to the course of American sociopolitical developments in the early twenty-first century.

- Explain the significance of Böll's use of unreliable narrators.

- What characteristics make clowns perceptive critics of social and moral deficiencies?

- In *Group Portrait with Lady*, does Leni defy or fulfill the implications of having been chosen "most German girl" in school?

- Discuss Böll's distinction between characters as "compositions" and characters as psychological creations.

POETRY:
Gedichte, 1972
Gedichte mit Collagen von Klaus Staeck, 1980

DRAMA:
Ein Schluck Erde, pb. 1962
Aussatz, pb. 1970

SCREENPLAY:
Deutschland im Herbst, 1978

NONFICTION:
Irisches Tagebuch, 1957 (*Irish Journal*, 1967)
Brief an einen jungen Katholiken, 1961
Frankfurter Vorlesungen, 1966
Hierzulande, 1967
Aufsätze, Kritiken, Reden, 1967
Neue politische und literarische Schriften, 1973
Schwierigkeiten mit der Brüderlichkeit, 1976
Missing Persons, and Other Essays, 1977
Einmischung erwünscht, 1977
Gefahren von falschen Brüdern, 1980
Spuren der Zeitgenossenschaft, 1980
Was soll aus dem Jungen bloss werden? Oder, Irgendwas mit Büchern, 1981 (*What's to Become of the Boy? Or, Something to Do with Books*, 1984)
Vermintes Gelände, 1982
Bild, Bonn, Boenisch, 1984

MISCELLANEOUS:
Heinrich Böll Werke, 1977-1979

About the Author

Conrad, Robert C. *Heinrich Böll*. Boston: Twayne, 1981.
Friedrichsmeyer, Erhard. *The Major Works of Heinrich Böll: A Critical Commentary*. New York: Monarch Press, 1974.
Heinrich Böll, on His Death: Selected Obituaries and the Last Interview. Translated by Patricia Crampton. Bonn, Germany: Inter Nationes, 1985.
Hook, Elizabeth Snyder. "Awakening from War: History, Trauma, and Testimony in Heinrich Böll." In *The Work of Memory: New Directions in the Study of German Society and Culture*, edited by Alon Confino and Peter Fritzshe. Urbana: University of Illinois Press, 2002.
MacPherson, Enid. *A Student's Guide to Böll*. London: Heineman, 1972.
Reid, J. H. "Heinrich Böll: From Modernism to Post-Modernism and Beyond." In *The Modern German Novel*, edited by Keith Bullivant. Leamington Spa, England: Oswald Wolff Books, 1987.
_____. "Private and Public Filters: Memories of War in Heinrich Böll's Fiction and Nonfiction." In *European Memories of the Second World War*, edited by Helmut Peitsch, Charles Burdett, and Claire Gorrar. New York: Berghahn Books, 1999.
Sokel, Walter Herbert. "Perspective and Dualism in the Novels of Böll." In *The Contemporary Novel in German*, edited by Robert R. Heitner. Austin: University of Texas Press, 1967.
Thomas, R. Hinton, and Wilfried van der Will. *The German Novel and the Affluent Society*. Toronto: University of Toronto Press, 1968.

© Washington Post; reprinted by permission of
the D.C. Public Library

JORGE LUIS BORGES

Born: Buenos Aires, Argentina
August 24, 1899
Died: Geneva, Switzerland
June 14, 1986

Borges's labyrinthine, esoteric short fiction and his innovative style have earned him an international reputation as one of the most significant contributors to twentieth century literature.

BIOGRAPHY

Born in Buenos Aires, Argentina, on August 24, 1899, to Jorge Guillermo Borges and Leonor Acevedo de Borges, Jorge Luis Borges (BAWR-hays) belonged to a well-off family. His father was of English descent. The young Borges appears to have enjoyed a relatively happy childhood and the security of a close-knit Latin American family. Under the nurturing influence of his family, Borges began to write at a very early age. He read voraciously from his father's personal library, which was rich in adventure tales by English authors such as Rudyard Kipling. Stories about distant lands and wild animals of the East shaped Borges's childhood imagination. This curiosity was later to develop into more serious pursuits of study in the areas of Eastern religions and philosophies. Borges was introduced to the benefits of private study from the beginning, not receiving any formal public education until the age of nine. This faith in self-education was to remain with him until he died.

In 1914, the Borges family was traveling in Europe when World War I began and was forced to extend its stay in Geneva, Switzerland, for four years. It was there that Borges attended secondary school and was first introduced to French and German languages and literatures, as well as to the works of European authors such as Heinrich Heine, Charles

Baudelaire, and Arthur Schopenhauer. Between 1919 and 1921, Borges and his family spent much of their time in Spain, where Borges produced his first poems and also met a group of young Spanish writers and poets who called themselves the Ultraístas. The Ultraístas, reacting against the Romanticism of the nineteenth century, had formed their own literary movement known as Ultraísmo. This movement was to be of some influence both in Borges's own career and in Argentina's literary growth during the 1920's. In 1921, the family returned to Buenos Aires, where Borges resumed his writing career. His early publications consisted mainly of poetry, manifestos, literary reviews, and a collection of essays. Some of these works exhibit traces of the tenets of Ultraísmo, such as the central use of metaphor, an art-for-art's-sake attitude, and an apolitical public stance, which Borges espoused for most of his life.

In the mid-1920's, Borges was closely associated with another avant-garde literary group known as the Martinfierrista group. Like the Ultraístas, this new group professed a disengaged aesthetic attitude, viewed literary activity mostly as an intellectual game, and was opposed by a more committed, leftist group of writers. Although Borges seems to have maintained an aloofness from political events, there is not enough evidence available to prove that he was personally detached from political reality, since he exhibited a characteristic reserve and shyness in discussing personal or political subjects.

Throughout the 1920's and the 1930's, Borges continued to write and publish poetry and essays.

At this time the subjects that seem to have absorbed him most are love, time, and memory, and some of his early poems are nationalistic and romantic in flavor. The economic depression of the early 1930's and the major political changes that were sweeping Argentina under a conservative regime, however, seem to have left their mark on Borges. He dealt with the crisis by developing an art that was self-absorbed and evasive of political reality. His writing became increasingly intellectualized and esoteric, and at the same time he grew interested in mystic belief systems such as Gnosticism and the Kabbala. Through his study of these systems of thought he developed a personal ethos of philosophic mysticism, which is often reflected in his fiction.

The 1940's are probably the most significant decade in Borges's career, for it was during this period that he published much of the short prose fiction that was to bring him international fame in his later years. His first collection of stories arrived in 1941 and was later included in a larger anthology, *Ficciones, 1935-1944* (1944; English translation, 1962). The short stories (some critics prefer the term "essayistic fiction" to describe Borges's short fiction) for which Borges is now renowned are to be found in *Ficciones* and in a later collection, *El Aleph* (1949, 1952; translated in *The Aleph, and Other Stories, 1933-1969*, 1970).

Because of a difference of views with the Juan Perón regime that had come into power in 1946, Borges lost his job as a librarian in Buenos Aires and was forced to spend the following decade as a teacher and lecturer at private institutions. Once Perón was removed from power in 1955, Borges's career opportunities improved considerably. He was offered the directorship of the National Library in 1955 and in 1956 was appointed professor of English literature at the University of Buenos Aires. In the same year he also was awarded the coveted National Prize for Literature; in 1961, he won the Fomentor Prize, which he shared with Samuel Beckett in a tie. By the mid-1960's he had won worldwide acclaim, and his work was being widely published in translation. In 1968, Borges returned from his travels abroad to life in Buenos Aires and was married for a period of three years to Elsa Astete Millán. The marriage ended in a divorce in 1970.

In 1960, Borges had embarked on a new phase of his career with the publication of a collection of prose and poetry called *El hacedor* (1960; *Dreamtigers*, 1964). Throughout the 1960's and the 1970's, Borges repeatedly turned to poetry as a medium of expression and published a number of collections of both poetry and prose. His literary production began to wane during the last decade of his life, but he continued to travel and lecture. In 1984, he again visited Europe, this time accompanied by his traveling companion, Maria Kodama, whom he married in 1986. Already suffering from almost complete blindness, he had developed cancer of the liver as well. He died in Geneva on June 14, 1986.

ANALYSIS

Borges is often included among writers described as postmodernists. Postmodernism, a literary movement whose influence has steadily increased since the middle of the twentieth century, is characterized by literature that meditates upon the processes of its own construction. Because of their inherent self-reflectiveness and circularity, Borges's stories provide a good example of such "metafiction." Borges is also known for his innovative literary techniques and an austere, polished craftsmanship.

The avant-garde intellectuals of early twentieth century Argentina, including Borges, conceived of literary activity as intellectual play. In Borges's "La lotería en Babilonia" ("The Babylon Lottery"), for example, the lottery is an intellectual construct, conceived by an unknown brain, which seduces people into risking their fates by playing with chance. Stories such as this one seem to emphasize that life—like its fictional counterpart, literature—is an arbitrary construction based purely on coincidence. Many of Borges's detective-type stories, such as "El jardín de senderos que se bifurcan" ("The Garden of Forking Paths") and "La muerte y la brújula" ("Death and the Compass"), emphasize equally the gamelike nature of everyday reality by their insistence on a mysterious relationship between life and accident. In such stories, Borges spoofs spy fiction and parodies other literary genres.

Borges repeatedly draws attention to the fact that literature is imitation and can be nothing but inventive repetition. In a typical story, "Examen de la obra de Herbert Quain" ("An Examination of the Work of Herbert Quain"), the narrator discusses the work of a fictitious writer whose experiments lead him to invent plots that repeat themselves in symmetrical structures. Borges uses stories such as this one in a dual way: He displays his interest in symmetry, invention, and the story-within-the-story structure and at the same time adopts a tongue-in-cheek critical attitude toward academic critics by mimicking them through his erudite, pretentious narrators. He thus combines serious meditations on the nature of fiction with a subtle and refined sense of humor.

In a more serious vein, Borges explores the relationship between the real world and its more fabulous counterparts. Two major metaphors that allow him to intermingle reality with imagination are the labyrinth and the mirror. Both of these appear in many of the stories included in *Ficciones* and *The Aleph, and Other Stories*. In "Los dos reyes y los dos labertinos" ("The Two Kings and Their Two Labyrinths"), which appeared in *The Aleph, and Other Stories*, the labyrinth is both a maze and a desert—a space within which one can lose one's way, or perhaps an intellectual problem that can be resolved only with great difficulty.

While the labyrinth suggests artifice, the mirror invokes duplication. In one of the stories from *Ficciones*, "La biblioteca de Babel" ("The Library of Babel"), a large library becomes an allegory of the universe. At the entrance to the library hangs a mirror, which may suggest the illusory nature of the universe or the possibility of having access to a duplicate world such as that of fiction. Such aspects of Borges's stories point to the influence of Hindu and Buddhist philosophies, in which the world is viewed as "Maya" or delusion, something ephemeral that can be shattered at any time.

What is paradoxical about much of Borges's philosophy is that it offers a two-pronged system of conception. On the one hand, Borges insists that twentieth century writers can do nothing but repeat ideas and plots that have already been presented in one form or another. Like literary activity, reality is for Borges both repetitive and cyclical. Paradoxically, however, repetition does not imply monotony, for the human being has the ability to be infinitely inventive in the rearrangement of previously acquired patterns of knowledge. Therefore, the possibilities available in any one lifetime are rich and multitudinous, even though the choosing of any one path may imply the foregoing of others.

The cyclical nature of the universe and of time is represented in many of the stories in *Ficciones*. In "Las ruinas circulares" ("The Circular Ruins") the protagonist discovers that the reality in which he envisioned another being is in fact a dream in which he himself has been projected by some greater dreamer. Such patterns of infinite regression are represented through the idea of the Creator-behind-the-Creator. In "El acercamiento a Almotásim" ("The Approach to Al-Mu'tasim"), the narrator's search for an omniscient God leads him to the idea that "the Almighty is also in search of Someone, and *that* Someone in search of some superior Someone (or merely indispensable or equal Someone), and thus on to the end—or better, the endlessness—of Time, or on and on in some cyclical form."

Borges's fascination with dreams and magic and with their power to lend a mythic quality to reality is not surprising, since he is the inheritor of a Latin American literary tradition that has had an ongoing interest in the fantastic as well as the occult. Concurrently, Borges's fiction has had its impact on other major Latin American writers, such as Gabriel Garcia Márquez and Julio Cortázar, as well as on writers as far removed geographically from Borges as Salman Rushdie. Borges's interest in the occult was more than a playful diversion. He undertook serious study of mystic belief systems such as the Kabbala and Gnosticism and adopted many of these ideas in his own writing. In Borges's fiction, the world of the fantastic duplicates and interrupts the real world. Yet he never lets the reader lose sight of the fabricated quality of fiction and, by extension, of reality. The intellectual and sometimes esoteric density that is thus created forces the reader to participate actively in the process of fabrication.

Finally, for Borges myth and mystery are never very far from philosophy. The allure of some of the mystical aspects of Middle Eastern and Eastern traditions seems to lie in the fact that they reinforce his own conception of the universe as a chance happening. Such a universe has all the qualities of a well-constructed dream and, like a dream, is susceptible to disappearance if left to the whims of a capricious God.

"TLÖN, UQBAR, ORBIS TERTIUS"

First published: 1940 (collected in *Ficciones*, 1962)

Type of work: Short story

An imaginary universe called Tlön, based on an idealistic philosophy, begins to rule everyday reality.

"Tlön, Uqbar, Orbis Tertius," which first appeared in the literary magazine *Sur* in 1940, is one of Borges's best-known stories. Because of its documentary style, which provides detailed "facts" about an imaginary universe, the text defies the term "short story" and, like many of Borges's other texts, verges on essayistic fiction. The story begins with the first-person narrator describing a conversation that he has had with his friend, Bioy Casares, during which his friend mentions a place called Uqbar, presumably discussed in the *Anglo-American Cyclopaedia*, a reprint of the *Encyclopaedia Britannica*. After some futile searching, the unusual article is found in a deviant and pirated copy of the same encyclopedia. The description of Uqbar, a mysterious city supposedly located in Asia Minor, seems deliberately vague. The narrator and his friend fail to establish whether such a place really exists, and the problem remains unresolved for two years. After this period, the narrator comes across another, equally mystifying encyclopedia that tells of a planet called Tlön, describing in some detail its culture, philosophy, language, and literature.

In the description of the planet and its idealistic philosophy, the reader can find some typically Borgesian ideas. The language spoken on Tlön includes verbs and adjectives but no nouns, because the existence of nouns would point to a materialistic and empirical conception of the universe, something that is anathema to the inhabitants of Tlön. Because the inhabitants also deny the possibility of reduction or classification, the only science that flourishes on the planet is psychology. Similarly, various schools of thought have redefined the notion of linear time, either rejecting it completely or injecting a fantastic aspect into it. One school of thought conceives of time as a vague memory of the past, while another insists that all people live in two duplicate time zones simultaneously. In many such examples, Borges is playing with some of the idealistic notions proffered by the eighteenth century philosopher George Berkeley. As is usual in any reading of Borges, the seriousness of these ideas is undercut through the use of irony and playfulness.

An idea that appeals especially to Borges is the possibility of creating objects through force of imagination, which is what the people of Tlön are able to do. These objects, or "hrönir" as they are called, at first the products of absentmindedness, are later deliberately created in order to modify reality. Through the concept of the "hrönir" Borges delves into the powers of intellectual activity. By imagining objects, the people of Tlön are able to transform their environment to suit their idealistic conception of reality. This activity, then, is very similar to that of writers, who also create fantastic environments that supplement the one available in the real world.

This association between the inhabitants of Tlön and writers of fiction becomes apparent in the postscript to the story. In this final summation the narrator describes how, some years later, forty volumes of an encyclopedia of Tlön are discovered. Among the facts revealed is that Tlön is the fabulous brainchild of a seventeenth century secret society, which has circulated the idea of Tlön's supposed existence through literature. In nineteenth century North America, an atheistic millionaire named Ezra Buckley expands on the original idea of a utopian city and turns it into an entire planet. Through these documentary details the narrator disassembles the mystery of Tlön and the various encyclopedias. In a typically Borgesian conceit, however, one enigma is unveiled only to posit another. For the dissemination of rational explanations occurs simultaneously with the discovery of certain mysterious objects that have secretly entered the real world. These include a magnetic compass from Tlön found among the table service of a princess and a heavy metal cone discovered by the narrator himself. The thought products or "hrönir" of a fictional world have begun to impinge upon the smooth rationalism and empiricism of reality. Finally, fiction and reality merge, first because it is impossible to keep them distinct, but second because reality welcomes the intrusion of an idealized world into its seamy present.

"THE GARDEN OF FORKING PATHS"

First published: "El jardín de senderos que se bifurcan," 1941 (collected in *Ficciones*, 1962)

Type of work: Short story

In this spoof of a spy story, the labyrinthine plot becomes the symbol of a mazelike universe where multiple time zones and destinies coexist.

In "The Garden of Forking Paths," Borges indulges in one of his common literary pastimes, the writing of spoof detective fiction. The story has all the necessary elements of a spy story: secret agents, guns, murder, mystery, drama, and an intricate plot that rushes the reader toward the resolution of the puzzle. Borges, however, is not as concerned with writing good spy fiction as he is with showing how an imitation of a spy story can be used for purposes other than the final demystification of the plot.

The plot concerns the escapades of its Chinese protagonist, Yu Tsun, a German spy. His task, while on a secret mission in England in the middle of World War I, is somehow to communicate to his German chief the name of a British town that is to be targeted by the Germans. Yu Tsun devises a clever plan that leads him to murder a man by the name of Stephen Albert, the last name of the murdered man being the name of the British town to be bombed. Pursuing Yu Tsun is a British agent, Richard Madden, who arrests him immediately after the murder but is unable to prevent the information from reaching Berlin.

Most of the story is told in the first person by the narrator, Yu Tsun, who is awaiting his execution at the end of the story. What adds to the intrigue of this interesting scheme of events are a series of coincidences and a labyrinth to be found at the heart of the story. Albert, the victim of the plot, happens to be a sinologist who lives in surroundings reminiscent of China. When Yu Tsun reaches his house in the countryside, he is mistakenly identified by Albert as a Chinese consul and so welcomed inside the house. Albert also happens to have occupied himself with unraveling the mystery of a labyrinth, whose construction is credited to Ts'ui Pen, an il-

lustrious writer and the ancestor of the narrator. Albert has resolved the enigma of the maze by discovering that the maze is not a building but the large, chaotic novel authored by Ts'ui Pen. In this novel, characters live not one but multiple destinies. Refuting the fact that every choice presented to the human being in one lifetime presumes the abandoning of all other alternative choices, the Chinese writer has tried to create a work in which all possibilities coexist in a multiplicity of time zones. The inspiring image for the novel is a garden of forking paths, in which bifurcating paths lead to different places but also sometimes converge.

Both the labyrinthine book and the garden become symbolic of a chaotic universe in which all

possibilities are available. Various destinies are realized in overlapping time zones. The metaphor of the labyrinth is a central one in much of Borges's fiction. It represents the idea of wandering and being lost in an unfathomable universe, sometimes following paths that converge with those already known, at other times retreading previously familiar tracks. The labyrinth incorporates the richness of endless possibilities available in infinite lifetimes. Seemingly dissatisfied with the definition of time as uniform and absolute, Borges attempts in this story, as he does in "Tlön, Uqbar, Orbis Tertius," to dwell on other possible ways of conceiving of it. The plot of Borges's own story is also a maze. The reader resolves the puzzle by following at the heels of the narrator and the writer of the tale. These cerebral journeys that make up literary activity form the backbone of Borges's aesthetic.

"Pierre Menard, Author of the *Quixote*"

First published: "Pierre Menard, autor del Quijote," 1939 (collected in *Ficciones,* 1962)

Type of work: Short story

This work is a tongue-in-cheek story about a fictitious twentieth century writer who uses memory and imagination in his attempt to rewrite Don Quixote de la Mancha *in its original form.*

In "Pierre Menard, Author of the *Quixote,*" Borges combines a sophisticated sense of humor, directed toward the scholasticism of the academic, with one of his favorite images—that of the simulacrum. The story begins as a eulogy written in the first person and dedicated to the memory of an admirable French author, Pierre Menard. The narrator first provides a list of the author's visible works in a rather pompous, academic style; the narrator often invokes his literary authority by dropping names of famous writers or providing documentary proof through the citation of very real authors or journals in his footnotes. The insertion of footnotes for the purpose of creating an impression of assumed authority is a much-used technique in Borges's stories. In this story the footnotes add to the general irony, since Borges uses them to mock academic critics. He mimics the style of bookish scholars who catalog literary works and associate themselves with reputable names in order to give themselves some stature as literary critics. Borges implies that such critics remain well on the outskirts of literary activity. Through such spoofs of literary techniques and genres, he invites the reader to participate in a playful activity that exposes the pretentiousness of some brands of scholarship.

From the imitation of bombastic critics and styles, Borges proceeds to another form of imitation. Menard, the eulogized writer, is credited with another set of "subterranean" works, one of which is an attempted imitation of Miguel de Cervantes's *El ingenioso hidalgo don Quixote de la Mancha* (1605, 1615; *Don Quixote de la Mancha,* 1612-1620). The reader is led to another typically Borgesian idea.

Since, according to Borges, everything that seeks to amaze has already been said before, there are no longer any new stories left to narrate. Rearrangement of old plots in new patterns is the only available type of creativity that writers in the twentieth century can enjoy. Therefore, he suggests the fabrication of simulacrums, or copies, of original tales. These copies will be different from the originals because they will rearrange facts, color them, or throw a new light on them through the use of an ironic or humorous tone.

The fictitious French author, Menard, who decides to rewrite *Don Quixote de la Mancha* three hundred years after its original publication, takes this Borgesian device even further. Menard does not want to rearrange the story of Quixote or to imitate its style in a modern tale. Rather, he wants to succeed at creating an identical story, a book that will duplicate the original in every minute detail. Any thought of creating a mechanical transcription is of course rejected at the outset. At first, Menard conceives the plan of immersing himself completely in the seventeenth century world of Cervantes. He decides to learn Spanish, become a Catholic, and fight the Moors and the Turks—in other words, experience the life of Cervantes in order to become Cervantes. This plan, however, does not seem challenging enough to the rather eccentric French writer, who then conceives an even more difficult method. Since by being Cervantes it would be relatively easier to write the book that Cervantes had written, Menard undertakes the task of creating a copy of the original work while he remains Pierre Menard. Having read the original work in childhood, he will depend entirely on his hazy memory of the work and his imaginative powers to reconstruct *Don Quixote de la Mancha* word for word. He succeeds, according to the narrator, at creating an exact replica of two complete chapters and a fragment of a third one.

The narrator then provides excerpts from Menard's and Cervantes's works and comments that Menard has created a new text that is infinitely richer and subtler than the original. Considering the fact that Menard's sentences are exact duplicates of those of Cervantes, the suggestion that Menard's work differs so radically from the original is funny yet not completely gratuitous. Although the passages to be compared are identical, the narrator draws the reader's attention to the fact that the more recently composed text is the work of a man who was culturally, geographically, and historically removed from his predecessor. The same words, written in the twentieth century, are bound to lead to new critical interpretations as well as the presumption of different authorial intentions. The narrator, placed in the role of a reader, is thus able to perceive subtle differences between excerpts that on the surface are exact replicas of each other. The reader's perception and interpretation, then, is as important a tool in the construction of fiction as the ability of the writer to fabricate these texts. In this very postmodern story, Borges undoes the traditional opposition between reader and writer, showing how both can achieve new variations of a text and how both play a role in the creation of fiction.

"FUNES, THE MEMORIOUS"

First published: "Funes el memorioso," 1944 (collected in *Ficciones,* 1962)
Type of work: Short story

The relationship between memory and abstract thought is invoked through a character who develops an infallible photographic memory.

Ireneo Funes, in the short story "Funes, the Memorious," is a young Uruguayan lad with an unusual gift. Known to be rather eccentric in his personal lifestyle, Funes is also famous in his province for always being able to tell the exact time without looking at a watch. After an accident in which he slips from his horse and sustains a concussion, Funes is crippled. This tragic loss of his physical capacities, however, does not seem to bother him, because he has been compensated in a rather amazing way. After his concussion, Funes develops the startling intellectual capacity for memorizing an infinite number of facts, names, and images that he has seen or read. This photographic memory includes the ability to reconstruct his own dreams in minute detail. In other words, Funes is unable to forget anything that his mind has observed even once.

The powers of his infallible memory are recounted to the first-person narrator when the narrator visits Funes in order to reclaim several Latin texts that he had earlier lent to Funes. With absolutely no prior knowledge of Latin, Funes is able to read and memorize the texts in their entirety. He provides other prodigious examples of his gift: He can perceive and remember exact changes in moving scenes—a herd of cattle in a pass, an innumerable number of stars in the sky, all the details of a stallion's mane, every leaf on every tree that he has ever seen. The burden of such an infinite memory, however, turns Funes into an insomniac. Although he can remember every precise detail from his past experience, he is unable to generalize about facts or to abstract himself from reality in any way. Finally, the narrator relates that Funes, who used to spend most of his time lying on a cot in a dark room, meditating upon his marvelous memories, dies of a pulmonary congestion.

Through the strange character of Funes, Borges dwells on the nature of language and the relationship between memory and thought. Funes's ability to remember everything presupposes his inability to forget anything. The gift of memory is thus at once a curse, its ominous aspects suggested through the funereal and unfortunate associations of the name "Funes." Borges indicates that imagination and creativity begin with the ability to think in abstract terms, to rise above precise details, and to condense impressions into thought. These things Funes is never able to do, for his photographic mind keeps him firmly entrenched in detail. He is unable to perform reductions, to idealize or to abstract other realities from the ones at his disposal. In fact, he compares his own mind to a garbage bin into which all kinds of useful and useless facts get thrown together. Borges suggests that in order to be able to create, one must first be able to select certain items and forget others, so that imaginary situations can be posited. It is thus an imperfect memory that lets the writer become a fabricator, someone who can forget and, subsequently, create.

SUMMARY

Combining some unusual literary techniques with a refined wit, Jorge Luis Borges insisted on the fictionality of fiction—something fabricated and artificial. Many of Borges's stories are true "artifices," carefully wrought intellectual exercises that involve clever conceits. Borges is thus a truly postmodern writer, as interested in the process of construction as in the final product itself. Through the use of metaphors such as the labyrinth and the mirror and a highly cerebral style, Borges offers the reader a unique philosophy that denies the division between the real and the unreal worlds.

Anu Aneja

BIBLIOGRAPHY

By the Author

SHORT FICTION:

Historia universal de la infamia, 1935 (*A Universal History of Infamy*, 1972)

El jardín de senderos que se bifurcan, 1941

Seis problemas para don Isidro Parodi, 1942 (with Adolfo Bioy Casares, under joint pseudonym H. Bustos Domecq; *Six Problems for Don Isidro Parodi*, 1981)

Ficciones, 1935-1944, 1944 (English translation, 1962)

Dos fantasías memorables, 1946 (with Bioy Casares, under joint pseudonym Domecq)

El Aleph, 1949, 1952 (translated in *The Aleph, and Other Stories, 1933-1969*, 1970)

La muerte y la brújula, 1951

La hermana de Eloísa, 1955 (with Luisa Mercedes Levinson)

Cuentos, 1958

Crónicas de Bustos Domecq, 1967 (with Bioy Casares; *Chronicles of Bustos Domecq*, 1976)

El matrero, 1970

El informe de Brodie, 1970 (*Doctor Brodie's Report*, 1972)

El congreso, 1971 (*The Congress*, 1974)

El libro de arena, 1975 (*The Book of Sand*, 1977)

Narraciones, 1980

LONG FICTION:

Un modelo para la muerte, 1946 (with Adolfo Bioy Casares, under joint pseudonym B. Suárez Lynch)

POETRY:

Fervor de Buenos Aires, 1923, 1969

Luna de enfrente, 1925

Cuaderno San Martín, 1929

Poemas, 1923-1943, 1943

Poemas, 1923-1953, 1954

Obra poética, 1923-1958, 1958

Obra poética, 1923-1964, 1964

Seis poemas escandinavos, 1966

Siete poemas, 1967

Elogio de la sombra, 1969 (*In Praise of Darkness*, 1974)

DISCUSSION TOPICS

- Explain why some critics call Jorge Luis Borges's short stories "essayistic fiction."

- In what ways does the postmodernistic concern with the processes of literature's construction resemble the manner in which other activities are studied today?

- Are Borges's labyrinths constructed difficulties or a reflection of the complexities of modern life? Give reasons for your answer.

- Elaborate either a positive or negative response to the following: Playfulness, one of the qualities of Borges's fiction, is an impediment to success in serious literary work.

- Consider whether the discussions of Borges's fiction assist the reader in also understanding his poetry.

Jorge Luis Borges

El otro, el mismo, 1969
El oro de los tigres, 1972 (translated in *The Gold of Tigers: Selected Later Poems*, 1977)
La rosa profunda, 1975 (translated in *The Gold of Tigers*)
La moneda de hierro, 1976
Historia de la noche, 1977
La cifra, 1981
Los conjurados, 1985
Selected Poems, 1999

SCREENPLAYS:
"Los orilleros" y "El paraíso de los creyentes," 1955 (with Bioy Casares)
Les Autres, 1974 (with Bioy Casares and Hugo Santiago)

NONFICTION:
Inquisiciones, 1925
El tamaño de mi esperanza, 1926
El idioma de los argentinos, 1928
Figari, 1930
Evaristo Carriego, 1930 (English translation, 1984)
Discusión, 1932
Las Kennigar, 1933
Historia de la eternidad, 1936
Nueva refutación del tiempo, 1947
Aspectos de la literatura gauchesca, 1950
Antiguas literaturas germánicas, 1951 (with Delia Ingenieros; revised as *Literaturas germánicas medievales*, 1966, with Maria Esther Vásquez)
Otras Inquisiciones, 1952 (*Other Inquisitions*, 1964)
El "Martin Fierro," 1953 (with Margarita Guerrero)
Leopoldo Lugones, 1955 (with Betina Edelberg)
Manual de zoología fantástica, 1957 (with Guerrero; *The Imaginary Zoo*, 1969; revised as *El libro de los seres imaginarios*, 1967, *The Book of Imaginary Beings*, 1969)
La poesía gauchesca, 1960
Introducción a la literatura norteamericana, 1967 (with Esther Zemborain de Torres; *An Introduction to American Literature*, 1971)
Prólogos, 1975
Libro de sueños, 1976
Cosmogonías, 1976
Qué es el budismo?, 1976 (with Alicia Jurado)
Siete noches, 1980 (*Seven Nights*, 1984)
Nueve ensayos dantescos, 1982
This Craft of Verse, 2000
The Total Library: Non-Fiction, 1922-1986, 2001 (Eliot Weinberger, editor)

EDITED TEXTS:
Antología clásica de la literatura argentina, 1937
Antología de la literatura fantástica, 1940 (with Adolfo Bioy Casares and Silvia Ocampo)
Antología poética argentina, 1941 (with Bioy Casares and Ocampo)
El compadrito: Su destino, sus barrios, su música, 1945, 1968 (with Silvina Bullrich)
Poesía gauchesca, 1955 (with Bioy Casares; 2 volumes)
Libro del cielo y del infierno, 1960, 1975 (with Bioy Casares)
Versos, 1972 (by Evaristo Carriego)

Antología poética, 1982 (by Franciso de Quevedo)
Antología poética, 1982 (by Leopoldo Lugones)
El amigo de la muerte, 1984 (by Pedro Antonio de Alarcón)

TRANSLATIONS:
Orlando, 1937 (of Virginia Woolf's novel)
La metamórfosis, 1938 (of Franz Kafka's novel *Die Verwandlung*)
Un bárbaro en Asia, 1941 (of Henri Michaux's travel notes)
Bartleby, el escribiente, 1943 (of Herman Melville's novella *Bartleby the Scrivener*)
Los mejores cuentos policiales, 1943 (with Bioy Casares; of detective stories by various authors)
Los mejores cuentos policiales, segunda serie, 1951 (with Bioy Casares; of detective stories by various authors)
Cuentos breves y extraordinarios, 1955, 1973 (with Bioy Casares; of short stories by various authors; *Extraordinary Tales*, 1973)
Las palmeras salvajes, 1956 (of William Faulkner's novel *The Wild Palms*)
Hojas de hierba, 1969 (of Walt Whitman's *Leaves of Grass*)

MISCELLANEOUS:
Obras completas, 1953-1967 (10 volumes)
El hacedor (1960; *Dreamtigers*, 1964)
Antología personal, 1961 (*A Personal Anthology*, 1967)
Labyrinths: Selected Stories, and Other Writings, 1962, 1964
Nueva antología personal, 1968
Selected Poems, 1923-1967, 1972 (also includes prose)
Adrogue, 1977
Obras completas en colaboración, 1979 (with others)
Borges: A Reader, 1981
Atlas, 1984 (with María Kodama; English translation, 1985)

About the Author

Bell-Villada, Gene H. *Borges and His Fiction: A Guide to His Mind and Art*. Chapel Hill: University of North Carolina Press, 1981.
Di Giovanni, Norman Thomas. *The Lesson of the Master: On Borges and His Work*. New York: Continuum, 2003.
Lindstrom, Naomi. *Jorge Luis Borges: A Study of the Short Fiction*. Boston: Twayne, 1990.
Rodríguez Monegal, Emir. *Jorge Luis Borges: A Literary Biography*. New York: Dutton, 1978.
Stabb, Martin S. *Borges Revisited*. Boston: Twayne, 1991.
_____. *Jorge Luis Borges*. New York: Twayne, 1970.
Sturrock, John. *Paper Tigers: The Ideal Fictions of Jorge Luis Borges*. Oxford, England: Clarendon Press, 1977.
Williamson, Edwin. *Borges, a Life*. New York: Viking, 2004.
Wilson, Jason. *Jorge Luis Borges*. London: Reaktion Books, 2006.

ELIZABETH BOWEN

Library of Congress

Born: Dublin, Ireland
June 7, 1899
Died: London, England
February 22, 1973

Known best for her novels, Bowen was an astute and subtle student of human nature, especially in conflicts between young people and adults.

BIOGRAPHY

Elizabeth Dorothea Cole Bowen (BOH-uhn) was born in Dublin, Ireland, on June 7, 1899. Her parents were Henry Cole Bowen and Florence Isabella Pomeroy (Colley) Bowen. Both of them were Anglo-Irish, giving Elizabeth a Protestant, land-owning heritage. Her father, a barrister, inherited Bowen's Court, which was built in the eighteenth century and in which Elizabeth lived as a young girl. In 1930, upon the death of her father, she inherited the family estate. When Elizabeth was thirteen years old, her mother died. After her father's health deteriorated, she spent several years living with various relatives. Her mother's death, her father's precarious health, and her lack of a permanent, stable home all had a strong impact on the way that Bowen developed, both as a person and as a writer.

Bowen's education began at Downe House, Kent, England. She also studied at the London County Council School of Art, and she soon began to write short stories. Her first collection, *Encounters*, was published in 1923. In the same year, she married Alan Charles Cameron, a graduate of Oxford and a World War I veteran. He began a long career in educational administration through his appointment, in 1925, as secretary for education in the city of Oxford.

By 1927, Bowen was an established writer and spent part of each year in one of her three residences: London's Chelsea section, Bowen's Court, and a home in Italy. In addition to writing ten novels and several collections of short stories, Bowen lectured and taught in Italy, England, and the United States. She also wrote literary criticism, book reviews, radio scripts, and autobiographical pieces, while also working for the Ministry of Information and as an air-raid warden in London during World War II.

Bowen's novels include *The Hotel* (1927), *The Last September* (1929), *Friends and Relations* (1931), *To the North* (1932), *The House in Paris* (1935), *The Death of the Heart* (1938), *The Heat of the Day* (1949), *A World of Love* (1955), *The Little Girls* (1964), and *Eva Trout* (1968). Among her short story collections are *Encounters* (1923), *The Demon Lover* (1945; published in the United States as *Ivy Gripped the Steps, and Other Stories*, 1946), and *A Day in the Dark, and Other Stories* (1965). Her nonfiction work includes *Bowen's Court* (1942), *Seven Winters* (1942), *English Novelists* (1946), and *Afterthought: Pieces About Writing* (1962). Most of Bowen's works were published in the United States shortly after they appeared in England.

Some of the many honors that she received include being named Commander, Order of the British Empire, receiving honorary degrees from Trinity College, Dublin, and from Oxford, and being designated a Companion of Literature of the Royal Society of Literature.

Having returned to Ireland after the end of World War II, Bowen and her husband lived at Bowen's Court for only a brief time. Alan Cameron died in 1952. Bowen continued to live at Bowen's Court for a few more years and wrote *A World of Love* there. She could not afford to maintain the old place, however, and returned to England in 1960. She died on February 22, 1973, in London, after one last trip to Ireland in 1973.

During her lifetime, Bowen enjoyed generally favorable, although by no means unanimous, critical acclaim. Rose Macaulay, reviewing *A World of Love*, wrote that it was "rather fascinating, though not to everyone." Many critics thought *The Death of the Heart* was her best novel; some even considered it one of the best English novels of the twentieth century. Victoria Glendinning, who wrote a biography of Bowen in 1978, thought she was one of the ten most important fiction writers in English. Even before her death, however, Bowen's popularity had begun to decline and her books were hard to find. In the 1970's, however, they were reissued in paperback, and a new generation of readers found at least some of them fascinating and entertaining.

ANALYSIS

In Bowen's novels and short stories, certain subjects and themes are represented, though with a variety of viewpoints and plots. Bowen was interested in the ways in which persons and events from the past can affect, control, and even destroy the living. Her Anglo-Irish heritage gave her a special understanding of this subject. She was particularly sensitive to displacement, a feeling of alienation, a helplessness in the face of what has occurred before. Bowen's "romances" contained the usual elements of love, conflict, and mystery, but the dramas that unfold in her works contain both tragedy and comedy.

Adolescence is a frequent subject in Bowen's fiction; many of her characters are young persons struggling to become adults and often struggling with adults, who represent the past. The older generation has usually come to terms with the past and attempts to impose its own worldliness on those who are yet in a state of hope and faith, in the kind of innocence that Bowen describes in *The Death of the Heart*. At one point, she says that the innocent are "incurable strangers to the world, they never cease to exact a heroic happiness." That could also be said of Jane in *A World of Love* and of the young characters in Bowen's other novels.

Bowen's use of houses and landscape is a pre-dominant feature of her narratives. The ramshackle house in *A World of Love* is exactly the right setting for the unfolding of this romance, which is almost a ghost story, in which the past imposes itself on all the main characters. In *The Death of the Heart*, two sharply contrasting houses form the essential background for Portia's struggle. The elegantly furnished, immaculate house in London is a place where feelings are unexpressed and where frank, open communication is unknown. In sharp contrast is Waikiki, the seaside house to which Portia has been sent while Thomas and Anna take an April holiday in Capri. Life at Waikiki is noisy, spontaneous, and as common as the life in the London house is formal and aristocratic. In both houses, Portia is an outsider; her separateness is emphasized by the alien atmosphere of each house.

In Bowen's books, the characters talk to one another rather than act; there is very little real action in her fiction. Rather, through conversations that are often ambiguous and restrained, hiding as much as they reveal, the story unfolds with a delicate subtlety that challenges the reader to discover what the story really means. Irony is another characteristic of Bowen's style. The wit and humor in her novels depend on the discrepancies between what the characters think and say and what other characters reveal about them. There is irony, too, in what they expect and what they receive. For example, the cruel irony of Eddie's betrayal of Portia is typical of the way that Bowen resolves her characters' fates. She does not, however, always use irony to highlight disappointment. In *A World of Love*, Jane gives up her ghostly lover just before falling in love with a real young man when she least expects that to happen.

Bowen's style is highly descriptive; her scenes are visible, and the atmosphere in which they take place is palpable. Objects are important images of the emotions being felt but not expressed. At Montefort, the setting of *A World of Love*, rooms are described meticulously and vividly, not in long passages but in carefully selected and telling details.

Another aspect of Bowen's style is her occasionally convoluted sentence structure. Her tendency to twist syntax was a delight to some of her readers and an affectation and annoyance to others. For example, in *A World of Love*, the author, in describing Maud, the younger sister, says, "Nothing, or al-

Elizabeth Bowen

most nothing, made Maud not young, not a child throughout." That is the kind of sentence that may leave the reader confused as to what the author means. On the other hand, Bowen's work has a poetic quality that many critics and other readers have noticed. Her language is allusive, precise, suggestive, and highly dependent on the implied, the unspoken but intensely felt truth.

The psychological insight that is perhaps Bowen's most notable characteristic is suggested by a remark made by St. Quentin, a Bowen character and a novelist, quite obviously speaking for Bowen, the novelist: "I swear that each of us keeps, battened down inside himself, a sort of lunatic giant—impossible socially, but full-scale—and that it's the knockings and batterings we sometimes hear in each other that keeps our intercourse from utter banality."

THE DEATH OF THE HEART

First published: 1938
Type of work: Novel

An orphaned sixteen-year-old girl goes to London and, through cruel betrayal, loses her innocence.

Portia Quayne is the sixteen-year-old heroine of *The Death of the Heart*, which begins soon after she arrives in London. Her father and mother having died within a few years of each other, Portia must now live with her father's son, Thomas Quayne, and his wife Anna. Thomas is a middle-aged, successful, reserved businessman who is unable to form close personal relationships with anyone, although he does love his wife in his own aloof and undemonstrative way. Anna is a stylish, elegant woman whose principal interest is making herself and her house beautiful. She entertains frequently, but she, too, has no close relationships, though she appears to have a certain cool, impersonal attachment to her husband. Both are embarrassed and uncomfortable at the appearance of Portia, the child of the elder Quayne's disgrace and second marriage.

Into this house comes Portia, who does everything that she can to please the Quaynes, being obedient, well-mannered, and quiet. She observes them minutely and records in a diary her thoughts about them, as well as the uninteresting events of her life, which consist primarily of attending an expensive, exclusive establishment where French lessons, lectures, and excursions are offered to a small group of girls. Portia does not know that Anna has discovered her diary. Worse, Anna discusses the diary with St. Quentin, a novelist and one of her several bachelor friends. Anna is upset by Portia's insights and candid observations, but she is too resentful of  the slight disruption caused by Portia's presence to feel any real pity or concern for her.

Portia is bewildered by the lack of open, shared feeling in this household. She believes that she is the only one who does not understand what is beneath the genteel, snobbish surface of the Quaynes' lives. Two other characters add to Portia's puzzlement. One is Matchett, the housekeeper, a woman who worked for the first Mrs. Quayne and who knows a considerable amount about the family but who reveals only as much as she chooses to reveal in response to Portia's attempts to make a connection with the only family left to her. Matchett is a perfect servant—conscientious, discreet, authoritarian, and snobbish. Her principal interest is the house and maintaining it in perfect order as she has always done. Like the Quaynes, she does not open herself to receive the affection of the lonely, seeking girl. The other character who is important to Portia, and who also disappoints her by being too self-centered and manipulative, is Eddie. At twenty-three, he recognizes Portia's innocence but is unmoved by her need for love; he has too many needs of his own.

Portia encounters a very different household when she is sent to Seale-on-Sea to stay with Anna's former governess while Thomas and Anna escape to Capri. Mrs. Heccomb is kind and her two stepchildren, young adults Dickie and Daphne, are as cool and self-centered as the Quaynes and Eddie are, but at Waikiki life is full of events, and Portia is

332

allowed to participate in the activities of the family. She shops and goes to church with Mrs. Heccomb; she goes walking, dancing, and to the films with the two young people. When Eddie comes, quite surprisingly, to visit Portia at Waikiki, he is immediately accepted by the others, but Portia is still just an observer. Just as she is imagining that her love for Eddie is reciprocated, she observes him holding hands with Daphne at the movies. Disillusioned, she returns to London, where she is further betrayed by learning that Anna has not only read her diary but also discussed it with St. Quentin; in fact, it is he who tells Portia about this duplicity.

The betrayals by Eddie and Anna push Portia to run away from the Quaynes. She goes to the hotel of Major Brutt, another bachelor friend of Anna; he is an honorable, sensible, responsible man and convinces her that he must let the Quaynes know where she is. Whether or not she will return to them, she says, depends on what they do. They send Matchett in a cab to retrieve her, and the book ends as Matchett arrives at the door of the hotel.

The reader is not told what Portia decides, but one can assume that she will return because she has nowhere else to go. The question of what will eventually become of Portia is also left unanswered. The real point of the story is that Portia's ignorance of the world—her innocence—has ended. It remains only for the reader to discover the meaning of the novel's ambiguous title. One can be fairly sure that Portia's heart is not "dead," for her sense of hurt and disillusionment is too intense to suggest that she no longer yearns for understanding and love. On the other hand, one can easily see that the adults around her *have* undergone a "death of the heart." Each one has shut himself or herself off from others, has refused to acknowledge the deep needs of others, is self-protective and deceitful. These people—Thomas, Anna, Eddie, St. Quentin, and Matchett—have all played a part in what happens to Portia, and one can only speculate on whether the damage that they have done to her through their lack of real concern and caring will result in Portia becoming like them.

A WORLD OF LOVE

First published: 1955
Type of work: Novel

In a small country house in Ireland, five related characters live in a world of illusion and fantasy dominated by a ghostlike presence.

Bowen wrote *A World of Love* a few years after returning from England to Bowen's Court, her ancestral home in Ireland. A dilapidated and deserted farmhouse nearby served as a model for Montefort, the setting of *A World of Love*. The owner of Montefort is Antonia Montefort, a photographer in her fifties, who lives in London and only occasionally visits the house that she inherited from her cousin Guy. Killed in World War I when he was twenty, Guy had been loved by Antonia as well as by Lilia, his seventeen-year-old fiancé, and quite possibly by one or more other women. Out of pity for Lilia, who should have inherited the house, Antonia arranged Lilia's marriage to Fred Danby, an illegitimate cousin of Guy and Antonia. Feeling responsible for this marriage, Antonia gave Lilia and Fred the use of the "manor" in return for its maintenance, an obligation that Fred diligently though not very successfully tries to fulfill. Meanwhile, Lilia, ostensibly the housekeeper, dreams of escaping from her dull, discontented, and stifling life. The Danbys have two children, both girls. Jane is now twenty and Maud is twelve.

The action of the novel takes place during two days in the summer of the early 1950's. Life in this isolated, seemingly half-asleep house is dreamy, unreal, and filled with fantasy, especially to Jane and Maud. They are not alike or close to each other, but they share a tendency to live in their imaginations, and the house gives them plenty of material with which to get through the uneventful days. Jane, who has completed her education under Antonia's sponsorship, is uncertain what she will do next. In the attic one day, she finds a bundle of love letters written by Guy to an unnamed lady. There is also a beautiful Edwardian dress, which Jane wears as she wanders in and out of the house, reading the letters, imagining that she is the one to whom they were addressed. This fantasy is the central "event" of the novel, affecting each of the three women at

Montefort in terms of their relation to Guy. Their relations with each other and with the past form the subject of the book.

The sense of Guy's presence dominates the lives of Antonia, Lilia, and Jane in the days after Jane's discovery of the letters. Jane's imagined love of Guy

becomes more real to her than the life that actually surrounds her. When she goes to a dinner party at a neighboring castle, she gulps her first martinis and then, seeing a spare place at the table, imagines that Guy is sitting there. To her, Guy is more real than the hostess and the guests, who seem to be merely actors in a drama performed for her benefit. Jane returns to reality when she learns that Guy did not write the love letters to her mother, as she had suspected, nor to her, as she had imagined.

Guy also appears to Antonia, who experiences a moment when Guy seems to be near her, thus restoring to her an awareness of herself; that, in turn, gives her the ability to make her presence felt by the others in the house, restoring to her a sense of importance that she had lost during her years of feeling abandoned by her beloved cousin. She now feels reunited with Guy instead of separated from him. The moment does not last, of course, but its effect does.

Lilia, whose life was made most uncertain and dependent by Guy's loss, also has a moment when she senses that Guy has returned. The house has been pervaded by this feeling that an apparition is present. When she goes out to the garden to meet him, she finds her husband, Fred, who, by handing her Guy's letters, makes it possible for her to renounce her dead and faithless lover and accept a real love.

Even Maud falls under the spell for a while. With her ever-present imaginary companion, Gay David, Maud unconsciously parodies the experiences of the three women. By stealing the letters from the place where Jane has hidden them, Maud sets the course of the novel back toward reality, which is fully realized when the two girls are driven by a chauffeur to meet a young man, a friend of the neighboring Lady Latterly, who gave the dinner party. Maud is very much in present reality as she sees for the first time an airplane landing. Yet it is left to Jane to go beyond the present moment and, without realizing it, into the future, as she and the young man catch sight of each other and immediately fall in love.

SUMMARY

Elizabeth Bowen was a prolific writer from the time that she published her first fiction. She was considered an important and original author by readers who shared her taste for the understated and the poetic. They admired her patient probing of the psychological aspects of her characters. Speaking through her characters, she revealed her insights through such images as "the lunatic giant" mentioned by St. Quentin in *The Death of the Heart.* That noisy, crazy, internal figure is the one to which Bowen paid the most attention.

The American scholar and critic Edwin J. Kenney pointed out that all Bowen's books deal with the isolated and self-destructive capacities of innocent heroines in disordered circumstances. The crisis of identity recurs in all of her work and makes a unified whole of the novels and short stories. A somewhat eccentric and oblique style set her apart from all but a few writers of her time, notably the novelists Virginia Woolf and Henry James. Her affinity with them in style, structure, and subject matter placed her in very distinguished company, among the outstanding writers of the twentieth century.

Natalie Harper

BIBLIOGRAPHY

By the Author

LONG FICTION:
The Hotel, 1927
The Last September, 1929
Friends and Relations, 1931
To the North, 1932
The House in Paris, 1935
The Death of the Heart, 1938
The Heat of the Day, 1949
A World of Love, 1955
The Little Girls, 1964
Eva Trout, 1968

SHORT FICTION:
Encounters, 1923
Ann Lee's, and Other Stories, 1926
Joining Charles, 1929
The Cat Jumps, and Other Stories, 1934
Look at All Those Roses, 1941
The Demon Lover, 1945 (pb. in U.S. as *Ivy Gripped the Steps, and Other Stories,* 1946)
The Early Stories, 1951
Stories by Elizabeth Bowen, 1959
A Day in the Dark, and Other Stories, 1965
Elizabeth Bowen's Irish Stories, 1978
The Collected Stories of Elizabeth Bowen, 1980

DRAMA:
Castle Anna, pr. 1948 (with John Perry)

NONFICTION:
Bowen's Court, 1942
Seven Winters, 1942
English Novelists, 1946
Collected Impressions, 1950
The Shelbourne: A Center of Dublin Life for More than a Century, 1951
A Time in Rome, 1960
Afterthought: Pieces About Writing, 1962
Pictures and Conversations, 1975
The Mulberry Tree: Writings of Elizabeth Bowen, 1986 (Hermione Lee, eitor)

CHILDREN'S LITERATURE:
The Good Tiger, 1965

About the Author

Austin, Allan, ed. *Elizabeth Bowen.* Boston: Twayne, 1989.
Bennett, Andrew, and Nicholas Royle. *Elizabeth Bowen and the Dissolution of the Novel: Still Lives.* New York: St. Martin's Press, 1995.

DISCUSSION TOPICS

- How might Elizabeth Bowen's sensitivity to the complexity of Irish social history be accounted for?

- Consider how Bowen's skill at dialogue, rather than action, helps move the plot along in *The Death of the Heart* or in one of her other novels.

- Weigh the advantages and disadvantages of Bowen's grammatical and syntactical challenges to the reader.

- Explain why, in *The Death of the Heart,* Matchett's qualities make her "a perfect servant."

- Biographer Victoria Glendinning ranked Bowen as one of the ten most important fiction writers in English. Challenge or defend this ranking by comparing Bowen with other fiction writers in English.

Bloom, Harold, ed. *Elizabeth Bowen*. New York: Chelsea House, 1987.

Coles, Robert. *Irony in the Mind's Life*. New York: New Directions, 1974.

Corcoran, Neil. *Elizabeth Bowen: The Enforced Return*. New York: Oxford University Press, 2004.

Craig, Patricia. *Elizabeth Bowen*. New York: Penguin Books, 1986.

Ellmann, Maud. *Elizabeth Bowen: The Shadow Across the Page*. Edinburgh: Edinburgh University Press, 2003.

Glendinning, Victoria. *Elizabeth Bowen*. New York: Alfred A. Knopf, 1988.

Lassner, Phyllis. *Elizabeth Bowen*. New York: Macmillan, 1990.

BERTOLT BRECHT

Born: Augsburg, Germany
February 10, 1898
Died: East Berlin, East Germany (now Berlin, Germany)
August 14, 1956

Brecht was Germany's leading modern dramatist and a central influence on Western drama after World War II.

BIOGRAPHY

Even though Bertolt Brecht (brehkt), born Eugen Berthold Brecht, composed several ballads in his early twenties that told of his having been descended from shrewd, ruthless peasants, his genealogy was solidly middle class and could be traced back to the sixteenth century. He was born on February 10, 1898, in Augsburg, Germany. His father, Berthold Friedrich Brecht, was managing director of a paper mill in Augsburg. The father was Catholic, and his wife, Sophie, was Protestant; both Bertolt and his younger brother, Walter, were reared in their mother's faith and primarily by her. Brecht's boyhood and adolescence were marked by self-confidence, quick-mindedness, cunning, and vitality—all characteristics that kept him in good stead throughout his life. His skill in manipulating people and his suppleness in pursuing his goals were also evident from his youth.

During World War I, Brecht began medical studies at the University of Munich to delay an early conscription call-up; however, the only medical lectures that he attended were those dealing with venereal diseases. Instead, he studied theater history and met Frank Wedekind, who not only wrote notorious, expressionistic plays advocating sexual liberation but also composed and sang ballads with aggressive bravado. Imitating Wedekind, Brecht performed his own ballads in the coffeehouses and cabarets of Munich. In 1922, he wrote a play, *Baal* (wr., pb. 1922, pr. 1923; English translation, 1963), about an amoral, bohemian bard-balladeer who cruelly exploits, and then discards, friends and lovers of both sexes. Baal's only care is for the natural world, whose beauty he celebrates in raw, eloquent

lyrics. That same year, Brecht also wrote *Trommeln in der Nacht* (wr. 1919-1920, pr., pb. 1922; *Drums in the Night*, 1961), a powerful pacifist drama whose protagonist is a disillusioned veteran returning to a Berlin dominated by war profiteers.

Perhaps the best of Brecht's early works was *Im Dickicht der Städte* (pr. 1923; *In the Jungle of Cities*, 1960). Two men, Shlink and Garga, engage in a seemingly motiveless duel of wills. Shlink, a Malaysian lumber dealer, seeks to buy Garga's soul but is himself shown to be a victim—one whose skin has been so toughened by life that he can no longer feel. He stages his battle with Garga to penetrate his own shell of indifference.

Brecht moved to Berlin in 1924 and became a celebrated personality in that city's culturally brilliant postwar jungle. He shortened his first name to "Bert" and established for himself a part-intellectual, part-proletarian persona. His trademarks were a seminarian's tonsorial haircut, steel-rimmed spectacles, two days' growth of beard, a leather jacket, a trucker's cap, a cheap but large cigar, and chronic rudeness. People found him either charismatic or repulsive; many women found him irresistible. He charmed the beautiful singer-actress Marianne Zoff in the early 1920's. They married in November, 1922, had a daughter in 1923, but separated that year and divorced in 1927. He was to have many mistresses, of whom the most cherished were Elisabeth Hauptmann, Margarete Steffin, and Ruth Berlau.

The most important woman in Brecht's life was the Vienna-born actress Helene Weigel. She was Jewish, strongly Marxist, and staunchly feminist. They met in 1923, married in 1929, and had a son,

Stefan, in 1924, and a daughter, Barbara, in 1930. Weigel's marvelously expressive face and superbly disciplined acting skills caused many theater critics to call her the best actress of her time on the German-speaking stage. Her greatest successes were in the title roles of Brecht's *Die Mutter* (pr., pb. 1932; *The Mother*, 1965) and *Mutter Courage und ihre Kinder* (pr. 1941, pb. 1949; *Mother Courage and Her Children*, 1941).

A central problem for students of Brecht is his adherence to Communism and its effect on his work. Clearly, from youth onward, he revolted against the middle-class values that led Germany to a wasteful war, bitter defeat, extreme socioeconomic disorder in the 1920's, and Adolf Hitler's rise to power in the early 1930's. What drew Brecht to Marxism was largely its antagonism toward Germany's business and military circles. His adherence to Communism remained, nonetheless, consistently idiosyncratic—equally distasteful to the official Soviet cultural apparatus, to the House Committee on Un-American Activities, and to the rigid party-liners who ran East Germany after World War II.

In his best plays, Brecht rises above his mixture of cynicism-cum-Communism. For example, in *Der gute Mensch von Sezuan* (wr. 1938-1940, pr. 1943, pb. 1953; *The Good Woman of Setzuan*, 1948) the heroine, Shen Te, is naturally loving, selfless, and motherly; she finds fulfillment in giving and thrives on sharing her feelings and goods. Unfortunately for her, the world repays her virtues with greed, betrayal, envy, spite, and ruthless exploitation. Hence she needs to call, with increasing frequency, on the services of her calculating male "cousin," Shui Ta, who meets the world on its own level of meanness and deception. Shui Ta turns out to be Shen Te masked, the other half of her personality, which she needs to protect her interests, yet also the half that denies Shen Te her essential identity.

When the National Socialists, commonly called Nazis, took over Germany's regime in 1933, Brecht had to flee for his life. In fifteen years of exile, he, his wife, their two children, and always at least one of his mistresses lived in various Central European countries, then in Denmark, Sweden, Finland, and, from 1941 to 1947, Southern California's Santa Monica. Remarkably, wherever he was and however scant his circumstances, Brecht continued to produce plays and occasional poems at full pres-

sure. He dragged his ménages after him, ruthlessly exploited the devotion of his intimates, cut his losses, and wrote his most masterful plays in exile: *The Good Woman of Setzuan, Herr Puntila und sein Knecht, Matti* (wr. 1940, pr. 1948, pb. 1951; *Mr. Puntila and His Hired Man, Matti*, 1976), *Mother Courage and Her Children*, and *Der kaukasische Kreidekreis* (wr. 1944-1945, pr. 1948 in English; pb. 1949, pr. 1958 in German; *The Caucasian Chalk Circle*, 1948).

By and large, the United States failed to impress, let alone inspire, Brecht. He frequented a narrow circle of German and Austrian refugee writers and performers and made only two important friends outside that orbit: the British-born actor Charles Laughton, who collaborated closely with him on a revised version of *Leben des Galilei* (first version wr. 1938-1939, pr. 1943; second version, in English, wr. 1945-1947, pr. 1947; third version, in German, pr., pb. 1955, revised pb. 1957; *The Life of Galileo*, 1947), and the critic-scholar Eric Bentley, who became the authorized American translator and occasional director of Brecht's works. In October, 1947, Brecht was forced, by way of a subpoena, to testify before the House Committee on Un-American Activites. Accused of having composed Communist poems, he was cleared of pro-Communist charges by the committee. A few days later, Brecht returned permanently to Europe.

Arriving there as a stateless radical, he soon surrounded himself with safeguards: Austrian citizenship, a West German publisher, and a Swiss bank account. Then he accepted the leadership of the East Berlin repertory troupe the Berliner Ensemble and fashioned it into possibly the world's finest theatrical company of the late 1940's and 1950's. Brecht supervised a unit of more than 250 actors and supporting staff and directed his own plays in productions rehearsed from three to five months. He became the grand old man of East German culture.

On June 17, 1953, workers in East Berlin demonstrated against increased production norms; Russian tanks quickly quelled the unrest. Brecht thereupon wrote a letter to Walter Ulbricht, first secretary of the East German Communist Party, generally siding with the strikers but also declaring his fundamental loyalty to the Communist regime. Ulbricht published only the sentence expressing Brecht's attachment to the party, thereby causing

Brecht to be widely attacked in the West as a burned-out coward of questionable integrity. Increasingly disillusioned with East Germany's course, worn out by the enormous strains to which he was subjected, Brecht died of coronary thrombosis on August 14, 1956, in East Berlin.

ANALYSIS

Brecht's status as Germany's greatest twentieth century playwright is by now securely established. He joins the pantheon of his country's most commanding dramatists, which includes Friedrich Schiller, Heinrich von Kleist, Johann Wolfgang von Goethe, Georg Buechner, and Gerhart Hauptmann. Moreover, he is also a distinguished poet, with an astonishingly wide lyric range spanning folk ballads, Rimbaudesque prose poems, political epistles, and luminously concrete sonnets. Additionally, he is a provocative theorist of drama, whose concept of theatrical presentation has had enormous influence.

To address Brecht's dramaturgy first: He had nothing but contempt for what he called illusionist, bourgeois, Aristotelian theater. He scorned all devices of composition and production that sought to seduce an audience into responding empathically to the events on stage, into identifying with one or more of the characters. He sought to produce the opposite effect, one of estrangement or distancing, which he called *Verfremdung*, the process of alienating. He wanted the audience not to identify strongly with the characters, not to be transported emotionally by the actions on stage. Instead, he wished to initiate contemplation and critical judgment in his spectators, to have them remain aware that they were witnessing "nothing but" a play on whose meaning they were invited to exercise their critical intelligence during the performance rather than after it.

To deliver his audience from what he regarded as the captivity of illusion and bring it to a state of social reform, Brecht rejected many of the hitherto unquestioned criteria of dramatic art. He sought to avoid a firmly coherent and climactic structure in his plays, instead unfolding the action in numerous loosely connected episodes that he termed "epic form." He instructed his actors to remain detached from the personages that they portrayed, instead telling them to play openly to the public in the theater, making their roles commentaries rather than

representations. He had brief synopses, often songs, at the beginning of each scene; they were intended to empty the following action of suspense. Instead of eliciting strong emotions to purge the spectators of pity and terror, Brecht sought to stress the unheroic, the grotesque, and the farcical, with his characters often speaking in colloquial, and even low, language.

Nonetheless, despite Brecht's intense efforts to achieve distance and estrangement, to make his theater a school for educating the audience to revolutionary acts, he usually succeeded as a dramatist in proportion to his failure as a didactic theoretician. The differences between illusionist and epic theater turn out to be ones of degree rather than direct opposition. After all, in no theater does complete identification of the spectators with the characters occur, or they would rush on stage to save Desdemona from Othello. In no theater can there be complete detachment of the spectators from the drama, or they would doze off or walk out.

Brecht's plays, despite his strenuous efforts to circumvent the emotional response of his audience by the negation of illusion, are charged with the energies of his moral and political passions. They have the effect of enthralling and, at best, deeply moving those who witness them. In his finest dramas, though he wished only to hone his audience to critical keenness, he also moved it to tears and wonder and laughter. Though he sought to shock his audience with sardonic humor and savage indignation, he could not help letting his compassion flood through self-imposed dikes of ferocious cynicism. Though he concentrated on such vices as greed, envy, brutality, and disloyalty in many of his works, he also rose above these pessimistic indictments. In such great achievements as *The Good Woman of Setzuan, Mother Courage and Her Children, The Caucasian Chalk Circle*, and *The Life of Galileo*, he presented immortal images of vulnerability, decency, and sacrifice; he dramatized a world where sold souls do not always stay sold, and where the promptings of humaneness sometimes conquer the dictates of ideology. The disproof of much of Brecht's theorizing, then, came through his art as a playwright—an art that richly gratified the audience's hunger for sympathy, identification, and, thus, illusion.

Brecht is a divided, often enigmatic, writer whose works, for all of their extreme left-wing ideology, remain enticing and elusive. His basic vision of life is harrowing, fascinated by, in his early plays, cruelty, determination, bestiality, irrationalism, and blind instinctualism. A hysteria of violence hovers at the margins of his early dramas (as well as poems), an awareness that humankind's will is weak and malleable and that its nature is savage, brutal, and often uncontrollable. Should a character speak of love, loyalty, friendship, honor, progress, or religion, the chances are that he is merely masking a corrupt and greedy deal.

Yet Brecht's works also often have a raffishly humane aspect that charms and beguiles his public. Almost all of his characters find themselves repelled by their base instincts and seek a state of calm beyond the turmoil of their appetites. All of Brecht's later characters, such as Galileo, Courage, Shen Te and Shui Ta, the two Annas in *Die Sieben Todsünden der Kleinbürger* (pr. 1933, pb. 1959; *The Seven Deadly Sins*, 1961), and Puntila drunk and Puntila sober, are split, vacillating between reason and instinct, the true self and the pseudoself, survival and self-sacrifice. The mature Brecht often shows human impulses as healthy, kindly, courteous, and loving, while reminding the audience that society is selfishly competitive and ultimately evil.

THE THREEPENNY OPERA

First produced: *Die Dreigroschenoper*, 1928 (first published, 1929; English translation, 1949)
Type of work: Play

This work is a Marxist reinterpretation of John Gay's ballad opera, starring a businessman-gangster.

The Threepenny Opera, written exactly two hundred years after John Gay's *The Beggar's Opera* (pr., pb. 1728), follows its model closely in plot and in the names of its characters. Like Brecht's Berlin, Gay's eighteenth century London underwent a period of expansion and consolidation, with a Whig government rotten with corruption. Gay's opera chiefly satirizes the aristocracy's manners and morals, although it also mocks marriage, politics, theatrical conventions, the prison system, and

many professions. By providing the highwayman Macheath with the dash of a courtier, and whores with the grace of ladies, Gay indicts the vices of the upper class without needing to bring a single upper-class personage on stage.

Brecht adopts Gay's ironic inversion of high and low life but aims, in place of the no-longer-vital aristocracy, at Germany's triumphant, smug, powerful bourgeoisie. The criminal highwayman Macheath is called "Mac the Knife" (Mackie Messer), and while he is a thief, arsonist, rapist, and murderer, he also has the habits of a middle-class entrepreneur, keeping books, worshiping efficiency, and insisting on business discipline by his gang. His thieves are in competition with big business and the banks; they are defeated by the more predatory, shrewder, better-financed Jonathan Peachum. As he stands before the gallows, in what seems to be his farewell address, Mackie laments that he is a small fish about to be swallowed by a bigger one:

> Ladies and gentlemen. You see before you a declining representative of a declining social group. We lower-middle-class artisans who work with humble jemmies on small shopkeepers' cash registers are being swallowed up by big corporations backed by the banks. What's a jemmy compared with a stock certificate? What's breaking into a bank compared with founding a bank?

In Brecht's cynical, Marxist equation, the petty bourgeois equals the petty larcenist, while the tycoon finds his counterpart in Peachum, who licenses all the beggars in London and forces them to pay him 70 percent of their weekly take. Peachum transforms healthy men into deformed and pitiful creatures through the application of artificial limbs, eye patches, and the like—all carefully calculated to evoke the limited charitable impulses of the rich. Thus, if Mackie exemplifies the relationship between crime and business, Peachum highlights the relationship between the selfish capitalist ethic and the sacrificial morality of Christianity. Both Mackie and Peachum agree, in one of Brecht's most famous statements, that eating comes first, then morality. Brecht suggests that Christianity and capitalism are really in the same ultimately corrupt league.

Brecht's satiric attack on the bourgeoisie extends to its conventions of marriage, romantic love, and male camaraderie. Mac the Knife's wedding to Polly Peachum is a typical middle-class banquet, featuring toasts, gifts, bad jokes, and gorging guests—except that it takes place in a stable and all the furnishings are stolen. Romantic love is reduced to lust and betrayal, with the relationship of Mackie and Jinny Jenny replete with pimping, whoring, sexual disease, and betrayal.

The play's action follows a complicated network of double crosses: Macheath betrays Polly, Lucy Brown, and his gang; the whores betray Macheath twice; Peachum not only informs against Macheath but also sabotages his daughter's chances for romantic bliss; and the plot climaxes with Mackie's betrayal to the authorities by his supposed friend, the high sheriff of London, Tiger Brown. The Brown-Macheath friendship, added by Brecht to Gay's plot, features a Kiplingesque ballad of their army bonding but is actually based on commercial advantage: Mackie gives Brown the goods on other criminals, while Brown, collecting a third of the reward, in turn provides police protection for Macheath.

Brecht sees every individual betrayed by an aggregation of other individuals, as well as by his own nature. Mackie, after all, commits consistent self-betrayals by following his compulsive libido and is brought down by his womanizing.

The Threepenny Opera is a second-rate achievement on Brecht's part: Macheath is too winning a charmer to persuade the audience that he is a reprehensible criminal. More significantly, Brecht's play fails to resolve a fundamental dilemma: Does human evil stem from an evil system (capitalism), or are there fundamental evils in human nature that systems merely reflect? The work's glory is Kurt Weill's brilliant music, which displays a high level of wit and rhythmic vitality. Thanks mainly to Weill, *The Threepenny Opera* is probably Brecht's most frequently mounted play.

MOTHER COURAGE AND HER CHILDREN

First produced: *Mutter Courage und ihre Kinder,* 1941 (first published, 1949; English translation, 1941)

Type of work: Play

Anna Fierling, nicknamed Mother Courage, lives by the war as a small trader but pays her dues by losing all three of her children.

Brecht completed *Mother Courage and Her Children* in November, 1939, with its theme of the harrowing and devastating effects of a European war paralleling the outbreak of World War II in September of that year. Its world premiere did not take place until 1941, in Zurich, Switzerland, starring the fine actress Therese Giehse. In 1949, an even finer actress, Brecht's wife Helene Weigel, assumed the central role for what was to be her most celebrated triumph. The work's subtitle, *A Chronicle of the Thirty Years' War,* indicates that it deals with the feast of death that bore down on much of Europe from 1618 to 1648, solving no problems and settling no issues.

Having identified business with gangsterism in *The Threepenny Opera,* Brecht now identifies business with war. He seeks to present a relentlessly Marxist indictment of the economic causes of war. In his production notes, he states that the work is designed to demonstrate that "war, which is a continuation of business by other means, makes the human virtues fatal even to their possessors." In the drama's atmosphere of rape, pillage, and meaningless killing, with Protestants and Catholics slaughtering one another for a generation, all human ideals degenerate into hypocritical cant, while heroism shatters into splinters of cruelty, madness, greed, or absurdity. The play is bitterly pacifist, with all the featured characters living off the war yet remaining blind to the penalties that it demands, as most of them pay with their lives.

The play's protagonist, Anna Fierling, is a canteen owner known more familiarly as Mother Courage. Brecht took the name from a character who appeared in two novels, *Der abenteuerlich Simplicissimus* (1688; *The Adventurous Simplicissimus,* 1912) and *Lebensbeschreibung der Ertzbetrügerin und Land-*

störtzerin Courasche (1670; *Courage: The Adventuress,* 1964), both written by the German novelist Hans Jakob Christoffel von Grimmelshausen. Whereas Grimmelshausen's heroine is a seductive, hedonistic, childless harlot of illegitimate but aristocratic birth, Brecht's Courage is a salty, opportunistic, self-serving businesswoman, a shameless profiteer who cashes in on the troops' needs for alcohol and clothing; another character calls her "a hyena of the battlefield." Shrewd, sardonic, and skeptical, she is a full-blooded personification of her creator's antiheroic view of life.

During twelve scenes that take place from 1624 to 1636, the reader/spectator follows Anna Fierling's wagon as she makes her living from the war yet believes she can keep her grown children out of it. Each child is by a different father, and each represents one virtue in excess and is consequently killed by it. Swiss Cheese, honest but stupid, is entrusted with the cashbox as paymaster of a Protestant regiment; when he is captured by the Catholics, he refuses to surrender the money and is riddled by eleven bullets. His mother could have saved him, but only at the price of pawning her wagon, on which she and her daughter depend for their livelihood. The mother concludes prolonged bouts of bargaining with the realization, "I believe—I haggled too long."

The other son, Eiliff, is brave—a virtue in wartime but a liability during an interlude of peace, when he murders innocent peasants who wished only to protect their cattle. He discovers that law and morality are relative, shifting their ground to accommodate society's needs.

Fierling's daughter, Kattrin, mute and disfigured, is the incarnation of kindness, compassion, and love, achieving allegorical grandeur. Yet in this merciless war she is shot down from the wagon's roof by soldiers attempting a surprise attack, as she beats her drum to warn the besieged town and thereby save children's lives. Her grand gesture succeeds, but at the cost of her life. The scene dramatizing Kattrin's heroism has the prolonged excitement and suspense of melodrama, substituting passionate persuasion and spectator empathy for Brecht's satiric dialectic and strategy of distancing.

Courage herself is one of Brecht's most contradictory and perplexing characters. She is in turn admirable and despicable, with more extreme traits than any other of his protagonists. As Eric Bentley has pointed out, she is tough, honest, resilient, and courageous, but also cold, cunning, rigid, and cowardly. She concludes business deals in the back room while her children die, yet all of her transactions are undertaken for their sake. Her philosophy is to concede defeat on such large issues as the war itself, while trying to prosper as a small business entrepreneur. Brecht intends her as a vice figure in a morality play but cannot control his affection for her as she transcends his design. He tries to condemn her as a vicious Falstaff, yet his drama stresses her single-minded determination to survive.

While it is true that Courage has haggled while her children die, it is also true that her loss of them is desolately tragic. A pathetic victim of wrong dreams, she must end the play by harnessing herself to her inhuman fourth child—her wagon—to trudge after the troops as the stage begins to turn in an accelerating vortex of crazed misery. Both her smallness and her greatness are memorable in the last scene of this masterpiece.

The Life of Galileo

First produced: *Leben des Galilei,* 1943 (first published, 1955; English translation, 1947)

Type of work: Play

One of history's greatest scientists exhibits both admirable strengths and deplorable weaknesses.

The Life of Galileo is the most heavily reworked of Brecht's plays, occupying his interim attention during the last nineteen years of his life. He began writing it in German in 1938 while in Denmark, with the great physicist Niels Bohr checking the accuracy of Brecht's astronomical and physical descriptions. This version was the one produced in Zurich in 1943. After he had moved to Southern California, Brecht befriended the actor Charles Laughton, and from 1944 to 1947 they collaborated on a new version in a unique mixture of mostly German and some English. This new text changes Galileo's character from that of a guileful hero who recants to safeguard his scientific discoveries to a coward who betrays the truth and later castigates himself for having compromised his scientific calling. The explosion of the first nuclear bombs over Japanese cities strongly affected Brecht's characterization of his protagonist. The Laughton version, starring Laughton in the central role, was produced in Los Angeles and then in New York in 1947, though with small success. In 1953, Brecht and some members of the Berliner Ensemble created a third version in German, using what they considered to be the best portions of previous texts. This construction was the one staged in 1955; it is generally regarded as the standard text.

The Life of Galileo is written in chronicle form, with fifteen scenes taking the scientist from 1609, when he is forty-five, to 1637, when he is seventy-four. In the first scene, he is a lecturer at the University of Padua, living with his daughter Virginia and housekeeper, Mrs. Sarti, whose intelligent son, Andrea, becomes his favorite pupil. Frustrated because he is underpaid, Galileo accepts better conditions at the court of the Medici in Florence. There his findings tend to prove the heliocentric theories of Nicolaus Copernicus, while the Church insists on adhering to the earth-centered Ptolemaic cosmology. The Holy Office forbids Galileo to pursue his research, but when a liberal mathematician becomes the next pope, Galileo resumes his work. His hopes for the dissemination of his theories are short-lived: He is summoned before the Inquisition, is threatened with torture, and recants his views. For the rest of his life, Galileo remains the Holy Office's prisoner. When Andrea Sarti visits him in 1637, however, Galileo gives him the "Discorsi" to smuggle out of Italy, while also bitterly denouncing himself for his cowardice.

Galileo tells Andrea that, had he resisted the Inquisition, "scientists might have developed something like the physicians' Hippocratic oath, the vow to use their knowledge only for the good of mankind." This unequivocal self-condemnation sharpens the split nature of the great scientist. For Brecht, Galileo is not only a masterly scholar and

teacher, an intellectual locksmith picking at rusty incrustations of Ptolemaic tradition, but also a self-indulgent sensualist who loves to gorge himself with food and wine. After his recantation, his disciples are disillusioned with their master. Responds Galileo drily, "Unhappy the land that needs a hero." Such a view echoes Brecht's own sentiments, and his Galileo is in important respects a canny self-portrait. Like Galileo, Brecht employed all of his cunning and compromised with the authorities so that he could persist in his work. Moreover, the Galileo who lashes himself for his failure of nerve may represent Brecht's self-evaluation and self-condemnation. For one brief stage in his foxy life, Brecht may have been seized by the seductive notion of absolutely intransigent morality. It did not last.

The Life of Galileo is the subtlest of Brecht's dramas, challenging readers and audiences with its muted, yet constrained, force and its divided focus: It is a play about both the suffocation of free intellectual inquiry and the alleged sociopolitical irresponsibility of purely scientific inquiry. Next to Courage, Galileo is the most complex of Brecht's characters, compassionate to his students yet brutal to his pious daughter, brilliantly charismatic yet also selfishly opportunistic, driven by a Faustian passion for knowledge yet gluttonous for personal comforts. The play is marvelously organic, with each scene serving an indispensable purpose, each character integrated meaningfully into its structure, while the language unites historical accuracy with elegant irony. It is one of the wonders of the modern theater.

THE CAUCASIAN CHALK CIRCLE

First produced: 1948 (first published, 1949; first produced in German as *Der kaukasische Kreidekreis*, 1958)

Type of work: Play

In this mellow morality play, virtue and justice triumph in an otherwise harsh world.

The Caucasian Chalk Circle is Brecht's most cheerful and charming play, offered as a moral lesson with deference to the techniques of both the Oriental and the Elizabethan theater. Its structure is intricate, and more distanced, or epic, than that of any other Brechtian play. Several plots run through it, all merging at the end.

Plot 1 is set in the Russian province of Georgia, where members of two collective farms meet to resolve a dispute about a tract of land. Plot 2 is a story of flight. The peasant Grusha is forced to flee a Caucasian city as a result of usurpation and revolt. Having saved the abandoned child of the dead governor's wife, she risks her life for her maternal instinct, passing over dangerous bridges, marrying an apparently dying man (who then revives to plague her), and almost sacrificing her lover, Simon, who is returning from the civil war. After two years, a counterrevolt returns the governor's party to power, and the governor's widow claims her estate, which she can obtain only as the mother of the legal heir. Her soldiers find Grusha and the infant and bring them to trial. As the storyteller, who distances the text in epic fashion, sings, "She who had borne him demanded the child./ She who had raised him faced trial./ Who will decide the case?"

The judge is Azdak, one of the finest rogues in dramatic literature. Plot 3 features him as a brilliant Lord of Misrule. Having been appointed magistrate as a consequence of a prank, he used bourgeois, Marxist legal chicanery to pass down antibourgeois, Marxist legal decisions. He is a drunk, lecher, and monumental bribe taker, yet he always manages to arrive at humane and fair decisions, acting according to the spirit of justice while ignoring the letter of the law.

In plot 4, the play's separate actions neatly converge, finding their moment of impact in a marvelous courtroom scene. Azdak awards Grusha the child in a chalk-circle test that enacts the biblical legend with inverse results: The woman who has been a nurturing mother obtains custody rather than the biological but unfeeling mother; moreover, Azdak divorces Grusha from her husband so that she and Simon can marry. The disputed land is awarded to the fruit growers, who can use it better than its previous, goat-breeding owners.

The play is a parable that poses and resolves a set of basic issues: legal justice versus practical justice, morality versus expediency, reason versus sentiment, and, as stated, the claims of the adoptive mother versus those of the natural mother. Yet the work is singularly lacking in didacticism and offers a wealth of theatrically striking episodes, while the lyrical language of the storyteller's narration is suitably balanced by starkly realistic, earthy idioms.

SUMMARY

Like his greatest characters, Shen Te, Grusha, Azdak, Puntila, Courage, and Galileo, Bertolt Brecht is a survivor. He survived fifteen years of exile in the 1930's and 1940's; he survived harrowing stresses of migration, poverty, personal crises, grubby internecine rivalries, the bitter pathos of Adolf Hitler's demonic enmity toward culture, and Joseph Stalin's betrayal of left-wing idealism. Wherever he was, however sour his circumstances, he managed to produce an impressive volume of distinguished plays, poems, and provocative essays on dramaturgy at full steam. Like his literary/scientific alter ego, Galileo, he employed his sly tenacity to persist in his work.

No theatrical writer since Henrik Ibsen, August Strindberg, and Anton Chekhov has achieved as many masterpieces as Brecht: *The Good Woman of Setzuan, The Caucasian Chalk Circle, Mother Courage and Her Children*, and *The Life of Galileo* are assuredly among modernism's dramatic peaks. Brecht's only rival as the leading Western playwright of the middle and late twentieth century is Samuel Beckett.

Gerhard Brand

BIBLIOGRAPHY

By the Author

DRAMA:
Die Hochzeit, wr. 1919, pr. 1926, pb. 1953 (as *Die Keinbürgerhochzeit; The Wedding*, 1970)
Trommeln in der Nacht, wr. 1919-1920, pr., pb. 1922 (*Drums in the Night*, 1961)
Baal, wr., pb. 1922, pr. 1923 (English translation, 1963)

Im Dickicht der Städte, pr. 1923 (*In the Jungle of Cities*, 1960)

Leben Eduards des Zweiten von England, pr., pb. 1924 (with Lion Feuchtwanger; based on Christopher Marlowe's play *Edward II*; *Edward II*, 1966)

Mann ist Mann, pr. 1926, pb. 1927 (*A Man's a Man*, 1961)

Die Dreigroschenoper, pr. 1928, pb. 1929 (libretto; based on John Gay's play *The Beggar's Opera*; *The Threepenny Opera*, 1949)

Der Ozeanflug, pr., pb. 1929 (radio play; *The Flight of the Lindberghs*, 1930)

Das Badener Lehrstück vom Einverständnis, pr. 1929, pb. 1930 (*The Didactic Play of Baden: On Consent*, 1960)

Happy End, pr. 1929, pb. 1958 (libretto; lyrics with Elisabeth Hauptmann; English translation, 1972)

Aufstieg und Fall der Stadt Mahagonny, pb. 1929, pr. 1930 (libretto; *Rise and Fall of the City of Mahagonny*, 1957)

Der Jasager, pr. 1930, pb. 1931 (based on the Japanese Nō play *Taniko*; *He Who Said Yes*, 1946)

Die Massnahme, pr. 1930, pb. 1931 (libretto; *The Measures Taken*, 1960)

Die Ausnahme und die Regel, wr. 1930, pb. 1937, pr. 1938 (*The Exception and the Rule*, 1954)

Der Neinsager, pb. 1931 (*He Who Said No*, 1946)

Die heilige Johanna der Schlachthöfe, pb. 1931, pr. 1932 (radio play), pr. 1959 (staged) (*St. Joan of the Stockyards*, 1956)

Die Mutter, pr., pb., 1932 (based on Maxim Gorky's novel *Mat*; *The Mother*, 1965)

Die Sieben Todsünden der Kleinbürger, pr. 1933, pb. 1959 (cantata; *The Seven Deadly Sins*, 1961)

Die Horatier und die Kuriatier, wr. 1934, pb. 1938, pr. 1958 (*The Horatians and the Curatians*, 1947)

Die Rundköpfe und die Spitzköpfe, pr. 1935, pb. 1936 (based on William Shakespeare's play *Measure for Measure*; *The Roundheads and the Peakheads*, 1937)

Die Gewehre der Frau Carrar, pr., pb. 1937 (*Señora Carrar's Rifles*, 1938)

Furcht und Elend des dritten Reiches, pr. 1938 (in French), pr. 1945 (in English), pb. 1945 (in German) (*The Private Life of the Master Race*, 1944)

Leben des Galilei, first version wr. 1938-1939, pr. 1943, second version, in English, wr. 1945-1947, pr. 1947; third version, in German, pr., pb. 1955, revised pb. 1957 (*The Life of Galileo*, 1947; better known as *Galileo*)

Der gute Mensch von Sezuan, wr. 1938-1940, pr. 1943, pb. 1953 (*The Good Woman of Setzuan*, 1948)

Das Verhör des Lukullus, pr. 1940 (radio play), pb. 1940, pr. 1951 (staged) (libretto; *The Trial of Lucullus*, 1943)

Herr Puntila und sein Knecht, Matti, wr. 1940, pr. 1948, pb. 1951 (*Mr. Puntila and His Hired Man, Matti*, 1976)

Mutter Courage und ihre Kinder, pr. 1941, pb. 1949 (*Mother Courage and Her Children*, 1941); based on Hans Jakob Christoffel von Grimmelshausen's *Der abenteuerlich Simplicissimus*, 1688 (*The Adventurous Simplicissimus*, 1912) and *Lebensbeschreibung der Ertzbetrügerin und Landstörtzerin Courasche*, 1670 (*Courage: The Adventuress*, 1964)

Der aufhaltsame Aufstieg des Arturo Ui, wr. 1941, pb. 1957, pr. 1958 (*The Resistible Rise of Arturo Ui*, 1972)

DISCUSSION TOPICS

- Consider the unfairness involved in the considerable criticism of Bertolt Brecht's Communist convictions while Europe was being wracked by Fascist and Nazi forces.

- With such organizations as the House Committee on Un-American Activities so important in the 1950's, why was 1956 such an unfortunate time for Brecht to die?

- Consider Brecht's place among the poets of Germany.

- What traits dominate the mother figure in Brecht's plays?

- What explanation might be given for the extraordinary popularity of Brecht's *The Threepenny Opera* in the United States?

- Did the success of Brecht's most important plays result because of, or in spite of, his relentless hostility toward business?

- Which merits of Brecht's *The Life of Galileo* give this play a chance to remain "one of the wonders of the modern theater"?

Die Gesichte der Simone Machard, wr. 1941-1943, pb. 1956, pr. 1957 (with Feuchtwanger; *The Visions of Simone Machard*, 1961)

Schweyk im zweiten Weltkrieg, wr. 1941-1943, pr. 1957 (in Polish), pb. 1957, pr. 1958 (in German; based on Jaroslav Hašek's novel *Osudy dobrého vojáka š vejka za svetove války*; *Schweyk in the Second War*, 1975)

Der kaukasische Kreidekreis, wr. 1944-1945, pr. 1948 (in English), pb. 1949, pr. 1958 (in German; based on Li Hsing-dao's play *The Circle of Chalk*; *The Caucasian Chalk Circle*, 1948)

Die Antigone des Sophokles, pr., pb. 1948 (*Sophocles' Antigone*, 1990)

Die Tage der Commune, wr. 1948-1949, pr. 1956, pb. 1957 (based on Nordahl Grieg's *Nederlaget*; *The Days of the Commune*, 1971)

Der Hofmeister, pr. 1950, pb. 1951 (adaptation of Jacob Lenz's *Der Hofmeister*; *The Tutor*, 1972)

Turandot: Oder, Der Kongress der Weisswäscher, wr. 1950-1954, pr. 1970

Der Prozess der Jeanne d'Arc zu Rouen, 1431, pr. 1952, pb. 1959 (based on Anna Seghers' radio play; *The Trial of Jeanne d'Arc at Rouen, 1431*, 1972)

Coriolan, wr. 1952-1953, pb. 1959 (adaptation of William Shakespeare's play *Coriolanus*; *Coriolanus*, 1972)

Don Juan, pr. 1953, pb. 1959 (adaptation of Molière's play; English translation, 1972)

Pauken und Trompeten, pb. 1956 (adaptation of George Farquhar's *The Recruiting Officer*; *Trumpets and Drums*, 1972)

SCREENPLAYS:
Kuhle Wampe, 1932 (English translation, 1933)
Hangmen Also Die, 1943
Das Lied der Ströme, 1954
Herr Puntila und sein Knecht, Matti, 1955

LONG FICTION:
Der Dreigroschenroman, 1934 (*The Threepenny Novel*, 1937, 1956)
Die Geschäfte des Herrn Julius Caesar, 1956

SHORT FICTION:
Geschichten vom Herrn Keuner, 1930, 1958 (*Stories of Mr. Keuner*, 2001)
Kalendergeschichten, 1948 (*Tales from the Calendar*, 1961)
Prosa, 1965 (5 volumes)
Me-ti: Buch der Wendungen, 1965
Bertolt Brecht Short Stories, 1921-1946, 1983 (translation of *Geschichten*, volume 11 of *Gesammelte Werke*)
Collected Stories, 1998

POETRY:
Hauspostille, 1927, 1951 (*Manual of Piety*, 1966)
Lieder, Gedichte, Chöre, 1934 (*Songs, Poems, Choruses*, 1976)
Svendborger Gedichte, 1939 (*Svendborg Poems*, 1976)
Selected Poems, 1947
Hundert Gedichte, 1951 (*A Hundred Poems*, 1976)
Gedichte und Lieder, 1956 (*Poems and Songs*, 1976)
Gedichte, 1960-1965 (9 volumes)
Bertolt Brecht: Poems, 1913-1956, 1976 (includes *Buckower Elegies*)
Bad Time for Poetry: 152 Poems and Songs, 1995

NONFICTION:
Der Messingkauf, 1937-1951 (*The Messingkauf Dialogues*, 1965)
Arbeitsjournal, 1938-1955, 1973 (3 volumes; *Bertolt Brecht Journals*, 1993)
Kleines Organon für das Theater, 1948 (*A Little Organum for the Theater*, 1951)
Schriften zum Theater, 1963-1964 (7 volumes)

Brecht on Theatre, 1964
Autobiographische Aufzeichnungen, 1920-1954, 1975 (partial translation *Diaries, 1920-1922*, 1979)
Letters, 1990
Brecht on Film and Radio, 2000

MISCELLANEOUS:
Gesammelte Werke, 1967 (20 volumes)

About the Author

Bentley, Eric. *The Brecht Commentaries: 1943-1980.* New York: Grove Press, 1981.

Clark, Mark W. *Beyond Catastrophe: German Intellectuals and Cultural Renewal After World War II, 1945-1955.* Lanham, Md.: Lexington Books, 2006.

Demetz, Peter, ed. *Brecht: A Collection of Critical Essays.* Englewood Cliffs, N.J.: Prentice-Hall, 1962.

Esslin, Martin. *Brecht: The Man and His Work.* 1960. Rev. ed. Garden City, N.Y.: Doubleday, 1971.

Hayman, Ronald. *Brecht: A Biography.* New York: Oxford University Press, 1983.

Lyons, Charles R. *Bertolt Brecht: The Despair and the Polemic.* Carbondale: Southern Illinois University Press, 1968.

Morley, Michael. *Brecht: A Study.* London: Heinemann, 1977.

Thomson, Peter, and Glendyr Sacks, eds. *The Cambridge Companion to Brecht.* New York: Cambridge University Press, 2006.

Unwin, Stephen. *A Guide to the Plays of Bertolt Brecht.* London: Methuen, 2005.

ANDRÉ BRINK

Born: Vrede, Orange Free State, South Africa
May 29, 1935

Among the first Afrikaner writers to win international acclaim, Brink is best known for his intimate portrayals of Afrikaner life, which are seamlessly placed within the larger context of the fight of blacks, Cape Coloureds, and other nonwhites to win political freedom.

BIOGRAPHY

André Phillipus Brink was the first of four children born to a local Afrikaner magistrate and a schoolteacher on May 29, 1935, in the Orange Free State, South Africa. The Afrikaners are descendants of seventeenth century Dutch and Huguenot immigrants who settled three main areas in what is today South Africa. Brink's parents shared their home region's strict Dutch Reformed Church's Calvinistic religious beliefs and evinced the Afrikaner suspicion of and disdain for the Bantu (black) and Cape Coloured (mixed race) peoples of Southern Africa.

Growing up in a household where his father's judicial work moved them from place to place in the Free State, Brink was exposed at an early age to the Afrikaner Nationalist Party politics espoused by his father and his friends, especially their distrust of the British rulers of South Africa, a remembrance focusing on past grievances, including the Boer War of 1899-1902, wherein Afrikaners were killed in great numbers and placed in the first of the world's concentration camps. His father and mother were, in their own way, exemplary citizens—dutiful, highly religious conformists careful about doing or saying anything out of the ordinary, and his siblings followed their lead. Brink was the only family member who would openly rebel against apartheid.

Brink went on to study Afrikaans and Dutch literature at South Africa's highly conservative Potchefstroom University from 1956 to 1959. Feeling in need of a more worldly perspective than that afforded him by Potchefstroom, he elected to study at the Sorbonne in Paris, which he attended from 1959 to 1961. His encounters with French manners and mores, in addition to the opinions of contemporary European writers, led him to see his native land in new ways. In fact, the bohemianism and the literary existentialism of Parisian intellectuals allowed him to find creative ways to break with his restrictive Afrikaner upbringing. It was in Paris that he became conversant with major Continental directions in writing, and he would incorporate European depictions of explicit sexuality and violence into his work.

After graduating from the Sorbonne, Brink returned to South Africa to study for degrees in literature at Rhodes University in Grahamstown, a place he would call home for three decades. His early Rhodes years marked his emergence as a major writer and member of the Sestigers Movement (literally, "people of the '60's") in literature, a rebellious group of young people who decried the apartheid policies that treated blacks as subhumans without rights. He went on to teach for many years at both Rhodes University and the University of Cape Town, the latter eventually awarding him the rank of professor of literature emeritus.

Brink published his first novel, written in Afrikaans, *Lobola vir die lewe*, in 1962, but it was not until the publication of another Afrikaans work, *Kennis van die aand* (1973; *Looking on Darkness*, 1974), that the South African government finally saw how subversive his writing was and banned it, the first Afrikaans novel ever to be so treated. Though banned in his own nation for his political views, Brink's subsequent novels and essays began to receive world renown; his fiction earned critical acclaim for its depiction of daily Afrikaner life, with its complex codes of conduct, its passionate beliefs based on fear and narrowness of mental horizon, its intense loyalties, and its betrayals by those whose eyes were open to the truth. He shocked some readers and many establishment critics with his emphasis on the most overt violence, as well as his depiction of vivid sexual encounters between men and women of different races and the homoerotic undercurrents lurking in the dealings of male Afrikaners.

In 1975, Brink published the controversial novel *'N Omblik in die wind* (1975; *An Instant in the Wind*, 1976), and he subsequently produced two major novels of protest, *Gerugte van Reën* (1978; *Rumours of Rain*, 1978) and *'N droë wit seison* (1979; *A Dry White Season*, 1979), both of which were banned in South Africa. The 1980's brought forth such impressive novelistic explorations of modern South Africa as *Houd-den-bek* (1982; *A Chain of Voices*, 1982), *Die muur van die pes* (1984; *The Wall of the Plague*, 1984), *States of Emergency* (1988), and *Die eerste lewe van Adamastor* (1988; *The First Life of Adamastor*, 1993, also known as *Cape of Storms*). In the 1990's, the decade marked by the apartheid system's destruction, Brink published several additional novels, including *An Act of Terror* (1991) and *Inteendeel* (1993; *On the Contrary*, 1993), and edited *SA, 27 April 1994: An Author's Diary* (1994). In the twenty-first century, Brink wrote the noted novels *Donkermaan* (2000; *The Rights of Desire*, 2000), *Anderkant die stilte* (2002; *The Other Side of Silence*, 2002), and *Praying Mantis* (2005). In addition to writing novels, he has translated many works of other authors into Afrikaans, and he has written critically lauded plays and essays.

His major novels and other literary works and his great help in bringing Afrikaner literature into the modern world have earned for him three South African Central News Agency (CNA) Awards for his work in both English and Afrikaans; honorary doctorates from noted South African and European universities; the Herzog Prize for theater; Britain's Martin Luther King Memorial Prize for literature; Italy's Premio Mondello award; and France's highly prestigious Legion d'Honneur, to name some of the most significant honors. Additionally, he has been nominated for the Nobel Prize in Literature and was twice on the short list for one of Britain's most important literary awards, the Man Booker Prize.

ANALYSIS

Brink possesses the restless spirit of a rebel and innovator whose ideas led him to confrontations with South African authorities during the apartheid era. He is at his best depicting the rural districts he knew as a boy, where white girls and boys often had as best friends the very same black girls and boys from whom they would wall off themselves in adult life. Yet despite the dictates of the old and now dismantled apartheid system, the whites, even as adults, would sometimes surprise themselves by falling in lust—or even in love—with someone of another race. Brink also is at his best when he graphically portrays the human costs resulting from the onerous apartheid laws—the beatings, the jailings, and the state-sanctioned murders.

In his earliest novels written in Afrikaans, Brink portrays those who, being at emotional and spiritual odds with fellow Afrikaners, find ways to divorce themselves from the country's soul-killing narrowness. During the apartheid period, people like Brink and those characters who resembled him followed their own internal countercultural compass and found themselves aliens in their own land, persons no longer considered part of the "white tribe" in which they had been raised.

Brink, in a large sense, envisions himself to be the true Afrikaner chronicler of the long, slow decline of white South African power and authority and the rise of a multicultural nation in its place. Through flashbacks, uninvolved narrators, diary entries, and other methods of showcasing the failures of apartheid's pass laws and immorality acts, its violence and brutality, and its more subtle means of coercing conformity, his aim is to depict how even the most determined efforts to maintain the status quo, to keep fear at bay through the dehumanizing of those perceived as "different," are bound to collapse when subversive events, such as love arising between those of differing ethnicity, relentlessly works against the creaky, jerry-built apartheid structure, eventually causing it to collapse.

RUMOURS OF RAIN

First published: *Gerugte van Reën,* 1978
   (English translation, 1978)
Type of work: Novel

A world-weary and rich Afrikaner business executive experiences an existential dilemma that forces him to reconsider the realities of apartheid.

Martin Mynhardt's ties to his family farm in the Eastern Cape of Good Hope could form a barrier to the acquisitive desires of a land-hungry company that wants to own and control the region outright. Yet Martin is not the sort of person to sentimentalize his roots or to care much about the effect of the farm's loss on family members and their black retainers.

There are, however, two people in Martin's world whom he does actually care for—far more than he cares for his emotionally estranged wife, Elise, or his angry, disillusioned son, Louis: namely, his old childhood friend and companion, the political revolutionary Bernard, and his lovely wife—and Martin's last lover—Bea, an Italian expatriate and political activist who came to South Africa at a young age. Martin's existential dilemma is whether to help his old friends by hiding important writings that Bernard pleads with Martin to take with him, thereby putting Martin's life in mortal danger as an enemy of the South African state, or to sell out his friends and resume some semblance of his previous politically uninvolved life. Martin then is faced with the hardest of choices: Should he once again turn traitor to Bernard—since Martin already betrayed Bernard by falling in love with Bea—and destroy everything Bernard had attempted to do with his life by turning state's evidence, or should he invite certain death by being seen as Bernard and Bea's accomplice in treason against the state?

Thus, this novel is about the loyalties of the heart, things people ignore only at their peril: Martin's long-standing marriage to Elise, interrupted over the years by various infidelities; his emotional ties to and sense of responsibility for his son Louis, a soldier in South Africa's losing fight against Angola, with whom he has not fostered a good father-son relationship; Bernard's love for Bea that is coupled with his inability to put her before his own powerful political aspirations; Bea's deep love for her husband, set alongside her physical desire for Martin's lovemaking sessions with her; and Martin's loyalty to his own boyhood and the family and farm that were at its center, versus the need for business allies who may come in handy in the future. In *Rumours of Rain,* love is a choice and is juxtaposed with decisions that betray it.

All of Martin's allegiances are tested by events he never saw coming. For instance, as South Africa's once seemingly unified, apparently strong facade develops cracks through participation in border wars and skirmishes, such as the conflict with Angola, young men like Louis are drafted into hellish and ill-conceived conflicts of attrition. Martin, wanting very much to see his "white tribe" winning, fails to be able to envision the failure of that enterprise, something of which Louis could apprise him, if he would only ask, for Louis has participated in war, unlike his father and other Afrikaners who cheer on the troops from their own safe and secure vantage point far from the front lines.

Linked in Martin's mind with Bernard's final day in court, before he is taken away by the thugs who run South Africa, is the death of his father, who though learned never found ways to leave behind his distorted Afrikaner concept of the world; readers readily see that same stubborn determination in Martin to be true to the traditional Afrikaner ways of thinking and doing. Yet Martin, unlike his father, who lived when apartheid was at its peak, cannot hang on to the past though he tries, just as he literally cannot hang onto his family's farm. Historical forces now dictate that he open his closed mind to a new world order, one that has engulfed his nation, and yet he never really does.

Bernard, however, is the true cycle-breaker of the piece—the true rebel, passionate and self-denying in his search for a transformed, reconfigured South Africa where all people can be free. He is the one at novel's end who is the agent of political change—that "rain" from the book's title that will fall hard and fast on this spiritually and morally drought-stricken place, a stream of destruction that brings new life. Yet Martin, almost despite himself, ends up becoming one with the redemptive flood of political action advocated by Bernard and Bea, and he gives up his life to the higher cause they espouse. Readers do see him as redeemed from what had been a bigoted, sorry, shallow, selfish, and morally diminished existence.

A DRY WHITE SEASON

First published: *'N droë wit seison,* 1979
 (English translation, 1979)
Type of work: Novel

A white teacher's quest for authenticity leads him to abandon family and friends to fight the racist South African apartheid system in order to find justice for a black man and his son who were murdered by that system.

In *A Dry White Season,* a successful novel which became a successful motion picture, Brink visits familiar terrain, namely Afrikaner South Africa (as opposed to British South Africa) at a time of moral and spiritual drought just prior to the coming of the storms of change that will bring this nation rain and renewal. As did his earlier novel, *Rumours of Rain,* Brink's *A Dry White Season* gives readers a white South African protagonist, but this time one more in keeping with Brink's own actively subversive nature, as well as one in tune with Steve Biko, a real-life hero who died after being tortured and killed while in the custody of the South African police at the very time this novel was written.

Unlike the narrator in *Rumours of Rain,* the generally self-seeking businessman Martin Mynhardt, this book concerns Ben du Toit, who from his student days has been an agent of resistance against the powers fostering the injustice he sees festering in his country. When Ben finds that Jonathan, the son of his school's gardener, Gordon Ngubene, has had his skin deeply scored six times by a knife while being detained by police on suspicion of being part of a minor melee, he becomes enraged. Jonathan Ngubene has been supported by Ben and is a kind of son to him, so this act of brutality against Jona-

than is appalling to Ben. Things, however, get worse when Ben finds that Gordon, the boy's father, has disappeared after he searched for his son, who was in police custody. Gordon vanishes into the police state netherworld of apartheid secrecy, and Ben finds he must investigate Gordon's fate, something that brings on his own destruction and martyrdom.

In this novel, Brink manages to deliver the physicality of his native South Africa, especially in his descriptions of all of those squalid, stinking, rotting, dangerous black townships, like Soweto, where the poor black majority of South Africans attempt to survive, but also in the glorious revealed splendor of that country's veld lands with its famous animal denizens. Yet another sight, one even more memorable, is revealed when the curtain is parted and readers see state lock-ups filled with the detritus of despairing convicts, places where torture is a daily occurrence. Here is the state's fearsome underbelly, a place where fear breeds hatred toward the feared. On the other hand, Brink also gives readers glimpses of humanity among the worst of these guards and torturers, seeing them as vulnerable persons whose pathetic lives are bound up in fear of "the Other," here represented best by Gordon, Jonathan, and then Ben.

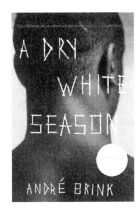

Brink's readers function as both judge and jury for the old apartheid state of South Africa in the world's courthouse of opinion. As prosecuting attorney, the author could be seen to say to them, as any good prosecutor would, "Here is the system we Afrikaners have assembled, and this terrible system does not deserve to live another day!"

SUMMARY

Within each of his works, André Brink depicts the brutal South African apartheid government apparatus from the viewpoints of victims, as well as their victimizers. At his most effective, as in *Rumours of Rain* and *A Dry White Season,* he compellingly demonstrates that even the most disinterested, self-serving, passive Afrikaner can suddenly find himself (and it is almost always a man) in a life and death struggle when someone he loves is in grave peril after having broken the laws of the apartheid state. He also manages to convey how essentially fragile that state, with all its projected power and authority, actually is when victims stand up to it and expose it to the world—people like for-

mer Robben Island prisoner Nelson Mandela. Replacing the heretofore reactionary nation of South Africa with the rainbow-hued South Africa of Mandela is part of what Brink is about in his subversive novels, and he succeeds in helping to bring about incredible change.

John D. Raymer

BIBLIOGRAPHY

By the Author

LONG FICTION:
Lobola vir die lewe, 1962
Die ambassadeur, 1963 (*The Ambassador*, 1964; better known as *File on a Diplomat*)
Miskien nooit: 'N Somerspel, 1967
Kennis van die aand, 1973 (*Looking on Darkness*, 1974)
'N Omblik in die wind, 1975 (*An Instant in the Wind*, 1976)
Gerugte van Reën, 1978 (*Rumours of Rain*, 1978)
'N droë wit seison, 1979 (*A Dry White Season*, 1979)
Houd-den-bek, 1982 (*A Chain of Voices*, 1982)
Die muur van die pes, 1984 (*The Wall of the Plague*, 1984)
Die eerste lewe van Adamastor, 1988 (novella; *The First Life of Adamastor*, 1993; also known as *Cape of Storms*)
States of Emergency, 1988
An Act of Terror, 1991
Inteendeel, 1993 (*On the Contrary*, 1993)
Sandkastele, 1995 (*Imaginings of Sand*, 1996)
Duiwelskloof, 1998 (*Devil's Valley*, 1998)
Donkermaan, 2000 (*The Rights of Desire*, 2000)
Anderkant die stilte, 2002 (*The Other Side of Silence*, 2002)
Before I Forget, 2004
Praying Mantis, 2005

SHORT FICTION:
Die meul teen die hang, 1958
Rooi, 1965 (with others)
Oom Kootjie Emmer, 1973
'N Emmertjie wyn: 'N versameling dopstories, 1981
Oom Kootjie Emmer en die nuwe bediling: 'N stinkstorie, 1983
Loopdoppies: Nog dopstories, 1984
Mal, en ander stories: 'N Omnibus van humor, 1995

DISCUSSION TOPICS

- What crimes does André Brink find that Afrikaners have committed against their own country?

- How does Brink enable readers to see how all people allow themselves to act on false impressions of those different from themselves?

- In Brink's view, what should come first in life: the people who are closest to you or the causes in which you deeply believe?

- What does Brink see as being his duty as an Afrikaner writer? Is it different from what a writer of any other nationality would envision?

- According to Brink, why are Afrikaners not able to fully feel a part of the continent in which they live?

- Are Afrikaners in these novels tribal in their thinking?

NONFICTION:

Mapmakers: Writing in a State of Siege, 1983 (better known as *Writing in a State of Siege*)
Destabilising Shakespeare, 1996
Reinventing a Continent: Writing and Politics in South Africa, 1982-1995, 1996
The Novel: Language and Narrative from Cervantes to Calvino, 1998

EDITED TEXTS:

A Land Apart: A Contemporary South African Reader, 1987 (with J. M. Coetzee)
SA, 27 April 1994: An Author's Diary, 1994
27 April: One Year Later, 1995
Groot verseboek, 2000, 2000

About the Author

Brink, André. "An Uneasy Freedom: Dangers of Political Management of Culture in South Africa." *The Times Literary Supplement*, September 24, 1993, p. 13.

Brown, Duncan, and Bruno van Dyk, eds. *Exchanges: South African Writing in Transition.* Pietermaritzburg, South Africa: University of Natal Press, 1991.

Jolly, Rosemary June. *Colonization, Violence, and Narration in White South African Writing: André Brink, Breyten Breytenback, and J. M. Coetzee.* Athens: Ohio University Press, 1996.

Wheatcroft, Geoffrey. "A Talk with André Brink." *The New York Times Book Review*, June 13, 1982, pp. 14-15.

"Writing Against Big Brother: Notes on Apocalyptic Fiction in South Africa." *World Literature Today* 58, no. 2 (1984): 89-94.

CHARLOTTE BRONTË

Born: Thornton, Yorkshire, England
   April 21, 1816
Died: Haworth, Yorkshire, England
   March 31, 1855

In isolated circumstances, Brontë produced Jane Eyre, *a work that was to have tremendous influence on the Victorian reading public.*

BIOGRAPHY

Charlotte Brontë (BRAHN-tee) was born in Thornton, England, on April 21, 1816, the third daughter of Maria Branwell Brontë and the Reverend Patrick Brontë. The family rapidly increased to include a son, Branwell, and two more daughters, Emily and Anne. Shortly after moving to the village of Haworth, situated high in the moors of West Yorkshire, the children experienced the first of many tragedies: In September, 1821, their mother died of a lingering illness. To help take care of the children, Maria Branwell's older sister Elizabeth came to live with the family; her strict Methodist ways and somewhat unsympathetic nature were a gloomy influence on the grieving, lonely youngsters.

Finding some sympathy in one another's company was not to provide solace for long. The two oldest Brontë daughters, Maria and Elizabeth, were sent to school, followed soon after by Charlotte and Emily. Weakened by bouts of measles and whooping cough and subjected to the poor diet of the school, Maria and Elizabeth were particularly susceptible to the illnesses that were epidemic at the time. Within months, both had been sent home from school, and by June, 1825, both had died. The younger children remained at home, being schooled by their father and forging the close literary relationships that were to inform their future endeavors.

In June of 1826, Patrick Brontë brought home a set of twelve wooden soldiers as a gift for Branwell. Already accustomed to making up stories in the style of *Blackwood's Magazine,* the children quickly named the soldiers after popular heroes and began to identify with their favorite characters. They created an imaginary land over which they ruled as the four "Genies." The two older children, Charlotte and Branwell, began collaborating on stories about the land of "Angria," about which they wrote every day in minuscule books. From these early productions came Charlotte's desire to be a novelist and Branwell's belief that he would become a great poet in the style of Lord Byron.

In 1831, Brontë again went to school, this time at Roe Head, a happy environment where she made lifelong friends with two other pupils, Ellen Nussey and Mary Taylor. She was fond of her teacher, and she seemed to accept the occupation for which she was being trained, that of governess. By the time she was nineteen, she had been offered the opportunity to teach at Roe Head, thereby earning free schooling for one of her sisters. Her letters from this period indicate her frustration with teaching; her only real pleasure seemed to come from the continued collaboration with Branwell. Yet Brontë suspected that even this satisfaction was temporary after she received a response to a letter that she had written in 1836 to Robert Southey, the poet laureate of England. He was discouraging about a literary career and warned her that she might become unfit for any other work if she spent too much time daydreaming. Brontë seemed to accept this advice, and she left Roe Head vowing to put her fantasy world behind her.

By 1839, Brontë herself was realizing the dangers of indulging for too long in imaginative escapism. After turning down two marriage proposals from men for whom she was temperamentally unsuited, she began to reject the extravagant romanticism of her imaginary characters and turned to the question of how to support herself. Much of the discretionary income of the Brontë family went to support Branwell's education and desire to become an artist or poet, and Emily seemed emotionally incapable of living away from her home and familiar moors, so Charlotte was determined to find practical employment. She took a position as private governess to a wealthy family but found the situation exhausting and degrading. Her experiences with the Sidgwick family provided much of the material for *Jane Eyre* (1847) but were otherwise unproductive.

Realizing that her education was insufficient to obtain a first-class teaching position, Brontë traveled to Brussels in 1842 to study French at the Pensionnat Heger, a small private school. Her lessons were interrupted by her aunt's death in November of that year, but she made enough progress to be asked to return to the Pensionnat as a teacher in 1843. She soon developed romantic feelings for the master of the school, Clementin Heger. She expressed her passion for him in letters that she wrote after her return to Haworth in 1844, but Heger, married, could not respond. Ironically, her depression over this unrequited love was deepened by the disturbing behavior of Branwell, who left a tutoring job in disgrace after having an affair with his employer's wife. Other aspects of Branwell's behavior—his bragging, his drunken carousing, his experiments with opium—all seemed evidence of the dangerous romanticism inherent in his adolescent aspirations to a poetic life.

Nonetheless, it was in 1844 that Brontë began her most productive period as a writer. With new maturity and seriousness of intent, she wrote her first novel, *The Professor* (1857), which was destined to be rejected by six publishers. Using the pseudonym Currer Bell, she published a collection of poetry with her sisters, *Poems by Currer, Ellis, and Acton Bell* (1846), and then, while Anne and Emily worked on their novels, she produced *Jane Eyre* (1847). This book, extremely popular at the time,

was to gain her the fame she experienced in her later life.

The year 1848 included Brontë's supreme enjoyment at reading good reviews of *Jane Eyre* and the pleasure of making herself known to her London publishers. This public triumph, however, was countered by private tragedy: Branwell, weakened by his intemperate behavior, contracted tuberculosis and rapidly died. Brontë collapsed emotionally and physically after his death, and, though needing care herself, she began to observe signs of tuberculosis in Emily. Emily refused to discuss her obvious illness or accept medical care. Before the year was over, she, too, had died, and there were suspicions that Anne was infected with the disease as well.

In 1849, Brontë published *Shirley*, a novel whose main character reflects aspects of Emily Brontë's personality. In an attempt to save Anne's life, Brontë traveled with her to Scarborough, where the air was deemed healthy for victims of tuberculosis. The effort came too late, and Anne died while visiting the seaside resort. Brontë traveled again to London and met William Makepeace Thackeray, the leading literary figure of the time, and in 1850 she became friends with Elizabeth Gaskell, a significant Victorian novelist who was to become Brontë's first biographer. Throughout this period of mourning, Brontë kept writing.

Villette, Brontë's last complete novel, was published in 1853. In 1854, she decided to marry Arthur Bell Nicholls, who worked as her father's curate. After taking a wedding trip to Ireland to meet Nicholls's relatives, she began work on another novel, *Emma*, which was published in *Cornhill Magazine* in 1860 (it is often reprinted in editions of *The Professor*). Brontë found great satisfaction in her marriage to Nicholls, despite having resisted his proposals for years. They seemed destined for a happy future, until she became ill. Already worn out by pregnancy, Brontë took a poorly timed walk on a stormy day, and her condition rapidly worsened. She died in Haworth on March 31, 1855, leaving her husband to see to the long-delayed publication of *The Professor*.

ANALYSIS

Brontë learned her craft from the available literature of the day and through practice. In childhood, she imitated the style of literary magazines and popular fiction while writing stories, plays, and poems with her brother and sisters. In these collaborative productions, she often chose to create the persona of a historical hero—a particular favorite was the duke of Wellington—and tried to speak in the elevated, stylized language that she imagined was appropriate to such distinguished public figures. The effort, although a considerable amount of imaginative fun, resulted in characters who sounded bombastic and unnatural.

In her mature fiction—four novels and an unfinished fragment of a fifth—Brontë found greater success creating narrators who shared a measure of her life experience. The most autobiographical of her novels, *Jane Eyre* and *Villette*, focus on the private world of women and their restricted choices in male-dominated Victorian society. Narrated by female characters, both *Jane Eyre* and *Villette* make use of the popular nineteenth century motif of the orphaned child who must make his or her own way in an antagonistic world. Brontë also successfully exploited elements of the romance novel and the gothic novel when she constructed her plots. Jane Eyre discovers a madwoman concealed in the attic of her employer's mansion, and Lucy Snowe (the narrator of *Villette*) is frightened by the recurrent appearance of a ghost who haunts her school.

Feminist critics have been extremely interested in Brontë's work because it exposes the limitations placed on women's lives in the nineteenth century. Women of the respectable middle class had very few ways of earning their keep. Marrying, teaching, or serving as secretary-companion to a wealthy woman were nearly the only choices that a moderately educated woman could expect to have. Brontë, though not an outspoken feminist, regretted that women were not encouraged to make the same kinds of contributions as men and were often treated as intellectually inferior. Her characters, male or female, demand respect as individuals and strive to work in conditions where their potential will be fully realized.

Brontë's ideas about nature were shaped by the Romantic poets and her life in the Yorkshire moors. In her novels, cities tend to be places of corruption, where human beings conspire against or neglect one another. Outdoors, there is a purifying element that allows people to approach one another honestly, and natural forces often act to promote correct moral behavior. Brontë makes use of the pathetic fallacy—nature mimicking human

feeling—and personifies nature in various ways, most notably when the moon becomes a mother figure in *Jane Eyre*. Both techniques emphasize Brontë's view that the landscape plays an important role in determining human action.

JANE EYRE

First published: 1847
Type of work: Novel

An orphaned, friendless governess achieves independence and finds contentment in marriage to her former employer.

Jane Eyre appealed to the Victorian reading public on both sides of the Atlantic. Published under a pseudonym, the novel had its London enthusiasts at first speculating about the real author, then marveling at the achievement of a little-known, isolated vicar's daughter from Yorkshire. In America, the plot and narrative technique of *Jane Eyre* were quickly imitated by women writers hoping to capitalize on the novel's popularity. The plot contains many elements to capture and maintain the reader's attention: an abused orphan who rebels successfully against her oppressors, a mystery involving screams in the attic and a burning bed, a marriage stopped at the altar, sensual temptation and moral victory, and the reformation of a good man gone wrong.

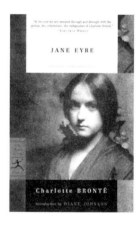

The appeal of the book is not dependent solely on a lively plot; Jane Eyre herself is an engaging character. Unwilling to accept others' definitions of her as an unattractive, dependent relation, Jane asserts herself against those who treat her badly. Faced with unpleasant cousins and oppressive schoolteachers, Jane fights for what she thinks is right. She is made to feel that her passionate responses are a character flaw, but the reader is made to see that her rebelliousness is appropriate.

In a book that explores the conflict between individual and society, it is not surprising that there are a number of structural oppositions as well. Jane's worldly cousins, the Reeds, are countered by her intellectual cousins, the Riverses. The tyrannical schoolmaster, Mr. Brocklehurst, is paired with the soothing headmistress, Miss Temple. Most important is the contrast between the two proposals of marriage that Jane receives, and the men who make them: Mr. Rochester recognizes Jane's true character, but he would pamper and oppress her with riches; St. John Rivers respects Jane's intellectual capabilities and self-control, but he would withhold true love and expect Jane to destroy her health doing difficult missionary work in India. Jane is able to resist both of them because she has developed a healthy sense of self-worth and has risen above the abuse she received as a child. Her emotional independence is matched by an unexpected inheritance, which alleviates Jane's need to work in subservient positions. Thus strengthened, Jane can return to Rochester after his first wife dies. The physical mutilation he has undergone—blinding and loss of an arm—makes him dependent on Jane for more than amusement. In a marriage of mutual respect and support, Jane's self-image can continue to prosper.

VILLETTE

First published: 1853
Type of work: Novel

Orphaned and nearly friendless, a young Englishwoman seeks to earn a living by teaching in a Belgian school.

In *Villette*, Brontë once again tells the story from the point of view of an autobiographical narrator. Unlike *Jane Eyre*, however, the narrator of *Villette*, Lucy Snowe, is neither entirely reliable nor likable. Her unpleasant nature and habit of withholding information from the reader is responsible for the lack of critical consensus about *Villette*. While some literary scholars see the novel as a well-constructed discourse on the repressive nature of Victorian society, others view it as a disordered representation of a neurotic character. The mixed response to

Villette was evident in the first reviews it received, and it never achieved the popularity of *Jane Eyre*.

There are marked similarities between *Villette* and *Jane Eyre*. Both narrators are orphans, both teach to earn their livings, and both consider themselves unattractive. In both novels, Brontë drew on her own experience to create a realistic setting; indeed, *Villette* is placed in the same Belgian territory as Brontë's first novel, *The Professor*. Yet *Villette* differs from the previous novels in a number of important ways. Formally, the shifting focus, plot coincidences, and length of

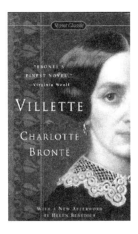

time that passes between Lucy's narration and the events that she recounts all challenge the conventions of the realistic novel. This departure is particularly evident in the ending, when Lucy refuses to explain what has happened to her fiancé, Paul Emanuel, and instead tells the reader to imagine that she has been reunited with him and has embarked on a blissful life. The reality, which Lucy condescendingly assumes the reader is too sentimental to accept, is that Paul has been drowned in a violent storm at sea.

Lucy's open ending of her story points to another important difference between *Villette* and earlier Brontë novels: The delineation of the narrator's character is such that she cannot be trusted. Like Jane Eyre, Lucy feels that her inner self is not expressed or evident in her passive, public existence. Unlike Jane, however, she does not rebel against this disjunction; instead, she manipulates it in order to satisfy her voyeuristic impulses. Powerless, Lucy gains perverse pleasure in thinking that she is more observant about others than they are about her. She works at disguising her true character, an effort that fails only with Paul, the man whom she eventually comes to love.

Lucy Snowe, named carefully by Brontë to suggest her cold personality and buried life, emphasizes those experiences that support her assertion that fate has deprived her of any kind of happiness. She hastily summarizes her childhood, spent happily with a godmother, and begins a detailed account of her life at the time of her first employment as companion to an old woman who has mourned a dead lover for thirty years. From this melancholy position, Lucy takes a job as teacher to the youngest children in a Belgian girls' school. Strongly biased against Catholics, she finds herself alone in a Catholic country with an imperfect grasp of the language and contempt for the moral corruption that she perceives in her pupils and fellow teachers. Isolated in such a way, it is small wonder that she has an emotional and physical breakdown.

Her illness serves to reunite her with her godmother and former friends, who now live in Villette, and Lucy is tempted to enjoy the life of ease that they offer. Instead, she returns to the company of Madame Beck, the director of the school, who spies on Lucy, and Paul, a sarcastic, small man who seems to discern Lucy's true nature. He recognizes her passivity for what it is, a condescending voyeurism, and he stimulates Lucy to bring her true talents to the surface. Under his sometimes savage tutelage, Lucy demonstrates significant intellectual and dramatic capabilities, and she seems less afraid of expressing her feelings. Yet Brontë was not content to write another novel with the conventional happy ending; Paul and Lucy never do marry, and Lucy, writing the book near the end of a long life, is careful not to revise her initial self-portrait as someone whom fate has deprived of happiness. What Brontë allows the reader to see, however, is that Lucy's psychological inability to act on her own behalf and her repressed anger at what she calls fate have partially created her circumstances. At the same time, Lucy has survived with a measure of dignity as the director of her own school. With both financial and emotional independence, Lucy suggests that there are possibilities for women other than marriage or degrading subservience to an employer.

SUMMARY

Charlotte Brontë's contribution to the Victorian novel was one of character, not one of plot or technical innovation. Her most vivid creation is the autobiographical narrator of *Jane Eyre*, a character who relates her story in an entertaining fashion and establishes that it is personality, rather than wealth or physical appeal, that makes an interesting heroine. By the time she wrote *Villette*, Brontë was more overt in her challenges to literary convention, a tendency that makes that novel more problematic and promising for contemporary literary scholars.

Gweneth A. Dunleavy

BIBLIOGRAPHY

By the Author

LONG FICTION:
Jane Eyre, 1847
Shirley, 1849
Villette, 1853
The Professor, 1857

POETRY:
Poems by Currer, Ellis, and Acton Bell, 1846 (with Emily Brontë and Anne Brontë)
The Complete Poems of Charlotte Brontë, 1923

CHILDREN'S LITERATURE:
The Twelve Adventurers, and Other Stories, 1925 (C. K. Shorter and C. W. Hatfield, editors)
Legends of Angria, 1933 (Fannie E. Ratchford, comp.)
The Search After Happiness, 1969
Five Novelettes, 1971 (Winifred Gérin, editor)
The Secret and Lily Hart, 1979 (William Holtz, editor)

MISCELLANEOUS:

The Shakespeare Head Brontë, 1931-1938 (19 volumes; T. J. Wise and J. A. Symington, editors)

About the Author

Alexander, Christine. *The Early Writings of Charlotte Brontë*. Oxford, England: Basil Blackwell, 1983.

Eagleton, Terry. *Myths of Power: A Marxist Study of the Brontës*. London: Macmillan, 1975.

Gaskell, Elizabeth. *The Life of Charlotte Brontë*. Edited and with an introduction by Angus Easson. New York: Oxford University Press, 1996.

Gérin, Winifred. *Charlotte Brontë: The Evolution of Genius*. Oxford, England: Oxford University Press, 1967.

Gilbert, Sandra, and Susan Gubar. *The Madwoman in the Attic*. New Haven, Conn.: Yale University Press, 1979.

Glen, Heather, ed. *The Cambridge Companion to the Brontës*. New York: Cambridge University Press, 2002.

Ingham, Patricia. *The Brontës*. New York: Oxford University Press, 2006.

Moglen, Helene. *Charlotte Brontë: The Self Conceived*. New York: W. W. Norton, 1976.

Plasa, Carl. *Charlotte Brontë*. New York: Palgrave Macmillan, 2004.

Torgerson, Beth E. *Reading the Brontë Body: Disease, Desire, and the Constraints of Culture*. New York: Palgrave Macmillan, 2005.

DISCUSSION TOPICS

- Does Charlotte Brontë's father or his children themselves deserve more credit for their creativity as youngsters?

- How do major characters in Brontë's novels mirror the author's extraordinary ability to overcome obstacles to her creative achievements?

- Explain Brontë's knowledge of Romantic poets and her keenness for art as bases for her depiction of nature in her novels.

- What combination of personal traits makes Jane Eyre such a successful heroine?

- Discuss whether *Villette* deserves a higher rank in English fiction than it has received.

EMILY BRONTË

Born: Thornton, Yorkshire, England
July 30, 1818
Died: Haworth, Yorkshire, England
December 19, 1848

Known chiefly for her inspiring novel Wuthering Heights, *Brontë is also recognized for her imaginative poetry.*

Library of Congress

BIOGRAPHY

Emily Jane Brontë (BRAHN-tee) was born on July 30, 1818, in Thornton, Yorkshire, England, the fifth of six children, five of whom were girls. Her father, Patrick Brontë, was an industrious Irish clergyman who accepted a permanent post at St. Michael and All Angels Church when Emily was two years old. Her mother, Maria Branwell, a Cornish merchant's daughter, died shortly after the move to Haworth, after which her devout and capable sister Elizabeth Branwell joined the family to care for the Brontë children.

Growing up in the parsonage shaped Brontë's life enormously. She was secluded from all but her family. The few accounts to be had of Brontë's character confirm that she was outwardly reserved, almost incommunicative, but inwardly she experienced a freedom and power of imagination that was anything but reserved. Brontë was attached to few things in her lifetime—her household, the moor, and her own imaginative world—but from these she was inseparable.

Brontë had little formal education. The few times that she left home were injurious to her. In 1824, at the age of six, Brontë and her sister Charlotte followed the two eldest girls, Maria and Elizabeth, to the Clergy Daughters' School at Cowan. Within a year, all had returned, Maria and Eliza-

beth subsequently dying of typhoid and consumption caused by the harsh conditions experienced at the school (a period later described in Charlotte's novel *Jane Eyre*, 1847). After that, Brontë was tutored at home in her father's study and exposed to a wide variety of literature, including the works of William Shakespeare, John Milton's *Paradise Lost* (1667, 1674), the novels and poetry of Sir Walter Scott, and the works of the Romantic poets, such as William Wordsworth, Percy Bysshe Shelley, and Lord Byron. She also had access to the Border country ballads from Scotland, political journals (*Blackwood's Magazine*), and local tales.

Brontë's first efforts as a writer began at the age of eleven. Her muse came to her in the form of a wooden toy soldier brought home in a box for her brother, Patrick Branwell. Together, the Brontë children began the ongoing creation of imagined worlds and the adventures of their newfound heroes. Brontë's was the world of "Gondal," an island kingdom in the South Pacific, complete with a history of political struggle and passionate intrigue. Many of her 193 poems originated in this imaginative but highly developed kingdom.

In 1831, Brontë briefly attended Roe Head School, where her sister Charlotte was governess. Intensely homesick, she was soon replaced by her younger sister, Anne. Seven years later, Brontë left home again to teach at Law Hill near Halifax, this time enduring only six months away from home. She left for a final time in 1842 to attend a school in Brussels with Charlotte, as part of their dream to open a school of their own in Haworth. Brontë's faculty for both music and languages proved enormous in Brussels, but she was forced to leave abruptly after a year, when Elizabeth Branwell died. Brontë chose never to return, remaining at Haworth until her death in 1848.

Brontë's poetry was first published in 1845, more than fifteen years after she began writing, and long since the girls had stopped sharing their work. A manuscript of her Gondal poems was discovered by Charlotte, who was delighted and stirred by the unusually bold style of her sister's work. Emily herself stormed at the invasion of her privacy and only gradually was persuaded to contribute the poems to a joint publication of all three sisters' poetry, *Poems by Currer, Ellis, and Acton Bell* (1846). Pseudonyms neutral in gender were used so that the sisters' work could not be judged solely on that basis, and all ties to the world of Gondal were omitted, erasing any possible aspects of childishness from the poems. Only two copies sold, despite the careful preparation and hard work put into the venture. Stimulated, rather than disheartened, by the experience, the three women began writing novels.

Between October, 1845, and June, 1846, Brontë wrote her great, and only, novel, *Wuthering Heights* (1847), a romance that has its roots in the Gondal poetry. Unfortunately, *Wuthering Heights* received attention mainly in connection with Charlotte's novel *Jane Eyre*, whose simultaneous appearance led to public confusion about the authorship of both novels. Some critics maintained that *Wuthering Heights* was a previous, inferior effort of Currer (Charlotte) Bell, condemning it as rough and brutal next to the more refined and humane *Jane Eyre*.

Brontë did not live to write another novel or see the strength of her one work acknowledged by more than her family and perhaps one critic. In 1848, her brother, Patrick Branwell, who had already succumbed to alcohol and opium, died of consumption. Brontë caught cold at her brother's funeral and never recovered. She died on December 19, 1848, in Haworth, Yorkshire, England.

ANALYSIS

Brontë shared much with the Romantic poets, whose works she had read during childhood. Underlying all of her own poetry and prose is the Romantic ideal of transcendence, the desire to rise above the domain of time and space that encompasses ordinary human experience. Brontë's works are filled with human passion and longing that drive toward this goal. In its emotional turmoil, the love between Heathcliff and Catherine in *Wuthering Heights* exceeds the boundaries of the mortal world and endures beyond the grave. This lack of established borders between life and death provides much of the excitement in the novel, as characters communicate as ghosts and in dreams through the veil of time, in a setting that simultaneously assumes supernatural qualities.

Brontë's poetry expresses the longing for freedom from the chains of mortality, depicting life as "cold captivity" (in "The Caged Bird") and death as liberation of the soul. The subject of one of her most renowned poems, "No Coward Soul Is Mine," is her Romantic desire for a mystical union with the deity, whom Brontë saw as the God both within and without her. In Brontë's poetry, crossing over the lines of the mortal world establishes a resonance, exemplified in "Remembrance," where speakers, events, and audience exist in different realms: for example, in the distant past, in the present, and in the realm beyond death. All of Brontë's poetry and prose is highly imaginative, which points to a final means to freedom in her work: the world of imagination, a gift more highly prized by the Romantics than reason.

Another important Romantic element in Brontë's work is nature. Growing up in the stormy northern England countryside, Brontë knew the great potential of the tempestuous moorland weather to communicate the vast range of human emotions. Brontë uses the outer world of nature as a metaphor for human nature, that is, as something heavily symbolic, carrying an equivalence to a person's inner world. There is interplay and even interchange between Brontë's characters and the natural elements. In *Wuthering Heights*, Lockwood's surreal dream of Catherine Earnshaw's ghost on a stormy night is prompted by the wildly knocking branch against the window pane, which becomes a "little, ice-cold hand!" when he reaches for it. Heathcliff himself assumes enough aspects of the moor in his brutal, remorseless nature that he becomes inextricable from it. The dynamic role of nature also adds much excitement to the action in the drama, continually energizing the characters.

For all the passionate overflow of Brontë's created worlds, her presentation is highly controlled, giving her work unexpected power and intensity. This aspect of her writing stems not only from the nature of the themes that she explores but even more from her own skill in delivering the material. The narrative of *Wuthering Heights* is a complex chronological layering, yet Brontë delivers it cleanly and ingenuously, as the narrator is brought under Heathcliff's roof by the storm and, in a single night, brings three names, three dates, and the ghost of Catherine Linton into view. Likewise, Nelly, the housekeeper who relates the tale to Lockwood, quotes the characters directly without encumbering interpretation or embellishment. Brontë's own description is always vivid and striking, with no extra words spent, moving her plot forward at a delightfully exciting pace.

Brontë's poetry exhibits the simplicity and austerity inherent in her style. She uses ordinary, uncomplicated language, direct address, and subtle methods, such as the repetition of single words or alliteration, to create moods and deepen their effects, often achieving a profound lucidity. Even the pauses in her lines work to expand or command a mood, as exemplified by her poem "No Coward Soul Is Mine" with her words to the immortal deity who "Changes, sustains, dissolves, creates, and rears." These singly delivered, sibilant words demand the slow pace of deliberation and awe. Likewise, Brontë constructs her literature from natural materials. As a result, her images endure humbly yet vividly in the memory. The correspondence posited in Brontë's poem "Love and Friendship" between love and the seasonal rose-briar and between the evergreen holly and friendship is simple, yet powerfully effective. In "The Bluebell," a single bluebell that can remedy homesickness for the more passionate "purple heath" of the moor quietly persists in miniature.

Brontë communicates her own fierce independence, as well as her well-known mystical yearning for transcendence, in all of her work, from her young poems of the childhood world of Gondal to the rich harvest of her single novel, *Wuthering Heights*. In all Brontë's work, it is apparent that her attachment to the natural world is always as strong as her desire to transcend it. This enigma of individuality that seeks to go beyond itself was the one that Brontë chose to write from and live through. It is this concern that haunts her poetry and lives unsettled and restless in her novel.

WUTHERING HEIGHTS

First published: 1847
Type of work: Novel

A jilted lover's passion becomes a storm of vengeance in the wild moorland of northern England.

First published in 1847, *Wuthering Heights* is an enduring gothic romance filled with intrigue and terror. It is set in the northern England countryside, where the weather fluctuates in sudden extremes and where bogs can open underfoot of unsuspecting night venturers. Under this atmospheric dome of brooding unpredictability, Brontë explores the violent and unpredictable elements of human passion. The story revolves around the tempestuous romance between Heathcliff, an orphan who is taken home to Wuthering Heights on impulse, and Catherine Earnshaw, a strong-willed girl whose mother died delivering her and who becomes Heathcliff's close companion.

The setting is central to the novel. Both action and characters can be understood in terms of two households. Wuthering Heights, overtaken by the sinister usurper, Heathcliff, becomes a dark, winter world of precipitous acts that lead to brutality, vengeance, and social alienation. What Wuthering Heights lacks in history, education, and gregari-

ousness is supplied by the more springlike Thrushcross Grange, where the fair-haired Lintons live in the human world of reason, order, and gentleness. Unfortunately, these less passionate mortals are subject to the indifferent forces of nature, dying in childbirth and of consumption too easily. They are subject to Heathcliff's wrath as well, losing all assets and independence to him.

Brontë uses the element of unpredictability to spur the action in *Wuthering Heights*, which adds excitement and suspense at every turn and enlivens the characters by infusing them with the characteristic storminess of the moorland weather. Seemingly chance events gather like ominous clouds to create the passionate tale of Heathcliff and Catherine. They are brought together by chance and are left to roam the moor together, far from the world of shelter and discipline, when Catherine's father dies, leaving her tyrannical brother, Hindley, in charge. Accident also accounts for Catherine's introduction to the more refined world of Thrushcross Grange, when she is bitten by a watchdog while spying on her cousins, who then rescue her. Even Heathcliff's angry departure and vowed vengeance is the result of eavesdropping, hearing only what he could mistake for rejection, and not Catherine's true feelings for him.

In Heathcliff's character, Brontë explores the great destructive potential of unrestrained passion. In him, human emotion is uncontrollable and deadly. In the ghostly union of Catherine and Heathcliff beyond the grave, however, Brontë suggests the metaphysical nature of love and the potential of passion to project itself beyond the physical realm of existence.

The ending of *Wuthering Heights* depicts Brontë's final answer to the theme of destructive passion—the answer of mercy and forgiveness, which Brontë holds to be the supreme quality in human beings. Hareton, whom Heathcliff once unwittingly saved from death and then forever after abused, forgives his captor for everything. This forgiveness is accompanied by the mercy that Catherine Linton shows Hareton, teaching him to read after years of mocking his ignorance. Together, these acts of grace nullify the deadly effects of their keeper, who dies soon afterward. The passion of winter becomes the compromise of spring; the storm has passed, and life continues in harmony at last.

"REMEMBRANCE"

First published: 1846 (collected in *Poems by Currer, Ellis, and Acton Bell*, 1846)
Type of work: Poem

A woman mourns the death of her lover, fifteen years later.

"Remembrance" is one of Brontë's well-known poems, one originally from the world of Gondal that Brontë created with her sister Anne at a young age. This poem is an elegy, a sorrowful lament for the dead. Queen Rosina Alcona speaks directly to her lost love, the emperor Julius Brenzaida, fifteen years after his assassination, in yearning that does not recognize the limits of time and space. Such an emotional state is typical in Brontë's poems, as is the simplicity and earnestness of the lines. The key feature of her style is repetition:

> Cold in the earth—and the deep snow piled
>   above thee!
> Far, far removed, cold in the dreary grave!
> Have I forgot, my Only Love, to love thee,
> Severed at last by Time's all-severing wave?

Brontë repeats single words, such as "cold," throughout the poem, insisting on their effect, but only subtly. When the repetition occurs in each line ("cold," "far," "love," and "sever"), a resonance is established that expresses the unfilled span of fifteen years through which the speaker's words must travel.

Brontë also uses assonance, the less obvious repetition of vowel sounds, as in the second stanza line, "Over the mountains, on that northern shore." She uses alliteration to unify the speaker's experience of life and death, sorrow and joy, as well. In the sixth stanza, "days of golden dreams" are tied to the "despair [that] was powerless to destroy" by strong consonant alliteration. To further the emotional effect of joy turned to sorrow, "destroy" is rhymed with "joy" in the last line of the stanza.

The pauses that occur at the ends of the lines are unusually long. This effect certainly adds to the resonance and feeling of words that must travel a long way, perhaps never reaching the listener except by the web of quiet persistence that exists in repetition. This is the memorableness of Brontë's poems, that they linger like faint strains of music.

Summary

Emily Brontë is a master at exploring human emotion. In the annals of world literature, her status is unique. Her standing as a major novelist rests on the merits of *Wuthering Heights*, yet no examination of English fiction can afford to ignore it. The book's character and settings are embedded within the heritage of Western culture. Her poetry, infused with the Romantic ideal of transcendence, depicts the soul's desire to travel beyond the limits of time and space in order to find liberation.

The moorland in which she grew up gave her a language of expression that is powerful as well as beautiful. Charlotte Brontë best expresses the originality and power of Emily's work:

> With time and labour, the crag took human shape; and there it stands, colossal, dark, and frowning, half statue, half rock: in the former sense, terrible and goblinlike; in the latter, almost beautiful, for its colouring of mellow grey, and moorland moss clothes it; and heath, with its blooming bells and balmy fragrance, grows faithfully close to the giant's foot.

Jennifer McLeod

Bibliography

By the Author

LONG FICTION:
Wuthering Heights, 1847

POETRY:
Poems by Currer, Ellis, and Acton Bell, 1846 (with Charlotte and Anne Brontë)
The Complete Poems of Emily Jane Brontë, 1941 (C. W. Hatfield, editor)
Gondal's Queen: A Novel in Verse by Emily Jane Brontë, 1955 (Fannie E. Ratchford, editor)

NONFICTION:
Five Essays Written in French, 1948 (Lorine White Nagel, translator)
The Brontë Letters, 1954 (Muriel Spark, editor)

About the Author

Bernard, Robert. *Emily Brontë*. New York: Oxford University Press, 2002.
Duthie, Enid Lowry. *The Brontës and Nature*. New York: St. Martin's Press, 1986.
Frank, Katherine. *A Chainless Soul: A Life of Emily Brontë*. Boston: Houghton Mifflin, 1990.
Gérin, Winifred. *Emily Brontë: A Biography*. Oxford, England: Clarendon Press, 1971.
Gezari, Janet. *Last Things: Emily Brontë's Poems*. Oxford, England: Oxford University Press, 2007.
Glen, Heather, ed. *The Cambridge Companion to the Brontës*. New York: Cambridge University Press, 2002.
Ingham, Patricia. *The Brontës*. New York: Oxford University Press, 2006.
Knoepflmacher, U. C. *Emily Brontë: Wuthering Heights*. New York: Cambridge University Press, 1989.
Torgerson, Beth E. *Reading the Brontë Body: Disease, Desire, and the Constraints of Culture*. New York: Palgrave Macmillan, 2005.
Winnifrith, Tom J., and Edward Chitham, eds. *Brontë Facts and Brontë Problems*. London: Macmillan, 1983.

Discussion Topics

- Would a child sharing the personal traits of Emily Brontë receive proper encouragement in the type of school she would be most likely to attend today?

- Explain whether Gondal was primarily an exercise of Brontë's imagination or something that she perceived as a reality.

- Does the term "gothic novel" apply to *Wuthering Heights*?

- Is *Wuthering Heights* a greater novel than *Jane Eyre*? Substantiate your claim.

- Does Brontë's fondness for music contribute substantially to *Wuthering Heights*?

- As in other arts, repetition can be a flaw or an asset in poetry. How does Brontë make it work?

RUPERT BROOKE

Born: Rugby, Warwickshire, England
August 3, 1887
Died: Aboard a hospital ship in the Aegean Sea
April 23, 1915

A poet and writer of some prominence before World War I, Brooke wrote war poems, particularly "The Soldier," that captured the patriotic idealism of the generation of young soldiers who died in the early months of that conflict.

Library of Congress

BIOGRAPHY

Rupert Chawner Brooke was born in Rugby, England, on August 3, 1887. His father, William Parker Brooke, was an instructor of classics at Rugby School, one of the most prestigious of England's public schools, but it was Mary Ruth Cotterill, Rupert's mother, who dominated the family. Young Brooke, the middle child among three brothers, attended Rugby School, playing cricket and football, excelling in English, winning prizes for his poetry, and becoming Head Boy. Many of his contemporaries were attracted to his personality; others noted his tall, blond physique, reminiscent of a young Apollo.

From Rugby, Brooke entered King's College, Cambridge, where, under the influence of more modern writers and intellectuals, he abandoned some of the Decadent fin de siècle postures found in his earlier poetry. He also made friends among some of England's most famous political and artistic families: the Asquiths, Darwins, Oliviers, and Stracheys. Freed from the day-to-day influence of his family, he joined the socialist Fabian Society and university dramatic groups; he also began writing for the *Cambridge Review*, a university journal with a national reputation. During his Cambridge years, from 1906 to 1909, he wrote at least sixty poems, about a third of which were printed in his first volume of poetry, *Poems*, in 1911.

Failure to receive a first-class degree and the complications of emotional exhaustion prompted Brooke to leave Cambridge for the small village of Grantchester, just a few miles distant but far enough from the attractions of the university city. His friends and acquaintances congregated around him there, and his time at the Old Vicarage, his principal residence in Grantchester, assumed almost mythic proportions, although he lived there principally for only two years. In addition to his poetry, Brooke became an accomplished literary critic; he particularly admired Robert Browning and John Donne, and although always opposing free verse, he praised the poetry of Ezra Pound. He also wrote a dissertation on the Elizabethan dramatist John Webster. Virginia Woolf, a friend, noted Brooke's wide literary knowledge and disciplined work habits.

Poems included fifty poems from both his younger years and after his university days. The volume was widely reviewed and well received, considering that it was the author's first book. In early 1912, however, Brooke suffered a breakdown, compounded by both personal and professional considerations. His literary career, his dependency on his changing circle of acquaintances, his relationship with his mother, and his other emotional attachments led him to fear that he was becoming insane. Nevertheless, during this period he wrote one of his most famous poems, "The Old Vicarage, Grantchester." By the end of the year, apparently recovered, he was again engaged in several literary projects.

In 1913, Brooke traveled to Canada, the United States, and the islands of the South Pacific. Initially, his response to the culture of the Western Hemisphere was mainly dismissive, but the California cities of San Francisco and Berkeley pleased him, and his three months in Tahiti led to some of his best love poems. He had also begun working with Edward Marsh on the first of a series of anthologies of modern poets. Known as "Georgian Poetry," the first volume appeared in 1913. Later, the term came to denote a certain artificial vacuousness, but the initial volume included, in addition to poems by Brooke, work by D. H. Lawrence, John Masefield, Robert Graves, Isaac Rosenberg, and Siegfried Sassoon.

By the time of Brooke's return to England in the spring of 1914, his circle included not only his university friendships at Cambridge and Grantchester but also the major writers and artists of the day. In addition, he was on close terms with the prime minister, Herbert Asquith, and Winston Churchill, first lord of the admiralty. Still young, his future seemed bright as a poet or literary critic, even perchance a politician. On the day after his twenty-seventh birthday, however, Great Britain entered World War I, and Brooke soon sought an officer's commission. During the winter of 1914-1915, he wrote a series of sonnets on the war, published in *1914, and Other Poems* (1915), in which he idealized sacrificing one's life for one's country. Many of his contemporaries had already gone to the Western Front, where thousands were dying in what came to be called "no man's land," and in early 1915 Brooke's Royal Naval Division was ordered to take part in the Dardanelles campaign against Turkey, Germany's ally. In spite of Brooke's robust appearance, his health had always been problematic, and before his unit entered combat he became ill with fever and died on a hospital ship in the Aegean Sea on April 23, 1915, England's St. George's Day. Even before his death, his poem "The Soldier" had been read during services in Westminster Abbey. Churchill wrote of Brooke's death and sacrifice in Brooke's obituary in *The Times* of London. Brooke's apotheosis had begun.

ANALYSIS

Brooke's facility with verse manifested itself early in his youth, and his technical abilities were fully developed before leaving Cambridge. Influenced by Browning's use of common language and ordinary personalities, so unlike the poetry of fellow Victorians Alfred, Lord Tennyson, and William Morris, Brooke freely borrowed from and parodied the style and content not only of Browning and Tennyson but also of A. E. Housman and Algernon Charles Swinburne. He mastered the dramatic sonnet form and wrote numerous poems in what has been called a narrative idyll style. Whatever his form, Brooke chose to write in traditional meter rather than experiment in the free-verse approach of Pound and T. S. Eliot. Brooke's reliance upon such forms is perhaps one reason why his reputation declined among critics, but it also explains in part why he remained popular among general readers.

Brooke's mature literary life was relatively brief. If he early mastered the forms of poetry, the subject matter of his works and the "voice" of his poems evolved from his boyhood days at Rugby and his years at Cambridge until his death while still in his twenties. Although he worked and reworked his material, his willingness to exclude so many of his early efforts from his first published volume of poetry in 1911 suggests that he realized that many of his poems were not of the highest quality. The collected poems form a rather slight volume, and in terms of mere quantity Brooke could be categorized as a minor poet.

Critics have also complained that Brooke too often intruded sentimentality and artificiality into many of his poems. In poems such as "Ante Aram," Brooke resorts to archaic diction, convoluted syntax, and vague, romantic description. The resulting language is more Victorian, more Tennysonian, than expected, given Brooke's avowed aim of a new poetry for the new century, and hardly reflects his praise of Browning's use of the common speech of the common people.

One of the most apparent elements throughout Brooke's work is his preoccupation with death, particularly the death of the young. His idealized notion of the sacrificial death appears out of place in the violent historical context of the twentieth century, but it could have resulted from Brooke's youth: Death can hold a morbid fascination for the young, who have no sense of their own mortality. Perhaps he was also influenced by the Decadent writers who interested him while still a schoolboy. Yet the paradigm for this theme may be Brooke's own personality; among his last poems, "The Soldier" can be seen as a culmination of his quest for death.

Brooke's poems also frequently connect death with love. In "Mummia," he describes the ancient Egyptians drinking the dust of mummies to achieve a state of sexual ecstasy. In the same way, he says that the poet has "sucked all lovers of all time/ To rarify ecstasy," citing famous lovers such as Helen, Juliet, and Cleopatra, whose tragic lives immortalized their passion. This romantic vision of death as the culmination of love contrasts with poems such as "The Funeral of Youth: Threnody," where Brooke tells in allegorical fashion the sad lament of those friends of Youth who came to his burial. He includes among these such figures as Laughter, Pride, Joy, Lust, Folly, Grief, Sorrow, Wisdom, Passion, and others who met again at Youth's funeral, "All except only Love. Love had died long ago." Death, in this poem, brings the loss of love, rather than its ultimate fulfillment. At other times, death results in the transmutation of love into a kind of Platonic ideal, as in "Tiare Tahiti," written during his travels in the South Pacific. He notes that, after death,

> Instead of lovers, Love shall be;
> For hearts, Immutability;
> And there, on the Ideal Reef,
> Thunders the Everlasting Sea!

Brooke, however, was not always the youthful romanticist or idealist ruminating about death and love. Like Browning, he could also be very much the realist, sometimes punctuating this realism with humor and irony, too much so for some of his contemporaries. Both his publisher and Edward Marsh, his close friend and adviser, objected to the inclusion of two of his sonnets in his first book of poems. In "Libido," where Brooke writes of sexual conquest, not romantic love, the phrase "your remembered smell most agony" was felt by Marsh and others to be in bad taste. In "A Channel Passage," the narrator tries to remember his lover in order to avoid becoming physically sick while crossing the English Channel.

Finally, if critics have often rightly criticized Brooke for idealizing the sacrificial death of youth, he could also write of the end of youthful idealism brought about by age. In a reference to Homer's tale of the Trojan Wars, Brooke shows, in "Menelaus and Helen," husband and wife at the end of their lives:

> Often he wonders why on earth he went
> Troyward, or why poor Paris ever came.
> Oft she weeps, gummy-eyed and impotent;
> Her dry shanks twist at Paris' mumbled name.
> So Menelaus nagged; and Helen cried;
> And Paris slept on by Scamander side.

Brooke never reached the age of Helen and Menelaus; instead, he died at age twenty-seven, to be immortalized like Achilles or the young Apollo, whom so many believed that he resembled.

"THE OLD VICARAGE, GRANTCHESTER"

First published: 1916 (collected in *Collected Poems*, 1916)
Type of work: Poem

The poem records the exiled poet's reflections and remembrances of his home in England.

"The Old Vicarage, Grantchester" was written by Brooke while in Berlin in 1912. After initially titling the poem "Home" and then "The Sentimental Exile," the author eventually chose the name of his occasional residence near Cambridge. One of Brooke's most famous poems, its references can be overly obscure because of the many specific Cambridge locations and English traditions to which the poem refers. Some have seen it as sentimentally nostalgic, which it is, while others have recognized its satiric and sometimes cruel humor.

Using octosyllabics—a meter often favored by Brooke—the author writes of Grantchester and other nearby villages in what has been called a seriocomic style. It is very much a poem of "place," the place where Brooke composed the work, Berlin, and the contrast of that German world ("Here am I, sweating, sick, and hot") with his home in England. Yet it is more than just the longing of an exile for his home, nostalgically imagined. The landscape of Cambridgeshire is reproduced in the poem, but Brooke, the academic, populates this English world with allusions and references from history and myth. He compares the countryside to a kind of Greek Arcadia, home to nymphs and fauns, and refers to such famous literary figures as Lord Byron, Geoffrey Chaucer, and Tennyson. Homesick for England, a land "Where men with Splendid Hearts may go," it is Grantchester, in particular, that he desires.

If the poem is nostalgic and sentimental, however, it is also satiric in its treatment of the Cambridgeshire landscape. In wishing to be in Grantchester, Brooke compares its virtues with those of other nearby towns and villages. In a series of wry couplets, Brooke pokes sly fun at the inhabitants of neighboring villages, whom he contrasts with those in Grantchester. The people of Cambridge are said to be "urban, squat, and packed with guile," while oaths—or worse—are flung at visitors to Over and Trumpington. He complains that "Ditton girls are mean and dirty,/ And there's none in Harston under thirty," but Grantchester is described as a place of "peace and holy quiet." Even the residents of Grantchester, however, are not immune to Brooke's teasing; in a line that is perhaps only half in jest, given his own bouts of depression, he adds that "when they get to feeling old,/ They up and shoot themselves, I'm told."

Yet there is also a seriousness in the poem underneath its comedic elements. In his conclusion, Brooke asks a series of rhetorical questions:

> Say, is there Beauty yet to find?
> And Certainty? and Quiet kind?
> Deep meadows yet, for to forget
> The lies, and truths, and pain? . . . oh! yet
> Stands the Church clock at ten to three?
> And is there honey still for tea?

The poet longs for the remembered, if imagined, permanence of Grantchester, but he also sadly and whimsically recognizes even its ultimate impermanence and transience. Written only two years before the outbreak of World War I, the poem foreshadows the world that will be forever lost as a result of that conflict.

"THE SOLDIER"

First published: 1915 (collected in *1914, and Other Poems*, 1915)
Type of work: Poem

Envisioning the narrator's probable death in war, the poem reflects his idealism and patriotic self-sacrifice.

"The Soldier" was one of five sonnets that Brooke composed shortly after the beginning of World War I and published in 1915 with the title *1914, and Other Poems*. Written in two stanzas, an octet of eight lines and a sestet of six lines, it is by far his most famous poem, expressing the idealism common throughout the nations of Europe as they eagerly marched to battle in 1914 and felt by Brooke before his own death in April, 1915.

The well-known opening lines represented this romantic notion of consecration through sacrifice by showing the speaker's transformation after death: "there's some corner of a foreign field/ That is for ever England." 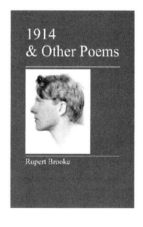 In retrospect, to others the poem came to epitomize the misguided and self-satisfied naïveté that died in the trenches of "no man's land." The real war of ugly and often futile death was captured not in Brooke's work but in the poems by his English contemporaries, such as Wilfred Owen's "Dulce et decorum est."

Yet "The Soldier" is more an elegy of sacrifice than a poem about modern war. It is true that Brooke died before going into battle, but his friendships with English statesman Winston Churchill and other high-ranking politicians had given him knowledge about the destructiveness that industry and technology would bring to the battlefield. There is nothing of that kind of war in the poem. There is also nothing about the reality of dying; the first-person narrator ignores the stench of corpses on the battlefield, instead envisioning a death that transfigures him into an idealized world.

This is not simply any world, however, for "The Soldier" is a poem about Brooke's feelings for England, particularly the rural English countryside of Cambridgeshire. His burial place, though in some foreign land, will become a part of England, but not the England of cities and factories. It was the landscape of natural England that made and formed the poet, and he waxes lyrical about the beauties of English flowers, rivers, and sunshine, elements that have formed him in his youth.

Brooke believed that his England was worthy of sacrifice. This patriotic element in "The Soldier" reflects the strong strain of nationalism existing throughout Western civilization in the late nineteenth and early twentieth centuries. As traditional religion had become more personal and individual, nationalism and patriotism had become the religion of the public community, and "The Soldier" reflects those passions. In the second stanza, Brooke refers to "the eternal mind," a Platonic reference, where the dust of the narrator had become a mere "pulse," but a pulse that

> Gives somewhere back the thoughts by
>   England given;
> Her sights and sounds; dreams happy as her day;
>   And laughter, learnt of friends; and
>   gentleness,
>   In hearts at peace, under an English
>   heaven.

Brooke's soldier—as Brooke himself—was eagerly willing to sacrifice everything, even his life, for the Eden of England. It struck a strong chord in the early days of World War I. By the end of the war in 1918, with ten million dead, other poets were striking other chords, less idealistic, less self-sacrificing, and less patriotic.

SUMMARY

Unfortunately, perhaps, Rupert Brooke is remembered primarily for one poem, "The Soldier," a poem that most critics agree was not among his finest accomplishments. His patriotic elegy to sacrifice, coinciding with his youthful death, turned Brooke into a monument to youth, to idealism, to a past that no longer existed after the Great War was over. Brooke saw himself and his poetry as a progressive step beyond that of his Victorian predecessors. Paradoxically, he now too often seems part of a world of rural innocence that has long since disappeared. If Brooke had lived, it is impossible to say that he would have become a major poet, but his early death obscured his legacy of poetic realism, irony, humor, intelligence, and passion, which is also found in his writings.

Eugene Larson

BIBLIOGRAPHY

By the Author

POETRY:
Poems, 1911
1914, and Other Poems, 1915
Collected Poems, 1915, 1916
Complete Poems, 1932
The Poetical Works of Rupert Brooke, 1946 (Geoffrey Keynes, editor)

DRAMA:
Lithuania, pb. 1935 (one act)

NONFICTION:
Letters from America, 1916
John Webster and the Elizabethan Drama, 1916
The Prose of Rupert Brooke, 1956
The Letters of Rupert Brooke, 1968

Friends and Apostles: The Correspondence of Rupert Brooke and James Strachey, 1905-1915, 1998 (Keith Hale, editor)

About the Author

Bloom, Harold, ed. *Poets of World War I: Rupert Brooke and Siegfried Sassoon*. Philadelphia: Chelsea House, 2003.

Delany, Robert. *The Neo-Pagans*. London: Macmillan, 1987.

Hassall, Christopher. *Rupert Brooke: A Biography*. London: Faber & Faber, 1964.

Jones, Nigel. *Rupert Brooke: Life, Death, and Myth*. London: Richard Cohen Books, 1999.

Lehmann, John. *Rupert Brooke: His Life and His Legend*. London: Weidenfeld & Nicolson, 1980.

Pearsall, Robert Brainard. *Rupert Brooke: The Man and the Poet*. Amsterdam: Rodopi, 1974.

Quinn, Patrick, ed. *British Poets of the Great War: Brooke, Rosenberg, Thomas, a Documentary Volume*. Vol. 216 in *Dictionary of Literary Biography*. Detroit: Gale Group, 2000.

Ross, Robert H. *The Georgian Revolt*. Carbondale: Southern Illinois University Press, 1965.

Stallworthy, Jon. *Great Poets of World War I: Poetry from the Great War*. New York: Carroll & Graf, 2002.

DISCUSSION TOPICS

- What did the development of Rupert Brooke's dramatic skill owe to his study of Robert Browning? What did it owe to John Donne?

- To what extent does Brooke's poetic reputation rest on his personal qualities and adventures?

- In what respects was Brooke a late Victorian poet?

- Can nostalgia and satire coexist successfully in the same poem? Does your answer apply to "The Old Vicarage, Grantchester"?

- Relate Brooke's "The Soldier" to the poetic tradition—familiar in William Shakespeare, Browning, and others—of celebrating England.

ANITA BROOKNER

Born: London, England
July 16, 1928

Brookner's novels depict the painful experiences of intelligent, sensitive, and lonely women and men who try to find love in a world of greed and selfishness.

BIOGRAPHY

Anita Brookner was born in London, England, on July 16, 1928; some references wrongly report the year as 1938. Her parents were Newson Brookner, a Polish immigrant and businessman, and Maude Schiska Brookner, who had been an opera singer before her marriage.

Brookner and her parents lived with her grandmother, part of an extended Polish Jewish family that included many aunts, uncles, and cousins. As a child she read many books by the great nineteenth century English novelist Charles Dickens. She was brought up according to Jewish traditions but because of her delicate health was never asked to learn Hebrew. Although Brookner is not religious and although she was born and reared in London, she thinks her upbringing may have caused her to feel like an outsider in English society. Critics think that many of the heroines of her novels reflect their author's sense of estrangement.

She attended James Allen's Girls' School in Dulwich, a pleasant section of London south of the Thames River. She earned a bachelor of arts degree in French literature at King's College of the University of London. She then studied art history at the Courtauld Institute of Art, also in London, where she was awarded a doctorate. She had traveled to Paris, France, conducting research to write her dissertation, which she later revised for publication as *Greuze: The Rise and Fall of an Eighteenth-Century Phenomenon* (1972).

Brookner had a distinguished career as an art historian before turning to fiction. She taught first from 1959 to 1964 as a visiting lecturer at the University of Reading in England and after 1964 at the Courtauld Institute. In 1967-1968, she was the first woman to hold the distinguished post of Slade Pro-

fessor of Art at Cambridge University. She has published several highly acclaimed works on art history, mainly on French painting of the late eighteenth and early nineteenth centuries.

Brookner began her career as a novelist when she was about fifty years old. She later told an interviewer that she was unhappy and thought that by writing a novel she would be forced to think carefully about her own life. Her first novel, *The Debut* (1981; published in England as *A Start in Life*, 1981), is generally regarded as autobiographical.

Thereafter, she published one novel a year. Her career can be seen in stages. *The Debut, Providence* (1982), and *Look at Me* (1983) center on the experiences of younger women growing up in London, beginning careers, and searching for love. In *Hotel du Lac* (1984), Brookner begins to write about older women and to construct more complicated stories. *Hotel du Lac*'s central character is a writer, and, like *Look at Me*, the novel questions the relationship of fiction to life. In 1984, *Hotel du Lac* won the prestigious Booker-McConnell Prize, and a film version was released in 1986.

Most of Brookner's later novels also have women as central characters, but they are middle-aged or older. These novels tend to expand her range in other ways as well. They often focus on families and their problems. Blanche Vernon in *The Misalliance* (1986; published in England as *A Misalliance*, 1986) has been divorced; Fay Langdon in *Brief Lives* (1990) is a widow. *Family and Friends* (1985) was something new for Brookner; it tells the story of a whole family, including two brothers, over a period of years and takes the reader as far afield as Hollywood. *Latecomers* (1988) also deals with two families, at the center of which are two male friends, marking Brookner's continuing ex-

371

ploration of male characters. In *Lewis Percy* (1989) and in *A Private View* (1994) the central characters are also male. Other novels she wrote in the 1990's include *A Closed Eye* (1991), *Fraud* (1992), and *A Family Romance* (1993).

When she was teaching, Brookner wrote her novels during summer holidays and mainly in her office at the Courtauld Institute. In 1987, she retired from teaching in order to devote her time to writing, including essays, introductions, and reviews. Brookner, who remained unmarried, settled in a small apartment overlooking a square in Chelsea, a fashionable district in London.

In 1990, Brookner received the title Commander, Order of the British Empire. Her professional achievements earned for Brookner such awards as honorary degrees from Smith College and the University of Loughborough. Criticizing Brookner's body of work as repetitive, Oxford University's Encaenia committee, which selects honorary doctorate recipients, repeatedly decided not to honor Brookner with that recognition despite colleagues' support after she won the Booker-McConnell Prize. Cambridge's women's college, New Hall, and King's College London both designated Brookner a Fellow. Her novel *Making Things Better* (2002; published in England as *The Next Big Thing*, 2002) was included on the Man Booker Prize long list in 2002. *The Bay of Angels* (2001) received the 2003 International IMPAC Dublin Literary Award.

During the early twenty-first century, Brookner continued to explore relationships between grown children and parents, especially daughters with their mothers, and friends in novels, including *The Rules of Engagement* (2003) and *Leaving Home* (2005). She also wrote the nonfiction book *Romanticism and Its Discontents* (2000).

ANALYSIS

Brookner has acknowledged that *The Debut* is autobiographical and that her novels taken together are sometimes seen as a massive work of self-analysis. Her intelligent and lonely heroines are often considered to be versions of Brookner herself. There is a recognizable Brookner woman and Brookner world.

Her novels are told in the present; flashbacks transport the reader to a character's youth and give a family's history. Brookner often employs sus-

pense. In *Hotel du Lac*, the reader does not find out why Edith left England until halfway through the novel; at the beginning of *Fraud*, Anna has mysteriously disappeared and does not surface for several chapters. Although most of Brookner's novels take place in London, some characters go abroad, mainly to France, and many (like Brookner herself) have important roots in central Europe.

Readers are introduced to London circles not often depicted in fiction. Most characters are financially comfortable. Many, like Francis Hinton in *Look at Me* and Anna Durrant in *Fraud*, have inherited wealth. On the other hand, Hartmann and Fibich in *Latecomers* are successful business partners. Brookner's earlier heroines are often both attracted to and repulsed by a well-off, happy, and conventional family, such as the Benedicts in *Look at Me* and the Livingstones in *A Friend from England* (1987). In most of these cases, readers enter these characters' spacious apartments, with their warm rooms expensively and heavily furnished in a taste that seems oppressively bland and old-fashioned.

Most readers and critics focus upon the Brookner heroine. No matter what her age, she thinks of the past, of her restricted childhood or of her blighted days as a young woman. She is intelligent, literate, and given to unblinking self-analysis and self-appraisal. She is acceptable looking, but not strikingly beautiful—some might call her plain. All these qualities make her think of herself as an exile.

Although the Brookner woman of the early novels is lonely and alone, she is a keen observer of the material objects that surround her and of the appearance and character of the people she meets. She wants to participate in life and is attracted to happy circles of what seem to her normal people. She yearns for marriage to a perfect man. She is disappointed.

Women in the later novels share many of these traits. Even though they marry, they still hope for love. Blanche in *The Misalliance* is deserted for a younger woman; Fay in *Brief Lives* lives for her married lover; and in *A Closed Eye*, Harriet yearns for but does not get Jack.

Readers and critics have charged that Brookner's women lack the assertiveness that is admired in the heroines of many contemporary novels. Although some, like Anna in *Fraud*, do assert themselves, most cannot change their relations with other people any more than they can change the drab decor of their apartments. Why do Brookner's women not break out of their restrictive worlds? Their worlds are powerful webs of obligations to their parents and of their personal limitations. In her later novels, these obligations combine with inertia and the complications of husbands, other women, children, and lovers. The ties are simple, but strong; the women do not break free. Even so, a mystery remains. Brookner's central characters seem to live in magic circles they cannot step out of. They resemble figures in a legend, imprisoned by a sorcerer's spell or a parent's curse. Perhaps the spell is simply that even though the characters know that dreams rarely come true, they also know that to give up those dreams is death.

Brookner creates a marvelous gallery of supporting characters. Her heroines fall for a variety of charming and vital men who always prefer beautiful, spoiled women, like Mousie and Sally in *The Misalliance* and Yvette of *Latecomers*. There are wise and sympathetic older women, like Molly Edwards in *The Debut*, the loyal Millie Savage in *Brief Lives*, and the no-nonsense Mrs. Marsh in *Fraud*. Some figures are absurd, like the acrobat Vadim in *Providence* and the charming Toto in *Latecomers*. Others are grotesques, from the scorpion-like Alix in *Look at Me* and the satanic Mr. Neville in *Hotel du Lac* to Fay's gin-swilling mother-in-law in *Brief Lives*, the exasperating Dolly in *A Family Romance*, and Katy Gibb, the vulgar New Age practitioner in *A Private View*. Many of these supporting characters know what the central characters seem unable to comprehend: that beautiful, greedy, selfish people always win, and virtuous, innocent people always lose.

Brookner mostly used boys and men as secondary characters in her early books. She began to depict more completely examined male protagonists in such novels as *Latecomers*, in which two Jewish males, Thomas Hartmann and Thomas Fibich, are exiles from Germany, somewhat like Julius Herz in *Making Things Better*, but experience greater extremes of suffering because of direct repercussions from the Holocaust. Like her women, Brookner's male characters are often isolated emotionally and physically, experiencing discouragement or despair when their desires are unattainable or unrequited. Brookner foreshadows Julius Herz's infatuation with his cousin Fanny Bauer in *Altered States*

(1996), in which Alan Sherwood desires his cousin Sarah Miller, who shares similar personality characteristics with Fanny. Unlike Julius, Alan's obsession becomes tragic when his wife Angela commits suicide after Alan abandons her.

Offering the similar themes and literary styles that she uses to portray her female characters, Brookner's male-driven novels explore characters' psychological responses by revealing what they are thinking and how they justify their behavior or passivity as they face losses and rejection. She explores changing gender roles in society and men's reactions when some female characters have successful careers and do not rely on men for financial support but still desire romantic interaction, although often imposing boundaries.

Some critics claim that Brookner's novels are really conventional romances. Although Brookner is aware of the attraction of romances, the endings of her novels are never conventionally happy. The conflicts in her novels may seem to be only those of innocent people against an evil world. In Brookner's hands, however, these personal conflicts reflect the profound cultural shock of the past two centuries, the clash of the hopes of Romanticism with the real world. Early novels dramatize this conflict rather simply, but as Brookner has matured as a novelist, her sympathies have grown wider, encompassing groups of men and women engaged in lives of hope, disappointment, and some success.

Few of Brookner's characters, male or female, often limited by assumptions, pretensions, or emotions, achieve complete autonomy and cling to people and places that comfort but are not always good for them. Brookner effectively establishes somber tones when these characters, confined by familial or romantic duties and expectations, remain unfulfilled and powerless and often on the periphery unless a catalyst provokes them to become more selfish and less selfless in an attempt to fill their emptiness.

Although several of her novels are told by their central characters (*Look at Me, A Friend in England, Brief Lives,* and *A Private View*), most of them employ limited omniscience. *Hotel du Lac* is a mixture of devices. For the most part, a narrator restricts the reader to Edith's mind, but significant exceptions hint at Mr. Neville's satanic powers. Edith's unsent letters are first-person commentaries on the action. *Family and Friends* is also unusual; it contains very little conversation, and its story is told almost entirely by a narrator.

Brookner has said that although she revises her first drafts very little, she prides herself on being lucid. Critics praise her prose for other qualities as well. It is studded with apt allusions to novels (English, American, French, and Russian) and to the visual arts. These references can become symbolic, as in descriptions of paintings in *The Misalliance*.

Her words describe the surface of life precisely and lovingly: furniture, clothes, art objects, food. Her metaphors and similes are surprising and expressive: Edith's room is "veal-colored" in *Hotel du Lac*, and Lewis Percy's potential mother-in-law watches him "with the stillness of a lizard." Moreover, the reader always senses a sophisticated and joyful play of wit and intelligence while reading Brookner.

THE DEBUT

First published: 1981
Type of work: Novel

An older woman remembers how her family thwarted her hopes for love.

In *The Debut*, Brookner's first novel, the reader meets Dr. Ruth Weiss when she is a teacher of French literature in a university. She is forty years old and dresses in an old-fashioned way. From the beginning, Brookner evokes one of her major themes: the relation of stories to actual life. The narrator tells the reader enigmatically that Ruth's life has been blighted by literature. Her students and colleagues are not aware of her past, which was intense and adventurous. The reader is taken back to Ruth's past.

Ruth grows up in London as the only child of irresponsible parents—her English mother a fading actress and her European Jewish father a philandering book dealer. After her sensible grandmother dies, their household, with the help of a slovenly housekeeper, Mrs. Cutler, degenerates into shambles. Ruth, an intelligent girl, takes refuge in books; their stories and their happy endings become real to her. She believes that real girls, like Cinderella, get to the ball. Ruth believes that virtue is rewarded, as in the endings of novels by Charles Dickens. Like most of the central female figures of Brookner's later novels, she is a lonely, rather plain, timid, thoughtful young woman. Even as a university student, she makes only a few friends; her attempt to make dinner for an attractive man is a disaster.

In her university work, she is fascinated by the French writer Honoré de Balzac, whose novels tell her unpleasant truths about life. She learns that vice succeeds more often than virtue and that good looks count for a lot. Her studies draw her to Paris (like Brookner), where life takes a turn for the better. She meets a worldly English couple who convince her to cut and style her marvelous red hair (Brookner herself is red-haired) and to dress fashionably. She begins to live a life of selfish pleasure. Then she meets the famous Professor Duplessis and falls in love. The professor is a renowned Balzac scholar; though married and much older than she, he is tender and considerate. Ruth's happiness is at its peak when the professor comes for a meal in her marvelous new apartment. A telephone message calls her home: Her parents' lives have been shattered by a violent quarrel. They need her, and she makes a dismal trip back to London.

She returns to a diminished life. She gives up her new, liberated personality and reverts to her earlier role as timid daughter. Her mother dies. Even though her father suffers a stroke, he lingers on for many years, with Ruth as his housekeeper. She gets a university job and prospers. She contracts a loveless marriage, but her husband is killed in an accident. The reader is returned to the Dr. Ruth Weiss of the first chapter, a typical Brookner heroine: a lonely, sensitive, intelligent forty-year-old academic who once hoped that life would have a happy ending but whose consolation is that she once had adventures that seemed as intense as those in any novel.

LOOK AT ME

First published: 1983
Type of work: Novel

Frances Hinton tries to enter a glamorous world and find love, but she is defeated.

The story of *Look at Me*, Brookner's third novel, is told in the first person by its central character, Frances Hinton. She is an efficient young librarian at a medical institute in London. Like other Brookner heroines, she is lonely. Her parents are both dead, and she lives on in the comfortable family apartment with their housekeeper. Perhaps because she knows she is not beautiful, perhaps because of a previous unhappy love affair at which she hints, Frances classifies herself (also like so many of Brookner's heroines) as an observer of life, not a participant. She shows readers her powers of observation in describing the odd people she knows and promises to use them as a writer of entertaining, sharply satirical fiction. She has had a story or two published, and she contemplates a novel.

Behind Frances the observer is Frances the woman who longs to be a participant in life. She longs to cry out: "Look at me!" She wants excitement and finds it in the friendship of Nick Fraser, a handsome doctor who works at the institute, and Alix, his beautiful wife. They are a perfect couple, handsome and attractive, though Alix gradually emerges as the more powerful of the two. She is domineering and self-centered, but Frances is willing to be dominated and realizes (like Ruth in *The Debut*) that Alix's selfishness and greed are what life's participants possess. Far from turning away, Frances attaches herself to the Frasers with her eyes open.

Frances also hopes for love. Through Nick and Alix's efforts, Frances is thrown together with Dr. James Anstey, who also works at the institute. Grad-

ually they develop a close friendship—perhaps love. Each evening after leaving the Frasers, they walk across Hyde Park to Frances's apartment and sit quietly together. Without acknowledging that she is in love, Frances feels more and more like a participant in life, less like an observer and less like a writer.

Things go sour. In an ugly scene at a restaurant, Frances realizes that James has become the lover of the Frasers' friend Maria, that he is another essentially selfish person, and that she is fated to remain an observer. At the end of the novel, Frances prepares to take revenge by writing satirical, entertaining novels about persons like the Frasers and James Anstey. (Brookner herself suggested that revenge may be one of her motives for writing.) The first-person novel, in fact, is presented as Frances's revenge. Yet part of her still cannot resist people like Nick and Alix. She will seek them out in order to make notes for her fiction.

HOTEL DU LAC

First published: 1984
Type of work: Novel

Edith, a writer of romances with happy endings, refuses the temptation of a possible happy ending in her own life.

At the beginning of *Hotel du Lac* (hotel of the lake), Edith Hope is thirty-nine years old. As usual in Brookner novels, she is less than beautiful. She is shy, meek, intelligent, and lonely. She is beginning an unexplained exile at an exclusive hotel on the banks of Lake Geneva in Switzerland.

Like Frances in *Look at Me*, she is a writer, but she is more than simply a satiric observer. In this novel, Brookner expands on the relationship of real life to fiction. Edith is an established writer of romances; she knows how to write stories with happy endings. She divides people into hares and tortoises: The hares are beautiful, selfish, and loved, like Nick and Alix in *Look at Me*; tortoises are meek, plain, and unloved, like Ruth in *The Debut*. Even though in real life the hares always win, Edith knows that her romances are popular because the women who read them are tortoises, and in her books the tortoises always win. Hares do not read books; they are too busy having fun.

The characters of *Hotel du Lac* are not so easily categorized, although Edith's descriptions of them are brilliant and amusing. The pencil-thin Monica and an aging countess may be tortoises. A grotesque old lady and her plump, seductive daughter seem like hares. The elegant and charming Philip Neville is clearly not a tortoise. After Edith, the professional novelist, invents plots for them, however, she discovers her fictions are nothing like their true stories.

Edith herself is not exactly a tortoise. She has participated in life. From the beginning, Edith reveals part of her story in letters (unmailed) to David, a married man who has been her lover. Halfway through the novel, the reader learns why Edith is in Switzerland: She had to get out of town after leaving her fiancé waiting at the church. At the end of the novel, she is tempted to escape her lonely life forever when Philip Neville offers her a luxurious, loveless marriage. She rejects him and returns home to uncertainty.

Like other Brookner heroines, she has yearned for true love and lost it, but that does not mean she has given up on fiction. In a final letter, she tells David that she has always believed in the happy endings of her romance novels, though she now suspects they are not for her.

MAKING THINGS BETTER

First published: 2002 (pb. in England as *The Next Big Thing*, 2002)
Type of work: Novel

Julius Herz contemplates how to proceed after he is forced into an abrupt, unplanned retirement.

Making Things Better opens with Julius Herz, age seventy-three, dreaming of his narcissistic cousin Fanny Bauer, whom he has romantically desired but been denied since childhood. Much of this narrative peers inside Julius's thoughts, revealing his backstory while chronicling his present. A German exile, a frequent figure in Brookner's fiction, Julius has lived in London since his Jewish family de-

parted Berlin when he was fourteen during the 1930's. A benefactor, Mr. Ostrovski, provided Julius's parents, Willy and Trude Herz, a flat and income from his music store.

This novel's American title is embedded in the text as Julius attempts to makes conditions tolerable by dutifully serving his controlling parents and maintaining contact with his older brother, Freddy, a gifted violinist who resides in a hospice after a mental breakdown. That exile enabled Freddy to escape his parents' expectations. Trapped in a dreamlike existence, Julius neglects his desires, including his wife, Josie, who divorces him. Instead of seeking autonomous employment, Julius works in the music store with his father, settling into a tranquilizing routine that helps him grieve as the sole survivor after his parents' and brother's deaths.

Ostrovski sells the property where Julius works and lives, forcing Julius to make decisions. Julius adjusts to newfound idleness by leasing a flat and strolling to shops, galleries, and parks. As times passes, aging Julius measures life in the terms of his lease commitment, assuming he might die before renewing it. The text repeats this novel's British title, referring to dying being the next significant event for older people.

Brookner's choice of Julius's German surname, Herz, meaning heart, symbolizes his geriatric concerns, both emotional and physical. He meets Josie for lunches but values her friendship rather than attempting to reconnect romantically with her. Julius is aroused by his unattainable new neighbor, Sophie Clay, a young career woman. He longs for love, particularly with Fanny. When he experiences alarming heart flutters, Julius seeks help from an aloof physician who prescribes medication and ignores Julius's comments about Sigmund Freud. Ted Bishop, Julius's housecleaner, shares a cautionary tale in which an elderly airline passenger experiences a dire medical situation, foreshadowing Julius's future.

Julius goes to Paris, desiring to see a Eugène

Delacroix painting that had impressed him as a young man. His memories offer revelations of freedoms he had briefly savored there in the past. At home, he gets rid of heirlooms, particularly family photographs. After not communicating with him for years, Fanny sends Julius letters, pleading for him to help her with legal troubles. Provoked, Julius responds, telling Fanny she is self-centered and should read Thomas Mann's *Buddenbrooks* (1901; English translation, 1924), which examines family relationships. Destroying those angry notes, Julius mails kinder messages, suggesting they retreat to Beau Rivage, the Swiss hotel where he had unsuccessfully proposed to Fanny thirty years earlier. As Julius, wholeheartedly pursuing his desires instead of submitting to others, prepares to board the airplane, he ironically suffers an attack, accidentally dropping and stepping on his heart pills. Julius moves forward, his fate and destination unclear, to experience the next significant phase of his life, either his demise or his renewal.

SUMMARY

Anita Brookner has created a number of distinctive novels. Her central characters usually are intelligent and sensitive women who yearn for love. The mood of the novels is somewhat somber because these women are foiled by many things: their own timidity, the restraints of family, and the self-centered greed of other people. Some of her later novels focus on male characters as well and describe the workings of more than one family. Readers get to know these characters well because of Brookner's deft analyses of their motives and attitudes, as well as her descriptions of the surfaces of their lives. If the stories are unhappy, Brookner's style is not: It is witty and imaginative.

Although some reviewers criticize Brookner's novels as being redundant, other critics emphasize that Brookner does not repeatedly create the same plots and characters but introduces new perceptions presented through people and settings familiar to her. They maintain that her evolving insights enrich her literary style with each novel she writes. While detractors dismiss Brookner's fiction as lacking sufficient literary substance, many scholars and readers recognize its qualities that merit continued attention.

George Soule; updated by Elizabeth D. Schafer

BIBLIOGRAPHY

By the Author

LONG FICTION:
The Debut, 1981 (pb. in England as *A Start in Life*, 1981)
Providence, 1982
Look at Me, 1983
Hotel du Lac, 1984
Family and Friends, 1985
The Misalliance, 1986 (pb. in England as *A Misalliance*, 1986)
A Friend from England, 1987
Latecomers, 1988
Lewis Percy, 1989
Brief Lives, 1990
A Closed Eye, 1991
Fraud, 1992
A Family Romance, 1993 (pb. in U.S. as *Dolly*, 1993)
A Private View, 1994
Incidents in the Rue Laugier, 1995
Altered States, 1996
Visitors, 1997
Falling Slowly, 1998

Undue Influence, 1999
The Bay of Angels, 2001
Making Things Better, 2002 (pb. in England as *The Next Big Thing,* 2002)
The Rules of Engagement, 2003
Leaving Home, 2005

NONFICTION:
Watteau, 1968
The Genius of the Future, Studies in French Art Criticism: Diderot, Stendhal, Baudelaire, Zola, the Brothers Goncourt, Huysmans, 1971
Greuze: The Rise and Fall of an Eighteenth-Century Phenomenon, 1972
Jacques-Louis David, 1980
Soundings, 1997
Romanticism and Its Discontents, 2000

TRANSLATIONS:
Utrillo, 1960 (of Waldemar George's biography)
The Fauves, 1962 (of Jean Paul Crespelle's book)
Gaugin, 1962 (of Maximilien Gauthier's book)

About the Author

Fullbrook, Kate. "Anita Brookner: On Reaching for the Sun." In *British Women Writing Fiction,* edited by Abby H. P. Werlock. Tuscaloosa: University of Alabama Press, 2000.

Hosmer, Robert E., Jr. "Paradigm and Passage: The Fiction of Anita Brookner." In *Contemporary British Women Writers: Narrative Strategies,* edited by Hosmer. New York: St. Martin's Press, 1993.

Malcolm, Cheryl Alexander. *Understanding Anita Brookner.* Columbia: University of South Carolina Press, 2002.

Piehler, Liana F. *Spatial Dynamics and Female Development in Victorian Art and Novels: Creating a Woman's Space.* New York: Peter Lang, 2003.

Sadler, Lynn Veach. *Anita Brookner.* Boston: Twayne, 1990.

Skinner, John. *The Fictions of Anita Brookner: Illusions of Romance.* New York: St. Martin's Press, 1992.

Soule, George. *Four British Women Novelists: Anita Brookner, Margaret Drabble, Iris Murdoch, Barbara Pym, an Annotated and Critical Secondary Bibliography.* Lanham, Md.: Scarecrow Press, 1998.

DISCUSSION TOPICS

- How does the theme of exile shape Anita Brookner's characters and affect their behavior and perceptions of cultural differences?

- Analyze how Brookner's descriptions of residences and domestic life reveal characters' mind-sets. Contrast how several of her characters define their concept of home.

- Discuss the significance of childhood memories to Brookner's characters and how the literary device of flashbacks either deepens or distracts from her characterizations and plots.

- How effective is Brookner's inclusion of characters' letters, both mailed and unsent, as a literary style?

- Compare characters' resignation and conformity to traditional gender and familial roles. How do themes of love, sacrifice, and disappointment permeate Brookner's novels?

- Examine how references to art and literature enhance the themes in Brookner's fiction. Discuss how possessing keen intellects strengthens or diminishes her characters' lives.

- Analyze how despair seems essential for character development in Brookner's works.

- Discuss Brookner's use of humor and how it balances her dramatic storytelling.

Elizabeth Barrett Browning

Library of Congress

Born: Coxhoe Hall, County Durham, England
March 6, 1806
Died: Florence, Italy
June 29, 1861

As a nineteenth century English poet, Barrett Browning is recognized as a major literary artist and is considered an originator of a feminine poetic tradition.

BIOGRAPHY

Elizabeth Barrett was born on March 6, 1806, the eldest child of Mary Graham Clark and Edward Barrett Moulton-Barrett. She spent her childhood at Hope End, an estate owned by her parents, located in Herefordshire, England. She was a bright, intelligent child who grew up with the advantages of living in an upper-middle-class family, advantages made possible by her father's plantations in Jamaica. According to an essay she wrote when she was fourteen, she claims to have wanted to be a poet from the age of four. Poetry remained her lifelong ambition.

Barrett's early life revolved around her family. Her mother was a submissive Victorian wife dedicated to her husband and children. She encouraged Barrett by copying and saving her daughter's early attempts at writing. Her father was a man with a tyrannical nature who imposed his will on the family. At the age of eight, Barrett wrote two birthday odes, one to her mother and one to her father. She portrayed women as loving and kind, but without power, and men as powerful and God-like. Although she remained devoted to her parents, neither parent served as a model for an aspiring female poet. She had to look elsewhere for the inspiration that she required to reach her goal.

Barrett found three main sources of encouragement through her commitment to reading and studying: the Romantic poets, especially Lord Byron, the radical feminist writings of Mary Wollstonecraft Shelley, and Greek language and literature. Her success in teaching herself the Greek language was one of the most extraordinary accomplishments of her early years. Since Victorian girls were not sent to school, all Barrett's knowledge was gained by self-study and her desire to learn. The two subjects to which she committed herself were poetry and Greek, although she taught herself other subjects, including Latin. Through her efforts, she became an acknowledged expert in her favorite subjects. Her first major poem, *The Battle of Marathon* (privately published by her father in 1820), written at the age of fourteen, is modeled after the Greek Homeric epic poem form. Its subject is an early Greek battle.

At fifteen, Barrett and two of her sisters became ill, and it was feared that she would die. She was sent to Gloucester for medical treatment and remained there for a year. She did not fully recover. The cause of her illness has never been determined. For many years, it was believed to be an emotional rather than a physical disorder, although it has been suggested that she suffered from tuberculosis. Her family blamed a fall from a horse, which injured her back. Whatever the cause, she became an invalid and a recluse. More than ever, her life was restricted to her family circle and the books that she loved. She devoted herself to writing.

In 1826, Barrett published her first serious book of poetry, *An Essay on Mind, with Other Poems*. Although published anonymously, it marked her first attempt to address a larger audience. The book also resulted in two important friendships. In response to *An Essay on Mind, with Other Poems*, she received a letter from Uvedale Price, an eighty-year-old man who asked her to review the proofs of his book on ancient Greek pronunciation. He praised her poems and approved of her latest work, "The Development of Genius," a poem to which her father objected and which she did not finish. Price encouraged her and provided the support that she needed to overcome her father's displeasure. Hugh Stuart Boyd, a blind classical scholar, also sent her a letter of praise. She began spending her time reading Greek to him, and he helped her to continue her study of the language and literature.

The years 1828 through 1832 were marked by setbacks in Barrett's personal life and a curbing of her literary production. In 1828, her mother died. Price died the following year. In 1832, her father had to sell his Hope End estate due to losses experienced in his Jamaican plantations. The family began a series of moves to various rented houses, ending in Wimpole Street, London, in 1838. With her mother's death and the loss of her friendships with Price and Boyd, Barrett became even more reclusive. In 1833, she published *Prometheus Bound, Translated from the Greek of Aeschylus: And Miscellaneous Poems*. With the publication of *The Seraphim, and Other Poems* (1838), she finally achieved critical and popular acclaim. The reviewers found the poems intelligent and learned. Her ballads were particularly popular. It was this book that established her reputation in the United States.

In 1844, she published *Poems*. The four years that Barrett spent writing the poems were filled with sickness and sorrow. She had contracted a disease of the lungs and was forced to lived in Torquay, France, because of its milder climate. In 1840, her brother Sam died from a fever, and her favorite brother, Edward, died in a sailing accident in the bay of Torquay. Her father believed Barrett had caused Edward's death, since Edward was visiting her when he died. She suffered intense grief, sorrow, and guilt. In 1841, she returned to Wimpole Street, where she retreated to her room to live the life of an absolute recluse. She refused to see anyone. Her doctors advised her not to change her clothes, so she continually wore a black dress, silk in the summer, velvet in the winter. During this period, she wrote the poems that established her as one of the major poets of her time.

Perhaps even more important than the acclaim she achieved with the publication of *Poems* was a letter of admiration she received from a fellow poet. In January, 1845, Robert Browning wrote Barrett, "I love your verse with all my heart . . . and I love you too" (*The Letters of Robert Browning and Elizabeth Barrett Barrett, 1845-1846*, published in 1898). This letter was the beginning of one of the most romantic love stories of all time. They continued to correspond until May, when he came to visit her. They were secretly married in September, 1846, and left England to establish their home in Italy.

Their marriage was a happy one. They influenced each other's poetry. Elizabeth Barrett Browning's *Poems* (1850), which includes *Sonnets from the Portuguese*, is a sonnet sequence of forty-four poems representing their relationship. During her married years, she continued writing poetry, including her epic poem of feminine struggle *Aurora Leigh* (1856). In 1849, at the age of forty-three, she bore her only child, Robert Weidemann. Barrett Browning died from a lung disorder, probably tuberculosis, in Florence, Italy, on June 29, 1861.

ANALYSIS

Elizabeth Barrett Browning is a poet remembered for all the wrong reasons. Reclusive for most of her life, publicity shy, and extremely reserved, she is primarily known today as the heroine of an unbelievably romantic and public love story, Rudolf Besier's *The Barretts of Wimpole Street* (1930); a 1934 film and its 1957 remake, have also been released under that title. A serious poet aspiring to her own place in Western poetic tradition, she is regarded as the conventional love poet of *Sonnets from the Portuguese* who celebrates the power of conjugal love and monogamous marriage. As an advocate for women's rights, she is seen as a mere appendage of her more famous husband. Politically conservative, born into aristocracy, and appalled by what she considered the inhumanity of modern industrial society, she has been viewed as a spokeswoman for radical political upheaval. Finally, though a woman who believed in the natural superiority of men, Barrett Browning is admired as an early proponent of equal rights for women.

These discrepancies between the person, the poetry, and the reputation are not merely the result of confusion or ignorance. Barrett Browning is an extremely difficult author, whose work is complex, experimental, and individual. Her use of poetic form to subvert poetic expectation and tradition makes her work interesting and significant but requires reflective readers and critical examination if it is to be understood. The study of her work is important for an understanding of the time in which she wrote and for her poetic achievement.

Barrett Browning was an extremely prolific author who began writing prose and poetry as a child and continued actively writing until she died at the age of fifty-five. She demonstrates a serious concern for the world around her, an unflinching ability to analyze her own feelings and motivation, a love of language, a desire to experiment and create a new poetry, and a conception of poetry as a moral force in the affairs of men and women.

Barrett Browning is also one of the first major poets to articulate the themes and concerns of Victorian England and the developing industrial world. The value of work, the awareness of alienation and human isolation, the loss of conventional religious faith, the conflict between religion and science, the function of art, the ambiguous relationship between society and nature, the conflict between free will and fate, the relationship between men and women, and the place and value of culture are subjects that absorbed Victorian writers and intellectuals. These themes are found throughout Barrett Browning's poetry. She anticipates the emptiness and feelings of alienation expressed by Matthew Arnold; writes medieval ballads and experiments with epic and sonnet forms, as did Alfred, Lord Tennyson, and Dante Gabriel Rossetti; uses dramatic monologues much like Robert Browning; and addresses the political and social issues of her time, as did many of her male contemporaries. Yet she is an original, innovative poet who presents her own well-considered, informed views in a highly developed, artistic form.

Barrett Browning's most lasting contribution to poetry and literature is her imaginative adoption of traditional poetic forms to new subject matter, her struggle and final success in establishing the female voice as a poetic possibility, her belief in poetry as a moral agent in the affairs of men and women, and her persistency in the belief that life has meaning and purpose. Poems such as "Rhyme of the Duchess May," "Lady Geraldine's Courtship," and "Bertha in the Lane" extend the ballad form to include the ambivalent position of women rather than the traditional subject of masculine heroism. *The Cry of the Children* (1844), "Crowned and Buried," and "The Runaway Slave at Pilgrim's Point" address the controversial topics of child labor, Napoleon I's return from exile, and slavery. They extend the province of poetry to contemporary political issues. In *Sonnets from the Portuguese*, she not only adopts a form previously reserved for the male expression of love but also creates one of the most accomplished and beautiful sonnet sequences in the English language. Finally, in *Aurora Leigh*, she creates a successful epic poem about the struggle of a woman to achieve a life of her own on equal terms with society and men.

Barrett Browning believed that a poet was an important moral influence in the world. Accepting the Romantic vision of the poet as prophet, she appropriated the vision and resolved restoration of values destroyed by the marketplace. She saw the underside of an industrial society in the prevalence of ignorance, crime, prostitution, and exhaustion. For Barrett Browning, the poet served as the link between the everyday values of commonplace life and the possibility of transcendent consciousness. In the materialistic world of Victorian England and the modern industrial world, she believed that there was a desperate need for a contemporary prophet-poet to restore the values preempted by the factories and the mines. Humanity required a poet who would embrace the joy and pain of human existence and confront the conditions and reality of the world. Barrett Browning saw herself as the prophet-poet in a debased, lost, industrial world, crying, like the children in her poem *The Cry of the Children*, for hope and compassion.

THE CRY OF THE CHILDREN

First published: 1844
Type of work: Poem

The plight of Victorian children working in a factory is exposed by their lament of the drudgery and hopelessness of their lives.

The Cry of the Children is representative not only of Barrett Browning's political poetry but also of her work in general. It contains themes and images that can be found throughout her work. The use of language, meter, and rhyme in the poem demonstrates her innovative poetics and singular style.

It is problematic that Barrett Browning actually heard the cry of the children whom she so eloquently laments in her poem. She wrote *The Cry of the Children* after reading a report on the employment of children in mines and manufactories. A master of language, she evokes its emotional power to engender a response of outrage in her readers. The poem is intentionally didactic, political in purpose as well as subject matter. It is an expression of her own alienation and abhorrence of industrial society seen through the eyes and feelings of factory children, represented as innocence betrayed and used by political and economic interests for selfish purposes.

Throughout the poem, demonic images of a Factory Hell are contrasted with the Heaven of the English countryside, the inferno of industrialism with the bliss of a land-based society. The children are implored to leave the mine and city for the serenity of meadow and country. The grinding, droning mechanism of industrial society destroys the promise and hope of human life. Barrett Browning was concerned with the fate of a society that exploited human life for profit, and she ends her poem with an indictment of industrial society.

The reader is made to experience the dreariness of the factory inferno by Barrett Browning's use of language, as she describes the harrowing reality of the "droning, turning" factory wheels, relentlessly grinding the children's spirit and life as it molds its goods. The factory is depicted as a perversion of nature, a literal Hell seen as the absence and corruption of the natural world. Instead of the world revolving around the sun, the sky turns—as the wheels, similarly, turn. Barrett Browning's use of words ending in "ing" and containing long vowel sounds—"moaning," "droning," "turning," "burning"—invokes the monotony and despair of this awful abyss of industry.

The "Children" of the poem are silenced by the sound of the wheels turning, seek the silence of death as their only means of escape, and, finally, are reduced to a mere "sob in the silence" in a vain effort to curse. The struggle to speak is a constant theme in the poem, a motif that vies with the oppression of the factory and the plight of the children. The repetition of the phrase, "say the children" makes it a key element in the very structure of the poem. Words of speech and silence are used throughout—"hear," "ask," "listen," "sing," "answer," "quiet," "silent," "still," "words," "speechless," "preach," "stifle." The hopelessness of the children's plight is partially caused by their inability to be heard or to express themselves. They are oppressed and exploited because they are not authorized to speak. In the end, even God is unable to hear their feeble attempts at prayer.

SONNETS FROM THE PORTUGUESE

First published: 1850 (collected in *Poems, 1850*)
Type of work: Poems

This sequence contains forty-four sonnets written in the Petrarchan sonnet form and treating romantic love in a long poem from a woman's perspective.

Sonnets from the Portuguese is Barrett Browning's most enduring and popular poem, although it has been undervalued by critics. The sequence of sonnets was new and experimental when it was written. It adopted a poetic form and subject matter reserved for the expression of male amatory experience and depicted modern life and domestic events in a traditionally high literary form used to express the pursuit of ideal love and the poet's failure to translate it into the actual world. Instead, Barrett Browning replaced the male poetic voice with her own and related the feelings that she experienced during Robert Browning's courtship. The sonnets bring together the voice of a woman and the voice of the poet and make them one. They not only relate a courtship between a man and a woman but also relate the transformation of a woman into a poet. They authorize the woman to be a poet and ponder the problem of being both the object and the subject of love and poetic thought.

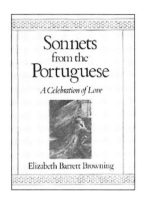

For a full understanding of the poems, it must be remembered that they are a sequence that forms a complete work describing a process that ends with achieved love and realized poetic power. Helen Cooper, in *Elizabeth Barrett Browning: Woman and Artist* (1988), divides the poems into three groups: woman seen as the object of a man's desire and love (Sonnets 1 and 2), the woman struggling to free herself from being objectified and maintaining her own subjectivity (Sonnets 3 through 40), and the woman achieving her own subjectivity while accepting the man's love (Sonnets 41 through 44). This grouping reveals the two themes addressed in the sonnets: the development of a mature love based on mutual respect and the quest of the poet-artist for her own voice and authority.

Barrett Browning wrote the sonnets to record her feelings during her courtship. At the time, she was living in her father's house and subject to his will. He had forbidden any of his children to marry, and, as a dutiful daughter, Elizabeth obeyed him until she married Robert at the age of forty. The sonnets are an honest portrayal of her struggle with the prospect of love and marriage, which were not easily accepted by her because of age and her father's demands. Many critics in her own time and later consider the poems too personal. They view them as a form of private love letters that should not have been published. In large part, their popularity is due to Barrett Browning's lack of pretense and sincere expression of her own experiences of love. Many readers have shared these experiences with her and find joy in their poetic expression. Although the emotions in the sonnets validate their sincerity, and though they are based on her own courtship, these considerations hide the true achievement that she accomplished in writing the sonnets. They are complex, crafted, artistic poems, written in a difficult form, employing original conceits and metaphors. They are not the simple emotional writings of a woman in love but the realized work of an accomplished poet performing at the height of her powers.

SUMMARY

Elizabeth Barrett Browning is a preeminent poet of the nineteenth century whose work belongs in the mainstream of Western poetic tradition. Her work is more significant and influential than is generally accepted. She is a pivotal writer in the transition from a Romantic to a modern sensibility, appropriating the outlook and perspective of her precursors, adapting them to her own time and situation, and preserving them for the future. Not only is she the first poet in a tradition of female poets, but she has also earned her place in the larger tradition of English poetry, which includes men and women.

Herbert Northcote

BIBLIOGRAPHY

By the Author

POETRY:
The Battle of Marathon, 1820
An Essay on Mind, with Other Poems, 1826
The Seraphim, and Other Poems, 1838
Poems, 1844
The Cry of the Children, 1844

Poems, 1850 (including *Sonnets from the Portuguese*)
Casa Guidi Windows, 1851
Aurora Leigh, 1856
Poems Before Congress, 1860
Last Poems, 1862

NONFICTION:

The Letters of Elizabeth Barrett Browning, 1897
The Letters of Robert Browning and Elizabeth Barrett Barrett, 1845-1846, 1898
Diary by E. B. B.: The Unpublished Diary of Elizabeth Barrett Browning, 1831-1832, 1969 (Philip Kelley and Ronald Hudson, editors)

MISCELLANEOUS:

Prometheus Bound, Translated from the Greek of Aeschylus: And Miscellaneous Poems, 1833

About the Author

Avery, Simon, and Rebecca Stott. *Elizabeth Barrett Browning.* New York: Longman, 2003.

Besier, Rudolf. *The Barretts of Wimpole Street: A Comedy in Five Acts.* Boston: Little, Brown, 1930.

Bloom, Harold, ed. *Elizabeth Barrett Browning.* Philadelphia: Chelsea House, 2002.

Cooper, Helen. *Elizabeth Barrett Browning: Woman and Artist.* Chapel Hill: University of North Carolina Press, 1988.

David, Deirdre. *Intellectual Women and Victorian Patriarchy.* Ithaca, N.Y.: Cornell University Press, 1987.

Garrett, Martin, ed. *Elizabeth Barrett Browning and Robert Browning: Interviews and Recollections.* New York: St. Martin's Press, 2000.

Gilbert, Sandra M., and Susan Gubar. *The Madwoman in the Attic.* New Haven, Conn.: Yale University Press, 1984.

Leighton, Angela. *Elizabeth Barrett Browning.* Edited by Sue Roe. Bloomington: Indiana University Press, 1986.

Mermin, Dorothy. *Elizabeth Barrett Browning: The Origins of a New Poetry.* Chicago: University of Chicago Press, 1989.

Pollock, Mary Sanders. *Elizabeth Barrett and Robert Browning: A Creative Partnership.* Burlington, Vt.: Ashgate, 2003.

Radley, Virginia I. *Elizabeth Barrett Browning.* New York: Twayne, 1972.

DISCUSSION TOPICS

- Explain how a consideration of Elizabeth Barrett Browning's early life rebuffs the inclination of critics to regard her as an "appendage" to her husband.

- Show how Barrett Browning's literary work is a better guide to understanding relationships between men and women than the famous romance between her and Robert Browning.

- Is *Aurora Leigh* truly an epic? What epic traits does it exemplify?

- Substantiate the assertion that Barrett Browning displayed "innovative poetics" in *The Cry of the Children*.

- Considering the lengthy tradition of sonnet sequences before *Sonnets from the Portuguese*, what features of Barrett Browning's sequence justify calling it "new and experimental"?

Library of Congress

ROBERT BROWNING

Born: Camberwell, England
        May 7, 1812
Died: Venice, Italy
        December 12, 1889

Widely recognized as one of the two greatest poets of Victorian England (with Alfred, Lord Tennyson), Browning produced some of the best dramatic poetry of all time and influenced modern poets.

BIOGRAPHY

Robert Browning was born on May 7, 1812, in Camberwell, a suburb of London, England, to Robert and Sara Anna Wiedemann Browning. His father was a senior clerk in the Bank of England and a conservative, unambitious, bookish man closer in temperament to a scholar than to a businessman. His mother, a Scottish gentlewoman, reared her son to love the Church, music, gardening, and nature. Growing up in the urban middle class, Browning had one sister, to whom he paid a lifelong devotion. From 1820 to 1826, he attended a boarding school. In 1828, he enrolled in the recently opened University of London, but he withdrew after only a few months. His main education came from tutors and his father's ample library.

In the view of many, Browning's young adulthood was an essentially irresponsible time, as he preferred to stay at home rather than work or attend school. At home, he read Alexander Pope's *The Iliad of Homer* (1715-1720), the Romantic poets in general, and a favorite who became his idol, the poet Percy Bysshe Shelley. Around 1824, Browning wrote "Incondita," a volume of poetry in imitation of Lord Byron. When his parents could not get the manuscript published, he destroyed it. Only two poems from this collection have survived.

Thus, Browning's occupation became that of poet. His whole family seemed to indulge him.

When his first poem, *Pauline*, finally appeared in 1833, his aunt paid for its publication. Anonymously printed, the poem received little notice, and no record can be obtained proving that it sold a single copy. In fact, most critics view *Pauline* as a typical Romantic poem characterized by excessive self-indulgence.

During the next few years, Browning journeyed to Russia (1834) and produced two long poems–*Paracelsus* (1835), set in the Renaissance, and *Sordello* (1840), set in medieval Italy. Although both poems were critical failures, taken together with his trip they indicate that Browning was learning to move beyond himself, to develop aesthetic distance from his subject.

From 1837 to 1847, Browning turned to playwriting. Determined to make a career change to dramatist and inspired by actor-manager William Charles Macready, Browning threw himself into his ambition. *Strafford* (pr., pb. 1837) was performed for five nights in 1837 before it closed, and his play *Luria* was published in 1846. None of his plays made money, and he finally abandoned the theater. That is not to say, however, that the period was wasted. During that time, William Shakespeare replaced Shelley as Browning's literary guiding light, and Browning mastered some of the basic dramatic techniques that later made his poetry great.

In 1841, concurrent with his outpouring of drama, Browning began writing a series of eight "shilling" pamphlets. Titled *Bells and Pomegranates* (1841-1846) for the hem of a Hebrew high priest's garment, all were issued at his father's expense. Originally intending to make each pamphlet a play, Browning had such faith in his newly acquired dramatic ability that he included a few poems. *Pippa Passes* (1841), the first of these poems, eventually became very popular. The poem, complete with monologues and scenes, tells the tale of a factory girl's yearly holiday and her song, which influences others into action and morality.

The strength of the ensuing poems was the dramatic monologue, a form that Browning did not invent but that he did perfect by adding a psychological dimension. *Dramatic Lyrics* (1842) contains his first real successes in this format, with such notable poems as "My Last Duchess," "Porphyria's Lover," and "Soliloquy of the Spanish Cloister." *Dramatic Romances and Lyrics* (1845) delivered "The Bishop Orders His Tomb at Saint Praxed's Church." Although few of these volumes sold well immediately, critics and a segment of the public began to appreciate his psychological insights into people and his grasp of historical periods. Influenced, too, by John Donne, Browning had achieved objectivity, ridding himself of his indulgent Romantic angst.

The most famous portion of Browning's life also occurred during this period, and it was directly occasioned by his new type of poetry. One person expressing admiration for his talents was the famed English poet and invalid Elizabeth Barrett. Thus began one of the great factual love stories in Western culture. Her father, dedicated to keeping his children unmarried, dominated her, using her poor health to make her into a recluse. In January, 1845, Browning began to correspond with her. Barrett expressed herself and her growing love for Browning poetically in *Sonnets from the Portuguese*, published in *Poems* (1850). After more than a year and a half of courtship, Browning secretly married her, without her father's permission, in St. Marylebone Church on September 12, 1846. With his new wife, her dog, and her maid, Browning hastened to Italy, their new home.

Flourishing in the society of Rome and Florence, Elizabeth seemed healthier, and Browning began to publish his finest work. *Men and Women*, which many people consider to be his best single volume, appeared in 1855 and became his first popular success. *Dramatis Personae* was published in 1864. During this period, Elizabeth produced a son, and, using Italian materials, Browning himself achieved great fame. Yet tragedy struck as the sickly

Elizabeth died in 1861. Browning buried her in Florence, took his son, Robert "Pen" Browning, home, and never returned to the city that he loved.

For the next two decades, Browning continued to produce collections of poetry at the rate of one every year and a half. Socially, he gave dinners for many of the literary luminaries of his day, and he had a great many honorary degrees conferred upon him. His poetry lost some of its freshness, and his voice occasionally weakened. Yet his poems still sparkled with moments of greatness.

From 1888 to 1894, his *The Poetical Works of Robert Browning* was published in seventeen volumes, and he supervised the last edition himself. In 1889, his last work, *Asolando*, appeared, and in the fall of that same year he journeyed back to Italy. While walking on the Lido in Venice, where he was staying with Pen and his wife, he caught a cold. He died on December 12, 1889, in Venice. His body was returned to England, where he received his most prestigious honor, burial in the Poets' Corner of Westminster Abbey. Born into the heyday of Romanticism, he died at the time that the Victorian era was itself expiring.

ANALYSIS

During his lifetime, Browning was probably appreciated most for his optimistic themes about humankind in a pessimistic era. Typically, Browning offers this self-portrait at the end of the epilogue to *Asolando*: "One who never turned his back but marched breast forward/ Never doubted clouds would break./ Never dreamed, though right were worsted, wrong would triumph." Retrospect, however, reveals a greater legacy and a more profound influence, especially on later generations of poets. When Browning began writing, Romanticism dominated poetry with all of its effusive self-indulgence, its confessional nature, its overwhelming *Weltschmerz*—its supreme subjectivity and preoccupation with the individual poet's emotional state of being. By the time he died, Browning had demonstrated that poetry could be intensely dramatic, profoundly psychological, and simultaneously insightful.

Browning's insistence on the poet's detachment and devotion to the dramatic ideal was his enduring literary legacy and his greatest influence on future poets, such as T. S. Eliot. In his advertisement published on the second page of *Dramatic Lyrics*, Browning announced his credo, his preference for "poetry always dramatic in principle, and so many utterances of so many imaginary persons, not mine." More precisely, Browning refined, though he did not invent, a poetic genre called the dramatic monologue. Browning's poems of this type are essentially speeches by a single person. Unlike a soliloquy, however, a listener/audience is present, though never speaking. As a result, as in real life, the speaker offers no guarantee of telling the truth. As with all drama, the speech is set at a particular place, is about a specific subject, and contains a conflict with some opposing force. The ultimate thrust of a Browning monologue is character insight; the speaker, no matter what the apparent subject of the monologue, always reveals the essence of his or her personality. Thus, there is usually a sense of dramatic irony. Browning's major contribution to the dramatic monologue, then, is to demonstrate its psychological potential; the chief motives, the very soul of the speaker, are laid bare.

Browning, then, is the harbinger of the modern literary preoccupation with the mysteries of the psyche. He reveals both the breadth and the depth of the human mind, and these insights range from the normal to the abnormal. Browning, for example, originally classified one of his earlier poems, "Porphyria's Lover," under the heading "Madhouse Cells." The poem, coldly narrated by a man who has only a moment ago finished strangling his lover, shows Browning's willingness to explore that other side of the human mind, the dark side. Moreover, Browning is willing to plumb the depths beyond the conscious mind. Occasionally, when his poems seem incomprehensible, his characters are gripped by irrational impulses and speak from their unconscious.

Of course, not all of Browning's seemingly obscure lines can be traced to the minds of his characters. After the hours in his father's library and his journeys to Italy, his knowledge was immense, and he frequently uses allusions to history, the Bible, and the classics. In "The Bishop Orders His Tomb at Saint Praxed's Church," for example, Browning displays an awareness of church ritual, Greek mythology, and marble. Also, he was a great experimenter. He used metrical variations and often unnatural syntax. He was fond of beginning his poems in mid-speech and situation. "My Last Duchess" commences as the Duke of Ferrara is only fifty-

six lines from finishing a long interview with the count's emissary. Browning shuns logical transitions, preferring to jump from one thought to the next as most people do in everyday speech. He often discards pronouns.

Another notable characteristic of Browning's verse is his detachment. Like many of the realists of his day, he refrained from the moral judgment of his characters, thus eschewing the didactic theory of art. Nowhere in "Porphyria's Lover," for example, does Browning intrude to pronounce the homicidal lover evil or a sociopath. If there are judgments to be made, Browning leaves that task to his readers. Thus, Browning occasionally went against the oversimplified Victorian morality of art.

As both Browning's intense love affair with Elizabeth Barrett and the title of one volume, *Men and Women*, suggest, he was very much interested in the relationship of the sexes, especially in the high plane of love. Perhaps partially because he was forced to woo Barrett at first from a distance, Browning became profoundly reflective about romantic love. Even a cursory reading of his poetry reveals that he had several theories about man-woman relationships, and these theories, combined with the intense psychological reality of his characters, suggest why he is viewed as one of the great love poets in English. Interestingly, some of his great love lyrics were written before he met his wife and after she had died. When the eponymous speaker of "Rabbi Ben Ezra" argues, "Grow old along with me! / The best is yet to be," one must realize that the lines were composed after Elizabeth had died and therefore express wishful thinking. Also, Browning's love lyrics express not only the joy of love but also its failures. "Meeting at Night" is coupled with "Parting at Morning," wherein the male lover must leave the woman whom he loves to return to the "world of men."

One notable idea often finding expression in Browning is how often love can be replaced by a preoccupation with material things. In "My Last Duchess," the Duke of Ferrara has reduced the woman whom he had married to a work of art, where she is now even less treasured than a bronze statue. In "The Bishop Orders His Tomb at Saint Praxed's Church," the dying bishop has replaced his original love of God with things—a wine press, classical manuscripts, and villas.

Another typical theme in Browning is the supremacy of romantic love. Perhaps the best example of this idea occurs in "Love Among the Ruins." The palace of the prince and the prince's power are in ruins, the soldiers and their war machines have vanished, and Browning concludes that despite their "triumphs" and "glories," "love is best." True love for Browning was part and parcel of spiritual love.

What, then, is the poet's role in the midst of love and psychology? Perhaps Browning best states his poetic credo in "Fra Lippo Lippi" by using the persona as his mouthpiece: "this world . . . means intensely, and means good." In his "Essay on Percy Bysshe Shelley," Browning elaborated upon this notion of the poet finding the "good." The poet must have a "great moral purpose," must search the world around him, for, paradoxically, the greatest spiritual elevation occurs when the poet immerses himself in the things of this world. Often Browning's optimism is misunderstood. Good comes not in the actual attainment of higher things, often love, but also in the attempt. Failure and disappointment are secondary if the attempt is made.

"My Last Duchess"

First published: 1842 (collected in *Dramatic Lyrics*, 1842)
Type of work: Poem

The Duke of Ferrara reveals himself to be a selfish, jealous man desiring to control other people's lives.

"My Last Duchess" is probably Browning's most popular and most anthologized poem. The poem first appeared in 1842 in *Dramatic Lyrics*, which is contained in *Bells and Pomegranates* (1841-1846). Perhaps the major reason for the fame of "My Last Duchess" is that it is probably the finest example of Browning's dramatic monologue. In it, he paints a devastating self-portrait of royalty, a portrait that doubtless reveals more of the duke's personality than Ferrara intends. In fact, the irony is profound, for with each word spoken in an attempt to criticize his last duchess, the duke ironically reveals his utterly detestable nature and how far he is from seeing it himself.

Before the subtleties of "My Last Duchess" can be grasped, the basic elements of this dramatic monologue must be understood. The only speaker is the Duke of Ferrara. The listener, who, offstage, asks about the smile of the last duchess in the portrait, is silent during the entire poem. The listener is the emissary of a count and is helping to negotiate a marriage between the count's daughter and the duke. The time is probably the Italian Renaissance, though Browning does not so specify. The location is the duke's palace, probably upstairs in some art gallery, since the duke points to two nearby art objects. The two men are about to join the "company below" (line 47), so the fifty-six lines of the poem represent the end of the duke's negotiating, his final terms.

Since the thrust of a Browning dramatic monologue is psychological self-characterization, what kind of man does the duke reveal himself to be? Surely, he is a very jealous man. He brags that he has had the duchess's portrait made by Fra Pandolf. Why would he hire a monk, obviously noted for his sacred art, to paint a secular portrait? The duke admits, "'twas not/ Her husband's presence only, called that spot/ Of joy into the Duchess' cheek" (lines 13-15). Then he notes that "perhaps/ Fra Pandolf chanced to say" (lines 15-16) and provides two exact quotations. The suggestion is strong that he observed the whole enterprise. He gave Fra Pandolf only a day to finish the expensive commissioned art. Pandolf is a painter so notable that the duke drops the artist's name. Probably, he chose Pandolf because, as a man of the cloth, the good brother would have taken a vow of chastity. Yet the duke's jealousy was so powerful that he observed this chaste painter with his wife in order to be sure. Later, the duke implies that the duchess was the kind of woman who had to be watched, for she had a heart "too easily impressed" (line 23), and "her looks went everywhere" (line 24). Yet the evidence that he uses to corroborate this charge— her love of sunsets, the cherry bough with which she was presented, her pet white mule—suggests only that she was a natural woman who preferred the simple pleasures.

The duke's pride and selfishness are also revealed. He is very proud of his family name, for, as he describes his marriage to his last duchess, he states that he gave her "My gift of a nine-hundred-years-old name" (line 33). Yet he never once mentions love or his willingness to emerge from his own ego. Instead, he emphasizes that it is his curtain, his portrait, his name, his "commands" (line 45), and his sculpture. Tellingly, within fifty-six lines he uses seventeen first-person pronouns.

Undoubtedly, though, the most dominant feature of the duke's personality is a godlike desire for total control of his environment: "I said/ 'Fra Pandolf' by design" (lines 5-6). Browning reveals this trait by bracketing the poem with artistic images of control. As noted above, the painting of Fra Pandolf portrait reveals how the duke orchestrates the situation. Moreover, even now the duke controls the emissary's perception of the last duchess. Everything that the listener hears about her is filtered through the mind and voice of the duke. The emissary cannot even look at her portrait without the duke opening a curtain that he has had placed in front of the painting.

The final artistic image is most revealing. The last word in the duke's negotiations is further evidence of his desire for control. He compels the emissary to focus attention on another commissioned objet d'art: "Notice Neptune, though,/ Taming a sea-horse, thought a rarity/ Which Claus of Innsbruck cast in bronze for me!" (lines 54-56). Once again, the commissioned art is a sort of Rorschach test—it reveals a great deal about the personality of the commissioner. The thrust of the art object is dominance—the duke desires to be Neptune, god of the sea, taming a small, beautiful sea creature in what would obviously be no contest. In other words, the duke sees himself as a god who has tamed/will tame his duchess.

As earlier indicated, the duke has always associated his last duchess with beautiful things of nature. Like Neptune, the duke rules his kingdom, Ferrara, with an iron fist. When he grew tired of his last duchess, he says, "I gave commands" (line 45), and her smiles "stopped together" (line 46). Since the duke says that in her portrait the last duchess is "looking as if she were alive" (line 2), the suggestion is strong that, like the god that he would be, the duke has exercised the power over life and death.

The key critical question in "My Last Duchess" focuses on the duke's motivation. Why would a man so obviously desiring marriage to the count's daughter reveal himself in such negative terms? Critics take opposing views: Some characterize him

as "shrewd"; others, as "witless." A related critical question considers the duke's impending marriage: Why would a man who has had so much trouble with his first duchess want a second wife?

The answers to both questions seem to lie in the duke's godlike self-image. Interestingly, for a man preoccupied with his nine-hundred-year-old name, nowhere does he mention progeny, and without children there will be no one to carry on the family name. Importantly, he uses a series of terminative images, all emphasizing the end of the cycle of life, to describe his last duchess—the sunset ends the day, the breaking of the bough ends the life of the cherry (also a sexual reference), the white mule is the end of its line (mules then could not reproduce within the breed), and whiteness as a color associated with sterility. Could it be that the duke, since he uses these images, employs his last duchess as a scapegoat and that he is the one who is sterile? Thus, his object in procuring the "fair daughter's self" (line 52) is children. No doubt, for a man who likes commissioned artwork, the "dowry" (line 51) will help defray his expenses. Perhaps the duke, like another Renaissance figure, Henry VIII, will run through a series of brides because he is unable to see the flaws in his own personality.

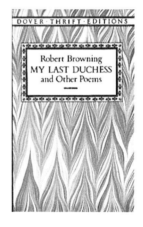

Stylistically, Browning has written a tour de force. The fifty-six lines are all in iambic pentameter couplets. The couplet form is quite formal in English poetry, and this pattern suggests the formal nature of the duke and control. Interestingly, unlike the traditional neoclassic heroic couplet, where lines are end-stopped, Browning favors enjambment, and the run-on line suggests the duke's inability to control everything—his inability to be a god.

Historically, readers have wondered about two things. Is the duke based on a real person? Some have suggested Vespasiano Gonzaga, duke of Sabbioneta, while others favor Alfonso II, fifth and last duke of Ferrara. Second, in his lifetime Browning was often asked what really happened to the duke's last duchess. Finally, Browning was forced to say, "the commands were that she should be put to death . . . or he might have had her shut up in a convent."

"THE BISHOP ORDERS HIS TOMB AT SAINT PRAXED'S CHURCH"

First published: 1845 (collected in *Dramatic Romances and Lyrics*, 1845)
Type of work: Poem

The dying bishop reveals himself to be more concerned with maintaining his materialism than admitting his many sins.

"The Bishop Orders His Tomb at Saint Praxed's Church" was printed in 1845 in *Hood's Magazine* and later that same year in *Dramatic Romances and Lyrics*, which is contained in *Bells and Pomegranates* (1841-1846). It was probably suggested by Browning's visit to Italy the previous year. Although an actual Saint Praxed's church exists in Rome, no bishop from "15—," the poem's dateline, is buried there, but the bishop in the poem typifies the bishops of the era.

The poem is another fine example of Browning's mastery of the dramatic monologue form. The speaker is the church's bishop, who is "dying by degrees" (line 11). His silent audience is his "Nephews—sons mine" (line 3). Actually, "nephews" is a historic euphemism for illegitimate sons, and only on his death is the bishop finally willing to acknowledge his paternity. The setting is Saint Praxed's church: More specifically, the bishop seems to be lying up front, to the right of the pulpit, and near the choir loft. The situation is simple: With not much time left, the bishop is negotiating with his "sons" to do something that he cannot—to ensure that he will be buried in a marble tomb as befits his position in the church hierarchy.

As with "My Last Duchess," the speaker ironically creates a self-portrait very different from what he intends. Because the bishop nears death, he can no longer control his words and thus reveals a man somewhat less than a paragon of virtue, a very flawed human who has hypocritically violated his clerical vows. As a representative of the Roman Catholic church, he suggests that the institution has failed, having been corrupted by materialistic, secular concerns.

One measure of a cleric's righteousness has always been how he avoids the seven deadly sins. Browning provides an ironic "confession" in which the bishop admits to them all. Wrath is one of the deadly sins. Dying, the bishop is still angry at Gandolf, his predecessor, who has claimed a better burial site in the church. As his negotiations with his sons prove unsuccessful, the dying bishop becomes increasingly angry at them. He also asks God to curse Gandolf.

Another sin is pride. Though the bishop begins his 122 lines with a warning about vanity, he is proud of many things, especially his possessions, and the fact that he won his boys' mother away from Gandolf. Yet he still envies (the third sin) his predecessor for that burial site.

Gluttony is manifest in a general sense by the sheer number of his possessions and in a gustatory sense by the way that he depicts the sacrament of communion; once dead, he will feast his eyes on a perpetual banquet, "God made and eaten all day long" (line 82). Greed is revealed with his last wish and his possessions. He desires his tomb to be made of basalt (a hard, dark-colored rock), as compared to his predecessor's cheap and "paltry onion-stone" (line 31). The bishop's legacy is mostly materialistic. Seeing that his sons are not acceding to his dying wishes, he offers his possessions as a bribe. He has accumulated a vineyard, a huge lapis lazuli stone, villas, horses, Greek manuscripts, and mistresses. Of course, as a priest he at one time took a vow of poverty.

Perhaps his greatest sin, however, is lechery. Having also taken a vow of chastity, he has also taken several mistresses and has fathered children by at least one of them. Quite often he commingles the sacred and the sexual. The lapis lazuli is described as "Blue as a vein o'er the Madonna's breast" (line 44). On the horizontal surface of his tomb, he wants etched in bronze a bas-relief of pans and nymphs, Christ delivering the Sermon on the Mount, Moses with the Ten Commandments, and "one Pan/ Ready to twitch the Nymph's last garment off" (lines 60-61). Furthermore, Browning emphasizes the ironic distance between the bishop's sexual activity and what the cleric should be by the name of the very church that the bishop serves and represents. St. Praxed was a second century virgin martyr who converted to Christianity and gave her worldly possessions to the poor. The bishop is a sixteenth century nonvirgin who has never practiced self-sacrifice and has unofficially converted from Christianity to mammonism. He now obviously worships all the worldly goods that he can accumulate.

One helpful way of reading this poem is as an ironic sermon. After all, the bishop typically begins his address with a biblical quotation, the words from the book of Ecclesiastes 1:2, and the rest of the poem is an ironic portrayal of his own vain self-estimation, complete with moral illustrations. As a religious person, the bishop should doubtless consider this moment as an occasion for confession—to explain what he did, to acknowledge its sinfulness, and to ask for forgiveness. Instead, he dies as vain and as self-deluded as he has lived. His final thoughts dwell upon the carnal beauty of his mistress and the envy that evoked in his archrival. Browning's final irony, then, is overwhelming. The bishop is not a servant of God but of Dionysus, the pagan god of fertility and sexuality.

"MEETING AT NIGHT" AND "PARTING AT MORNING"

First published: 1845 (collected in *Dramatic Romances and Lyrics,* 1845)
Type of work: Poems

Romantic passion is brief, and lovers must return to the real world.

"Meeting at Night" and "Parting at Morning" are companion poems that are best read as one poem. They were first published in *Dramatic Romances and Lyrics* under the general title "Night and Morning," which suggests that Browning saw them as part of a natural, inevitable cycle.

When the poems first appeared, they were criticized as being immoral because they describe lovers rendezvousing for a night of passion, then going their separate ways. Early critics worried that the man and woman, because of the clandestine nature of the tryst, are not married. In any event,

there is much of Browning in this poem, for, like its lovers, Elizabeth Barrett and he had to meet secretly.

Although early critics debated the poems' use of pronouns, Browning said that in both poems the man—the "me" of "Parting at Morning," line 4—is speaking, detailing his night with his lover. The real strength of the poems is Browning's mastery of imagery. Every line in both poems employs some specific image in an attempt to stimulate a particular sense. Browning's subject is a favorite, love between men and women, but only a close examination of the imagery reveals the exact nature of that love.

What Browning meticulously communicates in these poems is the physical nature of love. The images constantly refer to the senses of smell, taste, touch, and hearing, as well as sensations of heat, light, and kinesthesia. Browning's artistry lies in his indirection. Never does the speaker say that their relationship is deeply sexual; he implies it. The description of the journey becomes a sort of emotional topography. Life apart for the lovers is like the land, black and gray with only a little light. They are each halves of the moon. Yet as he gets closer to the woman, his senses come alive, even commingle: the "warm sea-scented beach" (line 7) appeals to three senses simultaneously. When they join, like the boat's prow in the "slushy sand" (line 6), there is a sudden spurt of love.

While he communicates the emotions of the ecstatic moment, Browning also suggests that they are fleeting, like the night, and inevitably the male must return to the "world of men" ("Parting at Morning," line 4). Browning said that the first poem argues that "raptures are self-sufficient and enduring," while the second contends "how fleeting" is that belief.

SUMMARY

Robert Browning stands as the transitional English poet between the supreme subjectivity of the Romantics and the subtleties of modern poetry. He masterfully showed the dramatic and psychological possibilities of verse. In the Victorian era of sexual reticence and profound doubt, he demonstrated the power of human passion and the prevalence of the human spirit.

Hal Charles

BIBLIOGRAPHY

By the Author

POETRY:

Pauline, 1833

Paracelsus, 1835

Sordello, 1840

Bells and Pomegranates, 1841-1846 (published in eight parts and contains *Dramatic Lyrics,* 1842; and *Dramatic Romances and Lyrics,* 1845)

Christmas Eve and Easter Day, 1850

Men and Women, 1855 (2 volumes)

Dramatis Personae, 1864

The Ring and the Book, 1868-1869 (4 volumes)

Prince Hohenstiel-Schwangau: Saviour of Society, 1871

Balaustion's Adventure, 1871

Fifine at the Fair, 1872

Red Cotton Nightcap Country: Or, Turf and Towers, 1873

The Inn Album, 1875

Aristophanes' Apology, 1875

Pacchiarotto and How He Worked in Distemper, 1876

The Agamemnon of Aeschylus, 1877 (drama translation in verse)

La Saisiaz, and The Two Poets of Croisac, 1878

Dramatic Idyls, 1879-1880 (in two parts)

Jocoseria, 1883

Ferishtah's Fancies, 1884

Parleyings with Certain People of Importance in Their Day, 1887

The Poetical Works of Robert Browning, 1888-1894 (17 volumes)

Asolando, 1889

Robert Browning: The Poems, 1981 (2 volumes)

DRAMA:

Strafford, pr., pb. 1837

Pippa Passes, pb. 1841

King Victor and King Charles, pb. 1842

A Blot in the 'Scutcheon, pr., pb. 1843

The Return of the Druses, pb. 1843

Colombe's Birthday, pb. 1844, pr. 1853

Luria, pb. 1846

A Soul's Tragedy, pb. 1846

NONFICTION:

The Letters of Robert Browning and Elizabeth Barrett Barrett, 1845-1846, 1926 (Robert B. Browning, editor)

Intimate Glimpses from Browning's Letter File: Selected from Letters in the Baylor University Browning Collection, 1934.

Browning's Essay on Chatterton, 1948 (Donald A. Smalley, editor)

DISCUSSION TOPICS

- What did Robert Browning learn from his study of Percy Bysshe Shelley's poetry?

- In regard to Browning, what do you understand the phrase "indulgent Romantic angst" to mean?

- How does the monologue form of Browning's dramatic poems differentiate them from plays?

- To what extent might the tones and emphases used in reading of "My Last Justice" aloud affect its interpretation?

- Should we understand the duke in "My Last Duchess" as "shrewd" or "witless" in his obvious revelation of himself to his visitor?

- How does one explain Browning's fondness for rhymed couplets when he so often seems to be undermining their effect with enjambments and rhythmical variations?

- What seems to be the best way of understanding the motivation of the bishop in "The Bishop Orders His Tomb at Saint Praxed's Church"?

New Letters of Robert Browning, 1950 (W. C. DeVane and Kenneth L. Knickerbocker, editors)
The Letters of Robert Browning and Elizabeth Barrett Barrett, 1845-1846, 1969 (Elvan Kintner, editor)

MISCELLANEOUS:
The Works of Robert Browning, 1912 (10 volumes; F. C. Kenyon, editor)
The Complete Works of Robert Browning, 1969-1999 (16 volumes)

About the Author

Browning, Robert. *Robert Browning's Poetry: Authoritative Texts, Criticism*. Selected and edited by James F. Loucks and Andrew M. Stauffer. 2d ed. New York: W. W. Norton, 2007.

Drew, Philip. *The Poetry of Browning: A Critical Introduction*. London: Methuen, 1970.

Garrett, Martin, ed. *Elizabeth Barrett Browning and Robert Browning: Interviews and Recollections*. New York: St. Martin's Press, 2000.

Hawlin, Stefan. *The Complete Critical Guide to Robert Browning*. New York: Routledge, 2002.

Irvine, William, and Park Honan. *The Book, the Ring, and the Poet: A Biography of Robert Browning*. New York: McGraw-Hill, 1974.

Kennedy, Richard S., and Donald S. Hair. *The Dramatic Imagination of Robert Browning: A Literary Life*. Columbia: University of Missouri Press, 2007.

King, Roma, Jr. *The Focusing Artifice: The Poetry of Robert Browning*. Athens: Ohio University Press, 1968.

Pollock, Mary Sanders. *Elizabeth Barrett and Robert Browning: A Creative Partnership*. Burlington, Vt.: Ashgate, 2003.

MIKHAIL BULGAKOV

Born: Kiev, Ukraine, Russian Empire (now in Ukraine)
  May 15, 1891
Died: Moscow, Soviet Union (now in Russia)
  March 10, 1940

Bulgakov's plays and novels draw on both fantasy and realism to portray life in the early Soviet Union and to comment on the human condition. While regarded primarily as a playwright in his own lifetime, Bulgakov became best known in succeeding years as the author of the grim comic masterpiece, his novel The Master and Margarita.

BIOGRAPHY

Mikhail Afanasyevich Bulgakov (bewl-GAH-kuhf) was born in the Ukrainian city of Kiev, then part of the Russian empire, in 1891. Although Kiev was an ancient seat of Russian civilization, Ukraine was a distinct province of the Russian empire with its own sense of identity. Bulgakov's family was of Russian ethnicity, however, and solidly situated in Kiev's middle-class intelligentsia. His father, A. I. Bulgakov, came from a line of theologians and was himself a professor at the Kiev Theological Academy. His mother was both religious and intellectual and played a large part in the education of Mikhail and his six brothers and sisters. At home, Bulgakov developed an interest in religion that lasted into the officially atheistic Communist years of his country, influencing his writings.

A. I. Bulgakov died in 1907, when Mikhail was only sixteen. His widowed mother supported the family, becoming a teacher and secretary at a society for the advancement of learning. At an early age, then, the future writer experienced the life of the struggling middle class.

Bulgakov's literary tastes and understanding were formed in school, as well as at home. His teachers at the First Kiev Gymnasium, which he attended from 1901 to 1904, encouraged him to read the great writers of Russian literature, including Alexander Pushkin, Nikolai Gogol, and Fyodor Dostoevski. After graduating from the gymnasium, he went on to study medicine at St. Vladimir University, completing his degree in 1916. While a student, he married his first wife, Tatiana Lappa, in 1913.

The young doctor finished his education to begin a professional life in the midst of war and revolution; Russia had been embroiled in World War I since 1914. Bulgakov practiced medicine for a time at the Kiev Military Hospital and then was transferred to be the only doctor in a small village in Smolensk province. His observations of peasant life became the basis for a short-story collection that he wrote in the 1920's, *Zapiski iunogo vracha* (1963; *A Country Doctor's Notebook*, 1975).

The Bolsheviks, led by Vladimir Ilich Lenin, took power in Petrograd (later Leningrad) in late 1917. They pulled the Russian empire, soon renamed the Union of Soviet Socialist Republics, out of World War I but waged a bloody civil war to unite the country under their government. Bulgakov returned to Kiev in 1918 to start a medical practice there, in time to see Ukraine torn by fighting among German occupation forces, Bolshevik Red Army soldiers, anti-Bolshevik White Army fighters, and Ukrainian separatists, among others. His first novel, *Belaya gvardiya* (1927, 1929; *The White Guard*, 1971), was a fictional treatment of the civil war in Kiev.

The White Army, needing physicians, drafted Bulgakov in 1919. He became seriously ill after the Whites sent him to the North Caucasus. It was apparently during his illness that he decided to leave medicine and take up writing as his career. His first plays appeared during his time in the Caucasus.

In 1921, as the civil war drew to an end with the Red Army victorious, Bulgakov moved to Moscow and attempted to earn a living by writing plays and short pieces for newspapers. His wife, Tatiana, moved with him, but the couple divorced in 1924 and he later married Lyubov Belozerskaya. It was in his early years in Moscow that he began work on *The White Guard*, part of which he published in the journal *Rossiia* in 1925. The Moscow Art Theater asked him to create a dramatic version of the story, so he rewrote his tale of civil war in Kiev as the play *Dni Turbinykh* (pb. 1955; *Days of the Turbins*, 1934), which was performed in 1926. Although many Bolsheviks disliked Bulgakov's sympathetic portrayal of White Army officers, the country's emerging dictator, Joseph Stalin, enjoyed it and approved it as politically acceptable. Although Bulgakov achieved recognition as a playwright, during these same years in Moscow he wrote other important works of fiction, including the acclaimed short novel *Sobache serdtse* (wr. 1925, pb. 1968, reliable text, 1969; *The Heart of a Dog*, 1968).

Bulgakov's plays became popular, but their often satirical character aroused the suspicions of the Bolsheviks, who became known in the years after the civil war as the Communist Party. He wrote more than thirty plays, but only ten have survived. *Days of the Turbins* was followed by *Zoykina kvartira* (pr. 1926, pb. 1971; *Zoya's Apartment*, 1970), which was popular but is not regarded as one of Bulgakov's better works. His play *Bagrovy ostrov* (pr. 1928, pb. 1968; *The Crimson Island*, 1972), an adaptation of one of his short stories, was also well received by the Moscow public. However, *Beg* (wr. 1928, pr. 1957, pb. 1962; *Flight*, 1969) was not produced until 1957 because Soviet officials decided it praised emigrating White Army generals. The satirical character of his work repeatedly got him into trouble, and in 1929 all of his plays were banned.

After the ban, Bulgakov decided he could not stay in Russia if he could not work, and he wrote to the Soviet government requesting permission to leave the country. Stalin replied with a personal telephone call and permitted Bulgakov to obtain work as an assistant producer at the Moscow Arts Theater. The Soviet dictator, who frequently gave more favorable treatment to writers than to other citizens, kept Bulgakov from being executed or sent to a prison camp but did not allow the author to resume publishing his work.

From 1928 until the end of his life, Bulgakov worked on his masterpiece, the novel *Master i Margarita* (wr. 1928-1940; pb. 1966-1967, censored version; 1973, uncensored version; *The Master and Margarita*, 1967). His third wife, Elena Shilovskaya, whom he married in 1932 after divorcing Lyubov Belozerskaya, encouraged him as he worked on this novel while his physical and mental health worsened. The novel was finished, but it was not published during Bulgakov's lifetime. He was completing a satirical novel on his experiences in the theater, *Teatralny roman* (1965; *Black Snow: A Theatrical Novel*, 1967), when he died of a kidney disease in Moscow in 1940.

ANALYSIS

Mikhail Bulgakov lived and worked in a world in rapid transformation, with the traditional and the revolutionary, the tragic and the comic, the mundane and the fantastic, and the secular and the religious continually colliding. His writing reflects these juxtaposed opposites, and this makes it difficult to place him in a literary category. Many of Bulgakov's works are marked by complex plot structures and narrative techniques that weave together different levels of storytelling. The plays, stories, and novels he produced also show the variety of his literary influences. They combine, in different degrees, the grim satire of early nineteenth century Russian author Nikolai Gogol and the moral realism of the late nineteenth century master Fyodor Dostoevski. Bulgakov was an admirer of science fiction, and his imaginative flights were inspired by the English author H. G. Wells. His early theological background led him to bring biblical themes and concepts into his work.

All of Bulgakov's work, even the most fantastic, contains a large element of autobiography, but it is always autobiography that mixes episodes in the external world, perceptions, and thoughts. *A Country Doctor's Notebook*, for example, is a series of fictionalized vignettes of his own experiences as a medical man in the countryside. It consists of tragicomic stories told by a first-person narrator. This narrator is an introspective individual, much given to spending time in his own thoughts, which superimposes an individual psychology on a world of events. Realistic enough to document early nineteenth century medical practices, the observations occur in the mind of a narrator readily stimulated to fantasy.

The White Guard similarly grew out of Bulgakov's own life. The Turbin family, around whom he structured the tale of the coming of war to Kiev, was based on Bulgakov's own family. Aleksei Turbin is clearly based on Bulgakov himself. In the novel's alternation between scenes of home life and battle scenes, the writer offered his own experience of the impact of history on the life of a single family and the life of a city. Again, however, the autobiography goes beyond historical realism and enters into a psychological level. The novel shuttles rapidly across scenes and episodes, at times possessing a cinematic quality. Bits of disconnected dialogue and sound effects accompany this scene-shifting. The overall effect is one of a world that is shattering around the lives at the center of the story; it is an autobiography that tries to recount how it felt to be in a city at war.

Satire was another characteristic of Bulgakov's work, one that coexisted with his autobiographical inclination. It was through satire that another trait was expressed most forcefully—the use of imaginative fantasy. Some of the satire can be seen in his humorous approaches to country life in *A Country Doctor's Notebook*. However, the contradictions and bureaucratic character of Moscow life in the 1920's after the civil war moved him more toward writing in the satirical vein. The short stories he published in the mid-1920's, such as "Diavoliada" ("Diaboliad") and "Rokovye iaitsa" ("The Fatal Eggs"), brought together the sharp satire of Gogol with twentieth century science fiction. Influenced by the fiction of Wells, the latter story tells of a Russian zoologist who invents a ray that enables creatures born of eggs to increase their size and reproductive rate. Russia is affected by a disease that wipes out its chicken population, and eggs are imported from other countries to replace them. The ray is applied to the eggs to increase productivity, but by mistake the eggs treated are those of reptiles rather than chickens and the country is attacked by an army of giant snakes and crocodiles. The Soviet worship of ever-increasing productivity and efficiency and the problem of unforeseen consequences are here mocked in the guise of science fiction. The satire was also pronounced in many of Bulgakov's plays; *The Crimson Island*, for example, satirized Soviet censorship.

THE HEART OF A DOG

First published: *Sobache serdtse*, wr. 1925; pb. 1968; reliable text, 1969 (English translation, 1968)
Type of work: Novella

After transplanting human organs into a stray dog, a scientist is troubled as the dog takes on human characteristics

The Heart of a Dog is often regarded as science fiction or satirical fantasy. The novella tells the tale of Sharik, a stray dog who has been brought in for experimentation by the scientist Philip Philipovich Preobrazhensky. The experimenter specializes in transplanting the organs of animals into humans and vice versa.

The work moves with a constantly shifting perspective, jumping from the dog's point of view to Preobrazhensky's to that of an unseen narrator. It opens with the howling of the dog, who complains that he was scalded when a cook at the National Economic Council's canteen spilled boiling water on him. Sharik recounts his misfortune to himself. He had been foraging in the garbage outside the council building when the cook threw the water out. The style shows some of what has been called "stream of consciousness," as the dog thinks about the good life he could have enjoyed, rolling in the park, and about his present misfortune.

A girl finds the injured dog, and, without a break, the narrative slips from the dog's thoughts to a narrator outside the story. Then it returns to the dog, who sees Preobrazhensky in the street and imagines what the man is thinking. Preobrazhensky puts a leash on the dog and leads him away. Thus, the opening of the story introduces readers to the main characters and the technique of juxtaposing internal monologues and physical descriptions.

The tale continues with Sharik watching the professor, who is seeing patients at his apartment. Sharik bites a man whom Preobrazhensky has been rejuvenating with transplants, and the dog sees a woman in whom the doctor promises to transplant monkey ovaries. The dog also watches as Preobrazhensky is visited by a house management committee threatening to install more residents in the doctor's home. Preobrazhensky overcomes this problem by calling a powerful patient waiting for an operation and threatening to end his practice. The scientist dismisses the committee with sneering comments about the proletariat. In this way, the science-fiction elements of the story are placed alongside elements of Socialist Realism, sardonically portraying the redistribution of homes and rooms in newly socialist Russia, along with the corruption that accompanied these types of social experiments. Bulgakov is calling attention to the clumsy nature of economic and social experimentation in the same scenes in which he presents imaginary scientific experimentation.

Preobrazhensky eats well, and while sharing a meal with a fellow doctor he makes more derisive remarks about the proletariat and socialist ideals. The reader is never entirely sure whether Bulgakov might be agreeing, at least in part, with Preobrazhensky's sentiments toward the new Russia. When the fellow doctor accuses Preobrazhensky of sounding like a counterrevolutionary, Preobrazhensky shrugs off the accusation and pays his friend for the bite that Sharik has inflicted. Sharik, however, is in for his own surprise. Doctor Bormenthal, Preobrazhensky's associate, puts a cloth with a strange smell over the dog's nose, and then the two men lift the animal onto an operating table. In an eerie operation, they replace the dog's testicles and pituitary gland with those of a deceased man.

After the operation the narrative shifts again, starting as Preobrazhensky's notes on the operation and then becoming a journal of changes in Sharik, who becomes gradually more human. The former dog begins to speak and then to wear clothes; eventually, his outward appearance is completely human.

As Sharik moves closer toward humanity, he becomes more of a bother to Preobrazhensky. Eventually, the dog becomes not simply human but a human along the lines of Soviet slogans, albeit with some canine traits, such as scratching for fleas. He renames himself Polygraph Polygraphovich Sharikov and styles himself as an agent of the Moscow Cleansing Department, which has the job of eliminating cats and other small animals. Eventually, Preobrazhensky has to turn his creature back into a dog in order to have any peace.

THE MASTER AND MARGARITA

First published: *Master i Margarita*, wr. 1928-1940; pb. 1966-1967, censored version; 1973, uncensored version (English translation, 1967)

Type of work: Novel

Satan comes to Earth in Moscow during the Stalinist period and turns a novelist's mistress into a witch, thereby unintentionally saving the novelist from oppression

The Master and Margarita is generally regarded as Bulgakov's best work and as one of the masterpieces of world literature. It incorporates the satirical fantasy of *The Heart of a Dog* but carries this to a higher level of sophistication and artistry. Bulgakov began writing the book in 1928 but reported burning the first version of the manuscript in 1930, after one of his plays was banned. He later wrote a second version and finally finished a draft of a third version in 1937, but he continued working on this last draft until his death.

In the first scene of the book, two Soviet atheist literary men, Berlioz and the poet Ivan Nikolayevich Ponyryov, who has the pen name Bezdomny, meet a mysterious magician named Woland on a park bench in Moscow. Woland, who is Satan in disguise, interrupts a discussion of theology, prefiguring the eruption of the religious and magical into materialist Soviet official reality that will run throughout the book. Woland predicts that Berlioz's head will be cut off at a precise time later that morning. Numerous satirical references to Soviet life appear in the first chapter. For example, Berlioz is is the head of the MASSOLIT, a Soviet-style acronym for a writers' organization that could be rendered in English as "Lottalit." The initial chapter is entitled "Never Talk to Strangers," which would not only be good advice for the two men meeting Satan but also reflects Soviet paranoid propaganda about public enemies.

Following Bulgakov's technique of rapidly shifting setting, Woland begins talking about the meeting of Pontius Pilate and Yeshua Ha-Nozri (Jesus the Nazarene), and the story jumps back centuries to this meeting. This same story will also be found in the rejected manuscript of the Master's novel, and it will recur as a second level of narrative, or a story within a story, throughout the book. Drawing on his theological background, Bulgakov works apocryphal material about the life of Jesus into the narrative. The scene moves back to the three men in the park, where the two atheists are skeptical of Woland's account of the Gospel. However, Woland's authority seems to be verified when Berlioz is hit by a streetcar and beheaded, according to prediction.

Much of the rest of part 1 of the novel concerns the descent of Ivan Nikolayevich into madness, or confrontation with reality, until he is locked up in a hospital. There, in chapter 13, entitled "Enter the Hero," Ivan Nikolayevich meets the mysterious Master. In delaying the introduction of the hero for so long and then announcing that he is bringing in the protagonist, Bulgakov is making a point of playing with novelistic conventions. Stories of Woland as a magician and his Satanic familiars are interspersed with the movement toward the entrance of the Master, as are episodes from the strange gospel of Pilate.

If Bulgakov delays in presenting the Master, he waits even longer to introduce Margarita, who enters only in the second half of the book. Margarita, who may have been based on Bulgakov's third wife, Elena Shilovskaya, continues to support the Master and his novel, even in the face of his despair. She reaches a deal with Woland, or Satan, and becomes a witch, flying naked through the air. The climax of the novel occurs when Margarita attends Satan's grand ball at midnight on Good Friday, a reminder of the Master's novel about Yeshua and Pilate. At the ball she meets the great figures from history released from the ball. Offered one wish, she chooses to free the Master. Together, the Master and Margarita leave Moscow, its hypocrisy and corruption, with Satan.

BLACK SNOW: A THEATRICAL NOVEL

First published: *Teatralny roman*, 1965 (English translation, 1967)
Type of work: Novel

A writer experiences hypocrisy and difficulty while attempting to stage a dramatic adaptation of his novel

Black Snow displays both the autobiographical and the satirical components in Bulgakov's work. Written in the first person, it tells the story of Maxudov, the author of a novel who has been invited to write a play based on his novel, much as Bulgakov was asked to turn *The White Guard* into *Days of the Turbins*. The theater is clearly the Moscow Arts Theater of the 1930's, guided by Konstantin Stanislavsky, the originator of method acting. Bulgakov skewers the character representing Stanislavsky, whom he clearly found difficult during his own days at the Moscow Arts Theater.

The novel opens with the chapter "How It All Began," with Maxudov receiving a request for an interview from Xavier Borisovich Ilchin, the director of the Academy of Drama at the Independent Theater. With Bulgakov's typical fondness for playing with plot structures, however, this turns out not to be the beginning, since the story then shifts back to a previous time, when Maxudov was the proofreader for *The Shipping Gazette* and had written an unpublished novel in his spare time. He was about to commit suicide when he heard a performance of the opera *Faust* in a nearby room and was interrupted by a magazine editor, who wanted to publish his novel. For several chapters, Maxudov tells the story of his novel's publication and then suddenly returns to his meeting with Ilchin.

Instead of bringing success, the dramatization of Maxudov's novel is an endless series of farcical frustrations. Ultimately, Maxudov does commit suicide by throwing himself off a bridge. The narrative ends in an uncompleted sentence. However, Bulgakov includes an afterword explaining that Maxudov did not finish his novel because of his suicide. Was the novel really unfinished, or was Maxudov's failure to end the tale the real and intended ending of Bulgakov's novel about a story about a play based on a novel?

SUMMARY

Mikhail Bulgakov blended social and spiritual concerns in his work, satirizing the absurdities and injustices of Stalinist Russia while raising questions about the deeper meaning of life. In a society ruled by rigid bureaucracy and collectivism, Bulgakov affirmed the transcendent value of individuals and the lasting worth of art. He drew on many of the traditions of Russian literature and religion, but his fictions are modern and experimental in their structures and styles.

Carl L. Bankston III

DISCUSSION TOPICS

- What were some of the ways in which Mikhail Bulgakov's own life served as a basis for fiction in his novels and plays?

- Name some of the ways in which Bulgakov defied the conventions of fiction and discuss why he chose to do so.

- Religion occupies an important place in Bulgakov's writing, but he does not express conventional Christian views. How does Bulgakov offer an unorthodox approach to religion?

- How did Soviet communism affect Bulgakov's life and writings?

- What characteristics of Bulgakov's writings led the Soviet authorities to ban them?

- In works such as *The Heart of a Dog* and *The Master and Margarita*, Bulgakov made use of many of the themes found in works of fantasy and science fiction. What are some of these themes, and in what books and stories can they be found?

BIBLIOGRAPHY

By the Author

LONG FICTION:
Sobache serdtse, wr. 1925, pb. 1968, reliable text 1969 (novella; *The Heart of a Dog*, 1968)
Belaya gvardiya, 1927, 1929 (2 volumes; *The White Guard*, 1971)
Master i Margarita, wr. 1928-1940, censored version pb. 1966-1967, uncensored version 1973 (*The Master and Margarita*, 1967)
Teatralny roman, 1965 (*Black Snow: A Theatrical Novel*, 1967)

SHORT FICTION:
Diavoliada, 1925 (*Diaboliad, and Other Stories*, 1972)
Traktat o zhilishche, 1926 (*A Treatise on Housing*, 1972)
Zapiski iunogo vracha, 1963 (*A Country Doctor's Notebook*, 1975)
Notes on the Cuff, and Other Stories, 1991

DRAMA:
Dni Turbinykh, pr. 1926, pb. 1955 (adaptation of his novel *Belaya gvardiya*; *Days of the Turbins*, 1934)
Zoykina kvartira, pr. 1926, pb. 1971 (*Zoya's Apartment*, 1970)
Bagrovy ostrov, pr. 1928, pb. 1968 (adaptation of his short story; *The Crimson Island*, 1972)
Beg, wr. 1928, pr. 1957, pb. 1962 (*Flight*, 1969)
Kabala svyatosh, wr. 1929, pr. 1936, pb. 1962 (*A Cabal of Hypocrites*, 1972; also known as *Molière*)
Adam i Eva, wr. 1930-1931, pb. 1971 (*Adam and Eve*, 1971)
Blazhenstvo, wr. 1934, pb. 1966 (*Bliss*, 1976)

Posledniye dni (Pushkin), wr. 1934-1935, pr. 1943, pb. 1955 (*The Last Days*, 1976)
Ivan Vasilievich, wr. 1935, pb. 1965, pr. 1966 (English translation, 1974)
Rashel, wr. c. 1936, pb. 1972 (libretto; adaptation of Guy de Maupassant's short story "Mademoiselle Fifi")
Minin i Pozharskii, wr. 1936, pb. 1976 (libretto)
Batum, wr. 1938, pb. 1977
Don Kikhot, pr. 1941, pb. 1962
The Early Plays of Mikhail Bulgakov, pb. 1972
Six Plays, pb. 1991

NONFICTION:
Zhizn gospodina de Molyera, 1962 (*The Life of Monsieur de Molière*, 1970)

TRANSLATION:
L'Avare, 1936 (of Molière's play)

About the Author

Belozerskaya-Bulgakova, Lyubov. *My Life with Mikhail Bulgakov.* Translated by Margareta Thompson. Ann Arbor, Mich.: Ardis, 1983.

Curtis, J. A. E. *Bulgakov's Last Decade: The Writer as Hero.* New York: Cambridge University Press, 1987.

Drawicz, Andrzej. *Master and the Devil: A Study of Mikhail Bulgakov.* Translated by Kevin Windle. Lewiston, N.Y.: Edwin Mellen Press, 2001.

Haber, Edythe C. *Mikhail Bulgakov: The Early Years.* Cambridge, Mass.: Harvard University Press, 1998.

Milne, Lesley. *Mikhail Bulgakov: A Critical Biography.* New York: Cambridge University Press, 1990.

JOHN BUNYAN

Born: Elstow, Bedfordshire, England
      November, 10, 1628 (baptized)
Died: London, England
      August 31, 1688

A master of the plain style, Bunyan enriched English literature by producing allegorical prose works on the theme of religion and a spiritual autobiography.

BIOGRAPHY

John Bunyan (BUHN-yuhn), the son of Thomas Bunyan and his second wife, Margaret Bentley, was baptized on November 10, 1628, in the village of Elstow, near Bedford, England. Although his ancestors had been English yeoman farmers and small landowners in Bedfordshire, his father was a whitesmith or metal craftsman, suggesting that the family fortunes had declined over generations. Bunyan himself was apprenticed at his father's craft, though the designation changed to tinker, or mender of metal implements, and for many years he earned his living through his skill. The Bunyans were not destitute, nor were they forced to become itinerant craftsmen, for both Bunyan and his father owned a forge and workshop in Elstow. In his confessional autobiography, Bunyan lists activities of his youth as dancing, playing tip-cat, ringing church bells, and swearing—all of which he solemnly condemned.

He attended school, either in Elstow or in nearby Bedford, but it appears that he learned little beyond the ability to read and write English. His actual lifelong education was obtained through the King James Bible (1611), which he knew well enough to recall hundreds, perhaps thousands, of verses at will. He absorbed its style, its metaphors and symbols, its cadences, and its themes. In addition, he possessed a broad knowledge of Protestant religious works, including John Foxe's *The Book of Martyrs* (1563) and Martin Luther's *In epistolam Sancti Pauli ad Galatas commentarius* (1519; *Commentary on St. Paul's Epistle to the Galatians,* 1575). Throughout Bunyan's lifetime, England was undergoing sweeping changes in its society, politics, economics, and religion. Although these changes affected Bunyan's life profoundly, he hardly noted them except for the movement toward religious freedom.

In 1644, following the death of his mother and his father's remarriage, Bunyan enlisted in the parliamentary army in a regiment garrisoned at Newport Pagnall and commanded by Sir Samuel Luke. Historians have established that parliamentary armies of the time had religion as their main interest, with units expounding the scriptures, reading, and debating points of doctrine; Bunyan probably encountered a wide range of viewpoints among the Dissenters. A plan to send his company to Ireland did not come to fruition, and he had experienced no military engagements of importance when he was demobilized in 1646.

Bunyan married soon afterward, perhaps in 1648, and his wife's small dowry included two religious handbooks, *The Plaine Man's Pathway to Heaven* (1601), by Arthur Dent, and *The Practice of Piety* (1612), by Lewis Bayley. The Dent book employed the biblical journey metaphor that became prominent in Bunyan's own prose. Following a prolonged period of religious angst, narrated in his spiritual autobiography *Grace Abounding to the Chief of Sinners* (1666), Bunyan joined the Baptist Congregation at Bedford in 1653 and began evangelical preaching and religious tract writing, the first of these being pamphlets directed against the Quakers. Following the death of his first wife, who left him with four small children, he married again in 1659 and, with his devoted second wife, had two additional children.

A successful preacher who never prepared his sermons in advance, Bunyan attracted large crowds through his obvious sincerity, plain style, and fervor. After his fame spread, he was invited to preach in towns throughout the Midland counties and even in London. Barred from preaching in the established church, he addressed congregations in fields, barns, chapels, and forests. As he was not licensed, he was arrested in 1660 and imprisoned in the Bedford county jail, where he remained until 1672, sustaining himself and his family by making laces. Imprisonment was not a stern ordeal for him, and it is plain from his own account that his jailers sought to release him, provided that he would agree not to preach. This Bunyan steadfastly refused to do. He pointed out that while none could be absolutely certain of correctness in biblical interpretation, his own views were as plausible as the official ones. During his imprisonment he was permitted visits from friends and family, wrote prolifically, and was released for brief periods to visit others. The record shows that he attended unauthorized religious meetings during some of his leaves from prison. Following his release in 1672, he became the minister of the Bedford Congregation; he was then imprisoned again for several months, probably in 1676 and 1677. It is generally accepted that during this imprisonment he wrote his masterpiece *The Pilgrim's Progress from This World to That Which Is to Come* (part 1, 1678). *The Pilgrim's Progress from This World to That Which Is to Come, the Second Part* was published in 1684.

For the remainder of his life, Bunyan continued his ministry and prolific writing. In August, 1688, while riding on horseback from Reading to London after attempting to settle a dispute between a father and son, he experienced a chill. He died in London on August 31, 1688, and was buried in Bunhill Fields, the principal cemetery for Dissenters.

ANALYSIS

Beginning with the publication of *Some Gospel Truths Opened* (1656), a tract directed against the

Quakers, Bunyan was to produce numerous published works during his lifetime. All were religious in nature, though there is considerable variety within the general subject. Some are polemical and controversial, and a few concern broad religious doctrines; some are handbooks or guides for adults, while others instruct children. Since Bunyan did not publish his sermons, little evidence remains of his preaching, though two of his published titles appear to be sermons. Literary historians agree that only four of his works are of lasting interest, and three of these—*The Pilgrim's Progress*, *The Life and Death of Mr. Badman* (1680), and *The Holy War* (1682)—are allegories of religious life that center on the plight of the individual soul.

Bunyan's first significant prose work was his spiritual autobiography, *Grace Abounding to the Chief of Sinners*, a prominent example of a genre that goes back to the fifth century *Confessiones* (397-400; *Confessions*, 1620) of Saint Augustine. In simple and muscular prose, Bunyan gives a dramatized account of his spiritual development, his conversion, and the beginning of his ministry. Details of his daily life are scant, and his autobiography serves to illustrate the workings of God on Earth. To Bunyan, salvation is essentially a gripping drama featuring God and the Devil struggling for the individual soul. In accounting for his spiritual development, Bunyan lists evidences of his wickedness, actually trivial infractions, and attempts to elucidate the stages of his conversion.

At the center of Bunyan's narrative lies a recurring cyclic pattern of psychological interest, for life's journey does not occur in a direct line. Always anxious about salvation, the narrator falls into a deep depression, convinced that he is lost or, in one memorable instance, that he has committed the unpardonable sin. These periods last for days, weeks, or months. He sometimes hears voices telling him to "sell Christ" or urging him to doubt or curse God. Occasionally he hears a stern and wrathful voice from Heaven issuing a warning. Efforts to find support and reassurance from others prove fruitless. On one occasion he confesses to a wise old Christian man that he believes he has committed the unpardonable sin, and the old man agrees. After a period of profound gloom, however, he reads or recalls a biblical verse that gives him hope or relieves his anxiety. The depression passes, and he is reassured for a time, only to experience a later recurrence of the entire cycle. Finally, sometime during his late twenties, the cycles end. Assured of salvation, he begins his ministry.

With the publication of *The Pilgrim's Progress*, a richly imaginative depiction of the quest for salvation, Bunyan achieved lasting fame. The work saw numerous editions within his lifetime and, through translations into many languages, attained the status of a world classic.

In contrast to Christian's successful journey to Heaven in *The Pilgrim's Progress*, Bunyan's next allegorical work chronicles the destruction of a sinner. *The Life and Death of Mr. Badman* is cast in the form of a dialogue between Mr. Wiseman and Mr. Attentive, who does not simply listen but injects comments of his own and asks pointed questions. A notorious sinner from childhood, Mr. Badman seeks wealth through marriage, defrauds others throughout his life, and betrays all who trust him. A clear example of Bunyan's view of a hardened sinner, Mr. Badman grows increasingly vicious in his personal life. Following the death of his first wife, he marries a woman as evil as himself, but they soon part in acrimony. As if to stress that he no longer struggles against sin, he is granted a peaceful death.

In their narration, Mr. Wiseman and Mr. Attentive enrich the plot with brief sensationalized accounts of other sinners and their fates. Drawn from actual events of the time or from current stories, they emphasize the disastrous consequences of evil, and their authenticity is never questioned. In one account, a man is borne away violently by evil spirits after publicly drinking a toast to the Devil. In other accounts, a despondent man's suicide is recounted in vivid detail, while a poor village woman, having stolen two pence, swears that she is innocent and invites the ground to swallow her, whereupon witnesses see the ground open and bury her twelve feet deep. To supplement the instructional intent of the allegorical and brief stories, Mr. Wiseman quotes biblical verses directed toward Christian behavior and ethics, reinforcing the moral message.

The Holy War features a more complex allegorical plot than Bunyan's earlier works; scholars have demonstrated that the meaning of the work operates on several levels. On one level, Bunyan alludes to contemporary events in Bedford, where Puritan officeholders were being replaced by Royalists. In its description of sieges and drills, the work also reflects the English Civil War and Bunyan's experience as a soldier. Yet fundamentally the book presents a sweeping, comprehensive depiction of God's Providence as it applies to the world at large and the individual soul. The city, Mansoul, with five gates named for each of the senses, is established by El Shaddai (God). Diabolus besieges and captures the city, endowing it with a new charter and replacing the old city recorder, Mr. Conscience, with Mr. Forget-Good. El Shaddai dispatches an army to besiege and retake the city, at length placing Emmanuel (Christ) in command. Supported by a host of important personages—such as Mr. Alderman Atheism, Mr. Lustings, and Mr. Fornication—Diabolus mounts a strong resistance, but eventually the city falls. Once the rule of El Shaddai is restored, however, the city relapses into its evil ways, and Diabolus renews the war. Although he recaptures most of the city, he fails to retake the citadel at the center, which is defended by Emmanuel and his supporters.

THE PILGRIM'S PROGRESS

First published: Part 1, 1678; part 2, 1684
Type of work: Religious allegory

Rejecting his existence in the City of Destruction, Christian makes the long and arduous journey to the Heavenly City.

The Pilgrim's Progress, Bunyan's best-known work, narrates the protagonist Christian's journey to salvation. Made aware of his own mortality, Christian abandons the City of Destruction and begins his journey to the Heavenly City. The narrative takes the form of an allegorical dream vision and develops the theme of individual salvation through a highly consistent allegorical framework.

Urged on by Evangelist, Christian abandons his wife and children, stopping his ears with his fingers to silence their pleas, an indication that the journey to salvation must be an individual experience. The two companions whom he encounters along the way, Faithful and Hopeful, are actually facets of his own character. Once he has begun the journey, he reflects the character of the wayfaring, warring

Christian disciple, often tempted and often struggling but never abandoning the path.

Christian is not tempted by the worldly pleasures of Vanity Fair or by any pomp and ceremony associated with riches, nor is he swayed by the erroneous reasoning of Obstinate, Pliable, Sloth, or Mr. Worldly Wiseman or the shallow optimism apparent in characters such as Hypocrisy, Formality, and Ignorance. His serious temptations concern fear, doubt, and despair. At the journey's beginning he is mired in the Slough of Despond, escaping only after difficult exertions. He meets frightening monsters such as Pope and Pagan and battles the demoniac warrior Apollyon. Cast into a dungeon at Doubting Castle by Giant Despair, he can free himself only with a key called Promise. He must maintain constant vigilance in order to avoid being distracted from his goal in places such as the Valley of Ease and the Valley of Deceit.

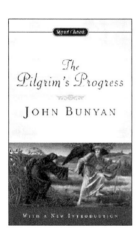

Yet the journey is not without its rewarding pauses and encouragements. At the outset his burden drops when he reaches the Cross, and at the House Beautiful he receives instruction and grace.

In the vicinity of Beulah Land, he meets the shepherds Knowledge, Watchful, Experience, and Sincere. As he approaches the River of Death near the end of the journey, he can see the Heavenly City beyond and is confident of his safe arrival.

The style of *The Pilgrim's Progress* makes the work accessible to readers of all levels. Bunyan employs simple diction and language, biblical images and metaphors, and repetition, all of which are suitable to his didactic purpose. In 1684, Bunyan published a second part of *The Pilgrim's Progress*, narrating the journey of Christian's wife, Christiana; her maid; and their children to Heaven. They are guided by the magnanimous Mr. Greatheart, whose presence makes the perils of the journey less intense.

SUMMARY

John Bunyan's writings brought him fame as a master allegorist and exponent of the plain style. While his works are informed with a powerfully consistent mythic vision, his arresting theme of individual salvation remains their most striking feature, a theme developed through strain and angst. His individualism, denying all but arbitrary grace, places the entire burden of salvation on the individual human. Even while realizing that most people would not play their part in the great drama successfully, he sought to illustrate how the individual's journey through life might best be made.

Stanley Archer

BIBLIOGRAPHY

By the Author

LONG FICTION:
Grace Abounding to the Chief of Sinners, 1666
The Pilgrim's Progress from This World to That Which Is to Come, 1678 (part 1)
The Life and Death of Mr. Badman, 1680
The Holy War, 1682
The Pilgrim's Progress from This World to That Which Is to Come, the Second Part, 1684

POETRY:
A Caution to Stir Up to Watch Against Sin, 1664
A Book for Boys and Girls: Or, Country Rhymes for Children, 1686
Discourse of the Building, Nature, Excellency, and Government of the House of God, 1688

NONFICTION:

Some Gospel Truths Opened, 1656

A Vindication . . . of Some Gospel Truths Opened, 1657

A Few Signs from Hell, 1658

The Doctrine of the Law and Grace Unfolded, 1659

Profitable Meditations Fitted to Man's Different Condition, 1661

I Will Pray with the Spirit, 1663

A Mapp Shewing the Order and Causes of Salvation and Damnation, 1664

One Thing Is Needful, 1665

The Holy City: Or, The New Jerusalem, 1665

A Confession of My Faith and a Reason for My Practice, 1671

A Defence of the Doctrine of Justification by Faith, 1672

A New and Useful Concordance to the Holy Bible, 1672

Saved by Grace, 1676

The Strait Gate: Or, The Great Difficulty of Going to Heaven, 1676

A Treatise of the Fear of God, 1679

A Holy Life, the Beauty of Christianity, 1684

Solomon's Temple Spiritualized: Or, Gospel Light Fecht Out of the Temple at Jerusalem, 1688

The Jerusalem Sinner Saved, 1688

DISCUSSION TOPICS

- John Bunyan possessed few, if any, of the early advantages many prospective writers possess. What resources buoyed the literary capacity of this tinker's son?

- Explain how Bunyan's *Grace Abounding to the Chief of Sinners* rises above its autobiographical form and becomes a book about the challenges of a religious quest.

- Give instances from *The Pilgrim's Progress* to exemplify Christian as a "wayfaring, warring Christian disciple."

- Characterize the "progress" of Bunyan's pilgrim.

- Full-blown allegory is not popular at present. How does one account for the forcefulness of Bunyan's allegory today?

About the Author

Davies, Michael. *Graceful Reading: Theology and Narrative in the Works of John Bunyan*. New York: Oxford University Press, 2002.

Dunan-Page, Anne. *Grace Overwhelming: John Bunyan, "The Pilgrim's Progress," and the Extremes of the Baptist Mind*. New York: Peter Lang, 2006.

Furlong, Monica. *Puritan's Progress*. New York: Coward, McCann & Geoghegan, 1975.

Hill, Christopher. *A Tinker and a Poor Man: John Bunyan and His Church, 1628-1688*. New York: Alfred A. Knopf, 1989.

Hofmeyr, Isabel. *The Portable Bunyan: A Transnational History of "The Pilgrim's Progress."* Princeton, N.J.: Princeton University Press, 2004.

Sadler, Lynn Veach. *John Bunyan*. Boston: G. K. Hall, 1979.

Talon, Henry A. *John Bunyan*. London: Longmans, Green, 1956.

Tindall, William York. *John Bunyan, Mechanick Preacher*. New York: Columbia University Press, 1934.

Winslow, Ola Elizabeth. *John Bunyan*. New York: Macmillan, 1961.

ANTHONY BURGESS

Born: Manchester, England
February 25, 1917
Died: London, England
November 25, 1993

One of the most prolific twentieth century British writers, Burgess is known for his linguistic prowess, his engaging plots, and his parodic, sometimes vicious, humor.

Monitor/Archive Photos

BIOGRAPHY

Anthony Burgess (BUR-juhs), christened John Burgess Wilson (Anthony was his confirmation name), was born on February 25, 1917, in Manchester, England, to Joseph and Elizabeth Burgess Wilson. In early 1919, an influenza epidemic killed Burgess's mother and his only sibling, a sister. In 1922, Burgess's father remarried. Anthony Burgess faulted his stepmother, Maggie Dwyer, with "an emotional coldness" that he believed marred his work and that many of the female characters in his novels exhibit.

Burgess attended a Catholic elementary school and received two scholarships to the Catholic preparatory school, Xaverian College, where he flourished, both artistically and intellectually. Though he attended Catholic schools, by sixteen he had rejected the Catholic church and its teachings; Catholicism remains, however, a recurrent subject in his fiction. Because he failed a physics course, Burgess was unable to enroll in music studies as he had wished, but he received his bachelor of arts, with honors, in English language and literature from the University of Manchester in June, 1940.

In October, 1940, Burgess joined the army, serving first in the Army Medical Corps, then in the Army Educational Corps. In January, 1942, he married Llewela Isherwood Jones, a Welsh economics student at the University of Manchester and a cousin of writer Christopher Isherwood. Throughout their long marriage, Llewela, or Lynne, as Burgess called her, was unfaithful, engaging in numerous casual affairs. This behavior, and Burgess's attitude toward it, undoubtedly contributed to the portrayals of faithless wives and the misogynism that appear in his fiction.

In 1944, while Burgess was stationed in Gibraltar, he received word that Llewela had been assaulted, according to her by American soldiers, resulting in her miscarriage and in physicians' orders that she never become pregnant again. Somewhat simplistically, Burgess blamed this attack for Llewela's increasing alcoholism and for her death, of cirrhosis of the liver, twenty-four years later. This attack was transformed into the attack on the fictional writer and his wife in Burgess's novel *A Clockwork Orange* (1962; reprinted with final chapter, 1986).

From 1946 to 1959, Burgess held various teaching posts, including one as an education officer in Malaya. His stay in Malaya was a turning point in his career: It is in Malaya that he began writing fiction. In 1956, his first novel, *Time for a Tiger,* the first novel in the Malayan Trilogy, was published. Since colonial servants were discouraged from writing fiction, he used the pen name Anthony Burgess. The trilogy's second and third installments, *The Enemy in the Blanket* and *Beds in the East,* appeared in 1958 and 1959, respectively; all three novels were published as *The Long Day Wanes* in 1965.

In 1959, Burgess collapsed while lecturing to his students, was sent back to London, and was diagnosed (so he consistently claimed) as suffering from a fatal brain tumor, with only a year to live. During this "terminal" year, his first year as a full-time writer, Burgess wrote five novels: *The Doctor Is Sick* (1960), *The Right to an Answer* (1960), *Devil of a State* (1961), *The Worm and the Ring* (1961), and *One Hand Clapping* (1961), the latter written under the pseudonym Joseph Kell. Burgess later complied with a request to review one of Kell's novels, claiming to have "assumed that the editor wanted a bit of a joke." Burgess's review created a controversy, with some critics charging that the author had deceitfully reviewed his own book, but Burgess's literary career was now firmly established. No sign or symptoms of a brain tumor ever subsequently appeared.

In 1962, Burgess published his most famous novel, *A Clockwork Orange*, as well as *The Wanting Seed*. In 1963, he published *Honey for the Bears* and another novel under the Kell pseudonym, *Inside Mr. Enderby*. His fictional biography, *Nothing Like the Sun: A Story of Shakespeare's Love-Life*, and *The Eve of Saint Venus* appeared in 1964, the same year that Liliana Macellari, a linguist at Cambridge University, and Burgess had a son, Andrew. His parody of Ian Fleming's James Bond series, *Tremor of Intent*, was published in 1966.

The year 1968 was a momentous one for Burgess. In March, his wife, Llewela, died. In October, Burgess married Liliana Macellari, the mother of his son. He published *Urgent Copy: Literary Studies*, *Enderby Outside*, and, in the United States, *Enderby* (which contained both *Mr. Enderby* and *Enderby Outside*). Burgess also permanently left England. From 1969 to 1973, he continued his prolific writing career, also serving as writer-in-residence and teaching creative writing at several universities in the United States.

Burgess's novel *MF* (1971) and director Stanley Kubrick's brilliant and faithful film adaptation of *A Clockwork Orange* appeared in the same year. From 1974 to 1986, Burgess published many books, among them *The Clockwork Testament: Or, Enderby's End* (1974), *Abba Abba* (1977), *Man of Nazareth* (1979), and *Enderby's Dark Lady* (1984). During this same period, Burgess wrote *Napoleon Symphony* (1974), his most experimental novel, which is elaborately patterned after Ludwig van Beethoven's *Eroica* symphony. *Earthly Powers*, his treatment of Roman Catholicism, appeared in 1980. In 1987, he published *Little Wilson and Big God*, the first volume of his projected three-volume autobiography. *The*

Devil's Mode, a collection of short stories, appeared in 1989; in 1990, the second installment of his autobiography, *You've Had Your Time*, was published.

Burgess died in London on November, 25, 1993, at the age of seventy-six.

ANALYSIS

Burgess seems not only fascinated with language but also obsessed with it. Though he claims to have avoided "overmuch word play and verbal oddity" in deference to his reading public, his novels are nevertheless filled, occasionally distractingly so, with wordplay. Sometimes, as in *A Clockwork Orange*, this playing with language creates a new language, one that becomes more powerful than English could have been for portraying the subject matter. When *A Clockwork Orange*'s gang member-narrator, Alex, describes "a bit of the ultra violence" as fine and "horrorshow," or describes as "sophistoes" two adolescent girls intent on seduction, the language defines Alex as much as, if not more than, his behavior does. In fact, in *A Clockwork Orange*, language is a character. Burgess also uses language effectively in *Nothing Like the Sun*, his fictional biography of William Shakespeare. In this novel Elizabethan language and idiom create a Shakespeare that no other rendering of language could have produced.

The language of Shakespeare, whom Burgess calls a "word-boy," involves the reader more intensely than traditional usage of English. In *The Eve of Saint Venus*, Burgess parodies overinflated poetic language, with language again becoming one of the characters of the novel. Burgess's Malayan Trilogy has been called "not so much plotted as it is orchestrated," and the integration of music with language is vital in his most experimental novel, *Napoleon Symphony*, in which he attempts to synthesize the language of the novel and the musical elements of Beethoven's *Eroica*. Though Burgess often calls unnecessary attention to his play with language and can overdo his linguistic games, he manages, in most of his work, to make language powerful, effective, and noticeable.

Burgess's work often deals with the duality of nature: good and evil, free will and determinism, romanticism and realism, comedy and tragedy. His characters must grapple with their behavior in terms of these dualities. In his attempt to discover his own beliefs, Hillier, in *Tremor of Intent*, has many debates with several characters on the nature of good and evil. The conflict and paradox of opposing forces pervade the three novels that constitute the Malayan Trilogy.

Kenneth Toomey, the homosexual narrator of *Earthly Powers*, wrestles with the question of good and evil. Toomey and the pope's discussions of good and evil and of free will and determinism form the philosophical backbone of the novel. Zverkov, a character in *Honey for the Bears*, represents philosophy and thought; Karamzin, of the same novel, represents force and physical strength. Like the characters in T. S. Eliot's *The Waste Land* (1922), the characters in Burgess's *One Hand Clapping* are confronted with the predicament of living a meaningful life in a spiritual and cultural desert. Alex, the narrator of *A Clockwork Orange*, complains about all the discussion and debate over good and evil; since no one ever tries to determine the essential source and nature of goodness, Alex claims that he does not understand the insistence on dissecting the nature of evil. Burgess seems as much a philosopher as a novelist, with his constant analysis of the duality of the nature of life, but it is these philosophical ruminations that lend depth to his work.

Sometimes subtle, but more often blatant if not slapstick, the comic elements of Burgess's work are essential Burgess. The violence and depravity of *A Clockwork Orange* are made palatable by its narrator's irrepressible sense of irony, lending humor to the most gruesome aspects of the novel. In the Malayan Trilogy, Burgess's engaging representation of life transforms depravity into comedy. The narrator of *The Right to an Answer* is cynical and ironic. *Devil of a State* is a farce, while *Honey for the Bears* is comic throughout. The comic elements of both *Earthly Powers* and *Tremor of Intent* are interwoven with philosophical musings on the nature of good and evil. The humor of Burgess's work is sometimes grotesque, often cynical, but usually integral to the fiction.

Sexuality, especially homosexuality, seems to be another obsession of Burgess. Many of the wives in his fiction are unfaithful: Hortense in *Earthly Powers*, Sheila in *The Doctor Is Sick*, Anne in *Nothing Like the Sun*, Mrs. Walters in *Tremor of Intent*, Belinda of *Honey for the Bears*, and Beatrice-Joanna of *The Wanting Seed*. Incest, and the potential for incest, also appears. Toomey often ponders the possibility

of a sexual liaison with his sister Hortense. Shakespeare's brother Richard has an affair with Shakespeare's wife, which constitutes a type of incest since she is Richard's sister-in-law. Hillier, in *Tremor of Intent*, often ruminates on his paternal yet sexual feelings toward Clara, with whom he does eventually have sex. *MF* also deals with the incestuous. Homosexuality often appears in Burgess's work. WS (Burgess's name for William Shakespeare) in *Nothing Like the Sun* becomes involved with his beautiful male sponsor. While in prison, Alex of *A Clockwork Orange* is forced to fend off an inmate to protect himself from homosexual advances. Alan in *Tremor of Intent* submits himself to a homosexual encounter in order to receive a stolen gun. The husband and wife of *Honey for the Bears* have an open marriage but are basically homosexual. Derek, the high government official of *The Wanting Seed*, is homosexual. Kenneth Toomey of *Earthly Powers* is a homosexual, and his sexual orientation is as much a concern of the novel as is the role of the church and God.

A CLOCKWORK ORANGE

First published: 1962
Type of work: Novel

In an unidentified future society, teenage Alex recalls his violent gang activities, his imprisonment, and his reformation.

Burgess's most memorable novel, *A Clockwork Orange*, cannot be discussed without addressing its language, "nadsat," a combination of Russian, English, and slang, which was invented for the novel and which catapults its narrator, Alex, into the reader's consciousness as few other books can. Alex invites readers along with him and his "droogs" (buddies) as they sit in a bar, eyeing the "devotchkas [girls] . . . dressed in the heighth of fashion" and wearing "make-up to match (rainbows round the glazzies [eyes], that is, and the rot [mouth] painted very wide)." He narrates their adventures as they do a bit of ultraviolence: They "razrez" a teacher's books to bits, then "tolchock" him and treat him to the "old bootcrush"; they come across Billyboy and his five droogs, which leads to a gang fight with "the nozh [knife], the oozy [chain], the britva [razor], not just fisties and boots"; they beat to death an old woman and her "pusscats."

Throughout part 1, the extreme violence of the novel is made palatable by the unusual language, which presents repulsive acts with strange, new words, drawing the reader into the book and into the violence itself. The language of the novel captures the reader and makes him or her one of Alex's "droogs," maintaining sympathy for Alex throughout his violent activities. When he rapes two ten-year-old girls in his room, he tells the reader that "this time they thought nothing fun and stopped creeching with high mirth, and had to submit to the strange and weird desires of Alexander the Large which . . . were choodessny and zammechat and very demanding. . . . But they were both very very drunken and could hardly feel very much." When he hints at his brutality toward his father and mother, he reveals that his father was "like humble mumble chumble." In addition to making the violence more acceptable, Alex's inclusion of biblical language, "Oh, my brothers," makes the narrator more than just an uneducated criminal; at times, in fact, Alex sounds suspiciously like a preacher addressing his congregation on the nature of good and evil. The language of *A Clockwork Orange*, innovative, powerful, and original, becomes almost like a character in the novel. The language not only distances the violence being described but also forces the reader to reevaluate that violence. Indeed, the language is one of the things that makes *A Clockwork Orange* so powerful.

The novel opens with the line "What's it going to be then, eh?" This question, which serves as the structure to open each of the novel's three sections, introduces the reader not only to the "humble narrator" Alex but also to one of the novel's major themes: the nature of free will. In part 2, Alex, who is only fifteen and who has been incarcerated for murdering the old woman with the cats, is subjected to reconditioning by the State. In this, "the real weepy and like tragic part of the story," the State tries to take away Alex's free will by making him ill when he views sex and violence, and also when he listens to Ludwig van Beethoven's *Ninth Symphony*, which had been a favorite of Alex after his violent activities. The nature of free will and determinism is one of Burgess's most oft-repeated themes; Alex and the prison chaplain, who constantly addresses Alex as "little 6655321" rather than by his name, discuss the fact that Alex is going "to be made into a good boy." Burgess's attack on behaviorists and on totalitarian states is obvious: Alex is made ill by drugs, is forced to view nauseatingly violent films, and is reduced to a sniveling, whining victim.

Part 3 presents the reader with a new, reformed Alex, an Alex without free will or freedom of choice, an Alex who has become a victim, and an Alex who ultimately tries to commit suicide. Something of a celebrity after his reconditioning by the State, Alex views a photograph of himself in the newspaper, looking "very gloomy and like scared, but that was really with the flashbulbs going pop pop all the time." Upon arrival home, Alex learns that his parents have

rented his room to a lodger and that he is no longer welcome there. All of his personal belongings were sold to pay for the upkeep of the orphaned cats of the woman Alex had murdered. Alex staggers away, only to encounter some of his former victims, who beat him and subject him to the same treatment to which he had originally subjected them.

Throughout, Burgess makes it clear that without freedom of choice and free will, even when that choice is used to commit evil, people become helpless victims of society and life. In his despair at his life without choice, Alex tries to commit suicide, leading the State to be accused of failure in its "criminal reform scheme" and to be accused of figurative murder, since the State has, indeed, murdered the real Alex. Alex's attempted suicide makes him feel "filled up again with clean." It also makes his parents repent for their abominable treatment of him after his release from prison. The government authorities try to restore Alex to his former, unreconditioned self.

Until 1986, the published novel excluded the final chapter, as did Stanley Kubrick's 1971 film, and the second to the last chapter ends with Alex's imagining himself doing some ultraviolence and his ironic comment, "I was cured all right." The final chapter, however, though often considered weak by American audiences or critics, reveals another of Burgess's important themes: an essentially optimistic view of humankind. Alex chooses to reject his formerly violent ways. He tells his audience, "And all it was was that I was young." Alex decides to grow up and have a family. Just as he had chosen to commit violence, with free will Alex can choose to avoid evil.

NOTHING LIKE THE SUN: A STORY OF SHAKESPEARE'S LOVE-LIFE

First published: 1964
Type of work: Novel

Set in Elizabethan England, and using Elizabethan language and idiom, this fictional account of William Shakespeare's love life concentrates on his sexual encounters.

In *Nothing Like the Sun: A Story of Shakespeare's Love-Life*, Anthony Burgess freely imagines the sexual exploits and love life of William Shakespeare. The protagonist, identified as WS throughout the novel, is seduced and forced into marriage with Anne Hathaway by her pregnancy. WS does not believe the child is his, and this establishes some of the themes of the novel: sexual infidelity, manipulation, and coercion. WS's relationship with his wife is not a happy one, and, despite the birth of twins, whom WS does claim as his own, he goes to London to work and live, rarely returning home to his wife and children, who live with WS's parents and siblings.

Away from home, WS becomes involved with his beautiful male sponsor, the earl of Southampton, Henry Wriothesly, to whom "Venus and Adonis" and the sonnets are dedicated. Like WS's wife, Southampton is also unfaithful to WS, which forces WS to seek the love of his "dark lady" in the arms of Fatimah, a beauty whom WS describes as neither black nor white, but "gold." Fatimah, greatly interested in WS's friends and acquaintances, eventually has an affair with Wriothesly. When WS discovers her infidelity, he returns to Stratford, only to find himself cuckolded by his own brother. WS returns to London. After a time, he takes Fatimah back. From her, WS contracts syphilis, which Fatimah contracted from Wriothesly. According to Burgess, this disease affects WS's worldview, leading, by implication, to the darker artistic vision of the tragedies.

Interwoven with WS's sexual exploits and disappointments is the milieu of Elizabethan England, Burgess shows his readers the effects of the plague, the struggles of the theaters, and the tempests of the playwrights and their players, all in the idiom and language of the Elizabethans. Burgess abundantly displays his linguistic ability and playfulness in *Nothing Like the Sun*. Many of the characters speak lines from Shakespeare's plays, and Burgess describes the environment, characters, and behavior in language that approximates that of the time period, lending a richness and complexity to the novel that would not have been comparable with contemporary English. The use of language is also of great importance to the "word-boy" WS, so the Elizabethan English in the novel becomes an appropriate metaphor for WS's struggles to form language that fits his view of the world and to express his deepest beliefs. To emphasize this importance of language, a few parts of the novel are written as a journal or as if they were excerpts from a drama.

As a sort of prologue (though not identified as such) before the novel proper, these words appear: "Mr. Burgess's farewell lecture to his special students . . . who complained that Shakespeare had nothing to give to the East. (Thanks for the farewell gift of three bottles of *samsu*. I will take a swig now. Delicious.)" In

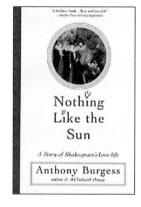

the epilogue, the reader is again introduced to this *samsu*-swigging persona, who enters the narrative of the novel only once or twice. The point of view in the epilogue immediately returns to that of WS, however, who is now dying, attended by his physician son-in-law. The viewpoint in *Nothing Like the Sun* is almost consistently that of WS, so it is unclear why Burgess's persona intrudes into the narrative, especially since Burgess does so infrequently and inconsequentially.

TREMOR OF INTENT

First published: 1966
Type of work: Novel

In this parody of the spy genre, secret agent Hillier is sent to reclaim a British scientist named Roper, and he encounters the villainous Theodorescu.

In the first part of Burgess's *Tremor of Intent*, the protagonist is a secret agent named Hillier, who wishes to retire and who suffers from the "two chronic diseases of gluttony and satyriasis." He recounts his memories of his childhood and young adult relationship with Roper, a British scientist. Hillier has been sent, on this last mission before retirement, to recover Roper from the Soviet Union.

Many of Burgess's standard themes appear in this part of the book: the role of the church and religion, the duality of good and evil, the nature of free will, and the infidelity of wives. Roper and Hillier address many of these topics themselves, but Roper also discusses the philosophical issues with others. Roper's wife, a German girl whom he married after World War II, is unfaithful, and Hillier, ostensibly in the name of Roper's honor, beats her lover (just before Hillier has sex with her himself). Though at the beginning of the novel Hillier is on a cruise ship on his way to recover Roper, it is not until part 2 that the action of the novel actually takes place on the cruise ship.

In part 2, where the parody of the spy genre begins in earnest, Hillier meets the siblings Alan and Clara Walters, who will aid him in his attempt to get Roper and who will save Hillier's life. Young Clara represents the innocent female in the novel, and, though Hillier will ultimately have relations with her, he spends much of the novel avoiding sexual contact with her, trying to convince himself that his feelings toward her are paternal. He readily admits his sexual feelings, however, for Miss Devi, the wicked woman of the genre; she is employed as secretary to the novel's villian, Mr. Theodorescu, a gluttonous, obese pederast.

Hillier engages in a gluttony contest with Theodorescu, and Burgess catalogs the foods they eat in great detail. Hillier also indulges in sexual antics with Miss Devi, leading to his being tricked (by drugs) into giving Theodorescu information, which the villain, as a neutral, plans to sell to the highest bidder. Burgess clearly condemns the villain Theodorescu for being a neutral. Apparently, not choosing sides, or choosing to be on all sides, is a crime in this novel; many of the other characters, but especially the young boy Alan, detest such neutrality.

In part 3, after Hillier finds Roper, he discovers that he himself is the one who has been duped: He has not been sent to rescue Roper after all, but to be killed. True to the genre, however, Hillier is saved. Burgess has the assassin engage in a philosophical discussion with Hillier and Roper, allowing them time to be rescued.

Hillier then finds Theodorescu, gorges the villain with information, and eliminates him. Hillier also has his long-anticipated sexual rendezvous with Clara. Even while parodying the genre, Burgess presents a plot with sufficient twists and surprises to retain the reader's interest. Though the sometimes lengthy discussions on good and evil or on the nature of choice may seem inappropriate, they can also be interpreted as Burgess's parody of the genre: His spies and villains deal with major philosophical issues even as they practice their craft.

In part 4, Burgess has Clara and Alan, who were essential components of Hillier's success in surviving his last assignment, come to visit Hillier, and the three of them briefly discuss some of the philosophical issues present in the early parts of the novel. Hillier, former spy, glutton, and satyr, has now, in the ultimate parody of the spy genre and in the ultimate representation of Burgess's essentially optimistic worldview, become a priest. Burgess does not play with language excessively in *Tremor of Intent* as he does in some of his other novels. His characters discuss his usual themes in great detail.

NAPOLEON SYMPHONY

First published: 1974
Type of work: Novel

In this fictionalized biography of Napoleon I, Burgess employs the structure of Ludwig van Beethoven's third symphony, the Eroica, *as a controlling literary device.*

When Beethoven began to work on his third symphony, the *Eroica*, he viewed the work as a tribute to Napoleon I. As he proceeded with the composition, however, he lost faith in Napoleon; Beethoven was so irked when Napoleon declared himself emperor of France that the composer ended up dedicating the *Eroica* not to Napoleon but to Prometheus. In *Napoleon Symphony*, Burgess merges his skill in writing with his highly developed knowledge of music to produce a tragicomical biography of the famed French general and emperor.

Like Beethoven's symphony, Burgess's novel is divided into movements, each of which focuses on a significant period in Napoleon's life. The novel is at once complex but eminently accessible to general readers. Readers with strong backgrounds in history and music will find hidden gems of meaning that might easily be missed by more casual readers. Less sophisticated readers, however, will delight in the basic story Burgess is telling and in the humor with which he tells it.

The novel covers Napoleon's life from the time he married Josephine to his death and some of the period following it. Just as Beethoven's symphony has four movements, so does Burgess's novel. In structuring it, Burgess played the *Eroica* over and over on his phonograph, timing each movement meticulously. He then worked out a way to make the sections of his novel proportionate to the movements of the symphony.

Following his death on the island of St. Helena, Burgess's Napoleon assumes Promethean proportions. Despite his defeat at Waterloo, Napoleon had moved relentlessly toward his ideal objective of uniting Europe, for which Burgess celebrates him. The greatest strength of *Napoleon Symphony* is that in structuring it parallel to the *Eroica*, Burgess succeeds in making the French emperor a rounded character. Readers see him as a conquering hero,

but they also are given access to him in his more personal moments.

In one section, Napoleon, who has no heir, is shown presiding over a family dinner. Most of the attendees at this dinner are fueled by greed. The salient question "What is in it for me?" underlies the motives of the people at this gathering. The irony of seeing a Napoleon who, although he could lead armies and shape empires, could not control his and Josephine's grasping relatives is not lost on readers.

EARTHLY POWERS

First published: 1980
Type of work: Novel

Against a backdrop of international events of the twentieth century, the homosexual author Kenneth Toomey narrates the story of his life.

Earthly Powers contains many of Burgess's favorite themes: the duality of nature, good versus evil, free will versus determinism, sexuality, and infidelity. The narrator, homosexual author Kenneth Toomey, becomes related, through the marriage of his sister Hortense, to the Catholic family Campanati, whose adopted son Carlo will one day become pope. Though future pontiff Carlo Campanati is rarely in the novel, when he is present, he and the narrator often argue about such philosophical issues as free will, choice, and the nature of a God who creates homosexuals and whose church condemns homosexuality.

Toomey is eighty-one years old at the start of the novel. When he attempts to end the relationship with his unfaithful lover-secretary Geoffrey, Geoffrey threatens blackmail. Geoffrey, however, is then forced to flee to avoid criminal prosecution for some crime he has committed. Early in the novel, Toomey is asked to corroborate a "miracle" supposedly performed by Carlo years earlier; to rid himself of Geoffrey, Toomey sends Geoffrey to Chicago to investigate the miracle.

The novel then explores Toomey's long life, including his various affairs and betrayals: with Val, who leaves him and who will one day become a poet; with Sir Richard Curry Burt, who involves

Toomey in a bizarre homosexual situation at a dock; with Ralph, an African American, who leaves Toomey to return to Africa and his black heritage; and with physician Phillip Shawcross, a platonic relationship that Toomey claims is his greatest love.

Like the wives in Burgess's other works, Toomey's male lovers in this novel are often unfaithful and frequently cruel. Toomey, like many of Burgess's characters, is obsessed with sexuality and often has incestuous thoughts about his sister Hortense, who seems to be the only woman with whom he would consider having a physical relationship. After her divorce, Hortense has a lesbian relationship, despite the fact that she had previously reviled Toomey for his homosexuality. At the end of the novel, Toomey and his sister Hortense are living together, as Mr. and Mrs. Toomey, and sleep in the same bedroom, though in separate beds.

Woven into the story of Toomey's relatively unhappy love life are the stories of his sister Hortense, who marries Domenico Campanati, the pontiff's brother, and who is unfaithful in order to give her sterile husband children; of Toomey's brother Tom, a comedian who dies, apparently from smoking-induced cancer; of Toomey's nephew John, who is killed in Africa, along with his wife, after Toomey helps finance a research trip for them; and of John's twin sister, Ann, whose own daughter Eve will become tragically involved with the person whom Carlo Campanati saved in the miracle performed so long ago. Toomey's life intersects not only with these characters but also with various literary and historical personages, some of whom are actually presented in the plot of the novel, and others who are mentioned only in passing: James Joyce, T. S. Eliot, George Orwell, Heinrich Himmler, and Joseph Goebbels, to name a few.

By the end of the novel, in a bizarre twist of the characters' fates, Toomey learns that the child miraculously saved by Carlo Campanati grew up to become Godfrey Manning, or God for short, a cult figure who poisons his entire congregation with cyanide but does not join his flock in this ultimate communion. Burgess's irony is deftly presented, especially in the final chapters of the novel. His homosexual narrator remains a relatively sympathetic character throughout *Earthly Powers*, and Burgess's plot successfully weaves the stories of all the characters together. Burgess does not engage in extensive linguistic wordplay or invent new language for this novel, as he does in many of his other books, but he does explore in depth his usual philosophical and theological issues: the nature of good and evil, the nature of free will and choice.

SUMMARY

The fiction of Anthony Burgess is a unique concoction of language and linguistic wordplay, philosophical discussions, grotesque details, comedy, and tragedy. Burgess's work is not of a consistently high quality; some of his novels are flawed, and his obsession with language can become intrusive and distracting. Nevertheless, Burgess's body of work shows a wide range of philosophical interests and diverse treatment of his subject matters, and it is a worthy representative of British literature. At his best, Burgess creates language that becomes a character in the fiction and that is greater than the characters or themes contained in the novels.

Sherri Szeman; updated by R. Baird Shuman

BIBLIOGRAPHY

By the Author

LONG FICTION:
Time for a Tiger, 1956
The Enemy in the Blanket, 1958
Beds in the East, 1959
The Right to an Answer, 1960
The Doctor Is Sick, 1960
The Worm and the Ring, 1961
Devil of a State, 1961

Anthony Burgess

One Hand Clapping, 1961 (as Joseph Kell)
A Clockwork Orange, 1962 (reprinted with final chapter, 1986)
The Wanting Seed, 1962
Inside Mr. Enderby, 1963 (as Kell)
Honey for the Bears, 1963
Nothing Like the Sun: A Story of Shakespeare's Love-Life, 1964
The Eve of Saint Venus, 1964
The Long Day Wanes, 1965 (includes *Time for a Tiger, The Enemy in the Blanket,* and *Beds in the East*)
A Vision of Battlements, 1965
Tremor of Intent, 1966
Enderby, 1968 (includes *Inside Mr. Enderby* and *Enderby Outside*)
Enderby Outside, 1968
MF, 1971
Napoleon Symphony, 1974
The Clockwork Testament: Or, Enderby's End, 1974
Moses: A Narrative, 1976
Beard's Roman Woman, 1976
Abba, Abba, 1977
1985, 1978
Man of Nazareth, 1979
Earthly Powers, 1980
The End of the World News, 1983
Enderby's Dark Lady, 1984
The Kingdom of the Wicked, 1985
The Pianoplayers, 1986
Any Old Iron, 1989
A Dead Man in Deptford, 1993
Byrne, 1995

SHORT FICTION:
The Devil's Mode, 1989

SCREENPLAY:
Jesus of Nazareth, 1977

TELEPLAY:
Moses the Lawgiver, 1976

NONFICTION:
English Literature: A Survey for Students, 1958 (as John Burgess Wilson)
The Novel Today, 1963
Language Made Plain, 1964
Here Comes Everybody: An Introduction to James Joyce for the Ordinary Reader, 1965 (pb. in U.S. as *Re Joyce,* 1965)
The Novel Now, 1967 (revised 1971)
Urgent Copy: Literary Studies, 1968
Shakespeare, 1970
Joysprick: An Introduction to the Language of James Joyce, 1972
Ernest Hemingway and His World, 1978

DISCUSSION TOPICS

- Anthony Burgess reveals a great deal about his attitude toward women in his writing. Discuss the attitudes that he reveals.

- What are the chief characteristics that Burgess's characters reveal in love relationships?

- Burgess is much concerned with such dichotomies as good and evil. Discuss the dichotomies that appear to motivate him most significantly.

- How does Burgess use humor to appeal to general readers of his work?

- Discuss Burgess's attitude toward religion as revealed in his writing.

414

On Going to Bed, 1982

This Man and Music, 1983

Flame into Being: The Life and Work of D. H. Lawrence, 1985

But Do Blondes Prefer Gentlemen? Homage to Qwert Yuiop, and Other Writings, 1986 (also known as *Homage to Qwert Yuiop*, 1985)

Little Wilson and Big God, 1987 (partly reprinted as *Childhood*, 1996)

You've Had Your Time, 1990

A Mouthful of Air: Languages, Languages—Especially English, 1992

One Man's Chorus: The Uncollected Writings, 1998

CHILDREN'S LITERATURE:

A Long Trip to Teatime, 1976

TRANSLATIONS:

The Man Who Robbed Poor-Boxes, 1965 (of Michel Servin's play)

Cyrano de Bergerac, 1971 (of Edmond Rostand's play)

Oedipus the King, 1972 (of Sophocles' play)

MISCELLANEOUS:

On Mozart: A Paean for Wolfgang, 1991

About the Author

Aggeler, Geoffrey, ed. *Critical Essays on Anthony Burgess.* Boston: G. K. Hall, 1986.

Biswell, Andrew. *The Real Life of Anthony Burgess.* London: Picador, 2005.

Bloom, Harold, ed. *Modern Critical Views: Anthony Burgess.* New York: Chelsea House, 1987.

Coale, Samuel. *Anthony Burgess.* New York: Frederick Ungar, 1981.

Farkas, A. I. *Will's Son and Jake's Peer: Anthony Burgess's Joycean Negotiations.* Budapest: Akademikiai Kiado, 2003.

Lewis, Roger. *Anthony Burgess.* New York: St. Martin's Press, 2004.

Morris, Robert . *The Consolations of Ambiguity: An Essay on the Novels of Anthony Burgess.* Columbia: University of Missouri Press, 1971.

Rozett, Martha Tuck. "Historical Novelists at Work: George Garrett and Anthony Burgess." In *Constructing a World: Shakespeare's England and the New Historical Fiction.* Albany, N.Y.: SUNY Press, 2003.

Smith, K. H. "Will! or Shakespeare in Hollywood: Anthony Burgess's Cinematic Presentation of Shakespearean Biography." In *Remaking Shakespeare: Performance Across Media, Genres, and Cultures*, edited by Pascale Aebisher, Edward Esche, and Nigel Wheale. Houndmills, England: Palgrave Macmillan, 2003.

Stinson, John J. *Anthony Burgess Revisited.* Boston: Twayne, 1991.

ROBERT BURNS

Born: Alloway, Ayrshire, Scotland
January 25, 1759
Died: Dumfries, Scotland
July 21, 1796

As the greatest of the Scottish poets, Burns composed lyrics, ballads, satires, and occasional verse that advanced the Romantic movement and remain part of the permanent literary heritage.

Library of Congress

BIOGRAPHY

Robert Burns was born on the family farm in the Ayrshire district of Scotland on January 25, 1759, to William Burnes (as the father spelled his name) and Agnes Broun. William, a poor tenant farmer, struggled to keep his family from poverty. At Mount Oliphant, Lochlie, and Mossgiel, as the family moved from one farm to another, the story of failure was the same, in spite of backbreaking toil. In every case, rents for the land were too costly. To supplement the family income, Burns tried to dress flax in Irvine, but he eventually returned to the farm in Mauchline parish, where his father died in 1784. In "The Cotter's Saturday Night," Burns romanticizes the nobility of his father in a nostalgic, deeply felt remembrance.

Burns's earliest schooling was from John Murdoch, a competent teacher hired by the farmers of the district; at Dalrymple, he studied at the parish school. Briefly in 1773, he was again a pupil at Murdoch's school at Ayr. In spite of the interruptions in his education, Burns was an apt scholar, and he was fortunate to have sound educators as his masters. He learned French well enough to read but not to speak in that language, studied mathematics with his uncle at Ballochneil in 1777, and studied elements of surveying under Hugh Rodger, schoolmaster at nearby Kirkoswald.

Before that time, Burns had been writing verse to various young women, among them Mary Campbell ("Highland Mary"), with whom he was having an affair, and who died in 1786. In 1788, he married Jean Armour, of Mauchline with whom he had four children. As early as 1785, he had begun "The Jolly Beggars." By 1786, he had collected enough early verse to publish his first book, *Poems, Chiefly in the Scottish Dialect*, which was printed in Kilmarnock, Scotland.

At first, Burns achieved a local reputation, but his fame as a supposedly unlettered bard soon grew. In Edinburgh, where he was lionized as a country genius by the aristocrats, he conducted himself with dignity. Two reprintings of his poems, with additions, appeared in 1787 and 1793. The volume was also published in London; within two years, pirated editions appeared in Dublin, Belfast, Philadelphia, and New York.

For the first edition of the Kilmarnock poems, he had received only twenty pounds, but for the second he earned the princely sum, to him, of four hundred pounds. With this money, he was able to travel briefly, buy property of his own, and settle down with Jean and their four children on a farm at Ellisland, near Dumfries. After a last unsatisfactory attempt to make the farm pay, Burns left with his family for Dumfries, where he accepted another appointment as an excise (tax) officer in 1791; he remained there for the rest of his life.

In spite of malicious gossip, his last five years were those of a respected townsman and celebrated poet. These years were burdened as well by illness, the toll of his early plowman's labors. Nevertheless, he continued writing and contributed three hundred songs to two collections of Scottish songs, James Johnson's *The Scots Musical Museum* (1787-1803) and George Thomson's *A Select Collection of Original Scottish Airs* (1793-1805). Burns died in Dumfries from rheumatic heart disease at the age of thirty-seven, on July 21, 1796.

ANALYSIS

In a letter to John Hamilton Reynolds on July 13, 1818, poet John Keats wrote of Burns:

> One song of Burns's is of more worth to you than all I could think for a whole year in his native country. His misery is a dead weight upon the nimbleness of one's quill—I tried to forget it—to drink toddy without any care—to write a merry sonnet—it won't do—he talked with bitches—he drank with blackguards, he was miserable—We can see horribly clear, in the works of such a man his whole life, as if we were God's spies.

Keats admires Burns's humanity, an expansiveness that elevates Burns's vision to those who, in William Shakespeare's words from *King Lear* (pr. c. 1605-1606, pb. 1608), are "God's spies." In his range, Burns indeed may be compared with such English poets of tolerance and humanity as Geoffrey Chaucer and Robert Browning; although his psychology and depth of understanding are less acute than those writers, his lyrical gifts are possibly purer. Burns's scope includes a wide range of types and literary conventions, from sketches on the "bitches" and "blackguards" in taverns or in churches, to the most elevated love songs, to rallying choruses for democratic solidarity. A poet of the people, Burns wrote so that "his whole life" became the subject of his art.

Burns's major poetry generally falls into five convenient groupings: drinking songs; love songs; satires, usually on Calvinistic rigors; democratic chants or songs; and verse narratives. In addition, he wrote miscellaneous verse epistles, mostly moralistic but sometimes aesthetic, and occasional pieces, usually to commemorate a particular event or to praise (sometimes flatter) a particular person. Among his most notable drinking songs are "The Jolly Beggars" and "Willy Brew'd a Peck of Maut." Examples of his love lyrics include "Ae Fond Kiss," "Highland Mary," "A Red, Red Rose," and "O, Once I Lov'd a Bonie Lass." Examples of the satires are "Holy Willie's Prayer," "Address to the Unco Guid," and "Address to the Deil." Among Burns's patriotic or democratic songs are "Scots, Wha Hae," "Is There for Honest Poverty," and the more Jacobean "A Dream" and "The Twa Dogs." His most famous verse narrative is "Tam O'Shanter." A good example of Burns's didactic verse treating his aesthetic is "Epistle to J. Lapraik." Taken together, these varieties of poetic subjects or types share the Burns signature of spontaneity, wit, freshness, sincerity, and vigor.

Usually classed among the "pre-Romantic" writers of the late eighteenth and early nineteenth centuries, Burns is in most regards a true Romantic. Like such major early Romantics as William Wordsworth, Samuel Taylor Coleridge, Lord Byron, and Percy Bysshe Shelley, Burns demonstrates in his verse extemporaneous effusion, directness, and lyricism; like them, he exalts the common man, delights in the rustic (or natural) beauties of the open countryside, and celebrates his own ego. To the extent that Burns is also influenced by neoclassical literary conventions, his verse is generally more tersely epigrammatical (except in comparison with much of Byron's work), less innovative in terms of experimentation with new meters or forms, and less directly concerned with transcendental emotions. Unlike the major Romantics who followed him, Burns eschewed blank verse and never attempted to write for the theater. These distinctions aside, Burns rightly takes his place with the still-greater poet William Blake as both forerunner and shaper of the Romantic impulse in Western literature.

"THE JOLLY BEGGARS"

First published: 1799 (collected in *The Canongate Burns*, 2001)

Type of work: Poem

Subtitled "A Cantata," this poem is a medley of rowdy, sometimes ribald, joyous drinking songs.

In "The Study of Poetry," Matthew Arnold, a severe critic of Burns in general, could not resist describing "The Jolly Beggars" favorably as a "puissant and splendid production." Literary antecedents of the work, which combines a medley of songs in a loose dramatic structure, go back to John Fletcher's *The Beggar's Bush* (before 1622) or to John Gay's *The Beggar's Opera* (pr., pb. 1728). Slightly more than a generation after Burns, the French poet Pierre-Jean de Béranger would write song-comedic productions such as "Les Gueux" ("The Beggars") and "Le Vieux Vagabond" ("The Old Vagabond"). However, nothing in Western literature can match Burns's production for energy, sly wit, and lyricism.

Suggested by a chance visit by the poet with two friends to the "doss house" (brothel) of Poosie Nansie (her real name was Agnes Gibson) in the Cowgate, Mauchline, "The Jolly Beggars" transforms the sordid reality of the original scene into a bawdy, lighthearted comedy. Challenging the prudery of his own day, Burns exalts a kind of rough, natural sensuality, without a trace of sniggering. Although joyous sex is a theme of the poem, its real message is that people must have liberty to live in the way that they wish. No more defiant yet witty lines have been written in defense of freedom:

> A fig for those by law protected!
> Liberty's a glorious feast!
> Courts for cowards were erected,
> Churches built to please the priest!

"A RED, RED ROSE"

First published: 1796 (collected in *The Canongate Burns*, 2001)
Type of work: Poem

The speaker in this well-beloved lyric bids his sweetheart farewell but promises to return to her.

"A Red, Red Rose," also titled in some anthologies according to its first line, "O, my luve is like a red, red rose," was written in 1794 and printed in 1796. The song may be enjoyed as a simple, unaffected effusion of sentiment, or it may be understood on a more complex level as a lover's promises that are full of contradictions, ironies, and paradoxes. The reader should keep in mind the fact that Burns constructed the poem, stanza by stanza, by "deconstructing" old songs and ballads to use

parts that he could revise and improve. For example, Burns's first stanza may be compared with his source, "The Wanton Wife of Castle Gate": "Her cheeks are like the roses/ That blossom fresh in June;/ O, she's like a new-strung instrument/ That's newly put in tune." Clearly, Burns's version is more delicate, while at the same time audaciously calculated. By emphasizing the absolute redness of the rose—the "red, red rose"—the poet demonstrates his seeming artlessness as a sign of sincerity. What other poet could rhyme "June" and "tune" without appearing hackneyed? With Burns the very simplicity of the language works toward an effect of absolute purity.

Readers who analyze the poem using the tools of New Criticism or other twentieth century critical approaches will observe, on the other hand, contradictory elements that seem to work against the speaker's innocent protestations of love. The first two lines of the second stanza do not complete an expected (or logical) thought: "So deep in luve am I" (that I cannot bear to leave my beloved). Instead, the speaker rhetorically protests his love through a series of preposterous boasts. His love will last until the seas go dry, until rocks melt with the sun; he will continue to love while the sands of life (in an hourglass) shall run. Yet so steadfast a lover, after all, is departing from his beloved, not staying by her side. For whatever reason, he is compelled to leave her rather than remain. His final exaggerated promise, that he will return to her, though the journey takes a thousand miles, seems farfetched, even ironically humorous: Instead of such a titanic effort, why should he not simply stay with her?

These paradoxical reflections, however, which change a reading of the poem from one of "pure" lyric to one of irony, are not so difficult to reconcile on the level of common sense. What lover has not exaggerated his or her emotions? Are these exaggerated promises of Burns's speaker any less sincere for being illogical? No matter how the reader resolves this issue, he or she cannot help but admire Burns's art in revising the meter of his source for the last stanza, an old song titled "The True Lover's Farewell": "Fare you well, my own true love/ And fare you well for a while,/ And I will be sure to return back again/ If I go ten thousand mile." Although Burns's revisions are minor, they reveal the difference in technique between a merely competent poet and a master.

"HOLY WILLIE'S PRAYER"

First published: 1789 (collected in *The Canongate Burns*, 2001)
Type of work: Poem

The poet satirizes Willie, who is far from "holy," caught in the act of prayer.

"Holy Willie's Prayer," written in 1785, was printed in 1789 and reprinted in 1799. It was one of the poet's favorite verses, and he sent a copy to his friend, the convivial preacher John M'Math, who had requested it, along with a dedicatory poem titled "Epistle to the Rev. John M'Math" (published in 1808). To M'Math he sent his "Argument" as background information:

Holy Willie was a rather oldish bachelor elder, in the parish of Mauchline, and much and justly famed for that polemical chattering which ends in tippling orthodoxy, and for that spiritualized bawdry which refines to liquorish devotion.

The real-life "Willie" whom Burns had in mind was William Fisher, a strict Presbyterian elder of the Mauchline church.

In his satire on religious fanaticism, Burns cleverly allows Willie to witness against himself. Willie's prayer, addressed to the deity of Calvinist doctrine, is really a self-serving plea to be forgiven for his own sins of sexual promiscuity (with Meg). Willie's God—more cruel than righteous—punishes sinners according to the doctrine of predestination of saints: Only a small number of "elect" souls, chosen before their births, will enter Heaven; the others, no matter their goodness, piety, or deeds, are condemned (predestined) to Hell. Willie exults in thoughts of revenge toward the miserable souls who are doomed to such eternal torment. The victims over whom he gloats are, from the reader's point of view, far less deserving of hellfire than Willie, a hypocrite, lecher, and demon of wrath.

In the "Epistle to the Rev. John M'Math," Burns defends his own simple creed as one superior to self-styled "holy" Willie's: "God knows, I'm no the thing I should be,/ Nor am I even the thing I could be,/ But twenty times I rather would be/ An atheist clean/ Than under gospel colors hid be,/ Just for a screen." His argument, he avers, is not against a be-

nign doctrine of Christianity with its reach of forgiveness for sincerely repented sins, but against the hypocrites and scoundrels "even wi' holy robes,/ But hellish spirit!"

"IS THERE FOR HONEST POVERTY"

First published: 1795 (collected in *The Canongate Burns*, 2001)
Type of work: Poem

This celebrated democratic poem advances claims for the simple dignity of the common man over those for class and caste.

"Is There for Honest Poverty" (also sometimes anthologized under the title "For A' That and A' That") was written in 1794, printed in 1795, and reprinted in 1799. Burns adapted the meter and the phrase "for a' that" from older songs. A Jacobite song published in 1750 has the following chorus: "For a' that and a' that,/ And twice as muckle's a' that,/ He's far beyond the seas the night/ Yet he'll be here for a' that." Also, in "The Jolly Beggars," Burns had used the popular refrain, although in a different context.

Although the poem is clear enough in its general outline—that the honest worth of men of goodwill, no matter what their social class, rank, or financial condition, outweighs the pretensions of caste or privilege—readers often have trouble understanding Burns's elliptical phrasing. His argument is that "honest poverty" has greater worth than the false pride of high social position. Symbols of rank—ribbons, stars, "and all that"—are superfluities. True merit is based upon "sense and worth," the "pith o' sense, and pride o' worth," not upon the "tinsel show" of fine clothing or the pretentiousness of fine dining.

Because Burns wants his reader to grasp the implied meanings of his poem, he often omits logical connectives between ideas. The beginning lines, with suggested additions, may be paraphrased as follows: (What) is there for honest poverty, that it hangs its head and all that (meaning, all that humility, all that false shame because of supposedly low status)? People pass by the coward slave (who lacks the authentic dignity of self-esteem); people dare to be poor for all that (in spite of "all that" lowly position implied by people's poverty).

Throughout the poem, Burns invites the reader to participate in interpreting the poem. He wants the reader to understand the elliptical expression "and a' that" in terms of one's own experiences with the class system. As for Burns's point of view, that is unambiguous. He hopes that men and women of goodwill in time will unite, so that "man to man, the world o'er/ Shall brithers be for a' that!"

TAM O'SHANTER

First published: 1791 (collected in *The Canongate Burns*, 2001)

Type of work: Poem

In this sustained narrative poem, a drunken befuddled Scottish farmer encounters witches, but he survives.

"Tam O'Shanter" was a favorite with Burns, who described the work in a letter to Mrs. Dunlop (April 11, 1791): "I look on *Tam O'Shanter* to be my standard performance in the poetical line." He goes on to say that his "spice of roguish waggery" shows a "force of genius and a finishing polish that I despair of ever excelling." The idea for the story came from several legends popular in the neighborhood of the poet's birthplace, which is within a mile of Alloway Kirk (church). One of Burns's friends, Francis Grose, sent him a prose account of the legend, one upon which Burns probably drew. If a reader compares the flat style of Grose with Burns's jolly version, then he or she can better assess the poet's talent. The conclusion of Grose's narrative is as follows: "the unsightly tailless condition of the vigorous steed was, to the last hour of the noble creature's life, an awful warning to the Carrick farmers not to stay too late in Ayr markets." Burns's rendering is: "Now, wha this tale o' truth shall read,/ Each man and mother's son take heed;/ Or cutty-sarks run in your mind,/ Think! ye may buy the joys o'er dear;/ Remember Tam O'Shanter's mare."

Tam himself may have been based loosely upon the character of Douglas Graham, whose father was a tenant at the farm of Shanter on the Carrick shore. Noted for his habits of drunkenness, Graham was, like Burns's hero, afflicted with a scolding wife. According to D. Auld of Ayre (whose story was taken from notes left at the Edinburgh University Library), a local tradition held that once, while Graham was carousing at the tavern, some local humorists plucked hairs from the tail of his horse, tethered outside the tavern door, until it resembled a stump. As Auld's account has it, the locals swore the next morning that the unfortunate horse had its tail depilated by witches.

Burns's narrative is that oxymoron, a rollicking ghost story. With gentle, tolerant humor, the poet moralizes over the foibles of Tam, commiserates with his good wife, Kate, and philosophizes on the brevity of human happiness. Most of the narrative is perfectly clear to readers, so long as they follow notes on the Scottish words glossed from a well-edited text. The matter of the "cutty-sark," however, confuses some. Burns has in mind, first, the short skirt worn by the most audacious of the witches; then he refers to the witch herself, when Tam blurts out, "Weel done, Cutty-sark"—meaning the hag who dances wearing the clothing. At this point in the narrative, Tam upsets the witches' frolic dances, and witches and warlocks chase after the hard-riding Tam to the keystone of the bridge. Why cannot the witches pursue Tam over the bridge? Because they must not approach water, symbol of Christian baptism and grace. Nannie, leading the witches' riotous pursuit, therefore can grasp only at poor Meg's tail as the horse reaches the safety of the bridge. Horse and rider are saved, but not the tail. So ends, with an appropriate moral, Burns's homily on the dangers of "inspiring bold John Barlycorn"—hard alcohol.

SUMMARY

In his "Epistle to J. Lapraik," Robert Burns modestly denies any pretensions to the highest ranks of poetry: "I am nae poet, in a sense,/ But just a rhymer like by chance./ An' hae to learning nae pretence;/ Yet, what the matter?/ Whene'er my Muse does on me glance,/ I jingle at her." Critics who have taken these casual words seriously, as a valid expression of Burns's aesthetic, have done the poet an injustice. His artistry is by no means that of "jingling" rhymes. Burns is a thinking sentimentalist, a writer who combines rationality with passion. Even his sentimentality is usually controlled by wit, irony, or plain common sense, so that his love poetry not only seems genuine, it is indeed a genuine expression of the poet's larger love of freedom—freedom to live honestly and to love openly, without the constraints of religious bigotry, social prudery, or political subjugation. In his love of freedom, Burns remains—over the centuries—a defiant voice against hypocrisy and cant, against meanness of spirit. Through his art, he shows his readers that freedom is joyous.

Leslie B. Mittleman

BIBLIOGRAPHY

By the Author

POETRY:
Poems, Chiefly in the Scottish Dialect, 1786 (Kilmarnock edition), 1787 (Edinburgh edition), 1793 (2 volumes)
The Canongate Burns, 2001 (Andrew Nobel and Patrick Scott Hogg, editors)

NONFICTION:
Journal of a Tour in the Highlands Made in 1787, 1834 (Allan Cunningham, editor)
Journal of the Border Tour, 1834 (Cunningham, editor)
The Letters of Robert Burns, 1931 (2 volumes; John De Lancey Ferguson, editor)

About the Author
Bentman, Raymond. *Robert Burns.* Boston: Twayne, 1987.
Carruthers, Gerard. *Robert Burns.* Tavistock, Devon, England: Northcote House, 2006.
Crawford, Thomas. *Burns: A Study of the Poems and Songs.* Stanford, Calif.: Stanford University Press, 1960.
Daiches, David. *Robert Burns and His World.* London: Thames & Hudson, 1971.
Ferguson, John DeLancey. *Pride and Passion: Robert Burns, 1759-1796.* 1939. Reprint. New York: Russell & Russell, 1964.
Grimble, Ian. *Robert Burns: An Illustrated Biography.* New York: P. Bedrick Books, 1986.
Lindsay, John Maurice. *The Burns Encyclopaedia.* New York: St. Martin's Press, 1980.
McGuirk, Carol. *Robert Burns and the Sentimental Era.* Athens: University of Georgia Press, 1985.
_____, ed. *Critical Essays on Robert Burns.* New York: G. K. Hall, 1998.
McIlvanney, Liam. *Burns the Radical: Poetry and Politics in Late Eighteenth-Century Scotland.* East Linton, Scotland: Tuckwell, 2002.
Stewart, William. *Robert Burns and the Common People.* New York: Haskell House, 1971.

DISCUSSION TOPICS

- What poetic habits of the eighteenth century does "pre-Romantic" Robert Burns share?
- Cite a few instances of Burns's successful appropriation of already familiar poetic images.
- Offer examples of Burns's capacity for observation of small yet telling aspects of nature.
- Although Burns's songs do not require music, many have been set to music. What qualities make them so musical?
- Show how "Holy Willie's Prayer" is a satire not just of religious hypocrisy but also of Calvinism.
- Are Burns's moral lapses as noteworthy as literary historians have tended to make them?

A. S. Byatt

Courtesy, Teos

Born: Sheffield, South Yorkshire, England
August 24, 1936

Byatt has bridged the gap between literary academia and popular fiction by creating characters and situations that are plausible, compelling, and sympathetic, and raising critical questions about the roles of literature, science, and faith in the contemporary world.

BIOGRAPHY

Antonia Susan Drabble was the first child born to lawyer John Frederick and his homemaker wife Kathleen Marie Bloor. The couple had received a Cambridge education and remained avid readers, encouraging their children's intellectual pursuits. A. S. Byatt (BI-uht) and her sister, Margaret Drabble, both rewarded their parents with prominent literary careers.

Like her parents, Byatt began her studies at Cambridge, where she graduated with honors in 1957. She then pursued postgraduate work at Bryn Mawr College in the United States for a year before returning to England to begin her doctoral studies in early English literature at Oxford. However, her marriage to Ian Charles Rayner Byatt in 1959 forced her to abandon the traditional path to an academic degree, since married women were not permitted to hold scholarships.

To satisfy her intellectual interests, Byatt began teaching part time while maintaining her household and giving birth to two children, Antonia and Charles. She also continued writing fiction, a habit she had begun while a university student, despite pressure from her professors to focus on criticism to the exclusion of more creative endeavors.

The two novels she started while at Cambridge and Bryn Mawr were soon to be published as *Shadow of a Sun* (1964; also known as *The Shadow of the Sun*, 1993) and *The Game* (1967). Between the two, she produced a collection of critical essays, *Degrees of Freedom: The Novels of Iris Murdoch* (1965), an extended study of Murdoch's work. Murdoch remains a major influence on Byatt's writing, along with Elizabeth Bowen and George Eliot, two other novelists who paint with a fine brush. Throughout Byatt's career, she has alternated the publication of fictional works with her criticism, including such works as *Wordsworth and Coleridge in Their Time* (1970; republished as *Unruly Times*, 1989) and *Passions of the Mind: Selected Writings* (1991).

In 1969, Byatt divorced her first husband and married Peter John Duffy, a businessman. Her second marriage produced two more children, Isabel and Miranda, but in 1972 her only son was killed in a car accident. For nearly a decade, she buried herself in English instruction, working with students at a local college. Even after *The Virgin in the Garden* was published in 1978, Byatt could not bring herself to quit teaching. Not until 1983 would she become a full-time writer.

While Byatt's previous work had not been unsuccessful, *The Virgin in the Garden* announced her presence as a literary personality to be reckoned with. Its lush, dense imagery is interwoven with sophisticated speculation on the nature of history, art, and education. The first in a tetralogy, which would eventually include *Still Life* (1985), *Babel Tower* (1996), and *A Whistling Woman* (2002), *The Virgin in the Garden* introduces its readers to the Potter family, particularly Frederica, a precocious intellect and avid reader, much like Byatt herself.

However, it was with the appearance of *Possession* (1990) that Byatt became one of the most best-loved figures in contemporary British letters. A blend of genres and periods, *Possession* mixes the Victorian literary landscape with the contemporary world of letters. Throughout the novel, Byatt intersperses selections purportedly written by nineteenth century poets, including her own skillful imitations of Robert Browning and Christina Rossetti, as well as fairy tales, letters, and diaries of Byatt's own invention. The narrative relies upon the conventions of romance, detective, and crime fiction to keep readers fascinated by the sometimes dark, often boring, underbelly of academia. *Possession* proved just how powerful Byatt's vast literary knowledge could be when it was used to create a brilliantly told story.

In addition to being a best seller that was adapted as a motion picture, *Possession* garnered Byatt the title of Commander of the Order of the British Empire. In 1999, after several more novels, short stories, and works of criticism, including *Angels and Insects: Two Novellas* (1992), *Babel Tower,* and *Imagining Characters: Six Conversations About Women Writers* (1995), Byatt was made Dame Commander. She was also awarded an honorary doctorate of letters degree from Cambridge, her seventh such award.

ANALYSIS

Byatt's fiction frequently depicts conflicts, sometimes violent, between siblings, spouses, or parents and their children. These episodes have been interpreted autobiographically by many critics. In particular, her first two novels, *Shadow of a Sun* and *The Game*, portray female characters suffocated by the aura of jealous competition exuded by the powerful male personalities who dominate them. Her latter work also explores the sibling rivalry that develops when two sisters enjoy varying degrees of success in their literary careers. While these plotlines may or may not have arisen from her personal experience, when developed with Byatt's subtlety and grace, they suggest broader literary themes beyond mere biography.

Although her early work was no doubt drawn from personal experience, beginning with *The Virgin in the Garden*, Byatt proved that she was more concerned with technique than content. She is particularly fascinated by the ways in which words can be manipulated on the page, much as artists

place paint on canvas. *Still Life* and *The Matisse Stories* (1993) represent her most conscious efforts to develop this technique. In both, she meditates upon color and light to establish moods.

Her work also examines the conflicting roles that her female characters must either fulfill or reject. Frederica, the main character in a quartet of novels featuring the Potter family, must divide her efforts in *Babel Tower* between caring for her son, divorcing her abusive husband, exploring an intensely fulfilling sexual relationship with John Ottaker, and teaching night school for a local adult education program. Her need to perform each of these tasks to the best of her ability and her fear that she will not be able to do so finally force her to find a creative outlet for the divided selves she feels powerless to unite. Although she prefers the companionship of males, she finds solace in the domesticity of her female roommate, a single mother like herself. The two establish a sort of domestic partnership that permits them both to find personal satisfaction beyond merely domestic labor.

The process of reading and writing is central to Byatt's fiction, which often features poets and scholars, such as the avid reader Frederica Potter or the academics Maud Bailey and Roland Michell, who study Victorian poetry in *Possession*. Behind Byatt's many technical details lurks always her solitary question: What purpose does literature serve? Clearly, she herself has not developed a satisfactory answer, since she continues to provide her readers with so many possibilities.

The Victorian era likewise fascinates Byatt, and several of her works have been set in that period. Specifically, she treats the era's conflict between faith and science, primarily in response to Charles Darwin's publication of *On the Origin of Species by Means of Natural Selection* (1859). Randolph Ash, the poet being studied in *Possession*, and William Adamson from "Morpho Eugenia" in *Angels and Insects* both find creative ways to analyze the biology of the natural world. Other characters whom Byatt treats sympathetically, such as Stephanie Potter Orton (*The Virgin in the Garden*), Maud Bailey (*Possession*), and Emily Tennyson Jesse ("The Conjugial Angel" in *Angels and Insects*) seek a spiritual outlook toward their world that is not tied dogmatically to any specific religious framework.

Despite both critical and popular acclaim, Byatt's fiction is sometimes criticized for being too dense, implying that her rich tangle of metaphors and allusions is too obscure and intricate for her readers to appreciate. Like the Victorians she imitates, Byatt will occasionally interrupt the narrative with authorial reflections. Hers, however, take on a particularly postmodern tone as she reflects on her desire to articulate meaning in a way her readers will comprehend and on her fear that language may block her efforts. Reaction to these reflections has been mixed; some critics enjoy the postmodern revelation of the wizard behind the screen, while others find it distracting. However, her skill at shaping characters and plots leaves much for even the naïve reader to enjoy, while the scholarly reader can revel in the complexity of her style.

THE VIRGIN IN THE GARDEN

First published: 1978
Type of work: Novel

Blesford Ride School celebrates the coronation of England's new queen, while the Potter family experiences passion, both sexual and spiritual.

Denser and more complicated than Byatt's previous books, *The Virgin in the Garden* appeared after a long period of personal turmoil that resulted in a sort of literary rebirth. The novel's time line spans the 1952-1953 academic year at Blesford Ride, and it is the first of four novels that will trace the fortunes of the Potter family alongside those of post-World War II England. Fictionally, this is the year in which Stephanie marries, Frederica attains the grades that determine her college choices, and Marcus suffers a nervous breakdown. Historically, Queen Elizabeth II succeeds her father as reigning monarch and accepts the coronation. In Byatt's novel, however, both the Potter family and 1950's England witness the rise of a new monarch: sexual relations.

The Potter's oldest daughter Stephanie resists her attraction to clergyman Daniel Orton as a way of reaffirming the intellectual aspirations that have been lagging since she began teaching grammar school. The middle child Frederica would love nothing more than to be swept off her feet by

teacher and playwright, Alexander Wedderburn. Alex's play depicting the life of Queen Elizabeth I, intended to usher in the era of her namesake, serves as a focal point for much of the novel's action and permits Frederica and Alexander a greater degree of intimacy than is perhaps advisable. The young woman's innocence is reaffirmed, however, through her shock and surprise at Alex's ongoing affair with the wife of the German master, Jenny Parry, and through her obliviousness to the relations between instructor Thomas Poole and her own classmate, Anthea Warburton, although both situations cast their dismal shadow over Frederica's own escapades.

In the midst of these tensions—sexual, emotional, and intellectual—the youngest Potter child, Marcus, withdraws into a world of his own, mentored by Lucas Simmonds, the math teacher, and thus the antithesis to the children's father, William Potter, head of the English department. Marcus is an intuitive young man who visualizes a complex network of images and is thus able to solve complicated mathematical problems, until his intuition is subjected to scrutiny. In an attempt to quantify his gift, Simmonds runs the boy through exercises that would now be called paranormal studies, all the while insinuating himself into the boy's innermost world. Eventually, the teacher makes a sexual advance toward Marcus that causes the older man to attempt suicide and leads the younger to suffer a mental collapse.

As unique as each situation may be, all reflect a facet of the same gem: unconsummated desire. For despite the rampant atmosphere of sexual activity, what is most interesting is all the sex that is not taking place. Stephanie and Daniel, despite their attraction for one another, fumble through the physicality of their relationship hampered by their private emotional and intellectual burdens. Alex's lover grows increasingly frustrated with the discomforts of stolen love, and her frustration renders him unable to satisfy her. Frederica's fumbling advances to her teacher could almost be comical were there not such serious repercussions to the corresponding behavior of her classmates and siblings.

For all of the tension, Byatt acknowledges that virginity may offer its own rewards, as in the case of Queen Elizabeth I, who withheld her favors to maintain title and control of her country. In general, however, Byatt treats sexual innocence much like spiritual faith that has not been tested. Both create a tremendous amount of irritation and excitability, but despite all of their rich promise, both remain infertile and barren; hence, the paradox of her title.

However, while sexual desire translates on one plane to spirituality, on another it equates to literary criticism. The innocence of Frederica's body is in stark contrast with the experience of her mind. The girl inherited a keen textual eye from her father, and yet, lacking the creative experience that someone like Alex possesses, can she read responsibly? By posing this complex question, *The Virgin in the Garden* differs from Byatt's previous two novels, and she has now landed in the world of postmodernism.

The contemporary reader will necessarily approach a text with a certain amount of knowledge, very much like the brilliantly educated and wickedly smart Frederica. The contemporary author might, like Stephanie, feel some hesitation at imposing the seemingly arbitrary limits necessitated by the narrative framework, although few contemporary critics seem as hesitant as Marcus is to expose the patterns. It will remain to later novels for Byatt to determine whether the contemporary reader, trapped within a dense network of literary theory, can continue to exist in an innocent state or whether only a creative act of one's own will finally initiate the reader into a realm of knowledge commensurate with the author.

POSSESSION

First published: 1990
Type of work: Novel

Previously undiscovered letters between two Victorian poets spark an intense interest on both sides of the Atlantic that culminates in grave robbery and a shocking revelation.

Ironically, Byatt's most popular novel, *Possession* is also the one most deeply imbued with literary scholarship, even if the world of belles lettres provides setting and motivation rather than metaphor and imagery. *Possession* is also the novel that most fully displays Byatt's impressive stylistic range in a virtuoso performance that combines narrative genres, including romance, detective, and crime fiction with poetic imitations of Robert Browning and Christina Rossetti, as well as journals, diaries, and letters in voices ranging from Scottish to American.

The idea of possession dominates the novel from the first chapter, as Roland Michell, an academic struggling to churn out an interpretation of obscure Victorian poet Randolph Ash for James Blackadder's "Ash Factory," stumbles upon a letter in the British National Library and decides to pocket it. Blackadder himself has charted out his own intellectual territory in the basement of the British Museum, where he has effectively imprisoned any scholar who would study Randolph Ash under his purported advisement, a convenient position from which he can monitor their publications. His American counterpart, Leonora Stern, has staked a similar claim for Ash contemporary Christabel LaMotte. Fellow American Mortimer P. Cropper fancies himself an Ash scholar, having written his biography, but proceeds as though knowledge were a commodity, available to the highest bidder.

Possessed in one way or another by each of these forceful personalities, Maud Bailey, director of the Women's Resource Center and herself an established LaMotte scholar, resists the giving of herself, fearful of having to abandon her identity. Intellectually, Bailey has chosen a corner of the world where she can work collaboratively with other like-minded scholars, outside of the competition on which Blackadder and others appear to thrive. Approached sexually by both Leonora Stern and Roland Michell, she holds their desires at bay even as she negotiates a successful working relationship with them.

She does, however, allow herself to be possessed by the past, along with Michell. He approaches her with the letters, believing that her extensive knowledge of LaMotte might provide him with some answers. Together, they embark on a journey across England and backwards through time to the days

when Ash and LaMotte were apparently embarking on the same tenuous relationship now unfolding between the contemporary pair. As they read letters and diaries, soak in the local landscapes, and interview distant relatives, both scholars find themselves enchanted by a past they had never imagined. Within the poetry by the purportedly happily married Ash and the purportedly lesbian LaMotte the reader may glimpse only the most transparent outline of a connection, one that apparently lies behind the tortured silent secret of the journals kept by Ash's wife, Ellen, as well as the apparent suicide of LaMotte's life partner, Blanche Glover.

As the novel progresses and the evidence mounts, so, too, does the suspense. The intellectual and financial stakes rise, to the point where Mortimer Cropper illegally exhumes Ash's corpse in order to expose his affair with LaMotte and thus shake the foundation of Victorian studies down to its very core. In a heart-pounding scene, he is caught, rain-soaked and mud-covered, by Bailey, Michell, and a host of others, who are all now privy to the secrets of the grave. From a locked box within the coffin, it is revealed that all evidence of the affair belongs legally and rightfully to Maud Bailey as a direct descendent of Maia Thomasine Bailey, formerly believed to be LaMotte's niece, now shown to be the illegitimate child of Ash's affair with LaMotte.

Maud learns to let down the glorious blond hair that proclaims her lineage and her desirability. She and Michell discover an equal partnership, while he abandons the world of academia to pursue his

own poetic talents. In an epilogue, Byatt concludes the story with the one aspect of it that could not be possessed: an individual's memory of an experience. Once upon a time, Ash met his daughter, who told him she wanted to be called May and that she did not care for poetry. He clipped a lock of her hair, and it was her braid that was buried with him, not LaMotte's, as had been supposed.

While the characters in the novel remain ignorant of this truth, Byatt's readers know the tale, and the irony of its inclusion forces them to question whether anything—artistic endeavors, personal identity, or familial relationships—can exist in this world without being public property. The epilogue, along with much else in the book, forces readers to question their own knowledge and assumptions, a task symbolized by Roland Michell. Initially engaged in an erudite quest to understand the influence of an obscure Enlightenment philosopher upon Ash's poem "Prosperina," by novel's end Michell is freed from the weight of the written record and able to approach literature with some self-assurance in his own power as both reader and author.

ANGELS AND INSECTS

First published: 1992
Type of work: Novellas

Two novellas explore nineteenth century attitudes toward science and spirituality as they reveal the passions by which the characters live, regardless of cultural standards or norms.

Angels and Insects consists of two novellas, "Morpho Eugenia" and "The Conjugial Angel," both of which are set in Victorian England just after mid-century, leading to speculation that the book continues several themes Byatt had left undeveloped in her earlier novel *Possession*. It would seem that the first story explores the scientific questions of the day while the second wrestles with the spiritual, but Byatt resists such neat thematic divides. The laboratory of Bredely Hall in the first novella resonates with the spiritual implications of Darwin's theory of natural selection, while in the second novella, sound scientific arguments are proffered in the living room of Tennyson's sister for the séances held there, thus twining the two themes together in a sort of Gordian knot.

The *Morpho Eugenia* is a species of exotic butterfly, one of the few relics salvaged by William Adamson when he was shipwrecked on his return from the Amazon. The Alabaster home seems to offer him a rebirth in a modern Garden of Eden. The father, Harald Alabaster, offers to support Adamson's research, while the two oldest boys spend their days on horseback, and three beautiful and eligible daughters are paraded before him. The most perfectly formed of these is also a Eugenia. In a dazzling scene, Adamson proposes to her in the family greenhouse as millions of live butterflies swirl around them.

Happily married, Adamson explores the land around the manor with the family's younger children and their governess, Mattie Crompton. Mattie's journals surprise him with her keen observations on the social behaviors of the insects they observe, much like those that keep Bredely Hall running with such precision, such as the daily efforts of the servants to dump the rat carcasses that collect in the kitchen. Meanwhile, Adamson's wife provides him with five new specimens to add to his collection: a son and four daughters.

Slowly, however, the knowledge dawns on Adamson that his real inheritance in England is not paradise, but the one gift shared by all of Adam's sons: the flawed nature of nature. Original sin, in its most primal state, revisits the household in the incestuous relationship maintained by Eugenia and her half brother, Edgar. William and Mattie use the earnings from their publications to escape beyond the smooth surface of the Alabaster household back to the Amazon world of the noble savage.

The characters in "The Conjugial Angel" are also searching for an escape of sorts. Through the séances they conduct, they hope to find answers to their most painful questions from the world beyond. Lilias Papagay, who literally lost her husband more than two decades ago when he set out to sea and never returned, invokes the spiritual plane through automatic writing, the receipt of messages from dead spirits. She works with her roommate, Sophy Sheekhy, a medium who has been plagued since her youth by visions of the dead. Together, they lead séances for Mrs. Hearnshaw, a desperate mother whose children have all died in infancy; Mr. Hawke, a spiritual "dabbler"; and for Captain and Mrs. Jesse.

Mrs. Jesse, formerly Emily Tennyson, had been engaged in her youth to Arthur Hallam, the best friend of her brother, Alfred, Lord Tennyson, who was historically the preeminent poet of the Victorian age. Alfred's grief over his friend's death is famously recorded in his seminal work, *In Memoriam* (1850). The poem makes him beloved of the British people but leaves Mrs. Jesse feeling as though her own process of mourning has been overshadowed. She hosts the séances, hoping to hear from Arthur, but when she finally does, she rejects his invitation to join with him after their death in the form of one Conjugial Angel, choosing instead the husband who comforted her in her long years of grief.

SUMMARY

Despite the occasional criticism for her weighty style, A. S. Byatt's dense, literary imagery, rich metaphors, and erudite store of knowledge balance beautifully with her engaging story lines and compelling characters, ensuring her a place not only among the best-selling authors but also within the world of academia. Always mindful of her responsibility as an author to remain true to her characters and to construct plots and situations only within the bounds of the plausible, she does not hesitate to remind her readers of the onus placed upon them to explore to the fullest potential of their own ingenuity as they interpret her work.

Byatt's firm convictions on topics ranging from female equality to the human craving for spirituality and creativity, when coupled with her vast imagination, find a passionate outpouring in language as visual, tactile, and otherwise sensorial as ink on a page can ever be. Notwithstanding her Victorian settings and characters, the questions she poses about faith and science, art and math, man and woman, will not be resolved for many hundreds of years to come.

L. Michelle Baker

BIBLIOGRAPHY

By the Author

LONG FICTION:

Shadow of a Sun, 1964 (also known as *The Shadow of the Sun,* 1993)
The Game, 1967
The Virgin in the Garden, 1978
Still Life, 1985
Possession, 1990
Angels and Insects: Two Novellas, 1992
Babel Tower, 1996
The Biographer's Tale, 2000
A Whistling Woman, 2002

SHORT FICTION:

Sugar, and Other Stories, 1987
The Matisse Stories, 1993
The Djinn in the Nightingale's Eye: Five Fairy Stories, 1997
Elementals: Stories of Fire and Ice, 1998
Little Black Book of Stories, 2003

NONFICTION:

Degrees of Freedom: The Novels of Iris Murdoch, 1965
Wordsworth and Coleridge in Their Time, 1970 (republished as *Unruly Times,* 1989)
Iris Murdoch, 1976
Passions of the Mind: Selected Writings, 1991
Imagining Characters: Six Conversations About Women Writers, 1995 (with Ignês Sodré)
On Histories and Stories: Selected Essays, 2000
Portraits in Fiction, 2001

EDITED TEXTS:

The Mill on the Floss, 1979 (by George Eliot)
Selected Essays, Poems, and Other Writings, 1989 (by Eliot)
Dramatic Monologues, 1990 (by Robert Browning)
The Oxford Book of English Short Stories, 1998

MISCELLANEOUS:

Vintage Byatt, 2004

DISCUSSION TOPICS

- What does A. S. Byatt define as a healthy balance between career success and emotional fulfillment for women?

- What does Byatt believe is the role of religion in contemporary culture? What distinctions does she draw between religion and faith, or spirituality?

- What themes are common to the two novellas in *Angels and Insects*?

- Identify a scene in either "Morpho Eugenia" or "The Conjugial Angel" that you believe is implausible. Justify its inclusion in or state how it detracts from the story.

- What solace do the characters in *The Virgin in the Garden* find in various types of artistic expression? Does Byatt appear to favor one creative endeavor, such as painting, over another, such as literature?

About the Author

Franken, Christien. *A. S. Byatt: Art, Authorship, Creativity.* Basingstoke, England: Palgrave, 2001.
Kelly, Kathleen Coyne. *A. S. Byatt.* New York: Twayne, 1996.
Parris, P. B., and Caryn McTighe Musil. "A. S. Byatt." In *British Novelists Since 1960: Second Series.* Vol. 194 in *Dictionary of Literary Biography.* Detroit: Thomson Gale, 1998.
Pereira, Margarida Estevez. "More than Words: The Elusive Language of A. S. Byatt's Visual Fiction." In *Writing and Seeing: Essays on Word and Image,* edited by Rui Carvalho Homem. Amsterdam: Rodopi, 2006.
Todd, Richard. *A. S. Byatt.* Plymouth, England: Northcote House, with British Council, 1997.
Walker, Jonathan. "An Interview with A. S. Byatt and Lawrence Norfolk." *Contemporary Literature* 47, no. 3 (Fall, 2006): 323-342.

LORD BYRON

Born: London, England
January 22, 1788
Died: Missolonghi, Greece
April 19, 1824

One of the major English Romantic poets, Byron, as satirist and as creator of the Romantic figure the "Byronic hero," also had a significant impact on nineteenth century European culture.

Library of Congress

BIOGRAPHY

George Gordon, later to become the sixth Lord Byron, was born January 22, 1788, in London, England, the son of Captain John "Mad Jack" Byron and Catherine Gordon of Gight, Scotland. Catherine was heiress to a small fortune, which her husband soon squandered. After the couple fled from creditors to France, Catherine left her philandering husband and moved to London. George Gordon was born with a clubbed right foot, an ailment that caused him much humiliation throughout his life but for which he attempted to compensate through athletic endeavors. The Byrons soon moved to Aberdeen, where Catherine could better afford to live on her modest allowance. Captain Byron died in France in 1791 at the age of thirty-six. His son would die at the same age.

After years of attending grammar schools in Aberdeen, George Gordon became the sixth Lord Byron upon the death of his granduncle in 1798. He moved to Newstead Abbey, Nottinghamshire, the Byron family seat, and the Byrons' lifestyle changed considerably. From 1801 to 1805, young Byron attended Harrow School, spending his vacations with his mother, who was alternately abusive and tender. In 1804, he began a correspondence with his half sister, Augusta Leigh, from whom he had been living separately since his infancy, thus

forming a close and complicated relationship that outlasted many others and that became the source of considerable scandal, in part accounting for the failure of his marriage and in part prompting Byron's self-exile to Europe. Entering Trinity College, Cambridge, in 1805, Byron formed other lasting alliances, most notably those of his dear friends John Cam Hobhouse and John Edleston. It was during this time that Byron began to form his ideals of the sanctity of political and personal liberty. In 1807, he published a volume of poems, *Hours of Idleness*, which was attacked in the *Edinburgh Review* An undistinguished student, Byron left Cambridge in 1808 with a master's degree.

In 1809, Byron took his seat in the House of Lords, often supporting liberal, unpopular causes. In this year, he also discovered and exploited his unrivaled knack for satire, publishing *English Bards and Scotch Reviewers*, in which he lashed out at the *Edinburgh Review* and criticized contemporaries Robert Southey, William Wordsworth, and others of the "Lake School" of poetry. Later in 1809, Byron left with his friend Hobhouse on a tour, not the customary Grand Tour of Western Europe, but a tour of Portugal, Spain, Albania, and Greece. This trip inspired him to begin *Childe Harold's Pilgrimage* (1812-1818; 1819), and he finished the first canto in Athens. In 1810, Byron finished the second canto of *Childe Harold's Pilgrimage*, traveling further in Turkey and Greece. Inspired by the Ovidian story of Hero and Leander, he swam the Hellespont on May 3, 1810, an accomplishment of which he boasted in a poem "Written After Swimming from Sestos to Abydos." He returned to England in

429

1811, shortly before his mother's death. Despite her unstable and often cruel treatment of him, the son mourned her loss, which was closely followed by the loss of two school friends.

In 1812, *Childe Harold's Pilgrimage* was published. "I awoke one morning and found myself famous," Byron wrote. Byron's fame, his extraordinary personal beauty, and the intriguing, dangerous image created by the public's insistence upon confusing the character of Harold with Byron himself attracted the attention of many women, and he engaged in numerous indiscreet affairs, notably with Lady Caroline Lamb, whose obsession with him would provoke him to escape into an ill-suited marriage with Annabella Milbanke in 1815. Meanwhile, in 1813, Byron also began an affair with Augusta Leigh, his half sister; he also published the first of his Oriental tales, *The Giaour* and *The Bride of Abydos*, and in the following year he published *The Corsair* and *Lara*. Annabella, who was intellectual but priggish, was frightened and appalled by Byron's cruelty, his sexual and behavioral eccentricities, and his excessive attention to Augusta. Seriously doubting his sanity, Lady Byron left her husband after only a year of marriage, taking their only daughter, Augusta Ada. In April of 1816, Byron again left England, this time never to return.

Byron spent the summer of 1816 in Switzerland with Percy Bysshe Shelley, the Romantic poet, Mary Godwin (later known as Mary Wollstonecraft Shelley, the author of *Frankenstein*, 1818), and her stepsister, Jane "Claire" Clairmont, with whom Byron had had a brief affair in England. He traveled some more through Italy and Switzerland with Hobhouse and published canto 3 of *Childe Harold's Pilgrimage* and *The Prisoner of Chillon, and Other Poems* (1816). The trip through the Alps inspired him to begin his verse play *Manfred* (pb. 1817, pr. 1834), the darkest treatment of his "Byronic hero." In 1817, Claire Clairmont and Byron had a daughter, Allegra. Byron spent most of 1817 traveling and living in Venice and other parts of Italy, completing *Manfred* and working on the fourth and final cantos of *Childe Harold's Pilgrimage*. It was also during this time that Byron luckily discovered the Italian poetic form of *ottava rima*, with which he experimented in writing *Beppo: A Venetian Story* (1818), a comic tale set in Venice.

In 1818, Byron began *Don Juan* (1819-1824; 1826). In 1819, he began his last major love affair, with Teresa, Countess of Guiccioli. The first two cantos of *Don Juan* were published in July, 1819. Public reception was one of outrage and cries of indecency and slander. In 1820, Byron lived in the Guiccioli palace in Ravenna, Italy, and wrote *Marino Faliero, Doge of Venice* (pr., pb. 1821), the first of his political dramas based on the five-part classical models. After the pope permitted Teresa's legal separation from her husband, Byron became more closely involved with her family's political activities, most significantly with the radical society known as the Carbonari, who conspired to revolt against Austrian dominance in Italy. This struggle was unsuccessful, and in 1821 the family was exiled to Pisa. Byron then turned his attention to the Greek cause of independence from Turkey.

In 1821, Byron also published *Cain: A Mystery* (pb. 1821) and cantos 3 through 5 of *Don Juan*, which, amid continued public disapproval, enjoyed tremendous sales. Joining Teresa and her family in Pisa, Byron was the source of extensive scandal back in England, and his friends, though admiring his genius, became increasingly concerned and admonishing about the license of his work. Disgusted with his publisher's reluctance to publish *Cain*, Byron changed publishers, allowing John Hunt to include *The Vision of Judgment* (1822) in the first issue of the literary journal *The Liberal*. In 1822, Byron mourned the death of both his daughter, Allegra, and his close friend Percy Bysshe Shelley. In 1823, Byron left for Greece with Teresa's brother, Pietro Gamba. He soon became severely ill, but left for Missolonghi, Greece, convinced of its strategic importance in the revolution. John Hunt published *Don Juan*, cantos 6 through 16. On his thirty-sixth birthday, Byron wrote "On This Day I Complete My Thirty-sixth Year." In Missolonghi, on April 19, 1824, Byron died, to this day a national hero in Greece. Denied burial with fellow great poets in Westminster Abbey because of his profligate lifestyle, Byron's body is buried in the family vault at Hucknall Torkard Church in Nottinghamshire, near Newstead.

ANALYSIS

Byron's popularity has not always corresponded to his critical appraisal. He stands apart from his fellow Romantic poets—William Wordsworth, Samuel Taylor Coleridge, Percy Bysshe Shelley, and John Keats—in his stubborn reverence for the poetic style of Restoration and Augustan writers such as John Dryden and Alexander Pope. Indeed, it was the eighteenth century propensity for wit and satire that was also Byron's forte. It is ironic, then, that Byron is in many ways considered to represent the epitome of the Romantic figure. Both personally and in many of his dark, tormented Romantic heroes, Byron created a cultural icon that had a significant impact on his society and the literary movement of his time, though it must be noted that, although the Byronic hero is certainly in part autobiographical, it represents only one aspect of a complex personality.

Perhaps the salient characteristic of Byron's work that assures his label as a consummate Romantic is his creation of the so-called Byronic hero. This character type appears in many variations in Byron's works but is generally based on such literary characters as Prometheus, John Milton's Satan, Johann Wolfgang von Goethe's Faust, and many popular sentimental heroes of the age—and, of course, on Byron himself. Though there are variations on this type—Harold, Cain, Manfred, the Giaour, Lara, Selim, and others—generally, the Byronic hero is a melancholy man of great and noble principles, with great courage of his convictions, and haunted by some secret past sin—usually a sin of illicit love, occasionally suggested to be incestuous. He is alienated, proud, and driven by his own turbulent passion.

Recurrent themes in Byron's work can be said to be subsumed under the larger category of nature versus civilization. Political oppression, military aggression, sexual repression, even the superficial restraints of a frivolous, silly English society—all go against the Romantic aspiration that Byron sees as inherent in human nature, and such oppression always yields disastrous results.

Byron, who appears to have had an almost innate love of liberty, was exposed in his extensive travels to markedly diverse cultures and experiences, thus giving him a unique perspective (and certainly a broader one than his contemporaries) on human nature and civilization. Witnessing the ravages of war, the demoralization of political oppression, and the violence of prejudice and hypocrisy particularly afforded Byron a rare insight into the weaknesses of his own English society. These political and societal flaws Byron exposed in many of his works, particularly in *Childe Harold's Pilgrim-*

age, Don Juan, and *The Vision of Judgment,* at the risk of great public disapproval and alienation and at great personal cost. The extent and the exotic nature of Byron's travels, in addition to his vivid descriptions of his experiences and his retelling of colorful folktales, additionally account for much of the popularity of Byron's works. His accounts of the virtually unexplored, mysterious land of Albania, for example, captivated the imagination of his insular English readers.

A common theme in Byron's work is certainly that of love in its many manifestations: illicit love, idyllic love, sexual repression, sexual decadence, thwarted love, marriage. Yet in all of its variations, this theme, too, is one of civilization and the discontentment it creates when it denies natural expressions of love. Probably the most touching of Byron's love stories is that of Don Juan and Haidee in canto 1 of *Don Juan.* The affair is innocent, natural, primitive, and therefore by society's standards immoral and unsanctified. Similarly, Don Juan's lack of proper sex education, despite his mother's otherwise vigorous intellectual rigors, in denying what is natural and inevitable, ironically destroys lives.

Byron also repeatedly rails against tyranny and political oppression of any kind. The recent turn of events resulting from the French Revolution and the despotic reign of Napoleon I, all of which in the beginning offered such promise, provided Byron with much fodder for condemning such acts of aggression. Yet in war Byron finds inspiration in those who fight to retain or protect their freedoms. His knowledge of political and military history—European, American, Asian, Mediterranean—was vast, his understanding profound.

Byron was a versatile poet, if not always an accomplished one. In addition to skillfully and poignantly handled romantic lyrics such as "She Walks in Beauty," "When We Two Parted," and the more famous epics, *Childe Harold's Pilgrimage* and *Don Juan,* Byron also completed lyrical dramas, a number of popular exotic and romantic tales, and satirical works on the literary and political foibles of his time. In terms of both style and structure, his indebtedness to his eighteenth century heroes Dryden and Pope has been given much critical attention. His philosophical and literary faith lay more in reason than in emotion; his preferred delivery was more often one of wit and satire than sentiment and self-indulgence.

CHILDE HAROLD'S PILGRIMAGE

First published: Cantos 1 and 2, 1812; canto 3, 1816; canto 4, 1818; the four cantos published together, 1819

Type of work: Poem

Attempting to escape the pangs of guilt resulting from his mysterious past, self-exiled Childe Harold flees to Europe and witnesses the beauties and horrors of other cultures.

Byron began *Childe Harold's Pilgrimage* on his first trip abroad, when he and Hobhouse toured Spain, Portugal, Albania, and Greece. It was originally titled *"Childe Burun"*; "Childe" refers to a young nobleman who has not yet officially taken his title, and "Burun" is an earlier form of Byron's own name. Inspired by his recent reading of Edmund Spenser's *The Faerie Queene* (1590, 1596), Byron chose to employ the nine-line Spenserian stanza for the major part of this work.

The first two cantos were published in 1812, and Byron's ensuing popularity among the social and literary circles of London was unprecedented, in part because the public insisted—with some accuracy and despite Byron's prefatory disclaimer to the contrary—upon identifying the intriguing Harold as Byron himself. Byron's own confusion of the two, however, is evident in his frequent dropping of the story line of the work to engage in repeated authorial digressions, which themselves intrude on the almost gratuitous plot. Harold is a young, though not inexperienced, Englishman who is compelled to flee Britain, although, the reader is told, it is in fact his own psyche he is trying to escape. The young man has a mysterious background, an unspeakably painful secret in his past. Perhaps, it is suggested, the secret is of some illicit love. With Harold, Byron introduces the first of his many Byronic heroes.

In canto 1, Harold leaves England, having lived a life of sensuous indulgence. He bids farewell to no friends or family, not even to his mother and sister, although he loves them both deeply. Landing in Portugal, Harold proceeds to visit various battlegrounds across Europe, thus giving Byron as narrator the opportunity to digress on historical,

political, and even moral issues of the recent Peninsular War in which England served to help the Spanish resist the French invasion, an event that portended the end of Napoleon I's tyranny. As he looks upon the towns that were devastated by Napoleon's army, Byron laments the loss of life and champions those who nobly fought for the preservation of liberty. Byron praises the courageous women of the Spanish province of Aragon who joined the men in resisting an invading French army. Though these women were not trained to be warriors, like the mythological Amazons, but were taught to love, they nevertheless proved themselves to be strong and brave; thus, Byron suggests, they emerge far more beautiful than the women of other countries such as England.

In Spain, Harold witnesses a Sunday bullfight in one of the most famous passages from *Childe Harold's Pilgrimage*, in which Byron is clearly at the same time fascinated and repelled by this violent yet graceful sport. Though Harold is moved by the beauty and song of the festivities around him, he cannot participate, for his pain alienates him from the joys of human activity. He remains a spectator. Singing a ballad, "To Inez," Harold mourns the futility of running away when it is his own "secret woe" that he is attempting to escape. Comparing himself to the "Wandering Jew" of medieval legend who, having mocked Christ, is doomed to roam the earth eternally, seeking the peace of death, Harold bemoans the "hell" that lies hidden in the human heart.

Canto 2 opens with a meditation upon the contributions of classical Greece, a salute prompted by Harold's visit to the Acropolis. As Harold views the ruins of Greece's high achievements, Byron interprets them as reflections of the present loss of Greek freedom, thus foreshadowing his later involvement in the cause of Greek independence. Descriptions of the mysterious land of Albania in this canto represent one of the earliest authentic representations of this exotic country by an Englishman.

Canto 3 begins with Byron sadly recalling his daughter, Ada, whom he has not seen since the breakup of his marriage. Byron returns to the story of Harold, first warning readers that the young hero has greatly changed since the publication of the first two cantos. During the interim, Byron has endured the painful separation and the scandal concerning his relationship with Augusta, all of which essentially forced him to leave England. His bitterness is evident in the far darker tone of canto 3, and the character of Harold and that of the narrator, never strikingly different in temperament, now are more clearly merged.

Still unable to completely detach himself from feeling the pangs of human compassion, Harold flees to the solitude of natural surroundings, finding nature to be the one true consoler. He feels a communication with the desert, the forest, the ocean, the mountains. Finding Harold at the site of the Battle of Waterloo, "the grave of France," Byron resumes the theme of Napoleon's despotism and takes the opportunity to examine tyranny in general. Praising the heroes of that fateful and momentous battle, Byron blames Napoleon's extremism, arguing that moderation would have prevented the disastrous results of a once noble plan. Harold then travels to Germany, where he still is not immune to feelings of love and joy, however fleeting.

Visiting the Swiss Alps leads Harold to the sites of other battles. Lake Leman (Lake Geneva) recalls to Byron the great French philosopher Jean-Jacques Rousseau, one of the forerunners of the Romantic movement. This section, it has often been noted, has a distinctly Shelleyan mood, and indeed Byron wrote it while visiting Percy Bysshe Shelley. Byron explores the pantheistic philosophies of William Wordsworth, Shelley, and Rousseau and expresses feelings of oneness with nature, though he ultimately rejects their ideas. These feelings, furthermore, lead him to consider his feelings of alienation in the world of humankind. Insisting that he is neither cynical nor completely disillusioned, Byron insists that he believes that there are one or two people who are "almost what they seem" and that happiness and goodness are possible. Byron concludes the canto as he begins it, lamenting his absence from Ada, imagining what it would be like to share in her development, to watch her grow.

Canto 4 takes Harold to Italy, at first to Venice, decaying yet still beautiful because its spirit is immortal. Byron confesses that he still has some love for his native country and that he hopes that he will be remembered there. If he dies on foreign soil, he confesses, his spirit will return to England. The canto concludes with Byron's famous apostrophe, or address, to the ocean.

DON JUAN

First published: Cantos 1 and 2, 1819; cantos 3 through 5, 1821; cantos 6 through 14, 1823; cantos 15 and 16, 1824; the 16 cantos published together, 1826

Type of work: Poem

Forced to flee his homeland, the ingenuous Spanish rogue finds love, tragedy, violence, hypocrisy, and wisdom on his world travels.

Don Juan is a unique approach to the already popular legend of the philandering womanizer immortalized in literary and operatic works. Byron's Don Juan, the name comically anglicized to rhyme with "new one" and "true one," is a passive character, in many ways a victim of predatory women, and more of a picaresque hero in his unwitting roguishness. Not only is he not the seductive, ruthless Don Juan of legend, he is also not a Byronic hero. That role falls more to the narrator of the comic epic, the two characters being more clearly distinguished than in Byron's *Childe Harold's Pilgrimage*.

In *Beppo: A Venetian Story*, Byron discovered the appropriateness of *ottava rima* to his own particular style and literary needs. This Italian stanzaic form had been exploited in the burlesque tales of Luigi Pulci, Francesco Berni, and Giovanni Battista Casti, but it was John Hookham Frere's (1817-1818) that revealed to Byron the seriocomic potential for this flexible form in the satirical piece he was planning. The colloquial, conversational style of *ottava rima* worked well with both the narrative line of Byron's mock epic and the serious digressions in which Byron rails against tyranny, hypocrisy, cant, sexual repression, and literary mercenaries.

Byron opens *Don Juan* with a dedication to his old nemesis, Robert Southey, who was at the time poet laureate. Byron hated Southey for his turncoat politics, for his spreading of rumors about Byron, and for his weak verse. The publication of the first two cantos in 1818 created scandal and outrage for the author. Although the names of publisher and author did not appear on the title page, Byron's identity was unmistakable. Even Byron's friends—Hobhouse and others—though admiring the genius of the work, were shocked and concerned about its language and content. The invectives against contemporaneous writers and against Lady Byron smacked of slander; his comments on political and theological issues bordered on sedition and blasphemy. Byron, arguing that this was in fact "the most moral of poems," remained steadfast against editing and censoring. The work, however, also received significant critical praise from such noteworthy giants as Percy Bysshe Shelley, German poet Johann Wolfgang von Goethe, and John Gibson Lockhart (Sir Walter Scott's son-in-law, writing under the pen name of "John Bull"). Byron found much strength and determination in these encouragements.

Byron's avowed purpose in *Don Juan* was to be "quietly facetious on everything." The narrative opens with sixteen-year-old naïf Don Juan, who innocently falls in love with Dona Julia, the young wife of Don Alfonso, a gentleman of fifty who has been linked romantically with Juan's mother, Dona Inez. Although Byron's poem is "epic" and he promises to observe the epic conventions of Aristotle and the classical authors, his hero is modern, of ordinary proportions and weaknesses. The plot

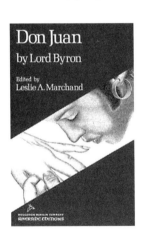

follows a line of at times almost stock farce, the lovers being discovered by Alfonso's spotting Juan's shoes under Julia's bed. At the end of the canto, Juan must flee Spain, the divorced Julia enters a convent, and the picaresque adventures of the young hero begin. Byron's narrator takes the opportunity during the story to comment on love, education, and marriage.

Juan is shipwrecked in canto 2 and, after a shocking encounter with cannibalism, is washed ashore in the Greek Cyclades and is rescued by the beautiful maiden, Haidee, with whom he shares an idyllic love in canto 3 until her pirate father, Lambro, returns in canto 4 and Juan is sold into Turkish slavery. Haidee dies of a broken heart. The Haidee passage is one of Byron's most poignant, his depiction of innocent love thwarted by exter-

nal, evil forces one of his most touching. Canto 5 finds Juan accompanied and befriended by Johnson, an English soldier of fortune, and the two are bought by a black eunuch who dresses Juan in women's clothes and takes him to the harem queen, Gulbayez, whose advances Juan rejects in deference to Haidee's memory. In canto 6, however, Juan spends a sensuous and loving night in the harem with Lolah, Katinka, Dudu, and the other odalisques but is unfortunately sentenced to death in the morning.

The epic takes on a more serious tone with cantos 7 and 8, in large part as a result of the significant changes in Byron's own life since the publication of the previous cantos. Juan and Johnson, who have managed to escape, join the Russian army, and Byron vehemently condemns war and military aggression. In cantos 9 and 10, Juan, now a war hero, meets Catherine the Great, who sends him to England. In the remaining cantos, 11 to 16, Byron satirizes English society. As a guest at the country estate of Lord Henry Amundeville, Norman Abbey (based on Byron's own Newstead Abbey), Juan is pursued by three women: Lord Henry's wife, the sophisticated and intellectual but self-centered Lady Adeline; the mysterious, gracious, graceful Countess Fitz-Fulke; and the silent but emotionally deep Aurora Raby. Much of the final canto concerns a social gathering and the identity of the mysterious ghost of the Black Friar, whom Juan sees at night.

At the time of his death in 1824, Byron was still working on *Don Juan* but had completed only a fragment of canto 17, which does not continue the story line.

THE PRISONER OF CHILLON

First published: 1816
Type of work: Poem

Imprisoned for religious and democratic sentiments, a priest watches his brothers die beside him but is inspired by a songbird and his own strong spirit.

The Prisoner of Chillon is a dramatic monologue written after Byron and Shelley visited the Castle of

Chillon in Switzerland, where a priest, François Bonivard, was imprisoned for six years for expressing democratic ideals rooted in his religious doctrine. Impressed by Bonivard's courageous and principled struggle against the cruelty and tyranny of his captors, Byron used the story to comment further on his already characteristic themes of isolation, liberty, oppression, and conviction.

The poem opens with the "Sonnet on Chillon," which reveals, both in content and in style, the influence of Shelley on Byron's work and thought at this time in his career. Byron celebrates the site of Bonivard's imprisonment as consecrated ground, and he praises in exalted and idealistic tones the futility of attempts to constrict the true and free spirit.

The remainder of the poem is told from the first-person perspective of Bonivard himself. Although Byron deviates somewhat from the historical record, this poem represents the first example of Byron using a real person as his protagonist. Bonivard's father and five of his brothers have already perished as a result of this persecution of their faith. Two of them were imprisoned with Bonivard: the youngest brother, sweet of disposition, with tears only for the pain of others; the older brother an active man, strong and courageous. Both of the brothers died while the three of them were chained to huge pillars in the dark Gothic dungeon. Alone and the last survivor of his family, Bonivard then fell into a deep despair, his senses dulled, losing any concept of time, unaware of darkness or light.

In an almost conventional Romantic moment, Bonivard's despair is interrupted by the arrival of a songbird. The prisoner speculates, with the last vestiges of optimism, that the bird may also have been imprisoned in a cage and has managed to escape. Perhaps, he speculates, the bird might in fact be his brother's soul visiting him with messages of hope. When the bird flies away, however, Bonivard feels more alone than ever. Yet miraculously, his captors begin to treat him with more compassion, allowing him to walk around in his cell unchained. He climbs up the wall, not to try to escape but merely to get a glimpse through the barred windows of the mountains once again. The beauty of this sight again makes his imprisonment seem even more unbearable. After an indeterminate length of time—days, months, even years—Bonivard is released.

The freedom is a hollow victory, however, since he has lost all that is dear to him, and he had come to consider the prison his home. Even the chains and the spiders seemed to be his friends.

THE VISION OF JUDGMENT

First published: 1822
Type of work: Poem

Upon the death of King George III, Satan and the Archangel Michael debate over possession of the tyrant's soul.

Byron had already mocked Robert Southey in *English Bards and Scotch Reviewers* (1809) and in his dedication to *Don Juan*, but his ridicule of Southey is at its pinnacle in *The Vision of Judgment*. Byron hated Southey for many reasons. He disapproved of the poetry of Southey and even the greater "Lake School" poets, William Wordsworth and Samuel Taylor Coleridge. He also resented Southey's turn to conservatism later in life, marked by his being made poet laureate in 1813. Moreover, Southey had spread vicious rumors about Byron's personal life. Upon the death of King George III, Southey, in his role as poet laureate, wrote a sycophantic celebration of George's glorious entry into heaven, *A Vision of Judgment* (1821). In this work, Southey lashed out at Byron, ascribing him to the "Satanic" school. Byron retorted with *The Vision of Judgment*. John Murray, Byron's publisher, was becoming increasingly fearful of the British disapproval of Byron's work, so Byron published the poem in the new literary journal *The Liberal*, edited by Byron and John Hunt, later Byron's new publisher.

In Byron's poem, Saint Peter waits, bored, by the gates of Heaven, his keys rusty and the lock dull with disuse. The angels have nothing to do but sing. Only the angel who records the names of souls lost to hell is overworked, even requesting additional help. Satan is so busy that his thirst for evil is almost quenched. The death of George III brings hypocritical mourning on earth, people drawn to the pomp without really caring about him. Upon hearing that King George III has died, Saint Peter recalls that the last royal entry into Heaven was by the beheaded King Louis XVI, who was admitted as a martyr by playing on the sympathy of the saints.

While the Archangel Michael and Satan debate over who will get the soul of George III, witnesses are called. These include one who praises George, obviously to flatter him, and the anonymous letter writer known as "Junius" who criticized George and who refuses to recant his writings. Then Southey arrives and starts to recite his *A Vision of Judgment*. By the fourth line, the angels and devils have fled in terror. At the fifth line, Saint Peter uses his keys to knock Southey into his lake. In the confusion, George slips unobserved into Heaven.

SUMMARY

Lord Byron's impact on nineteenth century European and American culture, both as a personal cultural figure and as a poet and satirist, cannot be exaggerated. Stylistically and formally, his work is more diverse than that of his fellow Romantics. Byron's curious and perhaps confusing blend of idealism and cynicism accounts in part for critical reluctance to assign to him the same label of Romantic as easily as to Wordsworth or Shelley. Yet in his idealistic, steadfast determination to pursue truth, to strip away the surface to expose cant, hypocrisy, and oppression, Byron was at once a reflection of his culture and an iconoclast.

Lou Thompson

BIBLIOGRAPHY

By the Author

POETRY:

Fugitive Pieces, 1806
Hours of Idleness, 1807
Poems on Various Occasions, 1807
Poems Original and Translated, 1808
English Bards and Scotch Reviewers, 1809
Hints from Horace, 1811
The Curse of Minerva, 1812
Childe Harold's Pilgrimage, Cantos 1-4, 1812-1818, 1819 (the 4 cantos published together)
The Bride of Abydos, 1813
Waltz: An Apostrophic Hymn, 1813
The Giaour, 1813
Ode to Napoleon Buonaparte, 1814
The Corsair, 1814
Lara, 1814
Hebrew Melodies Ancient and Modern, 1815
Poems, 1816
Monody on the Death of the Right Honourable R. B. Sheridan, 1816
The Prisoner of Chillon, and Other Poems, 1816
The Siege of Corinth, 1816
Parisina, 1816
The Lament of Tasso, 1817
Beppo: A Venetian Story, 1818
Mazeppa, 1819
Don Juan, Cantos 1-16, 1819-1824, 1826, (the 16 cantos published together)
The Prophecy of Dante, 1821
The Vision of Judgment, 1822

DISCUSSION TOPICS

- Is Lord Byron more of a Romantic figure than a Romantic poet? Justify your response.

- Consider the statement that *Don Juan* does not look as "immoral" today as it once was alleged to be.

- Do you agree or disagree with the assertion that *Childe Harold's Pilgrimage* is more travelogue than character study? Why?

- Byron was fond of difficult poetic stanzas, such as the *ottava rima* and the Spenserian stanza. How do his rhyming techniques contribute to his success at these forms?

- Assess Percy Bysshe Shelley's influence on Byron.

- Show why Byron deserves to be called an iconoclast.

The Age of Bronze, 1823
The Island, 1823
The Complete Poetical Works of Byron, 1980-1986 (5 volumes)

DRAMA:
Manfred, pb. 1817, pr. 1834 (verse play)
Marino Faliero, Doge of Venice, pr., pb. 1821 (verse play)
Cain: A Mystery, pb. 1821 (verse play)
Sardanapalus, pb. 1821, pr. 1834 (verse play)
The Two Foscari, pb. 1821, pr. 1837 (verse play)
Heaven and Earth, pb. 1822 (fragment; verse play)
Werner: Or, The Inheritance, pb. 1823, pr. 1830 (verse play)
The Deformed Transformed, pb. 1824 (fragment; verse play)

NONFICTION:
Letter to [John Murray] on the Rev. W. L. Bowles' Strictures on the Life and Writings of Pope, 1821
"A Letter to the Editor of 'My Grandmother's Review,'" 1822
The Blues: A Literary Eclogue, 1823
The Parliamentary Speeches of Lord Byron, 1824
Byron's Letters and Journals, 1973-1982 (12 volumes; Leslie A. Marchand, editor)

About the Author

Brewer, William D. *Contemporary Studies on Lord Byron*. Lewiston, N.Y.: Edwin Mellen Press, 2001.

Chew, Samuel. *The Dramas of Lord Byron*. Baltimore: Johns Hopkins University Press, 1915.

Eisler, Benita. *Byron: Child of Passion, Fool of Fame*. New York: Vintage Books, 2000.

Franklin, Caroline. *Byron*. New York: Routledge, 2007.

MacCarthy, Fiona. *Byron: Life and Legend*. New York: Farrar, Straus and Giroux, 2002.

McGann, Jerome J. *"Don Juan" in Context*. Chicago: University of Chicago Press, 1976.

Marchand, Leslie. *Byron's Poetry: A Critical Introduction*. Boston: Houghton Mifflin, 1965.

Rutherford, Andrew. *Byron: A Critical Study*. London: Oliver & Boyd, 1962.

Stabler, Jane, ed. *Palgrave Advances in Byron Studies*. New York: Palgrave Macmillan, 2007.

Thorslev, Peter, Jr. *The Byronic Hero: Types and Prototypes*. Minneapolis: University of Minnesota Press, 1962.

Trueblood, Paul G. *Lord Byron*. Boston: Twayne, 1977.

West, Paul, ed. *Byron: A Collection of Critical Essays*. Englewood Cliffs, N.J.: Prentice-Hall, 1963.

PEDRO CALDERÓN DE LA BARCA

Born: Madrid, Spain
  January 17, 1600
Died: Madrid, Spain
  May 25, 1681

Author of more than one hundred full-length plays and many one-act autos sacramentales *(religious, often allegorical plays), Calderón is considered one of the truly great dramatists of Spain's Golden Age.*

BIOGRAPHY

Pedro Calderón de la Barca (kahl-day-ROHN day lah BAHR-kah) was born in Madrid, Spain, on January 17, 1600, into a well-established Castilian family of the lesser nobility. He was the third child of Ana María de Henao and Diego Calderón de la Barca, who held a post at the Spanish court. The family therefore followed the king to Valladolid and then back to Madrid, where Calderón attended the Colegio Imperial, a Jesuit school, from 1608 to 1613. In 1610, his mother died suddenly, and his father died in 1615. His mother had wanted her son to become a priest, and his father encouraged him strongly to complete his studies. In 1614, Calderón had enrolled at the University of Alcalá de Henares. Then, in the years 1616 to 1620, he divided his time between Alcalá and the University of Salamanca, where he probably completed the degree in canonical law. His study of theology, logic, and scholastic philosophy may well have influenced his intellectual approach to the ideas presented in his plays. His early verses, which he entered in a poetry contest in 1620 in honor of the beatification of Saint Isadore, were considered worthy of praise by his great contemporary, the dramatist Lope de Vega Carpio, and his first play *Amor, honor y poder* (pr. 1623, pb. 1634; love, honor, and power) was performed in Madrid in 1623. During the next two years, he was probably a soldier in Italy and Flanders. This period is followed by a very productive period of playwriting. By 1630, he had

written fifteen plays, including *La dama duende* (wr. 1629, pr., pb. 1636; *The Phantom Lady*, 1664) and *El príncipe constante* (pr. 1629, pb. 1636; *The Constant Prince*, 1853).

Although the record of his life is quite sketchy for someone who lived within court society, two stories appear in discussions of Calderón's life. One is from his university period, when he is said to have been fined for having killed a relative of the duke of Frias (a case later settled out of court); the other tells of an escapade in which Calderón followed an actor, who had wounded his brother in a duel, into a convent. Complaints from the nuns caused him to be placed under house arrest for a few days.

By 1637, he had written almost all of his well-known secular plays, including his famous philosophical play *La vida es sueño* (pr. 1635, pb. 1636; *Life Is a Dream*, 1830), and when Lope de Vega died in 1635, Calderón became his successor as court dramatist. Twelve of his dramas were published in 1636 and another twelve in 1637. At the same time, he was appointed to the Order of Santiago. During a revolt against Spain in 1640, he was sent with his order to Catalonia. His portrayals in *El alcalde de Zalamea* (pr. 1643, pb. 1651; *The Mayor of Zalamea*, 1853) may have their origin in his experiences there. When ill health forced him to return to Madrid in 1642, he became a member of the household of the duke of Alba for four years. After his two brothers were killed and his mistress died within a short period, he resigned his post at court in 1650 and entered the priesthood in 1651. In the following period, he wrote many *autos sacramentales*, medieval allegorical dramas. He was chaplain in Toledo for a time and then was persuaded by the king to return to court in 1663, where he remained until his death. His plays were collected and edited: the third part with twelve plays in 1664, the fourth in 1672, and the fifth in 1677, which contains four plays that he disowned. His own list of dramas written in 1680 includes 110 secular plays and seventy *autos sacramentales*. It is said that at the time of his death he was in the process of writing a new *auto sacramentale*. He died on May 25, 1681, in Madrid, very much esteemed by his contemporaries as a great dramatist.

ANALYSIS

Calderón's literary productions fall squarely within a period in Spain during which the arts and literature reached their greatest glory, a period often referred to as the Golden Age and associated with the reign of Philip IV (1621-1665). When Calderón began writing his plays, Lope de Vega Carpio, the great dramatist and Calderón's predecessor at court, had already developed the prescribed form of the *comedia*, a three-act drama (not necessarily a comedy) written in verse. Lope de Vega's guidelines for composing the *comedia* are explained in *El arte neuvo de hacer comedias en este tiempo* (1609; *The New Art of Writing Plays*, 1914). Because of the tremendous influence of Lope de Vega on the theater of his time, Calderón also wrote using the established rules, composing carefully written plots and polished verse.

Calderón's style is marked by ornamentation, sometimes to the point of obscurity. A popular technique of this period, referred to as Gongorism (after a leading poet, Luis de Góngora y Argote), this style of writing was highly artificial and refined, using many figures of speech, mythological allusions, hyperbole, and archaic words, in addition to a complex syntax based on the Latin form. This style is often combined with conceptism, a cultivated play with ideas. Although this style presents difficulties for the modern audience, the seventeenth century Spanish audience expected and appreciated the skill behind such usage.

The *comedia* was a popular form of entertainment, involving questions of love, honor, and patriotism. In addition, the comic character provided comic relief in even serious dramas with scenes of mistaken identity or bumbling inability to understand a problem. The key, however, was action. Action was always preferred over subtle character development, and the plot itself involved major events of violence, such as murder, battles, even natural disasters. The conflict often set up a situation of good versus evil—for example, the peasant mayor defending his family's honor against an aristocratic captain's base actions in *The Mayor of Zalamea*, or the conflict between father and son in *Life Is a Dream*, successfully resolved when the son adopts the approved values of his father.

The plays of Calderón cover a whole range of variations. His poetic skill and religious sensitivity made him master of the *auto sacramentale*. In these allegorical plays, Calderón continued in the tradition of the medieval morality play, raising its artistic level. His scholastic background and dramatic skill combined to enable him to dramatize abstract theological concepts in a convincing way. A fine example of an earlier *auto sacramentale* is *El gran teatro del mundo* (wr. 1635, pr. 1649, pb. 1677; *The Great Theater of the World*, 1856). Throughout his life, these plays developed greater complexity, and late in his life the themes of the Fall and Redemption appear to be presented with a mature understanding and compassion toward human beings in their weakness. Some of Calderón's plays—*The Constant Prince*, about the devotion of Prince Ferdinand of Portugal, or the famous *El sitio de Breda* (pr. 1625, pb. 1636), based on events also depicted in Diego Velásquez's painting *Las lanzas*—present themes from history or a legend.

The court drama grew out of popular drama, and with the construction of the palace in the Buen Retiro, with its special theater, Calderón, too, wrote plays with spectacular staging effects and elaborate machinery and settings. Successfully developed court plays went beyond popular drama in combining drama with dance, music, and visual arts. Perhaps the best of these is *La hija del aire* (pr. 1653, pb. 1664; *The Daughter of the Air*, 1831), a two-part play of violence and passion based on the legend of a warrior queen of Babylon. Mythological themes dominate this art form, as can be seen by some of the titles, *Eco y Narciso* (wr. 1661, pb. 1688; Echo and Narcissus) and *La estatua de Prometeo* (wr. 1669, pb. 1683; the statue of Prometheus).

Calderón's bloody tragedies of honor were very popular with seventeenth century audiences, even if audiences today find the resolution of some of the honor conflicts shocking. For example, in *El médico de su honra* (pb. 1637; *The Surgeon of His Honor*, 1853), an innocent wife is murdered by her husband on the mere suspicion of dishonoring his name. The whole issue of honor and its defense must be seen in its seventeenth century context in order to be understood, but this play was intended to shock, showing perhaps Calderón's rejection of the rigid assumptions of the honor code, which led to such excesses.

Although Calderón was known for many types of serious plays, he was also a master of the light, amusing *comedia de capa y espada* (cloak-and-sword play). The name derives from the cloak and sword that were the marks of a gentleman of the time. These plays were pure entertainment—the theme was usually love along with its obstacles, intrigues, and misunderstandings, all written in charming, natural dialogue. The characters are paired sets of two or three gentlemen with their respective ladies and servants (confidants to their masters). The humorous *Casa con dos puertas, mala es de guardar* (wr. 1629, pr., pb. 1636; *A House with Two Doors Is Difficult to Guard*, 1737) is a good example.

Through the various forms that his dramas took, Calderón used the structure and poetic devices popular in his time, and, under Lope de Vega's influence, the development of characters was always subordinate to the action, producing a fast-moving, entertaining spectacle. In the case of the court play, especially, these elements often became quite elaborate. His plots are skillfully constructed, often with a struggle between opposing forces, and the themes are rarely simple; they are, rather, a group of related themes, all of which contribute to the plot.

Calderón's writing is characterized by various types of verse or meter depending on the use: soliloquies, for example, were often written in sonnet form; one of two types (called the *romance* and *redondilla*) was employed for dialogue and narration. Each change of meter changed the mood. Within his poetic style, Baroque techniques appear, such as the use of visual images drawn from nature and mythology, the use of simile and metaphor, parodies and plays on words, the contrast of light and shadow (chiaroscuro), and self-contradictory images (oxymorons). In all of his works, Calderón's skillful use of the themes, techniques, and style of his period mark him as a truly masterful dramatist.

LIFE IS A DREAM

First produced: *La vida es sueño*, 1635 (first published, 1636; English translation, 1830)
Type of work: Play

A young prince, imprisoned from childhood, is tested by his father to see if his reason and prudence will triumph over base instincts.

Usually recognized as Calderón's finest drama, *Life Is a Dream* premiered at the Royal Court of Spain. Its theme, revealed in the title, focuses on the instability of life and the illusory nature of the world. The story opens one night in the countryside between Poland and Russia, where Rosaura, a noblewoman disguised as a man, and her servant are journeying on foot after the loss of their horses. The opening lines give an example of Calderón's imagery and language:

> Are you the fabulous hippogriff running in
>   harness with the wind?
> Flameless thunderbolt, featherless bird, fish
>   without scales,
> Monster of the four elements without instinct to
>   check your headlong flight?

Rosaura's questions include mythological references and images of nature described out of character. The landscape itself reflects Rosaura's emotional upheaval. Amid the turbulence, she finds Segismundo's prison cave and hears his soliloquy of distress at the loss of his freedom. His guardian, Clotaldo, shown throughout the drama to be a man of integrity, sends the visitors away, but not before recognizing Rosaura as his daughter by the sword that she carries (which acts as a symbol of her family honor).

From the beginning, the first of several themes grouped together in this complex philosophical drama are introduced. Segismundo had been imprisoned by his father, King Basilio, who feared the predictions of the stars that his son would humiliate him and rule as a tyrant. Now, years later, he wonders if he has done right and decides to test the young man by drugging him and bringing him to the palace. In these luxurious surroundings, the inexperienced Segismundo shows his base nature by following his own pleasure and acting in a violent and insulting manner. When returned to his prison, he is told by Clotaldo that it was all a dream—a development that sets up a second theme complex in which dream and reality are confused, and in which deception and truth are indistinguishable to the protagonist. As Segismundo says in his famous lines:

> What is life? a delirium!
> What is life? illusion,
> A shadow, a fiction
> Whose greatest good is nothing,
> Because life is a dream!
> Even dreams are only dreams.

When freed by soldiers later, Segismundo proves that he has learned from his experience to control his passions and to do good, as Clotaldo has counseled, even in his dreams. At the end of the play, the prophecy has been fulfilled, as his father kneels at his son's feet—showing the strength of predestination. Yet a moment later, Segismundo wins his father's forgiveness and demonstrates forbearance and prudence in his final actions—showing his ability to use his freedom and free will wisely to counterbalance the pull of his destiny.

A second theme throughout the play, introduced in the first act, is the question of honor. Rosaura has been deceived and abandoned by Astolfo, nephew of the king. The two main characters meet in their hour of need and help each other: Rosaura inspires love in Segismundo and shows him the way to appropriate princely conduct, while he, in turn, restores her honor by marrying her to Astolfo, thus sacrificing his own wishes to the demands of society by restoring each person to his or her rightful place.

THE MAYOR OF ZALAMEA

First produced: *El alcalde de Zalamea*, 1643 (first published, 1651; English translation, 1853)
Type of work: Play

The mayor of Zalamea, a wealthy peasant, executes an aristocratic captain in the royal army for having dishonored his (the mayor's) daughter.

The theme of honor is central to the action of Calderón's much-admired play *The Mayor of Zalamea*. The plot is constructed around a conflict based on the contrast between the honorable and just peasant Pedro Crespo and the dishonorable deeds of the aristocratic Captain Alvaro. As the play opens, Crespo agrees to quarter Captain Alvaro in his home, but he takes the precaution of hiding his beautiful, unmarried daughter, Isabel, in the attic with a female companion. His curiosity aroused, Don Alvaro later manages to see Isabel and abduct her. She is rescued by her brother, but only after she has been raped and abandoned by the captain. In an effort to satisfy the requirements of the honor code, Crespo tries every means to get Don Alvaro to marry Isabel, even offering all of his wealth. The dramatic scene is particularly moving as Crespo acts sincerely and humanely to try to obtain justice. Yet even as he shows his nobility of character, the captain arrogantly refuses his offer and rejects his authority.

The question of legal jurisdiction now enters the play, as the aristocratic captain declares himself exempt from civilian authority. Coupled with this question is the theme of honor, which Crespo argues is a property of the soul, which belongs to God, even though Alvaro's life and possessions are in the service of the king. The honor question crosses the lines of rank and jurisdiction in his argument. At the height of the action, the commander, Don Lope de Figueroa, confronts Crespo angrily on the question of legal authority over Don Alvaro. The verse form expresses the anger as threats are exchanged.

The development of Pedro Crespo's character and demonstration of the qualities of prudence and a sense of justice are central to this play. The audience watches through the first two acts as his true character begins to emerge, until in act 3 he becomes an agent of social justice. In deciding to execute Don Alvaro, Crespo debates whether he should act as a father (in defense of family honor) or as the mayor of Zalamea (to obtain justice at a higher level). When he acts, he does so as mayor, and in his argument at the end he maintains that the two spheres of justice, military and civilian, are really all part of a higher law, the king's justice (representative of God's law).

SUMMARY

Pedro Calderón de la Barca proved himself a master of the many variations of dramatic art of his time. His style can be ornate, with imagery and mythological references, or simple and more direct, to reflect characters of society's lower classes.

His varied verse forms are suited to their use within the dialogue, and his plots are carefully constructed for dramatic effect.

Calderón's themes range from the religious and theological in his *autos sacramentales* to the witty and fast-moving stories of love and misadventure in his *comedias de capa y espada*. In his serious dramas, he focuses on larger issues, such as the problem of honor, dream and reality, deception and truth, freedom and predestination. With all of his dramas clearly anchored in the Spanish Golden Age, the force of allegory is often evident—showing the characters their rightful position within a society believed to be ordained by God.

Susan L. Piepke

BIBLIOGRAPHY

By the Author

DRAMA:

Amor, honor y poder, pr. 1623, pb. 1634

El sitio de Breda, pr. 1625, pb. 1636

El príncipe constante, pr. 1629, pb. 1636 (*The Constant Prince,* 1853)

Casa con dos puertas, mala es de guardar, wr. 1629, pr., pb. 1636 (*A House with Two Doors Is Difficult to Guard,* 1737)

La dama duende, wr. 1629, pr., pb. 1936 (*The Phantom Lady,* 1664)

Los cabellos de Absalón, wr. c. 1634, pb. 1684 (*The Crown of Absalom,* 1993)

La devoción de la cruz, pb. 1634, pr. 1643 (*The Devotion to the Cross,* 1832)

La vida es sueño, pr. 1635, pb. 1636 (*Life Is a Dream,* 1830)

El mayor encanto, amor, pr. 1635, pb. 1637 (*Love, the Greatest Enchantment,* 1870)

El gran teatro del mundo, wr. 1635, pr. 1649, pb. 1677 (*The Great Theater of the World,* 1856)

El médico de su honra, pb. 1637 (*The Surgeon of His Honor,* 1853)

A secreto agravio, secreta venganza, pb. 1637 (*Secret Vengeance for Secret Insult,* 1961)

El mágico prodigioso, pr. 1637, pb. 1663 (*The Wonder-Working Magician,* 1959)

El pintor de su deshonra, wr. 1640-1642, pb. 1650 (*The Painter of His Dishonor,* 1853)

El alcalde de Zalamea, pr. 1643, pb. 1651 (*The Mayor of Zalamea,* 1853)

La hija del aire, Parte I, pr. 1653, pb. 1664 (*The Daughter of the Air, Part I,* 1831)

DISCUSSION TOPICS

- If Pedro Calderón de la Barca is indeed a major writer of the Spanish Golden Age, what do his plays suggest about the literary traits that Spaniards of that age admired or expected?

- To what extent does the *auto sacramental* resemble English religious plays with which you are familiar?

- How does the theme of the Rosaura plot in *Life Is a Dream* relate to the plot involving Segismundo?

- Why must humans consider life as a dream?

- What features of *Life Is a Dream* seem most like comedy as William Shakespeare practiced it? What features seem significantly different?

La hija del aire, Parte II, pr. 1653, pb. 1664 (*The Daughter of the Air, Part II*, 1831)

El laurel de Apolo, pr. 1659, pb. 1664

La púrpura de la rosa, pr. 1660, pb. 1664

Eco y Narciso, wr. 1661, pb. 1688

Ni amor se libra de amor, pb. 1664

La estatua de Prometeo, wr. 1669, pb. 1683

Hado y divisa de Leonido y Marfisa, pr. 1680, pb. 1682

POETRY:

Psalle et sile, 1741

Poesías, 1845

Obra lírica, 1943

Sus mejores poesías, 1954

Poesías líricas en las obras dramáticas de Calderón, 1964

Los sonetos de Calderón en sus obras dramáticas, 1974

About the Author

Acker, Thomas S. *The Baroque Vortez: Velázquez, Calderón, and Grácian under Philip IV.* New York: P. Land, 2000.

Benabu, Isaac. *Reading for the Stage: Calderón and His Contemporaries.* Rochester, N.Y.: Tamesis, 2003.

Heigl, Michaela. *Theorizing Gender, Sexuality, and the Body in Calderonian Theater.* New Orleans: University Press of the South, 2001.

Hesse, Everett W. *Calderón de la Barca.* New York: Twayne, 1967.

McGaha, Michael D., ed. *Approaches to the Theater of Calderón.* Washington, D.C.: University of America Press, 1982.

Parker, Alexander A. *The Allegorical Drama of Calderón: An Introduction to the Autos Sacramentales.* Oxford, England: Dolphin Books, 1962.

_____. *The Mind and Art of Calderón: Essays on the Comedias.* Cambridge, England: Cambridge University Press, 1988.

Ter Horst, Robert. *Calderón: The Secular Plays.* Lexington: University Press of Kentucky, 1982.

Wardropper, Bruce W., ed. *Critical Essays on the Theatre of Calderón.* New York: New York University Press, 1965.

John Martin

MORLEY CALLAGHAN

Born: Toronto, Ontario, Canada
February 22, 1903
Died: Toronto, Ontario, Canada
August 25, 1990

Callaghan, one of the greatest Canadian fiction writers of the twentieth century, transcended the regional and national by handling universal themes in a compelling style.

BIOGRAPHY

Edward Morley Callaghan (KAL-uh-han) was born in Toronto, Ontario, Canada, to parents who were Roman Catholics of Irish descent. He attended public school, Riverdale Collegiate, and St. Michael's College of the University of Toronto. While in college, he did well in his studies, debated, boxed, played baseball and hockey, and was a part-time reporter on the Toronto *Daily Star.* In 1923, he met Ernest Hemingway, who was the European correspondent for the Toronto *Star Weekly* and who encouraged Callaghan's ambition to become a writer. After earning his B.A. in 1925, Callaghan attended Osgoode Law School in Toronto.

In 1926, he published two short stories and began to receive encouragement from the American literary figures Robert McAlmon and Ezra Pound. Callaghan visited New York City and met several important writers. Through the good offices of F. Scott Fitzgerald, Callaghan in 1928 met Maxwell Perkins, the brilliant editor at the publishing house of Charles Scribner's Sons in New York. Perkins became his loyal adviser, bought three of his stories for *Scribner's Magazine,* and accepted his novel *Strange Fugitive* (1928) and a collection of stories called *A Native Argosy* (1929). His short story "A Country Passion," about a couple's frustrations, was republished in *The Best Stories of 1928.* This was the first of many Callaghan pieces that were hon-

ored in The Best Stories series. Though called to the bar in 1928, Callaghan never practiced law.

In 1929, Callaghan married his college sweetheart, Loretto Florence Dee, and spent seven delightful months with her in Paris; much later, he reminisced in *That Summer in Paris: Memories of Tangled Friendships with Hemingway, Fitzgerald, and Some Others* (1963) about his time there. After a few restless months living on a Pennsylvania farm and in a New York hotel, Callaghan and his wife made Toronto their permanent home, beginning in 1930. By then Callaghan was established as a respected writer of long and short fiction. In addition to *Scribner's Magazine,* he eventually published in *The Atlantic Monthly, Cosmopolitan, Esquire, Harper's Bazaar, Maclean's, Saturday Evening Post, The New Yorker,* and *The Yale Review.*

Until World War II began, Callaghan's career was marked by steady writing and a sequence of excellent books. They are *It's Never Over* (1930, written in Paris), *No Man's Meat* (1931), *A Broken Journey* (1932), *Such Is My Beloved* (1934), *They Shall Inherit the Earth* (1935), *Now That April's Here, and Other Stories* (1936), and *More Joy in Heaven* (1937). Callaghan also wrote two plays in 1939 and began a monthly column a year later for *New World Magazine.* He continued with the column until 1948. In 1942, he was permitted to sail aboard a Canadian naval corvette, in preparation for writing a National Film Board script. A year later, he began work for the Canadian Broadcasting Corporation (CBC), starting with a talk show and continuing with quiz shows. He returned to novel writing in 1947. In 1948, two minor novels appeared, *Luke*

Baldwin's Vow, for children, and *The Varsity Story.* *The Loved and the Lost*, a Governor-General's Literary Award winner, was published in 1951, and *The Many Coloured Coat*, based on a 1955 story, appeared in 1960. Callaghan continued to produce stories, eventually writing more than one hundred, and he also published many nonfiction articles.

In 1950, Callaghan returned to the CBC with his own talk show and began to make guest appearances on television. In 1958, the *Star Weekly* dispatched him to Rome to report on the death of Pope Pius XII, and this experience led him to write his novel *A Passion in Rome* (1961).

In his last decades, the steady Callaghan made writing his life. He won more awards, including both the Canada Council Molson Prize and the Royal Bank of Canada Award in 1970. He enjoyed a beautiful home with his wife in Toronto and regular visits from admiring readers, critics, and fellow writers. His last novels include *A Fine and Private Place* (1975), *Close to the Sun Again* (1977), and *A Time for Judas* (1983); the latter novel is about Judas's finding a friend to record and preserve the story of Christ's need to be betrayed. Callaghan's beloved wife died in 1984. In subsequent years, he published his last two novels, *Our Lady of the Snows* (1985) and *A Wild Old Man on the Road* (1988).

ANALYSIS

Morley Callaghan's international literary reputation struggles against two curious adversities. The first resulted from the revelation that he had knocked down the burly Hemingway during a boxing match at a Parisian athletic club in 1929; a great deal of hoopla was made over this unimportant feat, which should have been quickly forgotten. In addition, his credibility as a significant international writer suffered because his fiction was often set in Toronto, causing many critics to dismiss him as merely a competent regional writer. Edmund Wilson, the distinguished and influential American critic, began a 1960 essay on Callaghan by saying that he "is today perhaps the most unjustly neglected novelist in the English-speaking world," and concluded wryly that this might be so because readers wonder whether any Toronto writer could be legitimately compared to Anton Chekhov and Ivan Turgenev—as White believed Callaghan should be.

Callaghan's fiction addresses many universal themes. Often, he uses characters who may be defined as ordinary people with dilemmas. He then dramatizes their suffering when they fail to make the "right" choices, which they often do because they lack anything resembling free will. He shows how the establishment breaks the hearts of the have-nots, the unfortunate, and the misfits in its midst. Callaghan also describes how people of goodwill must have, seize, add to, and strengthen their moral values to survive in a troubled world. Callaghan develops orderly, uncomplicated, suspenseful plots. He includes violence and muted sensuality, tangles people in permanent psychological conflict, and closes without passing judgment, leaving characters with little if any hope for happiness.

It's Never Over presents the consequences of the execution of a combat veteran who killed a policeman under mitigating circumstances. The murderer's sister wrecks her life, that of her brother's best friend, and that of the friend's girlfriend by clinging to a dead past that prevents her from having a living present or future.

No Man's Meat focuses on a triangular relationship. The staid, childless marriage of Bert and Teresa Beddoes is shattered when their friend Jean Allen, who has left her husband, comes to visit them. After a serene sunset over a peaceful Canadian lake, from which the three take no lesson, Bert and Jean shoot craps, while Teresa watches. Jean loses a final startling bet and sleeps with Bert to pay it off; Teresa does not protest but insists with "calmness" that the two sleep together. In the morning, Jean reveals why she left her husband. She can hardly stand a man's touch; she is a lesbian. She then departs with Teresa.

Such Is My Beloved has attracted increased attention in recent years. It's the story of an idealistic, young priest who falls in love with the idea of saving the souls of two prostitutes in his neighborhood. Though he has the best intentions, his innocence of social reality leads to negative consequences for all concerned.

Callaghan describes weather and street scenes in a painterly way and employs cinematic techniques. The opening paragraph of *Our Lady of the Snows*, for example, tells how on a certain Christmas Eve "big wet [snow] flakes" fall "on an old dilapidated neighborhood," and then zooms in on a nearby hotel and its loquacious bartender named

"Gil" Gilhooley. The novel also has autobiographical overtones, since Gil had ambitions to be a writer and is trying to come to terms with his brother's death. Callaghan's only sibling, an older brother, died in 1946. In *A Fine and Private Place*, Al and Lisa discuss details of the hit-and-run death of an enigmatic friend, a writer named Eugene Shore. Callaghan makes masterful use of clipped, simple dialogue that is at once realistic and heightened. Such dialogue is also reminiscent of cinema.

Callaghan often uses simple plot structures. *The Many Coloured Coat* features three central characters in an unnamed city that resembles Montreal. One character perceptively admires the other two, who are contrasted. A temptation generates a crime, a public trial, a conviction, and a suicide in prison. The fortunes of the surviving pair undergo inversion—one up-then-down, the other down-then-up. A second trial permits a private reconciliation of the two survivors.

Almost never presenting his action through omniscient narrators who explain things for the reader, Callaghan has his characters, especially in short stories, learn something significant at the climax. "Day by Day," for example, describes the consequence of a young wife's prayer that her husband may find contentment. He comes home, observes her spiritual enlightenment, becomes suspicious, and storms out. At the end of the story, "She had such a strange feeling of guilt. White-faced and still, she tried to ask herself what it was that was slowly driving them apart day by day." In "A Sick Call," a Catholic priest pays a requested visit to a sick former member of the church in order to provide spiritual comfort. In so doing, he bothers the woman's gruff young husband, whose love for her the priest wistfully sees as beautifully "staunch," though "pagan." The story ends: "As he [the priest] began to wonder about the nature of this beauty, for some reason he felt inexpressibly sad."

"TWO FISHERMEN"

First published: 1934, as "Who Is My Neighbor?" (collected in *Morley Callaghan's Stories*, 1959)
Type of work: Short story

A hangman comes to town on business, goes fishing with the local newspaper reporter before the execution, and confronts him afterward.

One of the two fishermen of the title is Michael Foster, a young journalist for a small-town newspaper called the *Examiner* who wants to work for a metropolitan paper instead. The other fisherman, K. Smith, has come to town to execute the well-liked Tom Delaney, who fought, was hurt by, and killed his wife's molester.

The story falls into two parts. The first part takes place in the evening; Foster finds Smith, borrows a boat, and rows him out onto the lake. They share a bottle and grow "neighborly." "Smitty" amusingly talks about his wife and children and then begins to discuss his work, "knowing he ought to be ashamed." Next day, soon after the execution, the two meet again. Smith, now formally dressed, gives Foster two fish he caught before dawn that morning. An upset crowd approaches and pelts Smith, and a flying rock cuts Smith's head. The inefficient sheriff intervenes and saves Smith. An irate citizen notices Foster's fish, grabs them, and hurls them toward Smith. Smith stares at his gift, in the dust; Foster, backing away, feels "hot with shame" for "betraying Smitty."

This story concerns injustice, friendship's limits, disloyalty, and the sad separation of work and play. Tom should not be hanged. Foster makes and loses a friend. Smith endures his job partly so he can fish in different places. The serenity of the lake implicitly mocks the characters' common inhumanity. A bleeding head, betrayal, and fish provide twisted Christian symbolism. When asked to select one of his stories for inclusion in *This Is My Best*, a 1942 collection of works by famous authors, Callaghan submitted "Two Fishermen." He might easily have chosen any of a dozen other splendid stories, but he rightly held this one in high regard.

THEY SHALL INHERIT THE EARTH

First published: 1935
Type of work: Novel

When a father and his estranged son are implicated in an only partly accidental drowning, frustrated hopes and wrecked lives result.

This novel, whose title derives from the Bible, tells the story of an egocentric, sinful man who learns repentance and gains forgiveness through the love of a meek woman. The plot involves interlocking activities of several characters. Andrew Aikenhead is a successful advertising agent. Andrew's mentally unbalanced first wife has died, and their son Michael, an infrequently employed engineer, resents his father's second marriage to Marthe Choate. Marthe's irresponsible son by her previous marriage, David, has tested the limits of Andrew's patience.

In a pathetic effort to improve matters, Andrew manages to persuade Michael to vacation with his family and a few friends at his lakeside home. David, who drinks excessively, harasses Sheila, Michael's sister and the fiancé of Ross, the physician son of Andrew's partner Jay Hillquist. After arguing noisily with Andrew, David goes boating with Michael in the dark. The two argue. David dives from the boat, swims around foolishly, becomes confused, and calls for help. Michael bruises him with an oar in an angry rescue attempt, then abandons him. The next day David's drowned body is found. Suspicion falls on Andrew, although the police lack evidence to prosecute. Michael, bitterly blaming his father for much of his life's trouble, fails to come forward with the truth.

Marthe leaves Andrew, who so declines that Jay dissolves their partnership. Sheila marries Ross but, fearing family madness, tells him she wants no children. Michael, on whom Callaghan concentrates, has four friends: Anna Prychoda, an unemployed dress designer; Huck Farr, a callous sensualist; Nathaniel Benjamin, a would-be teacher and a convert from Judaism to Christianity; and Bill Johnson, a loudmouthed communist. Michael finds no solace with Huck, despite their former camaraderie, especially when he observes Huck's campaign to seduce Anna. He finds no answers in religion through Nathaniel, none in politics through Bill, nor any in nature when he goes wolf hunting with Ross and observes slaughter.

Meek Anna becomes Michael's salvation. Falling awkwardly in love, they soon become intimate. When she shyly tells him she is pregnant and appears frightened by his initial silence, he explains: "I was just feeling glad, and I was trying to understand why I felt glad." Her reply is wondrous: "Then I'm glad too." At one point, Michael watches Anna peacefully sleeping and begins to understand:

> If to be poor in spirit meant to be without false pride, or be humble enough to forget oneself, then she was poor in spirit, for she gave herself to everything that touched her, she let herself be, she lost herself in the fullness of the world, and in losing herself she found the world, and she possessed her whole soul. People like her could have everything. They could inherit the earth.

Michael confesses his sin to Anna. She says that only meaningless justice would be served by his going to the police, that instead he should ask the prodigal son's forgiveness of the father. What follows this dramatic act, nicely underplayed by Callaghan, contains the seeds of a diminished contentment.

Callaghan handles details with consummate skill, creates many scenes as if for a film treatment, and conveys psychological realities by natural dialogue and by having his characters ponder what they want to say but cannot express. Misery results from misunderstanding, resentment, and misinterpretation but imperfectly articulated love points to a moral: "give all of yourself to help."

MORE JOY IN HEAVEN

First published: 1937
Type of work: Novel

A famous bank robber apparently reforms while serving a long prison term, but after a few months back in society, he is destroyed by the pressures of success.

Red Ryan was the actual person who served as the model for the hero of *More Joy in Heaven*. He was released from prison in 1935 after serving more

than ten years for grand theft. For a few months, Ryan was the toast of Toronto, but the fashion of his popularity passed and he reverted to his previous patterns. Ryan was finally killed by a police officer while attempting to rob a liquor store.

Callaghan's novel turns this true story into a version of the parable of the prodigal son. The fictional hero of *More Joy in Heaven*, Kip Caley, sees another side of life while serving his long prison term. His transformation is due largely to the help of a priest who is ministering there. Caley forgets the demands of his giant ego and finds new satisfaction in helping other inmates. He becomes a model prisoner, and through the intervention of a Canadian senator and other political figures, he is granted parole.

Unfortunately, his well-earned reputation for being reborn on the inside makes him a valuable commodity on the outside. The senator gets him a job as a greeter at a popular sports bar, which puts Caley back in contact with the fast-track world of heavy drinking, gambling, and prostitution. Shrewd entrepreneurs, political opportunists, and thrill seekers of various kinds pounce on him as soon as he is free.

Caley loses touch with Father Butler, who in prison had shown him a better way of life. Instead, Caley finds himself hobnobbing with a bishop of the church, whose devotion to the power of the institution leaves little time to care about any individual. A waitress named Julie, who has also been through some hard times, comes to love Caley for reasons that have nothing to do with his notoriety. She has to compete, however, with the senator's daughter, who wants only a fling with the famous former bank robber. Julie wins, but their love is not enough to stave off the inevitable tragedy.

The dream that catches fire in Caley's heart is to become a member of the parole board, which would allow him to continue on a larger scale the worthwhile work he had begun in prison. The dream is frustrated, however, by his own impatience and then vetoed by Judge Ford. This same judge had originally sentenced Caley and had opposed his early release. Judge Ford is untouched by mercy, pity, peace, or love. He sees nothing but the law. In one memorable passage, Ford is compared to the cynical former convict Whispering Joe Foley. They are portrayed as mirror images of each other, both addicted to the law. Ford can think only in terms of enforcing the law; Foley can think only in terms of breaking it.

The extremely romantic and dramatic ending leaves the reader with a better understanding of the impersonal forces that control society and destroy Kip Caley. Sympathy for Caley is qualified, however, by an appreciation of the tragic consequences of his kind of egomaniacal naïveté. The celebration to welcome back the prodigal son can become toxic if it continues too long.

THAT SUMMER IN PARIS

First published: 1963
Type of work: Memoir

Callaghan describes seven months in 1929 spent with his wife in Paris associating with expatriate writers and sharing their mostly carefree café life there.

Callaghan began *That Summer in Paris: Memories of Tangled Friendships with Hemingway, Fitzgerald, and Some Others* to correct the many stories generated by his outboxing Hemingway in Paris. The book, however, grew into a charming compilation of memories of Paris boulevards, commentary, and conversations with American writers, editors, and publishers. The book falls into thirds, followed by a coda. In the first third, Callaghan details his newspaper work in Toronto, meeting Hemingway there, and conferring with members of the literati in New York. Callaghan presents himself as an eager young author, ready for advice but also rather cocksure.

The Callaghans arrive in Paris in April. Callaghan, recalling numerous experiences with remarkable objectivity, offers vignettes of Parisian life before the economic collapse and war that were to come. He reveres Paris as "a lighted place where the imagination was free," that people "have to make room for . . . in their thoughts even if they never visit them." Distancing himself from the French writers he observes, he calls one trio "French cutups" and André Gide "a second-rate novelist." Some Americans fare no better. Gertrude Stein's abstract prose is "nonsense." A host spoils his generous treatment of Americans with gossip and cruel behavior. Through this host, however, Callaghan meets James Joyce, whom he esteems above all other living writers, whose wife he meets and likes, and in whose home he is entertained. Callaghan also reveres Hemingway and hopes to meet F. Scott Fitzgerald through him. Callaghan does meet "Scott" later.

Callaghan summarizes more adventures with celebrities and phonies, describes far too much drinking, and carefully reports his boxing match with Hemingway. Fitzgerald, who timed the match, in innocent excitement let a three-minute round run on, which allowed Callaghan to floor Hemingway, who bellowed that Fitzgerald had done it purposely to see him humiliated. Callaghan concludes that Hemingway had to be the winner in everything. The episode ruined the already shaky

friendship between Fitzgerald and Hemingway, whom Callaghan crisply analyzes: "[Hemingway's] quality for moving others to make legends out of his life may have been as tragic a flaw as was Scott's instinct for courting humiliation from his inferiors."

The book's last chapters serve as an epilogue. After enjoying a trip to Versailles and Chartres with Hemingway, the Callaghans return, via London and Dublin, to their home in Toronto. Embroiled at once in inaccurate reports of his boxing victory, Callaghan tries honorably but without success to set the record straight by publishing an explanation in the newspapers.

Callaghan, who took pains to disparage the seventeenth century love of balance and form seen at Versailles, avoids compositional symmetry in this book. It has two chapters of three pages each and one of nineteen. He makes casual generalizations concerning life and art. Some of his critical observations could, of course, be the result of hindsight. *That Summer in Paris* is now a classic remembrance of Paris in 1929.

SUMMARY

Morley Callaghan, a remarkably intelligent and enduring man of letters, transcended his Canadian borders. His is the work of a great writer rather than a great regional writer. At his best, he portrays ordinary people caught in situations too hard to wriggle out of with much grace; yet, his characters try and in trying merit nonjudgmental love. Callaghan invites his readers to approach these characters, get inside their personalities, and agree that words are often inadequate to do more than suggest the depths of their all-too-human quandaries.

Robert L. Gale; updated by Steven Lehman

BIBLIOGRAPHY

By the Author

LONG FICTION:
Strange Fugitive, 1928
It's Never Over, 1930
No Man's Meat, 1931 (novella)
A Broken Journey, 1932
Such Is My Beloved, 1934

They Shall Inherit the Earth, 1935
More Joy in Heaven, 1937
The Varsity Story, 1948
The Loved and the Lost, 1951
The Many Coloured Coat, 1960
A Passion in Rome, 1961
A Fine and Private Place, 1975
Season of the Witch, 1976
Close to the Sun Again, 1977
"No Man's Meat," and "The Enchanted Pimp," 1978
A Time for Judas, 1983
Our Lady of the Snows, 1985
A Wild Old Man on the Road, 1988

SHORT FICTION:
A Native Argosy, 1929
Now That April's Here, and Other Stories, 1936
Morley Callaghan's Stories, 1959
The Lost and Found Stories of Morley Callaghan, 1985

DRAMA:
Turn Home Again, pr. 1940 (also known as *Going Home*)
To Tell the Truth, pr. 1949
Season of the Witch, pb. 1976

NONFICTION:
That Summer in Paris: Memories of Tangled Friendships with Hemingway, Fitzgerald, and Some Others, 1963
Winter, 1974

CHILDREN'S LITERATURE:
Luke Baldwin's Vow, 1948

DISCUSSION TOPICS

- How does Red Ryan, the historical model for Kip Caley, compare to the fictional character who is the protagonist of Morley Callaghan's *More Joy in Heaven*?

- Peggy's innocence in *The Loved and the Lost* is referred to as malignant. Explain this unusual combination of ideas in this novel and/or other works of Callaghan.

- Describe the conflict between Christianity and the church in *Such Is My Beloved*.

- How has Callaghan's friendship with Ernest Hemingway affected his literary reputation over the years?

- How does the parable of the prodigal son relate to the themes of *More Joy in Heaven* and *They Shall Inherit the Earth*?

- What aspects of Callaghan's work do you find to be especially Canadian?

- Callaghan's style has been criticized as "corny" in recent years. Do you agree? Provide examples to support your view one way or the other.

- Explain how ordinary people suffer from their dealings with the establishment in three of Callaghan's works.

About the Author

Boire, Gary A. *Morley Callaghan: Literary Anarchist.* Toronto: ECW Press, 1994.

Callaghan, Barry. *Barrelhouse Kings: A Memoir.* Toronto: McArthur, 1998.

Conron, Brandon. *Morley Callaghan.* New York: Twayne, 1966.

Kendle, Judith. "Morley Callaghan." In *The Annotated Bibliography of Canada's Major Authors*, edited by Robert Lecker and Jack David. Downsview, Ont.: ECW Press, 1984.

Nischik, Reingard M., ed. *The Canadian Short Story: Interpretations.* Rochester, N.Y.: Camden House, 2007.

Pell, Barbara Helen. *Faith and Fiction: A Theological Critique of the Narrative Strategies of Hugh MacLennan and Morley Callaghan.* Waterloo, Ont.: Published for the Canadian Corporation for Studies in Religion by Wilfrid Laurier University Press, 1998.

Stains, David, ed. *The Callaghan Symposium.* Ottawa, Ont.: University of Ottawa Press, 1981.

Sutherland, Fraser. *The Style of Innocence: A Study of Hemingway and Callaghan.* Toronto: Clarke, Irwin, 1972.

Wilson, Edmund. *O Canada: An American's Notes on Canadian Culture.* New York: Farrar, Straus & Giroux, 1965.

Woodcock, George. *Moral Predicament: Morley Callaghan's "More Joy in Heaven."* Toronto: ECW Press, 1993.

ITALO CALVINO

Born: Santiago de las Vegas, Cuba
October 15, 1923
Died: Siena, Italy
September 19, 1985

With quirky humanism and imaginative style, internationally acclaimed storyteller Calvino breathed life into traditional and innovative narrative forms by skillfully blending reality, fantasy, and wit.

© Jerry Bauer

BIOGRAPHY

Italo Calvino (kahl-VEE-noh) was born in Santiago de las Vegas, Cuba, near Havana, on October 15, 1923, to parents who were well into middle age. Agricultural scientists, they returned to the ancestral farm on the Italian Riviera when Calvino was two. Their intellectual openness, enlightened skepticism, and enthusiasm for scientific method deeply influenced Calvino's later artistic development.

After a rather lonely adolescence, Calvino left San Remo to study agronomy at the University of Turin in 1941. Drafted into the national army two years later, he immediately deserted to join the Italian Resistance and fight Fascism. When World War II ended in 1945, he returned to Turin, changed his major from agronomy to English literature (his thesis was on Joseph Conrad), completed his degree, and began writing fiction. His first novel, *Il sentiero dei nidi di ragno* (1947, 1957, 1965; *The Path to the Nest of Spiders*, 1956), a realistic story about an orphan's wartime adventures with a band of partisans, first appeared in 1947. It won the Riccione literary prize in 1947 and much critical praise. His many short stories, some of which in the collection *Gli amore difficili* (1970; *Difficult Loves*, 1984), also earned acclaim.

In his mid-twenties, Calvino took a position with the Einaudi publishing house. The staff there included novelists Elio Vittorini, Cesare Pavese, and Natalia Levi Ginzburg—all leaders in Italy's intellectual vanguard. They introduced Calvino to the neorealist literary movement and encouraged his increasingly active participation in politics. Under their tutelage, Calvino found the late 1940's and the 1950's especially productive.

Besides his editorship at Einaudi (a position he kept until his death), he directed a literary journal with Vittorini, served on the staff of Italy's official Communist newspaper, and contributed many polemical articles to *Il politecnico*. He also produced an amazing amount of fiction, most of which boldly entered fantastic territory. Three of his four historical fantasy works—the novellas *Il visconte dimezzato* (1952; *The Cloven Viscount*, 1962), *Il barone rampante* (1957; *The Baron in the Trees*, 1959), and *Il cavaliere inesistente* (1959; *The Non-Existent Knight*, 1962)—are from this period. They constitute some of his most celebrated and characteristic works.

Calvino took special delight in reading and studying fables. By editing and retelling some two hundred regional folktales in *Fiabe italiane: Raccolte della tradizione popolare durante gli ultimi cento anni e transcritte in lingua dai vari dialetti* (1956; *Italian Fables*, 1959; also translated as *Italian Folktales*, 1980), Calvino entertained readers of all ages and contributed significantly to folklore scholarship. This absorption in storytelling's ancient roots also stimulated him to produce some modern counterparts; several of these are collected in *La giornata d'uno scrutatore* (1963; *The Watcher, and Other Stories*, 1971). These contemporary parables testify to Calvino's own political and social disenchantment (he quit the Communist Party around 1958).

Realistic and popular elements also pervade the

comic vignettes of *Marcovaldo: Ovvero, Le stagioni in città* (1963; *Marcovaldo: Or, The Seasons in the City*, 1983), in which Marcovaldo, an impoverished peasant, moves his family to the big city. Ironically, he spends more time and money trying to recapture the life he abandoned than in improving his lot. As in much of Calvino's work, an essentially tragic view of life underlies the humorous and gently resigned spirit of the narratives.

Calvino moved to Paris in 1964, where he met and married an Argentinean translator for the United Nations Educational, Scientific, and Cultural Organization (UNESCO) that same year; the couple had a daughter in 1965. Calvino remained in Paris for sixteen years, during which time friendships with internationally recognized intellectuals, such as anthropologist Claude Lévi-Strauss and literary critic Roland Barthes, greatly inspired his critical and creative writing. The finely crafted works from this period—*Le cosmicomiche* (1965; *Cosmicomics*, 1968), *Ti con zero* (1967; *t zero*, 1969), *Il castello dei destini incrociati* (1969, 1973; *The Castle of Crossed Destinies*, 1976), and *Le città invisibili* (1972; *Invisible Cities*, 1974)—are remarkable for their intellectual playfulness and literary inventiveness. In 1972, *Invisible Cities*, Calvino's final historical fantasy, captured the prestigious Feltrinelli Prize, Italy's equivalent of the Pulitzer Prize. The last novel Calvino wrote in Paris was *Se una notte d'inverno un viaggiatore* (1979; *If on a Winter's Night a Traveler*, 1981), a spirited parody of literary experiments, such as the French *nouveau roman* (New Novel), which appeared in 1979. The international success of this book secured Calvino's reputation as a major twentieth century author.

In 1980, Calvino and his family relocated to Rome. *Palomar*, his last novel, was published in 1983; the English translation, *Mr. Palomar*, appeared around the time of his death on September 19, 1985, in Siena, Italy, from a cerebral hemorrhage. As personal in its own way as was his first novel, *Mr. Palomar* is essentially an extended meditation on man and the cosmos. Its meticulous investigation of the complexities of human experience—whether physical, mental, or spiritual—is similar to the short stories in the posthumous *Sotto il sole giaguaro* (1986; *Under the Jaguar Sun*, 1988), where the senses of taste, hearing, and smell provide entry into the magical, ineffable, and grotesque dimensions of mundane existence.

ANALYSIS

Calvino's reputation as a master storyteller and innovative writer rests primarily on his success in fusing the traditional and original, the magical and mundane, the grotesque and ineffable—elements that are disparate, even contradictory. Generally, this literary alchemy is seen in two basic ways: If the story relates something real, Calvino will introduce magical or fantastic elements; if it describes the incredible or imaginary, he will present it in a nonchalantly realistic manner.

Because of the intricate interrelationship of the actual and the imaginary in his work, Calvino is considered both a realist and a fantasist. His brand of realism, however, is best described as neorealistic. Like realism and naturalism, neorealism depicts the world in an unidealized, concrete manner. Unlike these other literary genres, neorealism does not do so in order to present an impartial picture of reality; rather, it seeks to communicate a particular experience of that reality. Neorealism achieves this effect by revealing the elusive, intangible aspects of experience—the psychological, symbolic, or metaphysical dimensions, for example—residing within the physical and actual.

Calvino's imaginative perception of the real world is complemented by his rational interpretation of the fantastic. As he observes in an essay from *Una pietra sopra: Discorsi di letteratura e societa* (1980; *The Uses of Literature*, 1986):

> For me the main thing in a narrative is not the explanation of an extraordinary event, but the order of things that this extraordinary event produces in itself and around it; the pattern, the symmetry, the network of images deposited around it, as in the formation of a crystal.

Calvino refers frequently to the crystal to describe his own way of thinking and writing. In *Sulla fiaba* (1988; *Six Memos for the Next Millennium*, 1988), a collection of lectures that he was preparing at the time of his death, he remarks that the precision and geometric faceting of the crystal, and its ability to refract light, are what make it, for him, a model of perfection and an emblem of his work. In his writing, Calvino mimics the crystal's rationality, symmetry, and ability to combine endlessly in order to explore all the possible variations and alternatives of a given idea or argument. For him, the possible is as important as the real.

The "crystalline" features of Calvino's fiction are especially pronounced in works from his Parisian years. The complex permutations in *t zero*, the multiplicity of phenomena and interpretation in *Invisible Cities*, and the intricately woven interrelationships of characters, events, images, and ideas in *The Castle of Crossed Destinies* are clearly analogous to the faceted structure and systematic self-organization of crystals. Simultaneously rational and organic, this system offers Calvino a satisfying intellectual and artistic means of expressing and illuminating the entanglements of human life within an increasingly complex and unpredictable world.

The crystal's almost magical relationship with light is another significant quality. Applied to Calvino's fiction, lightness—one of the literary values he admired and discusses in *Six Memos for the Next Millennium*—suggests luminosity, elucidation, and weightlessness. Luminosity refers to visibility, or the exactness of Calvino's images. After observing that his stories generally grow out of an image or visualized concept, Calvino affirms that the visual image is "a way of attaining knowledge of the most profound meaning." In order to arrive at that meaning, he uses a procedure that strives to unite spontaneously generated images with the sequential logic of discursive thought. That is, in order to interpret images into words and then mold them into a narrative, he synthesizes intuition and reason, spontaneity and calculation, fantasy and fact.

Calvino's talent for elucidating contemporary reality often finds paradoxical expression in his historical novels. He sometimes takes a remarkable event as his departure point, such as Italian merchant Marco Polo's thirteenth century visit to Mongol emperor Kublai Khan's court in *Invisible Cities*, and interprets it in an original manner, which sheds light on contemporary issues. He also uses the literature of the past, such as Ludovico Ariosto's Renaissance epic *Orlando Furioso* (1516,

1521, 1532; English translation, 1591) and Miguel de Cervantes's satiric novel *El ingenioso hidalgo don Quixote de la Mancha* (1605, 1615; *Don Quixote de la Mancha*, 1612-1620), for example, to inspire and form his modern visions.

Calvino's respect for the past and for literary tradition rarely translates into mere imitation. In *Cosmicomics* and *t zero*, for example, he reverses the usual premise of the historical novel: Instead of using the past as a means for understanding the present, and instead of evoking a real, specific time and place from history, he employs modern scientific theories to fashion a fantastic, impossible past. This reconstruction achieves its unity through its first-person narrator, Qfwfq, an ageless, protean being who describes the formation of the cosmos, the evolution of life, and the perplexities of consciousness. With Qfwfq, Calvino not only gives abstract ideas, such as time and space, a narrative form, but, more importantly, elucidates important questions about the character of existence and the essence of being human.

It is this last question that raises the idea of light as weightlessness; while the tone of his work is accurately described as "light," it can hardly be called frivolous. This quality he prefers to characterize as a buoyant thoughtfulness adopted to ease the

> desperate and all-pervading oppression . . . in a human condition common to us all. . . . Whenever humanity seems condemned to heaviness . . . I have to change my approach, look at the world from a different perspective, with a different logic and with fresh methods of cognition and verification. . . . I look to ~~[literature and] science to nourish my visions in which all heaviness disappears.

Literature for Calvino is thus not a body of traditions or a special, artistic way of using words; it is rather "the search for lightness as a reaction to the weight of living." This search not only expresses humankind's existential needs but also affirms people's distinctly human values.

THE CLOVEN VISCOUNT

First published: *Il visconte dimezzato*, 1952
 (English translation, 1962)
Type of work: Novella

Split lengthwise by a cannonball, Medardo's good and evil halves generate various kinds of conflict, try to destroy each other, and are finally reunited.

The Cloven Viscount was rereleased in 1960 as part of the trilogy *I nostri antenati* (1960; *Our Ancestors*, 1980). Although the three novellas have no specifics in common, they are nonetheless connected by their similar exploration of concepts illuminating contemporary cultural crises. *The Cloven Viscount* probes ethics by interpreting literally the division of human good and evil; *The Baron in the Trees* explores the isolation and egocentricity of individuals; and *The Non-Existent Knight* examines the clash between the ideal and the real, between image and actuality.

The Cloven Viscount is deceptively simple. Participating in his first battle, Medardo is cloven in two by a cannonball. Patched by doctors, the recovered half returns to Terralba, immediately causes his father's death, and terrorizes the countryside; it is Medardo's evil self. Soon his good side returns. Inevitably, the two sides meet, duel, and, because of their wounds, are finally fused into "a whole man again, neither good nor bad, but a mixture of goodness and badness."

Clearly a parable on human nature, Medardo's division alludes to the archetypal struggle between good and evil. Yet Calvino offers alternate interpretations of this central dichotomy. In this story and its seventeenth century setting, Medardo's division refers to philosophical dualism—the human being perceived as mind and body, subject and object—a view formulated around 1640 by French philosopher René Descartes. Moreover, with the motifs of science and technology, Calvino further alludes to a twentieth century variation: human being and machine. Technology, like its creator, is both gift and curse; like Dr. Jekyll and Mr. Hyde, it possesses a formidable, ambiguous power.

To explore divisiveness and the ambiguities of duality, many other characters also contain contradictions: Pamela is chaste but earthy; Pietrochiodo is a destructive creator; Medardo's nephew, the narrator, is a high-born bastard. These variations and juxtapositions direct attention to what dualism, by nature, disregards—the inevitable "shades of gray." Such permutations also serve to effect a reversal in the sense of the terms of the dichotomy, as when the good Medardo is considered a worse evil than his counterpart. By exposing the complexity behind the supposed simplicity, Calvino emphasizes the integral unity of dichotomies: "Thus the days went by at Terralba, and our sensibilities became numbed, since we felt ourselves lost between an evil and a virtue equally inhuman." The paradoxical relationship of the two Medardos to Terralba's unusual members, especially the dour Huguenots and hedonistic lepers, provides a good example of the intersection of theme, structure, and technique in Calvino's work.

Unfortunately, "a whole Viscount is not enough to make all the world whole." Novels, like the situations they depict and the life they emulate, are, at least for Calvino, complex things incapable of giving easy answers. As the narrator melancholically reflects at the end: "I, though, amid all this fervor of wholeness, felt myself growing sadder and more lacking. Sometimes one who thinks himself incomplete is merely young."

THE BARON IN THE TREES

First published: *Il barone rampante*, 1957
 (English translation, 1959)
Type of work: Novella

A young baron, rebelling against the restraints of family and society, climbs into the treetops to live freely, vowing never to descend.

Calvino appropriately sets *The Baron in the Trees*, his tale of the rebellious and eccentric Baron Cosimo Rondo, in the late eighteenth century—the uneasy transitional period from Enlightenment to Romanticism. The elegance, inventiveness, and practicality with which Cosimo (only twelve when he climbs into the trees) adapts to and improves upon his condition illustrate the Enlightenment's faith in reason, progress, and perfectibility. Cosimo's self-indulgence, "superhuman tenacity," and feral lifestyle, on the other hand, suggest the egotism, extravagance, and primitivism of Romantic sensibility.

Elevated above the world, Cosimo enters a familiar reality made strange, in which "branches spread out like the tentacles of extraordinary animals, and the plants on the ground opened up stars of fretted leaves like the green skins of reptiles." Stranger yet are the people he encounters: ragamuffin fruit thieves, murderous Moors, plotting Jesuits, literate brigands, exiled Spaniards, and even the great Napoleon I himself. Each seems more curious than the other.

It is Cosimo who is the most unusual of the lot. As Biagio, the narrator and Cosimo's brother, remarks, the locals consider him mad: "I am not talking only of his determination to live up there, but of the various oddities of his character; and no one considered him other than an original." Original in his persistent aloofness and nonconformity, Cosimo is also unique for the many guises he assumes. Sometimes, for example, he portrays a savior, as when he extinguishes fires and assists peasants. Other times he is a destroyer, as when he causes his uncle's decapitation, his bandit friend's hanging, and his aged tutor's lifelong imprisonment. Most usually, however, he is a subversive: insurrection, a "Project for the Constitution of an Ideal State in the Trees," and freemasonry all play parts in his revolt against human organization.

Cosimo's eccentric individualism arouses both admiration and contempt, sympathy and incomprehension—an ambivalence particularly pronounced in his love affairs. His most complicated affair is with the perverse and haughty aristocrat Violante (Viola). Throughout the book, these two collide, mingle, and separate like a pair of natural, primeval forces. Cosimo's obstinate pride and ignorance of human feeling finally, irrevocably, clash with Viola's insatiable emotional appetite. As fiercely independent as Cosimo, Viola's individuality becomes too much for the customarily distant Cosimo; the inability to communicate and to accept another's individuality ultimately destroys their union.

Alone as never before, Cosimo vacillates between utterly wild, animalistic behavior and elaborately rational plans "for installing a world republic of men—equal, free, and just." Well past the age of sixty, he finally encounters a death that is as curious as his life and maintains his childhood vow. Although touchingly lyrical, his memorial, "Lived in trees—Always loved earth—Went into sky," only emphasizes his essential detachment from human life.

Paradoxically, however, Cosimo contributes his own special legacy to humanity. Restless spirit and witness to a great age, the "patriot on the treetops" achieves mythic stature. As his brother/biographer comments:

> [Cosimo] understood something else, something that was all-embracing, and he could not say it in words but only by living as he did. Only by being so frankly himself as he was till his death could he give something to all men.

INVISIBLE CITIES

First published: *Le città invisibili*, 1972
    (English translation, 1974)
Type of work: Novel

A young Marco Polo distracts the aging Kublai Khan with wild tales of cities he has seen in his travels—or are they reworked versions of the same city?

Despite being called a novel, *Invisible Cities* is not truly a novel. There is no plot or character development. Instead, it is a collection of about fifty-five short, highly impressionistic pastiches of arbitrarily named fantastic cities (such as Adelma, Berenice, Chloe, Diomira, Irene, Penthesilea, Phyllis, Raissa, Valdrada, Zirma, and Zobeide, to name a few), placed in a structure that is quite meticulous, yet rambling, that nearly mimics the structure of a full commercial novel.

The stories are set within the framework of a very loose dialogue wherein the famous Venetian explorer Marco Polo comes to the court of the legendary emperor Kublai Khan. While there, Polo is instructed to travel the empire and gather not gold or treasure but stories with which to regale the aging, and frequently impatient, conqueror with descriptions of every city he has visited on his long peregrinations through the Mongolian realm, as Khan is bored with his own messengers' stories.

Throughout the dialogue—and a true dialogue it is, as Khan and Polo are the only two characters in the work (although a case could be made that each city is also its own character)—the emperor expresses his belief that Polo is merely describing his home city of Venice in different and fanciful ways, ways that Polo could not use with honesty or impunity in his own land. Khan also occasionally believes that the cities Polo is describing do not exist at all, except in the Venetian explorer's imagination.

Upon a summary first reading, *Invisible Cities* could be considered a nice collection of prose works on imaginary cities. Indeed, during the interplay between the two characters it is difficult to tell whether the things Polo is describing represent differing aspects of a single city or different cities with the same aspect in each of them. However, it quickly becomes clear that while some passages are horribly contrived, the novel is larger in scope than mere descriptions of cities. It is a work that muses upon the concept of living in a city, the concept of home, and perhaps even the concept of belonging somewhere. Calvino's book is also a surreal and postmodern journey through the language of the imagination, a delicious mélange of psychological states, physical states, sensory states, transcendence, and more.

IF ON A WINTER'S NIGHT A TRAVELER

First published: *Se una notte d'inverno un viaggiatore,* 1979 (English translation, 1981)
Type of work: Novel

The Reader and the Other Reader attempt to read ten different books in ten different genres in libraries, bookstores, and government archives around the world. They also fall in love with each other and uncover an insidious plot by Apocryphers to replace real books with fake books.

This novel, which is definitely not a quick read, is considered an Oulipian work. Oulipo, the acronomym for Ouvrior de Littérature Potentielle (Workshop of Potential Literature), was founded on November 24, 1960, in France as a subcommittee of the Collège de Pataphysique by Raymond Queneau and François le Lionnais. This group of writers and mathematicians sought to create works using constrained techniques, such as repetition, switching every noun in a story with another noun, and writing without using a specific letter of the alphabet.

In *If on a Winter's Night a Traveler,* Calvino uses the constraint of repetitive experiences slightly differently. All the odd-numbered chapters are told in the second person and tell the reader what is happening in preparation for the next chapter. All the even-numbered chapters are chapters of the books that the protagonist is trying to read.

Near the end of the novel, the character Silas Flannery perhaps states what Calvino himself thought when writing this work: "I have had the idea of writing a novel composed only of beginnings of novels. The protagonist could be a Reader who is continually interrupted. The Reader buys the new novel A by the author Z. But it is a defective copy, he cannot go beyond the beginning. . . . He returns to the bookstore to have the volume exchanged . . . "

As the Reader continually tries to obtain a correct copy of the book that he wants to read, each time he encounters a problem: The chapters are all the same in one book, and the "replacement" is a totally different book altogether, although the pages after a certain point are all blank.

Calvino's skill is evident in this work, as each of the "novels" within the novel is written as though by a different author, with differing styles, tone, and prose. It is almost as though the author is daring readers to continue reading despite the abrupt endings, U-turns, and divergences. Despite the shuffling and shifting of stories, the end of the book ties up all the loose ends.

SUMMARY

Like his own forefathers, the Renaissance humanists, Italo Calvino finds material for his art wherever eye and mind pause, absorbed in contemplation or delight, and poses ageless questions about the nature of world and humanity. Calvino's own answer to the question "Who are we?" significantly reveals his artistic vision: "Who is each one of us, if not a combinatoria of experiences, information, books we have read, things imagined? Each life is an encyclopedia, a library, an inventory of objects." His translation of this comprehensive perception into vital new literary forms makes him one of the most original—and classical—authors of the twentieth century.

Terri Frongia; updated by Daryl F. Mallett

BIBLIOGRAPHY

By the Author

LONG FICTION:
Il sentiero dei nidi di ragno, 1947, 1957, 1965 (*The Path to the Nest of Spiders*, 1956)
Il visconte dimezzato, 1952 (novella; *The Cloven Viscount*, 1962)
Il barone rampante, 1957 (novella; *The Baron in the Trees*, 1959)
Il cavaliere inesistente, 1959 (novella; *The Non-Existent Knight*, 1962)
I nostri antenati, 1960 (*Our Ancestors*, 1980; includes *The Cloven Viscount*, *The Non-Existent Knight*, and *The Baron in the Trees*)
Il castello dei destini incrociati, 1969, 1973 (*The Castle of Crossed Destinies*, 1976)
Le città invisibili, 1972 (*Invisible Cities*, 1974)
Se una notte d'inverno un viaggiatore, 1979 (*If on a Winter's Night a Traveler*, 1981)
Palomar, 1983 (*Mr. Palomar*, 1985)

SHORT FICTION:
Ultimo viene il corvo, 1949 (partial translation as *Adam, One Afternoon, and Other Stories*, 1957)
La formica Argentina, 1952 (*The Argentine Ant*, 1957)
L'entrata in guerra, 1954
La nuvola di smog, 1958 (*Smog*, 1971)
I racconti, 1958
Marcovaldo: Ovvero, Le stagioni in città, 1963 (*Marcovaldo: Or, The Seasons in the City*, 1983)
La giornata d'uno scrutatore, 1963 (*The Watcher, and Other Stories*, 1971)

DISCUSSION TOPICS

- How was Italo Calvino's early exposure to Italian writers Elio Vittorini, Cesare Pavese, and Natalia Levi Ginzburg influential in his writing?

- Calvino's work has been compared to that of other writers like William Burroughs, Kurt Vonnegut, and John Barth. Do you agree or disagree and why?

- What is Oulipo? How does Calvino fit into the Oulipean movement?

- How does Calvino's work differ from other Oulipean writers, such as Georges Perec or Raymond Queneau?

- Does Calvino's influence show in any of the works of his "students," or writers whom he has influenced, such as Mario Rigoni Stern, Gianni Celati, or Andrea de Carlo?

Le cosmicomiche, 1965 (*Cosmicomics*, 1968)
Ti con zero, 1967 (*t zero*, 1969)
Gli amore difficili, 1970 (*Difficult Loves*, 1984)
Sotto il sole giaguaro, 1986 (*Under the Jaguar Sun*, 1988)

NONFICTION:

Una pietra sopra: Discorsi di letteratura e societa, 1980 (*The Uses of Literature*, 1986)
Collezione di sabbia, 1984
The Literature Machine: Essays, 1986
Sulla fiaba, 1988 (*Six Memos for the Next Millennium*, 1988)
Perché leggere i classici, 1991 (*Why Read the Classics?*, 1999)
Eremita a Parigi: Pagine autobiografiche, 1994 (*Hermit in Paris: Autobiographical Writings*, 2003)
Lettere: 1940-1985, 2000

EDITED TEXTS:

La letteratura americana e altri saggi, 1951
Fiabe italiane: Raccolte della tradizione popolare durante gli ultimi cento anni e transcritte in lingua dai vari dialetti, 1956 (*Italian Fables*, 1959; also translated as *Italian Folktales*, 1980)
Cesare Pavese: Lettere, 1926-1950, 1966
L'Uccel Belverde e altre fiabe italiane, 1972 (*Italian Folk Tales*, 1975)

About the Author

Bolongaro, Eugenio. *Italo Calvino and the Compass of Literature.* Toronto: University of Toronto Press, 2003.

Botta, Ann, and Domenico Scarpa. *Future Perfect: Italo Calvino and the Reinvention of the Literature.* Cava de Tirreni, Italy: Avagliano, 2002.

Cannon, JoAnn. *Italo Calvino: Writer and Critic.* Ravenna, Italy: Longo, 1981.

Carter, Albert H. *Italo Calvino: Metamorphoses of Fantasy.* Ann Arbor, Mich.: UMI Research Press, 1987.

Gabriele, Tommasina. *Italo Calvino: Eros and Language.* Rutherford, N.J.: Fairleigh Dickinson University Press, 1994.

Hume, Kathryn. *Calvino Fictions: Cogito and Cosmos.* Oxford, England: Clarendon Press, 1992.

Jeannet, Angela M. *Under the Radiant Sun and the Crescent Moon: Italo Calvino Storytelling.* Toronto: University of Toronto Press, 2000.

McLaughlin, M. L. *Italo Calvino.* Edinburgh: Edinburgh University Press, 1998.

Markey, Constance. *Italo Calvino: A Journey Toward Postmodernism.* Gainesville: University Press of Florida, 1999.

Olken, I. T. *With Pleated Eye and Garnet Wing: Symmetries of Italo Calvino.* Ann Arbor: University of Michigan Press, 1984.

Pilz, Kerstin. *Mapping Complexity: Literature and Science in the Works of Italo Calvino.* Leicester, England: Troubador, 2005.

Re, Lucia. *Calvino and the Age of Neorealism: Fables of Estrangement.* Stanford, Calif.: Stanford University Press, 1990.

Ricci, Franco, ed. *Calvino Revisited.* Ottawa, Ont.: Dovehouse Editions, 1989.

_____. *Painting with Words, Writing with Pictures: Word and Image in the Work of Italo Calvino.* Toronto, University of Toronto Press, 2001.

Weiss, Beno. *Understanding Italo Calvino.* Columbia: University of South Carolina Press, 1993.

LUIS DE CAMÕES

Born: Lisbon, Portugal
c. 1524
Died: Lisbon, Portugal
June 10, 1580

Camões wrote Portugal's great poetic epic, The Lusiads, *and is considered to be the founder and exemplar of Portuguese literature.*

Library of Congress

BIOGRAPHY

Luis de Camões (kuh-MOYNSH) is the preeminent poet of the Portuguese language, occupying a place in that language analogous to William Shakespeare in English or Dante in Italian in both the magnitude of his achievement and his influence upon Portuguese literature. Camões's epic of discovery and conquest *Os Lusíadas* (1572; *The Lusiads*, 1655) is the work for which he is most renowned, but his lyric poetry and plays have also commanded attention.

Luis Vaz de Camões, the son of Simão Vaz de Camões and Ana de Sá, was born in Lisbon, Portugal, around 1524. His family was well off but did not inhabit the upper reaches of the aristocracy. Camões's family was originally Galician in origin and had lived for some generations in the mountainous northern Portuguese town of Chaves. There are unsubstantiated rumors that some of his ancestors may have been converted Jews, but it is difficult to determine the validity of this claim.

His overseas travels aside, the details of Camões's life are hazy, and beyond a few known facts what is generally thought about Camões's biography is largely a product of scholarly conjecture. It is thought that Camões attended the newly relocated University of Coimbra, where his uncle Bento was the first chancellor. At Coimbra, Camões wrote *Enfatriões* (pr. 1540), a comic play in which the Greek gods assume human form. This play foreshadowed his juxtaposition of classical deities with contemporary characters in *The Lusiads*.

Camões arrived in Lisbon in the mid-1540's. He presented himself to King John III and wrote *Auto del-Rei Seleuco* (pr. 1542), a historical play based on domestic drama in the household of the Hellenistic monarchs of present-day Syria. On April 11, 1542, Camões first saw Caterina de Ataide in church, and that day changed his life forever. Caterina is believed to be the great love of his life and the object of his passionate love sonnets, where her name is encrypted as "Natercia." She returned his feelings, but Camões's relatively low status at court and a certain reputation for wildness of character did not allow Caterina to reciprocate openly the poet's ardor. His love inspired him to write sonnets that circulated privately, although they were printed posthumously in 1595 as *Rimas* (*The Lyrides*, 1803, 1884). Some critics also think he was in love with the king's daughter, the Infanta Maria, but there is no actual evidence for this.

In 1549, Camões made his first expedition outside Portugal; he was involved in a military foray into Morocco, where he lost an eye. Additional complications ensued on his return to Lisbon, where on June 24, 1552, he was accused of assaulting a cavalry officer, Gonçalves Borges. Camões was imprisoned, but he was released the following year after being pardoned by the king on the condition that he perform five years of military service abroad. Camões's voyage to India provided the empirical basis for his recounting of Vasco da Gama's voyage in *The Lusiads*.

Camões was the first major European writer to travel physically south of the equator. His distance from Caterina prompted him to write more sonnets. Camões is said to have been dissatisfied with his enforced Asian sojourn, not only because of its compulsory nature and his exile from his home country but also because of his distance from his Portuguese lover. However, as demonstrated in his poem "Barbara," Camões was not averse to the charms of ladies of the East whom he encountered on his voyage.

Camões was a keen observer of the places he traveled. His poem "Arabia Felix," although rife with classical framings of Arabian topography, contains insights that could not have been acquired other than by actual observation. Notably, in "Arabia Felix" Camões emphasizes how his experience with the places mentioned in the poem contradicted European idealizations of the exotic East.

Both Camões's personal experience and the Portuguese history he chronicled must be kept in mind when analyzing *The Lusiads*, which he began writing in the mid-1560's. The epic poem chronicles Vasco da Gama's voyage around Africa to India, although Camões himself spent far more time in Asia than in Africa. A traumatic and climactic event in his travels occurred in 1569, when he was on his way from Macao, the Portuguese enclave in China, to Goa, the equivalent enclave in India. His ship was wrecked off what are now the southern coasts of Vietnam and Cambodia; legendarily, he swam safely to shore while holding the manuscript of his unfinished epic.

Camões returned to Portugal in 1570 with the help of his friend Diogo do Couto. In 1572, *The Lusiads* was published, having been printed by Antonio Gonçalves over the course of the previous two years. The young king, Sebastian, the grandson of John III, was just reaching maturity and welcomed the publication of a national epic to buttress his rule and his ambitions to crusade against the Muslims. For the first time in his life, Camões was in official favor, and he briefly operated as a pillar of the Lisbon literary establishment, writing prose prefaces to a number of works by other writers.

This brief period of prosperity ended, however, after Sebastian was killed at the battle of Alcacer-Quibir in Morocco in 1578. Not only was the flower of Portugal's hope dead, but the rules of succession meant that, after a brief interval, the rule of Portugal would pass to King Philip II of Spain, leaving Spain and Portugal effectively united and the two empires effectively commingled. Camões died in 1580, four months after Philip assumed the throne.

ANALYSIS

Camões's ambitious epic *The Lusiads* has tended to overshadow his lyric poetry, but the same sensibility is evident in both. In sonnet 54, "Todas as almas tristes se mostravam," the sudden revelation of the poet's love for Caterina while he is in church, the sense of a general prayerfulness giving way to a more ardent and specific veneration of the beloved, is startling and forceful, even within the heightened rhetoric of sonnet conventions. In sonnet 314, "Se a ninguem tratais com desamor," he displays the resourcefulness of the lover in trying to read every sign of his beloved's conduct beneficially, seeing her very indifference to him as a kind of special favor. In sonnet 81, "Amor é um fogo que arde sem se ver," Camões contemplates the cessation of Caterina's treasured eyes and even envisages her bodily decomposition, or at least the stillness and coldness of her tomb. In "Alma minha gentl" (sonnet 18), on hearing of Caterina's death, the poet prays to join her, to be unconscious and insentient. The very ardor of his pleas, however, signifies his continued consciousness. He senses that his praise of Caterina is insufficient, yet the sonnet in which he expresses his admission is perhaps his greatest.

The Lusiads has an intimacy that is similar to Camões's lyric poetry. The epic is about real people who lived in the recent past, which differs from other Renaissance epics that concentrated on fictional, mythical, or biblical personages, or on figures, such as Godfrey of Bouillon (the hero of Torquato Tasso's *Gerusalemme liberata*, 1581; *Jerusalem Delivered*, 1600), who were sufficiently removed in time to be outside of living memory. The sense that the Portuguese, a previously obscure people, were now making their mark upon the world's destiny and the excitement that the country now had a national epic pervade the poem. The epic's depiction of non-European people was a novelty in its time, since most Portuguese people knew little or nothing about Asia and Africa.

Although written more than five hundred years ago, *The Lusiads* has continued to attract critical attention. Part of Camões's appeal to contemporary readers is his pronounced ambiguity on the subject of empire. This is clearly evident in book 4. As the Portuguese expedition sets sail, an old man sounds a cautionary note, warning of the negative implications of the nation's vaulting ambitions. This passage has long been read as Camões expressing reservations about the potential hubris of colonialism and exploration. Book 4 also contains a parallel passage about Adamastor, a mythological character invented by Camões who is similar to the giants and monsters in Greek mythology. Adamstor is the spirit of the Cape of Good Hope, which the voyagers must round on their way to the Indian Ocean. In later years, when the land around the cape was colonized and became South Africa, Adamastor became an important character in South African literature, epitomizing the Africans' recalcitrance to accept Eurocentric definitions of the continent.

The South African reading of Camões is the most obvious example of a difference in how he is read and interpreted in his native Portuguese and in English translations. Camões's life—his passions, his personal losses, and his sense of being a misfit in his own society—has received more attention in the Portuguese-speaking world. In the English-speaking world, however, the emphasis has been on Camões's contributions to the epic tradition, and, more recently, on the global and postcolonial implications of his work.

Richard Fanshawe in the seventeenth century, William Julius Mickle in the eighteenth century, Captain Sir Richard Francis Burton and Major Thomas Livingstone Mitchell in the nineteenth century, and Leonard Bacon, William Atkinson, and Landeg White in the twentieth century all translated Camões into English. Some critics and readers have complained that Camões's work suffers in its English translation because his translators did not live during the Renaissance. Nonetheless, *The Lusiads* has had a substantive if limited effect on several major English-language writers.

THE LUSIADS

First published: *Os Lusiadas,* 1572 (English translation, 1655)
Type of work: Poetry

The story of the Portuguese exploration of Africa and the Indian Ocean is told in the form of a traditional epic.

Vasco da Gama is the chief character in *The Lusiads,* but he is not its hero. The poem's title derives from Lusitania, the Roman name for the province that roughly encompasses present-day Portugal. The nation of Portugal and all of its people are the true heroes of this patriotic epic.

The Lusiads is written in *ottava rima,* a rhyme scheme of Italian origin that was commonly used in Renaissance epic poetry. An *ottava rima* stanza has eight lines with three rhymes, following the rhyme scheme *ababCC.* It is a flowing meter that allows the narrative to move smoothly, and the long, assonant rhymes have a kind of lulling quality.

The Lusiads begins in medias res, or in the middle of the action. Vasco da Gama and his Portuguese crewmen are in the East African kingdom of Malindi, having survived rough weather and an ambush. The local king encourages Gama to recite the history of the Portuguese people, which he does, going back to ancient times.

Gama tells the story of the Roman general Quintus Sertorius, whose successful rebellion drove a repressive regime out of Hispania (now Portugal and Spain). Gama then describes the growth of Portugal from a small principality to a significant European state. The story culminates in book 4, with the 1385 Battle of Aljubarrota, in which the Portuguese defeated the Spanish kingdom of Castile and restored the Portuguese monarch to the throne. Camões's patriotism is evident is his description of Portuguese general Nuno Álvares Pereira's victory over Spain:

O'er Tago's waves his gallant band he led,
And humbled Spain in every province bled;
Sevilia's standard in his spear he bore,
And Andulsia's ensigns kept in gore.
Low in the dust distresst Castilia mourned,
And bathed in tears each eye to heaven was turned
The orphans, widows, and the hoary sires;
And heaven relenting quench'd the raging fires
Of mutual hate. . . .

After this battle, the Portuguese were able to launch overseas explorations, and these initial voyages are delineated in the poem. Finally, Gama tells the story of his own voyage, his circumnavigation of the Cape of Good Hope, which the Portuguese called the Cape of Storms. It is here that the most supernatural elements of the poem appear: Adamastor and a maritime apparition. Along with these fantastic elements, book 4 also contains highly realistic details of a ravaging disease.

The Lusiads includes an account of the battle between the goddess Venus, who is a "divine" advocate on behalf of the Portuguese, and Bacchus, the patron god of Asia who tries to prevent the Portuguese from having a successful voyage. Bacchus represents both the irrationality of the non-European world and the limits of human daring and exploration that the Portuguese, through their bravery

and fortitude, are seeking to transcend. Despite the warm reception extended by the king of Malindi, some Asians and Africans resented the Portuguese exploration because it infringed upon the lives of the Muslims and Hindus who resided on these continents. Camões's poem depicts the introduction of Christianity to the non-European world as a result of the Portuguese and Spanish explorations of the fifteenth and sixteenth centuries.

Summary

When the Brazilian singer Caetano Veloso in his song "Lingua" says, "I like to feel my tongue touch the tongue of Luis de Camões," he is not only laying claim to an intimate contact with Portuguese literary tradition but also identifying himself with Camões as a bard and an artistic personality. In the twenty-first century, Camões is not merely a Portuguese national poet; he is a poet of the global Lusophone world, which includes Brazil, Angola, Mozambique, Guinea-Bissau, Cape Verde, and East Timor. The highest literary award for a writer in Portuguese is the Premio Luis de Camões, testifying to the poet's founding and indispensable role in worldwide Portuguese literary culture.

Nicholas Birns

Bibliography

By the Author

POETRY:
Os Lusíadas, 1572 (*The Lusiads*, 1655)
Cancioneiro, 1580
Rimas, 1595 (*The Lyrides*, 1803, 1884)
Selected Sonnets, 2005

DRAMA:
Enfatriões, pr. 1540
Auto del-Rei Seleuco, pr. 1542
Filodemo, pr. 1555

About the Author

Hart, Henry Hersch, *Luis de Camoëns and the Epic of the Lusiads.* Norman: University of Oklahoma Press, 1962.
Hower, Alfred, and Richard A. Preto-Rodas. *Empire in Transition: The Portuguese World in the Time of Camões.* Gainesville: University Presses of Florida, 1985.

Discussion Topics

- What is the principal preoccupation of Luis de Camões's lyric poetry?
- How did Camões's sojourn in Asia affect the subject matter of his writing?
- How does Camões's Portuguese nationality operate as his subject matter in *The Lusiads*?
- How is Camões seen differently in Portugal and in the English-speaking world?

Lipking, Lawrence. "The Genius of the Shore: *Lycidas*, Adamastor, and the Poetics of Nationalism." *PMLA: Publications of the Modern Language Association of America* 111 (March, 1996): 205-221.

Monteiro, George. *The Presence of Camões: Influences on the Literature of England, America, and Southern Africa.* Lexington: University Press of Kentucky, 1996.

Murrin, Michael. *History and Warfare in Renaissance Epic.* Chicago: University of Chicago Press, 1994.

Nicolopulos, James. *The Poetics of Empire in the Indies: Prophecy and Imitation in La Araucana and Os Lusíadas.* University Park: Pennsylvania State University Press, 2000.

Quint, David. *Epic and Empire: Politics and Generic Form from Virgil to Milton.* Princeton, N.J.: Princeton University Press, 1993.

Rajan, Balachandra. "*The Lusiads* and the Asian Reader." *English Studies in Canada* 23, no. 1 (March, 1997): 1-19.

Taylor, J. R., ed. *Luis de Camões, Epic and Lyric.* Manchester, England: Carcanet, 1990.

Vendler, Helen. "Camões the Sonneteer." *Portuguese Literary and Cultural Studies* 9 (Fall, 2002): 17-37.

ALBERT CAMUS

Born: Mondovi, Algeria
November 7, 1913
Died: Near Sens, France
January 4, 1960

A major force in France's intellectual life by the middle of the twentieth century, especially among those associated with existentialism, Camus was a leading novelist, short-story writer, philosopher, and playwright.

© The Nobel Foundation

BIOGRAPHY

Albert Camus (kah-MEW) was born on November 7, 1913, in Mondovi, a village in the interior of Algeria, which, since 1830, had been under the administration of France. Camus's father, Lucien, was a winery worker; his mother, Catherine Sintès, could not read or write. Shortly after the outbreak of World War I, Lucien Camus was mobilized in a North African regiment. Wounded at the First Battle of the Marne, he died on October 11, 1914, before Albert's first birthday. Catherine took the family to Belcourt, a working-class section of Algiers, to live with her mother, Marie Catherine Sintès. Catherine, who worked in a munitions factory and then as a cleaning woman, suffered a stroke that left her deaf and partially paralyzed. Albert lived with his mother, his older brother Lucien, and several relatives in a three-room apartment without electricity or running water, sharing a toilet with two other apartments.

At the local primary school, a teacher named Louis Germain took an interest in young Camus, providing him with extra instruction and entering him into competition for scholarships. As a subsidized day-boarder at a secondary school, Camus excelled in sports and began a lifelong friendship with teacher Jean Grenier, who encouraged him in his study of philosophy. In 1930, Camus developed the first symptoms of tuberculosis and moved out of his family apartment. In 1932, he published four articles in the Algerian journal *Sud*.

In 1934, Camus married Simone Hié, a fellow student, and also joined the Communist Party, which assigned him the task of proselytizing Muslims. Exempt from military service because of his lungs, he studied philosophy at the University of Algiers, financing his education through loans and a variety of odd jobs that included auto accessory salesman, municipal clerk, and research assistant with the university's meteorological service. Poor health, however, prevented him from pursuing a teaching career. His marriage was dissolved in 1936.

Cofounder of the blue-collar Théâtre du Travail, Camus collaborated in 1936 in writing the play *Révolte dans les Asturies* (revolt in the Asturias), the performance of which was banned. As an actor for Radio Algiers, he toured the countryside. In 1937, he began writing for the liberal newspaper *Alger-Républicain* and was expelled from the Communist Party in a dispute over policy. His first book, *L'Envers et l'endroit* (1937; "The Wrong Side and the Right Side," 1968), a collection of essays, was also published in 1937. In 1939, Camus cofounded the literary review *Rivages* and, when France declared war on Germany, attempted to enlist but was turned down because of his tuberculosis. He moved to Paris to work on the staff of *Paris-Soir*, relocating in the south of France when the Germans occupied the north. In December, 1940, he quit his job at *Paris-Soir* and returned to Algeria with his new wife, Francine Faure, a math teacher from Oran.

In 1942, to recover from an attack of tuberculosis, he traveled with Francine to Chambon-sur-Lignon in the mountains of central France. Camus remained there while Francine returned to Oran, and, after the Allied landing in North Africa, he became separated from her until the liberation of France. He joined the Resistance network Combat in the Lyons region. In 1942, he published his first novel, *L'Étranger* (1942; *The Stranger*, 1946), and his philosophical work *Le Mythe de Sisyphe* (1942; *The Myth of Sisyphus*, 1955). Camus moved to Paris, where he joined the editorial staff of Gallimard, a publishing house, and worked on the underground newspaper *Combat*, becoming its editor. His writings for *Combat* were published posthumously as *Camus à Combat: Éditoriaux et articles, 1944-1947* (2002; *Camus at Combat: Writing, 1944-1947*, 2006). He became acquainted with Jean-Paul Sartre and other influential intellectuals.

His play *Le Malentendu* (*The Misunderstanding*, pr., pb. 1948) was produced in Paris in 1944, after the city's liberation from German Occupation. In 1945, his play *Caligula* (wr. 1988-1939, pb. 1944, pr. 1945; English translation, 1948) was produced, and he visited Algeria to report on atrocities committed by the colonial French government. He also became father to twins, Jean and Catherine.

Camus visited the United States in 1946 and, the following year, published *La Peste* (1947; *The Plague*, 1948) to great acclaim. A 1948 production of *L'État de siège* (pr., pb. 1948; *State of Siege*, 1958) was not successful. Camus spoke out against French repression of a popular rebellion in Madagascar and in defense of Greek Communists who were sentenced to death. Through written deposition, he testified for the defense in a trial of Algerian nationalists. In 1951, publication of *L'Homme révolté* (*The Rebel*, 1956) provoked heated controversy and led to Camus's break with Sartre and other Marxist critics of his work.

After the 1954 outbreak of armed rebellion by Muslim Algerians against French administration, Camus became increasingly distraught over the escalating cycle of violence and reprisals. In 1955, he attempted to mediate a truce but was rebuffed. In 1956, he protested Soviet repression of the Hungarian Revolution and published *La Chute* (*The Fall*, 1957). In 1957, he published *L'Exil et le royaume*

(*Exile and the Kingdom*, 1958), a volume of short stories, and "Réflexions sur la guillotine" ("Reflections on the Guillotine"), a plea for the abolition of capital punishment. On October 17 of that year, Camus became the ninth Frenchman and second youngest author of any nationality to be awarded the Nobel Prize in Literature.

His health and mood fluctuating, Camus worked on *Le Premier Homme*, an autobiographical novel he never completed. On January 4, 1960, he was killed instantaneously when a car driven by his publisher Michel Gallimard crashed into a tree near the French village of Sens. Amid the wreckage was the working manuscript of *Le Premier Homme*, a slightly fictionalized account of Camus's own impoverished childhood in Belcourt. Though for a long time the author's heirs restricted access to the material, *Le Premier Homme* (1994; *The First Man*, 1995) was finally published more than three decades after his death.

ANALYSIS

When Camus received the Nobel Prize in 1957, the citation lauded him "for his important literary production, which with clear-sighted earnestness illuminated the problems of the human conscience in our times." Camus died less than three years later without augmenting what was a relatively meager oeuvre: three novels and a handful of plays, short stories, and essays. It is possible to read his entire life's work, including the posthumously published autobiographical fragment *Le Premier Homme*, in less time than it takes to absorb one novel by some of his more hermetic contemporaries.

Camus is widely read and fervently admired in a way few other twentieth century writers are. In a memoir of Robert F. Kennedy, journalist Jack Newfield recalls that the senator always traveled with a copy of Camus's writings: "He discovered Camus when he was thirty-eight, in the months of solitude and grief after his brother's death. By 1968 he had read, and re-read, all of Camus['s] essays, dramas and novels. But he more than just read Camus. He memorized him, meditated about him, quoted him and was changed by him."

Heir to the French tradition of literary crusaders, of activist authors like Michel de Montaigne, Voltaire, Victor Hugo, and Émile Zola, Camus is the lucid moral conscience of his era. His fiction, drama, and essays pose fundamental questions about individual identity and social bonds that cannot be ignored in the century that produced Auschwitz and Hiroshima. Camus served in the underground Resistance to the Nazi occupation of France and after the war refused to confine himself to a purely literary role. He became embroiled in many of the most tumultuous political controversies of the time—colonialism, capital punishment, racism, and East-West alliances. Even posthumously, he remains a public figure challenging his readers to a stringent standard of candor and compassion.

"A novel," wrote Camus in his review of Jean-Paul Sartre's novel *La Nausée* (1938; *Nausea*, 1949), "is never anything but a philosophy expressed in images." Camus's own novels are probably much more than just a philosophy expressed in images but they are never anything less. *The Stranger, The Plague,* and *The Fall* are among the most popular and esteemed books ever published in France; translated into dozens of languages, they remain not only in print but also in demand long after most other books of their era have been forgotten. Their appeal is less in plot and characterization than in the utter honesty with which they pose questions of personal, social, and cosmic identity. The scrupulously austere style that Camus honed was an embarrassment to the temptations of bogus rhetoric.

Camus came to Paris in the 1940's with a proletarian and Algerian background that set him apart from the erudite middle-class French intellectuals who befriended him. Along with Sartre, Simone de Beauvoir, and Maurice Merleau-Ponty, Camus emerged as one of the leaders of existentialism, a philosophical movement that was extremely popular following World War II. Existentialism has its roots in the writings of German philosophers, particularly Edmund Husserl, Karl Jaspers, and Martin Heidegger, though its legacy can be traced back through Friedrich Nietzsche and Søren Kierkegaard to as far as the pre-Socratic Greek Heraclitus. Never a systematic philosophy, existentialism was, in fact, a product of skepticism toward the intellectual arrogance of rational systems. Existentialism was the embodiment of a postwar zeitgeist cynical toward the shibboleths and values that had facilitated and camouflaged global catastrophe. It insisted that existence precedes essence, that noth-

ing is given—nothingness is the given. In the vast, indifferent universe, the individual is ineluctably responsible for creating his or her own identity. Five A's—alienation, absurdity, angst, anomie, and anxiety—seemed indispensable to the vocabulary of anyone who aspired to speak the language of existentialism, and there were many.

For a while, particularly in philosophical writings such as *The Myth of Sisyphus*, Camus was a very prominent existentialist voice, and the Algerian newcomer whom Sartre later called a "Cartesian of the absurd" became a frequent companion of Sartre and de Beauvoir during the heady days following the liberation of Paris. Camus, however, became increasingly uncomfortable in the role of high priest of the new cult of the posthumous God. Rejecting the faddishness of it all, he began emphasizing differences between his ideas and those of Sartre and insisted that he was not an existentialist. Following their feud in 1951, he no longer even called himself a friend of Sartre.

Whether or not they are technically "existentialist," and whether or not the term has ceased to have any clear definition, Camus's books are an embodiment of the attitudes of many Europeans at the middle of the twentieth century. Behind novels that are tolerant of everything but falsehood lies widespread bitterness over the failure of the crusade to save democracy in Spain, the fall of France's Third Republic, the Nazi genocide, and the prospects of nuclear annihilation.

"Phony" is Holden Caulfield's favorite term of derision in J. D. Salinger's *The Catcher in the Rye*, a popular novel published in 1951 during the peak of Camus's career, and the term applies as well to everything that Meursault, Rieux, and Clamence despise in Camus's fictional worlds. Camus, for whom metaphysical mutiny was a starting point for full awareness, saw a development in his own writings "from an attitude of solitary revolt to the recognition of a community whose struggles must be shared." The evolution of his work was cut short by a fatal automobile accident. What he did leave behind is a legacy that Sartre recognized in the eulogy he published three days after his erstwhile comrade's shocking death: "Camus could never cease to be one of the principal forces in our cultural domain, nor to represent, in his own way, the history of France and of this century."

THE STRANGER

First published: *L'Étranger,* 1942 (English translation, 1946)
Type of work: Novel

This terse account describes how a man kills a stranger and suffers the consequences of actions that he never intended or even understood.

The Stranger offers one of the most striking openings in modern fiction: "Mama died today. Or yesterday maybe, I don't know." Immediately introduced is a character, Meursault, so disconnected from chronology and other human beings that he is one of twentieth century literature's most memorable embodiments of alienation, of an absurdist world where social bonds are a sham. The British edition of Camus's first published novel translates the title as *The Outsider,* and Meursault indeed finds himself a marginal figure in a decentered universe where private and immediate sensations have displaced objective norms.

Meursault, an employee of a shipping company, participates in the rituals of his mother's funeral and, though he realizes he is supposed to be playing the role of bereaved son, cannot feel anything for the old woman's corpse. Shortly after returning to Algiers, Meursault goes to the beach, picks up a woman, Marie Cardona, and takes her to the movies and then to bed.

The following Sunday, Meursault and Marie are invited by Raymond Sintès, a raffish neighbor, to spend the day at the beach. During the outing, they are trailed and menaced by two Arab men who are apparently resentful of the way in which Raymond has abused a woman. During a solitary walk along the shore, Meursault encounters one of the Arabs again. It is oppressively hot, and the knife that the Arab wields glistens blindingly in the sun. Without premeditation or reflection, Meursault takes the gun that Raymond has given him and fires five shots into the stranger.

Narrated in Meursault's own affectless voice, *The Stranger* consists of two sections. The first recounts the events leading up to the fatal shooting, and the second reports its aftermath—Meursault's imprisonment, trial, conviction, and impending execution. Part 2 is in effect a commentary on part 1, an attempt to find coherence in one man's random actions. Marie, Raymond, the owner of the café that Meursault frequents, his mother's elderly friend, and others testify in court about the events in part 1. Both attorneys attempt to find some pattern. In the story that Meursault's lawyer tells, all the details paint the portrait of an innocent man acting in self-defense.

Yet the prosecutor finds a different design. For him, Meursault's callousness about his mother's death is symptomatic of a cold-blooded murderer, and it is that reading that the jury accepts when it sentences Meursault to death by guillotine. Meursault, however, rejects the specious patterns that both attorneys impose on events. He also refuses consolation from the prison chaplain, who offers him a kind of cosmic narrative in which everything is linked to a vast providential scheme.

Alone in his cell, Meursault realizes that despite the lies people tell to camouflage the truth, all are condemned to death. Uncomfortable with the florid rhetoric that distracts a reader from stark realities, he becomes a champion of candor. In his spare, honest style and his recognition that life is gratuitous and resistant to human attempts to catalog and rationalize it, Meursault is prepared to face extinction liberated from all illusions. He is, wrote Camus in 1955, "not a piece of social wreckage, but a poor and naked man enamored of a sun that leaves no shadows. Far from being bereft of all feeling, he is animated by a passion that is deep because it is stubborn, a passion for the absolute and for truth."

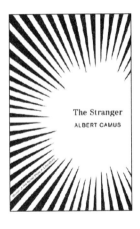

The Stranger
ALBERT CAMUS

THE PLAGUE

First published: *La Peste*, 1947 (English translation, 1948)

Type of work: Novel

Inhabitants of Oran, Algeria, are tested by an epidemic that devastates the city.

The Plague, which propelled Camus into international celebrity, is both an allegory of World War II and a universal meditation on human conduct and community. Organized into five sections, *The Plague* recounts the collective ordeal of Oran, Algeria, in the throes of an outbreak of bubonic plague. At the outset, even before the sudden proliferation of dead rats and sick humans that persuades reluctant officials to declare an epidemic, Oran is described as a drab, ugly city whose inhabitants are preoccupied with commerce.

Trapped within Oran after a quarantine is imposed are the novel's principal characters: Bernard Rieux, a physician separated from the ailing wife he sent to a sanatorium before the outbreak of the plague; Raymond Rambert, a Parisian journalist on assignment in Oran; Jean Tarrou, a stranger who takes an active part in opposing the epidemic; Joseph Grand, a municipal clerk obsessed with composing a perfect sentence; Paneloux, a Jesuit priest who delivers two crucial sermons during the course of the plague; and Cottard, a black-market opportunist.

Camus begins his novel with an epigraph from Daniel Defoe's *Robinson Crusoe* (1719) that invites readers to read the book as a veiled representation of something other than merely an epidemic in Oran. In a 1955 letter to critic Roland Barthes, the author specified the terms of the allegory; "*The Plague*, which I wanted to be read on a number of levels, nevertheless has as its obvious content the struggle of the European resistance movements against Nazism. The proof of this is that although the specific enemy is nowhere named, everyone in every European country recognized it."

The book is, moreover, a meditation on human solidarity and individual responsibility. What is the logical and ethical response to a universe in which suffering prevails and effort seems futile? In the first of two sermons strategically positioned in part 2

and part 4 of the five-part chronicle, Paneloux posits an anthropomorphic God who has sent the plague as retribution for human sin. After witnessing the agonizing death of an innocent child, however, Paneloux revises his theodicy to reconcile unmerited torment with belief in a logical and benevolent Providence.

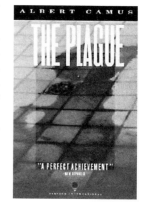

Tarrou, a magistrate's son who left home in revulsion over state executions, remains forever opposed to a scheme of things in which cruelty triumphs. His selfless, if hopeless, dedication to the struggle against the plague—both the actual disease and the metaphorical plague he contends is the human condition—offers a sharp contrast to the egoism of Cottard, who exploits the misfortunes of Oran for personal advantage. Rambert's initial reaction to the quarantine is concern for his personal happiness, for how he can escape from the city and return to Paris to the woman he loves. He learns, however, that his lot is also Oran's, and he stays in the city to make common cause with the victims of the plague.

Under such circumstances, the flamboyant individualism that enlivens traditional fiction is inappropriate, and the novel, conceding that readers crave heroes, nominates the lackluster Grand, whose grandness resides in selfless, bootless dedication to writing a perfect sentence and ending the plague:

> Yes, if it is a fact that people like to have examples given them, men of the type they call heroic, and if it is absolutely necessary that this narrative should include a "hero," the narrator commends to his readers, with, to his thinking, perfect justice, this insignificant and obscure hero who had to his credit only a little goodness of heart and a seemingly absurd ideal.

One of the novel's most striking features is its handling of narrative point of view. The story is told in meticulously neutral prose, from a perspective that seems detached from the experiences it recounts. Less than a dozen pages from the end, however, when the plague has subsided and the gates of Oran have been reopened, Rieux steps forward to confess that he has been the narrator all along. Though the text's preoccupation with exile and isolation are clearly the result of Rieux's own enforced separation from his ailing wife, he as narrator has taken great pains to present an impersonal "chronicle," the objective account of an honest witness. Writing himself into the story of his community is another way in which Rieux tries to overcome the solitude that is his lot as a widower and a human being.

In a universe in which "plague" is inexplicable and gratuitous, Rieux realizes that physicians are as ineffectual as anyone else. Yet he finds value in collective struggle, regardless of the outcome. The plague is never defeated. It merely, and mysteriously, recedes, and the reader is left with Rieux's realization that eternal vigilance is necessary against an indomitable foe.

THE FALL

First published: *La Chute,* 1956 (English translation, 1957)
Type of work: Novel

In an Amsterdam bar, a French lawyer imparts to a stranger his lessons in misanthropy.

The Fall is an extended monologue conducted over the course of five days by a man who calls himself Jean-Baptiste Clamence. The setting is Amsterdam, whose fogginess is miasmic and whose canals are likened to the concentric circles of hell. Like some infernal Ancient Mariner, the speaker attaches himself to a stranger who happens to wander into a raffish bar incongruously named Mexico City. A master of guile, Clamence deliberately piques the curiosity of his listener, who remains an unnamed "you." Gradually, cunningly, he implicates him—and the reader—in his diabolical tale. Clamence infers that his auditor is a successful Parisian lawyer in his forties, and he tailors his story to appeal to and expose the weaknesses of the stranger.

Clamence claims that he, too, used to live in Paris, where, as a widely respected magistrate, he exuded self-confidence. He then recounts an incident that forever undermined his certainties about personal worth.

One November evening, walking across a bridge, he heard the cry of a woman who had thrown herself into the river. His reaction was to deny that he had heard anything and to continue walking. He remains, however, haunted by that dying cry and the fact that he evaded responsibility toward another human being.

Written at a troubled time in Camus's own life, *The Fall* is the bitter fictional tirade of a brilliant misanthrope who dismisses civilization with a mordant epigram: "A single sentence will suffice for modern man: he fornicated and read the papers." Clamence admits that his name is a cunning alias. Like the biblical *vox clamans in deserto*, the narrator is a voice crying in the wilderness mocking specious hope for clemency toward universal guilt. "Every man testifies to the crime of all the others—that is my faith and my hope," declares Clamence. It is also the rationale for his narrative, a strategy of confessing his culpability and coercing the listener—and reader—into acknowledging and sharing it.

Duplicitous Clamence has assumed the function of what he calls "judge-penitent," a deft way of being both condemner and condemned. He eventually lures his listener to his apartment, where he reveals a stolen Van Eyck on the wall. The reader's knowledge of the purloined painting now implicates the reader, too, in the crime. The subject of the work, *The Just Judges*, reinforces the novel's theme of judgement even as it mocks the possibility of justice. It is not merely perverse bravado that impels Clamence to entrust his felonious secret to a stranger; he realizes that in a world devoid of innocence, no one dare judge anyone else. Yet he dreams of being apprehended, of finding release from his personal burden by a stroke of the guillotine. Jean-Baptiste longs for the decapitation that was the fate of his namesake John the Baptist:

> I would be decapitated, for instance, and I'd have no more fear of death; I'd be saved. Above the gathered crowd, you would hold up my still warm head, so that they could recognize themselves in it and could again dominate—an exemplar. All would be consummated; I should have brought to

469

a close, unseen and unknown, my career as a false prophet crying in the wilderness and refusing to come forth.

Such redemption never comes. *The Fall* portrays all as trapped in a fallen world. Like Sisyphus, Clamence is condemned to repeat his futile gestures. Every time he encounters another listener (and reader), he is compelled anew to spread his gospel of universal guilt, to confirm it by his very success in persuading readers to share his story.

"THE GUEST"

First published: "L'Hôte," 1957 (collected in *Exile and the Kingdom*, 1958)
Type of work: Short story

A schoolmaster living on a remote Algerian plateau is torn by an order to deliver an Arab prisoner to authorities.

To translate the French word *hôte*—someone who either gives or receives hospitality—into English, it is necessary to sacrifice its ambiguity. "The Guest," Camus's most frequently anthologized short story, focuses on a character who, suspended between giving and receiving, fails at hospitality. It could as accurately, or ironically, be translated as "The Host."

At the outset of "The Guest," Daru, a schoolmaster of European stock who was born in Algeria, observes two figures, one on horseback and one on foot, slowly make their way through the desolate, snowy landscape toward the schoolhouse where he lives, alone. Balducci, the man on horseback, is a gendarme, and he is accompanying an Arab who has been arrested for killing his own cousin.

Balducci explains that because of civil unrest Daru is being conscripted to convey the prisoner to the authorities in Tinguit, a town located a few hours' journey away, the next day. The teacher refuses this assignment, but Balducci leaves the unnamed Arab with him anyway. A reluctant host to an unwanted guest, Daru passes the night fitfully, fearful that the Arab might attack him and wishing for his escape. In the morning, the two set out for police headquarters in Tinguit. After walking a considerable distance but still two hours short of

their destination, Daru parts company with the Arab, telling him to proceed alone, either to turn himself in to the police in Tinguit or to seek refuge among sympathetic nomads. The teacher watches somberly as the Arab continues alone along the path to prison. On returning to his schoolhouse, Daru, who has tried not to take sides, discovers a message threatening revenge against him for having delivered the Arab to the authorities.

In "The Guest," the third of six short stories in a collection titled *Exile and the Kingdom*, Camus continues his examination of longing and alienation. The final word of the story, "alone," emphasizes the work's central theme of solitude. Just like the French Algerian Camus, who was rebuffed by both sides when he attempted in 1955 to mediate between France and the Algerian separatists, Daru finds himself condemned to solitude, uncomfortable either among his fellow colons or within the indigenous Arab community. A drawing of the four rivers of France on the schoolroom blackboard indicates that his job is to inculcate his North African pupils with the culture of a European colonial power. However, Daru's loyalties are not so much torn as eroded. The only bond that he feels is, ironically, with the vast, forbidding landscape that remains indifferent to the human beings who put in brief appearances. Like much of the rest of Camus's fiction, "The Guest" employs spare, incisive language to depict a universe of disconnected human beings who are tormented by the illusion of free choice.

THE MYTH OF SISYPHUS

First published: *Le Mythe de Sisyphe*, 1942 (English translation, 1955)
Type of Work: Essays

The Myth of Sisyphus is a meditation on an ancient Greek figure who, condemned for eternity to a futile task, is seen by Camus as representative of the human condition.

The Myth of Sisyphus, Camus's most explicit philosophical pronouncement, begins by dismissing all reflection that evades the question of why people live. "There is but one truly serious philosophical problem, and that is suicide," he declares. "Judging whether life is or is not worth living amounts to answering the fundamental question of philosophy."

The Myth of Sisyphus includes several miscellaneous pieces—a discussion of Franz Kafka, a self-interview on the responsibility of the artist, and four personal evocations of the landscape of Algeria that were also published elsewhere. The most remarkable and influential section of *The Myth of Sisyphus*, however, is its title essay. In it and the supporting chapters, Camus appropriates the ancient Greek story of the king of Corinth who was punished by the gods for failing to show them sufficient respect. Sisyphus is condemned for eternity to push a boulder up the side of a steep mountain. Whenever he is about to reach the summit, the boulder rolls back to the base, and Sisyphus is obliged to begin his endless, pointless task again.

Camus seizes on this myth as an emblem of the human condition. Life, he contends, is absurd. Devoid of purpose, existence is an endless, empty series of compulsive repetitions with no possibility of attaining a goal. Sisyphus becomes the prototype of the "absurd hero," a figure whose variations Camus traces in the roles of the philanderer, the actor, and the conqueror. Like Rieux, who rebels against a scheme of things he cannot accept but cannot change, Camus's Sisyphus is a figure of admirable futility: "His scorn of the gods, his hatred of death, and his passion for life won him that unspeakable penalty in which the whole being is exerted toward accomplishing nothing. This is the price that must be paid for the passions of this earth."

A literary meditation rather than a work of rigorous formal philosophy, *The Myth of Sisyphus* offers a vision of human contingency and self-authentication popularly associated with the term existentialism. It assumes a post-Nietzschean universe in which the obituary for God has been written. Refusing to accept external validation, Camus contends that individuals are responsible for their own situations. He insists that such responsibility begins with awareness, a consciousness that *The Myth of Sisyphus* is itself designed to encourage.

The essay "The Myth of Sisyphus" concludes with the provocative assertion that despite the futility and dreariness of his punitive task, Sisyphus is a figure of felicity:

> Sisyphus teaches the higher fidelity that negates the gods and raises rocks. He too concludes that all is well. This universe henceforth without a master seems to him neither sterile nor futile. Each atom of that stone, each mineral flake of that night-filled mountain, in itself forms a world. The struggle itself toward the heights is enough to fill a man's heart. One must imagine Sisyphus happy.

Sisyphus possesses the satisfaction of awareness, the modest pleasure of honest confrontation with the bleak conditions of his existence. It is a gloss on the life and works of Camus himself, an obsessively lucid author who refused the spurious consolations of actions and expressions that divert readers from the truth.

SUMMARY

More than most other authors, Albert Camus both reflected and shaped his zeitgeist, the spirit of an era plagued by tyranny, invasion, genocide, and colonialism. A child of the Algerian proletariat living among the Parisian intelligentsia and writing about human alienation, he stood both inside and outside history. He was a champion of lucidity and honesty in an age whose public rhetoric camouflaged savage realities. The sparely styled fiction, drama, and essays that Camus produced during a relatively brief career offer the paradox of tonic disillusionment, an exhilaration over candid contemplation of the absurd. In North America, perhaps even more than in France, Camus remains read and loved long after the works of many of his contemporaries have fallen out of favor and print.

Steven G. Kellman

BIBLIOGRAPHY

By the Author

LONG FICTION:

La Mort heureuse, wr. 1936-1938, pb. 1971 (*A Happy Death*, 1972)
L'Étranger, 1942 (*The Stranger*, 1946)
La Peste, 1947 (*The Plague*, 1948)
La Chute, 1956 (*The Fall*, 1957)
Le Premier Homme, 1994 (*The First Man*, 1995)

SHORT FICTION:

L'Exil et le royaume, 1957 (*Exile and the Kingdom*, 1958)

DRAMA:

Révolte dans les Asturies, pb. 1936 (with others)
Caligula, wr. 1938-1939, pb. 1944, pr. 1945 (English translation, 1948)
Le Malentendu, pr., pb. 1944 (*The Misunderstanding*, 1948)
L'État de siège, pr., pb. 1948 (*State of Siege*, 1958)
Les Justes, pr. 1949, pb. 1950 (*The Just Assassins*, 1958)
Caligula, and Three Other Plays, pb. 1958
Les Possédés, pr., pb. 1959 (adaptation of Fyodor Dostoevski's novel; *The Possessed*, 1960)

NONFICTION:

L'Envers et l'endroit, 1937 ("The Wrong Side and the Right Side," 1968)
Noces, 1938 ("Nuptials," 1968)
Le Mythe de Sisyphe, 1942 (*The Myth of Sisyphus*, 1955)
L'Homme révolté, 1951 (*The Rebel*, 1956)
L'Été, 1954 (*Summer*, 1968)
Carnets: Mai 1935-février 1942, 1962 (*Notebooks: 1935-1942*, 1963)
Carnets: Janvier 1942-mars 1951, 1964 (*Notebooks: 1942-1951*, 1965)
Lyrical and Critical Essays, 1968 (includes "The Wrong Side and the Right Side," "Nuptials," and "Summer")
Correspondance, 1939-1947, 2000
Camus à Combat: Éditoriaux et articles d'Albert Camus, 1944-1947, 2002 (*Camus at Combat: Writing, 1944-1947*, 2006)

DISCUSSION TOPICS

- Is it accurate or useful to consider the work of Albert Camus "existentialist"?

- How are Camus's Algerian origins reflected in his fiction?

- Why is Meursault executed in *The Stranger*?

- Why does Camus not reveal the identity of the narrator of *The Plague* until the novel's conclusion?

- What is the significance of the title *The Fall*?

- How does *The Myth of Sisyphus* help explicate some of Camus's fiction?

- What is going to happen to Daru after the final words of "The Guest"?

- How does Camus treat the theme of capital punishment?

- How does a tension between solidarity and solitude shape Camus's work?

About the Author

Bellman, Steven G. *"The Plague": Fiction and Resistance*. Boston: Twayne, 1993.

Bloom, Harold, ed. *Albert Camus*. New York: Chelsea House, 1989.

Carroll, David. *Albert Camus, the Algerian: Colonialism, Terrorism, Justice*. New York: Columbia University Press, 2007.

Ellison, David R. *Understanding Albert Camus*. Columbia: University of South Carolina Press, 1990.

Hughes, Edward J., ed. *The Cambridge Companion to Camus*. New York: Cambridge University Press, 2007.

Ironstone, Ronald. *Camus and Sartre: The Story of a Friendship and the Quarrel That Ended It*. Chicago: University of Chicago Press, 2003.

Knapp, Bettina L., ed. *Critical Essays on Albert Camus*. Boston: G. K. Hall, 1988.

Lottman, Herbert R. *Albert Camus: A Biography*. Garden City, N.Y.: Doubleday, 1979.

Todd, Olivier. *Albert Camus: A Life*. Translated by Benjamin Ivry. New York: Knopf, 1997.

PETER CAREY

Born: Bacchus Marsh, Victoria, Australia
May 7, 1943

In his fiction, Carey explores the nature of modern Australian identity, partly by creating origin myths for white Australia drawing on the nation's history, immigration, and land settlement, but also by experimenting with the nature of storytelling itself, showing how people constantly reinvent themselves through the stories they tell about themselves.

© Miriam Berkley

BIOGRAPHY

Peter Philip Carey was born on May 7, 1943, in Bacchus Marsh, Victoria, Australia, where his parents ran a General Motors dealership. He studied at the prestigious Geelong Grammar School between 1954 and 1960 before moving to Monash University in Melbourne to enroll in a science degree program, intending to major in chemistry and zoology. Boredom and a car accident cut short his studies, and he left the university to work for what he later described as an "eccentric" advertising agency. Two of his colleagues, the writers Barry Oakley and Morris Lurie, introduced him to a broad range of European and American literature. He read widely, particularly the work of James Joyce, Samuel Beckett, Franz Kafka, and William Faulkner, and by1964 he had begun to write fiction himself. In the next four years, he wrote several novels and a number of short stories. Although some of his early work was initially accepted for publication, it was later rejected and he remained unpublished as a novelist until 1981.

Carey traveled in Europe and the Middle East during the late 1960's, also spending two years in London before returning to Australia. He worked for a number of advertising agencies in Melbourne and Sydney and published a number of short stories which were later collected in *The Fat Man in History* (1974). In 1976, Carey joined an "alternative community" called Starlight at Yandina in Queensland. Here, he wrote the stories that were collected in *War Crimes* (1979), as well as *Bliss* (1981), his first published novel. Carey continued to work in advertising, setting up his own agency in 1980, until he left Australia in 1990 to settle in New York. Carey also directed the master of fine arts in creative writing program at Hunter College, part of the City University of New York.

Carey's move to New York, prompted by his wife's career as a theater director, drew criticism from some commentators, who wondered whether he had the right to speak from an Australian perspective while living outside the country. He has also courted controversy on other occasions, most notably in 1998, when he declined an invitation to meet Queen Elizabeth II after winning the Commonwealth Writers Prize. Many believed that this response was because of his Australian republican beliefs, although Carey cited family reasons. In fact, according to Carey, he had asked for the meeting to be postponed, and Buckingham Palace did reschedule it. More recently, Carey's novel *Theft: A Love Story* (2006) attracted adverse publicity when his former wife, Alison Summers, claimed he had created a particularly unpleasant minor character in order to take revenge upon her. Carey remained silent on the matter.

Carey has won numerous awards for his work. He received the Man Booker Prize twice, for *Oscar and Lucinda* (1988) in 1988 and *True History of the Kelly Gang* (2000) in 2001, and he has been shortlisted twice. He has won the Miles Franklin Award, given in Australia, on three occasions, for *Bliss, Os-*

car and Lucinda, and *Jack Maggs* (1997), and was short-listed on two other occasions.

ANALYSIS

Peter Carey once said, "my fictional project has always been the invention or discovery of my own country." His writing is shaped by an acute awareness that Australia's earliest white settlers were criminals cast out by their own country, cut adrift from their own history. Their dilemma is exemplified by Jack Maggs, who regards himself as an Englishman, but who can only remain English as long as he doesn't return to his home country. Carey's novels attempt to provide the voiceless former convicts with a new set of origin myths, to reflect their new circumstances, thus initiating a new cycle of history. This is important to Carey because Australians, as he has noted, really believe in failure and seek to deny the fact that their country's origins lie in the formation of penal colonies.

In the same way, there are no losers in Australia, only "battlers" who continue to struggle with seemingly insurmountable obstacles. Carey claims that Australians admire "battlers" more than those who actually succeed, and his fiction is populated with characters who have to deal with one setback after another. They are constantly on the brink of achieving success, only to lose everything at the last moment, often through their own incompetence. His careful portrayals of these people suggest a certain sympathy; however, he never shrinks from exploring the immensity of their self-deception. Ironically, the confidence-trickster in *Illywhacker* (1985) is the one character who fully understands his own capacity to deceive others, and even then he occasionally manages to deceive himself.

Carey is extremely skilled at providing a voice for those unable to speak for or to defend themselves. This is best illustrated in *True History of the Kelly Gang*, where Carey's close study of the language of Ned Kelly's Jerilderie letter allows him to tell Kelly's full story more vividly. Likewise, with *Jack Maggs*, Carey gives a convincing voice to an Englishman who has been away for a long time. However, Carey's skills extend beyond historical reconstruction, as shown in *Bliss* and *The Tax Inspector* (1991), where he reveals a flair for handling a complex ensemble of voices, while in *Theft* the narrative is shared between the Boone brothers, one of whom has learning problems. Only in the first-person framing narrative of *My Life as a Fake* (2003) does this skill seem to temporarily desert him, when he seems unable to create a convincing voice for Micks, the English poetry editor.

Carey employs a wide range of narrative techniques throughout his novels and constantly interrogates the nature of storytelling itself, as befits a man who is interested in providing his country with a set of histories. At times, Carey's narrators are aware of themselves as characters in novels and equally aware of their audiences, whom they directly address. In other instances, his characters are themselves storytellers, using their skills to come to terms with their lives, or else aware of the power of the printed word as a vehicle of expression.

Carey's great influences are Beckett, Faulkner, and Joyce; his narratives frequently appear to be chaotic or fragmentary, his characters acting at random rather than according to the dictates of a previously chosen plot. Carey notes the influence of postmodernism on his work, while *The Unusual Life of Tristan Smith* (1994) is clearly intended as homage to *The Life and Opinions of Tristram Shandy, Gent.* (1759-1767) by Laurence Sterne. Nonetheless, Carey's novels retain an overall narrative coherence; they often end abruptly, not always as the reader anticipates, but always in a way that, in retrospect, does provide closure and satisfaction.

OSCAR AND LUCINDA

First published: 1988
Type of work: Novel

An unconventional young couple, who have finally found love in the face of adversity, lose the chance of happiness together when the woman bets her fortune on the man's ability to deliver a glass church safely to its destination.

Oscar and Lucinda was the first of Peter Carey's novels to win the Man Booker Prize. The present-day first-person narrator tells the story of Oscar Hopkins and Lucinda Leplastrier, two young people who meet on board a ship sailing to Australia. The implication, from references made, is that the couple are the narrator's great-grandparents and that he or she is telling a love story. However, the truth is more complicated.

Lucinda, a wealthy heiress, is returning to Australia after carrying out research on the manufacture of glass in London. On a whim, once she had come into her fortune she bought a glassworks, which she is now attempting to run. Her efforts are confounded in part by the fact that her male employees, although they are willing to work for her, will not allow her in the factory and prefer to deal with her friend, the Reverend Hassett.

Accustomed to living on a farm in the bush with her father and mother, and latterly alone, Lucinda has found it hard to make friends in Sydney. Having bought the glassworks, she finds her way to the Reverend Hassett, an expert in the properties of glass though not its manufacture, and to the household of Mr. d'Abbs, her financial adviser, where she plays cards with him and his friends. Lucinda's unconventionality is not intentional, but all her life she has been used to taking care of herself, and she finds she does not fit comfortably into the role that society assigns wealthy young women. As a result, her visit to London, where she has called on her mother's old friends and correspondents, has been an unmitigated disaster.

Oscar Hopkins's father was a nonconformist preacher and naturalist who had brought up his son alone, according to his own unorthodox beliefs. Queerly dressed, physically and emotionally stunted, Oscar finally rebels by rejecting his father's religious beliefs and attaching himself to the local Church of England vicar. The church sponsors Oscar's degree at Oxford, where Oscar discovers his latent skill as a gambler. After he takes holy orders, the church determines to send him to Australia.

Oscar and Lucinda bond over their shared love of gambling. When Oscar arrives in Sydney, it is assumed by many that he is to be her husband. The men at the glassworks gladly accept him in a way that they have never accepted Lucinda. However, unable to articulate their feelings for one another, the two become confused about their desire for one another. Oscar is convinced that Lucinda loves the Reverend Hassett, who has been sent away to Boat Harbour because his bishop does not approve of his religious views, whereas Lucinda's determination to build the priest a church made out of glass is an attempt to encourage people to buy the buildings she wants to develop. Their work on the building brings Oscar and Lucinda together and they enjoy a period of happiness, although their relationship causes a scandal.

Their brief happiness is destroyed when Lucinda foolishly wagers her fortune on whether or not Oscar will be able to successfully deliver the building to the Reverend Hassett, convinced that he will succeed. However, Oscar's journey descends into farce as the expedition's leader determines to use the voyage to establish himself as a famous explorer. Pursuing his own agenda, he leads the expedition away from its intended route. On his arrival at Boat Harbour, Oscar, ill from the journey and emotionally naïve, is enticed into marriage by a local woman. After he dies by drowning, his wife claims Lucinda's fortune, and the reader finally understands that the narrator's great-grandmother is not the person they initially supposed. Lucinda has disappeared from the historical record without a trace.

True History of the Kelly Gang

First published: 2000
Type of work: Novel

A first-person account of the life of Ned Kelly, the Australian bushranger, in which he attempts to explain to his daughter how he was driven to break the law by the authorities.

True History of the Kelly Gang gives the bushranger Ned Kelly a chance to tell his own story in the form of a long letter to his daughter in San Francisco. Kelly's father was a former convict, transported to Tasmania; Kelly has no idea what his father's crime might have been. He met Kelly's mother, Ellen, in a town called Donnybrook, and they determined to marry. Her family, the Quinns, were habitual criminals who constantly drew the attention of the police. Ellen Quinn was unaware that her husband was a former criminal, but the police knew, subjected his family to much attention, and attempted to blackmail Ellen for sexual favors. Kelly's father is finally imprisoned when he takes the blame for young Kelly's theft and butchering of a cow, although he is in fact prosecuted for removing a brand from the hide. He is released as a favor after Kelly saves a local man's son from drowning, but he is a broken man and dies shortly after.

At twelve, Kelly finds himself the man of the family and struggles to lead a law-abiding life through farming and breaking horses. His mother, meanwhile, opens a drinking den and, it is suggested, also works as a prostitute. The family moves around, supported by the extended Quinn family, finally settling in the Glenrowan area, where they have bought some land and become "selectors," or settlers. However, they live in great poverty and remain targets for the local police. Young Ned is temporarily apprenticed to the bushranger Harry Power and is present when a number of crimes are committed. He serves several terms in prison for alleged cattle-rustling and other crimes.

The final period of his short but tumultuous life begins with an incident on the family property, when a policeman, Fitzpatrick, claims he was injured in a gunfight with members of the Kelly family. The Kelly family claim Fitzpatrick was knocked to the ground when he attempted to proposition Ned's sister Kate. Ned's mother is imprisoned, but Ned and his brother Dan go into hiding, where they are joined by two friends.

The police determine to track down the Kelly gang. Ned and his friends come across a group of police officers at Stringybark Creek, whom they disarm, killing one policeman, and then wait for the others to return. When they do, although one policeman proposes that the police should surrender, the others refuse, and there is a shootout in which all of the policemen are killed.

The Kelly gang then carry out a series of audacious bank raids, taking hostages but killing no one. They are finally betrayed by one of their friends when they arrive in Glenrowan. Knowing that a trainload of policemen is on its way to the town, the gang take hostages and pull up rail tracks in order to cause a train crash.

Ned Kelly's letter to his daughter ceases at this point, and his story is supplemented by a third-party account of the siege in which the Kelly Gang, all except Ned, are killed, and an account of Ned Kelly's hanging.

Throughout the narrative, Kelly is desperate to ensure that his daughter knows the truth about her father, and he attempts to justify his actions, as he did in the Jerilderie letter, by showing that the police and the authorities in Victoria treated the colonists unfairly and with great severity.

THEFT: A LOVE STORY

First published: 2006
Type of work: Novel

Michael "Butcher" Bones and his brother, Hugh "Slow" Bones, maintain an uneasy relationship as Michael attempts to resuscitate his flagging career as an artist while starting a new relationship with Marlene Leibovitz, an art historian.

Theft opens with artist Michael Bones, newly released from prison, discovering that he is to be sent to northern New South Wales to take care of an isolated property belonging to his biggest collector, Jean-Paul Milan, and also to act as caretaker to his slow-witted brother, Hugh Bones. The hope is that Michael will cut down on his drinking, as well as produce some new works. He has lost control of most of his work, as it was deemed to be marital assets during his divorce from his wife, and he was prosecuted for attempting to steal it back.

Michael is not particularly happy to be caring for his brother or to be exiled in Bellingen, let alone to be issued with a long list of maintenance tasks around the house. However, once Milan leaves, the brothers settle into a chaotic day-to-day routine, during which Michael more or less unintentionally vandalizes the house in the cause of his art, which is rather different in its production methods than his patron seems to suppose.

It is at this point that Marlene Leibovitz inadvertently enters the Bones brothers' lives, when, en route to visit their neighbor, Dozy Boylan, to authenticate a painting by Jacques Leibovitz, she is caught in a flood. Hugh and Marlene immediately establish a rapport, much to Michael's surprise. He meanwhile is astonished to learn that Boylan owns a painting by Leibovitz, as it was this artist who first inspired him to become an artist. When Marlene returns she tells Michael the story of how Lei-

bovitz's wife, Dominique, stole many of his half-finished works after his death and then altered and amended them, exercising *droit moral* (or moral rights) in order to control and authenticate them. Marlene, married to the artist's son, Olivier Leibovitz, now has the *droit moral* to control her father-in-law's work, and she is thus an immensely powerful woman in the art world.

Some time after Marlene's departure, Michael is surprised to receive a visit from the Sydney police, who seem convinced that he is in some way involved in the theft of Boylan's Leibovitz and who impound his latest work. He is already having trouble reestablishing his career, as the galleries do not want to know him, so this incident is a disaster for him. Unexpectedly, the brothers encounter Marlene Leibovitz again, and she rescues them, revealing that her husband has run away and is suspected of having stolen Boylan's painting, although he is physically incapable of touching any of his father's paintings because he hates them so much.

Michael and Hugh finally leave Australia and follow Marlene to New York. For a period, Michael, Marlene, and Hugh lead a golden life. Michael's art is recognized once again and he feels successful. Hugh enjoys the bustle of New York and makes friends. Marlene reveals her life story to Michael: She has deceived him and is really an Australian woman who fled a life of poverty and transformed herself, through hard work and study, into an expert on art, in order to catch Olivier Leibovitz.

Blinded by his growing love for her, Michael does not understand that Marlene, although she has enabled him to restart his artistic career, is also using him to help her authenticate forged Leibovitz paintings. When Olivier dies and she finally inherits the *droit moral* to control the paintings, Michael strongly suspects that Marlene encouraged Hugh to murder Olivier, and the brothers flee New York for Australia. However, Michael's past continues to haunt him.

SUMMARY

Peter Carey's novels address the issue of what it means to be Australian, particularly in regard to the paradox that the history of Australian settlement is so new, whereas the continent and its indigenous culture are so ancient. Likewise, he constantly seeks to give voice to the white colonists who have been expelled from their home country or who have fled, hoping to find a better life, and whose histories have been lost as a result. However meaningless and petty their lives may seem to outsiders, Carey's constantly reiterated point is that these are the people whose work made Australia what it is. Their lives are as just as important as those of the people whom history does remember, and his writing gives them a voice.

Maureen Kincaid Speller

BIBLIOGRAPHY

By the Author

LONG FICTION:
Bliss, 1981
Illywhacker, 1985
Oscar and Lucinda, 1988
The Tax Inspector, 1991
The Unusual Life of Tristan Smith, 1994
The Big Bazoohley, 1995

Peter Carey

Jack Maggs, 1997
True History of the Kelly Gang, 2000
My Life as a Fake, 2003
Theft: A Love Story, 2006
His Illegal Self, 2008

SHORT FICTION:
The Fat Man in History, 1974
War Crimes, 1979
The Fat Man in History, and Other Stories, 1981
Collected Stories, 1995

SCREENPLAY:
Bliss, 1985 (with Ray Lawrence; adaptation of his novel)

NONFICTION:
A Letter to Our Son, 1994
Thirty Days in Sydney: A Wildly Distorted Account, 2001
Wrong About Japan: A Father's Journey with His Son, 2005

About the Author

Gaile, Andre, ed. *Fabulating Beauty: Perspectives on the Fiction of Peter Carey.* New York: Rodopi Press, 2005.

Hassall, Anthony J. *Dancing on Hot Macadam: Peter Carey's Fiction.* Brisbane: University of Queensland Press, 1994.

Huggan, Graham. *Peter Carey.* New York: Oxford University Press, 1996.

DISCUSSION TOPICS

- How does Peter Carey's work contribute to a new myth of origin for Australia?

- Families are very important in Carey's work. Compare the role of family in *True History of the Kelly Gang* and *Theft.*

- Carey has lived outside Australia since he wrote *The Tax Inspector.* Has that affected his view of the country in later novels, and, if so, how?

- What is the difference between a loser and a battler, and how is this illustrated in Carey's novels?

- Carey has often referred to other novels in his work. Examine the influence of Charles Dickens's *Great Expectations* (1860-1861) on *Jack Maggs* and of Mary Wollstonecraft Shelley's *Frankenstein* (1818) on *My Life as a Fake.*